Jean Bodin

International Library of Essays in the History of Social and Political Thought
Series Editor: Tom Campbell

Titles in the Series:

Jean Bodin

Edited by

Julian H. Franklin

Columbia University, USA

ASHGATE

Published by
Ashgate Publishing Limited
Gower House
Croft Road
Aldershot
Hampshire GU11 3HR
England

Ashgate Publishing Company
Suite 420
101 Cherry Street
Burlington, VT 05401-4405
USA

Ashgate website: http://www.ashgate.com

British Library Cataloguing in Publication Data
Jean Bodin. - (International library of essays in the
    history of social and political thought)
    1.Bodin, Jean, 1530-1596 2.Bodin, Jean, 1530-1596 -
    Religion 3.Sovereignty
    I.Franklin, Julian H.
    320'.092

Library of Congress Cataloging-in-Publication Data
Jean Bodin / edited by Julian H. Franklin
        p. cm. – (International library of essays in the history of social and political thought)
    ISBN 0-7546-2545-1 (alk paper)
        1. Political science–Philosophy. 2. Social sciences–Philosophy. 3. Bodin, Jean,
    1530-1596. I.Franklin, Julian H. II. Series.

    JA71.J377 2006
    321'.6092–dc22

                                                                                    2006040754

ISBN 10: 0 7546 2545 1
ISBN 13: 978-0-7546-2545-2

Printed in Great Britain by TJ International Ltd, Padstow, Cornwall

Contents

PART IV RELIGION

PART V NATURAL PHILOSOPHY AND METHOD

PART VI THEORIES OF HISTORY

Acknowledgements

The editor and publishers wish to thank the following for permission to use copyright material.

Cambridge University Press for the essays: Julian H. Franklin (1991), 'Sovereignty and the Mixed Constitution: Bodin and his Critics', in J.H. Burns and Mark Goldie (eds) *The Cambridge History of Political Thought 1450-1700*, Cambridge: Cambridge University Press, pp. 298–328. Copyright © 1991 Cambridge University Press, reproduced with permission; Julian H. Franklin (1973), 'Bodin's Early Theory of Sovereignty' and 'The Shift to Absolutism' in Julian H. Franklin, *Jean Bodin and the Rise of Asbolutist Theory*, New York: Cambridge University Press, pp. 23–53. Copyright © 1973 Cambridge University Press, reproduced with permission; Julian H. Franklin (1973), 'Limitations on Absolute Authority', in Julian H. Franklin, *Jean Bodin and the Rise of Absolutist Theory*, New York: Cambridge University Press, pp. 70–92. Copyright © 1973 Cambridge University Press, reproduced with permission;Gary Remer (1994), 'Dialogues of Toleration: Erasmus and Bodin', *Review of Politics*, **56**, pp. 305–36. Copyright © 1973 The University of Notre Dame, published by Cambridge University Press, reprinted with permission.

Droz Publishing for the essay: Paul Lawrence Rose (1980), 'Introduction: The Enigma of Bodin's Religion', in Paul Lawrence Rose, *Bodin and the Great God of Nature: The Moral and Religious Universe of a Judaiser*, pp. 1–15.

Duke University Press for the essay: Denis P. O'Brien (2000), 'Bodin's Analysis of Inflation', *History of Political Economy*, **32**, pp. 267–92. Copyright © 2000 Duke University Press. All rights reserved. Used by permission of the publisher.

Imprint Academic for the essay: Julian H. Franklin (1986), 'Bodin and Locke on Consent to Taxation: A Brief Note and Observation', *History of Political Thought*, **7**, pp. 89–91. Copyright © 1986, Imprint Academic, Exeter, UK.

Marion Leathers Daniels Kuntz for the essay: Marion Leathers Daniels Kuntz (1975), 'Introduction: "Religious Views in His [Bodin's] Works" and "The *Colloquium Heptaplomeres* and the Sixteenth Century"', in Marion Leathers Daniels Kuntz (ed. and tr.), *Colloquium of the Seven about Secrets of the Sublime by Jean Bodin*, Princeton: Princeton University Press, pp. xxix–lxvi; lxxiii–lxxxi.

Princeton University Press for the essay: Ann Blair (1992), 'Introduction', in Ann Blair, *The Theater of Nature: Jean Bodin and Renaissance Science*, Princeton: Princeton University Press, pp. 3–13. Copyright © 1997 Princeton University Press. Reprinted by permission of Princeton University Press.

The University of Chicago Press for the essay: Owen Ulph (1947), 'Jean Bodin and the Estates-General of 1576', *Journal of Modern History*, **19**, pp. 289–96.

University of Pennsylvania Press for the essays: Kenneth D. McRae (1955), 'Ramist Tendencies in the Thought of Jean Bodin', *Journal of the History of Ideas*, **16**, pp. 306–23. Reprinted by permission of the University of Pennsylvania Press; Ann Blair (1992), 'Humanist Methods in Natural Philosophy: The Commonplace Book', *Journal of the History of Ideas*, **53**, pp. 541–51. Reprinted by permission of the University of Pennsylvania Press.

Series Preface

The International Library of Essays in the History of Social and Political Thought brings together collections of important essays dealing with the work of major figures in the history of social and political thought. The aim is to make accessible the complete text with the original pagination of those essays that should be read by all scholars working in that field. In each case, the selection is made from the extensive available literature by an established expert who has a keen sense of the continuing relevance of the history of social and political thought for contemporary theory and practice. The selection is made on the basis of the quality and enduring significance of the essays in question. Every volume has an introduction that places the selection made in the context of the wider literature, the historical period, the contemporary state of scholarship and the editor's particular interests.

TOM CAMPBELL
Series Editor
Centre for Applied Philosophy and Public Ethics (CAPPE)
Charles Sturt University
Canberra

Introduction

Jean Bodin, one of the most ambitious and prolific scholars of the later Renaissance, aimed at nothing less than to encompass all the disciplines (and pseudo-disciplines) of his age in a huge encyclopedia of knowledge. His involvement in the political struggles of the times notwithstanding, Bodin pursued this intellectual program with extraordinary constancy and notable success. By the time he died in 1596, he had made major contributions to historiography, philosophy of history, economic theory and history, political science, comparative public law and policy, philosophy of religion, comparative religion, and natural philosophy. Access to Bodin's writings, however, is often difficult for modern students. The intellectual style of the later Renaissance was marked less by systematic analysis of concepts than by massive erudition and adaptation which are sometimes difficult to mine. My aim in bringing together the essays which follow is to lower the barriers and ease the way. To this end, almost all of Bodin's major intellectual interests have been represented, the one exception of any significance being his work on witchcraft, which was all too influential. I have omitted it only because I am not aware of any suitable essay in English.

Bodin was born either in 1529 or 1530 at Angers and died in 1596. His family intended him for the priesthood, but he managed to secure his release from the Carmelite order in his teens and to obtain an excellent humanist education in Paris. He then studied civil (that is, Roman) law at the University of Toulouse where he aspired unsuccessfully to a professorship. By the 1560s he had turned to a political career and became a king's advocate in Paris. But he did not lag in his scholarly pursuits, and his book on history, published in 1566, was to win him the notice and favor of King Henry III who came to the throne in 1574. By 1571, now a noted humanist, Bodin became an aide and counselor to the Duke of Alençon, an ambitious member of the royal family, which made Bodin privy to the high politics of the time. And in 1576 he made a dramatic political move in his own person. At the Estates-General opened that year at Blois, Bodin attended as a deputy for the third estate of Vermandois. The Estates were opened during a shaky truce in the bitter civil war between the Catholic crown attempting to impose religious uniformity and a large Protestant minority in armed resistance. At Blois the king, clearly intent on a new campaign of forcible repression, requested subsidies, and Bodin became the spearhead of what was to become successful opposition to new taxation in the third estate. But his notoriety and success cost him the favor of Henry, although he continued to serve d'Alençon until the latter's death in 1584. He ended his career as a *procureur du roi* for Laon.

Bodin would face a cruel choice as the crown's representative at Laon. With the assasination of Henry III on 1589, civil war now raged between supporters of the Protestant Henry of Navarre (the future Henry IV) and the Catholic candidate, Antoine de Bourbon. Laon had been taken by the forces of the radical Catholic League which now demanded that the procurator, who was suspected of heresy, affirm his orthodoxy as a Catholic and declare the Catholic candidate for the throne. As a declared partisan of toleration, and as a connoisseur of the French law of succession which favored Henry of Navarre, Bodin might have been expected to resist. But faced with dire threats, he, like a great many French magistrates, succumbed and collaborated. It was not until Laon was liberated by Navarre that Bodin resumed his old positions.

At his own request, Bodin was buried as a Catholic. But this may have been pro forma. Throughout his life he had been something of a religious maverick and it is highly likely that his final religious preference was Judaism. He was surely a Judaizer, which was not unusual among philosopher-scholars of the later Renaissance. But his commitment could have gone even deeper, for there is strong evidence of a personal conversion. Some have even speculated that Bodin was returning to a secret Jewish tradition in his family, although this is generally dismissed as unlikely.

Sovereignty

Bodin is best known for his theory of sovereignty on which his contribution is original and historically important. The term *summum imperium* had appeared before in legal commentaries, but with varying and indeterminate content, while the vernacular *souverain* (in various spellings) was generally feudal in its associations. Bodin is the first to explore the idea exhaustively as the key juridical foundation of a centralized polity. The legal powers strictly necessary to the claim of sovereign authority are worked out in detail. Each of its prerogatives is widely illustrated from political systems past and present. And the principles of sovereignty then serve as the frame for a massive treatise of comparative public law and policy. This was his celebrated *Six livres de la république* (*Six Books of a Commonwealth*) which appeared in 1576 and had an immediate and deep impact on European political thought. Its systematic elaboration of the juridical function and legal institutions of sovereignty introduced a modernized doctrine of the state as a legal entity and initiated the scientific study of public law.

Bodin more or less correctly identified the essential prerogatives of governance, and above all the power to make law, which identified a sovereign authority. And he believed that these powers had to be concentrated in a single individual or corporate group if the state was to exist as a coherent entity. This was his celebrated doctrine of the indivisibility of sovereignty, which seemed to be empirically confirmed by most, if not all, of the many political systems past and present with which Bodin was familiar. And his belief that authority could not be ultimately divided, helped him to conclude that the ruling power in a proper state, including monarchies, could not be restrained institutionally. He was thus encouraged to contend for an absolutist interpretation not only of the French monarchy but of the Spanish and the English also. This, furthermore, was an ideological move of the highest importance in his time. It provided a conservative answer to the constitutionalist and resistance doctrines appearing in the wars of religion. Bodin did not deny, and indeed he earnestly insisted, that an absolute king was morally bound by the law of nature, which coincided with the law of God, as well as by certain fundamental laws on the legal status of the crown itself. But he was equally emphatic that even a tyrant was immune from lawful deposition if he held his office as a sovereign. The absolute sovereignty of a ruler, furthermore, seemed to rule out resistance not only by the civil law but by the law of God as well.

The massive detail and meandering style of Bodin's writing perhaps explain why his work on sovereignty has not been closely studied. I have therefore decided, reluctantly, to include two pieces of my own work as a scholarly introduction to this aspect of his thought. These deal with two central points about the genesis and application of his doctrine of sovereignty which require special introduction. First, most commentaries conclude too hastily that Bodin's interest in the concept of sovereignty was prompted by his fears of disorder at the height of the civil wars, that he came to the idea of undivided authority in the king of France as a program for political unity. In truth, however, Bodin had already come to the idea of indivisibility as early as 1566 when he published his *Methodus ad facilem historiarumm cognitionem* (*Method for the Easy Comprehension of History*). At that time, as I have tried to show (Franklin, Chapter 3), he came to that idea mainly from theoretical doubts as to formulae of a mixed republican constitution which he encountered in classical authors like Polybius. Yet at that juncture he was far from advancing any recipe for absolutism. Like most French commentators in the grand tradition, he viewed the French monarchy as limited even though unmixed, and he was actually more insistent on this point than most of his contemporaries. But his doctrine of sovereignty was not yet fully worked out. Ambiguities on the scope and juridical status of limitations on royal authority, and on the right of resistance to a tyrant had still to be cleared up. And I believe that this purely theoretical need to clarify the legal consequences of indivisibility has to be understood in order to appreciate the legal construction of Bodin's absolutism in the *République*. Ten years after the first edition of the *Methodus* France was in crisis, and Bodin, now deeply alarmed by the public disorders attendant on religious warfare, spoke with dark foreboding of the possible breakup of the French state in his preface of 1576. He must now have seen royal absolutism as the very anchor of stability. But theoretical reflection on the 'impossibility' of mixed government was also likely to have been a factor when he shifted to absolutism in 1576. The genesis and development of Bodin's doctrine of sovereignty is thus complex and that is one of the themes in Franklin (Chapter 3).

The second point is Bodin's portentous mistake in failing to recognize that sovereignty can indeed be divided between two corporate entities, and that its prerogatives can be separated and placed in different hands, as long as there are constitutional ground rules for coordinating their activities. This limitation of Bodin's thought is most often passed over by the commentaries, and I believe that my essay of 1991 (Franklin, Chapter 2), is a good way to see the problem in Bodin's own historical context. I here take up reactions to Bodin's theory among his near contemporaries, and most especially the strenuous efforts of German commentators to apply Bodin's idea of indivisible and absolute authority to the German Empire of the early seventeenth century. A whole generation of German jurists and publicists desperately attempted to describe the Emperor as an authentic sovereign in Bodin's sense, even though the constitution of the Empire was a strictly limited kingship or even a truly mixed constitution. The hopelessness of this quest ultimately inspired the brilliant and decisive critique of Bodin on the indivisibility of sovereignty by the German legal scholar, Christoph Besold. Hence these debates record early scientific interest in the logic of public law and at the same time illustrate the appeal of Bodin's doctrine to contemporaries.

J.U. Lewis Chapter 1, notes that Bodin's theory of sovereignty was the forerunner of positivist theories of law as the command of a superior running throughout the tradition from Hobbes to Austin and the analytic jurists of modern times. But Lewis also sounds an important note of caution. Unlike these later positivists, Bodin believed that the law of nature and the law of God were real sources of moral and legal values even though he did not find a way to integrate them with his theory of sovereign legislative authority.

Public Law

I have also argued that Bodin probably did not intend to distort the French tradition of 'tempered monarchy' even in his account of 1576. He most likely believed that his version of French institutions in the *République* was but a clarification of what he had written ten years before in the *Methodus*. The ambiguities on which the older view depended were now simply stripped away as he carried through his sharpened idea of indivisibility. Seeking consent of the Estates to royal legislation, which he once thought was often requisite, was now 'clarified' as wise policy merely rather than juridically necessary; the veto of the Parlements, which was formerly praised as the guarantor of limitations, was restated as purely suspensive.

With one rather curious exception on taxation, to be taken up below, the new account of French institutions was technically consistent with absolutism. Yet Bodin clearly expected that the government would function pretty much as he had thought ten years before. He never doubted that the crown would continue to observe all sorts of traditional limitations on the actual exercise of power and would observe the good old rules. As Ralph E. Giesey shows in Chapter 5, Bodin was deeply indebted to the medieval civil lawyers for his ideas as to how public authority is properly exercised. The medieval commentators on Roman civil law had worked up many procedural and substantive rules for the civil use of power, and Giesey traces Bodin's reliance on these sources not only in the text of the *République* but in its massive marginal annotations. Since the marginal citations to Roman law and medieval commentators are pre-modern in their format, making access to them difficult for Bodin students of the present time, Giesey's masterful use of them to illumine Bodin's doctrine is especially valuable.

Law in medieval and early modern times was not merely a set of rules for the practicing advocate. Like the jurists before him, Bodin thought of civil law as a science of society. But he would no longer limit his understanding of the Roman law to the dialectic method of the medieval commentators. Donald R. Kelley (Chapter 6) shows how Bodin's legal education was shaped by the new school of legal humanism of which the French had become the leading representatives. Exponents of the *mos gallicus* applied high philological technique to understand the original import, institutional setting, and social function of Roman legal rules. Some, disappointed by apparent incompleteness and lack of order in the inherited *Corpus Juris Civilis*, attempted to rework the system. Bodin, moreover, was among those who sought to expand the boundaries of jurisprudence even further. He early set out to create a system of public law that was not limited to Roman sources, but encompassed the best institutions of all known polities, past and present. This was a lifelong program, sketched out in Chapter 6 of the *Methodus* and developed at enormous length in the *République*. In his hopes of reducing this mass of material to some sort of system, Bodin resorted to the popular method of dichotomizing advanced by Peter Ramus, whose influence on Bodin is reviewed by Kenneth D. McRae (Chapter 4).

Political Economy

Closely connected to his theory of sovereignty are Bodin's views on taxation, which are at first surprising. Although he recognizes that the raising of new taxes is a form of legislation, which he presents as the most important prerogative of sovereignty, he holds in the *République* that even an absolute king cannot levy new taxes without the consent of the Estates. This, he maintains, follows from the law of nature, which enshrines the right of private property, and he finds the requirement of consent to be honored not only in England but in France, Spain, and every other proper monarchy. The only exception to this rule which he admits is an emergency so severe and sudden that the Estates cannot be assembled in time to address it. Martin Wolfe (Chapter 8), believes that this apparent contradiction in Bodin's theory of sovereignty was deliberate and that Bodin introduced it in order to promote popular willingness to support subsidies for Henry III. But it is more likely, I believe, that Bodin's main political concern was long term fiscal solvency. He still honored the medieval doctrine that a king should live off his own, that is, from the income of the royal domain. Making new taxation difficult, he may have thought, would put pressure on the crown to work toward redeeming its domain, many parts and incomes of which had been alienated.

In another essay (Franklin, Chapter 9), I have further argued that Bodin himself would have denied any inconsistency between his doctrine of consent to new taxation and his theory of sovereignty. He represented taxation as a taking of private property which was forbidden by the law of nature unless the proprietors consented. He was thus departing, mistakenly I think, from the received juridical tradition according to which the power to lay reasonable taxes is a necessity of government and an inherent part of its ordinary legislative power. If the state then, is an unmixed monarchy, the king is entitled to lay a reasonable tax without consent. Interestingly enough, the same mistake is to be found in Locke.

Bodin perhaps was tailoring his theory of sovereignty to fit his bold stand as a deputy of the third estate at Blois against agreeing to new taxation. Owen Ulph (Chapter 10), provides a full account of Bodin's strategy and tactics. He was adamantly opposed to the policy of repressing Protestant dissent and opposed a royal request for subsidies which everyone knew would be used to prosecute religious war. And when the king proposed instead to alienate yet more of the royal domain, Bodin led the Third Estate into opposition yet again.

Thus far we have been dealing more with law and fiscal policy than with economic theory. But there is one point of political economy on which Bodin made a notable and original contribution. In 1568 he advanced a quantity theory of money in order to explain the great French and European price inflation of the sixteenth century. The main cause, he argued, was not debasement of the coinage as was commonly maintained, but the importation of great quantities of precious metals into Europe from America which necessarily lowered the value of domestic coinage. A great deal of subtlety was required to make this connection as well as considerable ingenuity in illustrating it from the history of price movements in France. Denis P. O'Brien (Chapter 11), deals with the circumstances of Bodin's entry into the debate on this question, and points up both his originality and his sophistication.

Religion

The most remarkable of Bodin's works, and surely the most controversial in its time, is his *Colloquium of the Seven about Secrets of the Sublime* (*Colloquium Heptaplomeres de rerum sublimium arcanis subditis*). Completed around 1593, it was so heretical that Bodin dared not publish it in his lifetime. Indeed, no complete edition appeared until 1857, although manuscript copies were widely circulated in the scholarly underground during the seventeenth and eighteenth centuries. The text is a series of conversations among a natural theist, a skeptic, a Jew, a Muslim, a Catholic, a Lutheran, and a Zwinglian as to whether there is one true religion and if so how can it be recognized. Since each of the interlocutors finds no good reason to yield his grounds, they finally agree to disagree and separate in friendship. Bodin does not clearly identify himself with any of the seven positions and he apparently saw merits in all of them. But he seems to agree most of all with Judaism as the 'oldest' religion and the closest to the natural theism known to humans at the beginning.

This confrontation of religious diversity in the *Colloquium* is Bodin's own version of the religious universalism explored in the later Renaissance by adventurous intellectuals like Pico della Mirandola and Marsilio Ficino. Marion Leathers Daniels Kuntz, who published the first complete translation of the *Colloquium*, sets the historical context of this work in her essay entitled 'The *Colloquium Heptaplomeres* and the Sixteenth Century' (Chapter 12), and she also devotes a chapter to Bodin's theological views as does the essay by Christopher Baxter (Chapter 13). Neo-Platonism is a dominant theme in Bodin's religious views, and he is most strongly attracted to the Jewish neo-Platonist, Philo of Alexandria, who wrote around the end of the first century BCE.

The *Colloquium* not only documents Bodin's affinities to Judaism as his preferred form of monotheistic religion but most likely reflects an earlier conversion of some sort. The depth of his commitment to Judaism in the *Methodus*, in the *De la démonomanie des sorciers* (which deals with the detection and punishment of witches) and in the *Colloquium* is developed at length by Baxter. Maryanne Cline Horowitz (Chapter 14), brings all the evidence together to show that the case for Bodin's Judaism is strong. How, then, is Bodin's Judaizing related to his neo-Platonism? This is the issue taken up by Paul Lawrence Rose (Chapter 15), in his Introduction to *Bodin and the Great God of Nature: The Moral and Religious Universe of a Judaiser*. It is entitled 'The Enigma of Bodin's Religion'.

The universalism of the *Colloquium*, furthermore, is the final statement of continuing commitment to qualified religious toleration. In his earlier comments on this issue Bodin's stance on toleration seems strictly *politique* in that his decisive consideration for when toleration of religious dissent should be extended was the preservation of political cohesion rather than freedom of conscience. Toleration was a *pis aller* where a religious minority (like the Huguenots in France) was too strong to suppress without a civil war. But by the time of the *Colloquium* Bodin seems to have clothed this strictly political approach with a theological rationale. Sincere faith in any religion, he now maintained, was equally pleasing to God since all were variations on a common principle. Wise men could thus have no compunctions about worshiping the true God within the framework of the positive religion established in a given state. And if they did not challenge the established public worship, ordinary people would be likely to go along peacefully as well. This thesis, dealt with briefly in Baxter and Kuntz, is explored at length and related to other toleration doctrines of the time in Gary Remer's essay in Chapter 16, 'Dialogues of Toleration: Erasmus and Bodin'.

Humanist Method

The writers of the later Renaissance heavily depended on information and categories provided by the classics of antiquity which were then expanded by whatever sources they could get their hands on. Bodin, indeed, not only read prodigiously but made endless personal inquiries and interviews to inform himself on the political institutions of modern European and even Asian political traditions. Typical of humanist scholarship, his mode of research was to fill notebooks, or commonplace books, with odd bits of fact which were grouped together to support arguments the reader expected to use in the future. The aim of these collections was to achieve what Erasmus called *copia rerum,* or abundance of material, and Ann Blair has shown how Bodin uses this method of commonplace for his encyclopedic work on natural philosophy, the *Universae theatrum naturae* (*Theater of all nature*) which appeared in 1596. Her groundbreaking study of this work, and of Bodin's natural philosophy generally, is beyond our present focus. But Bodin recommends this method for all kinds of inquiry in the *Methodus*, which helps to explain the vastness and rather confused organization of the facts and opinions collected for his work on political and social science. Hence students of these areas of Bodin's thought will profit greatly from Blair's essay, 'Humanist Methods in Natural Philosophy: the Commonplace Book' (Chapter 17), which illustrates both the method of commonplaces and its limitations as a scientific procedure. I have also included, as Chapter 18, Blair's brief survey of Bodin's natural philosophy in intellectual history given in the 'Introduction' to her book, *The Theater of Nature: Jean Bodin and Renaissance Science.*

History

Bodin's interest in history is for the most part pragmatic. By amassing huge numbers of facts he hopes to discern general trends and even laws. The point of his *Methodus* is to show a potential reader of histories how to choose historians, how to evaluate them, how to draw profit from reading them, and the disciplines one has to know in order to appreciate their teachings. Among the principles he thinks a reader of histories should know is the influence of climate on the character of peoples and how it influences their political, religious, and cultural institutions. Bodin here is drawing on a long tradition of climatic and other geographic influences going back through the middle ages to Aristotle. But it has now been turned into a highly ambitious summary of customs and institutions throughout the world as Bodin knew it, and he anticipates Montesquieu in a number of his main ideas. The doctrine of climate is carried over pretty much unchanged from the *Methodus* to the *République* where even more evidence is assembled.

In the present day this approach to social science is no longer considered very helpful, and Bodin, writing in the sixteenth century, is often credulous as to facts as well as bizarre in conclusions. Bodin's ideas are perspiculously worked out by Marian J. Tooley (Chapter 20), who shows that Bodin's doctrine of climate was a collection and attempted synthesis of medieval ideas. The basic ideas of Bodin on climate and society are also briefly reviewed by John L. Brown in his essay entitled 'The Major Themes of the Methodus' (Chapter 19) which notes that the global patterns of climate were intended to indicate a world order of peoples, that is, a *respublica mundana* that was both political and economic. In the course of this essay, Brown also summarizes a number of themes on which Bodin is surprisingly original (if often erratic) – the idea of progress in the arts and sciences; the historical interpretation of myths, the use of philological evidence in studying history; and critical evaluation of various historians including Tacitus and Machiavelli.

Part I
Sovereignty

[1]

JEAN BODIN'S 'LOGIC OF SOVEREIGNTY'

J. U. LEWIS

University of Windsor, Ontario

I

IN our age people more often than not think of law as the 'command of a definite will or group of wills endowed with legitimate authority', and of the limits of law as being set by the volitions of men, expressed either formally in a constitution or by the 'unchartered limitations of public consent'.[1] This view is reflected in the 'authoritarian model of law',[2] and can be traced to the Roman dictum that 'the preference of the ruler is what has the force of law. . . .'[3] So widely is it accepted as an accurate and illuminating account of what law is that in some quarters, especially where analytical jurisprudence with its attendant disinterest in legal history holds sway,[4] the notion that legal authority is to be anchored to the obligation to command what *should* be commanded—that authority is to be exercised *sub lege*, as Bracton put it[5]—is thought to be incomprehensible. In many minds the phrase *sit pro voluntate ratio*, which explains that the sovereign's will must coincide with reason, is thought to have been wrongly quoted; that what one meant to say was *sit pro ratione voluntas*—the will of the sovereign takes the place of reason.[6]

The predominance of voluntaristic theories of law, however, is a relatively modern phenomenon. Indeed it was only with John Austin in the nineteenth century that the balance shifted decisively in favour of such theories.[7] For throughout the Middle Ages and well on up into the modern period the argument over whether law is an act of will or rule of reason was evenly fought.[8]

---

[1] E. Lewis, *Medieval Political Ideas* (London, 1954), p. 1.

[2] See A. P. d'Entreves, *The Notion of the State* (Oxford, 1967), Chap. 8.

[3] C. J. Friedrich, *Man and His Government: An Empirical Theory of Politics* (N.Y., 1963), p. 268.

[4] '. . . the lawyer's, or at any rate the English lawyer's, professional training tends to predispose him to look at the past from an unhistorical standpoint.' J. W. Gough, *Fundamental Law in English Constitutional History* (Oxford, 1961. 1st impression, 1955), p. 6.

[5] . . . *rex non debet esse sub homine sed sub Deo et sub lege, quia lex facit regem. De Legibus et Consuetudinibus Angliae*, I, 39.

[6] B. de Jouvenel, *Sovereignty* (Cambridge, 1957), pp. 209–11.

[7] Although of course the groundwork was laid earlier—e.g., by Hobbes. Cf. Jolowicz, *Lectures on Jurisprudence* (London, 1963), pp. 64 ff. on the beginnings of the idea of sovereignty in the Middle Ages.

[8] On the 'Eclipses and revivals' of natural law and its rival theories see A. Brecht, *Political Theory* (Princeton, 1959), pp. 138 ff. Cf. Davitt, *The Nature of Law* (London, 1953), Introduction, pp. 219 ff.

   Among the first thinkers in the modern era to grapple with the difficulties
inherent in this issue was the French lawyer and statesman, Jean Bodin,[1]
called 'the most powerful of French and perhaps all political thinkers of the
[sixteenth] century'.[2] There is some dispute as to how great his theoretical
innovations actually were, but a balanced assessment seems to be that in his
major work, *The Six Books of the Commonweale*, the thesis that the king is
above man-made law was for the first time fully and—although there is
dispute about this, too—systematically developed.[3] Some 'civilians'[4] and
even some theologians between the ninth and thirteenth centuries[5] had, it is
true, also said that law was the expression of a superior will; but in A. J.
Carlyle's words, 'we think it may properly be said' that Bodin's treatment of
the matter 'represents a much deeper and more dogmatic enunciation of the
conception' of sovereignty than had before been given.[6] The idea of sovereignty was not new; but what Bodin did to and with it was. His work was at
once the 'culmination of the claims of "imperialist" writers throughout the
Middle Ages who had sought to vindicate the position of the secular ruler
as independent of ecclesiastical authority'[7] and also the place in which the
idea of sovereignty was lifted out of the 'limbo of theology in which the
theory of divine right left it'[8] and placed within the context of secular constitutional theory.[9] Perhaps the closest any thinker came to Bodin in this
respect was Marsiglio of Padua, referred to by Clement VI as the 'worst

---

[1] For biographical data see K. D. McRae's introduction to *The Six Bookes of the Commonweale* (facsimile reprint of the English trans. of 1606, corrected and supplemented by comparison
with the French and Latin editions. Cambridge, Mass., 1962). Cf. Franklin, *Jean Bodin and the
16th-Century Revolution in the Methodology of Law and History* (N.Y., 1963), 1 ff.; and J. W.
Allen, *A History of Political Thought in the Sixteenth Century* (N.Y., 1960 (Univ. Paperbacks);
1st edn., 1928), pp. 394–9. The McRae edition is used throughout this paper with spelling and
syntax, except occasionally, modernized in passages quoted.

[2] Allen, op. cit., p. 394. Figgis ranks him behind Machiavelli. *Studies in Political Thought*
(Cambridge, 1923, 1st edn., 1907), p. 110.

[3] Allen thinks there is 'vast confusion' in Bodin's work. See his 'Jean Bodin' in F. J. C. Hearnshaw (ed.) *The Social and Political Ideas of Some Great Thinkers of the Sixteenth and Seventeenth
Centuries* (London, 1926), p. 42. Cf. Gough, op. cit., p. 403: Aristotle influenced the plan of the
earlier parts of the *Six Books* 'so far as there is one'.

[4] See G. L. Mosse, 'The Influence of Jean Bodin's *Republique* on English Political Thought',
Medievalia et Humanistica, Vol. 5 (1948), pp. 73–83. Cf. Franklin, op. cit., pp. 1 ff., 18 f., 33 ff.;
McRae, A3 ff.; A. J. (and R. W.) Carlyle, *A History of Mediaeval Political Theory in the West*
(London, 1936), pp. 6 and 417 ff.

[5] Davitt, op. cit., Pt. I.

[6] Carlyle, op. cit., pp. 419 f.; McRae, A3.

[7] Friedrich, op. cit., p. 549.

[8] Sabine, *A History of Political Theory* (London, 1963. 3rd edn.), p. 399. D'Entreves seems to
disagree: 'By the end of the Middle Ages the notion of the full independence of individual states
was almost universally accepted. . . . There lacked only a name to indicate clearly this conjunction of territorial and national independence with supreme power. The merit of having coined
that name belongs to Jean Bodin.' Op. cit., p. 99.

[9] Cf. McRae: 'It was he who first defined the state . . . in a way that was unmistakenly modern.
. . . Unlike previous theorists, Bodin made authority the central feature of his entire system of
politics.' A14.

heretic' he had ever read.[1] In his work were to be found all the elements of a theory of sovereignty; but the theory itself was lacking. Bodin provided it.[2]

The fundamental importance of Bodin's work to political and legal theory becomes apparent once it is understood that the chief difference between the modern and contemporary world of law on the one hand and the ancient and medieval systems on the other is the modern emphasis on legislation rather than custom as the chief source of law.[3] For as long as law was thought of primarily in terms of custom the question of authority was not a pressing one; the nature and function of the maker of law hardly arose. Custom is simply a 'rule or habit of action which is in fact used or observed . . . by some body or class of persons',[4] and it may in some cases stretch back beyond 'legal memory', beyond the time before which the memory of the law does not reach—which as far as Anglo-American law is concerned is 3 September 1189.[5]

When legislation becomes the core of a legal system, however, the situation changes radically. For legislation is 'that source of law which consists in the declaration of legal rules by a competent authority';[6] and with its use there arise the questions as to what constitutes 'authority' and what if any limitations are to be put upon it. Such questions comprise what Bertrand de Jouvenel calls the problem of 'the content and substance of decisions couched in the imperative'.[7] It is the problem of the nature and scope of sovereignty.[8]

A consideration of the nature of sovereignty and its relation to law and legal obligation must for two reasons begin with the thought of Jean Bodin. First, and from an historical standpoint, he claimed, 'probably with justice', as McIlwain says,[9] to have been the first man to understand it in terms of its

[1] Lewis, op. cit., p. 30. Another writer, Sir Thomas Smith, whose *De Republica Anglorum* was thought by Maitland and Pollock to be stressing a doctrine of sovereignty similar to Bodin's, actually was not. For the reasons, see Gough, op. cit., pp. 7–9.

[2] Lewis, loc. cit.

[3] D'Entreves, op. cit., pp. 89 and 93. Cf. Pound, *Jurisprudence* (St. Paul, 1959), Vol. I, pp. 62–109, esp. pp. 74 f.

[4] Pollock, 'The Nature and Meaning of Law', *Jurisprudence and Legal Essays*, A. L. Goodhart, ed. and intro. (London, 1963), p. 5.

[5] The coronation of Richard I. See Holdsworth, *Some Makers of English Law* (Cambridge, 1966. 1st edn. 1938), p. 8.

[6] *Salmond on Jurisprudence*, Fitzgerald edition (London, 1966), p. 115. This definition is not without difficulties. See Parker's edition of Salmond (1937), pp. 207 ff. But if it is further added here that whereas legislation consists of the formulation of rules for the future, adjudication determines how those rules are to be applied, it holds good. See, e.g., *Eastern Oil Refining Co. v. Court of Burgesses of Wallingford* 130 Conn. 606, 36 A2d 586 (1944); *State v. Huber* 129 W. Va. 198, 40 S.E. 2d 11, 18 (1946).

[7] Op. cit., p. 169.

[8] Sovereignty can be defined as 'that public authority which directs or orders what is to be done by each member associated, in relation to the end of the association'. *Cherokee Nation v. Southern Kansas R. Co.* 33 Fed. 900,906 (C.C.W.D. Ark. 1888).

[9] McIlwain, 'Sovereignty in the Present World', *History* (N.S.), Feb. and June, 1950, pp. 1 and 2.

legislative function.[1] Secondly, and with an eye to the theoretical problems inherent in the notion of sovereignty itself, Bodin attempts to overcome the dilemma that arises when the idea that lawmaking implies the existence of an authority that can establish law by its will clashes with the further idea that arbitrary sovereignty has no place in law.[2] The task undoubtedly caused him considerable strain, and Professor Allen was correct when he remarked that if 'you read certain modern writers you might suppose that Bodin's theory of sovereignty is a tolerably simple thing; you will not think so if you read Bodin'.[3] But the very difficulty met in seeking to understand his thought holds, in an odd way, a certain promise. To paraphrase H. L. A. Hart's 'tribute' to Austin, if he is wrong, the demonstration of where and why can prove to be a source of illumination.

In our own day political theorists have given various interpretations of Bodin's work. To some he seems to assert a doctrine of popular sovereignty, to others he is portrayed as a champion of monarchic absolutism.[4] But regardless of which way his work is read it is unanimously criticized as being internally inconsistent. His logic of sovereignty is said to be faulty, for he places limitations on the sovereign's power. Legal historians, too, have read his work; and the majority of them regard him as the well-spring of the tradition in law that flows through Hobbes and Austin to contemporary legal positivism and analytical jurisprudence.[5]

A purpose of this paper will be to examine these assessments of Bodin's thought. But before his logic of sovereignty can be tested its frame of reference must be understood.

II

The central theme in Bodin's *Six Books of the Commonweale*, to which everything he says contributes, is summed up in the following text:

We see . . . in the end of all edicts and laws these words, *Quia sic nobis placuit*, Because it hath so pleased us: to give us to understand that the laws of a sovereign

---

[1] Legal sovereignty, says Bryce, is the 'ultimate authority to make law'. He distinguishes it from political sovereignty, which is the ability to enforce obedience. *Studies in History and Jurisprudence* (London, 1901), Vol. II, pp. 505 f. The difficulties inherent in thinking of legal sovereignty independently of political sovereignty are not easily overcome. See H. W. R. Wade, 'The Basis of Legal Sovereignty', *Cambridge Law J.* (1955), pp. 172–97.

[2] The only 'real difficulty' connected with the topic of sovereignty, says Salmond, centres on the 'illimitable nature of legislative power'. *The First Principles of Jurisprudence* (London, 1893), p. 229.

[3] 'Jean Bodin' in Hearnshaw, op. cit., p. 44. In spite of the many references writers make to him, McRae writes, 'the scholar who has actually read Bodin is rare indeed'. A25.

[4] Allen, *Political Thought*, p. 443.

[5] E.g., Wu, *Jurisprudence* (St. Paul, 1958), p. 170; Brecht, op. cit., p. 183; Friedrich, op. cit., p. 552; Allen, 'Jean Bodin,' p. 49 f.; (but cf. 59 and *Political Thought*, p. 422); Lewis, op. cit., p. 30 f.

prince, although they be grounded upon good and lively reasons, depend never-theless upon nothing but his mere and frank good will.[1]

In such words historians of political theory see a breakdown of Bodin's logic of sovereignty: he appears in an inherently contradictory way to be saying both that law originates in the sovereign's will and also that it is dependent upon 'good' or right reason—almost as if he cannot decide in his own mind whether to side with Machiavelli or Sir Edward Coke.[2] Legal historians, on the other hand, have focused on the voluntaristic side of Bodin's doctrine of sovereignty, holding that all else he says is to be under-stood in its light.

When one reads Bodin's statement that anarchy is 'worse than the harshest tyranny in the world',[3] however, doubts about such interpretations of his thought are planted. For when it is recalled that Bodin's purpose in writing the *Six Books* was the essentially practical one of saving the French 'ship of state' from sinking,[4] it appears too facile to interpret his work in terms of concepts made second-nature to us by the overwhelming influences of legal positivism and power politics. And the doubts once planted begin to grow when it is discovered that Bodin's definitions of concepts such as 'sover-eignty', 'commonweale', and 'law' are, technically, definitions constructed in terms of final causality. A definition, he says, 'is nothing else than the very end and scope of the matter propounded. . .; he that knows not the end of the matter. . . is as far from hope of attaining thereunto as he is from hitting the mark who shoots at random'.[5] In other words, an understanding of what Bodin meant by 'sovereignty' and 'law' demands an understanding of what he thought the purpose of a sovereign ruler to be in the making of laws.

It is apparent from what we have so far seen Bodin say that he is inviting us to examine his basic view of reality. And unless we are prepared to accept the invitation we shall neither find the context that he himself has provided for his logic of sovereignty nor will we escape the fault of anachronistically interpreting that logic in nineteenth- and twentieth-century terms. Many today think of the universe as a whole as being comprised of closed, essenti-ally disordered, individual entities that are ordered and brought into inter-action with one another only by means of external forces.[6] This view constitutes the primal assumption operative in contemporary political and

[1] 92F.
[2] Some of the ways in which this indecision manifests itself are revealed by Allen in his con-cluding critique of Bodin's work, in 'Jean Bodin', pp. 49 f.
[3] A70 (in Preface to the first French edition).
[4] A69. See Franklin, op. cit., pp. 40 ff.   [5] 1B–D.
[6] See Merz, *A History of European Thought in the 19th Century* (Edinburgh, 1923, 4th edn.), Vol. I, p. 89; Hayek, *The Counter-Revolution of Science* (Glencoe, Ill., 1952), p. 207. Cf. Wild, 'Discussion: A Reply to Mr. Gale', *Philosophy and Phenomenological Research*, Vol. 21 (3); Frank, *The Philosophy of Science* (Englewood Cliffs, N.Y., 1958), p. 301.

legal theory.[1] But Bodin's world was not in any way like this, as his very terminology shows. 'The Great God of nature', he writes, 'harmonically composed this world [out] of matter and form, of which the one is maintained by the help of the other, and that by the proportion of equality and similitude combined and bound together'.[2] God is the 'most wise workman';[3] and he has so ordered the parts of the universe that every part is *intrinsically* ordered to every other, beginning from the 'celestial Spheres around which the planets move down to the earth, upon which the soil is joined to stones (by clay), stones to plants (by coral, which is a "stony plant"), plants to brute animals (by "Plantbeasts, which have feeling and emotion but yet take life by the roots") and brutes to men (by monkeys—"except we shall agree with Plato, who placed a woman in the middle between a man and a beast").[4] Men, be it noted, are slightly lower than the angels, being 'in part mortal and in part immortal'.[5]

Bodin places this view of reality at the very end of the *Six Books of the Commonweale*. It is also found in the Preface to the first French edition,[6] where in addition, the relation between his world-view and the nature of sovereignty and the purpose of law are treated in the outline that the remainder of the *Six Books* fills in:

> . . . just as the bond of nature . . . rules over the angels, so the angels rule over men, men over beasts, the soul over the body, Heaven over the earth, and reason over the appetites; so that whatever is less fitted to rule may be directed and guided by that which can protect and preserve it, in return for its obedience. . . .[7]

As might be expected, now, Bodin holds that society is natural to men, a position it might be noted, that serves to distinguish him sharply from Hobbes.[8] When God 'ingrafted reason in us [he] made men desirous of the company and society of man. . . .'[9] And, startlingly perhaps, what holds men together in society is love. It is 'the only foundation of all human and civil society, and much more requisite for the keeping and maintaining thereof than justice itself. . . .'[10] Bodin complements this understanding of the nature of society when he turns to consider the 'true end' of individual men. That end, he says, consists in contemplation, in knowing all things natural, human, and divine—and in referring that knowledge back unto God.[11] Thus in keeping with early Christian and medieval thought, but in

---

[1] Most especially in political and legal 'realism'. See K. Olivecrona, 'The Imperative Element in the Law', *Rutgers Law Review*, Vol. 12 (1964), p. 794. This assumption is given critical attention in M. Rooney, *Lawlessness, Law, and Sanction* (Washington, D.C., 1937).

[2] 792H.   [3] 792K.   [4] 792K–793B.   [5] 793C.

[6] The Preface to the second French edition, which is a letter to Gui du Faur and dated 29 Sept. 1577/8, does not deal with this topic. Nor does the Preface to the Latin editions, which deals with formal rather than substantive matters.   [7] A69.

[8] For Hobbes, '*Homo . . . non modo corpus naturale est, sed etiam civitatis, id est (ut ita loquar) corporis politici pars.*' *De homine*, Dedication. Cf. *Leviathan*, Chap. 37; *Elements of Law*, Dedication.   [9] 361D.   [10] 363E; cf. 363A–B.   [11] 4F.

sharp contrast to later modern and contemporary tendencies, the notions of 'society' and 'person' are seen by Bodin as correlative:

If we . . . confess [contemplation referred to God] to be the principal end of the most happy life of everyone in particular, we conclude that this is the felicity and end also of a Commonweale.[1]

There is, says Bodin, 'no difference between a good man and a good citizen . . .'.[2]

The context for Bodin's treatment of sovereignty is completed, finally, by one last point. It is that while all men have as their end the attainment of that happiness that comes from knowing God through his works, some among them have the special charge of being God's 'lieutenants'.[3] These are the kings and sovereign princes. Because their task is to serve 'the welfare of other men' while remaining, next unto God, 'greater or higher' than all other men, Bodin calls them 'images of God'.[4] With him, we next 'consider their majesty and power'.

III

Up to now Bodin's thought seems to be perfectly reflected in de Jouvenel's statement that it is essential that authority be 'independent of every human will, so that it may render complete obedience to reason alone. [For] it is the degree of its submission to reason which justifies the degree of its authority over men'.[5] Indeed, nothing we have seen him say so far vindicates Sabine's assertion that Bodin's concept of sovereignty 'logically places social, ethical, and religious relationships outside the bounds of political theory'.[6] For not only does Bodin explicity lash out against Machiavelli for 'supposing the state could exist without a moral basis and without religion'[7] but, and even more strongly, in Book I, chapter eight of the *Six Books* he writes that the greatest of all the Canonists, Innocent IV, had a profound understanding of the nature of sovereignty.[8] If one were to eliminate from Bodin's thought 'all his references to God, and its Princes as the lieutenants of God', thinks Allen,[9] 'the whole structure will stand unaltered'. More accurate, however, seems to be his statement in another place that a 'concept of sovereignty as actually creating right would have seemed to [Bodin] an atheistic blasphemy'.[10]

Clearly, then, the view that Bodin belongs at the beginning of the Hobbesian–Austinian tradition of political and legal theory needs reassessment. The elimination by some critics of his references to God and moral

---

[1] 4F. [2] 4H. [3] 153B. [4] 155E.
[5] Op. cit., p. 210. [6] Op. cit., p. 405.
[7] Allen, *Political Thought*, p. 402. [8] Cf. Figgis, op. cit., p. 110.
[9] *Political Thought*, p. 415 f. [10] 'Jean Bodin', p. 59.

J. U. LEWIS   213

values in the attempt to add the quality of consistency thought to be lacking in his logic of sovereignty does him an injustice. It is also unnecessary. His logic, as he developed it, has its own consistency.

In order to appreciate this point, two things need to be understood. The first is that Bodin's purpose in developing his political theory was, as mentioned above, a practical one. He was a *Politique,* an advocate of and fighter for tolerance of all sorts, especially for religious tolerance,[1] a 'practical inquirer into the political sickness of his time'.[2] As a *Politique* he 'saw in the royal power the mainstay of peace and order and . . . sought to raise the king, as the centre of national unity, above all religious sects and political parties'.[3] This point accounts almost entirely for his 'new' emphasis on sovereignty in political and legal theory.

The second point prerequisite to an understanding of Bodin's logic of sovereignty is this. Because he defines sovereignty as the 'most high, absolute, and perpetual power over the citizens and subjects of a Commonweale',[4] it is obvious from the outset that the limitations he places upon it cannot be found within the concept itself. If, therefore, one is to understand how he could place limitations upon the sovereign's power without contradicting himself, he must examine the way in which Bodin refers that power to the ends for which it, and the state as well, exist. And although it has been said that Bodin 'had no clear theory of the end of the state',[5] the result being a 'serious deficiency in his system',[6] his definition of the Commonweale as the 'right government of many families and of the things common amongst them',[7] and his statement that the contemplation of God, which is the 'principal end of the happy life of everyone in particular . . . and also of a Commonweale',[8] are surely clear enough. In their light, and viewed in terms of Bodin's practical concern to find a principle of unity that can hold together the ship of State and guarantee to its members a sufficient measure of religious freedom,[9] the following text can be seen to be a summary of his entire logic of sovereignty: '. . . nothing upon earth is greater or higher, next unto God, than the majesty of kings and sovereign princes, for they are . . . created his lieutenants for the welfare of other men'.[10]

Sovereignty constituted by majesty (*Maiestatem; Segnoria*),[11] limitations determined by purpose. Both are real to Bodin; and each plays a role in his thought. Thus, to weaken or ignore the ruler's sovereignty is to be left with the 'ill-digested opinion . . . that the prince is subject to his laws, . . . a thing

---

[1] Franklin, op. cit., p. 40 f.; McRae, A9 ff. But see below, n. 9.

[2] Laski, *The Foundations of Sovereignty* (London, 1921), p. 19.

[3] Sabine, op. cit., p. 399.   [4] 84H.

[5] Sabine, op. cit., p. 402.   [6] Ibid., p. 403.   [7] 84I.   [8] 4F.

[9] Atheists and comedians, however, were discriminated against by Bodin who assigned to them a Censor. Atheism, of course, weakened reverence to God, while comedians were the apprentices of 'all imprudence, looseness, whoredom, deceit. . . .' 644–6.

[10] 153B.   [11] 84H, 157E–158F; cf. McRae's Introduction, A15.

impossible by nature'. But, on the other hand, to exclude the notion of limitation upon that sovereignty is to confuse 'civil laws with the laws of nature, and of both jointly with the laws of God' so as to suppose that when the 'prince forbids killing or stealing or adultery that these are the prince's laws'.[1] And 'if we say that only he has absolute power who is subject to no law, then there is no sovereign prince in the world, seeing that all the princes of the earth are subject unto the laws of God, of nature, and of nations'.[2]

In order to see now exactly how and on what basis Bodin reconciles sovereignty with its limitations it is necessary to turn to his notion of law. For although his treatment of it seems incidental to the central aims of the *Six Books of the Commonweale*,[3] it is nevertheless in the things he says about law that his logic of sovereignty gains its vindication. Through a consideration of the definition of law it becomes clear that the limitations he places upon sovereignty are neither external nor non-essential, but serve intrinsically to complete it.[4]

IV

The chief reason why it is difficult for many writers to settle upon Bodin's place in the history of political and legal theory is that they treat his definition of law in Austinian, or at least positivistic, terms[5]—as if he defines law solely in terms of its source. The authority for this is taken to be Bodin's own assertion that 'law is nothing other than the commandment of a sovereign, using his sovereign power'.[6] Thus Arnold Brecht says that legal positivism in the sense of a 'theory that only those norms are juridically valid which have been established or recognized by the government of a sovereign state ... was inaugurated by Jean Bodin'.[7] Wu traces a direct line from Bodin to Hobbes to Austin,[8] as does E. Lewis.[9] Professor Gough writes that even Maitland and Sir Frederick Pollock took the same position.[10] Holdsworth adopts it as well.[11]

[1] 717B–C.   [2] 90I–K.

[3] There are two arguments for this view. (1) Bodin nowhere explicitly analyses the concept of law but simply sets down definitions. (2) When he does define law he does so in both value-free (108I) and value-laden (156H) terms, without, however, seeking to reconcile them.

[4] The need to look at his definition of law in order to understand his theory of sovereignty is clear from the definition of sovereignty itself, which is the 'power to give laws to all subjects without the consent of any. . . .' (159E, 161B). All other marks of sovereignty flow from this power. See 159E–180K.

[5] The failure to distinguish between legal positivism and analytical jurisprudence serves to increase the difficulty of determining Bodin's place in the history of legal and political thought. On that distinction and for an accurate description of each, see Hart, 'Positivism and the Separation of Law and Morals', *Harvard L. R.*, Vol. 71 (1958), p. 593, and Shuman, *Legal Positivism* (Detroit, 1963), pp. 12 ff.

[6] 108I–K; cf. 325E, 7–8.   [7] Op. cit., p. 183.

[8] Op. cit., p. 169 f.   [9] Op. cit., p. 31.

[10] Op. cit., p. 7.   [11] *A History of English Law* (London, 1924), Vol. IV, p. 196.

Now it is true that both Bodin and Austin define law as the command of a sovereign. But to take the wordings of their definitions by themselves is misleading. In the first place the two men wrote in different ages and with different aims in mind; and to lift Bodin's definition from its context and set it alongside Austin's is anachronistic. Secondly, whereas Austin's jurisprudence is professedly analytical in a technical sense, Bodin's *Six Books of the Commonweale* is not. Austin consciously wanted to delimit his definition of law to positive, man-made law; Bodin had no such thought. And while Austin purposely drove a wedge between his definition of law and the domain of morality, Bodin in one place defines law in terms of moral values. This is the definition overlooked or omitted by those who make Bodin a charter member of the schools of legal positivism and analytical jurisprudence; but it perhaps more surely than the definition quoted above mirrors his ideas about the relation between law and sovereignty. 'Law', he says in Book One of the *Six Books*, is the '*right* command of him, or them, which have sovereign power above others, without exception of person'.[1] That word, 'right', calls for a reconsideration of the thesis that Bodin is a positivist. For it signals to his readers that if they are to understand his definition of law and the relation it has to his concept of sovereignty, they will have to investigate not only what he says about the source of law but what he says about its end as well.

In Bodin's view the end of law is to secure order in the Commonweale.[2] He even goes so far as to say that it is 'better to have an evil Commonweale than none at all'.[3] But order, for Bodin, means justice;[4] and thus 'the first and chief law of all Commonweales is, The welfare of the people. . . .'[5] This is a medieval notion if ever there was one. Even more: it lies at the heart of all natural law theory; and Professor Gough puts the matter exactly when he says that for writers such as Bodin 'conformity with natural law was one of the recognized marks of the virtuous or constitutional ruler'.[6]

It was Bodin's conception of natural law that gave rise to the two restrictions that he places upon the sovereign's power. These are the *leges imperii*, or 'fundamental laws',[7] that bind the royal prerogative. According to the first, the sovereign must keep his promises to his subjects; for faith in him is the key to social order. The second restriction is that the property of private citizens is beyond the sovereign's reach. Even the power to tax needs their

---

[1] 156H. The entire definition is italicized in McRae.

[2] E.g., 316H–I, 364F, 503D.   [3] 469D.

[4] 500F–I, 501D f. The definition of justice is at 755C, line 9: 'The right division of rewards and punishments, and of that which of right unto every man belongeth.'

[5] 471A.   [6] Op. cit., p. 53.

[7] On the character of 'fundamental laws' in the sixteenth and seventeenth-centuries see Wormuth, *The Royal Prerogative* (Ithaca, N.Y., 1939), pp. 31–41.

consent[1]—a thoroughly modern view.[2] Thus he says that sovereigns are 'more stringently bound by divine and natural law than those subject to their rule'.[3] And when he adds that 'nearly all the masters of legal science have taught the contrary', it truly becomes difficult to see what connection his doctrine has to those of Hobbes or Austin. Professor Allen sums up the matter as follows:

To say that Bodin's main contribution to political thought was his conception of a sovereignty, absolute and unlimited, . . . is at once ambiguous and inaccurate. It is not true that [he] conceived of sovereignty as an unlimited right. . . . It existed only to subserve the ends for which the state existed. . . . He thought of all political sovereignty as necessarily and absolutely limited by the law of nature, the measure of which was the common consciousness of right and wrong. . . . [It] is wrong to obey [the sovereign] if he commands an injustice.[4]

It is only when Bodin looks at law from the standpoint of the authority that makes it does his doctrine appear to be positivistic. Yet in light of what we have seen him say about the end of law, the argument that because legal positivists emphasize the source rather than the content of law in determining its validity and because Bodin follows this course that therefore he is a legal positivist seems ill-conceived. For as noted above, his purpose in emphasizing the source of law is the extra-legal one of trying to steady the ship of State. This he does, however, without excluding considerations of the law's content, which, he insists, must be justice. Thus, although he says that law is a command of the sovereign, he also says, over and over, that sovereignty is limited. After all, even Aquinas says that the 'ability to compel is possessed by [the one] who has the right to inflict penalties (in the case of non-observance) and for this reason he alone can make laws'.[5] Yet Aquinas is hardly a positivist.

The important question, then, is whether sovereign rule is the sole criterion of legal validity. And just as it is not for Aquinas, neither is it for Bodin; both share the view that the ruler is sovereign only in the human sphere. Even in this instance, however, the ruler is sovereign only under God. What Bodin did want to emphasize, though, perhaps more than did Aquinas, was that, in his sphere, the ruler *was* sovereign. And although it may be intellectually embarrassing in our age of nation-States, in which it is assumed that law and morality are not only distinct but divorced, to think of legal sovereignty as limited, to Bodin the logic seemed consistent and, even, necessitated. Natural law was not in his mind the vague, unintelligible 'moral obligation' of today but the manifestation to men of God's will. Bodin's

[1] Bk. I, Chap. 8.

[2] In disputes with the government over taxation the citizen is favoured. See, e.g., 12 *U.S. Digest*, p. 679 at 'g'.

[3] A71 (Preface).   [4] *Political Thought*, 422.

[5] *Summa Theol.* 1–2, 90, 3. Cf. 92, 2, ad. 3; 2–2, 64, 3.

logic can thus be thought faulty only if the judgment that God exists is denied and if that denial is then read into his work. But then the concept of sovereignty itself becomes, in the peculiar phraseology of the nineteenth century, 'he who is competent to determine his own competence',[1] and limitations upon sovereignty become legal fictions.[2] Without the sorts of limitations upon sovereignty argued for by Bodin, however, political rule ceases to be a matter of law or of right, and its actual existence, whether induced by consent or force, comes to depend upon 'the mere physical fact of mastery'.[3]

But even granting that Bodin's logic of sovereignty be consistent, even assuming that he may have successfully reconciled the idea of sovereign rule with the notion that sovereignty has limitations, there still remains the question of why, in his mind, men have an obligation to obey the laws that the sovereign sets down. Does that obligation arise from the fact that the sovereign has made those laws?, or from the fact that the laws he has made are just? To put the question another way, does Bodin say that the foundation of legal obligation is the content, or the source, of laws?

V

From the very first page of the *Six Books of the Commonweale* it appears that Bodin locates the source of men's obligation to law in its content, in the justice that law embodies. A commonweale, he says, is a 'lawful government', and 'lawful' is equated with 'rightful'.[4] 'Right' in turn means in this context 'according to the laws of nature',[5] and upon this meaning rests Bodin's distinction between a king and a tyrant:

... a king conforms himself unto the laws of nature, which the tyrant at his pleasure treads under foot: the one respects religion, justice, faith; whereas the other regards neither God, faith, nor law: the one ... refers all his actions to the good of the Commonweale ...; whereas the other respects nothing more than his own particular profit, revenge, or pleasure. ... [6]

And again: 'it is not the law that makes the just and rightful government, but the true administration of justice. ...'[7]

Within the context of these statements it would seem necessary to say that the notion, expressed by Bodin himself, that a sovereign ruler is 'not subject to any law'[8] is only half complete and therefore misleading. And so it is; for Bodin also says that the sovereign must account to God and the laws of nature.[9] He cannot change those higher laws;[10] and so, Bodin writes, quoting

---

[1] Friedrich cites Jellinek in this regard, op. cit., p. 552, n. 13.
[2] See Wade, op. cit.   [3] McIlwain, op. cit., p. 9.
[4] 1B–D; cf. 84I–85E.   [5] 3A.   [6] 212F–213C.
[7] 243E.   [8] 88K.   [9] 86H, 89B–C.   [10] 104I.

Seneca with approval, when 'all things are lawful unto Caesar, even for that are they less lawful'.[1] The test of lawfulness, then, and of men's consequent obligation to obey the sovereign's commands seem to depend upon whether those commands are in accord with justice and 'reasonableness'.[2]

If this were the sum of Bodin's remarks about the nature of legal obligation his work would more properly belong to the tradition of a writer such as Sir Edward Coke rather than to that of Hobbes and Austin. But mixed in with those remarks, even at times side by side with them, are statements that appear to ground legal obligation primarily in the sovereign's will. For social and political order rather than justice is given a priority all through the *Six Books*; and there is nothing that can secure these so much as a strong will. This is why, as we have seen him say, Bodin prefers a tyranny to no rule at all, and why he even insists that though a sovereign be a tyrant he is still nevertheless a sovereign.[3]

Bodin's answer to the question about why men are obligated to obey laws is thus a disjointed one. Even he, says Professor Laski, seemed to be aware of this himself.[4] But to say that his answer is disjointed is not to say that it is confusing. A central thesis of this paper has been that Bodin's logic of sovereignty is sound; that there is nothing inconsistent in his view that a lawgiver is both sovereign and limited. Even God, he says, is bound by his promises,[5] and it is far from objectionable that Bodin should have attempted to hold on to the concept of authority while maintaining the proposition that the content of law should be expressive of justice in his attempt to explain why men are bound to obey their sovereign's commands.

It was in the attempt to bring these notions together, however, that Bodin seems to have failed. In saying this we have come full circle, for this point is best shown in the text with which we began our consideration of his doctrine of sovereignty.[6] That text bears repeating:

We see . . . at the end of all edicts and laws these words, *Quia sic nobis placuit*, Because it hath so pleased us: to give us to understand that the laws of a sovereign prince, although they be grounded in good and lively reasons, depend nevertheless upon nothing but his mere and frank good will.[7]

Bodin does, it is true, go on to reiterate the position that the ruler is bound by the 'laws of God and nature', but the split between the sovereign bound only by God and his subjects bound by his 'mere and frank good will' remains nevertheless. The sovereign's subjects, Bodin insists, are bound by his laws even though he be a tyrant: 'to proceed against him by way of justice, the subject has no such jurisdiction over his Sovereign prince, upon

---

[1] 104H.   [2] On reasonableness as a test of the law's validity, see 92I–K.
[3] 87E, 200G.   [4] Op. cit., p. 18.   [5] 107B.
[6] See page 209, above.   [7] 92F.

whom depends all power and authority to command'.[1] The disunity in such doctrine is no where better expressed than in Bodin's own statement that the sovereign's magistrate ought to 'discharge his conscience towards God, his duty towards his prince'.[2]

In his attempt to overcome the disjointed character of this theory of obligation Bodin provided a principle that could be said to bridge—although not, perhaps, to close—the gap that finds the sovereign, with his obligations to 'higher' law, on the one side and his subjects' obligations to his 'mere will' on the other. That principle, made much of by the Greeks and found, Bodin thinks, in Scripture as well, is this, that the sovereign should possess practical wisdom, or prudence. Nor is it simply that it would be expedient that he should possess this virtue. Human nature demands it. Bodin's reasoning is as follows.[3] 'Natural liberty is such', he says, that a man is not to be subject to anyone except God, nor to be under the command of any other than himself, that is to say, of his reason, which is to be 'always conformable unto the will of God'. This 'natural commandment of reason[4] . . . is the first, the greatest and most ancient that is: for before one can well command others he must first learn to command himself, giving unto Reason the sovereignty of command, and . . . his affections obedience' to it. The ruler, in sum, 'ought to refer all his judgments [to] . . . equity, religion or wisdom',[5] and to this end ought to have a counsellor to guide him.[6] The law does not 'make good Princes . . . in a Commonweale . . .; but [rather] upright reason and justice, engraven in the minds and souls of just Princes. . . .'[7]

With his notion that legal and political sovereignty is truly manifested only in the person of a wise and therefore just ruler, Bodin has clearly found a principle wide enough to allow him coherently to apply his understanding of the nature of obligation to both ruler and ruled. The wise sovereign occupies the centre tier in Bodin's model of the universal political hierarchy, rendering his obedience upwards to God and yet commanding the obedience of his subjects who are understood to be related to God through him. But the significance of this picture is not to be found in its symmetry. Bodin is firmly convinced that the general run of men are either incapable of practical wisdom or else are corrupt in practical affairs, possessing only cleverness instead.[8] Consequently, if the Commonweale is to have any hope at all of attaining and keeping order and justice, the ruler must be wise; for the wise man is 'the measure of right and wrong. . . .'[9] The man who 'speaks evil of his prince', therefore, 'does injury unto the majesty of God himself. . . .'[10]

---

[1] 222H. Even God accepts tyranny, he says. 223C–E.   [2] 325A.   [3] 14I–K.
[4] Reason is equated with the 'very light of nature' at 47B.
[5] 767E; cf. 257B: '. . . political wisdom should ever be joined with faith and justice'.
[6] 256G–K.   [7] 244G.
[8] This is strongly brought out in Bodin's treatment of the question of whether a magistrate should give up his post rather than follow a command he thinks to be unjust. 316H–I.
[9] 4H.   [10] 153B.

In view of this doctrine it becomes clear that the theory of obligation that Bodin formulated is internally consistent and in keeping with the order of the universe as he understood it only because of his insistence that the sovereign must be a wise and just ruler. It is because power is limited, not in spite of it, that his logic of sovereignty hangs together. Without the limitations not only it but his entire world-view would collapse. These could be removed, of course, and were—by Hobbes. But to point this out is not to imply that Bodin began a line of thought that Hobbes completed; it is to affirm, rather, that the two thinkers belong to altogether different, and incompatible, traditions.

VI

Bodin has been depicted in this study as one who sought to define law in terms not only of its source but of its content as well, and who defended the thesis that the concepts of justice and prudence are indispensable to the task of harmonizing the apparently incompatible notions that, while the sovereign's subjects owe their political and legal obedience only to his 'mere will', the sovereign on the other hand owes obedience to none but 'God and the laws of nature'. When read this way the proposition that Bodin originated a line of thought that was only modified by writers such as Hobbes and Austin is misleading at best. For although segments of his work can be severed from the whole and compared to statements made, for example, by Hobbes, his ideas are not restricted to the narrow confines of Hobbesian theory in which an emphasis on the source of law as its validating principle completely overpowers considerations of content.

That Bodin's thought is not so restricted is easily enough established by the facts that while his work was used by certain English royalists to stress the similarities between the French and English monarchies in their struggles with Parliament,[1] and while James I was looking—or thought he was looking —at England during his reign through the eyes of Bodin,[2] Le Bret in 1632 saw in Bodin's writings a doctrine that could be used against those who would divorce sovereignty from justice and right (*droit*).[3] Furthermore, while Sir Walter Raleigh changed Bodin's phrase 'right government' to 'certain government', thus reducing the limitations on sovereignty to purely pragmatic and voluntary checks,[4] Bodin's emphasis on the importance of the public good to the order and stability of the Commonweale was to echo in the writings of Maurice and Hooker.[5] And again, although Bodin may

---

[1] C. I. Smith, 'Jean Bodin and Comparative Law', *J. History of Ideas*, Vol. 25 (3), p. 417.
[2] H. M. Chew, 'King James I', Hearnshaw (ed.), op. cit., 105.
[3] Mosse, *The Struggle for Sovereignty in England* (E. Lansing, Mich., 1950), p. 31.
[4] Ibid., p. 42.   [5] Ibid., p. 33.

have influenced Hobbes and certainly was used by Sir Robert Filmer, who in his *Patriarcha* defended the royalist thesis that sovereignty was something 'fixed, immutable, and inherent in the nature of human society' against the Whigs who held that the right to govern was contractual and revocable by those who are governed,[1] he also directly influenced William Fullbeck, who in his *Direction or Preparative to the Study of Law* defined law as 'perfect reason',[2] a notion scorned by Hobbes.[3] Even Grotius read deeply of Bodin's work, and applied what he learned: that the concept of natural law was fundamental to the coherence and truth of political thought.[4] As time passed, however, writers began with increasing regularity to drop from their work Bodin's proposition that God's will and the laws of nature were limitations on sovereign power.[5]

In sum, from Bodin on there were two directions political and legal writers could go. They could, of course, pick up his definition of law in which all normative elements were lacking and follow Hobbes. On the other hand, they could accept his normative definition of law, in which law is said to be the '*right* command of him who has sovereign power', and then go on, after modernizing the concept of natural law in order to make it fit the then-current theories of constitutional law, to establish an ethical and not merely authoritarian foundation for political power.

There is, of course, no doubt that the first of these directions has been the one more often taken. So true is this that half a century ago Figgis was able to state that in political and legal matters all 'arguments but those of public policy are to a great extent laughed out of court'. Utility had become—and has remained—the test of legality; the 'theocratic and still more the juristic conception of political right [had] gone from the educated world'.[6] There are statements in Bodin's *Six Books* that can, if lifted out of context, be used to support the argument that he helped in this process; and it is even possible, if one does not look too closely, to see a similarity between Bodin's formal analysis of the sixteenth-century Estates General and French Parliaments and Austin's analysis of nineteenth-century custom and case law, or between Bodin's (admittedly unclear) notion that the power of sovereignty rests on its 'recognition' and H. L. A. Hart's view that recognition of a legal system is necessary to its existence. But such comparisons cannot be pushed too far; and it is in some ways just as easy, although less often done, to compare him with writers who stress the fundamental importance to law and politics of right rule.

[1] Filmer is cited in McRae, A64, n. 143.
[2] Stirling edition (London, 1829), pp. 5, 11.
[3] *Works* (Molesworth edition, 1840), Vol. VI, pp. 24–26.
[4] Franklin, op. cit., p. 73 f.
[5] Mosse, 'The Influence of Jean Bodin's *Republique*,' op. cit., p. 82 f.
[6] Op. cit., p. 12 f.

222   JEAN BODIN'S 'LOGIC OF SOVEREIGNTY'

The conclusion to be drawn from these remarks is that Bodin's importance is not to be found, in the last analysis, in the role he is alleged to have played in the positivistic and analytic traditions of legal and political theory but in the vigorous attempt he made, even while defining law primarily in terms of its source, to anchor that source to the demands of justice and reason. To read the *Six Books of the Commonweale* simply as a primer for an understanding of Hobbes instead of for the purpose of following Bodin's explorations into the ways that the power of legal and political sovereignty can be limited by the content of law itself is to lose sight of its worth. Nor would that loss be academic only. Bodin instinctively saw that a value-free definition of political and legal sovereignty, unrelated except by expediency to social purpose, is somehow inadequate. His intuition is being confirmed by a world grown too small for power politics.

[2]

Sovereignty and the mixed constitution: Bodin and his critics

JULIAN H. FRANKLIN

The account of sovereignty in the work of Jean Bodin was a major event in the development of European political thought. Bodin's precise definition of supreme authority, his determination of its scope, and his analysis of the functions that it logically entailed, helped turn public law into a scientific discipline. And the vast system of comparative public law and politics provided in his *Les Six Livres de la République* (1576) became the prototype for a whole new literary genre, which in the seventeenth century was cultivated most in Germany.

But Bodin's account of sovereignty was also the source of much confusion, since he was primarily responsible for introducing the seductive but erroneous notion that sovereignty is indivisible. It is true, of course, that every legal system, by its very definition as an authoritative method of resolving conflicts, must rest upon an ultimate legal norm or rule of recognition, which is the guarantee of unity. But when Bodin spoke about the unity of sovereignty, the power that he had in mind was not the constituent authority of the general community or the ultimate coordinating rule that the community had come to recognise, but the power, rather, of the ordinary agencies of government. He advanced, in other words, a theory of ruler sovereignty. His celebrated principle that sovereignty is indivisible thus meant that the high powers of government could not be shared by separate agents or distributed among them, but that all of them had to be entirely concentrated in a single individual or group.

This thesis was controversial even as applied to the more consolidated kingships of France, Spain, and England, and it was hopelessly at odds with the constitution of the German Empire and other monarchies of eastern Europe and Scandinavia. Yet so seductive was the idea of indivisibility that it remained a celebrated issue among academic jurists for at least a half-century after Bodin wrote. And even after the error was exposed, around

Sovereignty and the mixed constitution

the end of the first quarter of the seventeenth century, it lingered on in one form or another. In this chapter I shall deal only with the earlier and main phase of the controversy. I shall try to explain how Bodin's theory of sovereignty came about and how his confusion as to indivisibility was cleared up in the course of the debate on the locus of sovereignty in the German Empire.

i   Bodin's doctrine and its limitations

The idea that concentration of power in the ruler is an essential condition of the state as such might seem at first sight to have been absolutist in its inspiration, and Bodin, when he published the final version of his political doctrine in 1576, indeed argued that the king of France had all the power that a government could legitimately exercise and that apparent restraints on royal power were not constitutional requirements, but mere re-commendations of prudence and good government (Franklin 1973, pp. 54ff). Yet the earlier history of Bodin's thought suggests a somewhat different genesis. In his *Methodus ad facilem historiarum cognitionem* (1566), Bodin was not an absolutist, or was at least evasive on that subject, and his interest in the theory of sovereignty was clearly technical and quasi-academic (Franklin 1973, pp. 35ff).

In the earliest phase of his career as an aspiring teacher at the law school of Toulouse, Bodin had apparently undertaken to identify those powers of a sovereign that could not also be held as a right of office by ordinary magistrates (Franklin 1973, pp. 23–5). To say that a magistrate 'held' or 'had' a power by his right of office had been taken, by most medieval jurists, to mean that he could exercise that power according to his own discretion and without direct reliance on the king so long as he remained within whatever legal limits might apply. Not all powers were or needed to be held this way, of course. The public officer might be acting solely on delegated power subject to immediate control. But by medieval notions, that sort of officer was little better than a servant. High officers of state, who exercised some degree of *merum*, or pure, *imperium*, held their *imperium* by right. And since the *merum imperium* could include very high powers of the state, this conception of the right of office was naturally associated with a decentralised administration.[1]

With the growing consolidation of power in the French and other

---

1. For an historical survey of the issue of *merum imperium* in medieval and post-medieval legal theory going back to the thirteenth century, see Gilmore 1941.

Religion, civil government, and the debate on constitutions

Renaissance monarchies, this view of office was increasingly attacked, and most strenuously of all by Andrea Alciato, the great Italian legal humanist of the early sixteenth century, who held that the possession of *merum imperium* by right of office was a corruption of Roman civil law, that every power in the state, other than (abusive) feudal grants, was merely a right of exercise derived by delegation from the prince (Alciato 1582, cols 29ff). This opinion was obviously favourable to royal power. And given Bodin's constant preference for strong monarchical authority, one might have expected him to welcome Alciato's view.

But Bodin was also an erudite and cautious legal craftsman and throughout his career he constantly attempted to reconcile the new idea of royal dominance with the French juridical tradition of which he was a great admirer and connoisseur. Against Alciato, accordingly, and the whole tradition of juridical interpretation in which he stood, Bodin held that by the customary rule of public law in France, high magistrates could hold the *merum imperium* by right of office at least to the extent of imposing capital punishment. But against the medieval exponents of this view, he did not include those prerogatives that could make the magistrate a partner or rival of his prince. These could not be 'held', but could be exercised by delegation only (Bodin 1951b, pp. 174–6, 1961, pp. 432ff).

Unlike Alciato and his followers, accordingly, Bodin divided the *merum imperium* into a (minor) part that could be held by magistrates and a (major) part held only by the prince. And by this conservative route he was led, ironically, to a new and theoretically momentous question as to the character of sovereignty. He now sought to determine those powers that could not be held by magistrates, but only exercised, if the prince was to be accounted sovereign. Although this topic had sometimes been touched upon by other jurists of the time, Bodin was to treat the question in a more fundamental and systematic way than anyone before him. He now proceeded to derive the necessary rights, or 'marks', of sovereignty from the concept of supremacy itself. The question that he asked, in other words, was what prerogatives a political authority must hold exclusively if it is not to acknowledge a superior or equal in its territory.

Bodin's first reflections on this question almost surely go back to his early career as an academic jurist at the University of Toulouse (which he left in 1559 after failing to secure a permanent appointment). But the scope and depth of his investigation was decisively shaped by a far-reaching methodological commitment that carried him well beyond the conven-

Sovereignty and the mixed constitution

tional approach to legal studies. At some point of his Toulousan period,
Bodin concluded that issues of legal theory could not be settled in the
traditional fashion of the medieval civil lawyers by appeal to Roman
norms alone. The use of high philological technique in the study of the
Roman law by the great French school of legal humanism had prepared the
way for a methodological revolution in which Bodin became a leading
figure. The humanists, rejecting the medieval style of scholastic exegesis,
had attempted to get back to the original meaning of the Roman texts, and
to recover the underlying system of the Corpus Juris. But the further they
went, the more critical they became of Roman law itself. The Corpus Juris,
to list their main complaints, seemed incomplete in many areas, and most
especially in public law; Justinian had often been cryptic and inaccurate in
representing the best of Roman legal thought; many rules, some of which
seemed basic to the system, were peculiar to the Roman state and obsolete
for France; the Corpus Juris had not been arranged as a logically coherent
system, and could not be reduced to a system because of its defects and
omissions. The intellectual authority of Roman law was thereby shaken,
and this had a number of important repercussions (Franklin 1963, pp. 36ff).

One of these was a new appreciation of domestic legal custom
(Franklin 1973, pp. 37ff; cf. Kelley, 1970). But an additional motif,
especially strong in Bodin, was the idea of remedying deficiences in the
system of Roman law by consulting the materials of universal history
(Franklin 1963, pp. 59ff). This in large part was the theme of his *Methodus ad
facilem historiarum cognitionem*. The only way, says Bodin in the preface, to
construct a truly universal legal science is to compare 'all the laws of all, or
the most famous, states and to select the best variety'. A few years earlier,
perhaps while he was still at Toulouse, he had produced a grandiose design
for this comparison with his *Juris universi distributio* or *System of Law in its
Entirety*; and the *Methodus* presents a preliminary statement of his findings
for the area of public law in its very lengthy chapter vi.

In this fashion an enterprise that very likely started as an enquiry into the
specific prerogatives of the ancient Roman emperors and the kings of
France was transformed into a study of sovereignty in every kind of state.
In Bodin's design, the basis for comparing states, and explaining their
schemes of public law, was to determine and describe the locus of
sovereignty in each. He was thus required to work out common principles
of sovereignty that would apply to democracies and aristocracies as well as
monarchies, and to variants of each of these in different times and places.

Religion, civil government, and the debate on constitutions

One consequence of this was a comprehensive and general definition of the rights of sovereignty. The Corpus Juris offered virtually nothing on the theory of public powers since it was primarily a scheme of private law. And the lists of regalian powers used in feudal law were mainly catalogues of particular privileges. In Bodin's *Methodus*, however, the essential rights are distinguished and reduced to five main heads:

And so having compared the arguments of Aristotle, Polybius, Dionysius [of Halicarnassus], and the jurists – with each other and with the universal history of commonwealths – I find that supremacy in a commonwealth consists of five parts. The first and most important is appointing magistrates and assigning each one's duties; another is ordaining and repealing laws; a third is declaring and terminating war; a fourth is the right of hearing appeals from all magistrates in last resort; and the last is the power of life and death where the law itself has made no provision for flexibility or clemency. (Bodin 1951b, pp. 174–5)

This classification is not quite as modern as it seems. It becomes clear in the *République* that Bodin thinks of the legislative power (which he now puts first among the rights of sovereignty) as a very general power to command, so that it implicitly includes all others. Hence the modern distinction between legislation, as the making of a rule, and execution, as the application of a rule, is not yet fully grasped, and that confusion we shall see is costly. And yet Bodin makes a very important, and even decisive, step towards an adequate account of public powers.

A second consequence of Bodin's comparative enterprise was his celebrated claim that sovereignty is indivisible, which he seems to have come to only at this point. In seeking to determine the form of state for ancient Rome and certain other classical republics traditionally reputed mixed, Bodin was finally led to ask, in strictly juridical terms, for the locus of sovereignty in a mixed constitution – in a constitution, that is, wherein the sovereign was said to be compounded of monarchy, aristocracy, and democracy, or any two of these.

Thus put, the question was completely new, since Polybius, and other exponents of the mixed constitution, thought of it more as a balance of effective influence than as a legal formula for partnership in sovereignty. And Bodin's answer was that, beyond the three simple forms of state, 'no fourth had existed, or could even be imagined' (Bodin 1951b, p. 177). The difficulty with a mixed constitution, in other words, was not merely prudential or political. As Bodin saw it, the unity of a legal system seemed

Sovereignty and the mixed constitution

logically to require the unification of power in a single ruler or single ruling group (Franklin 1973, pp. 23ff).

This opinion is, of course, mistaken. Apart from federal decentralisation, which I leave aside for the purpose of this chapter, a constitution can be mixed either by sharing or by distribution. Where sovereignty is shared, the outcome is a compound polyarchy, the members of which, each retaining its identity within the whole, are the king, the senate, and the people, or any two of these, who may participate with different weights in different governmental functions. The idea of such a compound is not always easy to imagine. The President of the United States, for example, is, by virtue of his veto, a member of the legislature along with the two houses of Congress. Yet it is hard to imagine an act of legislation as the 'will' of such a complex entity, and more normal to think of it as an act of Congress subject, within certain limits, to approval by the President.

Where the constitutional principles of mixture are well understood, this way of speaking does not lead to theoretical confusion. But in the sixteenth century the mixed constitution had not yet been explored juridically, and where it occurred it was the legacy of traditional restraints and *ad hoc* adaptations that were not reflected in the legal terminology. In the limited monarchies of Europe, the king was still addressed as sovereign even though he might require the consent of the estates or other body for the conduct of some of his affairs, and commentators on the ancient Roman republic often passed over the traditional claims of the senate to a legislative veto.

Hence jurists of the sixteenth century were readily misled. The mixed systems of their own time or of the past were hard to grasp as authentic partnerships in sovereignty, while the mixtures they imagined and triumphantly proved to be impossible were irrelevant. Bodin, for example, assumes that the only sense in which a constitution might be mixed by sharing would be to give each of the partners the entirety of power simultaneously, which is of course juridically absurd:

But to institute the dominion of one, together with that of the few, and also with that of the many, simultaneously, is not only impossible but cannot even be imagined. For if sovereignty is by its nature indivisible, as we have shown above; how can it be allotted to one and to all at the same time? The first mark of sovereignty is to give law to all in general and to each in particular, and to command them. But will the citizens yield to being bound against their will when they, in turn, are empowered to coerce the person who commands them? If they

Religion, civil government, and the debate on constitutions

willingly obey their majesty collapses; and yet if both parties refuse to be commanded, and there is no one obeying or commanding, it will be anarchy rather than a commonwealth, which is worse than the cruelest tyranny.[2]

A second way of mixing constitutions (as distinct from sharing) is by distributing the rights of sovereignty to different partners separately. This entails express or implied coordinating rules by which the powers thus separated, and above all the legislative power, are adjusted to each other's functions. It supposes, more specifically, that the legislature, although supreme in making rules, cannot apply them and cannot control directly that authority which is constitutionally charged with execution. But this possibility was also difficult to recognise at the time that Bodin wrote. In the best known example of 'mixture', which was the classical Roman republic, the highest forms of executive and judicial power were joined with the legislative in the people, so that it was technically not mixed in this respect. In European monarchies executive and legislative power were linked in the person of the king. Indeed, even Locke, much later on, who recommended the separation of executive and legislative power and had an example of it in the English constitution, still thought that the former was naturally subject to the latter, and that the executive independence of the English king hinged on his legislative veto. Without that veto, Locke believed, the two houses of parliament would be entitled to make and unmake executives at will (Locke 1960, pp. 414–15).

Bodin's attempt to show that distribution must be futile as a scheme of mixture thus seems to start by holding that all other powers would be in conflict with the power to make law. And as though to complicate the issue, he adds, alongside the legislative, another all-inclusive power (as Bodin interprets it), which is the right of taking oaths of fealty. The

---

2. Bodin 1586, II.1, p. 176. The phrase 'as we have shown above (*ut antea demonstravimus*)' in this quotation probably refers to I.10, especially pp. 149–50, where Bodin, following Baldus and Cyno da Pistoia, observes portentously that a sovereign cannot share his power with a subject and still remain a sovereign. The implication seems to be that sharing somehow cancels sovereignty as such, as opposed to altering only the persons who hold it. This interpretation is confirmed by the passage just quoted.

In the French version, the original of which goes back to 1576, the result of this attempt to mix by sharing is described as democracy. 'And what individual can give the law, if he is himself constrained to take it from those to whom he gives it? The conclusion follows necessarily that, if no one in particular has the power to make law, and the power belongs to all together, the commonwealth is democratic.' *République*, II.1 (1961, p.254). One possible interpretation of this cryptic passage is suggested by Arnisaeus' comments on sharing, below p.321. The key clause in Bodin's passage would then be '… [if] the power belongs to all …' and the error would then consist in not seeing that 'all' do not participate equally or even directly, that the people and the aristocracy vote as corporations.

Sovereignty and the mixed constitution

breakdown of the attempted distribution follows from the conflict between these two powers, without excluding resistance also arising from the independent claims of all the rest. But no matter how the picture is construed, it is evident enough that Bodin is innocent of any notion of constitutional coordination of co-equal parts.

Let us produce, if that is possible, or at least let us imagine, a commonwealth in which the people would have the power to create magistrates, dispose of the public treasury, and to decide on life and death; while the nobility would be assigned the right of making laws, deciding war and peace, and levying taxes; and the citizens, collectively as well as individually, would be obliged to render an oath of fealty or homage to the king without exception of any other person, and the king, who is above all the other magistrates, would hear appeals in the last instance. By this method the rights of sovereignty will seem to be divided three ways: – the aristocrats and nobles will claim a part, the democrats and commoners a part, and the king will also claim a part – as a result of which a blend of royal power, aristocracy and democracy will seem to exist. But I deny that this ever was or can be done. For the aristocrats and nobility, who have the supreme power of making law – the power, that is, of laying commands and prohibitions on everyone – will use it to control the commoners and the prince, and will forbid homage to be rendered to the prince, while the prince will have bound everyone to swear to him and will permit obedience to no one but himself. And as each will vigorously wish to defend his own rights and not give up those he would assume, this arrangement will be incompatible with the nature of government in that the same actor that has the highest right of command would be forced to obey another who is yet his subject. This makes it clear that where the rights of sovereignty are divided between the prince and his subjects, a state of confusion must result in which the issue of supreme authority will always be decided by the force of arms until the highest power is in one man, in a few, or in the entire body of citizens.[3]

Bodin was thus confused about indivisibility, his greatest problems coming in trying to show that sovereignty could not be shared. His attempts to show that it was undivided in the Roman and other constitutions commonly regarded as mixed depended on a certain misunderstanding of their institutions. He failed to recognise the independent legislative function of the senate which thus shared power with the people in the earlier phase of the Roman constitution, and overlooked the powers of analogous councils in other ancient and modern city-states. On

---

3. Bodin 1586, II.1, p. 184. See also the sentence which follows directly after the passage on the sharing of sovereignty previously quoted: 'But if the people are given the power of making the laws and creating the magistrates, while all of the remaining powers are allowed to the senate or the magistrates, it will have to be acknowledged that the state is popular. For the power given to the senate and the magistrates is entrusted to them on loan and can be taken back at the people's command' (1586, II.1, p. 176).

Religion, civil government, and the debate on constitutions

the other hand, in treating contemporary European kingships, the thesis of undivided sovereignty was sustained by avoiding any clear definitions of the scope of public power. Only thus could Bodin account for the constitutional realities of the French kingship without acknowledging that sovereignty was shared.

For despite the centralisation and growth of royal power in the Renaissance, medieval notions of limited government still lingered on in French constitutional opinion. Commentators in the main tradition going back to Claude de Seyssel, held that the king of France, although sovereign and the source of all authority, was expected to act according to the law and not to change it without the advice of some semi-independent council like the high court, or *parlement* of Paris (Seyssel 1981, pt I, chs. viii–xii, pp. 49–58). Bodin not only accepted these restraints on royal power, but gave them even greater scope and weight. He held that a king of France could not change well-established law without the consent of the provincial or general estates, and that decrees in conflict with that law could be refused enforcement by the *parlements* (Franklin 1973, pp. 34ff).

The admission of these limitations seems at first sight to be in glaring conflict with Bodin's claim that sovereignty undivided was vested in the king. But when he wrote the *Methodus*, Bodin was implicitly working with a concept of limited supremacy. A king's authority, accordingly, could be sovereign yet less than absolute. He could be bound by fundamental law in the broader sense of well-established custom, which he could not change without consent. But if his regular powers were normally sufficient for the conduct of affairs and if nothing could be done apart from his initiative, he seemed nonetheless to be supreme. By such criteria a proper monarch like the king of France could be distinguished from the doge of Venice or the emperor of Germany, who were little more than figureheads, and might even be deposed for cause.

There is a certain common sense to this relaxed conception of supremacy, and it might be roughly workable.[4] But as the use of it in later writers shows, it is ultimately too flexible. The distinction between fundamental and ordinary law (which parallels the distinction between constituent and ordinary sovereignty) is legitimate, and indispensable, in constitutional theory. But where the scope of 'fundamental' becomes too indefinite and broad, the utility of sovereignty as a juridical concept is undermined. Bodin would have done better, therefore, to have defined the ruler's sovereignty as absolute (except with respect to the law of nature and

---

4. Which was once my own opinion: Franklin 1973, pp.38–40. But see Gierke 1966, p.161.

Sovereignty and the mixed constitution

fundamental law more narrowly defined), and have conceded that its functions were divided among the king, the *parlements*, and the estates.

But the incoherence in Bodin's theory of sovereignty was to be eliminated in a different way. By 1576, when his *République* appeared, he had come to the conclusion that sovereignty was absolute, by which he meant that a truly sovereign authority must have all the power that a state could legitimately exercise. To this extent the clarification of his doctrine was reasonable enough. But since Bodin continued to insist that sovereignty was indivisible, he concluded, necessarily but wrongly, that there had to exist in every commonwealth a single individual or group in which the entire power of the state was concentrated. Furthermore, since he had never doubted that the king of France was truly sovereign, it now seemed utterly clear that the king of France was absolute. And this applied to kings of England and of Spain as well.

Bodin was probably led to this revised idea of sovereignty by two considerations. One, almost surely, was further reflection on the logic of indivisibility, a thesis which had earlier been more or less intuitive. He must now have recognised that if there were legitimate acts of governance which a king could not perform without the consent of the estates or *parlement* then these consenting agents must have a share in his authority. Hence, consistent with the principle of indivisibility, he had to conclude that sovereignty was absolute, that the exercise of supreme authority could not be restrained within its territory by any independent agent. But Bodin would have been confirmed in this conclusion by another, more political, concern with the issue of resistance to a tyrant–king. At the time of the *Methodus* he had managed to avoid this question. Ten years later, however, in the midst of recurrent civil wars, the right of resistance was publicly asserted by the opponents of the crown, and Bodin, alarmed, construed it as a recipe for anarchy.[5] But the very key to resistance doctrine was the set of restraints on royal power that Bodin had earlier been inclined to admit. He must now have seen, at least intuitively, that binding restraints upon the ruler implied some sense in which the community was higher than the king and would have power to act against a tyrant. It would have been seen to follow, therefore, that the absolute power of the king of France and of every other proper sovereign was not only an analytic truth but the very foundation of political stability (Bodin 1961, Preface).

The outcome, accordingly, of Bodin's revised idea of sovereignty was

---

5. On French resistance theory see Franklin (ed.) 1969; and see Skinner 1978, II, ch. 7–9, on the more general doctrinal and political setting for assertions of a right of resistance and revolution in the period.

Religion, civil government, and the debate on constitutions

systematic elimination, in the *République*, of all enforceable limitations on the king's authority. This is not to say that there were no restrictions morally. Bodin strenuously insisted that absolute kings were subject to the law of nature – that they were bound to respect the liberty and property of free subjects, and that they were obligated by contracts entered into with private citizens. Bodin even managed to hold that, except in emergencies, new taxation required the consent of the estates if it was not to be a mere taking of the subject's property. But for violations of the law of nature the king was answerable to God alone, and was not required, in construing it, to have approval from the courts or the estates. Bodin believed that a prudent king would heed the remonstrations of the *parlement* and he recommended that the estates be frequently consulted. But these were in no way binding obligations. They were mere recommendations of humanity and prudence (Franklin 1973, pp. 79ff; Bodin 1961, pp. 149ff).

Bodin continued to believe that a king was also 'bound' by customary fundamental law. But this domain of law, which had been left vaguely broad in the *Methodus*, was now narrowed down to two arrangements – one prescribing the rule of succession to the throne, the other forbidding alienation of the royal domain without consent. Both rules were designed to keep the state intact, rather than to limit the royal right of governance. Their guarantee, moreover, was simply that attempted alterations or alienations by a sitting king would be disallowed upon his death. Hence neither the law of nature nor fundamental law could justify a challenge to absolute authority or resistance to a sitting king (Franklin 1973, pp. 70–9).

This systematic elimination of binding institutional restraints was a distortion of constitutional practice. But given the elements of ambiguity in the French tradition, the break was not easy to detect. The obligation of the king to keep existing law had always been presented tactfully. In the 1560s the obtaining of consent before changing well-established law was considered to be the normal and unvarying practice, but the invocation of absolute authority had not been totally excluded. The right of the estates had not been specified precisely in the older commentators; and there was even some uncertainty attaching to the status of the *parlements* (see Church 1941, ch. 3). They did not quite assert a veto on royal legislation, so much as a right of continued remonstration until such time as their complaints were heeded. Hence Bodin's change in 1576 would not have been obvious to many of his readers, and Bodin himself must have regarded his position in the *République* as a mere clarification of a doctrine he had always held.

As Bodin presented it, however, the idea of absolute kingship would not

Sovereignty and the mixed constitution

have seemed threatening to moderate contemporaries, and might have even been attractive. In one way or another he had managed to account for almost all the limitations that had been traditionally considered indispensable. And although he had undermined the legal force of checks upon the king, he still expected them to operate as in the past. He confidently believed that the complaints and administrative pressures of the magistrates would restrain impulsive rulers and he optimistically expected that the political value of the estates was sufficient to assure their consultation. Bodin's account of sovereignty would thus have appeared to be compatible with civilised and law-abiding government. Yet it seemed to provide an ironclad defence against any justification of resistance from below, which was to recommend it strongly in the troubled circumstances of the later sixteenth century (Bodin 1961, II.5, pp. 297ff).

ii   The question of sovereignty in the constitution of the German Empire

Hence, despite its basic error, Bodin's theory of sovereignty was received not only in France but in Spain and England also, where it was even less consistent with constitutional realities. In the epoch of resurgent royalism that followed the religious war, it was neither safe nor patriotic to question the logic of sovereignty. Jurists who continued to insist on the binding force of limitations generally abstained from challenge. They simply documented limits on the king while maintaining an attitude of reverence, and catalogued the legal precedents without speculation on the locus and character of sovereignty. It was only in the German Empire, where the monarch was universally and even officially acknowledged to be limited, that Bodin's central thesis posed an inescapable challenge to academic jurisprudence. And even here the issue was not clearly joined until the first decade of the seventeenth century.

Before this time the only knowledgeable answer to Bodin seems to have come from the French jurist, Vincent Cabot, who briefly yet lucidly set forth four formulas by which a mixed constitution could be instituted.

I shall not pursue these points further, since it is enough to have shown that there can be a mixed state and that it can come about in four ways, as is evident from what I have said. First, if one partner has one kind of supreme power, and another another; as when the king may constitute magistrates at his discretion, the aristocrats decide as to war and peace, and the people make the laws. Next, if they [all] have the same power but not with respect to the same persons, as in the

Religion, civil government, and the debate on constitutions

Roman republic where, as I said, the punishment of crimes committed in Italy was in the senate if they were done by provincials and in the people if by citizens. Further, if they [all] have the same power over the same persons, but one cannot act without the other; as if the prince could not establish magistrates, make law or complete any other act of supreme power without the senate and the people. Last, if one can do some things alone, and cannot do other things without consent, while the others alone cannot do anything. (Cabot 1752, p. 623)

Yet this first, very promising attempt was destined to have little influence. Apart from a passing reference to Poland, there is no comment on any European monarchy that might have sparked a controversy. Almost all of the illustrations are drawn from ancient Rome. Cabot, furthermore, does not diagnose the basis of Bodin's confusions, or offer an alternative theory of sovereignty, which alone was calculated to dispel the belief in indivisibility. Cabot, in short, was not yet part of a continuing debate; his ideas were not developed further by himself or noted, except occasionally, by later writers.

Among German writers, on the other hand, the issue raised by Bodin was more immediate and urgent. The emperor was more drastically restricted in his power than any of the kings of western Europe. Political power was decentralised among the individual 'estates'[6] of the empire – most epecially the Electors and the territorial princes, but also the cities which held directly of the emperor. And largely to guarantee these local privileges, limitations on the emperor by institutions representing the estates were extensive and jealously enforced. Not only was the emperor bound to make no law without the consent of the estates assembled in a diet, but some of his highest executive and judicial functions were jointly exercised with representatives of the estates in general or with the Seven Electors which, as the most preeminent estates, often acted on behalf of all. Appointment to vacant fiefs of the empire thus required consent of the estates, and cases in which an estate was a party under imperial law were heard not in the prince's court but in the high court of the empire in which the estates shared jurisdiction with the emperor. Most of these arrangements, along with others, were recorded in capitulations which had been undertaken by emperors at the time of their election and which thus afforded authoritative texts of fundamental law. The recesses, or ordinances, which embodied the legislation agreed to in a diet were often enacted in the name of estates together with the emperor.

---

6. The term 'estates' in German usage often refers to the individuals having independent powers in the empire, although sometimes also to groups of individuals having a common status (as in 'three estates'). In what follows the primary meaning will usually be clear from the context.

Sovereignty and the mixed constitution

In the sixteenth century, furthermore, these limitations were generally accepted by the legal commentators. It is sometimes suggested in the secondary literature that opinions on the status of the emperor, who was regularly a Catholic Habsburg, were divided along confessional lines – that Catholics tended to magnify the office with the Calvinists tending to be more militant on the rights of the estates and the Lutherans hewing to a conciliatory middle course. Such differences no doubt existed on the level of attitudes and programmes. But as to the basic facts of the German constitution there seems to have been little disagreement, at least among the more eminent and influential legal commentators. Since all of them were either professors at territorial universities or councillors to territorial princes and imperial cities, or both of these at once, they were hardly inclined to question the rights of the estates. In the first two decades of the seventeenth century, their accounts of constitutional restraints, not only in outline but also in detail, were pretty much the same. All agreed, moreover, that an emperor who defied restraints could be formally deposed for tyranny. The removal of Wenceslas in 1400 was generally taken without question as a precedent.

Yet these same commentators were by no means willing to embrace Bodin's conclusion that, strictly speaking, the German Empire was no longer a monarchy in any sense at all. Beginning with the Golden Bull and then with various electoral capitulations of the fifteenth century, the emperor, according to Bodin, had become utterly subject to the assembled estates, which, having acquired all the legislative power, could command the law as they saw fit and depose the emperor if he proved unwilling to comply. The emperor still retained the titles and honours of a king. But the German Empire, like the kingdoms of Denmark, Sweden, and Poland, was neither a monarchy, nor yet a mixed constitution, but a principate. The prince in these systems was but the first citizen and chief magistrate of an aristocratic state, who was properly compared with the doge of Venice, not a sovereign ruler like the king of France (Bodin 1961, II.6, pp. 321ff, II.1, pp. 262, 270).

German jurists and humanists writing around 1600, however, were not yet ready to make a cipher of the emperor. The territorial estates still looked to the empire for their common defence and for the settlement of disputes among them, for which purpose the emperor's initiative was needful, since the diet was primarily an instrument of limitation rather than of governance. Some independence of power in the emperor thus seemed residually useful; and in an age of resurgent royalism monarchical status for the emperor seemed also to be requisite for German dignity. Hence,

Religion, civil government, and the debate on constitutions

Bodin's equation of the emperor and the doge of Venice was offensive to patriotic and feudal sensibilities. Not all the commentators of all the different regions were equally sensitive in this respect, but none had reason to defend Bodin, while most had reason to oppose him. Indeed, with the one exception of Henning Arnisaeus, and that only partial, all the leading writers of the early 1600s insisted that the German emperor was a true monarch in some sense or another.

By thus asserting both monarchy and the right of the estates, the Germans were drawn into conflict with Bodin's theses on the indivisibility of sovereignty. The constitutional circumstances favouring such a confrontation were also present in other monarchies of central and northern Europe, which Bodin had also characterised as principates. But it was only in Germany that an intellectual culture existed which favoured theoretical elaboration of the issues. The first two decades of the seventeenth century marked the introduction of schools of public law in various sections of the empire. Beginning about 1600 a mass of brochures, dissertations, and treatises began to appear on politics and public law in general and German public law particularly, in which the analysis of sovereignty was inevitably a central topic.[7] By the middle 1620s, as we shall see, a satisfactory theory of mixed constitutions was finally presented (see below pp. 323ff). But this was only after much confusion and a number of false starts, a review of which will help to indicate the difficulties of the problem and the importance of its resolution.

Thus Johannes Althusius, although known as a critic of Bodin, endorsed his view on indivisibility. Bodin's real error, for Althusius, was his attribution of absolute power to the ruler, which the latter rejected as both immoral and inaccurate. An absolute power, he agreed, could indeed be found in every commonwealth. But for Althusius, here as so often transmitting the monarchomach position, that power was inalienably vested in the people and was held by the ruler only as a delegated power subject to conditions. This distinction between the constituent power of the people and the ordinary power of the ruler, or, as it would soon be called, between real and personal majesty, was an advance in the theory of sovereignty. But it did not dispose of the issue of indivisibility. For where,

---

7. On the development of schools of public law in this period, the classical account is Stintzing 1880–4, I.15.4ff. A brief but excellent recent account is Hoke 1968, pp. 17–39. For the history of doctrine the classical account is Stintzing 1880–4, II.17; Gierke 1966 *passim*; and Gierke 1957. For a concise modern survey see Hoke 1968, pp. 54–93, 152–64. A full treatment of the history of doctrines of sovereignty in German thought is Gross 1973, chs. 1–5.

Sovereignty and the mixed constitution

as in Germany, the prince was limited by law, he required the consent of
the estates not only for changes in the constitution, but for ordinary acts of
legislation, from which it followed, on Althusius' own account, that the
form of state, or personal majesty, was mixed. And indeed when Althusius
came to consider 'the forms of supreme magistrate' in the very last chapter
of his treatise, he was bound to admit that the German Empire, like the
French monarchy, contained an element of aristocracy. Yet he was still
unwilling, or perhaps unable, to understand such a kingship as prevailed in
Germany as a mixed constitution, and felt justified in calling it a monarchy
since that was the component which he took to be predominant.

Therefore, the kingdom of Germany or of France is a monarchy, even though the
power of the emperor or king is limited by the high court (*parlamento*) and the
councils of the realm. I have not denied this [monarchical status] in ch. 14 as
Arnisaeus thinks, in his *Doctrina Politica*, ch. 8. For even though there is something
of aristocracy in this French and German monarchy, or kingdom, that does not
mean that it ceases to be a monarchy. For the forms of commonwealth are to be
judged from the preeminent, prevailing, and predominant part.

(Althusius 1932, ch. 39, p. 404)

Institutional restraints upon the king are thus treated as moderations of
the royal principle rather than as alterations of the form. In practice no
systems ever is, or can be, pure, and all three components of monarchy,
aristocracy, and democracy will always be present, even though one of
them predominates and gives the state its name. This admixture of
components, furthermore, is desirable as well as unavoidable, since it works
against abuse of power, and the best arrangement, indeed, is a 'tempered'
monarchy more or less as in the German Empire (ch. 39, p. 405). But in
admitting this tempering of forms, Althusius does not acknowledge
mixture in the strict sense of the sharing or distribution of the rights of
(personal) sovereignty. Indeed, he comes close to rejecting it explicitly in a
critical comment on Cabot's four suggestions. 'I do not approve these
mixtures', says Althusius, 'nor do use and practice admit them, except
insofar as the people in the election of a king or supreme magistrate has
reserved certain powers to itself. That sort of mixture is the best, as I have
said. And such is thought to have existed in the Spartan commonwealth'
(ch. 39, p. 405).

The problem in Althusius is not that his account is wrong, but that the
concepts of predominance and tempering are non-technical and imprecise.
Political predominance does not exclude legal division of the rights of
sovereignty, since the powers may be shared unequally and in such a way

Religion, civil government, and the debate on constitutions

that one of the parties is situated more strategically for the advancement of its policies. Conversely, even where sovereignty is legally concentrated in a single individual or group, the pattern of effective influence need not correspond. And where, as in Germany, the tempering of monarchy depended on binding rules, as Althusius clearly thought, the limitation is not merely political but also constitutional, and the system is a mixture in one or more of the ways discriminated by Cabot.

It thus appears that Althusius' distinction between a tempered kingship and a mixed constitution simply cannot be technically maintained. In any event it could hardly be stretched to cover the German emperor. The 'certain powers' that the people had reserved, in Germany as well as Sparta, were so far-reaching as to threaten the very notion of the emperor's 'predominance' no matter how construed. The point is made against Althusius by Arnisaeus, who was Bodin's shrewdest and most independent follower among the German commentators. Arnisaeus, too, felt constrained to admit the existence of impurities and deviations in simple forms of states, but only insofar as they did not compromise the very form. Althusius, he thought, was one of those who had been too permissive in describing the monarchy of France. Along with the Huguenot resistance theorists, he had acknowledged reservations of power to the people that removed France from the ranks of monarchy:

A similar error is to be found in Junius Brutus, *Vindiciae contra tyrannos*, in Hotman's *De antiq. jur. Gallo*,[8] and in Althusius' *Politica*, c. 14, all of which exclude the French kingdom from the class of monarchies in that the first law of the kingdom as Hotman reports it in ch. 23 of his *De antiq. jur.* is that nothing bearing on the general condition of the kingdom can be decided by the king without authorisation of the public council.[9]

Unlike Althusius, Bartholomaeus Keckermann was willing to admit not only tempered forms of state but fully mixed constitutions in which each of the partners had an equal role. Yet he too was never led to break with Bodin on the indivisibility of sovereignty. Keckermann seems to have thought of mixture as a tempering of a simple form, which had been carried as far as it could go. But tempering or moderation, no matter whether the dose thereof was large or small, did not suggest to him, any

8. This refers to *De antiquo jure regni Galliae*, a posthumous edition of Hotman's *Francogallia*.
9. Arnisaeus 1606, VIII, pp. 159–60. For Althusius' embarrassed denial of this charge in the third edition of his *Politica* see p.313 above. Arnisaeus, it may be noted, achieved consistency in his own criterion of monarchy only by interpreting all of Hotman's limitations on the king of France as royal courtesies.

Sovereignty and the mixed constitution

more than to Althusius, a genuine sharing of the rights of majesty. Searching for a looser, more 'Bodinian' solution, Keckermann believed that he had found it in a distinction between state and government introduced for this purpose by none other than Bodin himself. Bodin, he claimed, had ultimately backed away from his strict rejection of the mixed constitution. He 'does not deny', says Keckermann, 'that one form may be tempered by another in its mode of government, as when a monarchy is aristocratic in its mode of government, or even democratic. But this is the very thing we want, namely that the simple forms of commonwealth can be moderated by each other' (Keckermann 1608, II.iv, p. 560).

This, however, is a serious misrepresentation of Bodin for whom the form of governance is not a modification of the form of state. The form of government, as distinguished from the state, is rather the pattern by which the sovereign distributes offices among the various classes of his subjects. Since the powers of these offices and the right to hold them are at the discretion of the sovereign, at least in strictest law, the form of government, no matter how desirable, is not a constitutional requirement. Although Bodin does not put it exactly in such words, his meaning is abundantly clear:

We will thus hold it for settled that the state of a commonwealth is always simple even if the [form of] government is contrary to the [form of] state. Thus monarchy is altogether opposite to a popular state, and yet sovereignty can be vested in a single prince who governs democratically, as I have said. This will not, however, introduce mixing (*confusion*) of a popular state with monarchy, which are indeed incompatible, but rather of monarchy with popular government, which is the most stable monarchy of all.[10]

With Keckermann, on the other hand, there is no distinction between the distribution of offices as an ordinary rule and as a constitutional requirement. His model of a monarchy governed aristocratically is the French system as it is described by François Hotman, the *Vindiciae contra tyrannos*, and Althusius; and this is also his model for the German Empire on which his comments are tactfully oblique (Keckermann 1608, II.iv, p. 563). Hence Keckermann, like many other writers after him, could eat his cake and have it too. He speaks of a mixed constitution. He describes a mixed constitution. But by misapplying Bodin's terminology, he is able to avoid speaking of divided sovereignty, and somehow manages to think of the state as monarchy. He merely fails to notice that the terms 'state' and

---

10. Bodin 1961, II.7, p.339, and compare 1586, II.7, p.234, for a slightly modified version in the Latin. See also 1961, pp.1013–14.

Religion, civil government, and the debate on constitutions

'government', in Bodin's usage, refer to different levels of authority, the first to the ownership of power and the second to the exercise thereof in accordance with the owner's will. Keckermann, therefore, admitted mixture but failed to see the implications for the theory of sovereignty.

A solution similar to Keckermann's was also proposed by Hermann Kirchner, the humanist and historian, who was among the most creative theorists of sovereignty in the first quarter of the seventeenth century. Kirchner's *Respublica* (1608) is the *locus classicus* for the principle of double majesty or the distinction between constituent power and the ordinary power of the state. That distinction is virtually present in Bodin, who speaks, in his *République*, of fundamental laws on the succession to the throne and on the inalienability of domain that an incumbent ruler cannot alter even though he is absolute for all ordinary purposes. Althusius, citing this as an implicit recognition of the people as the source of all authority, already spoke in passing of *duplex majestas*, or double majesty.[11] But he regularly preferred to reserve the term sovereignty or majesty for the constituent power of the people and to describe the power conceded to the government as *potestas administrationis*. With Kirchner the distinction is more clearly drawn and generalised in what was to become the standard terminology. There was in every commonwealth, he held, a *majestas realis*, or constituent supremacy, which always remains in the people as the source of all authority, and *majestas personalis*, or ordinary supremacy, which is delegated to the prince, or government, on whatever terms the people may prescribe.

Given the sharpness of this and other formulations in Kirchner, we might expect him to have read Bodin correctly as to state and government, and to describe the latter merely as administrative arrangements enacted by the holder of (personal) majesty. Yet when he offers an account of the mixed constitution, Kirchner makes the same mistake as Keckermann. 'But you will easily settle the issue', he informs his reader, 'if you hold that the state of a commonwealth differs from the principle of government and mode of administration, as did Bodin, indeed, when he saw that he had trapped himself. For he avowed it to be possible that the state could be royal and yet be governed democratically' (Kirchner 1614, p. 53).

Kirchner then goes on to describe the modern German Empire as a

---

11. Commenting on Bodin's unwitting admission of an ultimate layer of sovereignty on which the king's is based, he comments '. . . even according to Bodin there is a double majesty of the kingdom and of the king . . .' (1932, ch. 9, p. 93). But the term *duplex majestas* could have been borrowed from Kirchner.

Sovereignty and the mixed constitution

monarchy tempered by an aristocratic plan of government. 'And yet', he says,

the advice and consent of the aristocratic element, which serves the empire as rowers do a ship, takes nothing from its royal keel ... and does not diminish the authority of the royal power in promulgating laws but only graces and augments it ... And this is evidenced by the opinion of Bodin himself, who contends that the French kingdom is absolutely monarchical, ... although they never granted their kings absolute authority uncontrolled by law but rather tempered the course of royal governance with the advice and consent of assemblies and convocations, of the *parlements* and of the peers of France.   (p. 54)

That Kirchner here is thinking of consent as a binding requirement is indicated not only by his choice of words but by his citation of Hotman as his prime authority on French procedures (pp. 54, 94). And later on, the rule for Germany – as for England, Spain, and France – is said to be 'that the king may decide nothing pertaining to the state of the kingdom as a whole without the authority of the public council' (p. 94). Yet Kirchner somehow managed to persuade himself that Bodin too could be listed among those who ratified this formula. In Book III, ch. 1 of the *République*, Bodin held that a weighty senate is indispensable to a well-ordered monarchy. Kirchner cites this chapter without considering Bodin's express insistence that the proper role of a senate is advice and nothing more (p. 54).

By loose and careless use of Bodin's distinction between state and government, Kirchner felt able to account for mixture while still ignoring the divisibility of sovereignty, and to speak of the empire as an aristocratically governed monarchy by glossing over the question of a partnership in sovereign authority. Was personal majesty vested solely in the emperor? If so, how does one account for binding limitations in his mode of governance? Or if personal majesty was shared between the emperor and the estates, why, then, should the empire be called a monarchy? Given the looseness of the terminology, Kirchner's distinction between state and government allowed such questions to be bypassed.

So loose was it, indeed, that the distinction could be used to draw the very opposite conclusion! Kirchner had intended to account for mixture and was so understood by other writers of the time. But with just the slightest twist, his distinction between state and government could be made to show that the German monarchy was pure and even absolute, yet still without denying the facts of the imperial constitution! This, indeed, was the purpose for which Kirchner's argument on moderated monarchy was most often used. And one of the main architects of that adaptation was

Religion, civil government, and the debate on constitutions

Daniel Otto who was among the most prolific and ingenious commentators on the theory of sovereignty and the constitution of the empire in the
first quarter of the seventeenth century.

In an article of 1620, 'An mixtus detur reipublicae status?' ('Is There such
a Thing as a Mixed State?'), Otto denies that Kirchner, any more than the
others who defended mixture, have found a rationale, and he then
proceeds to turn the distinction between state and government against
them. The form of state, he observes, denotes the essence and substance of a
commonwealth; the form of administration merely indicates its quality.
But a change of qualities, or accidents, does not affect the essence of a thing,
so that Bodin was perfectly consistent in conceding the possibility, of
mixture in administration while denying it in the state itself. It thus follows
that Kirchner, Keckermann, and others who defended mixture in this way
have begged the question. And Otto felt able to conclude, triumphantly,
that the empire was a simple monarchy!

Since all of this is so, we confidently conclude that the modern empire is a
monarchical state, and a simple one at that, because not even a particle of the
imperial majesty is shared with the princes of the empire . . . And although in some
areas the state is tempered by aristocratic principles, it cannot on that account be
called aristocratic or mixed . . . It is clear enough from what has been said that the
mode of administration does not change the form of state. (Otto 1620, p. 652)

But Otto's dissent from Keckermann and Kirchner is simply a different
conclusion from the same mistake as to the distinction between state and
government. With Bodin, the function of those who assist the sovereignty
in governance is merely to advise or to carry out his orders. The consent of
the estates in Germany, however, which extended to almost all the great
affairs of state, was a constitutional requirement – a fact which Otto himself
does not deny, but rather openly admits!

For although there are many rights of majesty that the emperor cannot exercise
without the approval and consent of the imperial estates – as is evident from
imperial capitulations and from that clause so constantly used in imperial recesses,
darüber wir uns mit ihnen und sie hindwiderumb mit uns verglichen – yet nevertheless
monarchical power is not removed.

For what really counts, is whether the rights of supreme majesty are constrained,
or detracted from. The first of these surely diminishes absolute power, but does not
always cancel the existence of a supreme magistrate. The second leaves no
[supreme] magistrate at all, because there can be no [supreme] magistrate who is
lacking in the rights of sovereignty. (p. 653)

The sovereignty of the emperor is thus held to be constrained but not
defective, diminished in its absoluteness but still supreme. Yet sovereignty
constrained in matters of ordinary law is sovereignty shared, especially

Sovereignty and the mixed constitution

when it is limited as thoroughly and pervasively as it was in the German Empire. It thus turns out that Otto's talk about essence and qualities, substances and accidents, as applied to state and government, uses distinctions without a difference since the 'qualities' were prescribed and the 'accidents' constitutionally required.

There are two other assertions connected with Otto's view of the emperor's sovereignty that should perhaps be mentioned briefly. One is the argument that the feudal tenure of the German princes and the oath of fealty attached thereto imply subjection to the emperor and are inconsistent with their possession of a share of sovereignty. Yet Otto does not deny, and does not wish to deny, the hereditary status of the princes or the collective right of the estates. The language of subjection in the oaths that he cites is thus at odds with well-established constitutional norms, and should have been regarded as mostly ceremonial (p. 651). The second contention, more curious for modern readers, is that the emperor 'enjoyed' or somehow 'made use of' absolute authority. By this language Otto does not intend to deny constitutional limitations on the emperor. Like other champions of a German monarchy before him, he means merely that there are still certain areas of government in which the emperor can act alone without consent and at his own discretion. Otto suggestively notes that such power is the residual expression of an authority that was plenary in ancient Roman times. But he has no intention of denying that this 'absolute' authority has been narrowed in its scope and strictly delimited by law. 'We turn now', he says, in another of his essays,

to our Romano-German Emperor, and we ask whether he can still be considered absolute (*an etiamnum solutus dici possit*). The basis of doubt is that the emperor cannot exercise the rights of majesty without consent of the Electors and the estates . . . The basis of decision is that the absolute power conceded (*legibus soluta potestas concessa*) to the emperor has never been taken back *in toto*, either tactily or expressly . . . Hence he still enjoys that power. . .[12]

12. 'An princeps legibus sit solutus?' (1616, p.519). This use of 'absolute' is also to be found in Gottfried Antonius and Theodor Reinking. In the course of a complex polemic with Hermann Vulteius and his followers, Antonius assumed the position of a champion of mixture in the German constitution, the very point of which was to show that the emperor had 'absolute' power in some respects. 'Whatever was conceded to the emperors by Roman law, and has not subsequently been taken back tacitly or expressly, they still enjoy and use . . . In Roman law, however, the power conceded to the emperors was absolute . . . .nor can it be shown that it was ever tacitly or expressly taken back completely. Therefore, they still enjoy and use that power' (*De potestate Imperatoris*, in Antonius 1614, p. 625). For the position of Vulteius, who as early as 1599 attempted, almost allusively, to explain the German constitution by the state-government distinction, see *Ad titulos Codicis qui sunt de iurisdictione et foro competenti*, p. 511 (on III.xxiv.1.i of Code). For brief summations of the debate, which is often too confused for easy summary, see Stintzing 1880–4, I, pp. 462–3, II, p. 39; Hoke 1968, p.23; Gross 1973, pp.138–41. Reinkingk (1631, I, *classis* iii.xiii, no. 25–9) uses arguments similar to those of Antonius and Otto to glorify the emperor.

Religion, civil government, and the debate on constitutions

Otto's case for the sovereignty of the German emperor thus depends not so much on a misrepresentation of the constitutional relationships as on ambiguity of terms. But it must not be thought that this cluster of equivocations was peculiar to him. It was an attractive device for patriotic commentators who hoped to strengthen allegiance to the empire by enhancing the symbol of the emperor. Thus all the arguments we have noted in Otto are also to be found in Theodor Reinking whose loyalist treatise on the empire continued to be republished well into the eighteenth century.[13]

But the confusion of this period on the mixed constitution was not only the result of sentimental or patriotic attachment to the principle of monarchy in the German constitution. For there were at least two very highly sophisticated legal commentators who fully recognised the sharing of sovereignty in the German constitution yet could only think of it as a polyarchy rather than a mixture. The problem here was not that they failed to understand the legal relations among the partners of a mixed constitution. It was rather their inability to see that a mixed sovereign was a compound corporation in which at least one of the members was itself a corporate body. They thus assumed, mistakenly, that constitutions like the classical Roman or the contemporary German were properly described as (simple) polyarchies.

Thus Arnisaeus clearly recognised that in the early period of the classical Roman republic the legislative power was shared between the senate and the people. In Bodin, as we have noted, the formula by which the senate authorised and the people decided was denied or misinterpreted. But Arnisaeus treats this as a mode of mixture, or rather of attempted mixture, in which 'the same right of majesty is given separately to two or more estates, but to each one in a different way', so that neither has the whole of it (Arnisaeus 1606, viii, p. 163, cf. 1615, ii.vii, p. 875). And although he believed that such a system is likely to be unstable for political reasons, he does not find sharing or conjoint ownership of sovereignty to be formally inconsistent with the coordination of political authority.

But for this very reason, ironically, he refuses to admit that sovereignty held conjointly is a form of mixed constitution. In a mixed constitution, he assumes, the rights of sovereignty may well be separated and the separated rights distributed to different partners – which, indeed, is to construct a

---

13. Stintzing 1880–4, II, p. 40. For parallels to Otto's evasions in Reinking see, among other places, especially: 1631, I, *classis*, ii.1, nos. 56, 89, 137, 196.

Sovereignty and the mixed constitution

compound sovereign. But he believes that if a constitution is to be mixed
by means of sharing, this can only be if the entirety of any power or set of
powers is granted to each of the partners in the same way at the same time!
This, of course, is a juridical absurdity which is, however, absent from the
Roman scheme of legislation since power there was shared conjointly by
the senate and the people. But how, then, is that arrangement to be
classified? For Arnisaeus it is simply a version of polity in Aristotle's sense
because it seeks to balance the interests of the nobles and the commoners by
giving equal weight to each.

Yet in this [Roman] arrangement there is no mixture of commonwealths since
neither the senate nor the commoners control the rights of majesty, but these are
handed to each of them conjointly. Since, then, patricians and plebeians rule in
equal measure, how else portray this state than as a polity (*Rempublicam in specie*)?
For it is not the mode of administration (*modus dispensationis*) but the degree of
domination (*gradus dominationis*) that constitutes the form of a commonwealth, and
so long as the commoners and the nobles participate on an equal basis, they join
together into a true and legitimate commonwealth. An example may be taken
from the Roman republic, the gradual degeneration of which into a democracy
after the introduction of the tribunes is beyond all doubt . . . and yet the distinction
between the power (*potestatem*) of the commoners and the authority (*authoritatem*)
of the senate did not cease to exist up to the change of regime, or up to the age of
Livy, Florus, and Dio.   (1615, p. 876).

But this expansion of the concept of a polity leads to confusing
ambiguities. In a constitution mixed by sharing, like the Roman, the
constituent elements are separate corporations, each of which casts its vote
independently of the other. In the idea of polity as it is found in Aristotle,
on the other hand, sovereignty is located in a single assembly wherein all
participate as individuals although certain voting procedures are adopted to
promote a balanced outcome. It is thus a kind of moderate democracy
which, at least in its juridical principle, is very different from a mixed
constitution. Arnisaeus, indeed, is not unaware of the difference between
vote by order and vote by head. Speaking of polity (*respublica in specie*), he
notes the difficulty of maintaining the equality of nobles and people (which
is the very meaning of polity) where voting is individual, and then
continues:

Since it might not be possible in this manner to keep the patricians and the
commoners within the confines of a shared commonwealth because the commoners would be preponderant, Aristotle points out another way in *Politics* IV, chs.
8–9, which he calls *mixin* [mixing], or blending of oligarchy and democracy, and
in which he locates the nature of the polity (*reipublicae in specie*). If all the citizens are

Religion, civil government, and the debate on constitutions

admitted to the suffrage on a man by man basis, the majority may crush the minority, as has been said. But if the entire order of patricians is accorded a right equal to that of the entire order of commoners, without regard to the weight of numbers, then a form of shared commonwealth comes about in which the commoners can do no more than the nobility by virtue of their great numbers. There is, moreover, a distinction between this commonwealth and a mixed system, as we will show more fully in c.vi, sec. 1, since in a mixed commonwealth the rights of sovereignty are distributed among all the parts of the commonwealth, whereas in this they remain in all of them undivided, so that the first is a compound and this one mixed in such a way that it does not deviate from simplicity in its essence, given that to admit all the citizens into the government of the commonwealth on an equal footing (*aequo jure*) is the sign of a simple not a compound commonwealth. In a compound the king, the aristocrats, and the people each have different rights, but in this form all citizens of either order are regarded as having one and the same right. Aristotle, *Politics* IV ch. 9, has proposed both techniques since in either case all the citizens are admitted to partnership in the commonwealth, except in one way conjointly, in the other by separate rights (*divisim*). We will speak of both ways in our chapter on the mixed commonwealth. But here we will briefly note some things than can help to understand the polity. In this commonwealth, therefore, the order of the nobility – whether it has obtained this prerogative by virtue, by wealth, or by excellence of birth – ought to be distinguished from the order of the commoners so that in deliberations the opinion of a whole order may be heard, not that of individuals. (1615, II.v, pp. 825–6).

Arnisaeus here treats voting by order as but one more device of political moderation, rather than as a separate juridical form. His concept of polity, by thus embracing both a simple and a compound polyarchy, can refer to two quite different things, and becomes imprecise and ambiguous in its meaning. On the other hand, when he is dealing with the distribution of powers, Arnisaeus can be accurate. He describes the German constitution as a mixture of aristocracy and monarchy (with the monarchical element held preponderant in his account of 1606, and the aristocratic in his account of 1615) (1606, p. 183, 1615, II.vi.5, p. 1084). But the element of mixture here admitted is merely the reservation to the emperor of certain residual executive powers, which produces a separation, or distribution, of powers between the emperor and the diet. This Arnisaeus regards as an authentic and even desirable division of the rights of sovereignty. But insofar as there are powers that are shared, or held conjointly, he calls the outcome aristocracy since, for the reasons we have given, he can have no other term for it. Just as the partnership of nobles and people is 'polity', so that of king and nobles is 'aristocracy'.[14]

14. This is evident from the context as in 1615, II.vi.5, p. 1073. And in the same place there is a critical comment on Paurmeister which seems to agree that the term aristocracy is properly applied to the element of sharing in the German constitution.

Sovereignty and the mixed constitution

No less surprising, and similarly misleading, is the account by Tobias Paurmeister, whose *De jurisdictione Imperii Romani* is one of the most acute and influential treatises of this period on German public law. Paurmeister had no difficulty in recognising the shared jurisdiction of independent partners as an arrangement in which each of the partners had a veto. Speaking of the empire, he says,

The supreme power of the empire ... is distributed in two halves, one of which is held by Caesar, the other by the estates collectively. A division of this sort once existed between Caesar and the people, for Suetonius, writing about Caesar, notes that the power of the popular assemblies was divided [between them] – although in this case through separated areas of jurisdiction (*sed pro partibus divisis*). But now the entire power of the empire, except for the power of bestowing special rights and privileges, is shared, without divided jurisdiction (*pro partibus indivisis*), between the emperor and the estates. The half that belongs to the estates is distributed as three-sixths, of which the Electors have one, the Princes another ... and the senate of the imperial cities the third.   (Paurmeister 1608, II.ii, no. 20, pp. 342–3)

But although this idea of fifty-fifty sharing is later repeated in refuting Bodin's claim that sovereignty in the German constitution was entirely vested in the princes and the delegates of the cities, Paurmeister does not go on to a criticism of Bodin on the mixed constitution (II.ii. no. 34, pp. 356–7). On the contrary, in Book II, chapter i, he classifies the imperial system as an aristocracy or kind of oligarchy in accordance with a classification which holds that all regimes may be divided dichotomously into the rule of a few (oligarchy) and the rule of many (democracy) (II.i, nos. 7–9, 11–12, pp. 322, 324). This classification, much like Arnisaeus', is not exactly wrong, but it does not express, or even hint at, the fact of mixture in the German constitution, and might be readily taken to deny it. The terms oligarchy or aristocracy, then as well as now, would ordinarily convey the idea of a polyarchy in which those entitled to participate would vote not by corporation but by head, and it would therefore fail to indicate that the emperor in the German constitution had an independent share.

iii Besold and the mixed constitution

A clear understanding of the sharing of sovereignty and an adequate formula for the German constitution appear only with the work of Christoph Besold, who was the first to formulate the concept of a compound polyarchy. Besold seems to have put forward this conception in the first decade of the seventeenth century and then to have worked out the implications in the course of a running debate with Otto. His earlier statements are virtually inaccessible. But we are fortunate in having what

Religion, civil government, and the debate on constitutions

seems to be a complete as well as final version of his views in the form of an article, 'De reipublicae statu mixto', in a collection of his writings (1626).

Besold begins by observing that truly pure forms of state are almost never encountered in reality. But in contrast with Althusius, this does not lead him to propose that all systems be considered as virtually simple, but rather to insist that the mixed constitution is the most common form of state, and particularly so in modern Europe, in the monarchies of which the king is usually the prince of a mixed constitution (Besold 1626, p. 211).

The mixture of a constitution, furthermore, cannot be comprehended by the distinction between state and government, since the form of government exists *de facto* at the ruler's discretion, not as a *de jure* constitutional requirement. 'And surely if a commonwealth is defined not by law but by the mode of governance, then a master who embraces his servant in filial love would be his father not only in affection but in law, which no one will readily assert' (p. 211). Besold here refers approvingly to Otto's criticism of Kirchner and others who held similar views. But unlike Otto he is completely clear on the difference between arrangements of administrative convenience and requirements of fundamental law:

And if a king most often follows the advice of the estates of his realm and of the leading men among his people, the mode of ruling is no doubt aristocratic. But this is not to say that the form of the commonwealth is mixed unless it appears that sovereign power is shared with them in some degree. That happens only if the estates have the faculty not only of advising but also and at the same time of preventing and prohibiting; and the prince is bound to abide by their counsel or dissent. (p. 213)

By ignoring this difference, Otto has managed to conclude that a king could be constrained in his authority and the state remain a simple monarchy. But if a prince requires the consent of others for the ordinary conduct of affairs, it makes no sense to speak as if he ruled alone. 'He [Otto] thinks it to be a point of great importance', Besold comments, 'whether the rights of a supreme authority are constrained or taken away, etc., which I do not deny. For if they are constrained it is a mixture, and if taken away a pure aristocracy' (pp. 212–13).

Thus the rights of sovereignty had to be capable of being shared, Bodinian objections notwithstanding. The core of these objections, as they had been elaborated and refined by Otto in an attack upon Besold and others, was that the logical consequence of sharing sovereignty was to annihilate it altogether. And Besold's main contribution was to formulate the consequence of sharing as the institution of a compound polyarchy:

Sovereignty and the mixed constitution

It is never possible he [Otto] says, either in nature or even in imagination for supreme authority or majesty to be shared with an inferior and still remain supreme. It remains supreme, I answer, but not in one individual. It is rather in the whole body, or corporation, of those who rule (*archonton*) but in such a way that it is not distributed equally among the parts. The prince will be conceded some large degree of eminence (which will be larger, of course, than what the doge has in the Venetian commonwealth) or else it will be an aristocracy.   (p. 212)

The polyarchic outcome, furthermore, does not require that the king and the estates be equal partners. It can also exist where the king enjoys preeminence and is the focus of political allegiance. In a mixed constitution 'sovereignty is in the corporation (*collegium*) even though the head of that corporation, as often happens, may be above the other members in a variety of ways', and although the oath of allegiance may be rendered to the prince, it need not entail obedience to him outside his particular jurisdiction (p. 212). Even the emergency power of the prince, if such indeed exists, applies only to occasions that are foreseen by law and custom (p. 220). The components of the polyarchy, finally, are not individuals but orders, on which account it may be distinguished from democracy. Arnisaeus, Besold notes, refused to acknowledge the sharing of sovereignty as mixture:

And there seems to be some room for doubt here since a state of this kind, where all three forms of commonwealth are commingled without separation of the rights of sovereignty, may seem rather to be democracy. But in a democracy the majority decides; here the king, the nobles, and the commoners constitute three orders, and cast three votes, so that the majority of the people cannot preempt the others.
(p. 227)

In replying to Otto on the mixed constitution Besold is thinking of sovereignty shared between two or more partners in a compound polyarchy. But when he goes on to the German constitution, he notes that a state is also mixed when different rights of sovereignty are assigned to different agents. His purpose here is to account for the *reservata* of the German emperor, such as the right of hearing certain fiscal and feudal cases in his own tribunal as well as certain rights in foreign affairs and the conduct of warfare, which he could still exercise without the consent of the Electors or estates. Otto does not reach this issue because he managed to believe that all the rights of sovereignty belonged to the emperor alone. With Besold, on the other hand, the rights of sovereignty shared by the emperor and the estates belonged to a compound body that was juridically distinct from the emperor alone so that the issue of separated powers was readily confronted.

Religion, civil government, and the debate on constitutions

If Besold is brief on separation, it is largely because the issue had already been resolved by Arnisaeus, who at least in this respect had broken cleanly with Bodin. The parts of sovereignty are in some sense indivisible, Arnisaeus had observed, since no one of them can be exercised without the cooperation of the others. But this is not to say that these parts, although functionally inseparable, cannot be vested in separated agents so long as they are harmonised and coordinated by fundamental law.

For there are a number of powers and rights the union of which produces complete sovereignty. And although it is impossible for sovereignty as a whole and in its entirety to be shared among several agents, there is nothing to prevent its parts from being separated and distributed to several agents such that there is a fragment of sovereignty in each of them, and yet in the body as a whole complete and supreme sovereignty results from the union of the fragments of sovereignty coming together into one.   (Arnisaeus 1606, viii, pp. 164–5)

Bodin's mistake was that he not only failed to see this need for harmonisation but gave such scope to certain parts of sovereignty that they swallowed all the rest:

He [Bodin] concedes rights to the particular components such as carry with them the entirety of majesty, and this may not be done as we said a little while ago. Thus the power to make law on all topics cannot be given to some one component because power over everything goes with it. Nor can subjects be obligated to the king in all respects in this mixed commonwealth, because to do this is to lay the supreme power in the king's lap.   (p. 166).

Properly delimited and coordinated, therefore, the rights of sovereignty can be distributed among separate agents. And this is also the conclusion in Besold, who praises mixture of this sort as conducive to political stability:

The mixed state admits of many variations. Sometimes the rights of majesty are divided, as when the king has some of them and the senate some, or the optimates some and the commoners some. Sometimes they are shared, as when the king does not have them without the senate or the senate without the king, or when the commoners and the nobles enjoy them simultaneously. Sometimes the supreme power is tempered in other ways [outside of mixture]. In the first kind of mixed state, the rights of majesty are separated and different ones are assigned to different estates. This mixture seems to be the most finely balanced harmony, for some powers are best exercised by one person, such as the power of judging and imposing punishments, while there are others in which the participation of the orders or estates could hardly be denied without inequity. The right of undertaking a war is one of these perhaps, as well as others of a similar order.[15]
                                                        (Besold 1626, p. 213)

15. Besold, it may be noted, deals with the German constitution mainly as an example of distribution. He is not quite willing openly to list it under 'ephoristic' monarchies in which sovereignty is shared but does not rule that out (p.216). Poland is his first example of shared sovereignty, a form much

Sovereignty and the mixed constitution

Besold's refutation of Bodin and his followers was thus complete on all the main themes of indivisibility. And although he is perhaps indebted to Arnisaeus for his account of separation, his formulation of the more controversial principle of sharing seems to be original as well as luminous, and so decisive for a modern reader.[16] But in order to understand the difficulty of this question for contemporaries and their reluctance to acknowledge sharing as a form of mixture, it is worth showing how Otto, at least, attempted to maintain his view in the teeth of Besold's argument.

There had been, as we have said, a number of exchanges between Otto and Besold, and to a modern reader the first version of Besold's *De statu reipublicae mixto*, which must have appeared about 1620, should have left the question settled. But Otto in a last reply to Besold complained that the question had been begged. In his *De maiestate imperii et imperantis* of 1623, Otto contends that the concept of a compound polyarchy is not a mixture since power is in the whole and not the parts, and that it precludes the distribution of power to the parts which, Otto seems to think, is Besold's own criterion for mixture:

> In response to my [earlier] argument Besold replies that supreme authority continues [after sharing] but in a corporate body or college of rulers (*archonton*) rather than in one person. To which I reply that there is no mixture here and that this state in no way differs from a polyarchy, in which sovereignty is attributed to all collectively rather than to all as individuals. But let us go on. Even though (you say) the rights of majesty are entirely in the corporation, they can nonetheless be so divided that the king has some of them, and the senate some, or the aristocrats some and the commoners some; and the senate does not have them without the king, or the commoners and the nobles assert them simultaneously. But I reject this. If the rights of majesty are assigned to the corporation as such in a polyarchic state, I simply do not see how the same can be assigned to the individual parts.
>
> (Otto 1623, p. 31)

Otto's confusion here is twofold. In the first place, he blurs the difference between a simple and a compound polyarchy. This appears to be the same sort of error that we saw in Arnisaeus. But it is now more surprising, since it comes after Besold's clarification. In the second place, Otto utterly confuses *distribution* of the rights of sovereignty – in which some rights go to one partner and others to another – with *sharing* of the rights of sovereignty – in which the partners act together. But these two modes of mixture are clearly

recommended, he says, by Althusius, the *Vindiciae contra tyrannos*, Buchanan, and Hotman. The *reservata*, one should also note, are singled out by Antonius to show that the emperor is truly a monarch. See above p.319 n.12. And they are cited by Keckermann a one indication that the monarchical element predominates in the German mixture: 1608, II.iv, pp.570ff.

16. For another contemporary account see Frantzke 1621, which is a competent analysis of the sharing and distribution of the rights of majesty, and seems to be dependent on Besold and Arnisaeus.

Religion, civil government, and the debate on constitutions

and expressly distinguished in the passage from Besold Otto paraphrases (see p. 326). Besold never suggests that the same rights of sovereignty could be shared and divided among the same partners at the same time that would of course be logically absurd.

With the appearance, in Besold, of a theoretically decisive account of the divisibility of sovereignty in a mixed constitution, we bring this chapter to a close. This is not to suggest that all of Besold's conclusions were immediately or universally taken up. Almost to the end of the eighteenth century, there were theorists who continued to treat the obligation of a king to obtain consent to legislation as sovereignty limited rather than sovereignty shared (Gierke 1957, p. 154). And there were some who followed Pufendorf in holding that the several rights of sovereignty could not be separated, so that the German and even the English constitution were to be regarded not as proper states in which some individual or body ruled, but as irregular systems which were held together merely by comity among independent parts.[17] Yet such resistance notwithstanding, a change of perspective occurs around the end of the first quarter of the seventeenth century on which Besold's influence, although often indirect and difficult to measure, was no doubt considerable (Gierke 1957, p. 118). Around that time the German empire is deliberately expounded as a mixed constitution, in something close to Besold's usage of that term, by authoritative commentators on German public law (see esp. Hoke 1968, pt II). And among theorists of sovereignty, there is an unbroken succession, starting with Besold, in whom the sharing of sovereignty as well as the distribution of its parts are correctly identified as modes of mixture that are ultimately consistent with the coordination of governmental functions (Gierke 1957, pp. 155–6, 1966, p. 170ff).

17. Pufendorf 1934, pp. 1016ff, 1038–9, 1769, II.vii.9, pp. 693–5, II.viii.12, pp. 706–8; Gierke 1957, pp. 154–5.

[3]

Bodin's Early Theory of Sovereignty

Julian H. Franklin

Bodin's principle of sovereignty, as finally stated in the *République*, is the assertion that there must exist, in every ordered commonwealth, a single center of supreme authority and that this authority must necessarily be absolute. This proposition is presented as an analytic truth. By the very concept of a political order, a sovereign authority exists and must be absolute as well as indivisible.

But in an earlier work, Bodin presents the principle of sovereignty without the absolutist element, and this difference cannot be attributed to immaturity or inadvertence. The *Methodus ad facilem historiarum cognitionem* appeared in 1566, when Bodin was in his middle thirties, and was the fruit of some fifteen years of scholarly research in comparative history and jurisprudence. The purpose of the work was to provide the student or amateur of history with a critical and theoretical apparatus for reading historians with profit. One of the most important requirements, in Bodin's judgment, was to understand the nature of the state, the different types of states, the general causes of constitutional change, and the constitutions and changes of the most important political systems of the present and the past. Chapter VI of the *Methodus*, in which these themes are taken up, accounts for more than one-third of the bulk of the entire work and is really a treatise in itself. In the first part of this book within a book, which is very densely written, the principle of sovereignty and the doctrine of its indivisibility are stated and elaborately defended.

The thought of chapter VI of the *Methodus* is thus a mature and reasoned conception of the state, and in this early statement, absolutist elements are not only absent but are deliberately repudiated. Limited supremacy, subject to law and procedures of consent, is not only admitted as a proper form of sovereignty, but is described and recommended as the normal form of monarchy in Europe. The conception of the French kingship is a continuation and enthusiastic endorsement of the intellectual trend that we have seen in the preceding chapter. It is mistaken, therefore, to assume that the equation of supreme with absolute authority was an inherent or guiding component of Bodin's original inquiry. The absolutism of the *République* was something superadded, and in order to evaluate this change we must first understand the earlier conception.

Bodin's concern with the characteristics of supreme authority seems to have derived from very early studies on the inalienability of sovereignty in Roman

Jean Bodin

law. The generally accepted rule that sovereignty could not be alienated had
been ambiguous in medieval jurisprudence. In principle at least, the only valid
exceptions to the rule were grants of authority and privilege that did not
seriously impair the basic set of powers which each incumbent ruler was bound
to pass on to his successor. But the actual application of this rule was loose. In
order to account for the decentralized organization of the medieval Empire,
the legal commentators had devised all manner of ingenious formulae by
which they could acknowledge almost any alienation or prescription of the
Emperor's authority while still maintaining that imperial unity was somehow
unimpaired.[1]

The French civilians of the sixteenth century, who were thinking of the
king of France and not the German Emperor, had been far less permissive on
the prescription of sovereign prerogatives; they had been encouraged in this
point of view by new interpretations of the Roman sources developed by the
academic jurists. Beginning with the Italian commentator, Andrea Alciato,
the new school of humanist civilians had shown convincingly that medieval
views on alienation were often inconsistent with classic Roman usage.[2] By the
1550s, when Bodin was a student and young teacher at the law school of
Toulouse, the entire doctrine was in process of revision.

The questions posed were commonly taken up in the course of commentaries on titles of the *Digest* and the *Code* which dealt with the authority and
jurisdiction of magistrates. The technical problem was to define the kinds of
powers held by the different sorts of magistrates. But to decide the powers that
a magistrate might have was to take a position on the rights of sovereigns, at
least by implication.[3] The powers inseparable from sovereignty were all those
powers that a magistrate could never hold, or which he could legally exercise
only by a specific and revocable grant. Bodin's earliest efforts as a legal theorist
were almost surely intended as a contribution to this literature. Sometime
in the 1550s he composed a monograph, or pair of monographs, entitled *De
imperio et jurisdictione*. The manuscript, unpublished in his lifetime, was
burned at his request upon his death. But the title indicates a treatise on the

---

[1] For the adjustment of the idea of imperial sovereignty to the federal structure of the
Empire, see Cecil N. Sidney Woolf, *Bartolus of Sassoferrato* (Cambridge, 1913). The
counter-trends are developed in Peter N. Riesenberg, *The Inalienability of Sovereignty in
Medieval Political Thought* (New York, 1956).

[2] The most dramatic issue was the right of magistrates to 'hold' the *merum imperium*, or
'power of the sword', in permanent possession as a kind of usufruct. For an historical
survey of this celebrated controversy, which goes back to an alleged debate between Lothair
and Azo in the thirteenth century, see Myron P. Gilmore, *Argument from Roman Law in
Political Thought: 1200–1600* (Cambridge, Mass., 1941). For Alciato's revolutionary attack
on the dominant view that the high powers of *merum imperium* could be 'had' by
magistrates, see his *Paradoxa* (1518) in Andrea Alciato, *Opera* (Basel, 1582) IV, cols 29ff.

[3] One good example of the easy movement from one question to the other is Jean Gillot, *De
jurisdictione et imperio* (1537) in *Tractatus universi juris* (Venice, 1584–6) III. See also
Alciato, *Paradoxa*, vol. IV, col. 39, and Gilmore, *Argument from Roman Law*, ch. 2 *passim*.

Early theory of Sovereignty

law of magistracies, a surmise fully confirmed by allusions to the contents given by Bodin in the *Methodus*.[4]

These allusions also indicate that Bodin had already been led to general reflections on the character of sovereignty. His attempt to discover which prerogatives of government a ruler could not give away posed a question that was not directly answered by the legal texts. Since the *Corpus Juris* does not provide a list of sovereign prerogatives, it was almost useless for the purpose. The medievals had supplied this lack by incorporating the list of regalian privileges which had been claimed by Frederick I at the Diet of Roncaglia in 1158 and ratified by the Italian cities. But this was a list of feudal privileges unsuited to contemporary needs. For similar reasons French domestic custom was also unsuggestive. Here again there was no list of imprescriptible prerogatives, and most of the disputed points of law had to do with feudal rights of justice and taxation.

Bodin's contribution was to put the question of sovereign prerogatives in a more comprehensive way than anyone before him. He now attempted to derive the contents of supreme authority from the concept of supremacy itself. The question that he asked, in other words, was what prerogatives must be held by a political authority in order to say that it does not acknowledge a superior or equal in its territory.

The scope of this investigation was also affected by a crucial methodological decision. In the course of his Toulousan period, Bodin concluded that points of legal theory could not be settled by appeal to Roman norms alone. The use of philological techniques by the great French school of legal humanism had prepared the way for a methodological revolution in which Bodin became a leading figure. The more the humanists attempted to find the original meaning of the Roman texts, and to discern the underlying system of the *Corpus Juris*, the more they became critical of Roman law itself. The *Corpus Juris*, to list their main complaints,[5] seemed incomplete in many areas, and most especially in public law; Justinian and his compilers had often been cryptic and inaccurate in representing the best of Roman legal thought; many rules, some of

---

[4] *Methodus ad facilem historiarum cognitionem* (1566), Pierre Mesnard, ed., *Oeuvres philosophiques de Jean Bodin* (Paris, 1951) pp. 173, 175, 176. The first and third references are to a manuscript entitled *De imperio*. The second reference, which does not appear in the first edition, is to a work entitled *De jure imperio* [sic]. This would appear to be a mistaken rendition either of *De jure imperii*, or, more probably, of *De jurisdictione*. The latter title is much more appropriate to the context in which the citation appears, and it is mentioned along with *De imperio*, in a list of five manuscripts – all having titles suggestive of technical legal studies – that Bodin ordered to be burned at his death. The authority for this is Aegidius Menagius (Ménage), *Vita Petri Aerodii*, p. 143, cited in Roger Chauviré, *Jean Bodin, auteur de la République* (La Flèche, 1914) p. 95. Beatrice Reynolds also suggests *De jurisdictione* in her translation of the *Methodus*, *Method for the Easy Comprehension of History* (New York, 1945) p. 173, n. 52.

[5] For a survey of this anti-Romanist trend in humanist legal thought, see Julian H. Franklin, *Jean Bodin and the Sixteenth Century Revolution in the Methodology of Law and History* (New York, 1963) ch. III.

Jean Bodin

them basic to the system, were peculiar to the Roman state and obsolete for France; the *Corpus Juris* had not been arranged into a logically coherent system, and could not be because of its defects and omissions.[6]

One consequence of this critique was to strengthen that emphasis on domestic legal custom to which we alluded in the previous chapter. An additional motif, especially characteristic of Bodin, was the idea of remedying deficiences in Roman law by consulting the materials of universal history.[7] This, according to Bodin, was the only way to construct a truly universal legal science: to compare ' all the laws of all, or the most famous, states and to select the best variety '.[8]

Some years earlier, a grandiose design for this comparison had been projected in his *Juris universi distributio*, or *Sketch of Law in its Entirety*; and the sixth chapter of the *Methodus* of 1566 was a preliminary statement of his findings in the area of public law. In this fashion an inquiry originally focused on the special prerogatives of the king of France and the Emperor of ancient Rome was thus transformed into a study of sovereignty in every kind of state.

It is at this point, I would suggest, that Bodin was lured to the idea that sovereignty is indivisible. The premise in chapter vi of the *Methodus*, and throughout his examination of public law, is that sovereign authority has several forms, and is to be found not only in monarchies but also in republics. Bodin assumed, in other words, that the ' Senate ' in an aristocracy or the assembly of the people in a democracy had the same status with respect to other components of the commonwealth as that of the ruler in a monarchy.

But this equation is either mistaken or dangerously misleading. The idea of sovereignty is monarchical in connotation. It immediately suggests the ' sway ' or ' dominion ' of one person over others, the first ruling and the others being ruled. But in a pure democracy this relationship of ruler and subject does not obtain in any obvious or determinate sense. The entire society, as it were, is included in the ' subject ' of sovereignty. *Mutatis mutandis*, the same ' peculiarity ' applies to aristocracies as well.

The identification of the nobles or the people as ' the sovereign persons ' of republics is thus legitimate only by a legal fiction. If the nobles or the people are construed as a *persona ficta* or *moralis*, the procedures of decision-making can be cast into a ' royal ' form. The *persona ficta* can then be taken as the ruler of the general society, i.e., of all its parts in their individual capacities.

---

[6] All these themes are briefly mentioned by Bodin in the dedicatory epistle to the *Methodus*. The most elaborate critique is Hotman's *Antitribonian*, written one year later but not published until 1603.

[7] Thus Hotman, *Antitribonianus*, in *Variorum opuscula ad cultiorem jurisprudentiam adsequendam pertinentia* (Pisa, 1771), vol. vii, pp. 140ff and also François Baudouin, *De institutione historiae universae et ejus cum jurisprudentia conjunctione* Προλεγόμενων (1561) (Halle, 1726) p. 29.

[8] *Methodus*, Dedicatory epistle, Mesnard ed., p. 107 (2). Much the same thought is also expressed in the Dedicatory epistle to his *Juris universi distributio*, Pierre Mesnard ed., *Oeuvres philosophiques de Jean Bodin* (Paris, 1951), p. 71, which almost surely dates from his Toulousan period.

Early theory of Sovereignty

Bodin, however, moved from monarchical to other forms of state without examining this intervening step. Given the conventions of the time, his inadvertence was natural enough. In the tradition stemming from the ancients, the nobles or the people had always been treated as substantial entities. The people, for example, were most often envisaged as the ' poor ', and thus as one part of the society which ruled the rest in a democracy. Bodin, accordingly could look upon the nobles or the people as if they were a person, without observing that a legal fiction was implied.

For most purposes this omission was a purely technical defect that did not affect the substance of his argument. But one far-reaching consequence was Bodin's inability to comprehend the notion of a mixed constitution in the sense of a sovereign authority shared among the people, the nobles, and the king. From the standpoint of a theory of sovereignty, ' the sovereign ' of a mixed constitution would have to be described as a *persona ficta* composed of all three parts, with each part, or the members of each part, sharing in the making of ' the sovereign's ' decisions. This solution would soon be pointed out by Christopher Besold, who was one of the shrewdest of Bodin's early critics.[9]

But Bodin, having no theoretical conception of a corporate or fictive sovereign, was simply unable to imagine this. He was always thinking of ' the sovereign ' as one part of the society that rules the rest, according to the familiar model of a kingship. It seemed to follow, therefore, that if all three parts should share in sovereignty the entire relation of ruler and subject would evaporate, along with the state and sovereignty itself. That the outcome would be the same in a complete democracy, where all the people rule, escaped his notice utterly. The problem of division was always considered from the standpoint of a king, or as though the people or the nobles had the posture of a king.

The sharing of sovereignty could thus appear as a logical absurdity. By negating the relation of subjection, it seemed a negation of the state itself. Or to put it in another way, a mixed constitution seemed a contradiction in the

---

[9] *De majestate in genere ejusque juribus specialibus . . . accedit tractatio singularis de reipublicae statu mixto* (1618) in Christopher Besold, *Operis politici, editio nova* (Strasbourg, 1626) pp. 212ff. Besold is answering Daniel Ottho, who had attacked Besold and Bartholomaeus Keckermann for having defected from Bodin's position. Besold briefly summarizes and replies to seven arguments for indivisibility. His diagnosis of the error contained in all of them seems to be suggested in his reply to the first argument: ' It is never possible, he [Ottho] says, either in nature or even in imagination for supreme authority or majesty to be mixed with an inferior and still remain supreme. It remains supreme, I answer, but not in one individual. It is rather in the whole body or corporation (*collegio*) of those who rule (*archonton*) but in such a way that it is not distributed equally among the parts. The prince will be conceded some large degree of eminence (which will be larger, of course, than what the Doge has in the Venetian commonwealth) or else it will be an aristocracy ' (p. 212). A few sentences earlier Besold makes the decisive point that a mixed state is no less comprehensible than a simple aristocracy or democracy. ' As in a simple polyarchic state, majesty properly and integrally resides in that entire body which participates in majesty.'

Jean Bodin

adjective. A constitution is a ' state ' or ' condition ' of the sovereign authority. But a mixed constitution is a negation of authority as such, and thus a ' state ' of anarchy.

The fallacy in all of this is so transparent to the modern reader, and so profoundly foreign, that it is sometimes tempting to look for deeper lines of reasoning. For Bodin, on the other hand, the argument for indivisibility seemed so self-evident that he was hardly able to articulate his grounds. There is little argument at all in the *Methodus*, and the arguments later offered in the *République* involve such gross non-sequiturs that the modern reader often fails to see any connection whatsoever between premise and conclusion.

Thus one of Bodin's favourite arguments for indivisibility is based on the very simple observation that if a sovereign prince should share his power with a subject, he would no longer have the status of a sovereign:

Thus all [the jurists] agree that royal rights cannot be ceded, are inalienable, and cannot be prescribed by any tract of time. If a sovereign prince should share them with a subject, he makes a companion of his servitor, and in so doing is no longer sovereign. For the term sovereign, which refers to one who is above all subjects, cannot apply to someone who has made a companion of his servitor . . . The prince . . . cannot make a subject equal to himself without negating his own power.[10]

From a modern standpoint, the truth of this seems trite. Where sovereignty is shared by more than one, it cannot belong to one alone. But for Bodin the implications seemed momentous. For one thing, he seems to have thought that a king who would share his authority with others is no longer ' king ' in any sense at all, since he does not rule alone. Monarchy, accordingly, could not be mixed with other forms, for in the very act of mixture the monarchical element – or rule of one – would disappear! The further implication, virtually inarticulate, is that rule itself would disappear. If the king, in sharing power with his subjects, does not divest himself of all of it, there will be no highest power, and no authority at all!

Bodin, however, is sometimes more articulate, and comes very close to a clear expression of the fallacy in the following passage on the indivisibility of legislative power:

For if sovereignty is indivisible, as we have shown, how could it be shared by a prince, the nobles, and the people at the same time? The first mark of sovereignty is to give the law to subjects, and where then will be the subjects who obey, if they also have the power to make law? And what individual can give the law, if he is himself constrained to take it from those to whom he gives it? The conclusion follows necessarily, that, if no one in particular has the power to make law, and this power belongs to all together, the commonwealth is democratic.[11]

10 *Les six livres de la république* (1576) (Paris, 1583; reprinted by Scientia Verlag, Aalen, Germany, 1961) I, 10, 215 (155).
11 *Ibid.* pp. 254–5 (185).

Early theory of Sovereignty

The last sentence, in which the outcome of division is described, was to undergo an illuminating change in the Latin edition of 1586.[12] In the later version the outcome is described as anarchy, which was, no doubt, a better rendition of Bodin's underlying thought. But the closeness, in his mind, of democracy and anarchy nicely reveals the ultimate confusion. A regime in which all components participate in the making of decisions cannot be distinguished from anarchy, because it no longer displays the subjection of society to a natural person. Having no conception of a corporate sovereign, Bodin was ultimately unable to draw any stable distinction between a mixed constitution and democracy, and between either one of these and anarchy.[13]

Up to here we have been speaking of mixture or division only in the sense of sharing. From a modern standpoint the most obvious example would be the sharing of legislative power by two or more components of a compound legislature. But Bodin was also concerned to deny the possibility of distribution. This, from a modern standpoint, would be the separation of governmental functions, as when the executive or judicial power is divided from the legislative by being placed in separate hands. Although this position is not of immediate importance for Bodin's interpretation of French institutions, it is so interwoven with his other views on indivisibility that some examination of his thinking seems desirable.

The modern idea of separated powers depends on the rather subtle, and at first sight curious, thought that executive power can be simultaneously independent and subordinate. The subordination of executive to legislative is indispensable to the coordination of the legal system. But this subordination is not achieved through direct control by the legislative power. It depends on the fact that executive power stands to the legislative in the relationship of means to end. It is subordinated to the latter by the inherent nature of its function. Its independence, therefore, means that the legislative power is also restricted by its function. The legislative must be constitutionally forbidden to assume the role of the executive – either by direct expropriation of executive functions or by the issuance of particular decrees.

But the idea of fixed jurisdictional relationships was beyond Bodin's theoretical resources. When he thought of separated powers, he assumed that one or

---

[12] *De republica libri sex* (Paris, 1586) II, 1, p. 176.

[13] The tendency to identify monarchy with the essence of ' rule ' as such is nicely illustrated by. Bartholomaeus Keckermann, *Systema disciplinae politicae* (Hanover, 1607) p. 33: Monarchy is the simplest of political regimes because its essence is unity (*quia in unitate consistit*) and because it reduces the multitude of subjects to unity of a natural sort (*ad naturalem unitatem*).' This statement is particularly revealing because Keckermann is not an absolutist. He admits a right of resistance to any form of state, and he seems to prefer a mixed monarchy. Yet he is unable to comprehend division of sovereignty, and tried to accommodate the mixed constitution by applying Bodin's distinction between the form of government and the form of state. The result is a misinterpretation of Bodin and general confusion of the issue. See p. 560.

Jean Bodin

more of them must be inherently entitled to annex the jurisdictions of the rest. In the *Methodus* this control of jurisdictions may well have seemed inherent in the 'executive' power of 'creating magistrates and assigning each one's duties', which was then regarded as the 'first and most important mark of sovereignty'.[14] But no explanation was as yet attempted. Later on, in the *République*, the power to control all other jurisdictions seemed to be an inherent and inevitable aspect of the legislative power, and it is also discovered in the power of receiving oaths of fealty, which had now been added as a right of majesty. Both of these powers, therefore, would not only be in conflict with each other in a scheme of separated powers, but each would be in conflict with all others:

But, someone will say, can there not be a commonwealth in which the people create the officers, dispose of revenues, and grant pardons – which are three marks of sovereignty; and in which the nobility makes the laws, orders peace or war, and levies direct and indirect taxation – which are also marks of sovereignty; and in which there is, in addition, a royal magistrate above all others to whom the people as a whole and each person in particular renders faith and liege homage, and who judges in last resort without avenue of appeal or civil request? Would this not be to compose a commonwealth which is at once aristocratic, royal, and popular? I answer that no state like this was ever found, and that none can be made or even be imagined, seeing that the marks of sovereignty are indivisible. For he who will have the power to make law for all, that is to say, the power of commanding or forbidding what he pleases without any one being able to appeal from his commands or even to oppose them, he [I say] will forbid the others to make either war or peace, to levy taxes, or to render faith and homage without his leave. And he to whom fealty and liege homage are due, will obligate the nobility and the people to render obedience to no one but himself. And so will it always have to come to arms, until such time as sovereignty resides in the prince, in the lesser part of the people, or in all the people.[15]

In this passage the power to make law is considered to be absolute, which is in line with Bodin's later concept of supremacy. But I do not believe that the argument depends on this primarily. The obstacle to separated power is not located in the right of the legislative to make any decision that it wishes with respect to private persons, or subjects generally. It is found rather in its power to make laws affecting the rights of other jurisdictions.

Bodin, we may note incidentally, was also persuaded that every prerogative of sovereignty – like, for example, the right of hearing final appeals in civil and criminal cases – was somehow 'contained' in the power to make law, and that possession of the latter implied a claim to all the rest.[16] But his thoughts on this

[14] See below, p. 32.
[15] *République*, p. 266 (193–4).
[16] *Ibid.* pp. 223–4 (161–2). The absence of clear theoretical classification of governmental powers is characteristic of the tradition.

Early theory of Sovereignty

proposition, which may have influenced his doctrine of inseparability, are even less illuminating than the one that we have just described. The ultimate unity of powers is made to depend upon the fact that almost every governmental act involves the power of issuing a binding command. Since the legislative power is defined, in this context, as the power of issuing commands of every type, it is simply an abstract name for political authority in general. The functional differences between different sorts of power are simply ignored.

Once again, it might be tempting for a modern reader to look for something more. But here, too, the criticism of a near-contemporary may help to reassure us on that score. Early critics, like Besold and Henning Arnisaeus, generally accept the view that all governmental functions, in their highest aspects, are the ' parts ' of a power to command. They do not have a definite conception of functional relationships. But they do maintain that a corporate sovereign is possible if the parts of sovereignty are distributed in such a way that the rights of each component are restricted by the functions of the others. For this reason, Arnisaeus, who accepts Bodin's position on the impossibility of sharing sovereignty, will not go along with his doctrine of inseparability:

He [Bodin] concedes rights to the particular components such as carry with them the entirety of majesty, and this may not be done as we said a little while ago. Thus the power to make law on all topics cannot be given to some one component because power over everything goes with it. Nor can subjects be obligated to the king in all respects in this mixed commonwealth, because to do this is to lay the supreme power in the king's lap.[17]

Although Bodin's position on the ' mixed constitution ' seems naive from a modern point of view, it was natural and almost unavoidable at the time he actually wrote. In the sixteenth century, there were simply no materials that directly pointed to another view. Much had been said in Bodin's time about the advantages of a mixed constitution. But when he turned to the historical materials, he was unable to discover any clear example of divided sovereignty, or even any clear suggestion of what separation or division might entail.

In the humanist tradition the best-known example of the ' mixed constitution ' was the Roman Republic of classical antiquity. Because of Polybius and a whole host of later writers who elaborated on his point of view, it was the only constitution, traditionally reputed mixed, on which Bodin and his contemporaries were reasonably well informed. Ancient Athens was not regarded as a mixed constitution; Lycurgan Sparta was not known in significant detail; and the actual procedures of contemporary Venice were difficult to penetrate and were often represented in accordance with the Roman model.

Rome, then, was the crucial case. Yet the Roman constitution of Polybius' time was not a mixture, at least in strictest law, and Bodin was the first to

---

[17] Henning Arnisaeus, *Doctrina politica in genuinam methodum quae est Aristotelis reducta* (1606) in *Opera politica omnia* (Strasbourg, 1648) 1, p. 66.

Jean Bodin

see this clearly. In passage after passage, Polybius himself, and all the other commentators, had regularly attributed powers to the Roman people which amounted to juridical supremacy. Bodin could therefore see that on Polybius' own account, the position of the Roman people was legally analogous to the status of the king of France or the ancient Roman Emperor. The Roman constitution, therefore, was best represented as a ' pure democracy '; and Bodin was able to conclude, triumphantly, that Polybius and all the other ancients had been wrong in speaking of a mixture.

In one respect this criticism was ungenerous. When Polybius and the others spoke of mixture, they were not attempting to describe the basic juridical relationships of the Roman constitution, but the actual balance of effective political influence. To this extent, Bodin was misreading their usage of the term. Yet in the larger sense his own interpretation was superior in being more precise. He was perfectly willing to admit that the Roman Senate had exercised considerable influence, and this influence, he thought, had been highly beneficial to the Roman system.[18] But he was broadly right in holding that all the powers of the Senate were technically held on revocable delegation or sufferance of the people.[19] From a strictly legal standpoint, therefore, the Roman republic was a pure democracy.[20]

Thus the Roman constitution, ironically enough, was a confirmation of Bodin's position rather than a serious refutation. And the irony has many aspects. It is very likely that Bodin was led to formulate his principle of indivisibility by reflections on the Roman constitution, for he had no reason to make the point at all, except to rebut the traditional opinion. It is also very likely that his first formulation of the rights of sovereignty was directly suggested by none other than Polybius. In presenting his list of 1566, Bodin virtually announces this:

And so, having compared the arguments of Aristotle, Polybius, Dionysius [of Halicarnassus], and the jurists – with each other and with the universal history of public affairs – I find that supremacy in a commonwealth consists of five parts. The first and most important is creating magistrates and assigning each one's duties; another is ordaining and repealing laws; a third is declaring and terminating war; a fourth is the right of hearing appeals from all magistrates in last resort; and the last is the power of life and death where the law itself has made no provision for flexibility or clemency.[21]

Indeed, on close inspection, it turns out that this list was probably drawn up with a passage from Polybius in mind which must have been highly suggestive to Bodin as to the nature of the Roman constitution, since it purported to describe the powers of the Roman people. According to Polybius,

[18] *Methodus*, p. 179 (183).   [19] *Ibid.* p. 179 (184).
[20] *Ibid.* p. 177 (179): ' I therefore hold that the Roman state was surely popular in Polybius' time, and even more so in the time of Dionysius and Cicero '.
[21] *Ibid.* pp. 174–5 (172–3).

Early theory of Sovereignty

there is a part and a very important part left for the people. For it is the people which alone has the right to confer honors and inflict punishment ... [And] they are the only court that may try on capital charges ... Again it is the people who bestow office on the deserving, the noblest reward of virtue in a state; the people have the power of approving and rejecting laws: and what is most important of all, they deliberate on the question of war or peace.[22]

Bodin, studying this passage, could have hardly failed to note that the powers of the popular assembly, in the classical account of a mixed constitution, were the very powers required for supremacy.

There were of course certain periods of Roman history to which the idea of the republic as a pure democracy did not apply exactly. Prior to the third century B.C., and even later on occasion, the Senate still contended for its ancient privilege of authorizing legislation by the people. But the constitutional basis of this claim, and the legal effect of authorization, were unclear in Bodin's time; and there was similar obscurity surrounding analogous functions in the Senate of Lycurgan Sparta and the inner councils of contemporary Venice. Bodin could thus ignore the implications of a veto power in these bodies. He seems to have thought that their right of authorization was essentially advisory. In this respect at least, the functions of republican ' senates ' seemed to be much the same as those of a royal privy council.[23]

Hence, for all Bodin could see, there were no republican arrangements that contradicted the unity of sovereignty. Exceptions to the rule would later be collected by his early critics.[24] But I do not believe that he would have altered his opinion, even had he known of these. His confusion on indivisibility was so deeply rooted that nothing but a deliberate and eminently successful example to the contrary could have led him to perceive his error. His later sympathizers would dismiss all minor exceptions as ' impurities ', and deliberate exceptions as rare and monstrous abnormalities.[25] In the *République* such lines of defense are already anticipated.

[22] Polybius, *Histories*, W. R. Paton, trans., Loeb Classical Library (London 1923) III, pp. 301–3.

[23] *Methodus*, pp. 177–8 (180): ' Where then is the supposed aristocracy of Senators? If there is any, then it must exist in kingdoms also, since the council constituted by the prince has the same power (*parem potestatem*) as the Roman Senate. But to associate the council with the prince in power is not only foolish, but even a capital crime. The same is to be said about the Roman Senate, to which those writers give a share of power with the people, and thus associate the master of a state in partnership with his servants and agents.' But cf. *ibid.* p. 183 (194) where different degrees of power in senates are recognized and the issue of a veto is only barely avoided.

[24] Among the earliest critics was the French juridical humanist Vincent Cabot, whose demonstration of mixture in pre-Polybian phases of the Roman constitution was especially decisive and seems to have been highly influential for subsequent critics, most of whom were German. See Vincent Cabot, *Variarum juris publici et privati disputationum libri duo* (1598) in Gerard Meerman, ed., *Novus thesaurus juris civilis et canonici* (The Hague, 1751–3) IV, pp. 662–3.

[25] Among earlier writers, critical as well as friendly, the ' impurities ' of a constitution were not decisive for its classification so long as one of three components of the polity ' pre-

Jean Bodin

Bodin, finally, was fully persuaded that the principle of indivisibility was in no way incompatible with the French constitution as traditionally conceived.[26] In 1566, at least, he was not aware of any contradiction between the sovereign status of a king and the kinds of limitations upon royal power which we have described in the preceding chapter. Seyssel, reflecting on this scheme of limitations, had once declared that the French system ' participates in all three modes of political government ',[27] a notion that was guardedly taken over by Pasquier.[28] But the figure of mixture had never been intended literally as a legal division of supreme authority. Du Haillan, perhaps reacting to Bodin's disapproval of the figure, would soon be very careful to point out that it must not be taken as a denial of unitary sovereignty. The kings, he says,

of their own motion have established laws and officers by whose power and authority they [the kings] have voluntarily restrained and bridled their power, which is not on that account demeaned, diminished, or debased in any way. It has, on the contrary, been rendered more secure and ample, and more willingly supported. We do not say that France is a state composed of three modes of government, or that it is divided into three absolute and equal powers, each one in possession of its own authority. We say only that it seems to be so ... [and] there is a great difference between seeming and being.[29]

Hence Du Haillan, and presumably the other constitutionalists, did not think of institutional restraints as parts of sovereign authority. Limitations were intuitively regarded as checks external to sovereign authority, designed to keep it within proper bounds. From this perspective the constitutionalists felt able to maintain that the king of France was sovereign, and even absolute, while still insisting upon limitations.

With Bodin, of course, even the most figurative reference to a mixed constitution was suppressed.[30] The principle of mixture could properly apply to

ponderated '. Thus Cabot, *Variarum juris*, p. 623; Arnisaeus, *Doctrina politica*, p. 64; Besold, *De majestate*, p. 211; and Johannes Althusius, *Politica methodice digesta* (1603) (Cambridge, Mass., 1932) p. 405. Samuel Pufendorf, *On the Law of Nature and Nations* (1672) (1688 edition, C. H. and W. A. Oldfather, trans., Oxford, 1934) pp. 1040ff, discerns a whole class of deliberately ' irregular ' states held together by fragile comity among the parts rather than by any unifying legal principle. Cf. *République*, pp. 266–7 (194) and especially pp. 270–1 (198).

[26] The constitutionalism of the *Methodus* is sometimes understated as in Chauviré, *Jean Bodin*, pp. 271ff and De Caprariis, *Propaganda e pensiero politico*, pp. 362–3. The former regards it as a minor variation from the absolutism of the *République*, the latter as a mere gesture to traditional ideas. More accurate, in my opinion, are Beatrice Reynolds, *Proponents of Limited Monarchy in Sixteenth Century France : Francis Hotman and Jean Bodin* (New York, 1931) pp. 123–4; John L. Brown, *The Methodus ad Facilem Historiarum Cognitionem, A Critical Study* (Washington, D.C., 1939) pp. 120ff; and especially Jean Moreau-Reibel, *Jean Bodin et le droit public comparé dans ses rapports avec la philosophie de l'histoire* (Paris, 1933) pp. 66ff.

[27] Seyssel, *Prohème*, p. 80.

[28] *Recherches*, p. 56.   [29] *De l'estat et succez*, 156v.

[30] In *Methodus*, p. 177 (180), the thought is repudiated as not only ' foolish, but a capital crime '.

Early theory of Sovereignty

the mode in which authority is exercised, or what Bodin called the form of government. But it has no application to the form of state, or basic constitution which is the mode in which authority is ' owned '.[31] Yet even so, he felt fully able to assimilate the idea of binding limitations. Indeed, in some respects, Bodin's expression of this principle was even bolder than those we have previously considered. Dealing, as he was, with sovereignty in general, he was naturally led to resolve the issue more abstractly.

Almost at the beginning of his discussion of the types of monarchy, Bodin inquires whether it is possible and proper for a sovereign ruler to be subject to the law. He begins his answer negatively. There is perhaps a sense in which a sovereign must be superior to law in order to adapt it to a change in circumstances. But this conclusion is immediately qualified. A sovereign's superiority to law does not necessarily or properly imply that he is free to change it at his own discretion:

It is an honest way of speaking to hold, for the reasons we have given, that he who gives the law must be above the laws. But once the law is passed, and has been fully approved by the consent of all, why should the prince not be bound by the law he has established? This is the reason why the *Lex Cornelia Tribunitia* was adopted, which provided that praetors should be obligated by their edicts, and that a praetor could neither change nor abrogate his edict once it had been set [at the beginning of his term]. For as Asconius writes, it had been the custom of the praetors, arrogantly and at their own discretion, to issue decrees in conflict with their edicts. But the relation of a praetor to an edict is the same as that of a prince or a people to the law. Hence if it is only fair that he who makes a law for others should be bound by it himself, is it not even fairer that the prince or the people should be obligated by their own laws?

This is why the Roman people used to swear to a law that they had passed...
Since, therefore, the people was bound by its law until abrogation was more equitable, it follows that princes too are bound. Princes speak sophistically against the people when they say that their freedom from the law is so complete that they are not only above the laws, but are not obliged in any way, or, even more disgracefully, that what has pleased them has the force of law.[32]

The basic import of this argument is that a king's superiority to law is properly restricted to those occasions on which he has the consent of the community to change it. Since the ultimate sanction for an act of legislation is the general consent of the community, when that consent has been accomplished, the king is subject to his own enactments. In this sense a proper sovereign is supreme and limited at once.

There is, however, one hint of an exception to this principle for which some interpretation is required. Alluding to the Roman people, Bodin says that it was bound to the laws which it had passed only so long as they continued to

---

[31] *Ibid*. p. 168 (156). The distinction, only mentioned here, is elaborated at several points in the *République*, among which see especially II, 2, p. 272 (199–200).
[32] *Methodus*, p. 187 (203).

Jean Bodin

be equitable. By implication the grounds for abrogation could be determined by the people unilaterally, which might suggest that a king should be similarly empowered.

But it will soon be clear, from other things that Bodin says, that he did not intend this exception to be generalized. He is simply recognizing, half-confusedly, that in strictly democratic commonwealths the usual relationships of obligation are logically excluded by the nature of the sovereign. Where the sovereign body encompasses the whole community, the community does not appear as an independent entity which receives and ratifies the sovereign's enactments. This peculiarity of democratic commonwealths is elaborated in the *République*, and we may infer that Bodin was aware of it in 1566. In the later work, where he is speaking of absolute authority, he contends that the legislative power of a proper sovereign may never be restricted by a promise made to the community. He then points out that the absurdity of any such engagement is most clearly illustrated by the characteristics of a democratic sovereign :

If, then, it is useful that a sovereign prince, to govern well, should have the legislative power all to himself, it is even more expedient for the ruler in an aristocracy, and absolutely necessary for the people in a democratic state. For the monarch is distinguished from the people, and in an aristocratic state the nobles are distinguished from the common people, so that in both commonwealths there are two parties : one that holds the sovereignty on the one hand, and the people on the other. Hence the contentions arising between them on the rights of sovereignty, which are abeyant in a popular state. For if the prince or the nobles who hold the state are obliged to keep the laws, as some people think, and can make no law without the approval of the people or the Senate, then the law cannot be abrogated without the consent of the one body or the other, according to the rule of civil law. Nothing of this sort can occur in a popular state, because the people constitutes a single body and cannot be obligated to itself.[33]

In 1566, on the other hand, Bodin was apparently taking this peculiarity of democratic sovereigns as the exception rather than the norm. A sovereign monarch can and should be subject to the law; but a ruling people unfortunately cannot be, except by moral self-restraint. Bodin would like to hold that even democracies can tie their hands, but given his simple conception of community, he cannot see how this could be accomplished institutionally.

The main part of his discussion, however, centers on the forms of legitimate monarchy, among which two main classes are distinguished. Included in the first are all those rulers whom Aristotle had called lords or despots because they rule their subjects the way fathers rule their households, and because they hold their commonwealths as personal property. Examples of this sort are the kings of the Turks, the Persians, and the Abyssinians.

---

[33] *République*, i, 8, p. 143 (99).

Early theory of Sovereignty

Although these ' despotic ' kingships may be consistent with the law of nature so long as they are justly exercised, their legitimacy is only marginal.

In Bodin's delineation of this class, however, the concept of despotic kingship is not confined to systems of ' paternal ' rule. It is also extended, significantly enough, to any ruler who lays claim to absolute authority. Included, therefore, are the primitive or ' savage' kingships of the Scythians and Britons, and also, somewhat oddly, the contemporary Papacy since the Popes contend that they ' never tie their hands '.[34] The underlying thought, apparently, is that every sort of absolute authority, no matter what its social form, is the outgrowth or continuation of primitive rule or else a reversion to that form.

The second class of monarchies is portrayed, by contrast, as the correlate of full civility. With the passage of primitive conditions, the people or the nobles, reacting to tyrannical abuses, subjected kings to law in the course of violent struggles.[35] In European states this struggle and this outcome had been especially common because the peoples of the ' middle region ' are endowed with independent temperaments by the effects of geography and climate.[36]

The obligations of European princes, therefore, are grounded on long-established usage. But they do not depend on this alone. The rule of custom is explicitly confirmed by their oath of coronation, which is binding by the law of nature. This interpretation of the coronation oath as a universal guarantee was rather novel at the time. The coronation promise had been used to establish specific limitations like the inalienability of royal domain, and in the thought of Chasseneuz, as we have seen, it was closely associated with the confirmation of provincial customs. With Bodin, however, who admires Chasseneuz and may be pursuing his idea, the coronation promise goes to the basic legal order as a whole:

[W]hen they are inaugurated in the rites of coronation they swear a mighty oath in a form prescribed by the priests and by the notables of the kingdom by which the kings obligate themselves to govern the commonwealth according to the fundamental laws and equity (*ex legibus imperii et aequo bono*). But the coronation formula of our kings is not only especially outstanding for its language and antiquity; it seems to me to be the fairest of them all for the weight and gravity of what is said. And in this especially: that the prince, in the presence of the priests, swears by the immortal God that he will render due law and justice (*debitam legem et*

[34] *Methodus*, p. 187 (204). On primitive kingships, before the time that law was instituted, see p. 186 (201). [35] *Ibid*. p. 192 (215–16).

[36] *Ibid*. p. 192 (216–17): ' Since men of the middle region are born for the conduct of affairs, as we said in the preceding chapter, they all believe they have a claim to power, and the westerners most especially because they are more spirited than the orientals. Hence they [i.e. men of the middle region of the West] do not put up easily with tyranny. Either they compel the kings to keep the law (than which nothing more divine could be desired) or they throw the tyrants out of power and establish democratic or aristocratic states.' The influence of meridional and longitudinal situation on the ' natural temperament ' of peoples is described in chapter 5.

Jean Bodin

justitiam) to every order of society, and will judge with religion and integrity so far as in him lies. And once he has sworn he cannot easily violate his pledge, or if he could, he does not wish to. He is subject to the courts like any private individual (*jus enim illi dicitur ut privato cuique*), and he is held by the same laws. Moreover, he cannot uproot the laws proper to the kingdom as a whole, nor alter anything whatever in the practices and ancient custom of the regions without the consent of the Three Estates.[37]

This formulation is particularly bold because it uses the terminology of legal obligation. Whereas other writers of the time cautiously use the language of prediction, Bodin says the ruler ' cannot '. He is also more distinct than other commentators in saying, unequivocally, that the consent of the Estates is requisite for legislation. The only question is whether he is referring to the provincial or the general Estates. The context would suggest that he is mainly thinking of the former without intending to exclude the latter.

The preceding passage also indicates that established law is guaranteed by court review. In his elaboration of this point for France, Bodin's language is again unusually forceful:

Of all the fundamental laws of the realm none is more sacred than that which forbids any credit to the rescripts of our princes unless they are in conformity with equity and truth. On this account they are often repudiated by the magistrates, and for the same reason favors secured by importuning are of no advantage to the wicked. For the voice of the magistrates is often heard: that the prince can do nothing against the law.[38]

In this passage Bodin is referring to particular decrees. But in another and even more striking formulation, the same idea is extended to review of legislation by the sovereign courts. The passage should perhaps be quoted to illustrate the strength and direction of the trend that we described in the preceding chapter: ' The sovereign courts ', Bodin maintains,

take no account of laws unless they have approved them by their own promulgation; and they say they cannot be coerced. Yet custom, lapsing, goes astray. Would that they [the sovereign courts] would imitate the virtues of our forefathers, who would have yielded life before yielding their opinion.[39]

Thus in 1566 Bodin's idea of sovereignty was deliberately adapted to the French tradition of limited monarchy. An absolute authority might be legitimate in certain circumstances. But the civilized and proper form of sovereignty was supremacy within the law.

This notion of limited supremacy is not defined or reasoned through, and yet it was a workable conception even from the standpoint of consistency. In any legal order there is a range of discretionary powers which are anticipated by the law itself. The power of pardon and other forms of clemency are

[37] *Ibid.* p. 187 (204).
[38] *Ibid.* p. 208 (254).   [39] *Ibid.*

Early theory of Sovereignty

required in the interests of equity. The appointment of high executive officials, which colors administrative policy, requires some discretion in the choice of persons. The basic rules of law must be adapted to changing situations by quasi-legislative acts which, in modern terminology, are often called executive decrees. Where all of these prerogatives are vested in a single actor, it is meaningful to say that he is supreme within the limits of the law. A limited supreme authority would then be defined as one that possesses all of the discretionary powers that are normally required for the day-to-day conduct of affairs.

Along with this, however, a negative condition must be stipulated. Limited authority cannot be supreme if it is held at the pleasure of another. In Bodin's usage, the law by which the sovereign is bound cannot be changed except at his initiative, and thus with his approval. Furthermore, the review of his decisions by the courts is theoretically restricted in its scope. In principle, at least, his acts may not be disallowed unless there is clear trespass of a basic norm. Hence the complete definition of a limited supreme authority is one that is not responsible to any human agent for the use of its discretionary power, so long as it remains within the bounds of settled law, and it is this definition of supremacy that is implied by Bodin's usage.

Furthermore, the notion of limited supremacy was not so fluid and elastic as to erase the distinction between an actual ruler and a figurehead. Bodin was fully able, therefore, to distinguish princes who were truly sovereign from those whose titles were purely honorific. His main example of the latter was the status of the German Emperor. With the accumulation of restrictions, culminating in the Golden Bull, the imperial title seemed to have been voided of its original significance. Appointments by the Emperor were no longer at his own discretion but required approval by the Diet. In legislative matters, the Emperor was not only bound by the decision of the Diet, but could not prevent it from assembling, or compel it to assemble for matters he considered urgent. The Emperor, finally, could also be deposed.[40] For these and similar reasons, Bodin concluded that sovereign power had been finally transferred to the Diet, and that the German Empire was not a monarchy at all, but an aristocratic state. Like the Doge of Venice, and perhaps the kings of Denmark and Poland, the German Emperor was but the ' prince ' or first person of the commonwealth by virtue of precedence and etiquette. In the *République*, Bodin would call a system of this sort a ' principate '.[41]

---

[40] *Ibid.* pp. 188–9 (206–7).
[41] *République*, II, 5, pp. 301–2 (221). Besold, *De majestate*, p. 212, triumphantly concludes that, in admitting the category of a principate, Bodin has covertly acknowledged the possibility of mixture: ' And at certain points Bodin acknowledges principate as a kind of state intermediate between aristocracy and monarchy; and thus a form in some sort mixed.' But Besold's reading is, I think, too hasty. Some of the states that Bodin describes as principates should probably have been called mixed constitutions. But the category of principate is well-defined in principle, as for example in his comments on the Doge of Venice, *République*,

Jean Bodin

Whether this judgment was accurate or not for any particular regime is a question that need not detain us. The important point for present purposes is that Bodin, in the *Methodus*, made consistent use of a concept of limited supremacy, even though he never attempted to articulate it formally. To use Seyssel's expression, the form of sovereignty he recommended was ' neither too absolute nor too restrained '.[42] If the powers of the Turkish sultan were too complete for civil governance, the German Emperor was so restricted that he did not rule at all. The measure of a proper sovereign was thus the power of the king of France, who ruled, but ruled within the law.

Hence, despite his confusions as to indivisibility, Bodin's conception of supremacy in 1566 was flexible enough to account for the historical appearances. With the possible exception of the German Empire, where some distortion may have entered his account, his idea of undivided sovereignty was roughly adapted to all political systems as contemporaries knew and understood them. Above all it was completely adapted to the French constitutionalist tradition, which Bodin not only accepted but deliberately embraced.

I, 10, p. 219 (158). Bodin's error seems to lie less in the notion of a principate than in its application.

[42] More literally, ' not totally absolute, nor yet too much restrained ', Seyssel, *Monarchie de France*, p. 115.

The Shift to Absolutism

The absolutism of the *République*, accordingly, was not a direct and natural outgrowth of Bodin's earlier position. It was a sudden and dramatic shift which is best explained by a new political concern. It was, specifically, the outcome of his alarmed reaction to the revolutionary movement set off by the St Bartholomew's Day Massacre of 1572.

Open conflict between the state and the Calvinist reformers had been in preparation for over a decade. In the course of the 1560s the Huguenot churches had emerged as the unifying core of a formidable political alliance.[1] Although still a minority religion, Calvinism had won adherents in every part of France as well as in every social order, including members of the high aristocracy as well as fighting nobles of the countryside. In many towns, and in certain provinces and even entire regions, it often controlled the governmental apparatus, and could therefore establish military strong points. Locally, and sometimes nationally, it could often count on the support of Catholic ' malcontents ', who were sympathetic to the Huguenots on questions of economic and political reform.

There also existed a broad spectrum of ' peaceable Catholics ', reluctant to provoke a civil war, who were allied to the Huguenots on the issue of religious toleration. In the Estates of 1560–1 a majority of the nobles and the Third were probably in favour of some form of toleration. Indeed, as late as 1576–7 – despite heavy pressure from the government and active propaganda by the early Catholic League – the Estates could not be induced to take a serious stand in favor of repression. They would vote for religious uniformity in principle, but not for the subsidies needed to enforce it.

The Huguenot movement had thus become a formidable party, and by this very fact it was led to modify the attitude of passive resistance it had adopted in its early days. The Protestant confession in France was no longer a beleaguered sect of spiritual converts. The religious commitment of many of its new adherents was alloyed by worldly interests which were bound to be reflected in their sense of tactics. Continued insistence upon martyrdom as the sole response to persecution would thus have caused the movement to disintegrate. The religious leadership itself could not have insisted on that principle without aban-

[1] Among good accounts of the factional alignments of the civil wars are E. Armstrong, *The French Wars of Religion : Their Political Aspect* (London, 1904) and Romier, *Le Royaume de Catherine de Médicis*.

41

Jean Bodin

doning its hope that all of France would soon be brought within the ambit of its teaching. By the early 1560s the Huguenot party was cautiously moving towards a policy of meeting force with force, at least where provocation was extreme. The government, therefore, could no longer impose religious uniformity without protracted civil war.

This barrier to persecution was apparent to informed opinion and also to the government itself. From the standpoint of pure dynastic interest, the obvious strategy was toleration. But in the face of mounting Catholic pressures, that policy could be imposed only by a resolute and energetic king in control of all resources of the state; and in the 1560s the dynastic interest was weak. After the death of Henry II in 1559 the crown was transmitted first to Francis II and then to Charles IX, both of whom were minors at the time of their accession. Throughout the decade, therefore, the government was conducted by a regency which was badly split. The dynastic interest was represented by the queen mother, Catherine de Medici. Although she was inclined at times to toleration, her position was particularly weak since she was not only a woman but a foreigner. The Protestant interest was represented roughly by the Bourbons, or at least a section of that house. The Catholic interest was championed by the House of Guise, which was then the most powerful family of France apart from the ruling dynasty itself.

Governmental policy was thus a makeshift compromise that could not be effectively enforced. Beginning in 1562, the government repeatedly promised a limited degree of toleration. But its toleration edicts were never fully sincere and were often ignored or sabotaged by the judicial establishment. The result was intermittent civil war, with the government normally ranged upon the Catholic side.

In the 1560s the Huguenot response had been moderated ideologically. The Huguenot leadership still had lingering hopes that a peaceful solution could be found. The Counter-Reformation had not yet gathered full momentum, and the government was obviously inclined to some degree of toleration. For many reasons, furthermore, the Huguenots themselves were inclined to hew closely to legality as long as this seemed at all feasible. A modest posture was not only inherent in their moral attitudes; it was also a dictate of good tactics. As a minority party, the Huguenots could not afford to show impatience.

The leaders, therefore, publicly maintained, and perhaps believed at times, that aggression against them by the state was at the instigation of scheming Catholic princes who had imposed their will upon the regent and the king. Resort to arms could then be justified as resistance to a mere usurper. By this and similar pretexts, relations to the regent and the king could be tenuously maintained even in the midst of civil war. The Huguenots could defend their positions, and even go on the offensive, while still avoiding an open challenge

The shift to Absolutism

to the king's authority. In the 1560s restraint on both sides was so great that informed opinion was often tempted to believe, each time a truce had been concluded, that a peaceful settlement was possible.

But in 1572 a direct confrontation could no longer be avoided. Catherine, caught between two poles, had constantly tended to appease the stronger, Catholic side. This inclination, furthermore, was not only imposed by the balance of domestic forces, but by the strongest diplomatic reasons also, since she was deeply fearful of the prospect of a war with Catholic Spain. But the more she moved in the direction of the Catholics, the greater seemed the menace of the Huguenots. They gradually took on the aspect of a state within a state which balked her authority internally, and which carried on an independent, anti-Spanish foreign policy that was seemingly designed for the ruin of her dynasty. These suspicions were all the easier to hold since Catherine was simply too shallow, intellectually and morally, to appreciate the deeper religious and emotional forces that held the Huguenots together. So far as she could see, the opposition to her policy was the work of a factious, even treasonous conspiracy which ' ought ' to disappear and could be removed by force and fraud. In this fashion a weak and incompetent government finally decided on a criminal solution to its difficulties. The St Bartholomew's Day Massacre was designed to accomplish riddance of the Huguenots by assassination of their leaders.

The remnants of the Huguenots were thereby driven to more radical positions. The crime of 1572 could not be blamed on a usurper. It was publicly approved by Charles IX, who by then had come to his majority. Charles was thus the tyrant, and it was against him that the Huguenots took arms. This choice of larger grounds was partly a spontaneous expression of outrage and revulsion, but it was perhaps also a tactical necessity. The movement, badly stricken, might not have responded to less militant appeals.

The doctrine of legitimate resistance had been muted in the Calvinist tradition but was not completely absent. Scholastic concepts of resistance had been taken over by the Reformation, either directly or via republican versions current in Italian and German city-states. There were, of course, important modifications or refinements. Luther and Calvin had been sternly uncompromising in excluding resistance to established authority on the part of private individuals. If the title of a tyrant were otherwise legitimate, resistance by the ordinary subject was a violation of the law of God which forbade resistance to the higher powers. Exception was made for deliverers specially summoned to the task by God. For the ordinary private subject, however, there was no recourse but flight or martyrdom.

But resistance on the part of duly constituted powers underneath the tyrant was another matter. Since the high magistrates beneath the king could also be regarded as established powers who held their sword of God, they might use

Jean Bodin

it to defend His law.² Although Luther barely hints at this, and Calvin admits
it only guardedly, their reticence was perhaps more tactical than principled.
The idea was general in Reformation circles, and it was applied in last resort
by Luther's followers as well as Calvin's. In its *Admonition* of 1550, the rights
of lesser magistrates were invoked by the Lutheran town of Magdeburg to
justify resistance against Charles V.³ In a work of 1554 much the same idea
was mentioned by Calvin's disciple, Theodore Beza (de Bèze) who was to
become the spiritual leader of the Huguenots and, later on, the successor to
Calvin at Geneva.⁴

This earlier notion of the rights of lesser magistrates was vague and amor-
phous in its legal grounds. But in the 1570s it was given a firmer foundation in
the French tradition of limited monarchy. The resistance theories of Beza and
the Huguenots now depended on a radicalized version of the French constitution which was first developed in the *Francogallia* of François Hotman.

The *Francogallia* was an exploration of certain trends already present in
the French antiquarian tradition. Although published in 1573, and thus after
the St Bartholomew's Day Massacre, it was more than a *livre de circonstance*.
The form of the work, and one of its intentions, was a learned reconstruction
of French constitutional antiquities, the design for which was probably projected and partially fulfilled in the later 1560s as part of Hotman's general
program for a new study of French domestic law.⁵ It is difficult to say exactly
how radical his early findings were, since the *Francogallia* was finally put together, or perhaps rewritten, at Geneva after Hotman fled from Bourges in
order to escape assassination.

Hotman's version of the ancient constitution depended on two new discoveries, or emphases. One was the finding, massively documented from the
chroniclers, that the French kingship had been anciently elective. The other
was the showing that the public council of the realm, or ancient *Parlamentum*,
was coeval with the state itself. That some sort of folk assembly had existed
in the early days was also indicated by the chroniclers, and for an even earlier
period by Tacitus and Caesar. With Hotman, as with Du Haillan, these early
convocations were readily equated with the later Three Estates; and the Three

---

2 The fullest treatment is Richard R. Benert, ' Inferior Magistrates in Sixteenth-Century
Political and Legal Thought ', unpublished doctoral dissertation (University of Minnesota,
1967). For a brief survey, see Julian H. Franklin, *Constitutionalism and Resistance in the
Sixteenth Century* (New York, 1969) pp. 19–46.
3 *Ibid.* p. 31. See also Cynthia G. Shoenberger, ' The Confession of Magdeburg and the
Lutheran Doctrine of Resistance ', unpublished doctoral dissertation, Columbia, 1972,
especially chs. ii and v.
4 In his *De haereticis a civili magistratu puniendis.* See *ibid.* p. 98.
5 Ralph E. Giesey, ' Why and When Hotman Wrote the *Francogallia* ', *Bibliothèque
d'Humanisme et Renaissance*, xxix (1967) pp. 583–611. More recently J. H. M. Salmon has
been able to date important parts of the work from 1567. See *Times Literary Supplement*,
11 December 1969. A very full study of Hotman's intentions will soon be available in
Donald R. Kelley, *Hotman* (forthcoming).

The shift to Absolutism

Estates of Hotman's time were taken as a substitution for the people as a whole.

Putting these two main thoughts together, Hotman could contend that the ancient public council was not a creation of the kings, as the other antiquarians had held, but that kings were created by the people meeting in its council. The obligation of the king to remain within the law could then be understood as the condition of his elevation. The institution of election was thus a contract between king and people that was repeated with every new incumbent.

The proof that conditions were imposed, and also the fundamental content of these conditions, was regular supervision by the public council. Consultation by the king was required on every high affair, including not only legislation but the appointment of officials and decisions as to war and peace. The function of the council, furthermore, was not merely to approve or to permit, but seemingly also to decide. Hotman comes very close at times to saying that the public council was the seat of sovereignty.[6]

The institution of election, with which a royal promise was associated, also implied that a king could be rightfully deposed for flagrant violation of his office. Historical evidence in support of this contention was taken from the many instances in which kings of France had been driven from the throne. All of these, for Hotman, had been justified by tyrannical behavior or manifest incompetence and had somehow been sanctioned by the people. They were thus legitimate invocations of a right of deposition.

Despite alterations worked by time, the ancient constitution was supposed to have retained its basic shape. The institution of election had been gradually replaced by the ' Salic ' rule of primogenitive succession. But this, in Hotman's view, was not a change in the duties or status of the office, but only in the method of selecting an incumbent. The kingship was still transmitted by the people's will, which was now expressed in customary public law. At the time of Hugh Capet, furthermore, the offices of dukes and counts, which had been originally filled by election in the council, were given hereditary status. This, for Hotman, was a more serious diminution of the council's power, although he was not quite willing to call it illegitimate. The change, which the council was supposed to have approved, had not affected basic principles. The hereditary magistrates could still be regarded as the people's agents, since they held of the kingdom, not the king.

Most serious of all was the institution of the Parlement at Paris and the transfer to it of many high functions of the council together with its ancient name. Hotman, who as a legal reformer and a Huguenot despised the Parlements, branded their sovereign powers a usurpation, and all but overtly demanded

---

[6] Franklin, *Constitutionalism*, pp. 73, 86. A new variorum edition of the *Francogallia* edited by Ralph E. Giesey and translated by John H. M. Salmon is forthcoming in Cambridge.

Jean Bodin

restoration of the rights of the Estates. The Parlement of Paris was portrayed as a recent invention by the late Capetians designed to rid them of control by the Estates. It was not a Roman Senate but a ' counterfeit ', and was preferred to the Estates by scheming kings because it was easily corrupted and controlled.

Yet even so, held Hotman, the ancient constitution lived. The Estates had still to be assembled on matters of extraordinary import; and they were still entitled to remove a tyrant. But what if the Estates were prevented by the tyrant from assembling? Hotman's answer is pointedly conveyed by a highly colored version of the War of the Public Good against Louis XI, who was often cited as a tyrant by contemporaries. When Louis temporized in order to escape controls, the nobles took to arms and compelled him to assemble the Estates, which then took measures to reform the government. The implication, therefore, was that the higher magistrates, who held their office of the people, could initiate resistance in its name.

It was this conception of resistance that was now to be generalized and developed by the Huguenot theorists. Among the best known statements, the earliest and most incisive was Beza's *Droit des magistrats*, which was anonymously published early in 1574. Much the same idea is also to be found in the anonymous *Réveille Matin des François* published in that year, and also in Du Plessis-Mornay's *Vindiciae contra tyrannos*, which was probably begun about that time but was published, pseudonymously, only in 1579.

Hotman had already claimed that the right of holding public council was found not only in France but in many other kingdoms. Observing the great benefits derived from this arrangement in so many cases, he had claimed that the right of the council was required by the *jus gentium*, or common law of peoples. Beza now attempted to illustrate this right for every known kingdom considered to be civilized, and could thus conclude that a right so fundamental and so universal was based upon the law of nature. Not only must every legitimate kingship originate by free consent, but no community, in giving its consent, could be presumed to have agreed to absolute authority.[7] The absence of institutional restraints was presumptive proof of illegitimate coercion. It was inconsistent with rational and self-evident conditions of public welfare and the maintenance of justice. In this fashion the French constitution, as Hotman had understood it, was taken as a universal standard to which every other proper kingship was assimilated, and which was universally confirmed by experience and reason. In Beza's list of eminent parallels, special emphasis was laid on the English and Spanish constitutions.

For Beza, and all other reputable Huguenots, initiation of resistance by ordinary subjects was still forbidden absolutely. In this respect the French Calvinists differed from the Scotch and English, who were willing to admit individual resistance at least in last resort. According to Beza, the Estates alone

[7] *Ibid.* p. 107.

The shift to Absolutism

had the power to depose, and where the Estates could not assemble, or were hopelessly corrupt, the initiation of resistance belonged to the magistrates alone. But this was simply intended to prevent the ' excesses ' of democracy and to protect the Huguenots from the charge of general subversion of the social order. It was not understood as a serious bar to resistance in the existing circumstances. Beza generally assumed that the magistrates, confronted with a tyrant, would act in their corporate capacity. But he also implied that where the magistrates collectively have failed to do their duty, a single magistrate may sound the call to arms, especially if he occupies a major office of the kingdom as a whole. In the *Vindiciae contra tyrannos* these implications were explicitly endorsed.[8] Hence despite the ban on initiative by private subjects, a legitimate procedure could be found in almost any circumstance.

The general trend, indeed, was toward a constant radicalization of this aspect of the doctrine. The *Vindiciae contra tyrannos* was more permissive than the *Droit des magistrats,* and the writers of the later Catholic League, who built on Huguenot conceptions, were more permissive than their adversaries. Holding the majority position, they were less in need of giving reassurances.

On the substantive issues of this period, Bodin's position was generally liberal.[9] In the dedicatory letter to the *Methodus,* the reformist program of the Chancellor L'Hôpital is echoed in the call for the codification of French law, and Bodin's sympathy for other aspects of that program is broadly indicated in his discussion of the French regime. In the *République,* points of public policy are taken up at length, and in these chapters Bodin takes note of almost all the grievances, and embraces almost all the remedies, that were put forward in the *cahiers* of this period and that were taken up in reforming royal ordinances. Among other things, he attacks the sale of offices, the use of mercenary troops, and the custom of expensive gifts to favorites. Above all, he proposes that the burden of taxation, which he saw as a fundamental threat to political stability, should be gradually reduced through repurchase and improved administration of the crown's domain. In economic policy he was even in advance of contemporary thought in finding the key to French prosperity in natural and human resources rather than in precious metals.[10]

On the highly sensitive question of religious policy, Bodin was also liberal. Outwardly at least he was a Catholic. But his private religious meditations, which he dared not publish in his lifetime,[11] were an unusually daring as

[8] *Ibid.* p. 194.

[9] For a brief sketch of Bodin's overall position, see Julian H. Franklin, ' Jean Bodin ', *International Encyclopedia of the Social Sciences* (1968) 2, pp. 110–13.

[10] For the text of Bodin's tract on economic theory and commentary on it, see Henri Hauser, *La vie chère au XVIe siècle, La response de Jean Bodin à M. de Malestroit* (1568) (Paris, 1932). See *République,* VI, 2, for various references to this polemic against bullionism.

[11] The manuscript of the *Colloquium heptaplomeres de rerum sublimium arcanis abditis*

Jean Bodin

well as idiosyncratic development of the humanist tendency to deemphasize dogmatic conflicts. In the course of his restless effort to harmonize religious differences, he gradually came to that sense of their underlying unity which, in the sixteenth century, was the starting point for theories of toleration. The true, or natural, religion, in which Bodin believed, was his own combination of Jewish monotheism with neo-Platonizing speculation.[12] The different positive religions could then be understood as variations on this universal truth in the realm of sense impressions. They could not be refuted as mere errors since the evidence that each invoked on its behalf ultimately depended upon faith. Nor could they be branded as pernicious. Sincere worship in any of the positive religions, as distinct from mere superstitions, was acceptable to God. There was therefore no intrinsic reason to persecute religious dissenters as perverse or insincere. At the end of the *Colloquium heptaplomeres*, the seven interlocutors, representing the major religions, agree to disagree in friendly recognition of their differences.[13]

Bodin, however, was too impressed by the political advantages of religious uniformity to make religious freedom a fundamental right. On the practical level his recommendations were strictly ' politique '. Where religious uniformity existed, it ought to be maintained by law. To permit religious innovations would encourage the development of factions in the state. Where, on the other hand, a new religion was already present, and could no longer be removed by force except by endangering the state, toleration was the wiser course. In this situation the goal of religious uniformity was best promoted by a calculated blend of coercion and example. The king could show his disapproval of the new religion by keeping its adherents from positions of eminence and power. The mass of dissidents might then be persuaded to return, since it was the natural tendency of subjects to follow the example of their princes.[14] Outright persecution, on the other hand, would only confirm them in their opposition.[15]

Bodin's recommendations were thus substantially in line with the qualified and provisional toleration habitually proffered by the government in the truces of the civil war. It was not a generous policy, but in the circumstances of the

---

(1593?) was burned at Bodin's request upon his death, but unauthorized copies circulated in manuscript form. No printed version appeared until the nineteenth century, and no complete version until 1857.

12 On Bodin's religious thought in general, see Pierre Mesnard, ' La pensée religieuse de Bodin ', *Revue du seizième siècle*, XVI, 1929, pp. 71–121, and also Georg Roellenblek, *Offenbarung, Natur, und jüdische Überlieferung bei Jean Bodin* (Kassel, 1964), and also, ' Der Schluss des *Heptaplomeres* und die Begründung der Toleranz bei Bodin ', paper delivered at *Internationale Bodin Tagung* (Munich, 1970). The importance of Bodin's notorious belief in demons for his religious evolution is reappraised by C. R. Baxter, ' Jean Bodin's Daemon and his Conversion to Judaism ', paper delivered at *Internationale Bodin Tagung* (Munich, 1970).

13 *Colloquium heptaplomeres de rerum sublimium arcanis abditis*, L. Noack, ed. (Schwerin, 1857) p. 358.

14 *République*, III, 7, pp. 496–8 (380–2).   15 *Ibid*. IV, 7, p. 564 (537).

The shift to Absolutism

time it was probably the most that one could reasonably expect. Bodin, moreover, was sincere in his commitment. At the Estates of Blois he would be a stalwart opponent of religious war against the Huguenots.[16]

Bodin, then, was not too distant from the Huguenots on immediate political objectives, and this parallelism in his attitudes also extended to his moral evaluation of the royal court. To a large extent he accepted the Huguenot explanation of the St Bartholomew's Day Massacre, although he does not mention the event explicitly.

This appears from the preface to the *République*, which is grave and sombre in its tone. Confident as late as 1572, Bodin had been encouraged to believe that civil warfare had been permanently settled by the wise decree of a benevolent king whose words had been accepted in good faith by the more sober part of the community.[17] Now confidence had disappeared, and the ' shipwreck ' of the state could be envisaged. Two great errors that promote distrust are mentioned, one of which is the current doctrine of legitimate resistance. But the other, and the one discussed at greater length, is the mistake of those who ' instruct princes in the rules of injustice to insure their strength by tyranny, than which there could be no basis more ruinous to power '.[18] Machiavelli is the source of this mistake and is represented as the evil genius by whom such counsellors are guided. This portrayal is a striking change in Bodin's estimate. Machiavelli had been saluted in the *Methodus* as the first of the moderns to revive the ' civil science ' of the ancients.[19] Now he is singled out as the arch atheist and destroyer of commonwealths.[20]

Bodin does not say explicitly that these counsels had been adopted under Charles IX. But he is obviously alluding to a familiar contention of the Huguenots. On their account, Machiavelli was the ultimate architect of the St Bartholomew's Day Massacre. His poisonous teachings had been brought to France by Catherine de Medici along with her Italian counsellors. The crime of 1572 was thus the work, not only of a tyrant but of foreigners.[21]

[16] See below, pp. 90–1. Reformist and tolerationist motives could have played a role in Bodin's apparent involvement in the *Politique* conspiracy of 1574, although he could have been drawn into the plot simply as a result of his personal connections to the Duke of Alençon in whose service he was then engaged. The conspiracy, formed in anticipation of the death of Charles IX, was to bypass the rightful successor, Henry, Duke of Anjou (who was then also king of Poland) in favor of his more ' liberal ' younger brother, Francis, Duke of Alençon. On Bodin's apparent role, see A. Garosci, *Jean Bodin : politica e diritto nel Rinascimento francese* (Milan, 1934) p. 33, and especially Kenneth D. McRae, ' The Political Thought of Jean Bodin ' (unpublished doctoral dissertation, Harvard, 1953) pp. 57ff.

[17] *Methodus*, p. 211 (259). (This reference introduced only with edition of 1572.)

[18] *République*, preface.

[19] *Methodus*, p. 167 (153).

[20] *République*, preface.

[21] See Donald R. Kelley, ' Murd'rous Machiavel in France : A Post Mortem ', *Political Science Quarterly*, LXXXV, no. 4, December 1970, pp. 545–59. The best known Huguenot polemic is Innocent Gentillet, *Anti-Machiavel* (Geneva, 1576).

Jean Bodin

Bodin's shift to absolutism is thus surprising at first thought. Cautiously liberal on public policy and alarmed by the trend of royal tactics, he might have been expected to maintain a middle course and to lay even greater stress on institutional restraints. That he failed to do so is even more surprising in view of his earlier stance. Why did he now abandon a constitutional position that he had so firmly supported but a few years earlier? [22]

Bodin himself supplies no explanation because he saw no need to do so. In the *République* sovereign power is simply defined as absolute without any explanation of the grounds or any indication that a change in his position had occurred. For Bodin, apparently, the new definition of supremacy was but a clarification of what he had previously maintained, and he seems to have come to it intuitively. We can, however, make certain inferences as to the kinds of intellectual operations encompassed in that intuition.

The shift to absolutism was evidently occasioned by Bodin's profound unwillingness to acknowledge legitimate resistance. To deny the right of resistance with respect to a particular authority is to consider that authority as absolute. It can be argued that no legal obligation can be absolute. But that is to raise a different question. At the very least, Bodin was justified in thinking that if an authority was less than absolute, a right of resistance could not be denied.

In 1566 he had not examined the relation between resistance and limited supremacy. In one passage, he had suggested in passing that the right of deposition is incompatible with sovereignty. The existence of that right in Germany was one reason, very briefly mentioned, why the German Emperor was not a proper monarch. But for kingships like the French, which he believed were limited yet sovereign, the issue of ultimate obligation was evaded. In the manner characteristic of the antiquarians, he had used the language of prediction. He simply observed, approvingly, that tyrants have been frequently deposed.[23] The legal right of deposition had been therefore left ambiguous.

But in the 1570s the issue of resistance was presented as a working ideology that seemed to have dramatic consequences. Reflecting on the causes of the civil war, Bodin concluded that the mere belief of a community that it was entitled to resist a tyrant was inherently pernicious. We have indicated that in

---

[22] In 1572 Bodin undertook his one and only revision of the *Methodus* without introducing any substantial alteration of its constitutional perspective. There is even some evidence that he remained committed to his earlier view as late as 1573. After the election of Henry, Duke of Anjou (later Henry III of France), as king of Poland, Bodin was a member of the French delegation that welcomed the Polish ambassadors at Metz. Bodin may have written, or at least helped to compose, the address of Charles des Cars, which was strongly constitutionalist in tone. For a careful review of the evidence, see McRae, ' Political Thought ', p. 59, and also Moreau-Reibel, *Jean Bodin*, pp. 214–15, 273–4. We might also note that the tone of the *Politique* conspiracy of 1574, in which Bodin was implicated, was vaguely constitutionalist (see Georges Weill, *Les théories sur le pouvoir royal en France pendant les guerres de religion* [Paris, 1891] pp. 136ff) although Bodin's personal interest in this movement is unclear.   [23] *Methodus*, p. 192 (217).

The shift to Absolutism

the preface to the *République* he fixed on two great errors fatal to a commonwealth, one of which is addiction of the ruler to the arts of tyranny. The other is the mistake of those who propagate the doctrine of resistance:

But there are still others, directly hostile to these [counsellors of tyranny], who are no less dangerous and are maybe even more so. These are the ones who under the pretext of exemption from burdens and the people's liberty cause subjects to rebel against their natural princes, and thereby open the way to licentious anarchy, which is worse than the severest tyranny that ever was.[24]

The text of the *République* is even more explicit. To admit that resistance is legitimate is to encourage the subjects to rebel:

Many, indeed, would be the tyrants if it were allowable to kill them! The king who laid too many taxes would be a tyrant. The king who ordered anything the people didn't like would be a tyrant, on Aristotle's definition in the *Politics*. The king who kept guards for the safety of his life would be a tyrant. The king who punished conspirators against his state with death would be a tyrant. How could good princes be certain of their lives? [25]

Had the point been left at this, it would have been a simple judgment on political psychology. But Bodin took a further step. He intuitively concluded that the right of resistance in a people was inconsistent with sovereignty as such. If he had been able to articulate his argument, his reasoning might have gone like this:

A limited authority may be resisted;
A supreme authority acknowledges no superior or equal;
An authority which may be judged and deposed by its subjects acknowledges a superior;
Therefore, a limited authority cannot be supreme;
Supreme authority is absolute.

On this construction of his underlying thought, Bodin was simply extending his earlier judgment on the status of the German Emperor to every prince whose authority was limited. Since a true sovereign was irremovable, a prince was either absolute or he was not a sovereign at all. Although the argument is never stated in this order, the underlying logic is sometimes suggested in reverse. Particularly revealing is the following passage from the *République* on what kind of prince may be resisted:

[We] have to know whether the prince is absolutely sovereign (*absoluement souverain*), or whether he is not a sovereign. For if he is not absolutely sovereign, it follows necessarily that the sovereignty must be in the people or else the nobles. In this case, there is no doubt that it is licit to proceed against the tyrant.[26]

The questionable element in Bodin's intuition is the third premise of the argument as reconstructed, which asserts that the people is above a king if it has the power to depose him. A political authority that acknowledges a right

[24] *République*, preface.   [25] *Ibid.* II, 5, p. 307 (225).   [26] *Ibid.* II, 5, p. 301 (221).

Jean Bodin

of deposition in its subjects does not, by that alone, acknowledge a superior within the law. The right of deposition is not necessarily a power pursuant to law, in the sense of a judicial verdict. In the case of a limited monarchy, it is simply a declaration that the ruler has abandoned the rights and protections of his office by deliberate and flagrant transgression of the conditions of obedience. The right of resistance thus comes into play not by means of established procedures but in order to preserve them. Thus construed, it is consistent with supremacy, although not with absolute supremacy.

Yet Bodin's error is understandable enough. The logic of limited supremacy required considerable ingenuity. It was not developed until late in the seventeenth century, and even then it seemed to be extremely odd.[27] Writing in a less sophisticated period, Bodin could hardly have been expected to see it, and given his political preferences he had no reason to invent it. There is, indeed, no evidence that he was ever aware of any problem. It is not as though his earlier idea of sovereignty had been a reasoned concept which he then deliberately abandoned. His notion of limited supremacy had merely been implicit in his usage, and the issue of ultimate obligation had been left ambiguous.

It is important to point out, moreover, that the later equation of supreme with absolute was neither foolish nor utterly unworkable. The term ' supreme ' is sometimes used that way in ordinary discourse; and the concept can be adapted to limited monarchies and other constitutionalist systems by admitting division of supremacy. This perhaps is not the most illuminating way of looking at it. But it was the path adopted by many writers of the seventeenth century.[28]

Hence the main difficulty in Bodin's later theory is not so much the absolute definition of supremacy as the principle of indivisibility. Although the latter principle was wrong on almost any definition of supremacy, the new definition of supremacy made it less adaptable to France. Bodin, however, showed not the slightest inclination to rethink the principle, or even to revise its application. All the authorities that he had deemed sovereign in 1566 were still assumed to be so.

Yet, on the whole, the new conception of supremacy was added to his old identifications of the sovereign with surprisingly little embarrassment. His empirical demonstrations of the unity of governmental functions were not affected by the change, and his locations of the legislative power in city-states reputed mixed, and also in the German Empire, were no more wrong (or right) on the new conception than the old. The main problem in his former treatment of city-state arrangements was his failure to see the implication of a veto in certain forms of senatorial ' advice '. In the *République* he simply continued to ignore it.

The French constitution, and others like it, thus presented the most difficult problem, since Bodin had already organized the evidence to support a case for

[27] Samuel Pufendorf, *Law of Nature*, VII, 6, 10, pp. 1070ff.   [28] See below, note 29.

The shift to Absolutism

limitation. But there were certain factors, best called psychological, that helped to sustain him in a new interpretation.

We have already noted that no reputable commentator of the 1560s had seriously contended that the French constitution was a mixture. Bodin himself had never entertained this possibility, and saw no reason to entertain it now. He continued to believe that the king of France ' alone ' was sovereign and that every writer worth considering agreed on this. The only question now was to define more precisely what was meant by sovereignty. From this perspective, he need not have thought that his new version of the French constitution was a serious departure from what he had previously held. Persuaded now that absolute authority was an analytic implication of supremacy, he could have felt that he was simply removing an element of ambiguity which had become apparent on a deeper view of sovereignty.

By the 1570s, to be sure, the Huguenot theorists were beginning to develop a concept of divided sovereignty that was reasonably adequate to the constitution of a limited monarchy.[29] But Bodin would never see this point. Although many portions of the *République* were an implicit answer to the Huguenots, he paid surprisingly little attention to the specifics of their doctrine.[30] So far as he could see, the Huguenots were simply contending that sovereignty lay in the Estates, and many of their statements, at least in the early 1570s, could have easily been read that way.[31]

Hence, for all Bodin could see, there was nothing in the French tradition that clearly indicated an intermediate solution between popular sovereignty and absolutism. Given his new way of looking at the concept of supreme authority, and given also the element of ambiguity surrounding many of the legal precedents, his path towards an absolutist interpretation of the French constitution could not easily be halted by the evidence.

[29] On the distinction between the ' real ' sovereignty of the people and the ' personal ' sovereignty held of the people on condition by the prince, see especially Beza, *Right of Magistrates* in Franklin, *Constitutionalism and Resistance*, pp. 110–13, 128–9. For the subsequent history of this influential distinction, see Otto von Gierke, *Natural Law and the Theory of Society*, Ernest Barker trans. (Cambridge, 1934; reprinted Boston, 1957) pp. 54ff, and also John H. M. Salmon, *The French Religious Wars in English Political Thought* (Oxford, 1959) pp. 52ff.

[30] There is only one specific reference to any Huguenot writing. In *République*, I, 8, p. 137 (95) he speaks of those who have written on the ' devoir des magistrats ', which is probably a reference to Beza's anonymously published *Droit des magistrats*. The characterization is finished in a phrase, and nowhere in the *République* is the specific doctrine examined. The *Francogallia*, on the other hand, is discussed without being named only at the end of the *République* in a chapter dealing with the advantages of successive over elective kingship. Bodin seems reasonably clear on Hotman's position as to original election, but neither here nor elsewhere does he indicate direct familiarity with other aspects of the work. He may have known of it only at second hand through the refutations of Antoine Matharel. On Bodin's relation to the Huguenots, see John H. M. Salmon, ' Bodin and the Monarchomachs ', paper delivered at the *Internationale Bodin Tagung* (Munich, 1970).

[31] On the movement of the Huguenot doctrine from quasi-republicanism to limited monarchy, see below, p. 103.

[4]

RAMIST TENDENCIES IN THE THOUGHT OF JEAN BODIN
By Kenneth D. McRae

I

The decade of the 1540's saw the conservative elements in the University of Paris challenged on a fundamental issue. Its clearest manifestation was the revolt against the authority of Aristotle initiated by Peter Ramus.[1] The first salvo had been fired in 1536, when the twenty-one-year-old Ramus had triumphantly sustained his audacious master's thesis that whatever had been said by Aristotle was false.[2] When Ramus published his *Aristotelicae animadversiones* and *Institutiones dialecticae* in 1543, the struggle took a serious turn. The defenders of Aristotle in the University, enraged both by the violence of Ramus' attack and by his youthful presumption in outlining a new system of logic, sought and obtained a royal edict, dated March 10, 1543/4, which forbade Ramus to lecture in logic or philosophy. He remained free to discuss other subjects, however, and turned his attention to rhetoric, classical literature, and mathematics. When Francis I died in 1547, the Cardinal of Lorraine, Ramus' patron, obtained the rescission of the ban on philosophy. In 1551 Henry II created for Ramus a special chair in philosophy and eloquence at the Collège Royal, and thenceforth the stream of works from his pen was unbroken even by the vicissitudes of civil war until his death in the St. Bartholomew massacre of 1572.

In later years Ramus' attack was directed less against Aristotle himself than against what he felt to be the distorted Aristotelian doctrines of the medieval university tradition. One of the most persistent characteristics of the entire Ramist movement was its revolt against a scholastic subtlety which was alleged to have lost contact with the everyday world. Its keynotes were simplicity, practicality, and a constant insistence on never losing sight of things as they are. In this sense Ramism was an attempt at educational reform which reflected the increased importance attached to the world of action by

---

[1] Among the useful secondary works on Ramus' life and thought may be mentioned: C. Waddington, *Ramus (Pierre de la Ramée), sa vie, ses écrits et ses opinions* (Paris, 1855); F. P. Graves, *Peter Ramus and the Educational Reformation of the Sixteenth Century* (New York, 1912); Perry Miller, *The New England Mind: the Seventeenth Century* (New York, 1939); P. A. Duhamel, "The Logic and Rhetoric of Peter Ramus," *Modern Philology*, XLVI (1948–49), 163–171; W. J. Ong, "Peter Ramus and the Naming of Methodism," this *Journal*, XIV (1953), 235–248. I am much indebted to the Rev. Walter J. Ong, S.J., for several helpful suggestions concerning Ramism. He is not, of course, to be blamed for any of the facts or opinions stated below.

[2] " Quaecumque ab Aristotele dicta essent, commentitia esse." Waddington, *op. cit.*, 28.

the impatient Renaissance mind. The academic life was seen no longer as a career in itself, but as a preparation for useful public activities. Such an outlook demanded a new approach to the traditional *scholae,* and Ramus provided it. He and his followers desired to simplify the traditional academic disciplines as far as possible, and to eliminate everything unessential or artificial.

The key to reform was a reconstruction of formal logic, the foundation of the medieval university curriculum. Ramus had made a substantial beginning with the *Institutiones dialecticae,* and this phase of his work was virtually completed by the publication in 1555 of his *Dialectique,*[3] perhaps the first philosophical tract of any importance to appear in French. This brief work, which explained the Ramist system of logic in its simplest form, appeared in an astonishing number of editions and adaptations in several languages, and exerted an enormous influence for fully a century after its publication. Since the new logic was essentially a reclassification of the processes of thought, it was believed to be applicable to every other discipline. Ramus himself made it the basis of his treatises on French, Greek, and Latin grammar, mathematics, physics and metaphysics. His disciples extended its influence even further. Within a few years the techniques and aims of the Ramists found avid partisans in other universities, particularly in the Protestant countries, and the controversy they engendered was such that few educated Europeans in the second half of the sixteenth century can have remained unaware of them.

II

The career of Ramus in the University of Paris may seem to bear little relation to the thought of Jean Bodin, whose major studies in law, politics and history are remote from the former's interest in the traditional liberal arts. Nevertheless the paths of the two thinkers cross quite unmistakably during the formative years of the younger man. Bodin was born in 1529 or 1530, but his life is extremely difficult to trace until the later 1550's, when he was definitely studying law at Toulouse. In recent years his reputed stay in Geneva, possibly preceded by a trial for heresy at Paris in 1548, his supposed opposition to Jacques Cujas' candidacy for a chair of civil law in Toulouse, his alleged plagiarism of Adrian Turnebus' textual emendations of Oppian, and even his birthplace, long supposed to have been Angers, have been questions of warm dispute.[4] Yet despite all these uncer-

[3] References in this article are to the Latin edition, *Dialecticae libri duo* (Paris, 1556).

[4] See J. Moreau-Reibel, *Jean Bodin et le droit public comparé* (Paris, 1933); J. L. Brown, *The Methodus ad Facilem Historiarum Cognitionem of Jean Bodin* (Washington, 1939); H. Naef, " La Jeunesse de Bodin ou les conversions oubliées,"

KENNETH D. MCRAE

tainties there is one event in his early career which rests on the firm-est evidence: Bodin spent a few youthful years in Paris as a member of the Carmelite order engaged in the formal study of philosophy.

In January 1577/8, a formal inquiry was held, for reasons which the testimony does not make clear, into the status of a certain "frère Jehan Bodin," a former Carmelite brother. Three of his former col-leagues, who are styled doctors of theology in the University of Paris, testified that thirty-two years before the date of the inquiry they had known this particular Jean Bodin as a Carmelite from Angers; that he had lived with them at the Carmelite monastery in Paris; and that for about two years they had attended together a course of lectures in philosophy given by Guillaume Prévost, another brother of their order. Further, two of the deponents recalled that this Bodin had re-turned to Angers, whence word had reached Paris of his departure from the order.[5] This evidence seems incontestable. A certified copy of the original deposition was discovered in a bound volume of six-teenth- and seventeenth-century documents, some of which relate to Bodin's legal affairs at Laon. Moreover, it offers an unexpected and striking corroboration of the historian de Thou's statement, so often discounted by later writers, that Bodin had been a Carmelite in his youth.[6]

By subtracting thirty-two years from the date of the inquiry, we may date Bodin's studies in Paris somewhere between 1545 and 1550. Since he must have arrived on the scene only shortly after Ramus was peremptorily silenced insofar as philosophy was concerned, Bodin could scarcely have remained unaware of such a *cause célèbre*. No one with a mind so encyclopedically inclined as his demonstrably was could have been deterred by monastic considerations from the closest possible examination of the issue that had split the University. There is one factor which entitles us to speculate rather boldly on the con-nection between the two men. In 1545 Ramus took over the active administration of the Collège de Presle at the request of its aging prin-cipal, Nicolas Lesage, and on the latter's death a few years later he

---

Bibliothèque d'humanisme et renaissance, VIII (1946), 137–155; E. Droz, "Le Carme Jean Bodin, hérétique," *Ibid.*, X (1948), 77–94; J. Levron, *Jean Bodin et sa famille* (Angers, 1950) and "Jean Bodin, sieur de Saint-Amand ou Jean Bodin, originaire de Saint-Amand," *Ibid.*, X (1948), 69–76; P. Mesnard, "Jean Bodin à Toulouse," *Ibid.*, XII (1950), 77–121; P. Mesnard, "Un Rival heureux de Cujas et de Bodin, Etienne Forcadel," *Zeitschrift der Savigny-Stiftung für Rechtsgeschichte*, LXVII (1950), 440–458.

[5] A. Ponthieux, "Quelques documents inédits sur Jean Bodin," *Revue du seizième siècle*, XV (1928), 57–58.

[6] J. A. de Thou, *Historiarum sui temporis libri CXXXVIII*, 5 vols. (Geneva, 1626–1630), Book CXVII, Vol. V, p. 701.

became principal in name as well as in fact. His arrival elevated the college from a very mediocre status to a position of European renown. Unprecedented numbers of students thronged his lectures.[7] But it is arresting to note from old maps of the city that the Collège de Presle was situated not only in the rue des Carmes, but directly across that street from the Carmelite monastery. If physical propinquity is an argument of any importance at all, does it not suggest that the omnivorous young Carmelite from Angers was among the eager students, drawn from the entire University, who crowded the halls of the Collège de Presle to listen to Ramus?

Moreover, Bodin's early interest in philosophy continued throughout his life, as his later writings amply demonstrate. After 1560 he returned to Paris as an advocate, and any acquaintance with Ramist doctrines acquired as a student could hardly fail to be refreshed periodically by the continuing personal struggle between Ramus and his enemies in the University and by the growing stream of Ramist writings. In these circumstances it is reasonable to inquire whether the new movement had any appreciable effect upon Bodin's own thought, for so prolonged a controversy could scarcely fail to provoke some comment, either favorable or unfavorable. In fact, his viewpoint is expressed quite unequivocally, and an examination of Bodin's writings in the light of this general Ramist background of his early years indicates several points of contact, hitherto unexplored, which throw new light upon his general aims and methods.

III

In order to appreciate Bodin's use of Ramist concepts, we must first sketch very briefly certain features of the new logic. Ramus divided the subject into two sharply distinct compartments. The first, known as invention, was intended to lay bare the irreducible components which go to make up any proposition in much the same way that building blocks are used to construct a house. The second part, called disposition or judgment, concerned the proper use of these basic components, or arguments, as they were usually called, in the process of ratiocination.[8]

The technique to be used in invention was a skilful division of the given topic by successive stages, starting from the most general conception and progressing gradually to more detailed aspects. Regardless of the nature of the subject under discussion, Ramus insisted on reasoning deductively from general principles to particulars. The

[7] Waddington, *op. cit.*, 62–64.

[8] " Dialecticae partes duae sunt, inventio & judicium: Prima declarat singulas separare partes, unde sententia quaevis componitur: Secunda docet quibus generibus & modis disponantur omnia." *Dialectica,* 11.

KENNETH D. MCRAE

first step was always a brief definition in the most general terms, the purpose of which was to establish clearly the extent and limits of the subject, just as a surveyor measures off the boundaries of a parcel of land. True definition, as distinct from mere description, was always as brief as possible. Its function was to make clear the real essence of the thing being examined. Ramus believed that in most cases this could best be done by a simple classification according to genus and form, thereby starting a vogue for two-word definitions that was destined to enjoy immense popularity with his followers.[9]

The next step was a division of the subject defined into its principal compartments, technically known as *distributio*. This process could be carried out in several different ways, depending on the logical relationship between the parts and the whole.[10] Wherever possible the division was to be effected by a dichotomy which split the subject squarely down the centre, as it were, leaving two classes upon which the operation might be repeated. These rigid bifurcations, derived from Plato, are the most obvious identification tag of the Ramist technique. When one particular *distributio* was complete each of the classes so obtained was to be defined in turn and subdivided in the same way. It was an article of faith that when the division had been carried out properly to the furthest possible stage, all the arguments appropriate to the examination of the subject under study would become clearly evident by this simple exercise of human reason.

Keeping in mind this general technique for the discovery of arguments, let us turn now to a minor work of Bodin's which bears the significant title *Juris universi distributio*. First printed in 1578, it was conceived before 1566, for it is accurately described in the Dedication to the much better known *Methodus ad facilem historiarum cognitionem*. The *Distributio*, as we shall call it, is an attempt to establish a systematic framework for the art of jurisprudence. It opens with a definition of the subject in general.[11] This concept is then divided according to the Aristotelian four causes, which was the procedure recommended by Ramus to establish the primary division of a

---

[9] " Definiendi genera duo sunt, alterum proprie definitio, alterum descriptio nominatur. Definitio propria ex causis propriam, veramque rei naturam constituentibus explicat quid ipsa res sit, idque plerunque duobus vocabulis generis & formae caussas omnes propositae rei continentibus, quo pacto hominem definiemus animal rationale." *Institutionum dialecticarum libri III* (Paris, 1549), 80.

[10] " Distributio est totius in partes divisio: itaque tam multiplex sit necesse est distributio, quam varia totius & partium ratio sit. Optime vero & commodissime quadripertita ex causis, effectis, subjectis, adjunctis instituetur, ut intelligatur quibus e fontibus haec oriantur." *Ibid.*, 69. Cf. *Dialectica*, 100.

[11] " Jurisprudentia est ars tribuendi suum cuique, ad tuendam hominum societatem. . . ." Jean Bodin, *Oeuvres philosophiques* ed. P. Mesnard (Paris, 1951), I, 72. Henceforth this volume is referred to as *O.P.*, I.

subject.[12]   In this case the formal cause is law (*jus*) itself, which is in
turn defined and divided into two categories, natural and human.
Bodin explicitly rejects the more common threefold division based on
the Digest on the ground that "dichotomy is more convenient".[13]
Human law is either *jus gentium* or *jus civile,* but since the latter is
relevant only to a single nation, it is set aside as beyond the scope of
a true scientific discipline. *Jus gentium,* the law that is common to
all peoples, is Bodin's primary concern, and he subdivides it further.
The completed scheme for the division of *jus,* the formal cause of
jurisprudence, is shown in figure 1. Similar classifications are worked

Figure 1.

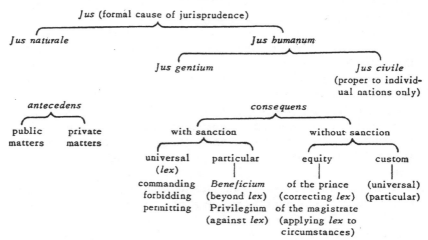

out for the material and efficient causes, and in the process such
typically Ramist terms as distribution from causes, from subjects, and
from adjuncts, are used repeatedly. In short, we find in the *Distributio* a complete classification of jurisprudence according to the precepts laid down in the first book of the Ramist logic.

   Now we must turn for a moment to the second part of the logic,
which is concerned with disposition or judgment. Disposition is defined as the proper arrangement of things discovered, i.e., of the arguments revealed by invention.[14] In the later *Dialectica* this function
was divided into three classes, enunciation, syllogism, and *methodus.*[15]

---

[12] *Inst. Dial.,* 69; *Dialectica,* 100-101.

[13] " Pervulgata divisio juris est in naturale, gentium, ac civile; sed commodius
est διχοτομεῖν, & unum uni quoad eius fieri potest opponere." *O.P.* I, 72.

[14] " Dispositio, est apta rerum inventarum collocatio." *Inst. Dial.* 89.   [15] *Dialectica,* 147–148.

The first consisted merely in linking one argument with another. It was to be used when the truth or falsehood of the matter to be judged was evident, for then a mere juxtaposition of arguments was sufficient to command universal agreement. It was in connection with these self-evident axioms that Ramus introduced the three rules of logic that became a rallying cry among his followers, the laws of universality, homogeneity, and catholicity. By the first, all precepts of all arts must be true without exception. By the second, precepts must be composed of arguments which agree naturally with one another. By the third, the relationship of the parts of a statement to one another is reciprocal, and may be demonstrated by cross-verification.[16] These rules were the basis of much abstract and tiresome discussion as to the proper relationship of the parts with one another and with the whole.

When a statement appeared to be of doubtful validity, its truth or falsehood was to be demonstrated by syllogism. This second type of disposition was essentially a simplified version of the traditional medieval form of disputation.

It is the third procedure, *methodus,* which is of the greatest interest here, for it was the most distinctively Ramist of the three. The fundamental notion involved is startling in its simplicity: when many precepts are under consideration at the same time, *methodus* is the technique required for arranging them in convenient order. Since the purpose of *methodus* was to facilitate the understanding and teaching of the material, the simplest notions were to precede, and the more difficult were to come later. Within the Ramist framework of knowledge this meant in effect that the most general concepts, such as definitions, as the most easily understood and the first to be noticed, would be placed first. The rest would be arranged according to their degree of generality, with examples, as the most special of all, at the end. Concepts of the same order of generality, such as the parts of a *distributio,* were to be discussed in the order in which they were propounded, so that the first to be noticed is to be placed first absolutely.[17] At first glance this procedure looks very much like invention under a new name, but there is one main difference. In *methodus* the main difficulty is not in making the proper division or *distributio,* but in selecting the most general precepts from a vast mass of undifferentiated data. Here the stress is overwhelmingly on arrangement, and the reader's convenience is the primary consideration. This form of *methodus,* Ramus claimed, was not only the fundamental logical technique common to all the sciences, but might be used for any body

[16] *Dialectica,* 171; 175. Cf. Miller, *op. cit.,* 141.
[17] *Inst. Dial.,* 133; *Dialectica,* 247–249.

of material " which we wish to teach easily and clearly." [18]

The procedure just described was called by Ramus *methodus doctrinae,* because it dealt with objective data of the sort found in the various disciplines. But there was a second type, called *methodus prudentiae,* which was intended to meet those situations where objective foundations were lacking by the use of human reason alone. [19] Ramus was far from specific in his treatment of this second type of *methodus,* which seems to have originated from his study of rhetoric. Its chief characteristic was that it " provides a plan for the arrangement of data according to the circumstances of persons, things, times and places." [20] Further discussion did not clarify this very much. The method of prudence merely advised finding another mode of procedure when the customary one was closed, just as a mariner driven off course by a storm carries on as best he can.

The very title of Bodin's *Methodus ad facilem historiarum cognitionem* is sufficient to suggest its connections with Ramism. Examination soon shows that the influence extends beyond the title. In the Dedication Bodin remarks that he has found three types of historical writing: discovery of data, arrangement of data in order, and elimination of errors. Further, he thinks it surprising that so many have found new materials while very few have arranged the discoveries scientifically. [21] He returns to this theme at the end of a Proemium which draws the reader's attention to the ease, delight and usefulness to be derived from histories. The advantages cited are the conventional ones used by many another writer, but he sums up with the rather startling statement that he has undertaken this work because, despite the abundance of historians, no one has yet explained the science and method of the subject. [22] Now in point of

---

[18] " Haec methodus in artibus bene traditis singularis & unica est . . . . Atque haec methodus non solum in materia artium & doctrinarum adhibetur, sed in omnibus rebus, quas facile & perspicue docere volumus." *Dialectica,* 248, 251.

[19] " Methodus, est multorum & variorum argumentorum dispositio: ea duplex est, altera doctrinae, altera prudentiae, non quod utraque prudentiae non sit, sed quod altera doctrinae & artis nihil fere habeat, sed ex hominis naturalis judicio prudentiaque pendeat." *Inst. Dial.,* 133.

[20] " . . . quae pro conditione personarum, rerum, temporum, locorum consilium disponendi dabit." *Ibid.,* 139.

[21] " Sed cum animadverterem triplex omnino scribendi genus esse; unum in rebus inveniendis, & materia suppeditanda: alterum in rebus ordine tradendis & forma perpoliendis: postremum in maculis veterum librorum eluendis: mirum mihi visum est tam multos esse, ac semper fuisse rerum inventores, qui vero res inventas arte ac ratione traderent, admodum paucos." *O.P.,* I, 107. In translating I have consulted the English translation by Beatrice Reynolds (New York, 1945).

[22] " Hujus ego scientiae utilitate incredibili ad hanc scriptionem adductus sum, cum magnam historicorum ubertatem & copiam animadverterem non deesse, qui tamen historiae artem ac methodum tradidisset, fuisse neminem." *Ibid.,* I, 114.

314   KENNETH D. MCRAE

fact Bodin had numerous predecessors in the field of historical method,[23] and he must have known the work of several of them. In the very next sentence he admits that some have written books about the construction of histories, but he compares these to some doctors "who, when all sorts of medicine have been suggested to the patient, return to their discussions about the making of medicines, instead of trying to explain the force and nature of the many that they have and to apply them to existing diseases. In the same way these men produce books on the writing of history, when all the books of antiquity and all libraries are full of historians, whom they might more usefully have studied and imitated, instead of indulging in rhetorical discussion of introductions, narration, and the excellence of words and sentences."[24]

Thus does Bodin dissociate himself from previous writers on historical method. His meaning seems clear enough. While others have written books about the composition of history, no one has yet done exactly what he proposes to do: to methodize *existing* historical materials after the fashion of the Ramists, with a view, no doubt, to their eventual application to contemporary situations. The ten chapters of the *Methodus* which follow this introductory statement constitute an explanation of how this ought to be done.

In accordance with Ramist principles, the opening sentence of the first chapter contains a two-word definition—history is truthful narration—and its division into three parts, human, natural and divine.[25] Bodin remarks that this division has been established by others, and does not feel obliged to defend it or modify it. Each of these branches of history may then be dichotomised into the universal and the particular. Although he admits the possibility of a fourth branch, mathematical history, the problem of division into parts remains a simple one. "And this is all," concludes the chapter, "concerning the division (*partitio*) of histories."[26]

The second chapter, which discusses the order in which histories ought to be read, opens with a passage which is extremely significant. In it Bodin insists that the same method is to be applied to history as is used in the sciences in general. Histories are to be read in the

[23] See the collection of treatises entitled *Artis historicae penus*, ed. J. Wolfius, 2 vols. (Basel, 1579); B. Reynolds, "Shifting Currents in Historical Criticism," this *Journal*, XIV (1953), pp. 471–492; J. L. Brown, *op. cit.*; E. Menke-Glueckert, *Die Geschichtschreibung der Reformation und Gegenreformation* (Osterwieck, 1912).

[24] *O.P.*, I, 114.

[25] "Historiae, id est verae narrationis, tria sunt genera: humanum, naturale, divinum." *Ibid.*

[26] *Ibid.*, 116.

appropriate order, like courses at a feast, in order to aid the understanding and the memory. To do this properly one must make use of the process known as analysis, which teaches the division of a subject into parts, and the harmonious coherence of the parts and the whole. No attempt is to be made to synthesize, for this is the task of expert historians.[27] This entire passage could almost have been written by Ramus himself, and the order described in the remainder of the chapter is that of moving from the most comprehensive works to the more specialized, from the general to the detailed. The first thing to be studied is a brief general table of the main events since the beginning of the world, such as is found in popular chronicles. Soon the reader graduates to more detailed accounts of universal history. Next he undertakes to study each of the more illustrious peoples in the order of their appearance in the chronological tables, and the same will later be done for the smaller, more obscure states. The final stage in learning human history is the study of the deeds of outstanding individuals. The same technique may be applied to natural and divine history. He emphasizes that this historical method is closely analogous to the study of cosmography, which proceeds by stages from the study of the universe as a whole to the elementary region, to geography (and the sciences of the other elements), to the study of particular areas and finally of individual places. "Not otherwise," he continues, "shall we divide and define universal history. For just as they are deceived who study regional maps before they have learned accurately the order of the whole universe and the relation of its parts between themselves and with the whole, so too they err no less who think they can understand individual histories before they have judged the order and sequence of universal history and of all times, displayed as though in a chart.

[27] "Quod in artium tradendarum ratione ac modo fieri solet, idem nobis est, opinor, in historiarum disciplina faciendum. neque enim satis est magnum historicorum cumulum domi habere, nisi cujusque usus & quo quisque ordine ac modo legi debeat intelligatur. & quemadmodum in epulis tametsi magna condimentorum suavitas est, nihil tamen insuavius si misceantur: ita quoque providendum erit, ne historiarum ordo confundatur: id est, ne postrema priore loco, vel media postremo, ad legendum proponantur. quod qui faciunt, non solum res gestas capere nullo modo possunt, sed etiam memoriae vim penitus labefactant: ut igitur plena sit & facilis historiarum scientia, principio adhibeatur praestans illa docendarum artium magistra, quae dicitur analysis: quae universum in partes secare, & partis cujusque particulas rursus dividere, totiusque ac partium cohaerentiam quasi concentum inter ipsa mira facilitate docet. nihil enim in synthesi nobis est elaborandum, cum historiarum fere omnium membra inter se apta sint, magnoque studio ab eruditis in unum veluti corpus coagmentata: sed imperite a nonnullis separantur. est autem partium ac totius tanta cohaerentia, ut si divellantur a se ipsa nullo modo constare possint." *Ibid.* Ramus stresses the Aristotelian distinction between *analysis* and *genesis,* or new composition, in the practice of dialectic. Cf. *Inst. Dial.,* Bk. III.

We shall use the same analysis for the particular history of each people." [28]

After this promising beginning, the *Methodus* strays widely from the strict Ramist pattern. The third chapter proposes to establish a set of topics of discussion, around which might be grouped the materials discovered in reading histories. These *loci communes,* as they were called, were frequently used in the sixteenth century as a means for systematic arrangement of materials, and they are not specifically a Ramist device. It is this topical arrangement which serves as a framework for the chapters on environment and government which constitute the most distinctive elements in his essay. Other chapters draw him into controversial issues discussed by other writers on history. Indeed, despite his protestation of originality of aim, Bodin is more directly influenced by his predecessors in the field of historical method than he cares to admit. In this respect the *Methodus* is less consistently Ramist than is the *Distributio,* which is a direct application to jurisprudence of the technique of the *Dialectica.*

For all its discrepancies, however, the *Methodus* should not be divorced from its Ramist context. Unlike many of the other treatises on historical method, it is an essay on the reading, not the writing, of history and as such it is solely concerned with the most effective utilisation of extant materials. By and large Bodin does not lose sight of his original intention to establish a simple, orderly arrangement of historical knowledge. The work is in no sense a treatise on historiography, nor was it intended to be a contribution to the philosophy of history. Modern critics who have discussed the *Methodus* from these viewpoints have all too frequently remained totally unaware of the logical operation which Bodin was attempting to execute.

Whether he succeeded in this primary aim is quite another matter. It is interesting to note that early in the seventeenth century the *Methodus* was sharply criticized from the point of view of method by Bartholomew Keckermann, who wrote, in addition to *schemata* of several other disciplines, an able but logic-ridden tract on the nature of history. Among other criticisms, Keckermann rejects Bodin's classification of history, deplores the lack of form and method in the *Methodus,* and generally insists that Bodin has not considered history logically enough.[29] He himself denies the existence of any special logical method peculiar to history, for history deals only with single events, and is therefore not a true discipline. History is merely a series of *examples* of general precepts, but the only method appropriate to the precepts themselves is that of the respective disciplines

---

[28] *O.P.,* I, 118.

[29] *De natura et proprietatibus historiae* (Hanover, 1610), 95–98, 153.

to which they belong, such as ethics, economics or politics. Accordingly the employment of *loci communes* in arranging historical data is fundamentally wrong " since *loci communes* are nothing but heads of method." [30]

Like most German scholars of his generation Keckermann was profoundly influenced by Ramism, but he was not particularly sympathetic towards it. In any case his more sophisticated view of historical method is hardly a fair refutation of the *Methodus*. Ramus himself had explicitly stated that the technique of *methodus* was applicable to any body of knowledge which is to be taught or studied, and not only to a true *ars* or *scientia*. Although Bodin does speak vaguely and perhaps carelessly of history as a *disciplina*, he had no intention of treating it as a science in itself. To his mind historical knowledge was primarily a means to the eventual attainment of a more ambitious design, the formulation of a true science of human behavior which would find its principles of organization in jurisprudence.

A modern reader might well wonder why Bodin saw fit to systematize law by means of a *distributio*, while treating history in terms of *methodus*. The answer lies in the Ramist logic. In applying the latter to any specific discipline, one must consider which parts of logic will be most appropriate. In law it seems clear that the heart of the problem is the discovery of the arguments, and that the most difficult task is that of making the successive divisions in the proper manner. Bodin himself hints at the difficulty in the Dedication to the *Distributio:* the division must be effected in such a way as to display at a glance the parts, their relationships among themselves and with the whole, and the nature of the totality, as is the rule in all disciplines.[31] History, by contrast, presents a different sort of problem, for it seems to bear some resemblance to grammar, the example chosen by Ramus himself to illustrate the use of *methodus*. In this subject, Ramus says, all the definitions, divisions and rules are present and proved at the start, though mixed together indiscriminately. " Here I ask what part of dialectic teaches me to arrange these confused precepts and reduce them to order." It will not be invention, for all the arguments are present. Nor will it be enunciation or syllo-

---

[30] *Ibid.,* 8-10.

[31] " Quod enim Plato dicere solebat, nihil divinius sibi videri quam apte dividere, eo pertinet, ut in recta divisione membrorum omnium perpetua sit, & continua quaedam series: tum ut alia ex aliis nexa, & omnia inter se apta colligataque uno possint & eodem aspectu videri, atque integri corporis formam prae se ferre. Ita fit ut respondeant extrema primis, media utrisque omnia omnibus, & facile intelligere quisque possit quid antecedat, quid sequatur. Haec illa est non modo artium tradendarum, sed etiam omnium scientiarum ratio communis." *O.P.,* I, 71.

318   KENNETH D. MCRAE

gism, for there is no controversy over the validity of the rules. Hence *methodus* must be the only technique that is called for.[32] One can almost imagine Bodin reaching the same conclusion with respect to the formless conglomeration of data uncovered by his prolonged labor in the field of history. Just as the *Distributio* demonstrates his familiarity with invention, the *Methodus* illustrates his reliance on disposition to bring a semblance of order into the chaotic records of human activity.

IV

It would be tedious to try to point out all the instances of Ramist doctrines in Bodin's other works. Besides, some of the most striking parallels lie in the general outlook of the two men, and this is difficult to illustrate by quotation. Consequently we shall merely note a few of the more interesting points in other works before attempting some more general conclusions.

Bodin's earliest known work, his translation with commentary of Oppian's *Cynegetica,* a didactic poem on hunting, seems to corroborate our hypothesis that his introduction to Ramism dates from his sojourn at Paris in the late 1540's. In the Dedication Bodin defends his choice of a poet so uninteresting to most modern readers on the specific ground that Oppian is concerned not so much with hunting and fishing as with the nature of animals and fishes; that his subject is not old wives' tales but complicated matters.[33] He feels that his desertion of " weightier studies " for poets of this type may be justified, " if only I am at liberty to gather the abundant fruits of philosophy and eloquence in them." [34] This in itself is suggestive of Ramist influences, but our suspicions are considerably strengthened by an examination of the commentary appended to the translation. As might be expected, many of Bodin's notes concern textual criticism, grammatical points, Greek antiquities and the identification of proper names, but there are some which develop a logical analysis of the poem in Ramist terms, and others embark on general discussion of philosophical questions. All in all, the edition of Oppian seems to exemplify precisely that union of philosophy and literature which was both advocated and practised by Ramus himself at this very period.[35]

[32] *Inst. dial.* 133–134; *Dialectica,* 250–251.

[33] " . . . non tam de venatione et piscatione quam de piscium et ferarum varia natura disputationem instituisse videatur. . . . Non est Oppianus ex eo poetarum genere, qui fabulas aniles caelo terraque consectantur, sed res arduas festivo ac perurbano poemate complectitur." *De venatione libri IIII* (Paris, 1555).   [34] *Ibid.,* Dedication.

[35] Waddington, *op. cit.,* 83–85.

In the *République* the traces of Ramism are less evident than in
the earlier works, but this may be due to the circumstances of its
composition. It was, from one viewpoint, a statement of the policy
and aspirations of the Politique party, an appeal addressed to Henry
III shortly after his accession, and much of the book was probably
written with a haste which left little scope for methodological niceties. Even so, however, the Ramist principle of *methodus* is at least
partially observed in its structure. The first book opens with a definition of the state, and the remainder of the book discusses the terms
of this definition in order.[36] The second book divides all states into
three types, and the third discusses the component parts of the state.
Though the fourth is intended to explain changes in states, it wanders
widely from this theme, and in general the organization of the last
three books is much less symmetrical than that of the first three.

When Bodin himself undertook the Latin translation of the work,
there was an opportunity for certain alterations, which he describes
in the Dedication. He had made these changes, he adds, in the interests of order: " that the last terms should correspond to the first,
the middle to both, and all to all; and that those which are deduced
from others and related and linked among themselves should be attached together in the same series. For in this way I thought it could
be understood more easily not only what things follow what, but also
what things are consistent with what." [37] Unfortunately a textual
comparison of two versions reveals how far he fell short of realizing
this logical ideal. Apart from the addition of one extra chapter, the
structural changes in the Latin edition are superficial only. While
many matters of detail are altered, Bodin's expressed desire for a more
lucid organization of his material is more valuable as an indication
of good intentions than as a statement of fact.

The *Universae naturae theatrum*, published only a few weeks before Bodin's death in 1596, demonstrates that his Ramist tendencies
were no mere youthful aberration. Next to the *Distributio*, the
Theatrum is perhaps the most thoroughly Ramist of any of his works.
Its aim is to provide a complete survey of the realm of natural science. In general it remains within the medieval Aristotelian framework, but many of Aristotle's specific precepts are rejected. It takes
the form of a dialogue between master and pupil, and this permits
Bodin to introduce through the mouth of the pupil certain traditional
doctrines taught in the schools, which are immediately rejected as

---

[36] " Republique est un droit gouvernement de plusieurs mesnages, & de ce qui
leur est commun, avec puissance souveraine." *Les six Livres de la Republique*
(Lyons, 1593), 1. However the " common property " is not discussed until Book VI.

[37] *De republica libri sex* (Paris, 1591). Dedicatory Epistle. The terminology is
almost identical to that used in the Dedication of the *Distributio*.

absurd by the master.[38]   In place of these must be substituted reason.[39]   Sometimes the appeal is to experience, " the mistress of all
things," [40] but this seems to amount to almost the same thing.   Even
more significant is the fact that when the work appeared in French
the translator saw fit to prepare an index, which the first edition lacks.
Deciding against the use of alphabetical tables, " which are more appropriate to words than to things," he chose the Ramist method " by
division of the things that are contained therein : . . since this doctrine is entirely philosophical, and cannot be understood well except
by definitions and divisions." [41]   Accordingly he reduced the entire
contents of the book to a series of tables in the Ramist style.

But lest it should be thought that we have speculated too rashly
in developing these parallels between Bodin and Ramus, there is one
more item to add to the evidence.   Bodin wrote a short tract in
French on the education of a prince which is known only in a Latin
translation made by the German Bornitius.   The latter describes with
care how the tract reached his hands, and there seems no reason to
doubt either its authenticity or his integrity.   This work expressly
declares the superiority of the Ramist logic above all other disciplines
as a general training for the youthful mind.[42]   As far as I know this
is the only time that Ramus is mentioned specifically in the whole of
Bodin's writings, but this one citation seems entirely adequate as a
coping-stone to an argument that rests so strongly on other evidence.

V

This Ramist background is not without considerable significance,
for it suggests an explanation of several persistent tendencies in
Bodin's thought.   In the first place, and perhaps most important, it
explains that carping and often unfair criticism of Aristotle which
runs like a continuous thread through the whole of Bodin's writings.
In attacking Aristotle while still sheltering beneath the Aristotelian
tradition, he was merely following the example of Ramus himself.
Secondly, it explains Bodin's diatribes against the grammarians' approach to knowledge.   Ramists claimed to be interested in " things "
rather than " words," and had little patience with the philological
aspect of humanist scholarship.   Bodin likewise vigorously shows his
disapproval of such methods and of those who practise them.[43]   Some

---

[38] For examples, see *Universae naturae theatrum* (Lyons, 1596), 470, 524–525,
578.   [39] " Rationibus oportet non autoritate disserere." *Ibid.*, 446. Cf. also 137.
[40] *Ibid.*, 249, 386.

[41] *Le Theatre de la nature universelle*, tr. F. de Fougerolles (Lyons, 1597), 917.

[42] ". . . tradenda est Rami Dialectica omnium optima, propterea quod haec ars
animum variarum dissertationum capacem reddat." *Consilia Johannis Bodini Galli,
& Fausti Longiani Itali, de principe recte instituendo* (Erfurt, 1603), fol. B2–B2v.

of his rancor undoubtedly stems from his clash with Turnebus over
the edition of Oppian, but it should not be forgotten that Ramus also
carried on a running quarrel with Turnebus during the early 1550's.[44]

Above all, Ramists insisted that knowledge is for use, and this
same concern for practical application lies behind Bodin's impatience
with poets who concern themselves with fantasy, with scholars like
Cujas who bury themselves in the historical study of Roman law,
and with political writers like Plato or Sir Thomas More who construct ideal commonwealths without reference to the possibility of
their attainment. Ramus never tired of insisting that experience is
a necessary foundation to any discipline. This too has its echo in
Bodin's repeated assertions that only those who mingled practice
with the appropriate theoretical foundations could properly comprehend any given discipline, whether law, history, government or natural science.[45] It may also help to explain Bodin's personal desertion
of academic life after 1560 for the career of a practising advocate before the Parlement of Paris. On the other hand, the Ramist background reveals why this passion for experience, this insistence on
first-hand observation of data, could never produce a genuinely in-
ductive approach to the social disciplines: the Ramist methodology
was irretrievably committed to a logical framework which commences
from general principles. As Bodin himself admits in one revealing
passage, the sciences may have been discovered by observation, but
once established they must be studied by analysis, which proceeds
from universals to particulars.[46]

There is one other rather general influence which Ramism may be
said to have exerted on Bodin's thought. The notion that the precepts of a science must be universally and necessarily true was part
of the Aristotelian heritage, but it was adopted by Ramus and raised
to prominence in the so-called *lex veritatis*. It is also one of Bodin's
most frequently repeated philosophical maxims, and it is quite likely
that he acquired it through Ramus, because he admits having learned

---

[43] *Methodus, O.P.*, I, 109, 141; *République*, Epistola Vido Fabro. It is to be
noted that Grotius termed Bodin "hominem rerum quam verborum studiosiorem,"
but he meant this as a reproach.—Letter to des Cordes, printed in R. Chauviré,
Jean Bodin, auteur de la République (Paris, 1914), 536.   [44] Waddington, *op. cit.*,
102–105.

[45] *Methodus, O.P.*, I, 108, 117–118, 127–128; *Consilia*, fol. B3; *Theatrum*, 141.

[46] "Ex quo quidem intelligitur artes omnes ac scientias a sensibili cognitione
coepisse, quam synthesim vocant: artes vero perceptas & cognitas ratione ac
methodo, id est, διὰ τῆς ἀναλύσεως tradi oportere, scilicet a simplicioribus, & univer-
salibus, ad individua & composita." *Theatrum*, 141. Ramus expresses the same
idea, citing Plato as his authority: "Plato in Philebo, cum ait omnes artes (quanvis
inventae sint inductione rerum specialium ad generales ascendendo) via tamen contraria tradendas esse, descendendo a summo genere ad multitudinem specierum in-
finitarum." *Dialectica*, 249.

KENNETH D. MCRAE

it from philosophers in his youth.[47]   However derived, the principle
plays an important part in his thought, for it underlies the attempt
to formulate a universal science of jurisprudence.   Interest in legal
methodology was characteristic of the age, and the desire to reduce
the confused sphere of law to a simplified system had already produced several essays in legal classification before the appearance of
the *Distributio*.   Nevertheless Bodin's brief contribution to the genre,
composed as it was before the appearance of the *Methodus* in 1566,
is among the earliest to reveal clear manifestations of Ramism.   To
this philosophical background we may attribute one important difference between the *Distributio* and its forerunners.   All previous
efforts in this direction had been directed towards systematisation of
the Roman civil code, and in the *Distributio* Bodin seizes upon this
particularist aspect of the movement to claim that his predecessors
in the field had fundamentally misconceived the whole idea of scientific method.[48]

He himself firmly believed that the proper field for the scientific
study of law is the universal law of all peoples, and this is what he
sought to discover.   The execution of his plan in its broadest sense
involved both *distributio* and *methodus*.   Into the framework established in the *Juris universi distributio* would be fitted the materials
gathered from a systematic study of history, as outlined in the *Methodus ad facilem historiarum cognitionem*.   Thus the corpus of universal law which was confidently expected to emerge from this vast
comparative inquest was to be founded on observed human behavior.
Those laws and customs which were found to be common to all
peoples were to constitute a normative standard, a guide to the
prudent management of human societies.   However since the art of
ruling men was not a pure *scientia* concerned with universals, but a
prudentia, it was therefore necessary to adjust the application of the
norm in accordance with the variable needs of " places, persons, and
times." [49]   But even these variations, he believed, could be reduced

[47] " At cum singula quae sunt infinita contemplaremur, plurima nobis omittenda
fuerunt, ut universa, id quod artium tradendarum proprium est, complecteremur.
Iam enim pridem adolescens contritum illud a philosophis acceperam, nullam rerum
singularum scientiam haberi." *De republica*, Dedication.

[48] ". . . eos qui artem illam ratione ac methodo tradere debuerant, juris civilis
artem fuisse professos: quo nihil est artium dignitate ac praestantia magis alienum:
cum artes ac scientiae sint universorum: jus autem civile proprium sit unius civitatis." *O.P.*, I, 71.   The same idea is developed at greater length in the Dedication
to the *Methodus*.   Cf. *O.P.*, I, 107.

[49] " Car l'un des plus grands, & peut estre le principal fondement des Republiques, est d'accommoder l'estat au naturel des citoyens, & les edicts & ordonnances
à la nature des lieux, des personnes, & du temps." *République*, 666.

to regular predictable patterns by careful study of the environment. Thus it may be suggested that what led Bodin to embark upon what is probably the most ambitious synthesis of political and social phenomena to be attempted since the time of Aristotle was his unquestioning faith in logical method. The source of this faith seems clear enough: it was derived from his youthful philosophical studies in the University of Paris, and more particularly from his contacts with Ramus, who believed the human mind capable of reducing all areas of knowledge to simple, orderly, easily comprehensible outlines.

It is best to insert here a word of caution. We have examined certain striking influences of Ramism on Bodin's thought, but it would be unwise to assume from this that Bodin may be counted among the active partisans in the struggle over methodology, or even that he was fully conscious of his debts to the new logic. He was not a thoroughgoing Ramist in the sense that Althusius, for example, obviously was.[50] The fact is that Bodin was too much of an eclectic to be classified as a faithful disciple of any one thinker, and in any case he was far less interested in logical niceties than in raw facts. He approached Ramism not as a theoretician but as a practician of the new techniques. Moreover, Ramism was a widespread phenomenon and a rather vague one. Because it owed much to the Aristotelian tradition out of which it grew, and because it claimed to be based upon man's natural reason, its distinctive characteristics are not always easily identified.

Nevertheless, despite these qualifications which must be made, the Ramist element in Bodin's thought seems important enough to justify the following conclusions. First, Bodin's early studies in philosophy exerted a greater influence upon his intellectual development than has been generally recognized. Secondly, in the contest between Aristotelians and Ramists at the University of Paris his sympathies were such as to make this philosophical training primarily a Ramist one. Thirdly, the traces of this early Ramist indoctrination are visible in many different aspects of his thought, some of which we have not examined here. Finally, Bodin's general fundamental approach to social and political theory, embodied in his conception of a universal law to be derived from a systematisation of total human experience, was to a considerable extent inspired by Ramist attempts to organize other branches of knowledge in the same way.

Nuffield College, Oxford.

[50] See the latter's *Politica methodice digesta,* ed. C. J. Friedrich (Cambridge, Mass., 1932).

Part II
Public Law

[5]

Medieval Jurisprudence in Bodin's Concept of Sovereignty

Ralph E. Giesey

To the dictum that Jean Bodin's *République* is a work more read about than read, I would like to add the following codicil by way of a general theme for the present essay: those who have read the work have read only the text. Anyone who has perused a significant portion of the French or Latin versions of the *République* might recall vaguely the existence of some marginal apparatus, but surely he would be surprised to be told that in some chapters one-third of the margin is filled with notes. Readers of Knolles' English translation will be almost totally ignorant of the marginalia, since all but a handful of the marginal notes were suppressed there.

The margins of the chapters which people are most likely to read, the two «sovereignty» chapters (Book I, charpters 8 and 10) are forty per-cent filled with notes. The pages from *Répub*. I, 8 reproduced at the end of this essay (p. 184 f.) only mildly exaggerate the usual situation.

The marginal apparatus of *Répub*. I, 8 is prone to be neglected, I surmise, because four-fifths of its citations deal with the Two Laws and late medieval commentaries upon them. Even scholars who are capable of identifying stylized references to Roman law and canon law might scorn spending the time to chase them down, for it is the opinion of many that the heaping up of «allegations» – an old technical term which I shall use to designate citations of the Two Laws and commentators [1] – is pure pedantry, used either ostentatiously to support the obvious or deceptively to camouflage the untenable.

One should hesitate to entertain such derogatory notions about Jean Bodin. He was trained in the humanistic school of Roman law jurisprudence *(mos gallicus)* which stressed antique historical content and scorned medieval jurists' penchants to make Roman law suit contemporary needs *(mos italicus)*. This makes strange, indeed, Bodin's massive application of late medieval jurisprudence to the most famous piece of all his writings. Book I, chapters 8 and 10 of the *République* have altogether about six hundred separate marginal citations of the Two Laws and

---

[1] The Oxford English Dictionary calls obsolete the definition of «allegation» as «quoting or citing a document or author», but it remains in good usage in French according to Littré's *Dictionnaire*. Best of all, see Du Cange, Gloss. lat. (s.v. allegare): «Allegationes partium rationes, quas reus et actor producunt.»

speaks for the second time about the inadequacies of his forerunners:
«But no one has defined just what is meant by absolute power – or better,
power freed from the law. For if we define it as freedom from all laws,
no prince at all could be known for sure to have sovereignty, since divine
law as well as natural law and even the law of nations – which is
grounded on either (or both) divine and natural law – are binding upon
all men.»[7] Only Bodin's Latin text, incidentally, brings out clearly the
verbal and spiritual nexus of «absolutism» in medieval arguments about
princeps legibus solutus.

That the prince must in principle be freed from obedience to civil law
follows necessarily from what Bodin considers to be the most important
aspect of sovereign power: the power to legislate. Civil legislation is the
willful creation of the sovereign. So, while the good ruler should obey all
laws – his own and his predecessors' – which are beneficial to the state,
he must be free to disregard and annul any of them according to the needs
of his country.[8] The passages driving home this point are the most cited
parts of the *République.* Whenever they stand alone, they do indeed
extol the «absolute» monarch.

What Bodin gives to the sovereign by way of absolute power, however,
he takes back in large measure (to his own way of thinking, at least) by
stating various exceptions. These are headed by the traditional medieval
notion that all earthly powers must be beneath divine and natural law.
This appears, for example, in the quotation just given and in the one to
be given just below. Less clear, however, is the origin of another exception: that the prince is bound by contracts. Contracts, it would seem, are
part of the civil law from which the prince is freed. This and a few
similar matters were singled out by Bodin when he composed a new
dedicatory letter for the third edition, in 1578. He laments that his
critics have charged him with giving inordinate power to the rule of a
single person: «For specifically in Book I, chapter 8 of my *République*
and frequently elsewhere, I have been the very first, even in the most
perilous times, to refute unhesitatingly the opinions of those who write

---

[7] «Quid autem sit absoluta, vel potius soluta lege potestas, nemo definit. Nam
si *legibus omnibus solutam* [Bodin's italics] definiamus, nulles omnino. princeps
iura maiestatis habere comperiatur, cum omnes teneat lex divina, lex item
naturae, tum etiam lex omnium gentium communis, quae a naturae legibus ac
divinis divisas habet rationes.» *Répub.* [7.28], 132.

[8] Of the many appropriate passages that could be cited to illustrate this, the
following is one of the best because Bodin calls it a maxim: «Et par ainsi nostre
maxime demeure, que le Prince n'est point subiect à ses loix, ny aux loix de ses
predecesseurs, mais bien à ses conventions [i.e., contracts] iustes & raisonnables,
& en l'observation desquelles les subiects en general ou en particulier ont
interest.» *Répub.,* 134.

of enlarging the rights of the treasury and the royal prerogative, on the ground that these men grant to kings an unlimited power, superior to divine and natural law. But what could be more in the interest of the people than what I have had the courage to write: that not even for kings is it lawful to levy taxes without the fullest consent of the citizens? Or of what importance is my other statement: that princes are more stringently bound by divine and natural law than those subject to their rule? Or that princes are bound by their contracts exactly as other citizens are? Yet nearly all the masters of legal science have taught the contrary.»[9]

Clearly Bodin did not consider himself an «absolutist» in the modern sense. The perusal of *Répub.* I, 8, bears out the contention that he did argue for limitations on royal power. More space is devoted to three such limitations than to any other matter: that the king is beneath divine and natural law, that he is forbidden to tax without consent, and that he is bound by his contracts *(pacta conventa)*.[10] In these sections, too, we find the greatest utilization of the texts of the Two Laws and of commentaries upon them. This conjunction of arguments for limited monarchy with intensive use of medieval legal allegations suggests that a spiritual bond exists between them.

---

[9] *République*, prefatory *Epistola*. I have followed the translation given by KENNETH McRae in his edition of Knolles' translation [7.44], p. A71.

[10] That the Prince is bound by contracts comes out less clearly in the French than in this Latin rendering: «Qui autem principes, legibus & pactis conventis solutos esse statuunt, nisi Dei praepotentis, ac naturae leges, tum etiam res ac rationes cum privatis justa conventione contractas excipiant, maximam immortali Deo, ac naturae injuriam inferunt»; *Répub.* [7.28], 153. Also, this passage: «nous pouvons tirer une autre reigle d'estat, c'est à sçavoir que le Prince souverain est tenu aux contracts par lui faicts, soit avec son subjeçt, soit avecques l'estranger; car puis qu'il est garant aux subiets des conventions & obligations mutuelles qu'ils ont les uns envers les autres, à plus forte raison est il debteur de justice en son faict»; ed. 1583, 152. See also above, note 8. MAX A. SHEPARD [110]. Sovereignty at the Crossroads: a Study of Bodin, Political Science Quarterly, 45 (1930), 590 ff., treats the problem of contracts well up to and including this summary sentence: «Contracts may not be laws in themselves, but the principle that contracts must be kept and that promises have binding force surely is a law and one derived directly from the law of nature» (591–592). But then Shepard wanders off into metaphysical speculations about contract as a kind of legal formalizing of the static social structure of the Middle Ages, which Bodin is supposed to imbibe still. Like many, Shepard understands too little about medieval jurisprudence.

II

Bodin's «anti-absolutism», such as it is, depends chiefly upon his feelings about the force of natural law in the world order, and upon the extension of natural law into temporal affairs. Natural law's force is something we must infer from Bodin's cosmology; it is largely taken for granted in *Répub.* I, 8.[11] The extension of natural law, however, is dealt with explicitly in a variety of instances in the text of that chapter. The corresponding marginal references refer most often to Roman, canon, and feudal law, along with the medieval commentaries upon them. We have, therefore, the apparently anomalous situation of natural law's being conflated with positive law. To understand how this happens is basic to the understanding of Bodin's concept of limited monarchy.

The opening chapters of the *Digest* define natural law in broad terms, and later chapters spell this out at length.[12] Several other places in the *Digest* and some in the *Code* give specific illustrations of the operation of natural law.[13] Likewise, the law of nations *(ius gentium)*, a category which Bodin did not differentiate from natural law in any meaningful way, is similarly defined and illustrated in the *Digest*.[14] These simple facts establish an important but easily overlooked consideration: Justinian's codification is not strictly a compilation of Roman civil law. Tribonian and his co-workers sought to locate what we would call the positive law of the Romans within the wider context of philosophy of law. The space devoted to this philosophical context is small, but its importance incalculable, for the dicta of the *Corpus Juris Civilis* con-

---

[11] See the papers in this volume of Mme. CHANTEUR, in general, and of Mr. BAXTER in relation to divine retribution in particular.

[12] *Digest* 1, 1, 1, 3: «Natural law is what nature teaches all animals ... not to the human species specially but all animals ... From it derives ... matrimony, ... child-bearing and education of children.» *Digest* 1, 1, 11: «There are many forms of the law. One form is the law of that which is equitable and good, as is natural law; another from, what is useful to all or to most in a given city, as is civil law.»

[13] E.g., *Digest* 12, 6, 14: «As it is only right, as a matter of natural law, that no one should become richer to the injury of another,» and *Digest* 2, 14, 1 (speaking of contracts): «The justice of this part of the Edict is founded on nature.»

[14] *Digest* 1, 1, 9 separates *ius gentium* from *ius civile* in much the same way that *Digest* 1, 1, 17 separates *ius naturale* from *ius civile:* i.e., that which befits a certain *civitas* is called *ius civile* whereas «what is established among all men by reason of nature, is observed by all and each and is called the law of nations as if it were the law observed by all people.» *Digest* 1, 1, 15 is very important for Bodin: «It was by this same *ius gentium* that war was introduced, nations were

cerning the confines of Roman civil law were taken to describe the limits of every nation's civil law. We should include also canon law and feudal law, which might be described as the civil law of the first and second estates of medieval society. Put another way, knowledge of Roman law in the totality of Justinian's compilation necessarily involved knowledge of the nature of natural law, because tiny but important fractions of the Corpus Juris Civilis dealt with that issue.

The commentaries of medieval legists abound in judgments about the borderlines between natural law, the law of nations, and civil law – as well, of course, as the superior category of divine law. Most of the argumentations drew upon *Corpus Juris Civilis* passages which make crucial distinctions. In time, the legists' interpretations far exceeded the primary passages in size, scope, and subtlety. This medieval apparatus began to develop a personality and character of its own. Statements about the extent of natural law were not gathered in one place, but remained scattered about in appropriate contexts. Some commentators, like Baldus, were more disposed than others to indulge in lofty philosophical observations. It took considerable experience, therefore, for a Renaissance lawyer like Bodin to assemble and impart order to the wide range of medieval juristic thought about natural law. Moreover, it might be difficult to recognize the result as a compendium of medieval thought, because Bodin's kind of philosophical synthesis was not the style of medieval jurists.

That Bodin quarried medieval arguments about the interpenetration of natural law and civil law does not mean that he slavishly followed or copied the medieval legists. He admired their works because they united actual legal practice with juristic theory in a way that his humanistic education had shunned. Bodin seems to have come to realize that some Bartolists possessed a strain of just that kind of philosophical humanism which the new school of Renaissance legal scholarship supposed they had lacked.

---

dinstinguished, kingdoms were established, rights of ownership were ascertained, boundaries were set to domains, buildings were erected, mutual traffic, purchase and sale, letting and hiring and obligations in general were set on foot, with the exception of a few of these last which were introduced by civil law»; translation of MONRO, I, 4. The final words of the last-quoted law touch upon the issue of «obligation», which Bodin argues vigorously (in *Répub.* I, 8) is a matter of natural law even thought the action in law with it is related is civil. From the law just cited, it is clear that obligation could be considered one of the «few of these last» introduced by civil law, although Bodin held the reverse.

III

By the count of separate citations in *Répub*. I, 8, Bartolus' student Baldus (d. 1400) is far ahead of all others with twenty-six. Bartolus himself is encountered fourteen times; the fifteenth-century civilian Alexander Tartagnus (d. 1477) and the canonist Panormitanus (Nicholaus de Tudeschis, d. 1445) twelve times each; and the canonist Felinus Sandaeus (d. 1503) fifteen times.

The last named, Felinus, is the most obscure member of this quintet of the *Répub*. I, 8's most cited authors. None, however, surpasses him in degree as a forerunner of the ideas in this chapter. Specifically, his long commentary on «Quae in ecclesiarum» *(Decretals, 1, 2, 7)* uses that law's concern with lay rulers' respect for the Church and its goods as a springboard to cover a score of major points concerning the sovereign's relations with his subjects' goods. These arguments fit perfectly Bodin's need to spell out the limits of the sovereign's *imperium* in public matters as against the subject's *dominium* over his own property. All three of the limits to princely power which Bodin in 1578 reminded his readers were involved in *Répub*. I, 8 are dealt with by Felinus: the prince bound by divine and natural law, by his own contracts, and by the need to have consent to taxation.[15]

Alexander Tartagnus' *Consilium 216* (in Book II of his collected *Consilia*) compares in importance with Felinus' commentary on «Quae in ecclesiarum». Alexander deals extensively with the question of the

---

[15] FELINUS SANDAEUS, *Commentaria in Lib. Decretalium*, on *Decretals* 1, 2, 7 («Quae in ecclesiarum»), ed. Basel 1567, 126 ff. The first and second conclusions show that secular princes and the Pope can both derogate divine law *ex causa* (the princes in cases of tolerating justifiable homicide, the Pope in dissolving marriage); the third conclusion begins by setting the general rule «Ex causa rationabili, & non aliter potest princeps statuere contra ea, quae sunt de iure naturali, vel gentium,» then gives more detailed applications: «etiam imperator non potest tollere ea, quae sunt de iure naturali, & sic non potest alicui auferre rem suam sine causa, quia licet habeat iurisdictionem in universo ...; etiam respectu bonorum infidelium nam sine causa nec Papa, nec imperator potest eis auferre bona ...; nec princeps, nec civitas potest aliquem privare dominio rei suae sine causa» (§§ 25–27); «licet ex causa princeps possit uni auferre rem suam, & dare alteri, tamen illud est verum dummodo solvat pretium rei ille, cui eam aufert [lex «ita si verberatum» is alleged a few lines later – cf. below, n. 21] (§ 28); «princeps, vel habens iura principis, non potest etiam cum causa auferre rem suam non sibi subjecto» (§ 30); «(princeps) possit revocare suum privilegium ... sed si non est privilegium, sed conventio, tunc non potest revocare, nisi secundum ipsius rei naturam» (§ 51). I have examined less than a third of this very important commentary.

Medieval Jurisprudence in Bodin's Concept of Sovereignty   *175*

prince's power versus the subject's possession of private goods.[16] His arguments pro and con develop the same kind of tension which Bodin strives to create between freedom and restriction in the sphere of princely activity. So, the prince may not in general disturb proprietary rights or ignore his own contracts, but for the sake of public utility he may do both. The emphasis falls upon exceptional circumstances which allow the prince to do things normally prohibited him, but the unvoiced assumption holds that usually the prince is strictly limited in these matters.

Alexander and Felinus are masters of applied Roman and canon law. They build upon the work of Italian jurisprudence during the previous two centuries. They move easily between the Two Laws, and embrace readily feudal law as codified in the *Libri Feudorum*. They may lack the originality of their predecessors, but for someone like Bodin (himself a late-comer to the medieval Italian tradition of jurisprudence) they have the convenience of synthesizing the older learning under topical headings which are directly applicable to public law. Not only do they give general principles a lapidary form, but also they provide abundant examples.

Baldus, Bodin's seemingly favorite commentator, provides many examples of how *trecento* Italian jurisprudence put specific limits upon princely «absolutism». A typical instance occurs in Consilium 363 of Book I of Baldus' collected *Consilia*. At issue is the disposition by a Duke (who possesses full regalian rights by imperial concession) of certain goods to one person, while the former owner disposes of them to someone else. Public *imperium* and private *dominium* seem to lock horns. *Dominium* wins, because it stems from *ius gentium* which stems from natural law which binds the ruler: «Indeed, the Duke for his part does not seem to be able to take away the rights of ownership of another person, since those rights come from the law of nations, as said in the laws ‹quoties› and ‹rescripta› (*Code* 1, 19, 2 & 7), whence the prince is beneath the natural law, as in the law ‹digna vox.›» (*Code* 1, 14, 4.)[17] Other matters, such as the right of the fisc and the force of contract are also brought to

---

[16] ALEXANDER TARTAGNUS, *Consiliorum libri*, II, 216 (ed. Venice 1597, 181v ff., esp. 182v for these quotations): «licet princeps non possit auferre dominium acquisitum ex contractu iuris gentium, secundum magis communem sententiam, tamen ex causa illud tollere potest, & maxime si sit causa publicam utilitatem respiciens (§§ 18–19) «et dicunt Doctores quod decretum, quod transivit in contractum, potest revocari ex causa respiciente publicam utilitatem» (§ 20); «quando Imperator rescribit propter publicam utilitatem ... tunc potest res privatorum auferre, eodem modo civitas.» (§ 21).

[17] «Quinimo ipse dux non videtur posse auferre dominium alterius, cum dominia sint de iure gen. ut not. in l. quot. & in l. rescripta. C. de precib. Impera. unde princeps est sub l. naturali. ut C. de leg. l. digna vox.» BALDUS, *Consilia*, I, 363 (ed. Frankfurt 1589, fol. 108); in *Répub.* I, 8, p. *157*.

bear on the question. In such well-reasoned and compact arguments as these by Baldus it is possible to appreciate how thoroughly the limits of public law were enunciated by the 14th century Italian legists.

The pages reproduced at the end of this essay contain a very complicated allegation which has a double lesson for the unwary: it reveals clearly Bodin's habit of slovenly writing or proofreading, and it illustrates the need always to consult the Latin as well as the French texts. Withal, when the problems are sorted out, we have a fine illustration of the process of alleging medieval legists. The critical phrases in each text have been underlined (the much greater length of the Latin, usually the more economical language, revealing at a glance the great changes wrought between 1576 and 1586), and the notes circled to faciliate locating them. The note I wish to deal with («2» in one text, «c» in the other) has had to be relocated in the Latin version. This can mislead the reader in itself, but the noteworthy difference really is in content of the marginalia: the French note, reversing the situation in the text, is twice as long as the Latin one. The Latin omits the latter part of the French, beginning with the words «Cum ansi. inco». Since these three words make no sense, they deprive the learned citations that follow of association with any author. When translating, Bodin may have been unable to unscramble the garbled reference and so have decided to eliminate the confusing parts. But the suppression only compounds the original blunder, as I shall show, because the part preserved – viz:, everything up to «Cum ansi. inco». – consists of false or misleading allegations, while the part cut out contains a true one.

If one is not duped by the words «raison naturelle» in the text of the French version, one should expect the marginal allegations to provide evidence of «eminent domain», i.e., the right of the sovereign power to acquire the goods of a private person for reasons of the public good. Heading the note is a reference to the law «Item si verberatum» (*Digest* 6, 1 15), a law which states three instances of restitution owed by a defendant who has profited wrongfully from the use of another's goods: if he should have had to sell the goods out of necessity, if it were a question of land since given to soldiers, and if it concerned a slave or animal since deceased or destroyed. None of this random series clearly involves eminent domain, although the case of land given to soldiers seems to have the greatest possibility of doing so.

The citations of Felinus (commentary on *Decretals* 2, 26, 12), Corneaus (*Consilium* 100) and Alexander (*Consilium* 15) which precede «Cum ansi. inco.» are not relevant to eminent domain, so that the Latin note is virtually a phantom. Among the things suppressed, however, is a reference to «consil. 216», which rings a bell because of the unusual significance which a consilium of that number by Alexander Tartagnus turned out to have a few pages earlier in Bodin's argument. There, at last, one finds the mysterious Digest 6, 1, 15 («Item si verberatum») cited in relationship to eminent domain, specifically as proof of the statement that «when the Emperor issues a rescript for the sake of public utility... he can in that case take the goods of private persons».[18] Alexander also hints that Bartolus is important for this doctrine. Going to Bartolus' commentary on *Digest 6, 1, 15* (which it would have been wise to do in any event), one finds this declaration: «The prince, for cause, can take my right or my property and give it to another; the same, I believe, is true in the public affairs of any city.»[19] Finally, on the lookout for other legists who mention «Item si verberatum», one soon discovers it in Felinus' commentary «Quae in ecclesiarum», so often cited by Bodin. Felinus says that public goodwill is a legitimate cause for the emperor's taking a subject's goods, as is found in the Digest's «Item si verberatum», «where the land of a third party is given for the use of soldiers as a matter of public goodwill».[20]

There is no doubt, therefore, that Bodin was arguing from a strong medieval tradition when he invoked «Item si verberatum». He did indeed garble his references. A proper allegation would have read: «Bar. in l. item si verberatum, de rei vindic. Felin in c. quae in eccles. de constitut. Alexand. lib 2. cons. 216.»[21]

IV

The juristic apparatus in the margins of *Répub.* I, 8 takes us regularly into the world of 14th and 15th century Italian legal theory and practice. The example from Baldus shows this *in nuce*. In the *République's*

---

[18] Quoted above in note 16.

[19] BARTOLUS OF SAXOFERRATO, *Prima super digesto veteri*, on *Digest* 6, 1, 15 (ed. Lyon 1533, fol. 173): «Item si verberatum. Si quis rem [the law being commented upon]. Possessor qui dicit necessitate distraxit tenetur solum ad pretium quod recipit... Ultimo not. quod princeps ex causa potest auferre ius meum seu rem meam et dare alteri; idem puto in republica alicuius civitatis.»

[20] § 27 of the source cited above, n. 15: «Causa autem legitima est favor publicus, per textum principalem in hac materia, in l. item si verberatum. ff. de rei ven. ubi fundus tertii datur ad usum militibus favore reipublicae.» (This is one answer to the riddle of which case of restitution mentioned in «Item si verberatum» is relevent to eminent domain.) For another citation of «Item si verberatum» by FELINUS, see next note.

[21] In FELINUS' passage quoted in the previous note the emphasis falls upon the right of eminent domain; but Felinus also cites «Item si verberatum» in a context stressing the recompense owed the deprived person (see above, n. 15). BARTOLUS' commentary, on the other hand, could serve different purposes for ALEXANDER and FELINUS; I suspect an earlier commentary known to all them but not to me.

text, however, Bodin relates not Italian but French juristic matters of
the later Middle Ages. So, in the reproduced pages at the end of this
essay, we find an incident from the reign of Louis XI used to illustrate
a general legal-political issue raised in the underlined passages. This
happens time and again, as Bodin strives to illustrate how French public
law during recent centuries had carried out the principles of royal limitations which he was enunciating. Bodin's whole process of reasoning can
be grasped, however, only by referring to the marginal apparatus. There
one finds theory and practice intimately united by the genius of the
Italian jurists, who argued about natural law and the law of nations in
the course of applying Roman and Canon law to the ruling powers of
their times. The limits which they set to princely absolutism can be found
just as early in France (Bodin showed in his text) as in Italy, but French
jurists were not as articulate about the theoretical side of the matter.
Withal, the *République's* text and marginalia are meant to be equal
representations of how natural law operated in two different late-
medieval sovereign realms as a check upon arbitrary princely rule. The
casual reader, who does not penetrate the evidence of the marginalia,
will miss the Italian aspect altogether. A full knowledge of Bodin's
allegations, on the other hand, reveals that the Italians were by far the
more sophisticated thinkers, and that the applied *Corpus Juris Civilis*
was the fundamental text. That compilation was not only a monument
of a dead civilization, but was potentially a creative force in modern
jurisprudence. Such a striking departure from Bodin's original view of
the medieval legal tradition suggests some unusual experience in his life.

V

It has often been noted that Bodin moved steadily towards absolutism
from the *Methodus* of 1566 to the *République* of 1576. The examples
from the République which we have examined, however, show Bodin
working for limited and not absolute monarchy. The quandary may be
resolved, I believe, by reference to Bodin's *curriculum vitae* as revealed
in this famous passage:

«When I was lecturing publicly on Roman Law at Toulouse [1550 to
1559] I deemed myself very wise to be one in company of young scholars,
and I thought that princes of the legal science like Bartolus, Baldus,
Alexander, Faber, Paulus, and Du Moulin – indeed, the entire corps of
judges and order of advocates – knew little or nothing at all. But after
I had been initiated into the mysteries of jurisprudence in the courts
and had gained experience in the day-by-day workings of the law, I
realized that a true and sound knowledge of it lay not in law-college

Medieval Jurisprudence in Bodin's Concept of Sovereignty   *179*

debates but in courtroom battles, not in the quantities of syllables but in the scales of justice and equity. Those who know nothing about the art of pleading remain in the greatest ignorance of Roman law. Indeed, who ventures to use the formula *«Ex facto consultus respondi»* [«I answer by citing such-and-such decision»] when nobody asks his opinion on a point of law? or invokes the refrain of the jurisconsults, *«Hoc Iure Utimur»* [«We are following such-and-such law»] when he knows not by what laws he is proceeding?»[22]

He goes on then to declare that all teachers should have practical experience, so that they could show the students what is useful before overburdening their minds with the plethora of law and customs then extant.

Bodin seems to be telling us that after his scholastic years in Toulouse, 1550–1559, and during the ones at the bar in Paris, 1559–1566, he discovered the world of the *mos italicus.* He found it in French courts, especially in the Parlement de Paris. There one had to know Bartolus, Baldus, and company. Not only were they cited, but their arguments carried great meaning for the student of political philosophy. On this basis Bodin could have changed his mind concerning the concept of sovereignty which he had outlined in the *Methodus.*

Although Bodin's *Methodus* appeared only in 1566, actually at the end of his years of practicing in Paris, it has been soundly argued that the work was composed earlier during the years in Toulouse.[23] It is infused with humanistic learning. Roman law enters only as knowledge conditioned by education according to the *mos gallicus.* The *Methodus'* section on sovereignty is a good example: it lacks completely the medieval juristic apparatus with which the corresponding chapter of the *République* is so replete.

The passage quoted above extolling Bartolus and other medieval com-

---

[22] My translation differs in emphasis but not in substance from those of KENNETH MCRAE [7.44] – who explains the context of the writing of this second preface of the *République* – and of JULIAN FRANKLIN [226] Jean Bodin and the Sixteenth Century Revolution in Methodology, New York 1963, 64.

[23] Cf. PIERRE MESNARD [174], Jean Bodin à Toulouse, *Bibliothèque d'Humanisme et Renaissance* 12 (1950), 50, 54, relying upon John L. Brown [140], The Methodus ad facilem historiarum cognitionem of Jean Bodin, Washington 1939 for demonstration. Brown's valuable and useful dissertation errs somewhat in its account of the relationship of the *Methodus* to the *République,* at least in respect to the legal apparatus that concerns us here. Brown quotes the MAITLAND passage cited at the end of my text as evidence of medieval Italian influence on the *Methodus,* which otherwise his own arguments go against (cf. p. 30), as certainly do mine. He gives the impression that the *République* is more philosophical and classical (cf. p. 153 ff.) without accounting for the extensive medieval apparatus.

mentators is found in the same new prefatory letter of the 1578 edition
of the *République* wherein we earlier saw Bodin harping upon the limits
to princely power set forth in the first edition of 1576. The link between
the medieval commentators and the limits of sovereignty, turns out
usually to be the operation of natural law in living juridical practice. We
may now speculate upon the broader implications of these facts for
Bodin's doctrine of sovereignty.

VI

Most commentators who defend Bodin as a constitutionally minded political thinker rely heavily upon the few passages in the *République* which
evoke *leges imperii,* or fundamental laws. For France this meant the
Salic Law, for example. But Bodin himself makes no effort to delineate
the proper nature of fundamental laws, and contradictions can be found
in what he does say about them.[24] By contrast, he elaborates upon natural
law's role in the actual operation of French public law at great length
and with considerable subtlety. The trick, seen simply, is to discover that
what appears often to be mere civil law actually is a manifestation of
natural law. The category of laws which are «seemingly civil, actually
natural» is, in my opinion, by far the most important element in whatever
case can be made for Bodin the constitutionalist.

Bodin magnifies the scope of natural law by closely associating it with
equity, and by stressing the difference between *lex* and *ius.* In a host of
instances of *lex* (law as command) which operate in the world of jurisprudence, the discriminating and learned eye will see that the principle
of *ius* (law as equity) is actually at stake.[25] If one were to imagine the
spheres of natural law and civil law as hierarchically arranged, then

---

[24] In a brief note, J. H. Burns [194], Sovereignty and Constitutional Law
in Bodin, *Political Studies* 7 (1959), 174–177, shows the complicated nature of
the problem of fundamental law in Bodin. (It is a good example, inter alia, of
the necessity of reading the Latin as well as the French texts.) Logically, things
belonging to the office of the sovereign cannot be changed by the sovereign; the
medieval distinction is crystal clear, and in effect Bodin is using it in the famous
passage where he refers to the Salic Law and other *leges imperii* (the point of
Burns' argument). But, on the whole, Bodin either does not understand or deliberately rejects the whole paraphernalia of the «two bodies» concepts of medieval political thought, (cf. Kantorowicz, as above n. 6). Bodin strives to root
power in the living incumbent, not in the abstract office. I have touched upon
these matters in The Juristic Basis of Dynastic Right to the French Throne
(= Transactions of the American Philosophical Society, LI: 5; Philadelphia,
1961), 11, n. 29 and 30–31.

[25] The classic lines are these: «mais il y a bien différence entre le droit & la

natural law would appear to dip down into and overlap civil law to a very large extent. A given law may appear to be both civil and natural. This makes little difference to the ordinary subject, since he is normally bound to both. But it makes a great difference to the prince, since he is *legibus solutus* only in respect to civil law and *legibus alligatus* in respect to natural law. The latter aspect preempts the former whenever they appear together.[26]

In the years of his practice in Paris, Bodin discovered the juristic actuality of *princeps legibus alligatus* which had been created by courts and commentators from the 13th century until his own day. Italian legists of the 14th and 15th centuries were especially important. They had been concerned to establish a workable constitution for independent communes by establishing juridical limitations upon the *segnoria* (the word, by the way, given as the Italian equivalent of *souveraineté* in the opening sentence of *Répub.* I, 8). When an Italian jurist observes that the prince differs not from an ordinary private person in respect to the binding force of contracts, he probably had in mind a despot whose princely legitimacy bears no comparison with transalpine monarchs who ruled by the grace of God. Still, the Italian legists' evidence that princely obligations such as contract were part of natural law dovetailed with contemporaneous French historical examples found in the registers of Parlement and elsewhere.[27]

Bodin's experience in the courts brought the realization that the guarantee of subjects' proprietary rights within the French juristic tradition imposed clear limitations upon the sovereign's power In the *République* he seems to see French history as the reverse of what François Hotman pictured it to be in the *Francogallia*. Hotman declared that

loy: l'un emporte rien que l'equité, la loy emporte commandement; car la loy n'est autre chose que le commandement du souverain, usant de sa puissance»; *Républ.* 155. This whole problem, nowadays, should be reviewed in the light of GUIDO KISCH's work on equity in Renaissance law, especially his *Erasmus und die Jurisprudenz seiner Zeit*, Basel 1960. See also Mme CHANTEUR's paper in this volume.

[26] Besides what Bodin himself claims (above, n. 9), I give this passage from SHEPARD [110], *Sovereignty*, 602–603, with which I concur exactly (but prefer *alligatus* to *tentus* as more idiomatic): «The general tone of his book, however, leads one to believe that he regarded the notion of a king *legibus tentus* as of at least as great significance as the idea of *legibus solutus*. Indeed, it seems correct to say that Bodin, in so far as he clearly faced the problem at all, reserved the force of the *legibus solutus* clause exclusively for those laws enacted inside the spere of the sovereign's restricted authority.»

[27] Besides the Registres du Parlement, Bodin's French historical examples are drawn from the *Olim* and JEAN LE COCQ's (Johannes Gallus') contemporary collection of royal edicts.

ancient constitutional limits upon kings had been abandoned, making it necessary to have a thoroughgoing reformation of institutions in order to recover the pristine virtuous state.[28] Bodin maintained that the existing juristic system imposed sufficient limitations upon the king. These are to be found *de facto* still argued in French courts; the *République*, one might say, aimed to render them *de jure* by revealing the underlying legal-philosophical principles.[29]

VII

Bodin's vision of legal restrictions upon the prince differs basically from the medieval idea of sovereignty, much as they would seem to have in common because of putting the king beneath the law in important respects. Medieval definitions of sovereignty proceeded by specific allocations of power to the ruler; he was given *certain* powers and no more. Bodin, contrariwise, granted the sovereign power *all* power except such and such. Bodin believed that he was a true adherent to limited monarchy, but by medieval standards this can be accepted only if one believes that the power which Bodin left to the king after imposing limitations upon him was not greater than the sum of specific powers typically allotted to the king by medieval political theory. On a theoretical level, this question must remain moot, but when considering the actualities of governance – where it is indisputable that Renaissance sovereigns had much greater potentiality to exert centralized authority than their predecessors had had, due to military and bureaucratic advances – it would seem much more risky to give all residual powers to the sovereign (even after having heeded natural law's domain) in the 16th century than at any earlier time.

---

[28] My views on HOTMAN's intent in the *Francogallia* are set forth in two articles in *Bibliothèque d'Humanisme et Renaissance* 29 (1967), 581–611, and 32 (1970), 41–56. J. H. M. SALMON's paper in the present volume goes much further, and still more on the Monarchomach influence on Bodin, and vice versa, appears in the introduction to *Francogallia* by FRANÇOIS HOTMAN, edited by Salmon and me, Cambridge Univ. Press 1972.

[29] I do not mean to say that Bodin was correct in his estimate of judicial restraint upon the French monarch in the later middle ages or in his own. He knew recent French history no better than Hotman knew early Frankish history – which is not to condemn either, since they lived several centuries before anywhere nearly precise history of the Middle Ages was had. So, my efforts to delineate Bodin's potential constitutionalism in the *République* does not conflict necessarily with the estimate of JULIAN FRANKLIN, in his paper in this volume, that Bodin was actually retreating from constitutionalism from the *Methodus* to the *République*.

If Bodin deemed himself an advocate of limited monarchy because of his extended application of natural law, then we may explain his later reputation as an absolutist in terms of the changing meaning of *ius naturale*. According to the millenia-old Aristotelian world system, which Bodin must have shared essentially with his contemporaries, the universe was rationally ordered as an hierarchy by the Creator. Natural law a first principle of that order, the very adhesive of the system. Violation of it had to bring anarchy, if not the wrath of God directly.[30] This applied as much to political and social matters as to physical ones. With the decline of this cosmology after the 16th century, however, natural law changed its character. In terms of the physical world it became more quantitatively defined, losing its character as a divine immanence, and in political terms it was ever increasingly equated with mere morality. If one reads Bodin's usage of *ius naturale* as meaning mere morality, then almost all meaningful checks upon the sovereign disappear, leaving him indeed *legibus solutus*, truly «absolute».[31]

There are, however, indications that Bodin's cosmology was not completely orthodox for his times. By embracing a voluntaristic philosophy, for example, Bodin did not have to consider God's creation of the world order as final and complete, but rather still amenable to change. If true that *ut deus, sic princeps*, then the innovative and generally creative role of the sovereign is vouchsafed. The king as judge is medieval; the king as legislator, modern. From judge to legislator denotes the shift from passive to active rulership, from a static to a dynamic state. In *Répub.* I, 8, we see this clearly manifested in passages where Bodin compares the king to God. The king is a creator, imitating God, not simply God's instrument to preserve God's own order.[32] The dilemma

---

[30] Cf. above, n. 11.

[31] SHEPARD [110], Sovereignty, 584 ff., sees the problem as one of whether *ius naturale* was «legal» (Bodin) or «moral» (Hobbes-Austin), with which many modern scholars agree; cf. e.g., SCHEUNER's paper in the present volume. This conforms with the view of W. H. GREENLEAF [238], Order, Empiricism and Politics, Oxford 1964 – expounded at greater length in his paper in the present volume – that Bodin's view was wholly that of the «political theory of order» (p. 134). For myself, I believe it necessary to stress that the sense of order, while certainly dominant, was beset by countervailing forces of the daemonic and the voluntaristic in Bodin's philosophy (as shown by the papers of BAXTER and ISNARDI-PARENTE in this volume).

[32] The classic passage constitutes the last sentence of *Répub.* I, 8: «Car si la justice est la fin de la loy, la loy œuvre du Prince, le Prince est image de Dieu, il faut par mesme suite de raison, que la loy du Prince soit faicte au modelle de la Loy de Dieu» (p. 161). Signora ISNARDI-PARENTE's paper in this volume cites other evidence of this kind of God-prince mimesis.

Equivalent Pages from Jean Bodin,

DE LA REPVBLIQVE. 157

foit iufte & raifonnable, foit par achet, ou efchange, ou
confifcation legitime, ou traittant paix auec l'ennemi, fi
autrement elle ne fe peut conclurre , qu'en prenant du
bien des particuliers pour la côferuation de l'eftat: quoy
que plufieurs①ne foyent pas de ceft aduis : mais la rai-
fon naturelle②veut que le public foit preferé au particulier, & que les fubiects relafchent nonfeulement leurs
iniures & vengeances, ains auffi leurs biês pour le falut
de la Republique : comme il fe fait ordinairement, & du
public au public, & du particulier à l'autre. Ainfi voyons
nous au traicté de Peronne, faict pour la deliurance du
Roy Louys x 1.prifonnier du Comte du Charolois qu'il
fut dit que le feigneur de Torci pourroit faire execu-
ter fon arreft contre le fieur de Saueufes. C'eft pourquoy
on a loué Thrafybule, lequel apres auoir chaffé les x x x.
tyrans d Athenes, fit crier l'oubliance generale de toutes pertes & iniures entre les particuliers, qui fut auffi
depuis publiee en Romme par le traicté faict entre les
coniurés d'vne part, & les partifans de Cefar d'autre. Et
toutesfois on doit chercher tous les moyens de recom-
penfer la perte des vns, auec le proffit des autres : & s'il
ne fe peut faire fans trouble, on doit prendre les deniers
de l'efpargne, ou en emprûter:côme fit Aratus③ qui em-
prunta foixante mil efcus, pour aider à r'embourfer ceux
qui auoyent efté bannis & chaffés de leurs biens, qui
eftoyent poffedés & prefcrits par longues annees.   Cef-
fant donc les caufes que i'ay dit, le Prince ne peut prendre ny donner le bien d'autruy, fans le confentement du
feigneur : & en tous les dons, graces, priuileges & actes
du Prince, toufiours la claufe, S A V F le droit d'autruy,
eft entenduc, ores qu'elle ne fuft exprimee. Et de faict ce
fte claufe appofee en l'inueftiture du Duché de Milan,
que fit l'Empereur Maximilian au Roy Louys x 1 1.fut
occafion de nouuelle guerre, pour le droit, que les Sfor-
ces pretendoyent au Duché, que l'Empereur n'auoit
peu, ny voulu donner.   Car de dire que les Princes font
feigneurs de tout, cela s'entend④de la droite feigneurie,
& iuftice fouueraine, demeurant à chacun la poffeffion
& propriété de fes biens. Ainfi difoit Seneque.⑤ *Ad reges*
poteftas omnium pertinet, ad fingulos proprietas : & peu aprés:
Omnia Rex imperio pôffidet, finguli dominio.   Et pour cefte
caufe

① Hoftien. in c̃ quanto. de iure iurand. Butrio, ibi.col. 2. Inno-cent. & Panorm. in cap.in noftra. de iniur.

②d.l. item fi ver beratum. Fel.in cap.cùm non li-ceat.col.5.de ref crip.Corne.côf. 100.li.j.Alex.c6 fil.15.li.col.2.Cû anfi.inco.l.53.& 158.col.j.& côfi. 161.col.3.& con-fi.106.li.3. & la-tiff.confi. 216.& conf.65.li.j. nu. 3.& côf. 126. nu. j.lib. 2.

③Poly.lib.2.

La force de la claufe. Sauf le droit d'autruy.

④Felin. in cap. quæ in ecclefia rum. de conft. col.11.Bal.conf. 563. fine lib. j. Iaf.in authent. quas actiones. de facrof. c. 4.l. in re actio. de rei vindic.afflic. in conft.Neapol. lib.4.tit.10.
⑤lib.7. c.4. & 5. de beneficiis.

Six Livres de la République [1576]
ed. Paris, 1583

République, Book 1, Chapter 8

DE REPVBLICA, LIB. I.   161

fit:fic enim Pliniusiunior, ad Traianum Auguſtum *(a) Plin. in Pa-*
*Vt enim,*inquit;*felicitatis eſt,poſſe quantū velis,ſic magnitudi-* *negyrico.*
*nis,velle quantum poßis.*hæcille : quibus verbis efficitur,
nihil Principes poſſe,quod natura turpe ſit,aut iniuſtum. Iam
vero inepteloquatur,qui potentiæ ſummæ tribuat,alie-
na diripere, aut prædari,aut vi ſtuprum inferre ; quæab
animofracto libidinis& cupiditatum iinpotentia profi-
ciſcuntur.Quod ſi Principi non licet mouere terminos,
quos Deus opt. max. cuius ipſeeſt imago viuens ac
ſpirans,ſempiternis naturæ legibus pepigit;neque certe
licebit,alteri detrahere ꝙ ſuum eſt , ſiueiuſta ratione,
ſiue coemptione,ſiue commutatione,ſiue legitima pre-
ſcriptione,ſiue fœdere cum amicis feriendo,ſiue pacis a- *(b)Hoſtienſis in*
ctione cum hoſtib.concipienda,ſi aliter pax iniri neque- *c. quanto. de*
at; quam privatorum detrimento,quorum bona ſæpe *iureiurando.*
hoſtib.frueda permittunt Principes pro ciuium ac Rei- *Butrio ibid.*
col.2.Innoc.
pub.ſalute:tametſi quibuſdam *(c)*placet,vt ſuū quiſqꜩ te- *in c.in noſtrā,*
neat,nec de bonis privatorū publice diminutio fiat:aut *de iniuriu.*
ſi vrget publica neceſſitas,ab vniverſis ſarciendū eſſe; ꝗ *(c) item ſi ver*
ſententia mihi probatur,ſi tamen commode id fieri poſ- *beratū, de rei*
vindic. Felin.
ſit.Sed cum ſalus privatorum,bona omnia civium , pa- *in c. cum non*
triæ ſalute contineantur, non ſolum privatas offenſio- *liceat.col.5.de*
nes,&acceptas ab hoſtibus contumelias, ſed etiam ſua *reſcript. Corn*
bona,privatos Reip.*(c)*non gravate concedere oportet: *conſ.100.lib.1*
nam fere ſemper pax habet aliquid iniquum, quod pu- *Alexand.lib.*
blica vtilitate compenſatur;&eo quidem iure populi o- *5.conſ.15.*
mnes vtuntur,vt non modo publica publicis ac privata *(d)Hoſtienſis*
in c.quāto,&
privatis,ſed etiam vtraꝗ vtriſqꜩ in pacis actione,mutu- *ibi Butrio ,de*
is vtilitatibus ac detrimentis ſarciantur. *iureiurando.*

Video pleroſqꜩ*(e)*iuris vtriuſqꜩ magiſtros,in ea ſentē- *DD poſt.In.o*
tia & eſſe,&fuiſſe,vim eorum fœderum , quibus exce- *cent.in cap.in*
noſtr.de iurei.
ptum eſt,ne vlla detrimentorum hincinde acceptorum *Bald.in l. vi-*
quæſtio habeatur,inanem eſſe,nec priuatis præiudiciū *nia.de in ius*
afferre,alio tamen iure vtimur : nam in pace Peronen- *voc. Caſtrer.ſ.*
ſi,vt Ludouicus x1.Rex Francorum, carceribus Caro- *in l.2. de pact.*
Mart. Laud.
li Burgundionum Comitis eriperetur, vno capite cau- *in tract.de cō-*
tum eſt,*Ne Tortio ſententiam curiæ Pariſiorum ; aduerſus Sa-* *fœder.q.1.*
                    L   *nuſium*

De Republica Libri Sex [1586]
ed. Frankfurt, 1591

of Bodin, then, is to want to preserve an eternal and natural order guaranteed by natural law, so that the sovereign's domain is small in measure as natural law's is great, but at the same time to empower earthly sovereigns to act creatively on earth as does God in the macrocosm. The points of contact between the original Creator's legislation, *ius naturale*, and the new legislator's creations, *ius civile*, play a vital role in Bodin's definition of sovereignty in *Répub.* I, 8. How they can be reconciled, on the other hand, is perhaps better seen elsewhere in the *République*, above all in the final chapter on cosmic harmonics.[33]

Those who followed in Bodin's footsteps, starting a generation later, are notable for their greater clarity in rendering his ideas: Paurmeister, Arnisaeus, Bornitius, Reinking, Besold, Althusius, Grotius.[34] None of these, I would guess, knew anything but the text of the *République*, because I doubt that many legal writers after 1600 *could* have studied the marginal allegations. For one thing, hardly any of the late medieval legists' works were printed after 1600, when the manner of teaching the law in the humanistic fashion completely took over. Even more significantly, the edition of the *Corpus Juris Civilis* with Accursius' *glossa ordinaria*, which had served as the basic legal text for over three centuries, gave way after 1600 to the new humanistic edition edited by Denys Godefroy. Bodin, therefore, belongs to the last generation which had a thorough experience with the older medieval tradition. He himself learned it not in the classroom (although that still could have been done in some schools in his time) but in the courtroom. After him, however, it is doubtful that anyone could find the great tradition of Bartolus and his followers in either the universities or the courts.

Since the medieval legal tradition became moribund soon after Bodin's time, while the idea of sovereignty which he had propagated had a remarkably vigorous growth, the scholar today could be tempted to leave Bodin's marginalia resting in limbo. First, however, he might do well to ponder these words of Maitland's: «But Baldus and Bartolus, Innocentius and Johannes Andreae, them he [the modern reader] has never been taught to tackle, and they are not to be tackled by the untaught. And yet they are important people, for political philosophy in its youth is apt to look like sublimated jurisprudence, and, even when it has grown in vigor and stature, it is often compelled to work with tools – social contract, for example – which have been sharpened, if not forged, in a legal smithy.»[35]

---

[33] See the brillant exposition by M. VILLEY, elsewhere in the present volume.

[34] See E. HANCKE, Bodin, Breslau 1894, 5, n. 2 and *passim* [48]; also, now, the paper of M. HOKE in the present volume.

[35] FREDERIC W. MAITLAND, Introduction to O. GIERKE, Political Theories of the Middle Age, Cambridge 1900, VIII.

[6]

The Development and Context of Bodin's Method

Donald R. Kelley

I. Bodin: Quid et Quotuplex

Jean Bodin is a many-sided figure who has been in recent years the subject of proliferating and increasingly specialized studies. The one persistent habit of Bodin scholars, it seems to me, has been to restrict themselves to one of two of these sides, which moreover are defined in terms of rather formal categories of political thought, historical method, law, geography, and the like. This habit is well illustrated by the agenda (though perhaps not the purpose) of the present conference, and I must confess that it has affected my own work. But I have for a long time been uncomfortably aware that Bodin's «method», like his «republic», is like no other, and that approaching him through modern compartments of knowledge is not only anachronistic but also somewhat distorting. In any case it is these convictions, which have proved stronger than my sense of scholarly caution, which have led to this experimental attempt to see Bodin in a somewhat broader perspective and more philosophic context.[1]

Bodin seems to present a historical paradox. On the one hand he was almost too typical of his age. «Humanist, jurist, astrologist», Etienne Fournol remarked, «here indeed is a man of the 16th century». On the other hand, and in a longer perspective, he was a man for many ages. «If he was one of the last of the legists», Fournol added, «he was also the first of the philosophes.»[2] Yet there is no real contradiction here, except to the extent that Bodin himself entertained extreme and conflicting views. For if he displayed the spirit, methods, and some of the substance of scholastic learning, he also rebelled against the restraints of conventional «authority» and set out quite deliberately to create a science of society that was, according to his lights, empirical as well as rational. Drawing

---

[1] In general this essay is a byproduct of my Foundations of Modern Historical Scholarship, New York 1970 and, in part, a justification for not including Bodin, except peripherally, in the constellation of érudits discussed there (though I confess that it was an interest in Bodin's work that provoked this book in the first place).

[2] FOURNOL [51] Bodin prédécesseur de Montesquieu, Paris 1896, 21, 27; cf. FOURNOL Sur quelques traités de droit public du XVI. siècle, Nouvelle revue historique de droit français et étranger 21 (1897), 298–325 [54].

upon the wisdom of the past, he tried to build a system for the future. «The republic never dies», ran the old maxim, and Bodin wanted to insure that his own *Republic* had a comparable longevity.

A man with a passion for the past and designs upon the future, Bodin does not seem to have been much at home in his own time; he might well have preferred to be a contemporary of St Thomas or of Descartes. For in an age of academic inhibition he was a boldly speculative thinker, in an age of doctrinal faction a philosophical syncretist, in an age of discriminating criticism a compulsive and rather credulous eclectic. Not satisfied merely with investigating the past, he sought to extract from it principles of universal and eternal import; not satisfied with determining rules of human behavior, he wanted to arrange them into a coherent system; not satisfied with analysing society in rational terms, he wanted to uncover the *arcana* of nature as well as of the imperium. These overreaching philosophical ambitions led him down strange and even forbidden paths and gave him an almost Faustian reputation. Small wonder that he inspired distrust among such careful scholars as Cujas and Scaliger. Several contemporaries suspected that Bodin literally did not quite belong to their world. According to François Pithou (who heard it from Claude Fauchet), «Bodin was a sorcerer».[3]

Bodin accepted no man as his master, though he learned from many; he belonged to no school of thought, though he attended several. His first intellectual allegiance was clearly to the legal profession, with all of its totems, taboos, and traditions. From the beginning, too, Bodin was attracted by the humanist movement and its concern for educational reform. Yet he submitted to the standards neither of the professional lawyer nor of the professional humanist. He shared neither the arrogance of the first, who insisted that his «science» was superior (*nobilior et dignior*) to all others, nor to the snobbery of the second, who seemed prize eloquence above doctrine.[4] On the contrary, to Bodin nothing human – or superhuman – was alien, and in effect he assumed the unity

---

[3] *Scaligerana, Pithoeana* .., Amsterdam 1740, I, 500. That Bodin shared some of Machiavelli's diabolical reputation is shown, e.g., by Antonio POSSEVINO's *Judicium de Nicola Machiavelli et Joannis Bodini scriptis* in his translation of the former's *Princeps*, Ursel 1600, 197. See also Mr. Baxter's paper on Bodin's «demon.» With all the books on Bodin there has been no satisfactory attempt to treat him as a philosopher.

[4] Two classic but seldom cited panegyrics of the «science» of law appear in CHASSENEUZ, *Catalogus gloriae mundi*, Paris 1529, pars X, passim, and JEAN CORRAS, *De Jure civili, in artem redigendo*, in the fundamental collection, *Tractatus universi juris*, Venice 1584, I, f. 62v. The various (sometimes «interdisciplinary») attempts of 16th century jurists to place law in the encyclopedia of arts and sciences deserve further investigation.

of all learning. If he preferred, in humanist fashion, to arrange this learning in a circular way *(encyclopaedia)* rather than according to a hierarchy, he did not hesitate to open this classical preserve to «barbarian» ideas. His attitude was at once inter-disciplinary and inter-cultural.

In general the pattern of Bodin's intellectual growth was one of exploring and charting large and distant fields of thought, but seldom of settling and cultivating them carefully. In particular his route led from a wide-ranging study of history, law, and philosophy to a system that embraced, while at the same time it transcended, all three. But Bodin rarely adopted other mens' views without transmuting them to suit his own goals, and so some of the most interesting features of his thought are not fully accessible through simple exegesis, conventional biography, or piecemeal *Quellenforschung*.[5] What I propose here is to supplement such studies (of which we have an abundance) by means of two related lines of inquiry: first to suggest, by comparison with views of contemporaries, certain features of his intellectual environment and certain scholarly traditions which helped to shape his historical and political philosophy; and second to reveal, by a kind of structural analysis, some of the changing configurations of his thought leading up to the *Republic*. What ever the merits of this approach, it seems to be in keeping with and perhaps even invited by Bodin's own «method», which likewise depended upon comparisons to locate essential, underlying principles, which likewise used logical rather than literal analysis to show these relationships, and which in general exhibited an *esprit de système* that seems to soar uncomfortably high above its alleged sources.

II. Bodin: Grammaticus

If Bodin had any single point of departure, it was the «new learning» of the Renaissance, for which his Toulouse oration of 1559 was an advertisement.[6] Here he rehearsed the story of the «translation of studies» from Italy to France, sponsored by that «father of letters», Francis I, with the help of Guillaume Budé, and given institutional embodiment in the royal

---

[5] So it would not be appropriate, even if it were possible, to cite here the vast and growing quantity of Bodiniana bearing upon such questions, though I should record my special debts to the work of MOREAU-REIBEL, BROWN, REYNOLDS, MESNARD, and CHURCH.

[6] *Oratio de instituenda in repub. juventute ad senatum populumque Tolosatem*, in *Œuvres philosophiques*, ed. PIERRE MESNARD, Paris 1951 [4.20], 9 ff; cf. LE ROY, *G. Budaei vita*, Paris 1540, 46 ff. The later parallels between the thought of these two is well known, having been discussed by J. B. BURY, ROGER CHAUVIRÉ, and others.

126   *Donald R. Kelley*

«College of Three Languages» established during the 1530's. This often
told tale was sanctioned by Budé himself and by his first biographer, Louis
Le Roy (who like Bodin was a graduate of the Toulouse law school and
later a professor in this same royal college), and by the time Bodin gave
his oration it had become quasi-official doctrine. But for Bodin and Le
Roy and indeed most scholars of their generation the «studies» thus
celebrated were exclusively neither ancient nor Italian; they were perforce
joined to and colored by the whole glorious tradition of the French
monarchy, barbarous and vernacular as it was. As a result the humanist
«encyclopedia» was expanded to include the entire cultural past of Europe
and came to resemble the usage of D'Alembert more closely than that of
Budé.[7] Being heir to such eclecticism, Bodin could hardly help breaking
out of the humanist mold.

Within the new learning Bodin attached special importance to the «new
jurisprudence», which was one of its byproducts and which had flourished
especially in France. This so-called *mos gallicus* had been pioneered by
Budé, had been introduced into the universities by Andrea Alciato, and
had been developed further by such «Alciatei» as François Connan, to
mention the three jurists specifically named by Bodin at this time. The
story of this phase of the humanist movement, a sort of companionpiece
to the Budé legend just referred to, was also told by Le Roy, this time in
his biography (again the first) of Connan.[8] Toulouse was not particularly
cordial to «legal humanism», but it was here nonetheless that Bodin, like
Cujas and Le Roy, became a devotee of this new school which, as he now
thought, had enriched the study of law with philosophy as well as with
classical learning. It is perhaps significant that already Bodin emphasized
the philosophical rather than the philological aspect of the «reformed
jurisprudence», that he gave no credit to the real founders of the school
(Lorenzo Valla and Angelo Poliziano), and that of all the distinguished
disciples of Alciato he singled out not one of the university jurists but a
practicing advocate interested in legal reform. Connan did repeat certain
humanist commonplaces, including strictures against a servile imitation
of Aristotle and the neglect of history and philology, but of all the pro-

---

[7] Budé himself, who helped to promote the Italianate «encyclopaedia», notably in his *Annotationes in Pandectas* of 1508 and his *De Philologia* of 1532,
spoke of a «Minerva Franciae» in the preface to his *De Asse* of 1515, where he
also celebrated the «translation of studies». Such naturalization of the classical
idea of culture is even more conspicuous in such vernacular works as Le Roy's
De la vicissitude ou varieté des choses, Paris 1575, and Etienne Pasquier's
Recherches de la France, Paris 1621, esp. book IX.

[8] *De Francisco Connano* ... (1553) in Connan's *Commentariorum juris civilis
libri X*, Naples 1724; cf. Bodin, *Oratio* [4.20], 17. One of the earliest full versions of this story appears in Pasquier, *Recherches*, X, 39.

ducts of the *mos gallicus* he was possibly the least typical excepting Bodin
himself.[9]

There has been much discussion of «legal humanism» in recent years,
but the subject is still in some confusion. The trouble is that we continue
to see the movement less in terms of its accomplishments than of its public
image, whether through the panegyrics of its friends, such as Cujas, or
through the invectives of its enemies, such as Alberico Gentili.[10] By Bodin's
time, in fact, the contrast between the *mores gallicus* and *italicus* was not
nearly so sharp as contemporary polemic suggests. On the one hand there
were many conventional jurists (*Bartolisti, doctores scholastici, doctores
italici* as they were variously, and almost always invidiously, called) who
not only possessed elegant literary tastes but who, like Charles Dumoulin,
«the glory of our profession», as Bodin referred to him, also had impressive philological skills and interests in textual emendation. On the other
hand there were humanists (*grammatici, encyclopedei, Vallenses, Alciatei,
Cujacii, docteurs humanistes,* and other epithets) who, like François
Hotman and indeed Alciato himself, did not hesitate to revert to a
basically scholastic method (and indeed for pedagogical purposes even
Cujas recommended a conservative approach).[11] What is more significant,
methodology was becoming a less divisive issue than ideology, especially
as expressed in the conflict between the Italians (also called *doctores
italici,* or *ultramontani,* here in a political, though still often derogatory,
sense) and the Gallicans (*doctores citamontani*).[12] This distinction cer-

---

[9] CONNAN, *Commentarii,* Praefatio: «Nec hujus causa mali sunt fuit doc-
torum penuria (qua enim in scientia plures) sed ignoratio docendi, cum hi nullam
artem scirent, neque Latinae linguae essent et historiae periti, quod utrumque
fuerat necessarium.»

[10] *De Juris interpretibus dialogi sex,* London 1582, attacking not only the
«encyclopedia» and Latin and Greek eloquence but dialectic and especially
history («Pomponius. Historia non est cur legat Juris interpretes»). One famous
reference to this conflict was made by a man who, like Bodin, rose above it:
FRANÇOIS HOTMAN, *Antibribonian,* Paris 1603, ch. 15 (p. 120). distinguishing
between «chauffoureurs, Bartholistes et barbares» and «Humanistes purifiez et
grammariens desquels aucuns [referring to Bodin?] mettent le docte François
Connan», for whose works Hotman himself had written a preface. The best and
most relevant recent survey is JULIAN H. FRANKLIN [226], Jean Bodin and the
Sixteenth Century Revolution in the Methodology of Law and History, New
York 1963, though there are some further qualifications to be made.

[11] JACQUES FLACH, Cujas, les glossateurs et les bartolistes, *Nouvelle revue
historique de droit français et étranger* 7 (1883), 205–32. These qualifications
have been well brought out by GUIDO KISCH, Humanismus und Jurisprudenz,
Basel 1955, 18 ff.

[12] A good example, again, is CHASSENEUZ, *Catalogus gloriae mundi,* V, 28,
referring to an imperialist view held by «canonistae ..., Bart. et omnes Itali, et

tainly meant more to Bodin himself, who was interested less in the language than in the concepts — less in making *restitutiones* than in discussing the *opiniones* — of civil law.

Nor was «legal humanism» itself a simple and coherent school of thought. Certain difficulties may be avoided by setting aside particular ideological overtones (such as the incidence and significance of «civic humanism» in legal scholarship, though this is indeed an interesting and almost totally neglected subject worth pursuing) and by regarding this movement in a more neutral fashion; that is, as a combination, in one way or another, of legal scholarship with the *studia humanitatis*, or better with the whole «encyclopedia» of subjects necessary for a proper, which is to say a historical, understanding of law.[13] It is also true that by the latter half of the 16th century there were few amateurs like Valla or Budé who had the temerity to interpret legal texts, and so there was a growing professional uniformity of standards. Nevertheless, within this professionalized tradition of legal humanism there were a number of distinguishable — and increasingly divergent — trends. Three of these were inherent in the civil law itself and were so described by François Baudouin just a year before Bodin's Toulouse oration. Just as the Digest title «de verborum significatione» required the jurist to know some philology, Baudouin wrote, so the title «de origine juris» demanded history and the title «de justitia et jure» demanded philosophy.[14] Each of these tendencies left a certain imprint on Bodin's thought.

In the first place there were the «pure grammarians» like Cujas and Antonio Agustín, whose principal interest was in separating Roman law from the jumbled Byzantine mosaic assembled by Tribonian and

---

ultramontani...,» in contrast to the «opinio contraria, quam doctores citramontani tenuerunt...,»

[13] Following here, in other words, the view of humanism taken by P. O. KRISTELLER in his various studies. It may be noticed that a major omission in the many discussions of «civic humanism» made and inspired by HANS BARON is the significance of civil law. As for the formal relations between jurisprudence and the «studia humanitatis», the most direct approach is through the various treatises on the best method of teaching law (see note 21), including those of LE DOUAREN, BARON, BAUDOUIN, HOTMAN, which are all in N. REUSNER, *Cynosura juris*, Spires 1588; also CORRAS (note 4), CUJAS (note 11), and MARIN LIBERGE, *De Artibus et disciplinis, quibus studiorum instructum et ornatum esse oportet*, Anjou 1592, among others; and through such counterattacks as those of GENTILI and GRIBALDI (the latter in Reusner). A study of this topic would be very useful.

[14] *Commentarius de Jurisprudentia Muciana* (1559), Halle 1729, «Epistola auctoris ad lectorem»; cf. LIBERGE, *De Artibus*, 4, attacking «perniciossimae eorum opinioni, qui sine philologia, philosophia, et antiquitatis cognitione juris scientiam et artem intelligi et doceri posse contendunt....»

Justinian's other editors, or at least in establishing a correct text of the Digest.[15] Their virtues included an often heroic erudition and an acute, indeed an unprecedented, sense of anachronism which permitted them to uncover many «Tribonianisms». Their conspicuous faults were a «trivial» concern with legal and literary vocabulary and a «juristic classicism», as a modern critic (Fritz Schulz) has called it, which not only deprived their work of some relevance but in its own way blocked a clear view of the development of, or changes in, civil law. Now Bodin was properly shocked by «Tribonian's crime» and the corruption of the texts of civil law, and he often relied upon the scholarship of modern critics. Yet he found it increasingly difficult to take seriously «those who would rather be called grammarians than jurists», a description which indeed fits his rival Cujas.[16] Toward the literary and antiquarian excesses of the «Cujacians», as Gentili called them, Bodin took precisely the same critical position as Alciato had taken toward Valla, the «emperor» of the grammarians.[17] Theirs was a game that Bodin would never play, though his understanding of Roman law certainly presupposed their work.

Secondly, there were the legal historians, and in fact it was to this circle – the fifth in Gentili's juridical Hades – that Bodin has often been consigned. More typical of this group were scholars like Baudouin and

---

[15] The symbol and relic as well as chief target of this school was the famous Florentine manuscript of the Digest, whose legendary provenance was repeated by many humanists, including BAUDOUIN, *Praefata de jure civili* (1545), in HEINECCIUS, col. 10; HOTMAN, *Antitribonian*, 124, and *Ex Indice universae historiae* in *Operum*, Geneva 1599, I, col. 1086; LIBERGE, *Universae juris historiae descriptio*, Poitou 1567, 95, as well as PASQUIER, *Recherches*, X, 33. The utility of this manuscript was also attacked by GENTILI, *De Juris interpretibus*, f. 92, who rejected it as an object of a kind of philological idolatry.

[16] *Oratio*, 9; cf. *Methodus ad facilem historiarum cognitionem*, prefatory letter to Jean Tessier [4.20], 108, 109, complaining again of the ineptitude of Justinian's editors and, at the same time, of the «pestis grammaticalis, in intimos omnium disciplinarum aditus usque coepit, ut pro philosophis, oratoribus, mathematicis, theologis: minutos de schola grammaticos fere cogamur.» Contrast this with the remark of FRANCOIS PITHOU about his mentor (*Scaligerana*, II 285): «Quand on vouloit mespriser Monsieur Cujas, on l'appeloit Grammarien, mais il s'en riot, et disait que telles gens estoient marris de ne l'estre pas.»

[17] ALCIATO, *Dispunctiones* (1518), III, 13, in *Opera omnia*, Frankfurt 1617, IV, 201. Even BAUDOUIN disassociated himself from the philological school; so in his *Commentarii de Pignoribus et hypothecis*, Basel 1563, 3, on the general usages of these terms, «Sed id grammaticis relinquo». Indeed, the question had been discussed at some length by VALLA, in his *Elegantiarum latinae linguae libri sex*, VI, 57 (on Digest, 20, 5, 1), and had been answered by ALCIATO, among others; the whole controversy has been assembled in C. A. DUKER, *Opuscula varia de Latinitate jurisconsultorum veterum*, Leiden 1711.

his disciple Marin Liberge, who came to regard civil law primarily as source material for the reconstruction of universal history. Baudouin had made important contributions to the study of early Roman law, especially that of the Republic, and to the search for «Tribonianisms»; and by 1559 these researches had led him to his grand design for an alliance between law and history. Moreover, when he published his *Method of History and its Conjunction with Jurisprudence* two years later, it was clear that history was to be the senior member of the partnership.[18] This was even more clearly the case with one of the later «methods» of history, that by Pierre Droit de Gaillard, who likewise proposed an alliance of law and history *(historiae et jurisprudentiae collatio)*. «All the law of the Romans and of other nations», he declared, «is nothing more than that part of history which describes the customs ... of each nation.»[19] It might be assumed that Bodin's own *Method of History*, which falls formally in this same genre *(artes historicae)*, would be in accord with this program, and indeed there are obvious similarities that have not gone unnoticed. And yet in certain more fundamental ways Bodin's work was irreconcilable with the others. Baudouin and his followers assumed, to take the most conspicuous example, that both law and history had to be understood in strictly chronological order. «Since later law abrogates earlier law», as Liberge explained, «we will commit many errors ... if we do not study history according to the sequence of times and keep the chronology of laws.»[20] To such scholarly scruples Bodin could not have been more indifferent; he quite deliberately sought a more rational and supratemporal (which is to say super-human) arrangement in which, on the contrary, the substance of history would be subsumed under the categories of law.

---

[18] One may follow this shift in emphasis from the *Scaevola* of 1558, where, attempting to recover the legal contributions of this family, he remarked («Lectori»), that «Jurisprudentia cum Romana historia, et historia cum Jurisprudentia Romana perpetuam conjunctionem, ut duas unius veluti corporis partes indivisas esse sentirem», to the *De Institutione historiae universae et ejus cum jurispurdentia conjunctione* of 1561, where he remarks (Strasbourg 1608, 189): «Ego quidem nondum satis statuere potui, plusne lucis historia ex Jurisprudentiae libris, an Jurisprudentia ex historicis monumentis accipiat.» I focus more directly on this school in: The Rise of Legal History, *History and Theory* X (1970).

[19] *De Utilitate et ordine historiarum praefatio*, to BAP. FULGOSIAS, *Factorum dictorumque memorabilem libri IX*, Paris 1578, a little essay «deprompta ex suis institutionibus historicis», that is, from his *Methode qu'on doit tenir en la lecture de l'histoire*, Paris 1579 – from which circumstance I have taken the liberty of translating BAUDOUIN's own *Institutio* as «method».

[20] *De Artibus*, 85, citing and practically paraphrasing BAUDOUIN, *De Institutione*, 227.

This brings us to the third group, which included such philosophical jurists as Connan, Hugues Doneau, and to some extent François le Douaren, who wanted to establish a rational system of jurisprudence on the basis of Roman law as reconstructed by philology. There was much talk about refashioning law into an art *(jus civile in artem redigendo)* or restoring it to the status of a science which it properly enjoyed; almost every jurist devised his own particular «method» in order to make civil law more intelligible; and almost all of the legal humanists of Bodin's generation wrote at least one essay «de ratione docendi juris civilis» (a genre which which may be traced back to Justinian's often cited edicts prefacing the Digest).[21] Such reforming efforts had philosophical as well as pedagogical motives, and nothing was more common for these jurists than to make analogies with such better organized arts as geometry and to introduce Aristotelian terminology. But in general civil law had its own rationale, and most jurists before the time of Domat and Vico contented themselves with adjusting the schemes established by Justinian. In his «methodical interpretation» of the Digest Le Douaren followed roughly the usual sequence of topics but elaborated on and changed the particular rubrics, introducing his own precepts and theory of textual criticism, while his young protégé Doneau did not hesitate to depart from the order of titles in the Digest as well.[22] So, even more radically perhaps,

---

[21] «Discussion about method was in the air» is the appropriately unspecific remark of J. L. BROWN in his fundamental study of Bodin's *Methodus*, which is still the best discussion of the subject. It seems to me that the role of Ramus has been much exaggerated in this connection, though it is difficult to disagree with the spezific link with the *Juris universi distributio*, if not the *Methodus*, argued by KENNETH Mc RAE [189, 228] in *Journal of the History of Ideas* 16 (1955), 306–23, and 24 (1963), 569–71. Useful for background is NEAL GILBERT, Renaissance Concepts of Method, New York 1956, 137 ff., but the subject of legal method needs to be investigated more thoroughly. Not quite to the point is F. EBRARD, Über Methode, Systeme, Dogmen in der Geschichte des Privatrechts, Zeitschrift für Schweizerische Geschichte 57 (1948), 95–136. There do seem to be some generally agreed-upon requirements for a proper «method». In one of the most extensive discussions CORAS (*De Jure civili*, f 59r) argues, among other things, that it must aim at «praecepta universalia», that it begin with «definitiones et divisiones», that it be in accord with «natura», and he goes on to make a very conventional analogy with geometry; see esp. ch. VIII, «De triplici methodo, resolutiva, compositiva, et definitiva», as well as the other works cited in note 13.

[22] *In Primam partem Pandectarum methodica enarratio*, in *Opera omnia*, Lucca 1765, I, 1; cf. *De Pandectarum compositione, ordine as methodo*, in *Opera*, IV, 47. An excellent discussion of these topics may be found ii EYSSELL, Doneau, Dijon 1860 and now in CHRISTOPH BERGFELD, Franciscus Connanus 1508–1551, Cologne 1968, the first useful treatment of this jurist so admired by Bodin.

did Connan, whose influential commentaries, published in 1557, included, among other things, comparative discussions of law and feudal institutions. Bodin shared the compulsion, common among jurists of his generation, to find a method which, through its mnemonic and logical virtues, would permit the construction of a system of universal law. And as usual Bodin would be satisfied with no one's handiwork but his own.

III. Bodin: Pragmaticus

In the seven years between his Toulouse oration and his *Methodus* Bodin was increasingly impressed by another tradition that was ultimately more significant than any variety of humanist jurisprudence. This was the practice of law and, inescapably, the Bartolist school on which it relied. At first Bodin had had the usual intellectual's contempt for the *pragmatici*, «those whom Cicero called mean and mercenary», as Hotman dismissed them at just this time. But in the course of his own legal career and especially the experiences of the wars of religion Bodin, like Hotman, came to prize the work of «those who have spent their lives serving the republic» above the «frivolities of the grammarians». He would agree with Baudouin's lofty ideal of «homo politicus, hoc est jurisconsultus».[23] Consequently, like Tiraqueau and others, he came to realize that the development of civil law had to be understood in terms of the later commentators as well as of the original sources. This was particularly necessary for public law, which classical jurists tended to avoid on principle. What is more, Bodin took very much the same attitude toward civil law as had the medieval commentators, regarding it as a treasury of accumulated wisdom (*rerum humanarum et divinarum notitia*, as Ulpian had defined it, if not *ratio scripta*) to be applied to contemporary problems. It was not without reason that Pasquier placed Bodin in «la chambre de Bartole italien».[24]

Yet it will not do simply to call Bodin a «neo-Bartolist». Although he had apparently graduated from academic to practical jurisprudence, he had not in fact merely substituted one tradition for another; as usual he tried to combine the best of both. In methodological terms, however, the Bartolists were hardly better off than the humanists. The crucial point

---

[23] BAUDOUIN, *Commentarius*, 20, and HOTMAN, *Jurisconsultus*, Basel 1559, 34. Cf. Bodin, *Methodus*, 134, attacking those «qui leviores Grammaticorum nugas malunt, quam gravissimas corum narrationes qui totum vitae suae tempus in Repub. gerenda consumpserunt». Here is the theme of «civic humanism», which may be traced back to Budé and especially to Valla (and perhaps earlier).

[24] PASQUIER, *Recherches*, 902.

The Development and Context of Bodin's Method 133

Bodin made, and not for the last time, in his *Distribution of Universal Law*: unlike all other arts and sciences civil law dealt not with a general subject but with the creation of a particular society, and neither the humanist nor the scholastic jurists had escaped this narrow Romanism.[25] If legal humanism was unacceptable because it dealt with trivial (that is, historical) questions and scorned contemporary legal practice, Bartolism was unacceptable because it failed to notice the limitations and mutability of civil law. Bodin valued the work of the humanists for giving a clear picture of Roman law and that of the Bartolists for insights into the nature of society and politics, but neither offered an adequate basis for constructing a system of jurisprudence or even for drawing general conclusions about institutions. In general, he assumed, it was a fallacy to think that the experience of any single national group was sufficient for political philosophy. This was one of the unspoken axioms of Bodin's method – that the universal was never adequately represented in the particular.

Underlying this assumption, however, was a particular bias as well as a general methodological insight; and here Bodin was indebted to another legal tradition, namely, that of the royal legists in France. Beholden as they were to civil and canon law, these French *avocats du roi* had, over some three centuries, fashioned their own ideology and acquired their own scholarly habits. Most significant for Bodin was their practically unanimous rejection of the «authority» of Roman law. While «ultramontane» jurists, including Alciato as well as Bartolus, had to believe that their emperor was lord of the world *(dominus mundi)* and that «his» law was universal, their French critics, including humanists like Cujas as well as Bartolists like Chasseneuz, were bound by the contradictory rule that «the king of France has no superior in temporal things».[26] Although the

---

[25] *Juris universi distributio* [4.20], 71, remarking, «cum artes ac scientiae sint universorum: jus autem civile proprium sit unius civitatis», and (p. 73), «Jus civile, quod unius aut alterius civitatis est proprium, nec in arte cadit». He makes the point still more clearly in the *Methodus*, 107: «At illi juris civilis, id est, singularis cuiusdam civitatis artem tradere sunt conati, quam sapienter, non disputo: nihil tamen artis dignitate ac praestantia potuit alienus cogitari. omitto quam sit absurdum, ex Romanis legibus, quae paulo momento mutabiles fuerunt, de universo jure statuere velle».

[26] CHASSENEUZ, *Catalogus gloriae mundi*, V, 28–29 (see note 4). «Habet multa jura et singularia privilegia, quae non habet alii principes» (f. 141r): the 208 *jura* listed, adding to the well known set compiled by JEAN FERRAULT, constitute a kind of empirical definition of sovereignty that anticipates Bodin's in many ways. (See the discussion in Mr. Franklin's paper.) His key *opiniones*, that «Imperator non est dominus mundi», and that «Rex Franciae [est] Princeps neminens recognoscens, et non subditus Imperatori», were intended directly to

doctrinal basis for this principle was canon law, much historical evidence could also be adduced to show that «the king of France was not subject to the emperor», as Chasseneuz argued, and that consequently «the emperor was not lord of the world». Bodin was in agreement both with this and with his further declaration that the French king «has many unique privileges that other princes do not have», and presumably the reverse held as well. It was for precisely this reason that, in order to discuss a topic like «sovereignty» in general and philosophic terms, it was necessary to resort to a comparative method.

In more general terms, too, French legists had rejected the idea that the Roman tradition was universal. «There are many nations that have never been subject to the empire», declared Charles de Grassaille, «whence the most correct conclusion that the emperor was never in possession of the world».[27] This was a position that had been taken not only by generations of commentators but also, as Cosmo Guymier pointed out a century earlier, by many historians. And if Roman law could not claim universal jurisdiction, how much more circumscribed was that feudal law (the *Consuetudines feudorum*) sanctioned by the medieval German emperors? Not only were these customs without authority in civil (as well as French) law, charged Dumoulin, but the empire itself was merely a local institution.[28] This was quite in accord with Bodin's pluralistic views. What he did in his *Methodus*, in effect, was to transform this legal attitude into a methodological principle, that no national tradition could claim to represent humanity as a whole. It was essentially this Gallican view of the empire (*illa monarchia non fuit universalis* was the phrase of Chasseneuz and Grassaille) that inspired Bodin to his attack upon the political and cultural imperialism of Rome, notably in his famous refutation of the theory of Four World Monarchies, though

contradict those expressed by such Italian jurists as ALCIATO (*In aliquot primae Digestorum ... titulos commentaria*, in *Opera*, I), who held that «Imperator est dominus torius orbis», and that «Rex Francorum recognoscat Imperatorem de jure in superiorem». For the medieval background (centering on Innocent III's *Per venerabilem*) see SERGIO MOCHI ONORY, Fonti canonistiche dell' idea moderno dello stato, Milan 1951, 96 ff.; F. CALASSO, I Glossatori et la teoria della Sovranità, Milan 1951; and GAINES POST, Studies in Medieval Legal Thought, Princeton 1964, 453 ff.

[27] *Regalium Franciae libri duo*, Paris 1545, 82, citing and repeating Chasseneuz as well as Ferrault; cf. *Pragmatica sanctio glossata per Cosmam Guymier*, Lyon 1488, f. 1r: «Franci nulli umquam fuerunt subjecti in temporalibus, ut probatur ex antiquis historiis ...»

[28] *Commentarii in parisienses ... consuetudines*, in *Opera omnia*, Paris 1681, I, 22; cf. GRASSAILLE, *Regalium*, 106, «Leges seu consuetudines feudorum non habent locum in Francia.»

as always he provided his own perspective and supported his thesis with evidence of his own choosing.[29]

A most interesting corollary of this anti-universalist (and anti-imperialist) orientation of Gallicans was the common tendency among French jurists to make comparisons between civil law and institutions, ancient and modern, and those of French society. There were several obvious reasons for this: first because French lawyers were in fact trained in one law in the universities (or two, but the distinction between civil and canon laws was increasingly blurred) and obliged to practice another in many courts; second because civil law was the only feasible model for, and alternative or corrective to, French customary law (for which indeed it was *jus commune* in the so-called provinces of written law); third because customary law logically fit into the civilian category of *jus non scriptum* or *consuetudo* and was often discussed in that context; and fourth because of the growing need (and market) for polemic urging the independence and even the superiority of the French monarchy and its traditions. French historiographers had long argued that the «fortune and virtue» of their kings were not inferior to those of the Roman emperors, but this was little more literary convention; in the 16th century this contrast was given substance through the study of legal institutional history.[30] It was just during Bodin's lifetime, in fact, that there arose a new kind of work devoted to the comparison of particular French offices, institutions, and laws with their Roman counterparts, real or supposed. It may be useful to offer a few examples of this literature, which merits further investigation in its own right as well as background for Bodin's thought.

On the one hand, and perhaps on the lowest level, was the work of the French feudists, who naturally had recourse to civil law as a standard of judgment and as a source of terminology and perhaps supplementary illustrations. This was most conspicuously true of that «prince of legists» Dumoulin, who was a master of every sort of law and who interlaced

---

[29] *Methodus*, ch. VII. Another casualty of Bodin's argument was the old medieval notion of the «translation of empire». With regard to Germany this has been treated extensively by W. Goez, Translatio Imperii, Tübingen 1958, but the interesting fortunes of the idea in Renaissance France await investigation.

[30] A striking example of this is the work of Du Haillan, who continued the conventional themes of Gaguin and Paolo Emilio, most conspicuously in his *De la Fortune et vertu de la France*, Paris 1570, which was a kind of advance announcement for his history of France – and whose *De l'Estat et succez des affaires de France*, Paris 1570, the first comprehensive history of French institutions, carried the somewhat invidious comparison of France and Rome into this area.

his commentaries with references to contemporary practice *(hodie, apud nos ...)*.[31] It was true as well of such lesser lights as Chasseneuz and Tiraqueau, who were among the first to bring something of humanist culture (though little of the philological method) to the study of customary law. Tiraqueau showed a particularly broad interest in the customs and institutions of other societies, and his biographer has suggested that, despite his indifference to any kind of system, his attitude not only resembled but even heralded that of Bodin. Still more impressive, it seems to me, is the work of Chasseneuz, who brought to bear upon the Burgundian custom a veritable encyclopedia of learning, philosophical and Biblical as well as historical and literary. His purpose was to enrich, perhaps to inflate, this vernacular text through comparisons with alien but logically similar concepts *(droits de justice* with the *jura meri imperii,* for example, and coutume itself with Roman conceptions of unwritten law).[32] He also tried to bring some order into customary law by the introduction (in Bartolist fashion) of Aristotelian categories such as genus and species for purposes of classification and the notion of final cause to explain the prooemium of this customal. Like Bodin, in short. Chasseneuz took an «unhistorical» approach, and like Bodin, too, he could claim a certain philosophical justification.

A similar pattern may be seen still more clearly in another, less traditional, kind of legal literature that emerged in the 16th century which may best be described as handbooks of administration. Among the most interesting of these are Vincent de la Loupe's *Origin of Dignities,* Bernard du Haillan's *State and Success of Affairs in France,* Lancelot de la Popelinière's *Admiral of France,* René Choppin's *Treatise on the Domain of France,* and Jean Duret's *Comparison of Roman Magistrates with French Officers,* which may all be located somewhere between the genre of technical legal monographes (like Jean de Montaigne's work on the parliament of Paris) and conventional historiography (like Du Haillan's history of France).[33] For these works reference to the Roman experience was both

---

[31] This point, which also deserves further investigation, was made by RALPH GIESEY [211], The Juristic Basis of Dynastic Right to the French Throne, Philadelphia 1961, a book which itself offers a useful study of comparative law (though this is not its main purpose) with respect to one major topic. On Tiraqueau see the remarks of JACQUES BREJON, André Tiraqueau (1488–1558), Paris 1937, introduction and p. 345.

[32] *Consuetudines ducatus Burgundiae,* Frankfurt 1572, especially the prooemium. Chasseneuz' work, too, would repay further investigation.

[33] The most striking, though by no means most significant, example is JEAN DURET, *L'Harmonie et conference des magistrats Romains avec les offices François, tant laiz, que Ecclesiastiques. Ou succinctement est traicté de l'origine, progrez et iurisdiction d'un chacun, selon que les loix Civiles, Romaines, et Fran-*

a literary convention and a professional necessity, if not a conditioned reflex. Use of a «comparative method» ranged from such far-fetched analogies as that of the «Salic law» with the Roman *lex regia* to the most sophisticated discussions of judicial organizations or of fiscal resources or of the influence of foreign institutions.

Finally, there were the works of French civilians, especially the humanists, who strayed from the texts of Roman law into digressions or obiter dicta on French institutions. This tendency, which is already obvious in Budé's seminal *Annotations on the Digest*, is illustrated most clearly in Eguinaire Baron's little known «bipartite commentary» on Justinian's Institutes (1550), which contains parallel discussions of Roman and French laws and offices.[34] «To the Roman *princeps* we compare the king of France, who follows the same general pattern of establishing and promulgating laws», he wrote, going on to compare the imperium with *haute justice*, for example, as well as to point out certain unique institutions, such as the Roman *patria potestas* and French laws of succession. Similar in intention, but considerably more schematic, were the various attempts to shape French law directly into a Roman mold, as in Pasquier's *Interpretation of the Institutes of Justinian* and in Louis le Caron's *Pandects of French Law*, which originated as a plan to translate the Digest but which ended as a treatise on comparative law. The same impulse may be seen in Le Caron's pioneering edition of the *Grand Customal of France*. Perhaps the best illustration of all is Hotman's notorious *Anti-Tribonian*, which revealed at length the fundamental differences between Roman and French society and, in its own invidious fashion, brilliantly applied a comparative method to a set of problems involving both legal reform and the interpretation of history.[35]

Many of the intellectual habits underlying such works were shared by Bodin, but as usual they were transformed and adapted to his more

çoises l'ont permis, sans obmission de l'histoire aux lieux propres ..., Lyons 1574, which, despite its patriotic tone does not hesitate to reject the theory of Trojan origins (f. 9v); among the authorities cited are included not only Grassaille and Gaguin, but also Budé, Le Douaren, and (f. 6v) «Cujacius et Hotomanus, duo amplissimo veteris ac novae jurisprudentia lumina».

[34] *Institutionum civilium ab Justiniano Caesare editarum libri IIII*, Poitou 1550, in tit. and IX. (p. 6, 32). Most interesting of all is the work of Louis Le Caron, who was at once a student of Baudouin and, with respect to customary law, of Dumoulin; I am publishing a fuller investigation of this scholar.

[35] It should be remarked that the «comparatist» point of view was inherent in the century old search for «Tribonianisms», which assumed a fundamental disagreement between classical Roman and Byzantine law (and society as well); indispensable for this subject is LUIGI PALAZZINI FINETTI, Storia della ricerca della interpolazioni nel corpus iuris giustinianeo, Milan 1953.

transcendent purposes. What he wanted was not simply to make comparisons between French and Roman institutions but to inquire into those of a multitude of societies and eventually to construct a legal system that would encompass them all. Just as one obtained a knowledge of a species through the investigation of individual specimens, so one could attain a knowledge of universal law through positive law – that is, of the *jus naturale* through the *jus gentium*.[36] In other words, just as Pico assumed that every philosophical or religious tradition reflected one aspect of a general and transcendent truth, so Bodin seemed to assume that the customs and laws of particular societies reflected, however imperfectly, one aspect of an ideal jurisprudence. The ultimate aim of Bodin's comparative method, it may be inferred, was likewise to achieve a kind of «perennial philosophy».

This may suggest something of the breadth of Bodin's vision, the profusion of his ideas, and perhaps the flexibility of his standards. Bodin had moved entirely beyond, and evidently lost interest in, the conventional dichotomy of the *mores gallicus* and *italicus* and indeed that between the *grammatici* and the *pragmatici*; and he admired scholars of both humanist and Bartolist persuasion. As examples of the first he commended Baron and Connan, of the second Tiraqueau, Chasseneuz, and Dumoulin. In one way or another they all combined formal knowledge with practical experience. But Bodin, needless to say, demanded still more, and no wonder Gentili threw up his hands. According to the composite portrait presented in the *Methodus*, the perfect jurist was a living encyclopedia possessing at once a knowledge of history and philosophy, an understanding of natural law and equity, a familiarity with the commentators, a competence in both Latin and Greek philology, and above all a proper «method» to organize this refractory mass of material.[37] Given such an intellectual appetite and given a special interest in public law, it was obvious that legal sources alone were insufficient and that only an intense investigation of the past would supply information about the *jus gentium* in Bodin's sense of the term. *In historia juris universi pars optima latet*: it was this axiom that, the essence of universal law would be found in history, that led Bodin to formulate his iconoclastic and yet curiously dogmatic *Method of History*.

---

[36] Bodin's statement of the method he wanted to follow in order to rise from the particular to the universal, that is, from history to political science, appears at the beginning of *Methodus*, ch. VI, which is essentially an early draft of the *Republic*: «utile visum mihi est, ad eam quam instituto methodum, philosophorum et historicorum de Republica disputationes inter se et majorum imperia, cum nostris comparare, ut omnibus inter se collatis, universa Rerum publicarum historia planius intelligatur».

[37] *Methodus*, 108–9.

IV. Bodin: Philosophistoricus

In this pivotal work, which looked at once back to his humanist sources of inspiration and forward to his system of political and social philosophy, Bodin set out to redefine the traditional «art of history». Unlike Baudouin he was not much interested in historical method in a modern sense, in *Quellenforschung* and *Quellenkritik*, and he never even distinguished very consistently between history as object *(actio)* and history as subject *(narratio)*. The main reason for this is that he was concerned not with the writing but with the reading of history: how to «pluck the flowers of history» and then arrange them in the best pattern, or in another image, how to extract from history its medicinal value. Although history was itself a form of memory, it could not in Bodin's view be grasped and retained by individuals in chronological order, that is, in its temporal disorder; it had to be arranged not according to the form of human experience *(ordo temporum* or *naturalis* in the conventional medieval formula)* but rather according to the form of human reason *(ordo artificialis)*.[33] Although history in a sense already held a position «above all sciences» *(supra scientias omnes)*, it had itself to be converted into a science by the imposition of a rigidly logical «method». Although history retained its connection with the trivium in Bodin's view, its partner was not grammar or rhetoric (as for Baudouin and most other humanists) but rather dialectic.

It was inevitable that the form taken by Bodin's method should be pedagogical, or rather, since the principal aim was «to assist the memory», mnemonic. More specifically, he adopted the model of humanist logic, with its emphasis on topical distribution for handy reference for the resolution of particular problems; and his purpose was literally to define historical commonplaces *(loci communes)* and, without much regard for context, to relocate historical evidence in a rational or at least utilitarian way. The almost obsessively analytical character of Bodin's thought may be suggested by one of those diagrams to popular in dialectical, legal, and even historical works of Bodin's age.[39] Although

---

[33] *Methodus*, 116: «Principio adhibeatur praestans illa docendarum artium magistra, quae dicitur analysis: quae universum in partes secare, et partis cujusque particulas rursus dividere, totiusque ac partium cohaerentiam quasi concentum inter ipsa mira facultate docet.» Cf. BAUDOUIN, *De Institutione*, 38; and in general, MARIE SCHULZ, Die Lehre von der historischen Methode, Berlin 1909, 98 ff.

[39] The accompanying diagrams (see p. 148-149) are somewhat simplified analyses of the basic argument of the three principal works discussed here (and of the *Methodus* by itself). The pattern is particularly clear in chapter III («De Locis

Bodin did not here follow the rigidly bifurcating pattern of Ramus in the *Methodus*, he did move from large to small categories by making distinctions and sub-distinctions, with the expectation, at least in theory, of arriving eventually at the smallest units of historical discourse, that is, the plans, works, and deeds of individual men. For Bodin, then, history was to be methodized by rearrangement into parallel and proliferating sets of categories, or rather topics, which would ultimately accomodate not merely arguments (as in humanist logic) but the phenomena of history itself. The result may not have been a «philosophy of history», but it was a very impressive looking conceptual aid.

Like Baudouin, Bodin made a fundamental distriction between universal and particular history. In this he was following not only the Polybian and Eusebian pattern but also the current conviction of Protestant historians that «history was to encompass all ages», as Melanchthon put it, that it should provide a« portrait of the human race».[40] This fashion was introduced into the «arts of history» by Christophe Milieu, who offered what was perhaps the most comprehensive of all descriptions of the *universitas* of history during that century, making room for social, political, and cultural history *(prudentia, principatus,* and *sapientia,* including *historia literaturae)* as well as natural history. Bodin made a similar analysis, but he related these stages of development to various levels of the human will *(voluntas),* which related first to the problem of sustinence *(necessitas),* then to comfort *(commoditas),* and finally to the products of leisure *(splendor* and *voluptas).*[41] These motives, taken together with the social and political devices for accomplishing them, constituted the general rubrics under which the stories of particular nations could all be fitted.

One of Bodin's principal disciples complained that he «should have thrown more light upon particular history rather than digressing so upon universal history».[42] Yet in a sense the Bodin of the *Methodus* was interested more in the species than in the genera of the historical world, more in the variety than in the uniformity of human nature, and perhaps

---

historiarum recte instituendis»). What follows here is largely a commentary on this teaching aid which I have extraced from Bodin's writings. It may be added that this sort of diagram was very common in Bodin's age, not only in the works of logicians like Ramus, but of jurists like Hotman *(Tabulae de criminibus* of 1543) and of authors of *artes historicae,* notably that of G. J. Vossius, *Ars historica,* Leiden 1623 (diagram C).

[40] Preface to *Chronicon Carionis,* in his *Opera (Corpus Reformatorum,* XII, col. 705 ff.). In general, see Adalbert Klempt, Die Säkularisierung der universalhistorischen Auffassung, Göttingen 1960 [205].

[41] Mylaeus, *De Scribenda universita rerum historia,* Basel 1551.

[42] La Popelinière, *Idee de l'histoire,* Paris 1599, 29.

more in the texture than in the structure of history. For his intelligible unit of study was not humanity but the national group. This was one reason why he was determined to demolish that myth of imperial historians, the theory of Four World Monarchies, which had established both a false universalism and a false uniformity of perspective. At the same time Bodin distrusted the particular national perspectives which arose from pride and ignorance. It was the question of national origins that furnished perhaps the most fertile field for the cultivation of legend and violation of chronology – and also for the exercise of historical criticism. In theory, that is, for in practice Bodin was still under the influence of the Celtic enthusiasm of the mid-16th century, which had touched scholars like Pasquier and moved Connan to suggest that even feudal institutions were by origin Gallic rather than German.[43] But the significant thing about Bodin's work was the continuing plea for a concentrated and controlled reading of the best historians.

Perhaps the most crucial, and certainly the most characteristic, aspect of Bodin's theory of history was his view of causation. Like Baudouin, Milieu, and others, he made a basic distinction between human and natural (leaving aside divine) history, corresponding of course to the three kinds of law. Unlike them he did not mind letting the human and natural spheres overlap, nor did he hesitate to introduce occult factors. There were three ways of accounting for the variety of human nature, Chasseneuz declared: that of the orthodox theologians (especially the Sorbonists), who attributed them simply to inherent qualities of the soul; that of the philosopheres and physiologists, who referred them to particular «complexions» which in turn were functions of the humors; and that of the astrologists – which Chasseneuz rejected – who traced them to the influence of the climata and location under the celestial sphere.[44] There was of course nothing revolutionary in bringing «natural» explanations into the field of human behavior. On the contrary, as Chasseneuz

---

[43] *Methodus*, 247. Cf. PASQUIER, *Recherches de la France*, I, 3; and CONNAN, *Commentarii*, II, 9. There is need for a study of this Celtic movement of the 1550's, noted briefly by MESNARD [4.20], 37, n. 10; there are some remarks in R. E. ASHER [186], The Attitude of French Writers of the Renaissance to Early French History (University of London, unpubl. Ph. D. thesis, 1955).

[44] *Catalogus gloriae mundi*, X; «Prima opinio est philosophantium et medicorum, quo complexioni attribuunt excellentiam ingenii ... Secunda ergo opinio, dicentium complexiones insequi climata et diversitatem coeli ... Omissa ergo opinione astrologorum, quae somnia et phantasmata recitat, ad tertiam opinionem veram, quae est theologorum, maxime Parisiensem, qui determinaverunt unam animam in naturalibus esse alia perfectiorem et excellentiorem, cui determinatione standum est.» And X, 18: «Scire est per causas cognoscere ... Legistae et canonistae cognoscunt per causas et rationes.»

and Coras stipulated, one of the basic characteristics of legal science was that it interpreted its subject in such terms, that is, *scire per causas*, which was a standard definition for science. But Bodin's conception of cause took him further and led him indeed into forbidden territory. Using the deterministic concepts of ancient (and medieval) medicine and astrology, Bodin sketched out a «geohistorical» science, which contained elements of anthropology and ethnography as well as sociology, and which seemed to fulfill the demand, made five years earlier by Baudouin, for an alliance between geography and history.[45]

In general Bodin's *Methodus* constituted an attempt to reduce the field of history to a hierarchical and branching set of topics in which historical information could be stored for use. The pattern may be quite simply diagrammed and the ingeniousness as well as the ambiguities this displayed. «History» itself he defined in three ways, or rather on three levels, though neither entirely explicitly nor entirely unequivocally. Most generally it was a true narrative *(vera narratio)*, and it could be pursued, as far as humanity is concerned, either on a universal plane or on a particular plane, that is, the history of nations, *(maximae respublicae)*, of cities *(minimae respublicae)*, or biography *(res gestae virorum)*. Secondly, history had to be understood from the point of view of the reader of the narration *(as cognitio)*, and this of course, as the principle subject of the book, required its own peculiar distribution. This included first the choosing *(delectus)* and classifying *(ordo et collectio)* of historical works in order to establish a basic reading list; and second the criticism *(judicium)* of these authors in terms of the auxiliary sciences of geography and chronology and in the light of what modern scholarship had to say about such problems as the theory of Four World Monarchies and myths of national origins. In these two ways Bodin discussed what may be called the subjective side of «history».

But the problem of historical knowledge was not one which Bodin was interested in pursuing further; and it was history in its third sense, history as «action» not thought *(res non verba*, in the conventional classical topos), that was to preoccupy him. The main thrust of his interest was clearly in the sphere of human action *(res humanae)*;[46] and the train of thought leading to the *Republic* appears unmistakeably in the third and sixth chapters The mechanism of history is explained here as the drive of human will toward increasingly civilized goals: that of indivi-

---

[45] *De Institutione*, 181. In general, M. J. TOOLEY [183], Bodin and the Mediaeval Theory of Climate, *Speculum* 28 (1953), 64–83; and A. MEUTEN, Bodins Theorie von der Beeinflussung des politischen Lebens der Staaten durch ihre geographische Lage, Bonn 1904 [58].

[46] Cf. BAUDOUIN, *De Institutione*, opening and closing paragraphs.

dual man toward the necessities of life and that of man in communities toward the comforts and pleasures of life, hence toward a political organization *(respublica)* that can insure these. Thence Bodin moved to the question of political power (the *imperium)*, its distribution and administration (through *concilium* and *executio)*, and the complex social and cultural pattern underlying it. Such were the categories of human action (including *consilia* and *dicta* as well as *acta)* in which historical knowledge, after being analysed, was to be deposited. For Bodin, in short, history was to be transformed into an applied science.

Whatever the source of inspiration for his logical analysis, it seems clear that jurisprudence remained the principal model for Bodin's codification of history. Both history and law were conventionally equated with wisdom («the knowledge of things human and divine»),[47] and it was natural that Bodin, like Baudouin, should want to bring the two into closer alignment. The difference was that Bodin set out to impose his own almost totalitarian format on both. In both cases he began with a general definition and then distinguished its parts *(jus quit sit, ejus divisio; quid historia sit et quotuplex);* in both cases he recognized three principle types (human, natural, and divine) and a particular as well as universal form (corresponding to national and universal history was *jus civile* and *jus gentium)*; in both cases he made a fundamental distinction between private and public (in history between man in community and man as citizen); and in both cases he wanted to find a scheme that would exhaust the substance of his subject (individual *leges* and, in a broad sense, individual *actiones).*[48] In general it is hard to disagree with the conclusion of one of Bodin's most devoted disciples that he was a «theoretical historian» *(historien contemplatif)* and that his book was in fact not a method of history at all but rather «method of law».[49]

---

[47] ULPIAN in Digest, 1, 1, 10: «Iuris prudentia est divinarum atque humanarum rerum notitia.» The Ciceronian formula was «sapientia est rerum humanarum divinarumque scientia» – on which see EUGENE RICE, The Renaissance Idea of Wisdom, Cambridge, Mass. 1958; it was applied to history, e.g., by BAUDOUIN, *De Institutione,* 9.

[48] Cf. *Juris universi distributio* [4.20], 72–73.

[49] LA POPELINIÈRE, *Histoire des histoires,* Paris 1599, 28, and see note 42. It may be noted that La Popelinière carried on, in several works, Bodin's concern with geo-history.

144   *Donald R. Kelley*

V. Bodin: Politicus

A «philosophistorian», according to Bodin, was one who combined the
narration of facts with precepts of wisdom.»[50] If we add that Bodin
ultimately hoped to dissolve narrative history altogether in his philosophic concoction, this prescription more than fits his work. Given his
hyper-rationalizing tendencies and his overriding interest in public law
(already evident in the *Methodus*), it is not surprising that he should
have left behind the earth-bound concerns of historical scholarship
(marginal as they were for him in any case) and moved into the higher
sphere of political science *(civilis disciplina)*. And so to his collection of
models Bodin added that of political philosophy, and especially Aristotle's. He proceeded with his usual idiosyncrasy, refusing either to be
bound by Aristotle's conclusions or to discard any of the material he had
accumulated previously; as before he simply moved on to a larger set
of categories to accomodate his sources. At the same time, needless to say,
the events of the 1560's and the early 1570's tended to sharpen his
interest in, while modifying his views about, some of the more explosive
issues of politics. Such was the path by which Bodin approached his
Republic, the first comprehensive study of political science, as Bodin
saw it, of modern times.

Among modern authors Bodin found few worthy of consideration and
only Machiavelli deserving of praise – and even then rather for his
pioneering effects that for his actual accomplishments. The similarities
between these men have often been pointed out, but as Bodin himself
suggested, the divergences may be more fundamental, especially by the
time the *Republic* appeared (1576), when Machiavelli's name had become
a synonym for hypocrisy, tyranny, and atheism. Yet there was more to
Bodin's charge that Machiavelli identified political science with tyrannical and irreligion ruses than simply the fashionable anti-Machiavelli-
anism of the aftermath of St Bartholomew.[51] For Bodin was also, at least
implicitly, objecting to the narrowness of Machiavelli's intellectual horizons and to the superficiality of his conception of politics. Although

---

[50] *Methodus*, 138: «Ut autem Geographistorici regiones cum historia: sic
Philosophistorici rerum gestarum narrationem cum sapientiae praeceptis cumu-
larent.»

[51] *Methodus*, 167; cf. preface to the first edition of the *Republic*, translated
by KENNETH D. MCRAE in the introduction (A 70) to his edition, Cambridge,
Mass., 1962 [7.44]. The view that Bodin was a «disciple» of Machiavelli was
taken by CHAUVIRÉ [76], 207, among others. The contrast between the two I
have elaborated upon in: Murd'rous Machiavel in France, *Political Science Quarterly* 85 (1970), 545–559.

Bodin and Machiavelli agreed upon some of the grand themes of political philosophy, such as the Polybian *anacyclosis,* and certainly shared the goal of constructing an intelligible science of politics, their modes of perceiving political reality were basically different and their respective methods in some ways irreconcilable.

The reasons for this go deeper than Bodin's obsession with system. To begin with there is an obvious contrast between their life situations. While Machiavelli was a political activist always concerned, directly or indirectly, with policy-making questions, Bodin never held comparable responsible office near the center of power, which seemed not only distant but, in keeping with official ideology, almost sacramental in character. While Machiavelli looked instinctively to the psychology of his fellow citizens, Bodin looked to the inherited traditions and the complex of institutions that circumscribed the actions of Frenchmen. It may be suspected, too, that whereas Machiavelli never lost his faith in the efficacy of individual action, Bodin naturally took a more pessimistic view – if not because of the political inertia of a structure as large and complex as the French monarchy, then surely because of the traumatic experiences of the religious wars. Most important of all, while Machiavelli had enjoyed military as well as diplomatic and administrative experience (and never distinguished too sharply between the arts of politics and of war), Bodin was a professional jurist little interested in diplomatic maneuvering and warfare (one of the few subjects, indeed, in which he was content to follow Machiavelli). In general Bodin worked in a much richer – and more inhibiting – context of legal, historical, and philosophical erudition, and he was by training and nature, if not by nationality, unable to separate politics from its legal and social environment.

In terms of method, then, Bodin and Machiavelli were literally worlds apart. As Bodin's most perceptive commentator summed it up. «The *Republic* is the work not so much of a great politique as of a great legist, the work of a successor not of Machiavelli but of Beaumanoir and Bartolus.»[52] Machiavelli's tendency was to concentrate upon individual motives and strategies, on discrete and even interchangeable factors, and on linear causal sequences. He viewed institutions, constitutional as well as religious, in a functional manner. He sought and usually found simple answers to simple questions; if not he could always take refuge in the old notion of fortune. And in applying the lessons of history he was normally content with easy analogies and accepted Roman experience as a sufficient model. By contrast Bodin could not discuss political change

---

[52] MOREAU-REIBEL [116], Jean Bodin et le droit public comparé, Paris 1933, 135.

without becoming involved in questions of social structure and relationships. Like Machiavelli he was concerned with questions of power, but
for him this entailed private as well as public law, which meant the
whole web of society from the family through the various corporate
groups, social classes, and administrative hierarchy up to the central
government. Between the citizen and the prince, in short, there were
many gradations which obscured the lines of force and which greatly
complicated the analysis of political transformation. Moreover, he assumed that any political situation or institution had to be understood in
terms of a total social structure, a specific geographic milieu, a variety
of customs, and a particular national tradition, if not (as in the case of
France) a multiplicity of traditions.

As Walter Ullmann remarked about the medieval civilians, «By view-
ing law as a social phenomenon, medieval jurisprudence was forced to
elucidate some basic principles about society, and thus was led to consider
topics which, under modern conditions, would be dealt with, not by the
lawyer, but by the sociologist.»[53] It was this school of thought above all
that distinguished Bodin from Machiavelli — and established him as one
of the founders of modern social science.

VI. Bodin: Dominus Factotum

In sum, to judge from the three works discussed here, it was Bodin's
intention to do for the *jus gentium* in a general sense what medieval
commentators had tried to do for the *jus civile*, that is, to rationalize
it, to resolve conflicts and inequities, and to adapt it to contemporary
problems; and ultimately he hoped thereby to formulate a social ideal
that would approximate the *jus naturale*. Clearly, it was such an ideal,
rather than any deep sympathy for humanist or legal erudition, that led
him to his total attack upon history, to his search for underlying physical
and especially geographical, principles underlying history, to his reassessment of Aristotelian political philosophy, and to his renowned «comparative method», if such indeed it was. In fact his method, to judge
from the *Republic*, seems designed mainly to keep all restrictions off the
riot of learning which he had gathered. Accepting no «law of citations»,
he was able to combine legal and philosophical «authorities» with historical and geographical evidence and so to disregard any distinction
between historical inference and political generalization, which often

[53] The Medieval Idea of Law as Represented by Lucas of Penna, London
1946, 163.

meant between descriptive and normative statements.[54] A curious and confused sort of «empiricism», reminiscent rather of a scholastic than a comparative approach. To this extent, indeed, it may be suggested that Bodin did not altogether escape the utopian impulse.

So we return, again and finally, to the somewhat unearthly quality of Bodin's thought. He ignored the standards of established «disciplines». He rejected, too, the temporal limitations of human history and tried to fix the accumulated experience of humanity into a transcendent system. These characteristics may help to explain how, to one trying to assess the historical significance of Bodin's thought, he seems to be a man belonging to several ages. On the one hand he appears to have the scholastic philosopher's unhistorical and indiscriminate attitude toward his authorities and his faith that an ideal system may be assembled merely by the proper arrangement and criticism of these. On the other hand he sometimes seems, as in his discussion of feudal institutions, to be attempting to find the «spirit of the laws» (*mens legum* was a civilian expression which in fact did imply an ideal, since it referred to the intention or spirit as distinct from the letter of the law)[55] through the comparison of the customs of various societies. In this sense Bodin may be regarded as a significant member of that as yet untraced tradition of social thought leading from the legists of the middle ages to the philosophes of the 18th century – a prime mover in that shifting of the Heavenly City (according to Carl Becker's notorious thesis) to its «earthly foundations». The author of a veritable «Summa of political philosophy», as Henri Baudrillart declared over a century ago, Bodin was nevertheless a «Montesquieu of the 16th century».[56]

This has been only a provisional discussion, but perhaps it may suggest ways of bringing together some of the disparate features of Bodin's thought and of resolving some of the contradictions which many commentators (though not Bodin himself) have found in his work. As the papers of this conference (especially those of Messrs. Giesey and Reulos and Mme Isnardi Parente) have made abundantly clear, Bodin had access to a practically unlimited range of sources as well as to the

---

[54] More specifically, I doubt that Bodin's use of legal citations in the *Republic* is any more orthodox than his discussion of the art of history (in the rhetorical tradition) is in the *Methodus*. This seems to me to be a fundamental and unanswered question: not what his sources were, but what he thought (or assumed) their function was in his system.

[55] See NICOLAS VALLA, *De Rebus dubiis* ... (in *Tractatus universi juris*, XVIII, f. 317v): «Mens ergo legis nihil aliud est, quam sententia et ratio ejus manifesta, ex qua vel obscura, vel ambigua ipsius legis dispositio declaratur, aut generalis et indefinitiva expenditur, aut restringitur.»

[56] BAUDRILLART [27], J. Bodin et son temps, Paris 1853, 109.

148   *Donald R. Kelley*

Diagram A.

Bodin's Method of History

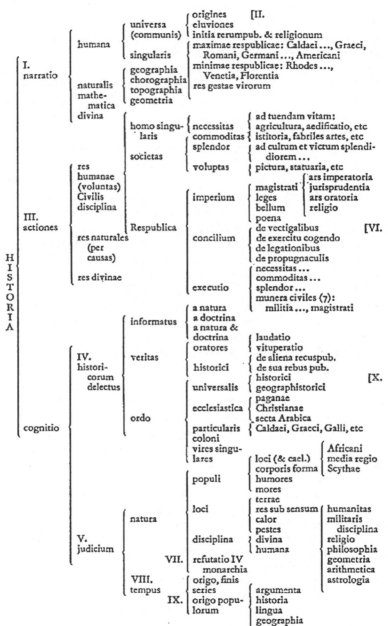

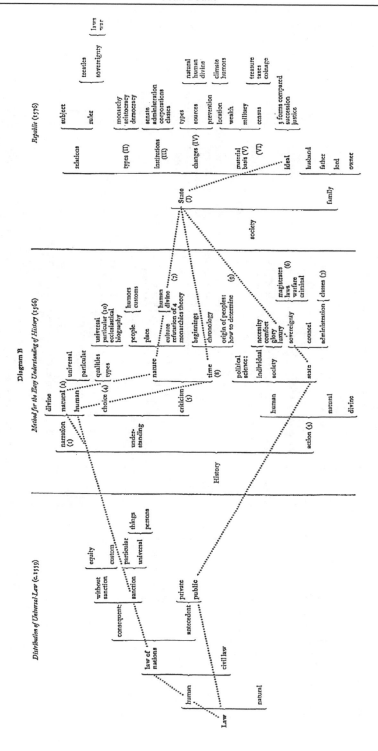

Diagram C

Vossius: SYNOPSIS

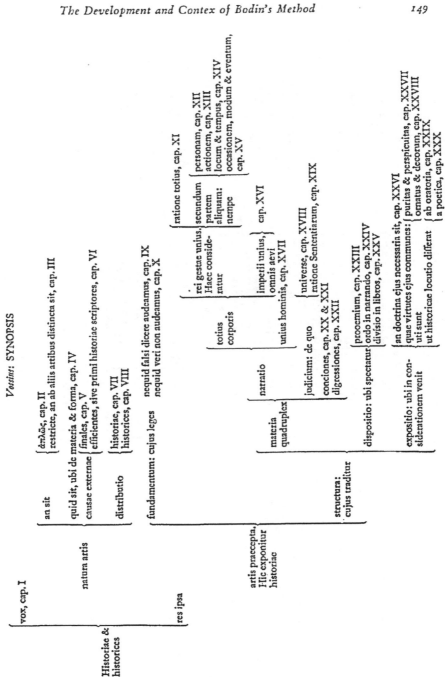

most challenging political and social paradoxes of modern times. Yet it is no less obvious that Bodin entertained an almost compulsive monism that drove him to accommodate this personal and vicarious experience in a single and coherent system.

This has been reflected in part by Bodin's fascination with the «old metaphysics of order» (as Mr. Greenleaf put it) and in the new logic of Ramus (as Mr. McRae has shown), with ancient notions of harmony (as Mr. Villey has explained) and with modern notions of tolerance through the reconciliation of opposites (as Mr. Roellenbleck has argued). Above all it has been exemplified by Bodin's struggles to reconcile old ideas of corporate and «constitutional» order with with a new view of absolute sovereignty (as has been indicated in different ways by Messrs. Salmon, Franklin, Polin, Scheuner, and others). To what extent particular works may be reconciled with Bodin's general though changing system may be debated, but (as I myself believe) his last and most neglected work, the *Theater of Universal Nature*, shows that his systematizing urge never deserted him. To set for himself such transcendent goals Bodin must indeed have cast himself in the role of prophet (as Mr. Baxter has suggested) if not of sorcerer. Nor can I think of any more plausible way of accounting for the wonder, suspicious as well as worshipful, which Bodin has inspired in generations of scholars down to the present day, present company included.

[7]

Limitations on Absolute Authority

Julian H. Franklin

The limitations acknowledged by Bodin were divided into two broad classes. Some were derivations from the law of nature and looked mainly to the protection of the rights of individuals. The others were positive fundamental laws which guaranteed the continuity and resources of the crown itself, and which Bodin refers to as *loix royales* or *leges imperii*. Since the theoretical issues posed by the latter are more complicated, it seems better to begin with them.

In the French tradition, the idea of fundamental law, if not the term itself, often included every form of constitutional restriction – procedural as well as substantive, positive as well as natural. Bodin's usage, consistent with his absolutism, is inevitably more specialized and narrow.[1] Only two fundamental laws are mentioned, both of which may be technically regarded as mere creations of a right in the successor. The law of succession to the throne, which is one fundamental law, is the rule that determines the successor. The law against alienation of the royal domain, which is the other fundamental law, establishes a right in the successor to undiminished use of all the resources of the office. Bodin correctly thought that both these rules were not only basic for political stability but were also fully compatible with absolutism.

It is with respect to the law of succession that the theoretical relationships are clearest. In any stable order there has to be a rule of continuity which is ultimately the same as the law that identifies the rightful sovereign. In republics, where the sovereign person is collective, the test of continuity, and indeed of legitimacy, is the rule of selection and form of procedure that identifies the ruling corporation. In monarchical states the same function is performed by the law of succession to the throne. It is the test by which a legitimate incumbent can be distinguished from a mere usurper.

Depending on the specific form of the monarchy, this rule may be a more or less severe restriction on the freedom of incumbents to name their own successors. In purely patrimonial kingships, the incumbent may be technically free to bestow the crown on whom he pleases, although he is obviously bound to some degree by the rule of consanguinity. In France, on the other hand, all rights of testamentary disposition were technically denied to the incumbent, since the crown descended automatically by primogeniture in the male line.

---

[1] There is a sharp distinction introduced between these two fundamental laws and other well-established rules of common law, which is not encountered in Seyssel and the antiquarians.

Limitations on Absolute Authority

With respect to naming a successor, the king of France was as fully limited as the king of an elective monarchy.

Yet even a restrictive rule is compatible with absolute authority. Absolute supremacy does not necessarily imply a right in its possessor to determine situations that arise when he has left the scene. He must, of course, have full juridical authority to determine situations in the present. But this is not affected by denial of his right to name an heir. In other words, the situation that the law of succession seeks to regulate is created by the ruler's death.

This consistency can also be looked at in another way. One test of absolute authority is its immunity from legitimate resistance. But the law of succession to the throne need not give rise, legitimately, to a preventive act of the community directed against the actual incumbent. If an incumbent should designate an heir who is other than the one prescribed by law, his designation is technically a nullity. A pretender, who might later attempt to succeed upon the will of that incumbent, could be rightfully opposed by the community, since he would be a mere usurper. But there could be no occasion for preventive action against the incumbent who made the designation. The sole mechanism for enforcement of the law of succession is the assertion of a claim by the successor that it designates.

In Bodin's formulation, the ideas that we have just set forth are introduced through a succinct but effective distinction between the powers of the royal office and the title of an incumbent to possession of that office. The royal office may be absolute and the incumbent to that office may make use of all its powers for the present. But where the law of succession is restrictive, the incumbent's title to these powers is but a life-possession, or a life-estate. The law of succession to the throne may thus be regarded as a kind of entail annexed to the crown in favour of some designated heir:

And as to laws, like the Salic law, that concern the state of the kingdom and its establishment; – since these are annexed and united to the crown, the prince cannot detract from them. And should he do so, his successor can also annul anything that has been done in prejudice of the royal laws on which the sovereign majesty is established and supported.[2]

No explanation is advanced as to how this annexation came about. But it follows from all that we have said that no special explanation is required. Once an order of succession has been fixed by custom, and in so far as it is firmly fixed, it is beyond the reach of each incumbent and beyond the reach of royal power generally. The Salic law would thus be a special custom of the realm, which differs from most other customs in that a king is impotent to alter it without the consent of the community.

Bodin therefore felt no need to discuss the derivation of the rule, except to show that it was not an outgrowth of original election. According to the

2 *République*, 1, 8, p. 137 (95).

Jean Bodin

Huguenots, as we have seen, the Salic law was an alteration, introduced by custom, of an earlier and original system of election, the traces of which could still be found in various aspects of the royal coronation. Strictly speaking, this derivation was not incompatible with absolutism. As Bodin himself had said, an elective kingship could be absolute. Nevertheless, the thesis of original election was so closely associated with a constitutionalist version of the history of France that Bodin attempted to oppose it at all costs. He had always thought that the Frankish monarchy in France had been instituted by a conquest,[3] and, faced with the challenge of the Huguenots, he clung to this idea with even more tenacity. Despite the evidence amassed by Hotman, he attempted to refute original election.[4]

Consistent with this view, moreover, Bodin is vigilantly on guard against any version of the coronation ceremony that might be taken as a vestige of original election.[5] According to an old tradition, the kings of France did not acquire full title to their office until they had been formally inaugurated. On this account, as Bodin notes, an interregnum would occur between the death of one incumbent and the installation of the next, in which the business of the state would have to be conducted in the people's name. Since such arrangements seemed too reminiscent of elective systems, he dismisses the tradition as erroneous, and is one of the first important commentators to endorse the maxim that the king never dies.[6] The transfer of power is thus supposed to be accomplished instantaneously without intervention by the public.

A related position that Bodin also scornfully attacked was the assimilation of the Salic law to the *lex regia* of imperial Rome. Certain French civilians of the sixteenth century, including some whose attitudes inclined toward absolutism, had found it convenient to assume that the kings of France received their powers from the Salic law in the same manner that the Roman emperors acquired theirs from the *lex regia*.[7] This might be taken to imply that in France, as in elective systems, the powers of a king reverted to the people on his death and were then conferred upon a new incumbent. In an anecdote,

---

[3] *Methodus*, p. 207 (252), p. 192 (215).

[4] *République*, VI, 5, pp. 983ff (729ff). Bodin's attempted refutation seems to depend on that of Antoine Matharel [with Jean Papire Masson], *Ad F. Hotomani Franco-galliam responsio* (1575).

[5] On the coronation ritual itself, see *ibid*. pp. 984–5 (pp. 730–2). For the opposing interpretation, constantly suggested by the Huguenots, see the *Vindiciae contra tyrannos*, in Franklin, *Constitutionalism and Resistance*, pp. 142ff.

[6] *République*, I, 8, p. 160 (112); III, 2, p. 386 (288); VI, 5, p. 986 (732). On Bodin's legal formula, see Ralph E. Giesey, *The Royal Coronation Ceremony in Renaissance France* (Geneva, 1960) p. 177. In actual practice, immediate exercise of power by the new incumbent had become the custom in the thirteenth century. But the idea of a kind of interregnum still lingered on, and is used in the *Vindiciae* (Franklin, p. 183) as an indication of original election.

[7] Thus Jean Ferrault, *Tractatus . . . iura seu privilegia aliqua regni Franciae continens* (1515), priv. no. 12, p. 344 (bound together with Grassaille, and continuously paginated beginning at page 319). The king alone, according to Ferrault, is entitled to enact a law 'because by an ancient royal law (*antiqua lege regia*), which is named the Salic law, every right and all power were transferred to the king '.

Limitations on Absolute Authority

approvingly recounted by Bodin, the use of the *lex regia* as an analogue for France is rebuked as a subversive utterance.[8]

There were certain situations, to be sure, in which intervention by the public could hardly be denied. Bodin apparently admits that, where a regency was needed, it ought to be approved by the Estates.[9] But this authorization was not an indication of a deeper or more fundamental right. In principle, at least, a regency was conducted in behalf of the incumbent who acquired title by successive right.[10] A more interesting question was posed by the extinction of a dynasty. If the last survivor failed to name an heir, the power passed to the Estates.[11] But this contingency apparently seemed so remote, and so refractory to legal treatment, that it is noted without special comment.

The second fundamental law was the inalienability of royal domain, which embraced the entire complex of valuable rights attaching to the royal treasury — such as public lands and forests; feudal dues and other rents; fees, fines, tolls, and confiscations; and all manner of established taxes. The inalienability of this domain had always been regarded as a fundamental rule of fiscal probity. The domain was supposed to have been set aside in order to provide a king with a source of annual income normally sufficient to defray the costs of government.[12] If the capital were squandered and the revenues reduced, the public was unnecessarily exposed to an increased burden of taxation. Alienation of domain, except in situations of emergency, was thus considered inherently unjust.

The rule of inalienability could also be regarded as a protection of the dynasty itself. If the usual sources of revenue were lost by the sales or gifts of an incumbent, his successors in the kingship would be forced to desperate and dangerous expedients, among which the most ruinous was new taxation since it so often led to revolution.[13] To alienate domain, accordingly, was directly to prejudice the interest and right of the successor. It was to sell or give away the very substance of his legacy.

From either standpoint, however, the rule of inalienability was consistent with absolute authority. Like the law of succession to the throne, the rule was prospective in its force with respect to a particular incumbent. Even on a strictly absolutist version of the rule, a king was not prevented from entire use of the domain as long as he remained in office, and, as long as he remained king, he could leave possession of the domain in the hands of anyone he wished. The only thing he could not do was to transfer right to the domain

---

[8] *République*, VI, 5, pp. 986–7 (733).   [9] *Ibid*. I, 8, p. 136 (95).

[10] But the right of the Estates to ratify a regency had often been invoked as an indication of ultimate authority. See, for example, the speech of Philip Pot at the Estates of Tours, reported in R. W. and A. J. Carlyle, *A History of Medieval Political Theory in the West*, 6 vols (Edinburgh and London, 1909–36) VI, pp. 176–7 and notes.

[11] *République*, VI, 5, p. 988 (734).

[12] *Ibid*. VI, 2, pp. 856–7 (650–1).   [13] *Ibid*. pp. 860–2 (653–4).

Jean Bodin

that would endure beyond his lifetime and bind his successors in the kingship. This limitation was no doubt severe, since it warned potential buyers of domain that their title would be insecure. Yet this defect of right in the incumbent was not, technically speaking, a limitation on absolute authority. It simply followed from his temporary possession of that absolute authority.

As with the law of succession, furthermore, a violation of the law of the domain was simply a legal nullity and could not justify preventive action on the part of the community. The mechanism of enforcement was the imprescriptible title of successors to assert their right of use.[14] The law of the domain, finally, could also be easily accounted for. It too was a special custom of the realm that was beyond the reach of particular incumbents.[15]

In the civilian-canonist tradition, all of these relationships are contained in the idea of the domain as a usufruct in public property, or even as a simple right of use, or as something analogous to the right of a husband to a dowry; and these comparisons are taken over by Bodin.[16] In all of these relationships of private law, the user of the property is unable to alienate the title, but in the case of usufruct at least the right of the ultimate owner to enforce this limitation is restricted to subsequent recovery. An illegal alienation, in other words, does not terminate the usufruct, so that the analogy carried over into public law implies no right of preventive action on the part of the community.[17] In

---

[14] *Ibid.* p. 857 (651).   [15] See Lemaire, *Lois fondamentales*, pp. 112–14.

[16] *République*, VI, 2, pp. 859–60 (652–3). Since these ideas were commonplaces no specific derivation need be sought, although it might be noted that Bodin refers readers to Choppin's *De domanio Franciae libri III*, which had appeared in 1574. Choppin's treatise is rich in comparative materials on which Bodin may well have drawn. We may also note that Bodin also mentions, as applicable to France, the Roman distinction between the *fiscus* of the Emperor, which was private property, and the *aerarium* of the state, which was public. This point is made by many commentators of the time in order to emphasize the public status of the domain and to claim for it the same protections accorded the *aerarium* in classical Roman law. However, there was no real parallel in France to the *fiscus*, since the patrimony of the dynasty was public domain.

[17] This implication of the analogy goes unmentioned in the medieval commentators, or at least in the ones that I have checked. It seems simply to have been assumed, and Bodin, repeating the tradition on this topic, saw no need to make the point explicit. But Barclay, writing slightly later, and dealing with the extreme situation where a sovereign alienated the entire kingdom to a foreigner, was to take a position that then moved Grotius to elaborate the point by way of answer. Barclay had said that where the entire kingdom was alienated, not only was the act illegal, but the king who sought to alienate was thereby deprived of his title to the kingdom. Grotius, more cautious, holds that the act is simply a nullity, and then goes on to argue that ' this is the view of the jurists in regard to a usufructuary, to whose position, we have said, that of such a king is analogous; by alienating his right to a third person the usufructuary effects nothing. And the statement that the usufruct reverts to the owner of the property must be construed in accordance with the period fixed by law.' *Law of War and Peace*, I, 4, 10, p. 157.

The last sentence of this passage refers to an apparent antinomy in Roman private law between *Institutes*, 2, 4, 3 and *Digest*, 23, 3, 66. According to the first, a usufruct does not revert to the ultimate owner of the property in the event of an attempted alienation by the fructuary; but the second passage could be read to hold the opposite since it says, in effect, that despite the attempted alienation, the usufruct reverts to the ultimate owner.

Limitations on Absolute Authority

private law the attempted alienation is simply a legal nullity which cannot debar the true proprietor or the designated successor to the usufruct from full enjoyment of the property at the time the usufruct expires. In public law this situation would occur only at the death of an incumbent king.

There were, inevitably, some exceptions to the rule of inalienability. Under French law there were two situations in which alienation was legitimate. One was the constitution of appanages, subject to conditions of reversion, for younger brothers of the reigning king. The other was sale of the domain, with provisions for repurchase, in order to raise money for a war emergency.[18] According to Bodin, and most other writers of the time, alienation in this second situation required the consent of the Estates.[19] Yet even this was compatible with absolutism. Consent was simply regarded as one of several conditions which, if properly met, would foreclose any claim by a successor. But if this or any other condition were ignored, the successor would be entitled to recover.

On the other hand, there were some provisions of French law for which this remedy did not suffice. According to the Edict of Moulins of 1566, donations of domain for a limited period of time, or the farming of taxes at rates below the market value, were to be considered alienations of domain, and the courts were enjoined to disallow them.[20] Since the purpose of such rules was to prevent donations on a temporary basis – to prevent, as it were, the transfer of the fruits of the domain as well as transfers of the title – the abuse that they attempted to prevent could not be compensated by subsequent recovery of use.[21] To this extent, Bodin's conception of inalienability was a weakening of the French tradition. Although he clearly disapproved alienation of the fruits, he did not specify this prohibition as a principle of fundamental law and could not have done so without endangering his absolutist principle.[22]

Grotius, ingeniously and also persuasively, I think, reads the second passage as if it said that, despite the alienation of the usufruct, the act is of no effect, and the usufruct will revert to the ultimate owner at the expiration of its term just as it would have, had no attempt at alienation occurred.

[18] Edict of Moulins, par. 1 in Isambert, *Recueil*, 14, p. 186. Hence in principle at least the rule of the sixteenth century is more restrictive than that suggested by the medieval commentators. The latter permitted alienations if the damage to the successor was not severe. See Bartolus on *Digest*, 43, 23, 3, *Commentarii*, v, f. 148v.   [19] *République*, vi, 2, p. 859 (652).

[20] Edict of Moulins, par. 5 in Isambert, *Recueil*, 14, p. 187.

[21] Unless perhaps by suit against the occupant for the value of his use, which would not, of course, be a sure remedy. The Edict of Moulins, it may be noted, frequently speaks of prevention by the courts, although this, from a purely royalist standpoint, would be a right conferred by statute and one that the king could override by a derogatory clause.

[22] But the idea of a duty in the king to conserve the fruits of the domain for public purposes was so traditional, that at one point he casually includes it: ' And so sovereign princes are not permitted to abuse the fruits and revenues of the domain, even if the commonwealth is at peace and completely free of debt, for they are not its fructuaries but its users (*usagers*, Lat. *usarii*) only, and once they have taken what they need for their household and the commonwealth, they must save the surplus for [future] public necessity.' *République*, vi, 2, p. 860 (653). See also i, 9, p. 182 (130).

Jean Bodin

The basic conception of these fundamental laws was also extended to the inalienability of sovereignty itself as distinguished from valuable domain. On this very complicated topic Bodin's remarks are curiously brief and fragmentary. But since his various positions are generally in accord with the received tradition, the major outlines may be stated.

One traditional question was whether full independence could be conceded by a ruler to particular subjects. Italian cities, for example, had claimed independent status by virtue of concessions from the Emperor. According to Bodin, any concession of this sort is an extreme alienation of domain, and, in principle at least, is forbidden absolutely:

Thus it was not in the power of the Emperors, or of any prince whatever, to alienate any part of the public domain, and least of all the rights of sovereign majesty, without it being always in the power of his successor to lay hands on it, just as a master may always retake his fugitive slave.[23]

Another and more difficult issue was whether the kingdom as a whole, or even a portion of the kingdom, could be ceded to a foreign prince either as an outright transfer or, more commonly, in the form of feudal dependency. For Bodin, the existence or non-existence of a restriction is made to depend on the specific character of the law of succession to the throne.

In kingships like the French, the consent of the community was needed for transfer of the kingdom as a whole, since the alienation would violate the Salic law. By somewhat more complicated reasoning, the prohibition of the Salic law would also prevent alienation of a portion of the kingdom without the consent of its lord, if not of its inhabitants. The transfer of a vassal without his own consent would violate the ruler's obligation to protect him.[24] It could not be accomplished by the ruler legally unless he were also entitled to transfer the kingship as a whole with all its rights and obligations, and this, as we have seen, is forbidden by the Salic law, unless of course the whole community consents:

And on this account it was decided that Philip the Fair, King of France, could not make Arthur, Duke of Brittany, the vassal of the King of England, against the wishes of the Duke, unless he [Philip] were to leave his entire kingdom to the King of England. But this he could not do without the consent of the Estates – and not even by his absolute authority despite what some have said.[25]

[23] *Ibid.* p. 182 (129).

[24] The use of feudal notions to develop a general obligation to protect is traced to Baldus by Peter N. Riesenberg, *Inalienability of Sovereignty in Medieval Political Thought* (New York. 1956) p. 136. Bodin's formulation follows this tradition and, perhaps for this reason, is more cautious and more narrowly feudal than some of the larger and more eloquent conceptions beginning to be developed in the period. Thus, Hotman, *Quaestiones illustres* (1573) in *Operum*, 11, pp. 847ff; and, slightly earlier, Fernando Vazquez de Menchaca (Vasquius), *Controversiarum illustrium . . . libri tres* (1564) (Valladolid, 1931), 1, 4 (vol. 1, pp. 148–9).

[25] *République*, 1, 9, p. 179 (127).

Limitations on Absolute Authority

According to Barclay, as we have noted,[26] extreme violation of this rule would justify preventive action on the part of the community. But this was not a problem that Bodin considered. He simply assumed that transfers made without consent were liable to subsequent recovery, which seemed adequate for all his purposes. The French public had some protection against permanent divisions of the realm through hasty actions by the kings, while the kings, in turn, were given a convenient pretext for repudiating cessions by their predecessors on the grounds that due procedures were omitted. It may also be noted that all of this would apply to elective kingships too, although Bodin neglects to point this out.

On the other hand, for ' hereditary ' kingships like the Spanish or the English, this protection is specifically denied.[27] An hereditary kingship, for Bodin, seems to have been one in which the law of succession to the crown was substantially the same as the law of intestate succession to private property, and in which the incumbent was perhaps technically entitled to vary the order of succession by his testament as long as he confined his choice to a member of the ruling family.[28] In such kingships the ' cause ' which established the right of a successor lay, as it were, in the progenitor. In ' successive ' kingships, on the other hand, of which the sole exemplar would seem to be the French, the ' cause ' of the successor's right was designation by a special public custom. One operational distinction between the first form of kingship and the second was whether women were permitted to succeed. In Spain and England, where the succession of women was permitted, succession to the throne seemed to follow the law of private inheritance. In France, on the other hand, the normal order of private inheritance was clearly overridden by the Salic law.

This distinction, which Bodin frequently invokes, was old in continental jurisprudence. French publicists, writing in the early 1400s, had rejected the concept of inheritance in order to protect the crown from various treaties on succession arising from the Hundred Years War.[29] By Bodin's time it was a commonplace of legal thought that a king of France, like the king of an elective monarchy, held his crown by public designation rather than hereditary right.

For some commentators, one consequence of this principle was that successors to the crown of France, unlike successors by inheritance, were not automatically obliged by the contracts and engagements of their predecessors.[30] This is the position that Bodin employs to deny the alienability of sovereignty in France. On the other hand, in Spain or England the king was not only

---

[26] See above, note 17.   [27] *République*, 1, 9, p. 179 (127).

[28] See note 31 below.

[29] For the development of the legal theory, see Ralph E. Giesey, *The Juristic Basis of Dynastic Right to the French Throne* (Philadelphia, 1961) *passim* and especially pp. 12ff on Jean de Terre Rouge, who was the key figure in the formulation of the legal doctrine. See also Lemaire, *Lois fondamentales*, pp. 54ff, and F. Olivier-Martin, *Histoire du droit français* (Paris, 1948) p. 310.   [30] See below, pp. 8off.

Jean Bodin

entitled to cede a portion of the kingdom to a foreigner, but could even transfer his entire realm, as in doing homage to a foreign prince. If an engagement
were made, the successor to the crown was obligated. Since the kingship was
a mere inheritance, consent of the Estates was not required.

It is hard to say exactly why Bodin insisted on this latter point. One possible
motive, suggested by the context, was to show that the king of France enjoyed
a security of title that no other king could claim. He may also have felt
that the conclusion was imposed upon him by the logic of a traditional
distinction.[31]

In any event, the result seems hopelessly inadequate. The rule was obviously
unworkable, since no king of Spain or England could be realistically expected
to acknowledge it, and even from a theoretical standpoint, it was inconsistent
with other things that Bodin held. He believed, for example, that the kings of
Spain or England were not entitled to alienate domain to subjects except in

---

[31] For clarification of this highly complicated technical distinction, see Giesey, *Dynastic Right*,
passim, as well as Grotius, *Law of War and Peace*, ii, 7, pp. 267ff, and Pufendorf, *Law
of Nature*, vii, 7, pp. 1093ff. But, in order to indicate what it is that Bodin is confused
about, a few very condensed observations may be offered here.

In Grotius and Pufendorf three main types of succession (other than election) are distinguished – patrimonial succession, in which the choice of a successor is left to the discretion of
the incumbent and in which the rule of intestate succession is followed where the incumbent
has made no designation; hereditary succession, in which the order of succession is legally
fixed according to degree of proximity to the deceased incumbent; and successive kingship
(or simple succession), in which the order of succession is legally fixed by lineal relationship
to a remote progenitor of the dynasty. Lineal succession may either be cognate lineal
succession (of which Castile is offered as the main example) or agnate lineal succession (which
is the French rule of primogeniture through the male line only).

The theoretical distinction between fixed and patrimonial succession is simple enough, but
the difference between hereditary and lineal succession is subtle and uncertain. From one
standpoint, lineal succession is merely a more precise determination of the proximity of
kinship relations to the incumbent and thus partakes of heredity. But from another standpoint, the successor by heredity is more like a private heir who, in Roman law, was a
substitute for his predecessor in all aspects, while the lineal successor was more like the
successor to a public office by election or appointment.

Bodin's confusions thus appear to be twofold. He does not distinguish clearly between
patrimonial and hereditary – in part perhaps because the theory of succession was less
well-developed in foreign countries. England, which Bodin believed to be hereditary, is a
good example, at least in the fifteenth and early sixteenth centuries. He was, furthermore,
unable to see the fundamental similarity in the legal status of hereditary and successive
kings. He fails to see that the right of the heir in a system of fixed inheritance precludes the
incumbent from alienating sovereignty or a portion of the sovereignty to another. He also
fails to see that an heir whose right is fixed by law, need not be regarded as a strictly
private heir and might thus be relieved of some of the obligations imposed on heirs by
private law. In Grotius and Pufendorf both of these points are resolved in favor of the
hereditary successor. It is assumed by these writers that in hereditary kingships, as distinguished from patrimonial kingships, the right of incumbents to dispose of the succession by
testament was eliminated by a public law which was imposed by the community at the time
the kingship was instituted. It is also assumed that by this same law the community intended,
and tacitly provided, that successors in the kingship should not be required to assume all
the obligations of a private heir but only those obligations consistent with their public duties.
On this latter assumption the status of an hereditary king is fully assimilated to that of a
successive king.

Limitations on Absolute Authority

situations of emergency, and it is hard to see how this could be reconciled with the possibility of ceding sovereignty to foreigners. There is no reason, given Bodin's principles, why the successor should be exempt from the engagements of his predecessor in the first case but obligated in the second.

Bodin, then, would have been better advised to treat succession to the crown of Spain or England in the same fashion as succession to the crown of France — as a designation arising from the law according to a rule of consanguinity. This would not only have removed the inconsistency; it would also have been more congenial to his general perspective.

But apart from this aberration, his views on fundamental law seem adequate. His interpretation of the law of succession and the law of domain, and his application of these rules to the inalienability of sovereignty, are broadly consistent with French and European norms. The rules are logically consistent since they are all derived from the concept of the kingship as a life-estate. And they are also compatible with absolutism in Bodin's meaning of that term.

The law of nature, as we have often pointed out, was not regarded by Bodin as an obligation of the ruler which the community was entitled to enforce. It was essentially a moral obligation binding solely on the ruler's conscience. But this is not to say that he looked upon the law of nature as an insignificant restraint. He obviously believed that the rule of justice was so inherent in the entire order of human and natural relationships that it could not be persistently defied without disastrous consequences. Nor did he think that the law of nature was completely unprotected institutionally. There were many ways anticipated in which the magistrates and judges of a kingdom could impose limitations on a king without resorting to overt defiance or inviting armed resistance. The law of nature was thus a force in social life, and it seemed important to Bodin to define its injunctions with precision.

In most of its aspects, the law of nature was inherently variable in application. As a guide to legislation, the specific meaning of the rule of justice depended on the circumstances.[32] As a guide to execution, or rule of fair procedure in criminal and civil proceedings,[33] it could vary greatly with the form of state. Less variable were rights of private property and claims related to that right. These were substantive restrictions on the state traditionally supposed to be universal and definite in content, and Bodin was thus required to define their basis and their scope.

The two main obligations on the ruler, both well-established in the civil law tradition, were to honor contracts made with private subjects (as well as contracts made with foreign princes) and to recognize a claim for compensation where he had done damage to the right of property either inadvertently or by invocation of eminent domain. If Bodin put somewhat greater emphasis on

[32] *République*, I, 8, pp. 151–2 (105–6).   [33] *Ibid*. VI, 6, pp. 1029–30 (768).

Jean Bodin

the obligation of contracts, it is in part because the issues were more complicated, and in part also because he was anxious to forestall misunderstanding.
Having held that engagements by a ruler to maintain existing law were not
completely binding, he could have been taken to imply that every royal contract was liable to the same flexibility. He wished, therefore, to make it very
clear that flexibility did not apply to contracts made with private individuals
to pay for loans, services, or goods from the general resources of the treasury.

The general obligation of the ruler to honor contracts of this sort was so well-
established in the civilian-canonist tradition that argument was hardly needed.
There were, however, points of controversy on interpretation. On one opinion,
which Bodin attributes to the canonists, the ruler's obligation by a contract
came solely from the law of nature, and was therefore less precise and binding
than the obligation of private parties under civil law, from which the ruler was
exempt. On this issue, Bodin adopts the stronger view, which seems to have
been taken by most of the civilians. Either the law of nature is as binding as
civil law in this respect, or else this is one respect in which the king, by virtue
of the law of nature, is bound by civil law.[34]

One other and more complicated question was the obligation of successor
kings to honor contracts entered into by their predecessors. The civilians of
the late thirteenth and early fourteenth centuries had been reticent and
cautious on this point. But they seem generally to have assumed that a
successor to the kingship was in much the same position as an heir in private
law. In assuming the status of his predecessor, he assumed the latter's
obligations.[35]

There were, however, certain obvious defects in this point of view. On the
theoretical level, the concept of inheritance could not be easily applied to elective kingships like the Empire. In its practical implications, the rule (in principle at least) gave no protection to the successor against irresponsible contracts
on the part of an incumbent or against claims that might arise from an
incumbent's frauds and delicts.

More congenial for Bodin's concerns, therefore, was a more sophisticated
line of reasoning that seems to have begun with Baldus. Distinguishing elective and successive princes, Baldus had contended that the latter only were
obligated directly by their predecessors, since it was from the predecessors
that office was acquired. The former, on the other hand – who received their
office from the public – could be obligated through the public only. In other
words, the incumbent to an elective kingship could bind his successor by a
contract only insofar as he could bind the public or the public treasury. The
test, accordingly, was whether the incumbent was acting 'in pursuance of his
dignity', – that is, in his public role as distinguished from his purely personal
capacity. There was one condition, however, on which even his frauds and

[34] *Ibid*. 1, 8, p. 153 (107).   [35] Carlyle and Carlyle, *Medieval Political Theory*, vi, p. 16.

Limitations on Absolute Authority

delicts could give rise to continuing obligations. If his misbehavior had actually enriched the public treasury, the successor, as the public's steward, was bound to honor claims for restitution. The public, and the king, were forbidden by the law of nature to profit from another's loss.[36]

By the sixteenth century, Baldus' treatment of elective kingship had been gradually extended to successive monarchies as well,[37] and in Bodin's work, the assimilation is unusually bold and clear.[38] Given the prevailing interpretation of the Salic law, theoretical grounds were readily available. Since the kings of France did not acquire office from their predecessors, but were designated by a public law, they could be said to have the same position with respect to contracts as that of an elective king. They could not be bound by an obligation of their predecessors unless it had been contracted for a public purpose or stemmed from enrichment of the treasury.[39]

Curiously enough, the protection of this rule was also extended to ' hereditary ' kingships like the Spanish and the English. At least on this topic – although not, as we have seen, in other contexts [40] – Bodin was willing to treat the usual order of succession in these systems as designations by a customary rule. Hence the only case in which the successor was completely bound was where he had actually received his kingdom by a testament.[41] There was one exception even here. Where a testament existed, and the person named was the designee of custom also, he could claim his title by the latter rule if he saw fit, and escape the obligations of a private heir. Such was the position of Edward VI, Mary, and Elizabeth I of England, all of whom came to the throne by the normal order of succession but had also been named in the testament of their father, Henry VIII. ' In this case ', says Bodin :

We must decide whether the designated heir wishes to accept the state in the capacity of heir or, renouncing the legacy of the testator, wishes to claim the crown by virtue of the custom and law of the land. In the first case the successor is bound by

---

[36] *Consilia sive responsa* (Venice, 1575) III, *cons.* 159, fos 45r–6r; and see also I, *cons.* 271, fos 81v–2r. The ramifications of these two *consilia*, and especially III, 159, are extremely rich. For wider commentary, see Ernst H. Kantorowicz, *The King's Two Bodies* (Princeton, 1957) pp. 398ff.

[37] But as late as the turn of the fifteenth century, Jason de Maino distinguished the rule of Baldus as applying only to elective kingships. Jason, apparently worried by the rule, claims with some relief that it cannot apply to a successive monarch : ' But . . . where kingdoms are transferred by succession, in the sense that the oldest son succeeds to the kingdom, duchy, or county, then, I think that, in so far as it is not incompatible with the general custom, the successor is bound to honor every compact and any agreement whatever just as if he were a private successor.' Commentary on *Digest*, I, 4, I, Jason de Maino, *In Primam Digesti Veteris Partem commentaria* (Venice, 1589) f. 23v.

On the other hand, Baldus himself, at least in the two *consilia* we have mentioned, does not draw the line this sharply, and may have envisaged an extension of the principle.

[38] Unusual in Bodin is his willingness to state, without evasion, that purely personal obligations do not continue. Cf. Rebuffi, comm. on *Digest*, I, I, 31, *Explicatio ad quatuor Pandectarum libros* (1549) (Lyon, 1589), p. 35, and Gregory of Toulouse, *De republica libri sex et viginti* (1596) (Frankfurt, 1609) 7, 20, 39, p. 312.   [39] *République*, I, 8, pp. 159–60 (111–12).

[40] See above, pp. 77–8.   [41] *République*, I, 8, p. 159 (111).

Jean Bodin

the acts and promises of his predecessor, as is any private heir. But in the second case he is not bound to the acts even if he [the predecessor] swore to them. For the predecessor's oath does not bind the successor, but the successor is bound to anything that may have turned to the kingdom's profit.[42]

The ' public' theory of successor obligations was thus extended almost universally. The only problem was to determine which of the predecessor's acts were purely personal, and which were genuinely public. This was not a problem that Bodin took lightly. Although he wanted to protect successors from capricious charges, he was intensely aware that continuity of lawfully contracted obligations was essential to the public credit. Repudiation of debts was sternly disapproved as a means of restoring fiscal solvency.[43]

From this standpoint the test of advantage to the public treasury was obviously too permissive as applied to public contracts. A potential creditor could have little assurance by this rule, since he could never tell, at the time he made a contract, whether it would turn out to the advantage of the treasury or if it did whether it would be so regarded by successor kings. Looked at from the other side, the test of advantage to the public could work a serious hardship on the state. A king who had a need to borrow would be seriously handicapped by his inability to pledge the public faith conclusively.

Either responding to this problem or else attempting to ensure justice for the creditor, Baldus had suggested a procedural solution. If the incumbent, in entering a contract, should specifically declare that he intended his successors to be bound, or that he was acting in the name of the state, he could thereby indicate that his act was being done in his public capacity and that the faith of the public was engaged.[44] There is some indication of a similar notion in Bodin, but, understandably enough, it is not a thought that he pursued. If the incumbent's declaration had always to be taken on its face, the successor could be bound too easily. Later writers would consider the incumbent's words as a presumptive indication of honest and reasonable intent, but would refuse to regard it as absolutely definitive.[45] Bodin achieves a similar result by holding that any engagement is binding on successors if the consequence is not too prejudicial.[46]

There was, however, one alternative which Bodin explores with respect to the validity of treaties. Observing that treaties by the king of France are subject to the same conditions of extinction as any of his other contracts, he holds that these limitations can be overcome if the treaty is publicly ratified:

If, then, the sovereign prince has made an engagement in his capacity as sovereign on a matter that concerns the state and profits it, the successors are bound. And much more are they bound if the agreement (*traicté*) was made with the consent of

---

[42] *Ibid.* p. 159 (112). [43] *Ibid.* VI, 2, p. 896 (676). And see below p. 83.
[44] Baldus, *Consilia*, III, 159, fos 45v–46r.
[45] Thus Grotius, *Law of War and Peace*, II, 14, 12, p. 387, and Pufendorf, *Law of Nature*, VIII, 10, 8, p. 1346. [46] *République*, I, 8, pp. 160–1 (113).

Limitations on Absolute Authority

the Estates, or the principal towns and communities, or the Parlements, or the princes and most eminent nobles. They [the successors] would then be bound even if the agreement (*traicté*) was disadvantageous to the public in view of the [pledged] faith and obligation of the subjects.[47]

Public ratification thus transforms the successors' obligation from a mere obligation not to profit from another's loss, if the agreement should prove advantageous, into one that is fully and strictly contractual. The idea, moreover, was potentially wider in its applications. Although Bodin is thinking mainly, and perhaps exclusively, of treaties, the notion could apply to contracts with a private subject through the usual procedure of verification by the Parlements. Bodin perhaps was using a similar idea when he insisted on public ratification to validate alienations of domain. In both situations the effect of ratification is to debar the successor from refusing to acknowledge the result.

The only difficulty with this solution is to explain the binding effect of public ratification. To say, as Bodin does, that the ' faith and obligation of the subjects ' is entailed might tend to compromise the principle of absolutism. For if the pledge of the public is decisive, it must be entitled to fulfill its obligation even against the wishes of the king. Perhaps Bodin should have said that solemn consultation of the public by the king gives clear indication that he deliberately and responsibly intends to act in his public capacity. The approval of the Estates or other body would be an attestation of this serious intent, and the result would be a modified and closely guarded version of Baldus' suggestion on solemn declarations.

Having thus indicated the rationale and qualifications of Bodin's rule on the obligation of successors, it is well to let him state them for himself:

But if the prince has contracted with a foreigner, or even with a subject on some matter of interest to the public, without the consent of those whom I have mentioned, then if the contract is highly prejudicial to the public, his successor in the state is not bound in any way, and all the less so if he succeeds by right of election. In that case one cannot say that he holds anything by virtue of his predecessor, as would be the case if he had come into the state by way of a gift (*résignation*). But if the acts of his predecessor have turned to the profit of the public, the successor is always bound by them, no matter in what capacity he takes the throne. Otherwise, he would be permitted to derive profit from another's loss by fraud or deviousness, and the commonwealth could perish in its time of need since no one would be willing to give aid, which result is against equity and natural reason.[48]

This passage, taken together with the others we have cited, form a rule of obligation that is designed to give every possible protection to the creditor, short of holding that every obligation of a king is permanently binding. Where

---

[47] *Ibid*. p. 160 (113).

[48] *Ibid*. pp. 160-1 (113). The special reference to elective kingship in this passage is not intended to be juridically restrictive. It is simply language carried over from the Italian civilians from whom Bodin derived his conceptual scheme.

Jean Bodin

ratification has occurred the right of the creditor or holder of alienated domain is fully guaranteed. Even without ratification, the right of the creditor is guaranteed if the result of the agreement was advantageous to the public. Bodin seems also to be suggesting that the contract may be binding on successors even where the outcome was unfavourable, if the engagement was solemnly made and the result was not too prejudicial. In every case, moreover, a lawful engagement is fully binding on the king who undertook it.

At the same time none of these rules (with the slight exception we have mentioned) is incompatible with absolute authority as Bodin understood it. Engagements entered into by incumbents are binding solely through the law of nature and not by consent of the community. Where consent is used to ensure the obligation of successors, it is permissive and corroborative rather than restrictive, and the right corroborated is that of the creditor, not of the community. The successor, finally, is not directly or immediately obligated by any act of the community or even by the act of his predecessor. He is obligated only indirectly by his ' natural ' duty to do justice and maintain the public credit. At no point, therefore, does the public have a right to act against him.

The security of private property against arbitrary seizure by the state, either by expropriation without a lawful pretext, or by taking for a public use without compensation to the owner, was overwhelmingly, if not quite universally, accepted in the civil law tradition. On a very literal reading of the phrase *omnia principis esse* (everything is the prince's) in *Code* 7, 37, 3, some of the glossators had maintained that the Emperor held title to all property. But in the main tradition the standard reply to his interpretation was Seneca's celebrated maxim: ' The king holds everything by public power, but ownership is in the hands of individuals (*omnia rex imperio possidet, singuli dominio*).' [49]

Bodin enthusiastically repeats this maxim as a defining norm of ' royal monarchy ' [50] and then insists that royal monarchy is virtually required by the law of nature. Systems in which the king is truly the proprietor of everything are called lordly or despotic monarchies, and their legitimacy is cast in doubt. [51] In the European tradition, the idea of an ' oriental ' kingship, in which the ruler had legal title to the persons and the possessions of his subjects, had always been treated as inherently uncivilized. [52] According to Bodin, despotic monarchy, like slavery, was a derogation from the law of nature usually arising from an act of conquest. But it was a practice that had occurred so

---

[49] Nicolini, *La proprietá*, pp. 107ff.   [50] *République*, 1, 8, p. 157 (110).

[51] In the *Methodus*, the states thus classified together are distinguished from the other class of monarchies because their rulers are above the law in general. The basis of demarcation has thus been significantly narrowed. See above, pp. 36–7. Bodin now refers to the despotic form as ' seigneurial ', or ' lordly ', to suggest the parallel with ownership of private property. The despotic king ' has ' everything not only by *imperium*, but also by *dominium* as well.

[52] For a succinct and lucid history of the concept of despotism as used by political thinkers from the Greeks to the middle of the nineteenth century, see Melvin Richter, ' The History of the Concept of Despotism ', *Dictionary of the History of Ideas* (forthcoming).

Limitations on Absolute Authority

often and had been accepted by so many peoples that he was not prepared to condemn it absolutely. It had to be regarded as something tolerated by the law of peoples.[53] Yet in admitting its legitimacy, Bodin observes that it is a kind of power that is liable to abuse, and that it is associated with barbaric times or places.

He is thus at pains to show that despotic title is absent in European king-ships, and ought not to be inferred from the formal status of the king as feudal overlord. He is willing to concede that the barbarian invaders of the Roman Empire established some semblance of despotic power. But they did so only partially, since they did not claim all the land, and usually respected the liberty of persons. As manners softened in the course of time, even this limited lordship was formerly restricted:

And it might be said that there is no monarch in Europe who does not claim direct lordship over all his subjects' goods, and that there is no individual who does not acknowledge that he holds his goods of the sovereign prince. But I say that this does not suffice to hold that the monarchy is lordly, in view of the fact that the subject is avowed by the prince as a true proprietor who may dispose of his goods, while the prince had only feudal lordship according to law (*droite seigneurie*). Besides there are many allodial holdings where he has neither property nor feudal lordship according to the law.[54]

Hence in all European kingdoms, there were rights of private property, not excluding possessions held in fief. Where these existed, the right of property could not be taken without violation of the law of nature. The sole exception to this rule, apart from punishments for crime,[55] was the taking of property for public use, where the public need was evident and where compensation was provided or promised. That the individual could be required to yield his property where public necessity demanded, was a well-established doctrine, and Bodin would probably have accepted most of the cases of necessity that were defined in the civil law tradition. Yet he appears reluctant to be too permissive. Only one example of public need is actually mentioned – defeat in war where confiscation of property is necessary in order to conclude a peace. But even then, compensation must be paid the owner, since the public may not profit from a member's loss. This requirement, although common in the juridical tradition, was not unanimous, and Bodin, insisting on this, is aware that he is rejecting opinion to the contrary.[56]

Within certain limits, it was also possible to hold that all these obligations of the ruler could be cited against him in the courts. Access to the courts for suits against the sovereign was a prominent feature of the French tradition to

---

[53] *République*, II, 2, pp. 273–4 (200–1), pp. 278–9 (203–4). On the legitimacy of slavery, which Bodin is even more reluctant to admit, see I, 5.

[54] *Ibid*. II, 2, p. 275 (201–2).

[55] Leaving aside of course such special rights of confiscation as the *droit d'aubaine* by which the inheritance of an unnaturalized foreigner passed to the sovereign. See *ibid*. I, 6, p. 94ff (65f).   [56] *Ibid*. I, 8, p. 157 (109).

Jean Bodin

which Bodin was much attracted. He even says that royal obligations are more rigorously construed in such proceedings than those of ordinary subjects. If the king should fail to answer through his procurators, no delay is granted and the verdict is awarded to the plaintiff. In disputes arising from a royal contract, the performance required of a king is more precise than what would be demanded of a private party, on the grounds that the king should be the exemplar of good faith.[57]

But the power of the courts to examine suits against the king becomes incompatible with absolute authority if carried to its logical extreme, and there are certain limitations on the power that Bodin mentions or implies. The power, to begin with, is a privilege rather than a right, since it is held only on the ruler's sufferance.[58] The king, no doubt, has an inherent obligation to do justice, and is required by the law of nature to grant some sort of hearing, either by himself or by his agents. But he is not required to give a magistrate the power to hear or to decide.

Even where the power is accorded and the verdict goes against the ruler, he is technically able to ignore it with impunity, since his person cannot be constrained. ' [T]he person of the sovereign is always excepted in civil law, no matter what power and authority he gives another; and he never gives so much to anyone, that he does not keep more himself '.[59] Or, to put it in yet another way, the presence of the sovereign utterly extinguishes the power of the magistrate and momentarily returns him to the status of a private person vis-à-vis the ruler.[60] If the verdict of an authorized hearing was defied without good cause, the king would be culpable of tyranny according to the law of nature. But the common law provides no remedy for this infraction.

We turn now to the final and most puzzling of Bodin's limitations, which is his rule on new taxation. In the course of arguing that the kings of England may legislate without consent, he pauses to consider the objection that this would not apply to new taxation:

But someone may say that the Estates [of England] do not suffer any imposition of extraordinary charges or subsidies unless they have been accorded and consented to in Parliament pursuant to the ordinance of Edward I in the great charter [Magna Carta?] by virtue of which the people have always prevailed against the kings. I reply that other kings have no more power than the king of England, because there is not a prince in all the world who has it in his power to levy taxes on subjects at his pleasure, any more than he has the power to take another's property, as Philippe de Commines wisely admonished at the Estates of Tours according to his *Mémoires*. Nevertheless, if the necessity is urgent, the prince should not wait for the Estates to assemble, or for the consent of the people, since

[57] *Ibid.* p. 153 (106–7), p. 158 (111).
[58] *Ibid.* p. 130 (90).
[59] *Ibid.* p. 123 (85).
[60] *Ibid.* p. 127 (88).

Limitations on Absolute Authority

their safety depends on the foresight and diligence of a wise prince. But we will speak of this in its proper place.[61]

Leaving aside for the moment the qualification included in the penultimate sentence of this passage, the basic rule is incompatible with absolute authority, although Bodin of course was not aware of this. He apparently believed that consent to new taxation was no more incompatible with absolutism than consent to alienation of domain or ratification of a treaty or a contract.

But if this was his idea, he was mistaken. In the other situations we have treated, such as alienation of domain, the legal function of consent was to transform provisional arrangements into a permanent obligation binding on successors. Consent to new taxation, on the other hand, would be required for action in the present, and for this reason it violates the principle of absolutism. In this situation the requirement of consent denies the power of a sovereign to act without another's leave, and would thus imply a right of resistance on the part of the community if the procedures of consent were not observed. Nor is this consequence obviated by the fact that a king is not required to wait upon consent in an emergency. Since this is the exception rather than the rule, clear abuse of the emergency provision would also justify resistance.

There was perhaps a deeper inadvertence on Bodin's part that reassured him. He could have thought that the obligation to consult, being based upon the law of nature, was enforceable by God alone and could give no occasion for legitimate resistance. But this solution is equally unworkable. The law of nature, as Bodin habitually interprets it, is confined to substantive requirements, and from a substantive standpoint the most that could be said about taxes is that the king is forbidden to impose them unless there is a public need.[62] Hence procedures of consent would not derive directly from the law of nature. They would have to follow from an inherent right of the community independently established by history and custom.

This conclusion can also be looked at from another angle. If consent to taxation were indeed required by the law of nature, Bodin's entire position would be undermined. Since the test of a legitimate tax is the existence of a public need, the right of consent in the community is a right of determining that need. But according to the law of nature, the existence of a proper public need is one test for any act of government, and especially an act of legislation. Hence, the rule of consent to new taxation would have to be extended universally.

On the question of taxation, therefore, Bodin was inconsistent, and it is an especially surprising inconsistency since he went out of his way, as it were, to introduce it. The idea of consent to new taxation was not so emphatic in the

---

[61] *Ibid.* p. 140 (96–7). The passage is partly inspired by Comines, *Mémoires*, J. Calmette and G. Durville eds., 3 vols (Paris, 1965) II, pp. 217ff (v, ch. 19).

[62] This, of course, is the traditional view of the civilians. See, for example, the opinion of Bartolus quoted in Carlyle and Carlyle, *Medieval Political Theory*, VI, p. 77.

Jean Bodin

French tradition that Bodin had special need to depart from his absolutist doctrine in order to acknowledge it. In medieval thought the basic attitude toward royal taxes was that they should not exist at all, since, in principle at least, the king was expected to live upon his own. Where new taxation was required for abnormal purposes, the need for consent was assumed and often stated.[63] But this idea had never been given the degree of institutional embodiment it was destined to receive in England. There was no clear parallel in France to a national body like the English Parliament, which habitually granted new taxation and insisted on that privilege as one condition for the perpetuation of its other powers. The Parlement of Paris had rarely attempted to assume that role, and the French Estates had never had the unity and continuity to explore that course persistently.

The French constitutionalist tradition, therefore, had not put special emphasis on consent to new taxation.[64] Insofar as consent was understood as a requirement, it was a mere implication of consent to legislation generally. Ironically enough, this failure to distinguish taxation as a special issue was also characteristic of Bodin's earlier work. At one point in the *Methodus* he considers, but tentatively rejects, the proposition that the power to tax is a prerogative of sovereignty.[65] But this has nothing to do with any special insistence on consent. It is simply a hesitant concession, later taken back,[66] that the ruler's power of taxation may be shared with other magistrates and local corporations. The question of consent is never taken up specifically.

In the *République*, accordingly, Bodin could have treated the levying of taxes like any other act of legislation. He could have said that consent was desirable and usual, but was not constitutionally required. And he could have supported this position by pointing to many exceptions from consent in France – and in England too, no doubt, had he seriously attempted to discover instances. We must assume, accordingly, that his insistence on consent to new taxation was the result of strong political motivations of a special sort.

Before attempting to explain this purpose, one other *caveat* seems useful. Bodin's motivations would not be correctly understood if constitutionalist objectives are imputed. Taken out of context, his rule of consent to new taxation might seem to intend a far-reaching role for the Estates. It might seem to envisage the use of this right by the Estates to extract institutional

---

[63] Comines, *Mémoires*, v, 19.

[64] Even in the Huguenots, it has no special prominence. The *Francogallia* barely touches on it, and *Vindiciae contra tyrannos* is brief. See Franklin, *Constitutionalism and Resistance*, pp. 60, 76.

[65] *Methodus*, p. 175 (173).

[66] *République*, I, 10, p. 244 (177). Bodin now says that taxes may be imposed and repealed by the sovereign ' alone '. But this is not incompatible with the requirement of consent in I, 8, p. 140 (96–7) and elsewhere. ' Alone ' in this context means to the exclusion of other magistrates. The king ' alone ' could ask the Estates for permission to enact. The verbal difficulties here will exemplify the kind of caution needed in reading ' absolutist ' statements dating from this period.

Limitations on Absolute Authority

concessions. This interpretation of his motives might seem to be corroborated by Bodin's own behavior at the Estates of Blois. It would thus appear that he was after all a secret constitutionalist. For, in view of the chronic imbalance of the royal budget and the near exhaustion of public credit, the government had become increasingly dependent upon new taxation. The crown, in a period of weakness, had been forced to assemble the Estates, and at each of the assemblies between 1560 and 1576 the Estates had attempted to make use of their financial leverage to encroach upon the crown's prerogatives. Bodin, in insisting on consent to new taxation, might thus appear to be endorsing such attempts.

But this appearance is misleading. The truth rather is that Bodin's purposes were purely fiscal and were utterly innocent of any grand constitutional design.[67] We have seen that he, like most contemporaries, was fully convinced that the king could and should live of his own – that the income from domain, in other words, was potentially sufficient to defray the costs of government. According to a recent reckoning, almost the entire domain had already been rented at a mere fraction of its market value. Had the rents been realistic, the yield, according to Bodin, would be 3,000,000 *livres* annually, which was enough not only to maintain the royal household but to pay the salaries of public officers without dipping into the return from ordinary and extraordinary imposts.[68] It followed, therefore, that the only sensible solution to the existing fiscal crisis was to redeem the domain by paying compensation to its holders, and to re-rent it at profitable levels and with adequate safeguards. To gather money for repurchase some new taxation might be needed, but almost everything could be accomplished by better management of the income from existing sources. If the king abstained from lavish gifts to favorites, suppressed unnecessary offices, and removed inefficiency and corruption in collections of his income,[69] funds could be accumulated for redemption of the crown's domain, and the burden of taxation, far from being raised, could be gradually reduced.[70]

These calculations were surely much too optimistic, but Bodin was probably right in his beliefs that without a solution of this sort the monarchy was ultimately doomed. It seemed to him that the burden of taxation was already intolerably high and utterly absurd, especially when measured by the English level. Were the burden to be raised still higher, rebellion must result. In his chapter on finances the king is constantly reminded that revolutions are more frequently caused by high taxation than by any other grievance.

[67] A fine treatment of Bodin's political and economic objectives, which also surveys previous attempts to explain the contradiction in his thought, is Martin Wolfe, ' Jean Bodin on Taxes: The Sovereignty-Taxes Paradox ', *Political Science Quarterly*, LXXXIII, no. 2, June 1968, pp. 268–84.

[68] *République*, VI, 2, pp. 862–3 (654).

[69] *Ibid*. pp. 901 (679), 903–5 (681–2), 908–9 (684).   [70] *Ibid*. p. 882 (666).

Jean Bodin

We may thus assume that Bodin's insistence on consent was designed to make new taxation as difficult as possible without excluding it entirely. Since new taxation might be needed temporarily to redeem the crown domain, and might otherwise be necessary in a time of dire need, Bodin is bound to acknowledge its legitimacy. But in view of the attendant dangers, he wishes to make sure that the power will not be used too frequently. Hence he introduces the consent of the Estates as a limiting condition. Since the Estates were notoriously hostile to taxation, they would not be likely to indulge a king's requests unless the need was evident and taxation was the only remedy.[71]

The rule of consent to new taxation was therefore intended as a kind of ' fundamental ' and quasi-automatic limitation on the fiscal power of the state itself. Bodin did not anticipate that the Estates would use the right to bind the power of the king in other areas of public policy and thus alter the institutional relationships on which absolute authority was founded. From this perspective, consent to new taxation could well have seemed to be consistent with his general constitutional conception.

In certain situations, as Bodin probably knew, the powers of consent could have an indirect effect on royal policy. One consequence of his tenacious and successful resistance to grants of new taxation at the Estates of Blois, and to alienations of domain, was to make war against the Huguenots more difficult. He was surely cognizant of this connection, and could hardly have been disapproving. But at no point was he prepared to countenance the use of fiscal leverage, or of any other resource of the Estates, to enhance their institutional position, even though an opportunity was offered that led, or seemed to lead, in this direction.

Almost from the very beginning of the Estates of Blois, proposals had been made for participation by the Estates in the preparation of the royal ordinance which the king, in accordance with tradition, would issue in answer to the *cahiers* and which would not be published until after the Estates had been dissolved. Among other features of the scheme was the appointment of a commission of thirty-six deputies, twelve from each of the three Estates, to collaborate with the Privy Council in passing judgment on the *cahiers*. Henry III, eager to gain support for subsidies, evasively agreed to go along.[72]

---

[71] Commenting on the ruinous consequences of public distributions in ancient republics, Bodin observes : ' That does not occur in a monarchy, since monarchs – who have no revenue more assured than that from the domain, and who have no right to tax their subjects without consent except in cases of urgent necessity – are not so prodigal with their domain.' *Ibid.* p. 863 (655).

[72] Jean Bodin, *Recueil de tout ce qui s'est négocié en la compagnie du tiers-état de France en l'assemblée générale des trois états, assigné par le roi en la ville de Blois au 15 novembre 1576*, in C.-H. Mayer; *Des États généraux et autres assemblées nationales* (Paris and The Hague, 1788) xiii (pp. 212–328), p. 223. Henry would have limited the commissioners to a purely advisory role, and he also rejected the proposal that all grievances unanimously accepted by all three of the Estates should be adopted automatically.

Limitations on Absolute Authority

Bodin, however, was bitterly and adamantly opposed. Much of his concern was immediately political. He feared that the twelve deputies chosen from the Third – in a weak minority position – would be tempted to concede too much and might even approve alienations of domain. Where, moreover, the grievances of the Third were directed against the other two Estates, he evidently expected that the Third would be more likely to get satisfaction if the king alone passed judgment than if the points of difference were submitted to a joint commission.[73] But he also argued that the absolute power of the sovereign, which he takes to be a given, would turn the joint commission into a cruel and dangerous illusion. The king, he implied, might use the commission to advance his own designs. But the commission would be unable to control the king, since the sovereign, having absolute authority, could treat its advice as he saw fit.[74]

Hence Bodin's opposition as a deputy at Blois was devoid of constitutionalist intentions.[75] Although he boldly championed the right of the Estates to withhold requested subsidies, he never challenged the absolute power of the ruler in any other area of public policy. The purpose of his opposition was simply to protect the Third Estate from an unnecessary increase in the burden of taxation, and also to deter the king himself from a course of fiscal and religious policy that he believed to be politically disastrous.

Thus understood, Bodin's insistence on consent was apparently consistent with his desire for a strong and independent kingship. If he failed to see legal inconsistency, it was very likely because he could not think of new taxation as an ordinary function of the state. It seemed so abnormal and perverse to him that he could not assimilate it to the kinds of powers that monarchs properly exerted. Hence in requiring consent to new taxation he ignored the larger implication.

But this larger implication was quickly noticed by his near contemporaries whose doctrine of the state was broadly similar. In Gregory of Toulouse and William Barclay, consent to new taxation is reduced to a prudential maxim.[76] The ruler is earnestly reminded that consultation of the Estates is the course of wisdom and decency. But he is also told that, in principle at least, he is free to levy taxes on his own determination of the public need. It is this interpre-

---

73 Owen Ulph, ' Jean Bodin and the Estates-General of 1576 ', *Journal of Modern History*, XIX, no. 4, December 1947 (pp. 289–96), pp. 295–6.

74 *Recueil*, pp. 277–80.

75 On two occasions [*République*, I, 8, p. 140 (97), III, 7, p. 501 (384)] Bodin remarks, incidentally, that the English Parliament usually meets more frequently than the Estates of other countries because the rule of consent to new taxation is there so well observed. It is just barely possible that he felt that emphasis on this rule for France would lead to a similar result, which he regarded as desirable (see below, p. 101). But beyond this he gives no indication of any political objective, and he would not have thought that more frequent Estates assemblies would alter the institutional relationships of king and Estates.

76 Claude Collot, *L'École doctrinale de droit public de Pont-à-Mousson* (Paris, 1965) p. 179.

Jean Bodin

tation, rather than Bodin's, which was to become the standard opinion among legal commentators of the seventeenth century. In Charles Loyseau, for instance, Bodin's view is carefully excluded.[77]

Overall, however, Bodin's position was consistent. With the one exception of consent to new taxation, he admitted no limitation on the sovereign which the community could be entitled to enforce. He anticipated some situations in which the act of an incumbent, done without consent, would not be binding on successors. But even then, the act of the community was corroborative rather than preventive.

At the same time, the incumbent ruler had full and sole possession of all the powers that were ordinarily required for conduct of his government. In some situations – like the alienation of domain in time of war, or the levying of taxes for emergencies – his capacity to act would be enhanced by community support. But in Bodin's view at least, these exceptions were narrowly defined, and applied only to extraordinary situations.

This, then, is what he meant by absolute authority. An absolute king had full possession of all the powers that a state could legitimately exercise, and even if he overstepped the bounds of higher law, he could not be lawfully resisted or deposed.

[77] Charles Loyseau, *Traité des Seigneuries* (1610) ch. 3, pp. 14, 16, in *Oeuvres* (Lyon, 1701). This is a revised version of the first edition (1608) in which Loyseau was still somewhat hesitant. See Myron P. Gilmore, ' Authority and Property in the Seventeenth Century: the First Edition of the *Traité des Seigneuries* of Charles Loyseau ', *Harvard Library Bulletin*, IV (1950) no. 2 (pp. 258–65) p. 260.

Part III
Political Economy

[8]

Jean Bodin on Taxes:
The Sovereignty-Taxes Paradox*

MARTIN WOLFE
University of Pennsylvania

What did Jean Bodin really intend to accomplish in writing his masterwork, the *Six Books on the Republic?* Several facets of this problem are still being debated by specialists in the history of political thought, but most would agree that his main purpose was to demonstrate that strong monarchy is the best of all forms of government, and that monarchy functions best when there are no limitations on the king's law-making functions except the king's own recognition of the guides imposed by natural and divine law. Bodin was the first to see clearly that the essence of a state is its sovereign power, and that sovereignty, while possessing many attributes, is most clearly marked off by the ability to "impose laws generally on all subjects regardless of their consent." Does this include the power to raise taxes on the monarch's own authority? Apparently not, though Bodin definitely names the taxing process as one of the aspects of "making and unmaking law"[1] and therefore as one of the "unique attributes of sovereign power"; and he emphatically denies the power to tax to all but the king. In an often-quoted passage, however, Bodin lays down the rule that "it is not within the competence of any prince in the world to levy taxes at will on his people," and he admits that parliaments must be allowed to "agree and consent" to all "extraordinary taxes or subsidies," by which he means any revenues

---

* Parts of this paper were read to the Middle Atlantic Conference of the Renaissance Society of America at the University of Delaware, Oct. 29, 1966.
[1] *Les six liures de la Republique de I. Bodin Angevin* (Paris, 1580), 223.

beyond the crown's traditional and patrimonial income. Here and in other passages where Bodin discusses the fiscal system it is clear that he does indeed believe that laws passed for the purpose of increasing the burden of taxes or even for continuing previous taxes must be subject to the consent of the Estates-General and of other representative institutions.[2]

Several scholars have tried their hand at explaining Bodin on taxes. Beatrice Reynolds feels that his apparently contradictory views demonstrate an extremely important fact about his general philosophy: that for all his emphasis on integral sovereignty Bodin was at heart a proponent of limited monarchy.[3] Roger Chauviré's position is that Bodin believes an Estates-General by its very nature to be respectful and loyal, unlikely ever to refuse the king anything within reason.[4] M. J. Tooley holds that for Bodin the state exists to provide a proper moral climate as well as to furnish the machinery for efficient government; since taxation can be used as an instrument for moral discipline it is proper for the king to resort to extraordinary imposts (especially on luxuries), though presumably these as well as other taxes had to be subject to approval by the Estates.[5] Friedrich Meinecke holds that there is no inconsistency here in Bodin's theory, since Bodin does allow the king the power to raise money on his own authority in an emergency.[6] In William Church's important work on Renaissance constitutional thought the point is made that Bodin extracted taxation from the sphere of sovereign power because taxation affects property rights and property rests on natural law, not human law.[7] J. W. Allen suggests that Bodin on taxes simply is inconsistent with Bodin on sovereignty.[8]

[2] *Republique*, 140, 244-45.

[3] Beatrice Reynolds, *Proponents of Limited Monarchy in Sixteenth Century France: Francis Hotman and Jean Bodin* (New York, 1931), 176, 185-86, 199-200.

[4] Roger Chauviré, *Jean Bodin, auteur de la 'République'* (Paris, 1914), 447-48.

[5] M. J. Tooley, *Six Books on the Commonwealth, by Jean Bodin* (New York, 1955), xxi, xxxvi-xxxviii.

[6] Friedrich Meinecke, *Machiavellism: The Doctrine of Raison d'Etat and its Place in Modern History* (London, 1957), 58.

[7] William F. Church, *Constitutional Thought in Sixteenth-Century France* (Cambridge, Mass., 1941), 234-37. See, also, Henri Baudrillart, *J. Bodin et son temps* (Paris, 1853), 274-75.

[8] J. W. Allen, *A History of Political Thought in the Sixteenth Century* (London, 1928), 419-21. For a more general discussion of internal contradic

I would like to present another view for consideration. There is indeed a contradiction in the theoretical components of his ideal state, but Bodin had another purpose than discovering the universal rules of government and formulating them in a consistent fashion. In writing on taxes especially, Bodin's main aim was to convince the crown that substantial reforms in the fiscal system were desperately needed in order to keep the country from being destroyed by the religious wars.

For our purpose it is important to emphasize that Bodin was more than a detached philosopher. In 1571, when he was already well known as the author of several works on jurisprudence as well as the famous *Method for the Easy Comprehension of History* (1566) and the even more renowned economics treatise, *Reply of Master Jean Bodin . . . to the Paradox of Monsieur de Malestroict* (1568), he took a post as privy counselor to the duke d'Alençon, a younger brother of the king. Alençon at the time was being courted enthusiastically by the moderate faction in France, a group later known as *politiques,* whose position can be defined roughly by stating that they believed national security and internal order to be more important than crushing the Huguenots and restoring France to one faith. A known moderate, Bodin narrowly escaped being butchered in the St. Bartholomew's Eve massacre of 1572.[9] Bodin's standing in court circles improved in 1574 when Henry III came to the throne; whatever else may be said about him, Henry III appreciated brains and intellectual courage. We know that on a few occasions the king invited Bodin to dine with him and to discuss problems of philosophy. Bodin enjoyed the high regard of many of his countrymen, too. In 1576, the year the *Republic* was published, he was elected a deputy to the crucially important Estates-General at Blois and played a major role there in the debate over taxes; in fact, for part of these meetings he functioned as *président* (speaker) for the Third Estate.[10] On this occasion he strongly resisted the crown's demand that the Estates-

---

tions in the political theory of the *Republic,* see George Sabine, *A History of Political Thought* (New York, 3d ed., 1961), Chap. XX.

[9] Chauviré, 35 and n. 3.

[10] *Relation iournaliere de tout ce qui s'est negotié en l'Assemblée Generale des Estats . . . en . . . Blois . . . de M. I. Bodin . . .* (Paris, 1614), 20 r°; 24 v°-25 r°; 31 r°; 40 r°.

General support the king's attempt to raise more revenues; this may have cost him further advancement.[11] He remained an adviser to Alençon, however, and accompanied him on a voyage to England at the time the duke was engaged in an elephantine flirtation with Queen Elizabeth I. Though the door to royal advancement was shut to him, Bodin continued to share with the king the conviction that strong monarchical government must be preserved and that it could be preserved if only the right formula could be found to keep the country's disruptive forces in check.

Six Books on the Republic attracted an enormous amount of attention when it appeared; it was published in no less than eleven editions in French, three in Latin, and one each in Italian, Spanish, and German, all while Bodin was still alive.[12] We know it had a crucial role in laying the foundations for the discipline of political science, just as his earlier *Reply to . . . Monsieur de Malestroict* heralded the birth of the sort of reasoning we call political economy. Though Bodin has a good deal to say on taxes, however, no one has ever claimed him as a founder of the science of public finance. The reason is all too obvious. Bodin's concept of how a well-managed fiscal system should operate seems curiously backward, and some of his proposals for reforming the French tax machine of his time seem strangely out of touch with reality.

I

Reference to taxes and suggestions for fiscal reform are scattered throughout the *Republic,* but the first three chapters of Book VI obviously constitute what Bodin regards as his important statement on public finance, here or in any of his writings. These three chapters, though, are quite different one from the other in scope and goal. The first is a quaint attempt to show that tax reform might be combined with a basic state-directed improvement in private morals, through establishing a censor in, as Bodin believed, the ancient tradition. The third chapter is a sort of addendum to Bodin's great work on price fluctuations and money, the *Reply . . . to Monsieur de Malestroict.* It demonstrates in a forceful way

---

[11] *Ibid.,* 21 v°-23 r°; 38 v°-39 r°. See also Chauviré, 66-68. In editions of the *Republic* after 1577, Bodin refers to this: in the 1580 edition, 485-86.
[12] See the list in Chauviré, 517-18.

the social and political as well as the economic evils of debasing money.[13]

Chapter 2 of Book VI, "On Public Finances," is Bodin's most important fiscal work for its arguments and for its relative length —in the 1580 edition it takes up fifty-eight of 1,060 pages. He begins this chapter by explaining that he is not concerned with the whole sphere of taxation, but only with "honest" revenues. There are plenty of "great experts on tax affairs," he says sarcastically, who know all there is to know concerning gouging money from the people in every conceivable manner. But Bodin is more interested, he says, in the common weal than in expediency. There follows a most surprising listing of what he calls "the seven sources of revenues which include all the possible sources that one can well imagine."[14] Item one is the royal traditional and patrimonial income, the *domaines* (that is, the crown's own rents, fines, seigneurial fees, and tolls); these Bodin emphatically regards as the most legal or "honest" source of funds, and he drags up massive humanist artillery to prove how, from the ancient Hebrews on, in well-ordered states part of the ruler's income had always been set aside to satisfy the needs of government. Items two through five strike us as hardly worth mentioning; he discusses income obtained through foreign conquest, through gifts from friends, by pensions from allies, and by the prince himself engaging in commerce. Tariffs he lists as revenue item number six; and *all* the main imposts on France, both direct and indirect—the *tailles*, excises, salt taxes, clerical tenths, and so on—are lumped together as item number seven.[15]

What is Bodin's purpose in presenting such a bizarre categorization? When he solemnly informs us that great kings of ancient Persia often lived from "voluntary presents," is he seriously suggesting that this is possible in late sixteenth-century France?[16]

---

[13] Beatrice Reynolds points to another contradiction in the theory of the ideal state here; in Book VI, Chap. 3, Bodin wants "the value and weight of money [to] be fixed, by means so secure that neither prince nor subject could alter it, even if he wished," while in Book I, Bodin places coinage among the attributes of sovereignty. *Proponents*, 169, 172.

[14] *Republique*, 856 ff.

[15] But in another place, p. 879, Bodin has the *tailles* as "ordinary." However, in this connection he seems to mean "ordinary" in that they were regular or annual, in contrast to "casual," that is, taxes raised only occasionally.

[16] *Republique*, 869.

Does he really expect the haughty kings of France to go into trade?[17] Do we have here merely a scholastic attempt to be exhaustive? Or (and this seems more likely) is Bodin suggesting that, since the crown has seven sources of income, it is feasible to reduce or even abolish the most bothersome of them, that is, the chief imposts? If this is correct, it is a rather unrealistic device, since all persons with some understanding of the realities of royal revenues (and this includes Bodin, who tells us himself that he was given access at times to the records of the Chambre des comptes)[18] certainly understood that the chief imposts in this era made up between two-thirds and four-fifths of royal income.[19]

Another element of an old-fashioned outlook on taxes in Bodin is his passionate opposition to any form of usury—so much so that he demands that the state refrain from borrowing at interest, no matter how reasonable the rate.[20] Again, writing in the hectic and expensive early years of Henry III's reign, he presumes to suggest that current deficits could be met in large part by increasing fines on wrong-doing—with the additional advantage, according to him, of raising the moral tone of the nation.[21] Perhaps with tongue in cheek, he advises the crown to tax judicial trials in order to dampen the enthusiasm of the French for suing each other.

Is it possible that such a keen observer could not understand that the modern state—that entity to the definition of which he contributed so much—was so vastly expensive to operate that it could never get along on the tiny and erratic resources he allowed it? Perhaps he could, but in fact he goes to considerable lengths to give the contrary impression. A large portion of Chapter 2, Book VI, "On Public Finances"—twelve pages out of fifty-eight —is taken up with arguing that the royal *domaines* could, with proper management, support not only the royal household but

---

[17] *Ibid.*, 873-74, 892.

[18] *Ibid.*, 905, 911. See, also, Beatrice Reynolds, *Method for the Easy Comprehension of History*, by John Bodin (New York, 1945), 256-57.

[19] J. J. Clamageran, *Histoire de l'impôt en France*, 3 Vols. (Paris, 1867-76), II, 196-98, 244. And see Bodin's own contemptuous treatment of those so impractical as to dream of cutting back revenues to the days of Louis XII (around 1500): *Republique*, 882-83.

[20] *Republique*, 893 ff. See, also, Paul Nancey, *Jean Bodin, économiste* (Bordeaux, 1942), 239-44.

[21] *Republique*, 887-89; see, also, 840.

also all the legitimate expenses of government, at least in normal years.[22] Bodin recognizes that virtually all the *domaines* had been sold off to meet past emergencies or to satisfy the demands of greedy courtiers; but his reaction to this situation was to complain that such grants had been illegal, since the *domaines* are not the crown's property to sell or give away; they are, so to speak, brought by the nation to the prince at the time of the coronation ceremony "like a dowry to a husband" to pay for both court expenses and "la chose publique."[23] Bodin brings up here some decidedly unconvincing figures to support his contention that if these traditional and proprietary revenues were all purchased back by the crown and handled in a businesslike fasion they would remove the need for taxation.

It is certainly true that in order to understand Bodin on taxes one must appreciate his position on the role of private property in society. This position is developed not in Book VI, but in earlier chapters on the family, property, and sovereignty. For Bodin, property rights are the glue that holds a successful commonwealth together. The middle ages viewed commonwealths as networks of mutual obligations and rights, networks formed by individuals and groups such as guilds, towns, and even larger associations like Estates, for their own protection and profit. But for Bodin a commonwealth is not an association of individuals or of these larger groups, but of households. Bodin sees the family as a "natural" unit; it existed before the first state and will outlast any and all of them. Therefore the family and things that nourish it belong to the area of natural law, not to be touched by any mortal, even the sovereign himself.

And it is property and property alone, according to Bodin, that binds the family together. It is his control over property that enables the head of the family to feed, clothe, and shelter the individuals in his family; and the father's ability to withhold sustenance from unworthy persons in the family is society's best deterrent against crime and immorality. This means that private property is not so much an institution in society as its very foun-

---

[22] Bodin apologizes here for not writing even more on the *domaines* and refers to a large and valuable recent work on the subject by his friend René Choppin.

[23] *Republique*, 859, 863.

dation. Since a commonwealth is a government over families, undermining property rights is, in effect, destroying the state. It follows
that private property cannot be taken by the state except through
carefully-defined legal processes or by the freely given consent of the
owners. Appropriating property through arbitrary taxation, therefore, is illegal; and when a sovereign relies on this form of income
he is in effect working for his own downfall. The power to tax is
indeed the power to destroy—to destroy the whole commonwealth.

When the king is moved by "urgent necessity" to ask his subjects for part of their property, therefore, he bears an awesome responsibility. In recognition of the seriousness of such a step he
must consult the peoples' representatives in local or national assemblies. Bodin carefully explains that the use of such parliaments
in no way reduces the powers of the ruler; rather, sovereign power
is enhanced when the people voluntarily associate themselves with
it. The ruler of England, for example, is no less sovereign when
he asks his parliament for tax grants.[24]

Bodin does not take up the problem of "the power of the purse
strings," by which parliaments can use their control over taxes to
force favors from the crown and so increase their powers in other,
non-fiscal areas, thereby still further reducing the exclusive sovereignty of the monarch. Bodin does recognize, however, that such
a phenomenon exists; and (in his section on how the king, though
above laws, must honor contracts to which he is a party) he comments on the fact that in Castile the crown has made concessions
to the Cortes in order to obtain tax grants. Even more disturbing is
the problem of what is to happen when a parliament refuses outright the crown's demand for more revenues. Bodin never really
faces up to such a shattering dilemma, but he must have realized
that long before his time the French state had reached the point
where stopping the flow of income from the chief imposts for
even a few months would have brought collapse. Unless Bodin's
ideal state is to have no relevance to the real world, it cannot have
both a monarch as sovereign as Bodin says he must be and a parliament participating in the levying of taxes.[25]

[24] *Ibid.*, 139-40. See, also, Church, 235 and n. 114; Philip Dur, "The Right
of Taxation in the Political Theory of the French Religious Wars," *Journal
of Modern History*, XVII (1945), 297.

[25] In Book I, Chap. 10, Bodin says, "If the prince can only make law with
the consent of a superior he is a subject; if of an equal he shares his sover-

It seems clear that Bodin did not want what we think of as a
limited monarchy. At one point he states emphatically that "When
edicts are ratified by Estates or parliaments, it is for the purpose
of obtaining obedience to them, and not because otherwise a sovereign prince could not validly make law."[26] Bodin specifically
rejects the radical notion, then coming into some prominence, that
sovereign power is derived from the people, who implicitly or
explicitly delegate it to the king. He denies that "consent plays
any part whatsoever in the obligations to obey." Bodin's king
must be the unique possessor of indivisible power; Bodin is fond
of saying that a sovereign prince who is subject to check by a
parliament is neither prince nor sovereign. Internal consistency in
political theory on sovereignty and taxation, therefore, is impossible for Bodin, except in the meaningless cases where a ruler
can truly manage on his domainial revenues only, or where a parliament automatically grants every request for imposts. Bodin's
own time provided many examples of parliaments which refused
to grant funds that rulers claimed they needed. And we have seen
that in 1576 Bodin himself was instrumental in the rejection by
the Estates-General at Blois of demands for a tax grant by Henry
III.

When an emergency prevents the crown from taking the time
to convene his parliament, of course, the king must take imposts
first and ask later; for, as Bodin has "a Roman senator of ancient
times" say, "nothing is more just than that which is necessary."[27]
But emergency levies imposed without consent do not bind the
community once the emergency is past.[28] Since the *tailles*, excises,
and salt taxes currently being collected had not been granted to
the crown in the recent past, it follows that they are illegal and
should be wiped out as soon as possible. Interpreted literally, this
position seems impossibly far-fetched, even for the most mor-
alistic of political philosophers.

Bodin's "model" of the government he prefers is not a purely
imaginary affair, a utopia. His state is derived from observations

eignty; if of an inferior, whether it be a council of magnates or of the people,
it is not he who is sovereign."

[26] *Republique*, 140.

[27] *Ibid.*, 863, 876, 895.

[28] *Ibid.*, 880, 882.

of the actual functioning and the real problems of states in his own day and in the past.[29] Though the real world contained no actual and complete example of his ideal state, he attempts to convince his readers of the validity of his views by furnishing them with intellectually defensible proof that the components of his "model" are feasible in the sense that if translated from the plane of theory to that of reality they would indeed provide optimum government. Let us admit that in this sense the fiscal aspects of Bodin's "model" are a failure, since they lead to important internal inconsistencies.

II

What remains to be discussed is whether these inconsistencies were simply an error, a mistake Bodin failed to notice or possibly never bothered to correct, or if Bodin had some other purpose in taking such a position on the taxing process. Whether Bodin understood that his views on taxing and sovereignty involve contradictions is a matter we probably never shall resolve. But it may well be that the limitations Bodin imposes on sovereignty when he discusses property and popular assemblies in his ideal state are quite consistent *in purpose* with the policies he urges on the crown in the chapters on public finance. If Bodin's larger goal in writing the *Republic* was not to be consistent, but "to find out the secret of stability in a politically unstable world" (M. J. Tooley), his statement that the Estates-General must participate in the taxing process makes some sense. Furthermore, when we look at Bodin on taxes from this point of view the details of his notions on how a fiscal system should operate seem less naïve. Bodin probably intended his observations on the taxing process in an ideal state to stand as a warning to Henry III that not only were the French dangerously antagonistic to his rule, but that, so far as tax grievances were concerned, they had every right to feel that way. Therefore the crown should embark on a program of tax reform not only because it would be correct politically, but also because it would be sound morally, or, if one prefers, "constitutionally."

By 1576 the Wars of Religion had divided France so badly that

[29] See the first chapter of Book I: "At the same time I do not want to sketch out an abstract and non-existent commonwealth, such as those imagined by Plato and Thomas More, the chancellor of England."

large sections of the country had cut themselves off from control by the crown and were being run by Huguenot assemblies and nobles; other provinces were under the effective control of Catholic war lords. While the crown remained weak, it seemed that some radical Huguenots would continue to build little Genevas all through France, and some Catholic zealots would continue to proclaim that they would never rest until the last ember of heresy was stamped out. It seems safe to conjecture that Bodin's most important concern at this time was not the development of internally consistent theories of government, but helping to preserve a strong and centralized monarchy in France.

As yet neither of the extreme factions had won over the great mass of Frenchmen, still mainly uncommitted or simply politically inert. This was the strength of the *politique* position. If the moderates remained convinced that strong monarchy was the best government, if the uncommitted masses were not goaded into supporting the malcontents, effective authority could be returned to the king's hands. As a patriotic and sensitive Frenchman, deeply worried about the safety and happiness of his country, what could Bodin do? As he says in the dedication of the 1580 edition of the *Republic,*

> Since the conservation of kingdoms and empires and of all peoples rests after God on good princes and wise rulers . . . everyone should aid them, by supporting their power, by carrying out their holy laws [and] by influencing their subjects by works and writings that add to the common weal of all in general and each in particular.

A successful king has to be a strong king; however, particularly in the crisis of the fifteen-seventies, the very existence of the monarchy depended on the king's being accepted as the good head of the best kind of government by his subjects, no matter what their religious beliefs or local loyalties. Taxing away property, as we have seen, was regarded by Bodin as an attack on the very foundations of the state. But Bodin could see that the breaking-point would come long before these foundations were eaten away through appropriation of so much private substance that families could no longer actually function. He must have known that what the king had to fear was not so much that taxes were in fact destroying

family strength and wealth as that families *believed* this dreadful
situation was being brought to pass. The mechanism of breakdown, in other words, would be not economic but political, not
bankruptcy but sedition.

If the records of the past teach us anything, Bodin says, it is
that "one cannot find more frequent upsets, seditions, and ruins
of commonwealths than because of excessive tax burdens and imposts."[30] And he proceeds to prove his point by listing a large
number of such disturbances, from ancient Corinth on. The king
must realize how disturbed people become over what they regard as
unjust taxing and profligate spending by the crown. Even in up-
risings where burdensome taxes are not a direct and obvious
cause, revolutions always "strip away all imposts, *tailles*, and subsidies as a sign of liberty."[31]

One of the greatest dangers facing a "prince exacteur," says
Bodin, is that by taxing everything in sight he is in danger of
acquiring a reputation as a tyrant.[32] Bodin refers here to what
must have been one of the more cherished stories about taxation
in the sixteenth century. Once the great emperor Vespasian, mull-
ing over new means of filling his treasury, hit on the scheme of
taxing the use of public urinals in Rome. His son Titus found
this to be a churlish sort of fiscal device, and let Vespasian know
it. Vespasian is supposed to have answered by thrusting under
Titus' nose a handful of coins obtained in this way, with the comment that while urinals might smell, money did not.[33] The modern
French, and presumably some of the Renaissance French, too,
would say the meaning of the story is that *l'argent n'a pas d'odeur*
("there is no such thing as tainted money"); but Bodin draws
from it a different moral. To him it demonstrates that there was
only a fine line between a "prince exacteur" and a ruler resented as
a tyrant.

[30] *Republique*, 881 f.

[31] *Ibid.*, 886.

[32] See also Book I, Chaps. 3 and 4, where in several places Bodin has as
one of the characteristics of tyranny "heavy taxes and imposts."

[33] *Republique*, 897. Another version is that rather than taxing the urinals,
Vespasian forced the public to use them, so he could sell the urine de-
posits to fullers and dyers. See R. L. La Barre, *Formulaire des esleuz* (Rouen.
1622), 392.

III

Some of Bodin's most biting comments are reserved for princes who use the stupid and harmful expedient of raising money by selling offices. Kings who sell positions in the judiciary, especially, are to be blamed for auctioning off something priceless, namely, justice. "They sell the commonwealth, they sell the blood of its subjects, they sell the laws." Kings who create and sell posts in the fiscal bureaucracy expose their subjects to vampires who think of nothing but gain. "It must be stated bluntly," says Bodin, "that the people are fed up with the petty thievery of such officials."[34]

A standard trick of tyrants, Bodin claims, is to attempt to turn wrath away from themselves by stirring up jealousies and antagonisms among the various interests in the nation. Thus the clergy and nobility in France always have been given tax concessions so that they do not side with the people on this issue. The poor, therefore, must bear most taxes, since even among townsmen only the poor pay, while the rich buy exemptions; and in the villages the rich peasants connive with officials to pass the burden on to the poor.[35] But the privileged groups are only deceiving themselves, since in reality if the king does not obtain sufficient cash from the poor he finds ways of tapping more favored groups or individuals. The clergy, for example, are forced to pay many *décimes* (tenths); the nobles "have to sell their goods . . . to make war at their own expense; [so everyone] pays *tailles* and imposts either directly or indirectly."[36] Instead of protecting the ruler from discontent, therefore, these unfair practices stir up more trouble than ever; and the first and principal cause of sedition is such inequity.[37] How is it, asks Bodin, that kings cannot see the obvious fact that people are terribly disturbed by fiscal operations that hurt some and enrich others?[38]

Bodin understands quite well that even in the best-run states

[34] *Republique*, 909-10. In fact, from the early sixteenth century on in France almost all judicial posts and every single one of the posts in the fiscal system was venal. See Chapter 10 of my forthcoming work, *The Tax System of Renaissance France.*

[35] *Republique*, 886-87.

[36] *Ibid.*, 886-87.

[37] *Ibid.*, Book IV, Chap. 4.

[38] *Ibid.*, 877. Bodin favored indirect taxes and especially tariffs, arguing that the rich and powerful found it too easy to dodge direct taxation. *Ibid.*, 887-90. See, also, Nancey, 123-43.

expensive emergencies will crop up, that armies do cost money, that exceptional methods must be taken at times to "faire argent promptement." He recognizes that "war is not paid for by talking (*par diëtte*) as a captain of ancient times says."[39] That is why it is such a wise practice to establish a war chest for emergencies, rather than relying on harmful expedients like venality, debasements, imposts, or, worst of all, alienation of the royal *domaines*.[40] If imposts must be levied, the people have to be shown that their tax money is being put to good use. The king must not invent some pretext or other to declare war, raise taxes for the war, and keep the revenues even when no fighting develops, as did "Denis le tyran" [Dionysius of Syracuse?].[41] Of course, if the enemy is really at the gates, "public welfare must be preferred to that of individuals, and . . . citizens should give up both their antagonisms and animosities, and their possessions, for the safety of the Republic."[42]

As in taxes, so in money; all power belongs to the king, therefore all responsibility is his. Let the king remember that Dante put Philip the Fair of France, an incorrigible debaser of the coinage, in the lower depths of hell as a common forger. If the king is scornful of his own reputation, let him at least consider that changing the alloy or the tale of coins is incredibly damaging to everyone. Nobody can be sure of where he stands; contracts, pensions, and rents all shift in value, and the taxes paid into the treasury buy less for the king, too. Furthermore, it is well known that courtiers learn about a debasement in advance and take advantage of their special knowledge to line their pockets through shady deals; the king's treasury, meanwhile, profits but little. In his third chapter of Book VI, "The Way to Prevent Money from being Debased or Counterfeited," Bodin works out some elaborate plans for making small change dependable and for establishing stable par values for gold and silver, one of the most worrisome problems besetting mint officials and the business community.

[39] *Republique*, 855.

[40] *Ibid.*, 906. See, also, his preliminary statement on the main purposes of public finance, 855.

[41] *Ibid.*, 878. This was a frequently used argument against proposed tax increases during the Renaissance, and undoubtedly figured in the decision of the delegates at Blois in 1576 to reject the crown's tax plans.

[42] *Ibid.*, Book I, Chap. 8.

Chapter 2 of Book VI, where Bodin takes up the expenditure side of the fiscal system, also is full of specific advice and warnings.[43] Paying off the soldiers should have first claim on the treasury after support of the royal household and works of charity. This will spare the villages the horrible depredations of resentful troops. Next on the list of expenditure priorities should come beneficial public works, in order to banish "the two great plagues of the Republic—unemployment and poverty."[44] Next the king should concern himself with fortifications, roads, canals, and colleges. He should stop building expensive châteaux; a prince who has built such monuments to "vainglory" has "used the blood of his subjects for building materials."[45]

Finally, there is a pathetic lecture to the crown in which Bodin seems to be trying to convince profligate Henry III that there is nothing incompatible between maintaining royal dignity and paying careful attention to the details of the country's finances. Kings who immerse themselves in financial administration find it quite as interesting as the roisterous and meaningless life at other courts.[46] The greatest monarch of all, says Bodin, Philip II of Spain, does not think it beneath him to check over carefully all budgets and accounts, thereby keeping his bureaucracy on its toes and sparing his country many a fiscal fraud. This does not mean that considerate and careful kings need live meanly; King Louis XI of France pinched his personal expenses so hard he wore patches on his cloak, but he also squeezed the people with the heaviest and most arbitrary taxes they ever had experienced.[47] Bodin even suggests, on rather slim authority, that rulers who were active and meticulous in managing records tended to be long-lived and to have time for everything; Henry III, it should be noted, was notorious for his fear of death.[48]

IV

Through petty arguments or solid ones, Bodin had to reach the king. Different editions of the *Republic* are dedicated to different

[43] *Ibid.*, 897 ff.

[44] *Ibid.*, 900.

[45] *Ibid.*, 901. The original phrase is even stronger: "maçonné du sang des subiects."

[46] *Ibid.*, 902-03.

[47] *Ibid.*, 909.

[48] *Ibid.*, 903.

persons, but it is obvious that, especially from Book IV on, the
work is aimed primarily at the king and his counselors.[49] Persuading the king to improve his "image" as the nation's ruler
probably was more important to Bodin than consistency in the
theoretical structure of his "well-ordered and absolute monarchy."
His writings on taxes, particularly, should not be interpreted as
a search for universal principles. Therefore the fact that they contain apparent contradictions in theory and naïve policy proposals
counts for less in assessing the value of what he has to say. Bodin's
problem was not how to improve his countrymen's knowledge of
the nature of the fiscal system, but how to persuade them to stop
pulling their country to pieces.

We have known for some time that Bodin had *politique* aims
in writing the *Republic*, that he intended it in large part as "a
defense of politics against parties" (George Sabine). It seems true,
in addition, that Bodin intended the *Republic* to protect the political system against the corrosive effects of blundering by the king,
particularly in the area of taxation.

If the interpretation put forward here is correct, the actual effect
of Bodin on taxes was far from his intent. The *Republic* brought
him increased prestige in intellectual circles, but no important
post in the royal administration. The king did try some fairly
important fiscal and monetary reforms during the next few years,
but the main outlines of the tax system remained exactly as before,
the burden of taxes increased, and popular anger over fiscal in-
justices continued to grow. After 1584 the political situation de-
teriorated at a sickening rate; and in 1588, when the king had the
chief Catholic leaders assassinated, a majority of the provinces
went over to outright rebellion.

Bodin on taxes may have had more influence, ironically, in
seventeenth-century England than in sixteenth-century France;
he was widely quoted by opponents of the Stuarts, who found in
the *Republic* arguments to support the old view that "the king
should live of his own." In Italy, Giovanni Botero, a famous

---

[49] It is true that Bodin sometimes gives a different impression. In the dedication to the 1576 edition he explains he has written in French (rather than
Latin) in order to be understood by "all born Frenchmen"; in the 1584 edition,
at a time when the collapse of the state seemed even more imminent, he says
in the dedication that though his work is written for all, he wants especially
to reach the nobility. Baudrillart, 223-24.

disciple of Bodin, followed step by step Bodin's thinking on the proper structure of royal revenues and on royal borrowing. But in France much of Bodin's thinking on the nature of sovereignty was incorporated in the increasingly fashionable arguments of those advocating divine-right monarchy, a philosophy of rulership Bodin would have spurned. By ignoring the first three chapters of Book VI, the proponents of divine-right monarchy were able to stand Bodin on his head and argue that, since sovereignty had to be indivisible, the king must have unlimited powers to impose taxes.[50] Succeeding generations were more interested in what they could carve out of Bodin's theory for their own purposes than in applying his specific policy recommendations.

[50] Church, 243-45, 254-57, 270 and n. 64, 331-32.

[9]

BODIN AND LOCKE ON CONSENT TO TAXATION: A BRIEF NOTE AND OBSERVATION*

Julian H. Franklin

In Book I, chapter 8 of his *République* Bodin holds that taxation without consent is a taking of the subject's property and is forbidden by the law of nature. His purpose here is to account for an institutional restraint on royal power while still maintaining that any monarch worthy of the name is absolute. The obligation to obtain consent to new taxation was so deeply rooted in the European tradition that Bodin was eager to accommodate it, and in any event he regarded it as a beneficial limitation. Yet Bodin was committed by his theory of sovereignty to the thesis that a proper ruler had to be invested with all the legislative power that a state could legitimately exercise, which is what he meant by 'absolute'. His solution, therefore, was to treat consent of the Estates to new taxation not as a sharing in the legislative power, which would imply divided sovereignty, but as a special procedure arising directly from the law of nature and the right of private property. '[T]here is not a prince in all the world', Bodin asserts, 'who has it in his power to levy taxes on subjects at his pleasure, any more than he has the power to take another's property.'[1] Taxation is thus implicitly understood as an extraordinary measure rather than an ordinary act of government, and the consent of the Estates as an exceptional procedure rather than a positive constitutional requirement.[2]

But this solution is based on a mistake. It overlooks the principle, which was known in the civil law tradition, that every citizen owes the government reasonable support.[3] A reasonable tax, accordingly, is not a 'taking' of property in a sense forbidden by the law of nature, and its legitimacy does not depend upon consent unless that is specially required by the constitution. A king who cannot tax without consent must thus be less than sovereign, which is one reason why Bodin's position on taxation was not taken over by succeeding absolutists.

But in his *Second Treatise*, secs. 138–40, Locke, the constitutionalist, makes the same error as Bodin, the absolutist. A few sections earlier, in a brief and even perfunctory discussion, Locke had included 'pure', or

---

*One reason for choosing this topic is that I first became interested in this question as the result of conversations I had some years ago with Professor Deane.

[1] Jean Bodin, *Six livres de la république* (Aalen, 1961), p. 140.

[2] Julian H. Franklin, *Jean Bodin and the Rise of Absolutist Theory* (Cambridge, 1973), pp. 86–92.

[3] See for example the opinion of Bartolus of Sassoferrato quoted in R.W. and A.J. Carlyle, *A History of Medieval Political Theory in the West* (Edinburgh and London, 1909–36), Vol. VI, p. 77.

'unmixed', monarchy and aristocracy as legitimate forms of government. He thus admitted regimes in which, by definition, the entirety of legislative power was concentrated in a single individual or ruling group. And yet as a committed constitutionalist, he was unwilling to admit a power to tax without the consent of the people or its representatives. Locke, accordingly, faced much the same dilemma as Bodin, and, possibly following Bodin's example, he now adopted a similar solution.[4]

The right to tax is accordingly separated from the power to make law and derived directly from consent. '[T]he prince or Senate', says Locke, 'however it may have power to make laws for the regulating of property between the subjects one amongst the other, yet can never have a power to take to themselves the whole or any part of the subjects property, without their own consent.'[5] The rationale for this is that the power to tax without consent is by its mere existence a negation of the right of private property and is therefore forbidden by the law of nature. Locke acknowledges in passing that every subject is obliged to help defray the costs of government in proportion to his means.[6] But that contribution, if exacted without the subject's own consent, is nonetheless condemned as a taking of his property. It is as though a king endowed with the power to lay taxes unilaterally would be entitled to take anything he fancied.

> For if anyone shall claim [holds Locke] a power to lay and levy taxes on the people, by his own authority, and without such consent of the people, he thereby invades the fundamental law of property, and subverts the end of government. For what property have I in that which another may by right take, when he pleases to himself?[7]

But the power to tax, as we have seen, is restricted by the law of nature even where it is vested solely in the prince. Locke, however, fails to note this, and one consequence of this mistake is a curious but fundamental inconsistency in his classification of constitutional forms. Since his distinction between the power to tax and the power to make law is ultimately unworkable, Locke's idea of a pure yet limited monarchy or aristocracy simply cannot be sustained. Where a king or Senate cannot tax without popular consent, an ordinary right of government is shared between the ruler and the people, and a regime so constituted has to be considered mixed.[8]

---

[4] The parallel to Bodin is almost never mentioned in the commentaries on Locke. One notable exception is John Plamenatz, *Man and Society* (London, 1963), Vol. I, p. 230 who does not, however, explore the underlying theoretical issue.

[5] John Locke, *Two Treatises of Government* (New York, 1965), sec. 139 (p. 407).

[6] *Ibid.*, sec. 140 (p. 408).

[7] *Ibid.*

[8] For the distinction in Locke between ordinary and constituent authority, see Julian H. Franklin, *John Locke and the Theory of Sovereignty* (Cambridge, 1978), pp. 93–4.

BODIN AND LOCKE ON CONSENT TO TAXATION 91

One other, even more dramatic consequence is a contradiction in Locke's doctrine of consent. His concept of taxation seems to require the consent of every single individual, which is anarchic and unworkable, while what Locke wishes to establish is the collective consent of the community given either directly or by elected representatives. At one point Locke makes the desperate move of equating these two rules. If the tax on a subject is to be legitimate, he says, 'it must be with his own consent, i.e. the consent of the majority, giving it either by themselves, or their representatives chosen by them'.[9] But this manoeuvre fails.[10] If a tax becomes legitimate only by an *ad hoc* waiver of a right of nature, it is a kind of voluntary gift on the part of the contributors, each one of which would have to give his own consent. An individual who wished to make his own decision could not be bound by the vote of a majority.

This contradiction in Locke's doctrine of taxation by consent could not have been removed (if Locke had noticed it) without a certain cost. He could not have excluded the consent of every individual without abandoning the attempted distinction between the power to make law and the power of taxation. And he could not have abandoned that distinction without giving up his idea of 'pure', or 'unmixed', monarchies and aristocracies in which, however, the ruler was forbidden to tax without consent. But this was a cost that Locke could readily have borne. Unlike Bodin, he was not committed to the indivisibility of sovereignty; he could have said that the power to tax, unshared with the people's representatives, was so fraught in practice with the risk of tyranny that it was not reasonable for a people to permit it. Locke's difficulties here accordingly stem less from dogma than from inadvertence.

Julian H. Franklin COLUMBIA UNIVERSITY

---

[9] *Ibid.*

[10] Other comments on this question in Locke include J.W. Gough, *John Locke's Political Philosophy* (Oxford, 1950), p. 69; C.B. Macpherson, *The Political Theory of Possessive Individualism* (Oxford, 1962), pp. 252–5; John Dunn, 'Consent in the Political Theory of John Locke', in *Life, Liberty and Property*, ed. Gordon Schochet (Belmont, California, 1971), pp. 129–61, pp. 146–50; Aldo Tassi, 'Two Notions of Consent in Locke's *Second Treatise*', *The Locke Newsletter*, no. 3, spring 1972, pp. 26–31; Geraint Parry, *John Locke* (London, 1978), pp. 120–1.

[10]

JEAN BODIN AND THE ESTATES-GENERAL OF 1576

OWEN ULPH

CONSIDERABLE attention has been devoted in the past to Jean Bodin's theory of sovereignty. Very little has been written, however, concerning his association with the estates-general which assembled at Blois in 1576, the same year in which the *Republic* first made its appearance. During the course of the deliberations of the assembly, Bodin, as deputy from the bailiwick of Vermandois, was afforded the opportunity to apply his principles to some of the most critical issues of the day. His experience, studied in relationship to his political and legal philosophy, sheds much light on the reasons why absolutist theories and practices gained acceptance by enlightened members of the third estate in sixteenth- and seventeenth-century France.

In addition to the extensive program of reform which the deputies hoped to bring about indirectly through the redaction of the *cahiers*, three major problems confronted the Estates-General of 1576. Their first task was to re-establish religious peace, the second to provide a remedy for the disorganized condition of the royal finances, and the third to devise a scheme to make effective the participation of the estates in the govern-ment of the kingdom. All three issues were interrelated, and on each one the views of Bodin were among the decisive factors which determined the eventual outcome of the deliberations of the deputies.

With respect to the settlement of the religious problem, the estates were free to support the conciliatory Edict of Beaulieu, which had been issued a few months prior to the convocation of the assembly in order to pacify the Huguenots.[1] In view of the widespread influence of the newly organized Holy League, however, such a policy threatened to secure peace with the Protestants only at the price of war with the Catholics. Many, consequently, advocated religious repression and sought to abolish civil war by exterminating all heterodox belief. Since the Protestants were not represented in the assembly and since the Holy League had done much to

[1] The Edict of Beaulieu, more popularly known as the Edict of Pacification, had been issued in accordance with the terms of the Peace of Monsieur concluded between Henry III and the Huguenots on May 6, 1576. The convocation of the estates-general of Blois was itself a concession granted to the Huguenots by Article 58 of the Edict (see F. A. ISAMBERT, *Recueil général des anciennes lois françaises depuis l'an 420 jusqu'à la révolution de 1789* [Paris, 1821–23], XIV, 298–99).

control the elections and opinions of the deputies, the latter policy seemed destined to be adopted by the estates. The king tended to support the program of the League, since it appeared to represent popular opinion, and Henry III, if he were doomed to have another war on his hands, elected to fight the minority rather than the majority. Moreover, he believed that, were the estates to declare the war, they would be forced to grant him the funds necessary for its conduct. A few deputies, however, under the leadership of Bodin, attempted from the beginning to promote a policy of religious toleration in conformity with the Edict of Beaulieu.

The clergy and nobility did not hesitate to declare in favor of religious unity. The third estate was not so easily convinced, and controversy arose in their earliest deliberations. During the separate sessions of the *gouvernement* of the Île de France, the deputies, who were mostly members of the League, drew up a *cahier* demanding the recognition of none but the Catholic religion in France. Pierre le Tourneur, an eloquent Parisian lawyer popularly known as Versoris, presented the *cahier* to the general assembly of the third estate for acceptance. Bodin opposed the motion by reading an article from the *cahier* of Vermandois in which the king was requested to preserve peace among his subjects and, within two years, to hold a national council to decide the religious question.[2] Bodin made clear to the assembly that they were faced with the task of choosing between religious unity and war, on the one hand, or toleration of the dissenting creed and peace, on the other. The choice was such a difficult one for the

deputies that the discussion was temporarily deferred.[3]

A few days later Versoris reopened the question and forced a decision from the estates. Bodin stated unequivocally that to accept the *cahier* of Paris was to vote for a declaration of war. In reply, the *gouvernement* of the Île de France modified its position and declared for the re-establishment of religious unity "by the most moderate and holy ways that His Majesty should advise." Thus amended, the ultimate decision was thrust upon the king, and Bodin reluctantly ceased to offer opposition.[4]

The deputies in favor of peace had exerted considerable influence, but they were unable to check those who were intent upon pressing the cause of religious unity. When the vote was taken on the proposed *cahier*, six *gouvernements*, Normandy, Champagne, Languedoc, Orléanais, Picardy, and Provence, supported the recommendation of the Île de France.[5] The five remaining *gouvernements*, Burgundy, Brittany, Guyenne, Lyonnais, and Dauphiné, declared that "the union of religion should be brought about by moderate and pacific ways," adding the specific words, "without war." The majority refused to accept this qualification and insisted upon the complete suppression of the reformed faith and the banishment of all officers of the Huguenot church. Bodin argued that the vote was unfair because of the inequality in size and population of the *gouvernements*. He pointed out that Provence possessed only two deputies whereas Guyenne possessed seventeen, yet the former enjoyed a voice equal to that of the latter in determining the decision.[6] His objections were disregarded.

[2] C. J. MAYER, "Journal de Bodin," *Des états généraux et autres assemblées nationales* (Paris, 1788) (hereafter cited as "BODIN, *Journal*"), XIII, 217.

[3] *Ibid.*, p. 218.

[4] *Ibid.*, p. 224.

[5] *Ibid.*, p. 227.

[6] *Ibid.*, p. 228.

JEAN BODIN AND THE ESTATES-GENERAL OF 1576

The action of the third estate amounted to a declaration of war on the Protestants. An immediate series of Huguenot victories dampened the enthusiasm of many of the deputies for war, but an even more decisive factor arose to cause them to question the wisdom of their premature zeal. This was the question of finance.

Since the meeting of the Estates-General of Orléans in 1561, the monetary needs of the crown had been mounting by four million livres per year. Many provincial estates had begun to resist crown demands, thus throwing the financial burden on the remaining provinces. The evil of inequitable distribution was added to an already intolerable tax situation. The estates of Blois faced a thorny problem.

On December 31, M. de Nicolai, first president of the chambre des comptes, presented a report describing the poor state of finances, which he attributed to the debts of the king's predecessors.[7] The deputies of the estates, "as the only true physicians of the state," were to find a remedy for the illness of the treasury. He requested the nomination of a commission for the purpose of reviewing accounts. In accordance with the request, each order chose twelve delegates to the commission, but the commission proved a farce. Very soon the appointed deputies realized that the true condition of the finances was being withheld from them and that their efforts were not being taken seriously by the crown.[8] They were even more irritated to learn that new taxes were being levied throughout the provinces without the consent of the estates. Nevertheless, on January 9 the commission delivered their report to the general assembly of the estates.[9] Much to the exasperation of the king and the

royal treasurers, the report was not a recommendation of means by which additional money could be raised but an explanation of why the finances were in the slovenly condition in which the estates found them. The commission considered the chief abuses to be the excessive expenditures of the king and his court and the diversion of state revenues at their source through the alienation of crown domain.[10]

The king was anxious for the estates to complete the drawing-up of the *cahiers* and for the third estate to vote the subsidies with which he could pay his most pressing debts, but every day seemed to retard rather than to advance the work of the deputies. Realization that the establishment of religious unity was to prove expensive caused the deputies to reflect more carefully on their course of action. They decided that, if war were to be carried on, its costs should be borne equally by the three orders.[11] This was not a theory concocted on the spur of the moment. Bodin had developed the thesis in his *Six books on the republic*. Taxes, he argued, should be distributed equitably "in order that rich and poor, noble and commoner, priest and laborer should all pay their share on taxable lands. The law should make exception of neither pontiff nor noble."[12] On January 9 and 10 he presented these views in the assembly of the third estate. The deputies agreed with Bodin, and the date marked the end of the accord which had prevailed among the three orders since their convocation.

The third estate continued to send delegates to confer with the representa-

[10] *Ibid.*, p. 239.

[11] *Ibid.*, p. 242.

[12] Jean BODIN, *Les six livres de la république* (Lyon, 1580) (hereafter cited as "*République*"), Book VI, chap. ii, p. 618.

[7] *Ibid.*, p. 230.   [8] *Ibid.*, p. 231.   [9] *Ibid.*, p. 237.

tives of the nobility and the clergy on the problem of the distribution of the tax burden but would not empower their delegates to make any decisions without referring to the general assembly of the order.[13] Action became paralyzed by the discord among the three estates. The third estate refused to make concessions until the other two orders had expressed a willingness to share a portion of the expense. "The privileged orders," said Bodin, "sought only the means to burden themselves upon the third estate."[14] At the same time the deputies invoked their mandates and maintained that they had come to the assembly at Bois instructed to seek a reduction in taxes, not to agree to new ones.[15]

Angered by the niggardliness of the estates, the king sought to frighten the deputies by describing the horrors being perpetrated on faithful Catholics by victorious Protestants. The constituents, he argued, expected their deputies to reestablish religious unity, and this could not be accomplished without money. The president of the third estate of the *gouvernement* of Bordeaux replied that religious unity did not necessarily mean religious war and that the problem should be settled "through councils and through the reform of abuses."[16] It was no longer possible for the third estate to avoid the fundamental issue. In the opening days of the assembly they had declared themselves in favor of the reestablishment of religious unity even at the risk of war. Now they were forced to renounce their earlier position and to reconsider the policy of Bodin.

A royal session of the estates-general was scheduled for January 17, 1577. In preparation for the occasion, the deputies

of the third estate instructed their orator, Versoris, to present the revised viewpoint to the crown. He was to reassert the desire for unity but was to state specifically that it should be accomplished "without war."[17] When Versoris delivered his speech, however, he was unable to bring himself to utter the restriction which was personally odious to him. His colleagues were extremely angered at the way in which the orator had betrayed them. In the gathering of the order which followed the royal session a small riot ensued in which Versoris and his patron, the provost of the Paris merchants, were forced to escape through a rear door of the assembly in order to save themselves from violence.[18] The incident served to discredit the deputation from the Île de France, chief spokesmen for the League, and to strengthen the supporters of Bodin.

For weeks the struggle between the king and the third estate over finance dragged on, with Bodin continuously advising the deputies to refuse an increase in taxation. His Majesty was begged "not to take the refusal of the third estate to respond to his demands in bad grace since the deputies were without the power to act otherwise."[19] The delegates from the Île de France "moved heaven and earth" to alter the decision of the third estate but without success. Bodin accused them of self-interest and defended the resistance of the third estate on the basis of concern for the welfare of the nation.

Meanwhile the king, in desperation,

---

[13] BODIN, *Journal*, p. 243.

[14] *Ibid.*, p. 247.

[15] *Ibid.*, p. 242.

[16] *Ibid.*, p. 250.

[17] *Ibid.*, p. 248.

[18] *Ibid.*, p. 263. See also P. de LESTOILE, *Journal*, I, 81, in J. F. MICHAUD and B. POUJOULAT, *Nouvelle collection des mémoires pour servir à l'histoire de France depuis le XIIIᵉ siècle jusqu'à la fin du XVIIIᵉ* (Paris, 1850).

[19] BODIN, *Journal*, p. 264.

JEAN BODIN AND THE ESTATES-GENERAL OF 1576

presented the assembly with a new project for raising money. The plan proposed that three hundred thousand livres be raised immediately by alienation of a portion of the royal domain. The clergy consented readily enough since alienation was a financial contrivance that did not tap their own wealth. The third estate, encouraged by Bodin, once more resisted. Through promises of gifts and pensions, the king attempted to corrupt a number of the deputies to work in his behalf. Hémar, president of the parlement of Bordeaux, and Bigot, a delegate from Normandy, were allegedly singled out and bribed to act as the king's spokesmen.[20] They defended alienation, said Bodin, "with a vigor that could only have come from personal interest." But Bodin again won the day. He pointed out that the domain was not the king's to give away, that he held it only in simple usage, and that it belonged to the people and could not be alienated without the consent of the estates. Since the estates lacked the mandate from their constituents to agree to such a proposal, alienation was out of the question. Even were the deputies so empowered, Bodin added, they would not yield without a detailed rendering of court accounts.[21] Bellièvre, a member of the privy council, urged the cause of alienation before the assembly on the ground that it was necessary to dispose of a part to save the whole. If the estates would not consent, they should, at least, provide other means for the relief of the state.[22]

On the surface the refusal of Bodin to admit the right of the crown to alienate domain appears as a limitation of sovereignty and hence as a logical inconsistency in his thinking. A number of argu-

ments existed, however, which enabled Bodin to rationalize his position into conformity with his concept of sovereignty. First of all, French legal theory since the fourteenth century had regarded the king as limited by two "fundamental laws," the Salic Law of succession and the prohibition of the alienation of domain. In so far as Bodin's theory of sovereignty was a theory of right as well as a theory of might, the sphere of royal power could, logically, be circumscribed by the "fundamental laws."[23] Moreover, the law against alienation was subject to varied interpretations. It had been generally understood since the meeting of the estates of 1439 to mean that the king could not alienate revenue-bearing property attached to the crown. In this specific sense it was interpreted by Bodin. By the end of the century, however, legal theorists were interpreting domain to mean sovereign power itself. Whether domain were identified with sovereign power in the abstract or were taken to mean actual property or territory, the theoretical result was the same. The very restriction of the power of the king became, paradoxically, a positive assertion of sovereignty. The king did not possess the power to divest the crown of power. If he were allowed to alienate territory, he would be surrendering his judicial, administrative, and fiscal rights in the detached areas to others—in other words, sharing sovereignty. According to Bodin, such action was inadmissible. His attack upon alienation of domain, viewed in this light, remained in accordance with his concept of undivided sovereignty and in line with his desire to check the privileges of the great seigneurs who stood ready to gain from alienation. The domain belonged to the republic and the

[20] *Ibid.*, p. 298.

[21] *Ibid.*, pp. 299–300.   [22] *Ibid.*, pp. 301–2.

[23] BODIN, *République*, Book I, chap. i, p. 3; chap. viii, pp. 88 and 95; and Book VI, chap. ii, p. 597.

republic belonged to the prince. The security of one was inconceivable without the security of the other.[24] The domain provided the means by which the prince fulfilled his functions; and should he alienate domain, he would deprive himself of the source of power. These views were summed up by Hémar, who likened the domain to "a wife whom the husband could not put aside at will."[25] The third estate resolved that, if money were needed, the crown could either borrow from the financial agents or sell the lands of the clergy.[26]

The estates, in the meantime, had completed the drawing-up of the *cahiers*, and on February 9 they were formally presented to the king.[27] The task of defending the *cahiers* before the privy council still remained. This brought to the fore the third major problem confronting the estates, that of establishing for themselves effective influence in the governance of the realm. The power of the privy council was strong in that those *cahiers* which the councilors saw fit to dismiss would have no chance to become incorporated in any subsequent ordinance that might be drafted in answer to national grievances. To combat this arbitrary power of the council, the estates had earlier won the right to be represented by their own delegates in the discussions which were to take place in council before the king on the subject of each individual *cahier*.

The initial move was made by members of the clergy, who approached the third estate on the matter of the election of the delegates to the council and the extent of the powers to be granted them. Both the nobility and the clergy were in favor of the customary committee of thirty-six, a delegate from each of the twelve *gouvernements* to be selected by each order. Immediately the old suspicions of the third estate were aroused. They were afraid that such a committee would place them in the position of a minority, and they repeated the old maxim that "two orders should have neither the power nor opportunity to bind the third."[28] Bodin opposed representation on the council altogether. Four hundred deputies, he insisted, were already too few to represent France effectively. To reduce the number to thirty-six was to turn the estates into "a thing in miniature."[29] The implication of this somewhat disingenuous logic seemed to be that if the French people could not be represented on the council en masse, it would be better for them not to be represented at all. Bodin argued that a small number of deputies, overawed by the presence of the king and a large number of great seigneurs, would quite likely do whatever their superiors wished. Had not this happened, he asked, under Louis XI? A large body, he concluded, could preserve independence of judgment, whereas a small one would frequently be forced to submit to the royal and seigneurial will and might prove too susceptible to corruption and intimidation. The danger was that the reluctant concessions of the abbreviated body might be construed to have popular ap-

[24] *Ibid.*, Book VI, chap. ii, pp. 596–601.

[25] BODIN, *Journal*, p. 302. It was the tradition of the estates that whoever was instructed to speak for them was obliged to express the opinions of the majority, even when the opinions were not the speaker's own. Although Hémar had defended alienation, he was forced to argue the opposing view before the king. The case in which Versoris betrayed his trust in a similar situation has already been observed (see above, p. 292).

[26] BODIN, *Journal*, p. 304.   [27] *Ibid.*, p. 275.

[28] *Ibid.*, p. 281; see also *République*, Book III, chap. vii, p. 338.

[29] BODIN, *Journal*, pp. 277–78.

proval since the council would, technically, represent the estates.

In addition to this argument, Bodin insisted further that, in the event that such a committee of thirty-six should be given power to determine, as members of the council, the fate of the *cahiers*, one order would be unable to avoid being bound, at least in some instances, by the other two. Even were the three orders in agreement, Bodin added as if by afterthought, the committee should not have the power to dictate to the king and his councilors.[30]

The question naturally arises: Why did Bodin champion the cause of the estates so stubbornly against the crown on the question of taxation and alienation and demonstrate, on the other hand, such apparent servility to the crown in the matter of the representation of the estates on the council? His arguments to the assembly fail to provide a satisfactory explanation, and his political theory seems no more adequate. It is true that Bodin regarded any hint of legislative power on the part of the estates as a limitation on sovereignty.[31] A committee of thirty-six with the authority to determine the provisions of an ordinance, he maintained, would thus become a lawmaking body. To Bodin this was incompatible with true sovereignty. Sovereignty he recognized as the unlimited authority to make law.[32] Sovereignty was indivisible. The mixed state, as a sovereign state, could not exist.[33]

To these arguments the opponents of Bodin replied that the power of the crown was in no way weakened by enhancing the position of the estates, that

the power of the crown was, in fact, greatest when enjoying the support of the community, and that if the king were independent of the views of the people the estates would never have been summoned in the first place. Representation of the estates on the council would be quite proper, for had not the king himself referred to the estates as his councilors?[34]

These views were as logical as those advanced by Bodin. In fact, Bodin's arguments on sovereignty were scarcely applicable to the situation. The presence of thirty-six delegates on a council which had the task of reviewing the *cahiers* could scarcely be considered a limitation on the sovereignty of the crown, even by the deputy himself. The council only influenced legislation. The actual ordinance was always issued in the name of the king. That fear of the estates' encroaching upon the legislative power of the crown was not the basic reason for Bodin's opposition is made certain by more concrete evidence. In order to circumvent the objections of Bodin, the Archbishop of Lyon proposed, as an alternative suggestion, the election of a committee to act simply in a consultative capacity, but the deputy from Vermandois was unable to agree even to this. The only procedure of which Bodin would approve was for the *cahiers* to be reviewed by the council without any interference from the delegates of the estates.[35]

The basis for Bodin's position must be explained on grounds more significant than theory. When Bodin resisted religious war, increased taxation, and alienation of royal domain, he spoke not for the estates-general as a whole but for the

---

[30] *Ibid.*, p. 279.

[31] BODIN, *République*, Book I, chap. viii, p. 96.

[32] *Ibid.*, chap. x, pp. 155–56.

[33] *Ibid.*, Book II, chap. i, pp. 175–76.

[34] LALOURCÉ and DUVAL, *Recueil de pièces originales et authentiques concernant la tenue des états généraux, 1560–1614* (Paris, 1788), V, 288.

[35] BODIN, *Journal*, p. 280.

third estate only. In supporting the committee of thirty-six, Bodin would have been forced to defend the interests of both the clergy and the nobility, which he had no desire to do. To allow such a council to influence the king and his advisers was to open the pathway to power of the very groups within society which his theory of sovereignty was designed to suppress. His fear of the nobility caused him to resist any trend toward parliamentary government in France. If the sovereign prince is subject to the estates," wrote Bodin, "he is neither prince nor sovereign, and the republic is neither a kingdom nor a monarchy, but a pure aristocracy of seigneurs in which the greater governs the lesser."[36] This statement is more than a reflection of the personal fears of a single deputy. It is a key to the explanation of the complete failure of parliamentary government in France under the Old Regime. In 1576, as on numerous previous and subsequent occasions, the estates-general neglected to take advantage of favorable opportunities to increase their powers at the expense of the crown because the third estate was unwilling to concede a share in sovereign power to an institution which might too easily be made to serve the interests of the privileged orders. Despite their antagonism to the religious and financial policies of the king, the deputies of the third estate could discover no way, within the framework of the existing constitu-

tion of France, to bridle his authority without augmenting the already offensive political influence of the clergy and nobility. Bodin's labored attempts to reconcile his attitude toward the king and the estates with his tenuous theories of sovereignty reflect the political dilemma of the middle classes in sixteenth-century France. The issue was not so much that representative government could not be made consistent with a theory of sovereignty but that representative government might represent the wrong people. The third estate surrendered their own opportunity to place constitutional checks upon the crown in order to thwart the ambitions of their rivals. The middle classes continued to look toward absolutism as the only alternative to anarchy and the exploitation of the nation's resources by the privileged orders.

Unable to change the opinions of members of the third estate, the nobility and clergy were forced to abandon their scheme. The question of representation of the estates on the council was dropped. Review of the *cahiers* was left to an unhampered council. The influence of the deputy from Vermandois on the estates of 1576 was probably not exaggerated when Henry III remarked to some of his minions that Bodin had led the estates around at his pleasure.[37]

UNIVERSITY OF NEVADA

---

[36] BODIN, *République*, Book I, chap. viii, p. 96

[37] *Ibid.*, Book III, chap. vii, p. 338; see also BODIN, *Journal*, p. 282.

[11]

Bodin's Analysis of Inflation

Denis P. O'Brien

The work of Jean Bodin (1530–1596) has been known to economists at least since the mid-nineteenth century (McCulloch [1862] 1995, 37), even though his wider fame, by far, lies in political philosophy. But there has been disagreement over precisely what Bodin achieved in his writings on economics.[1]

There is no disputing that the interest of his economic writing lies chiefly in his analysis of the causes of the inflation that was affecting France at the time that he published the two editions of his *Response to Malestroit* (1568 and 1578). But there is considerable dispute about the nature of his achievement. On one hand, we have J. A. Schumpeter

Correspondence may be addressed to Denis P. O'Brien, c/o Department of Economics, University of Durham, Durham DH1, 3HY, U.K. This reconsideration of Bodin's work has been inspired by the new translation of his *Response to the Paradoxes of Malestroit* ([1568/1578] 1997) by the late Henry Tudor and Dr. R. W. Dyson. This translation is unique in its incorporation of the texts of both the 1568 and 1578 editions of Bodin's *Response*. I am grateful to Professor John Creedy and Dr. Julia Stapleton for comments on earlier versions of this essay, and to Professor Roger Backhouse for drawing my attention to the disputed authorship of the *Discourse of the Common Weal*. At a later stage, comments from two anonymous referees were extremely helpful.

1. By far the greater part of the secondary literature relating to Bodin stems from French and German authors. The French contribution includes the work of Baudrillart (1853), Bodin de St. Laurent ([1907] 1970), Harsin (1928), Hauser (1932), and Servet (1994). The German contribution has paid more attention to the economic background to Bodin's work and in particular to the depreciation of the precious metals. Detailed references are in Hauser's (1932) introduction to Bodin's *Response* and in the excellent account in Spiegel 1991 (700–703). See Baudrillart 1853 (111–44) for a discussion of Bodin's life.

expressing the clear view that Bodin's "analysis needs but little readjustment or generosity of interpretation to be a correct diagnosis of the historical case as it presented itself in 1568. Even as regards general theoretical content, it is superior to much later work" (1954, 312). Similarly, in his study of Bodin's monetary thought, Bodin's descendant Jean Bodin de St. Laurent ([1907] 1970, 31–35), had no difficulty in crediting Bodin with the first correct statement of a metallist version of the quantity theory, while the distinguished French economic historian Henri Hauser (1932, xliv) expressed astonishment at those who denied Bodin's achievement in formulating, with remarkable clarity, a version of the quantity theory of money.

But on the other hand, scholars both inside and outside France have been inclined to downplay the extent of Bodin's achievement. Thus P. Harsin, in a controversial (Hauser 1932, ix–x) volume, dismissed Bodin's claim to pioneering achievement (1928, 31–44, esp. 40). After World War II, the Swedish economist Hugo Hegeland also denied Bodin credit, on the grounds that in 1568 the quantity theory was not as fully worked out as it was in later centuries; Hegeland also made the claim—which, as we shall see, is baseless—that Bodin believed "that the price level was solely a function of the quantity of money" (1951, 37n., 153).

The controversy has continued. A recent revisionist interpretation of Malestroit credits him with a formulation of the idea of money as a veil and, correspondingly, downplays Bodin's achievement (Servet 1994).

It is, however, worth emphasizing that neither critics nor proponents (with the exception of Hauser) call in evidence of their position a detailed examination of the text. It is my contention in this article, based on just such an examination, that the dismissal of Bodin's priority rests—where the grounds for such dismissal are clear at all—upon an inappropriate and incomplete statement of the quantity theory. If we identify the theory with five generally accepted propositions associated with it, however, Bodin does indeed have a strong claim to be regarded as the pioneer formulator of that theory.

By "the quantity theory of money," I take as understood the following propositions: (1) there is a *demand for money*, dependent primarily on the existing price and income levels; (2) there is a *supply of money* —in the historical context we are discussing this means specie; (3) the *money market clears*, with demand for money equal to its supply; (4) a disturbance to *either* demand or supply requires an adjustment in the price (or income) level to enable the money market to clear; (5) the direction of *causality* is from changes in the money supply to changes in the price level.

In the present context, an increase in the money supply is of key interest. In addition it should be recognized that, until quite recently, quantity theorists did not assume completely inelastic aggregate supply, so that there may also be some change in output associated with a change in the money supply.

While it is unreasonable to expect these five key points to be set out clearly by the earliest writers, formulating the issues in this way makes clear what we are seeking in Bodin's work, and indeed in that of other writers distant from us in time. The foundation upon which the analysis rests is the recognition that an increase in the money supply, whatever its source, is likely to raise the price level. As we shall see, Bodin has strong claims to have developed this line of argument earlier and better than anybody else.

We begin with an outline of the European experience of precious metal inflow and inflation (section 1). Next comes a sketch of the intellectual background enjoyed by Bodin (section 2). This is followed by an account of Malestroit's "Paradoxes" and Bodin's critique of these, in which he developed his analysis of the causes of inflation (section 3). This analysis is then set in the wider context of Bodin's economic thought, covering the gains from trade, Gresham's Law, and the demand for money (section 4). Finally we come to the harmful effects of inflation and Bodin's proposals for currency reform, which were designed to limit the damage (section 5). Section 6 concludes.

1. Inflation

Inflation in Europe

All governments are faced with a temptation to inflate the money supply to capture resources. The twentieth-century experience of this has been so all-pervasive that there is a developed literature on "inflation taxation" (Humphrey 1993, 190–91). Medieval monarchs, lacking the printing facilities of modern governments, resorted to the process of "debasement," which involved adding low-value metals to the coinage, spreading the supply of gold and silver further. Such a practice was widespread. The history of France contains many examples, and Henry VIII and his successors in England managed to debase the silver coinage to one-sixth of its silver content in thirty years (Heaton 1948, 250–55).

Debasement was essentially a national problem, however, and adjustment of the nominal exchange rate to reflect the different content of precious metals in different currencies could be relied on to contain within national boundaries at least most of the inflation thus generated. But the sixteenth century witnessed a different and far more fundamental monetary change: a huge increase in the supply of the precious metals themselves, resulting in an inflation that spread across national boundaries and raised prices throughout Europe. The relative value of commodities and the precious metals changed significantly. Thus the author of the hugely impressive study of the Spanish inflation estimated that prices in Spain rose by a factor of 4.1 during the sixteenth century (Hamilton 1934; see also Hauser 1932, xi–xix, xlvii–xlix). The index of grain prices for New Castille, calculated by Hamilton (1934, 390–91), rose from 37.05 in 1504 to 102.5 in 1568, the year in which Bodin published the first edition of his *Response*. Hamilton's composite index for silver prices rose from 33.26 in 1501 to 92.44 in 1568 and 137.23 in 1600 (Hamilton 1934, 493).

By modern standards this was a very moderate inflation. (British prices rose almost twenty times between the late 1940s and the early 1990s.) But the very insidiousness of the process made its causes harder to discern; Malestroit was undoubtedly misled into thinking debasement the more important problem, and it is Bodin who deserves credit for pinpointing the increase of precious metals as the real issue.

Of course, precious metals did not constitute the only means of payment. Boyer-Xambeu, Deleplace, and Gillard (1994) stress the important developments in payment by bills of exchange. But as they state, the use of credit instruments ("economising expedients," in later terminology) made the coins "all the more available for internal trade" (151). Indeed they make the point that "the bill of exchange did not exclude specie, which had a twofold function in intra-European trade: settling accounts and providing reference rates for exchange. The bill of exchange was a monetary instrument both because it replaced coins in international relations and because it depended on them in its relationship with the unit of account" (151). Thus, as under the gold standard, the bills were not independent of the metallic base.[2]

Inflation in France

The impact of the increase in precious metals was most direct, and earliest, on Spain, since the metal was coming from the Spanish colonies. But France, as an immediate neighbor linked by both trade and labor mobility, felt the impact quite soon.[3] There is no doubt that, whatever imperfections existed in Renaissance markets, there were very many ways in which the precious metals could find channels of circulation apart from the official ones, including loss, theft, and smuggling (Gillard 1994; Peronnet 1994, 48). The profit opportunities offered by arbitrage were strong enough to ensure that the New World precious metals spread from Spain by both official and unofficial channels. The official channels were connected, in part, with the pan-European ambitions of the Spanish monarchy (Vilar 1976, 187; Spooner 1972, 26–29).

In addition, there were the normal trade and payments resulting from a variety of factors that Bodin identifies, in particular French agricultural exports to Spain and remittances to France from Spain by migrant workers. Although Spain and Portugal attempted, in true mercantilist style, to keep full accounting records of the treasure coming in from the New World, a good deal of it will have entered by unofficial channels —"skimming" by those involved—not to mention the piracy that was official policy for Britain, Holland, and France in the sixteenth century (Davies 1994, 185).

---

2. See also De Roover 1953, 57–58. The importance of credit instruments has also been emphasized in the informative review of Boyer-Xambeu, Deleplace, and Gillard in Lowry 1996, 311–12. See also Gómez Camacho 1998, 537.

3. It should be acknowledged that some French economic historians dispute this. In particular, Boyer-Xambeu, Deleplace, and Gillard (1994, 178) contend that the increase in the precious metals was insignificant in relation to the French gross domestic product (GDP). However, since they compare only the precious metals arriving in the *last decade* of the sixteenth century with the French GDP, and since a figure for the French GDP in the sixteenth century (for which they give no precise figure or source) must, in any case, be highly speculative, not everyone will find such reservations persuasive. In any case, what would be immediately relevant would not be the total French GDP (however calculated) but that part of it passing through the market system.

272   History of Political Economy 32:2 (2000)

The end result of this activity was perceptible inflation in France.[4] As in the Spanish case, it was very modest by modern standards and thus, correspondingly, harder to analyze. Most estimates show prices rising by 2.5 or 3 times during the sixteenth century, though some acceleration seems to have occurred in the latter part of the century. Estimates by G. D'Avenel (1894) show rather larger rises in the value of land, but wage income lagged behind. A modern study by Phelps Brown and Hopkins (1959) indicates this clearly. Taking the third quarter of the fifteenth century, when prices had fallen, as the base (100), the price of land had risen to 338 by the middle of the next century, to 728 by the third quarter, and to 1,062 by the end of the century. The wage rate (in the official accounting currency of *livre tournois*), with the same base, had risen to 156, 179, and 258 over the same period (Phelps Brown and Hopkins 1959, 26). Earlier, Hauser (1932, xx), drawing on the work of Levasseur, had reported the price of wheat rising by a factor of 2.5 between the 1520s and the 1580s.[5]

This is representative of results obtained by a number of the earlier researchers, which were summarized by Bodin de St. Laurent ([1907] 1970, 4). This modest inflation thus sets the scene, in terms of contemporary economic experience, for Bodin's analysis of inflation. However, there is also a significant intellectual background to his thought.

2. Intellectual Background

The Scholastic Contribution

Sixteenth-century Spanish Scholasticism was an intellectually fertile background. According to Schumpeter, "The very high level of Spanish sixteenth-century economics was due chiefly to the scholastic contributions" (1954, 165). As Schumpeter recognized (1954, 101), the roots of what was to become the quantity theory of money are found in the writings of the Scholastic philosophers. Here the experience of debase-

---

4. For a violently opposed view, see Morineau 1985. However, it should be noted that even sympathetic critics refer to "la phobie de Michel Morineau pour un 'quantitativisme' " (Boyer-Xambeu, Deleplace, and Gillard 1988, 962).

5. The picture concerning inflation in France is obscured by a distinction to be made between the unit of account and money in circulation, with the former being the subject of official debasement. Some information, on what is itself a huge topic in detail, is in O'Brien 1997, 14–15. On the recoinage of 1577 in particular, see Boyer-Xambeu, Deleplace, and Gillard 1994, 191–93.

ment was significant; the analysis of this by Nicholas Oresme, who wrote about 1360, is of particular importance. For Oresme approached the valuation of metallic money in the same way as the valuation of other commodities. This had the important effect of making it subject to the analysis of the Just Price, which was a development of central importance (G. O'Brien 1920, 145–55; Gordon 1975, 188–95; see also Monroe [1924] 1966, 26, on Antonine). The Scholastic analysis of the Just Price had become, largely under the influence of Aquinas (1225–1274), an analysis of price in terms of "common estimation," thus pointing in the direction of subjective value theory. In this analysis the Just Price reflected competitive market valuation (where there was not fraud and monopoly), and it thus reflected relative scarcity. So what had become established in the universities of late medieval and Renaissance Europe was an analysis of value founded on relative scarcity, thus clearing the way for an analysis of changes in the values of precious metals that had become much less scarce.

Such ideas are found in the writings of the sixteenth-century Scholastics, notably Dominic de Soto and Luis Molina (Dempsey 1935).[6] Among these writers was one of particular importance to Bodin's background, Navarrus.

Navarrus

Martín de Azpilcueta Navarro (1493–1586) became a leading member of the school of Salamanca (Grice-Hutchinson 1952, 45; De Roover 1953, 175; Gordon 1975, 203; Gazier and Gazier 1978). Indeed, Marjorie Grice-Hutchinson (1952, 52, 95; 1978, 95) has claimed that the first clear statement of the quantity theory of money is in Navarrus's *Comentario Resolutorio de Usuras* (1556) (see also Gómez Camacho 1998, 554). Navarrus argues that relative scarcity determines the value of money, money being a commodity subject to the same analysis of relative scarcity as other commodities. Navarrus then explains

> that (other things being equal) in countries where there is a great scarcity of money all other saleable goods, and even the hands and labour of men, are given for less money than where it is abundant. Thus we see by experience that in France, where money is scarcer than in Spain, bread, wine, cloth, and labour are worth much less.

6. See also the outstanding essay by Gómez Camacho (1998).

274   History of Political Economy 32:2 (2000)

> And even in Spain, in times when money was scarcer, saleable goods
> and labour were given for very much less than after the discovery of
> the Indies, which flooded the country with gold and silver. The rea-
> son for this is that money is worth more where and when it is scarce
> than where and when it is abundant. (Translated in Grice-Hutchinson
> 1952, 94–95).

Thus Navarrus has stated clearly that the purchasing power of money
is inversely related to its quantity. He does not, however, claim (though
this claim has been made on his behalf [Grice-Hutchinson 1952, 56]
that Purchasing Power Parity exists. Indeed, given the impediments to
the distribution of the precious metals, this could only be a long-run
equilibrium position.

Bodin was exposed to the influence of these writings in two ways.
Firstly, he became a religious novice in his teens and was thus subjected
to the detailed intellectual training that would have been the norm
(Tooley 1955, vii–viii). After he abandoned the religious life, Bodin
studied law at Toulouse, where Navarrus had taught (Franklin 1968;
Hauser 1932, xxxvi–xliii), though it has been established by H. W.
Spiegel (1991, 90, 702) that there was a twenty-five-year gap between
Navarrus's departure from Toulouse and Bodin's arrival. But even if
Bodin was not directly taught by Navarrus, it is not credible that he
would have been uninfluenced by the work of a major writer in a tradition with which he was already familiar from his novitiate and who had
taught at the institution, no doubt within the memory of some individuals still there.

The Quantity Theory in the Sixteenth Century

While the major influences on the development of Bodin's thought would
have been economic experience and the Scholastic background, one has
to recognize that the quantity theory of money, at least in a rudimentary
form, was beginning to emerge at the time that he wrote (Gómez Camacho 1998, 536–54; Popescu 1998, 580, 582). Most writers will accept
that, objectively, Copernicus can claim priority (Spiegel 1991, 86–88).
But Copernicus did not go beyond the idea that "money usually depre-
ciates when it becomes too abundant" (Grice-Hutchinson 1952, 34),
and it is highly unlikely, as Hauser has pointed out, that Bodin owed
anything to Copernicus in this matter, even though references else-

where in his writings show that he was familiar with the astronomical theories of Copernicus. For, given the scholastic background he already had, Bodin had no need to read what Copernicus wrote about money. Apart from Copernicus, credit has also been given to Nöel du Fail. Bodin de St. Laurent, who drew attention to du Fail's work on the effects of the inflow of treasure, dated this at 1548, which would have given du Fail some priority over Bodin.[7] However, as Bodin de St. Laurent pointed out, du Fail offered a perception, not a developed argument, and in any case it now seems doubtful whether the 1548 work Bodin de St. Laurent cited contains the relevant material (Harsin 1928, 40n.1). At all events, there is no evidence that Bodin himself owed anything to du Fail, and it seems reasonable to conclude that his own, remarkably comprehensive treatment sprang from the Scholastic intellectual background combined with an exemplary concern with the available data, which will become apparent when we look in detail at his text.

An important piece of evidence concerning the scholastic influence on Bodin is indeed found in the condemnation of usury in his *Republic*. Bodin saw usury as a source of social inequality and political tension, but he based his condemnation squarely on religious sources (Bodin de St. Laurent [1907] 1970, 149–78). Bodin's monetary analysis, then, appeared, in true Scholastic style, as a critique (Bodin 1568, 1578). In this case it was a critique of two "paradoxes" put forward by Jean Cherruies (or Cherruier) "Seigneur de Mallestroit" [*sic*] one of the "conseillers-maîtres des comptes" (Servet 1994, 73). It is thus necessary to examine Malestroit's argument.[8]

3. The Debate

Malestroit's Paradoxes

Malestroit's first paradox is a claim that, although prices have risen in terms of the currency, following debasement, the prices of commodities have not risen at all in terms of the precious metals. The rises in price are thus simply changes in the unit of account, resulting from debase-

---

7. Bodin de St. Laurent has a useful review of precursors of Bodin, including Xenophon, Buridan, and Oresme as well as Copernicus and Nöel du Fail.

8. For the wider context of the debate, see Boyer-Xambeau, Deleplace, and Gillard 1994, 189–93.

276   History of Political Economy 32:2 (2000)

ment. He insists that prices have not risen in terms of the precious metals during the preceding three hundred years (41).[9] His prime exhibit in support of this claim is the steadiness, as he reports it, of the price of velvet in terms of precious metals, once changes in the precious metal content of the currency have been allowed for. More ambitiously, he extends the claim to perishable commodities, notably corn and wine.

Malestroit's second paradox seems incomprehensible at first sight. It is the claim "that a significant loss can be made on an ecu or other gold and silver money, although it is paid out at the same price as that at which it was received" (44). The essence of the argument is, however, that rents stated in silver terms now exchange for less gold than they used to, because they are specified in silver *coinage* which has become debased.

Malestroit's aim in publishing these paradoxes is not clear, although it was no doubt done in connection with his official position in the public finance machinery, and it may also have been designed to serve the monarchy by damping popular discontent. In advancing his arguments he was clearly hoping to persuade through demonstration of expertise; indeed, he employed a rhetorical technique similar to that later employed by Sir William Petty, which drew on itself the deserved satirical attention of Jonathan Swift (Letwin 1963, 128–40). The technique, as employed by Malestroit, involves describing in words a simple algebraic relationship using ratios. Then, as if by magic, a ratio implied, but not specified, by the verbal expression is appealed to to give an unexpected result. Thus let S/V be the silver price of velvet and S/G the silver price of gold. Then the ratio $\dfrac{\Delta S/\Delta V}{\Delta S/\Delta G}$ yields $\dfrac{\Delta G}{\Delta V}$, so that changes in the gold price of velvet can be expressed without being specified directly.[10] Such sleight of hand might well have been impressive in sixteenth-century France.

9. Page references both to Malestroit and to Bodin's *Response* are to the Tudor-Dyson translation, Bodin [1568/1578] 1997. I had intended to include also references to the Hauser edition (Hauser 1932). Unfortunately, Hauser 1932, which is a translation of the first (1568) edition of Bodin, is seriously inadequate with regard to the second (1578) edition variants included in an appendix, and I felt that an incomplete set of page references was of little use.

10. Thus, for instance, we find Malestroit stating that in 1328 1 gold ecu was worth 20 sols, and a measure (an "ell") of velvet was worth 4 "livres," which was worth 4 ecus. An ell when Malestroit was writing cost 10 livres, but 10 livres was still worth 4 ecus equal to 50 sols. "Therefore, the said ell of velvet is no dearer now than it was then" (quoted in Bodin [1568/1578] 1997, 41).

Bodin's Critique

In his *Response*, Bodin was able to destroy the factual basis of Male-stroit's argument. The essential points he established were these: First, Malestroit's use of data was faulty. Second, even after full and correct allowance had been made for debasement, this was completely inade-quate to explain the rises in price that had actually occurred.

On the first count Bodin was able to advance plausible reasons for doubting whether velvet was even known in fourteenth-century France (53–54). Given the central claim made by Malestroit about the steadi-ness of the price of velvet, this was a damaging point. Secondly, Bodin was aware that inflation had spread throughout Europe (57) and was able, on the basis of the data to which he had access, to identify rises in prices, in terms of the debased silver currency, by a factor of 20. In terms of gold currency, the price of corn had risen by a factor of 2 (55). Malestroit had identified a fivefold debasement, but the remainder of the change required explanation.

Bodin carefully based his view on price records with which, from his legal work, he was familiar. It is hardly surprising that he immediately encountered the problem that all economists faced until the pioneering work on the construction of widely based index numbers by William Stanley Jevons (1863) in the nineteenth century: how to represent a general price change.

Like a number of Jevons's predecessors, Bodin decided that the price of land would provide a good general measure of depreciation. It had the advantage of reflecting (through transfer earnings, though Bodin did not make this point) the prices of a range of commodities. It was, he argued, fixed in amount and of constant fertility in France (55). The price of land had trebled in the preceding fifty years in terms of gold coin, while the gold content of the ecu had fallen by only 10 percent. The implied inflation was thus around 2.7 times (56).

Casting around for measures of depreciation, Bodin inevitably intro-duced some confusion into the argument. Later in his *Response* he referred to a rise in the price of property in terms of gold of 3.5 times after correction for debasement (79–83). He also claimed that Crown lands had become worth as much in rental as they were once worth in outright purchase price. Employing the standard mathematics of the value of a perpetual flow (and assuming that the French Crown could borrow at 4 percent), this implies a 25-fold rise in price (Chiang 1984,

278   History of Political Economy 32:2 (2000)

462–64). This, however, results from the fact that rents had been specified in silver *coinage* so that the calculation indeed allows both for
debasement and for the fall in the value of silver. Land having risen in
price by more than commodities, this is consistent with the 20-fold
inflation referred to above.

Once the argument is disentangled, it becomes apparent that Bodin's
basic estimate of inflation purely in terms of precious metals was in
excess of 2.5 times, a remarkably accurate estimate, given the later
studies referred to above. In applying the Scholastic technique of criticism to Malestroit's paradoxes, Bodin had succeeded in establishing
that debasement was, on its own, not enough to explain the rise in
prices. In itself this was no mean achievement, demonstrating as it did
a remarkable grasp of data, a grasp that becomes even more apparent
when one looks at his discussion of coinage and exchange rates later in
the *Response*.[11]

But having thus established that Malestroit's claims were insupport-
able, Bodin was then faced with the next stage of his self-imposed task:
to explain the causes of the rise in prices. It is in this explanation that
the real distinction of his performance lies.

Bodin and the Causes of Inflation

Bodin attributed the rise in prices to five main causes. It is worth emphasizing that there are five such causes, in view of the claim by Hegeland
noted above that Bodin relied solely on changes in the quantity of
money. The five main causes are (1) "the abundance of gold and silver,
which is greater in this kingdom today than it has been in the last 400
years"; (2) monopolies; (3) "scarcity which is caused both by the
export trade and by waste"; (4) fashionable demand for luxuries; and
(5) debasement (59). Bodin identified the first cause as, quantitatively, the most important. The historical data (and Bodin was not
only enormously well read but also the author of an important work on
history [Reynolds 1945]) showed this clearly (59–60). Following the
Scholastic analysis, the value of the precious metals depended on relative scarcity, and the scarcity of both gold and silver, relative to the
supply of commodities, had changed significantly. One piece of evidence for this was the fact that in past centuries the precious metals had

11. For Bodin's methodology, see Baudrillart 1853, 145–68.

been in such short supply that there had been serious difficulties in raising ransom payments for captured royalty. Payments had improved to such an extent that even the difficulties of liquidity encountered in raising revenue for the French Crown had now disappeared. "If Monsieur de Malestroit consults the records of the *Chambre*, he will agree with me that more gold and silver has been found in France to meet the needs of the king and the commonwealth between 1515 and 1568 than could be found in the previous 200 years" (63). The key to the change in liquidity lay in the French balance of payments, which had improved remarkably. On one hand, an improvement in the terms of trade had resulted from Portugal's development of trade with the East, enabling France to buy products such as spices on better terms than those exacted by the Italians during their monopolization of this trade. On the other hand, the increase in French agricultural output following the arrival of more peaceful times had resulted in a significant rise in agricultural exports, earning gold and silver not only from Spain but also from northern Europe. Thus treasure that had come to Europe from the New World had found its way into France (62–65).

To the improvement on current account was added an inflow on capital account. This was connected with public sector borrowing; the French Crown paid high interest rates, and the City of Paris granted annuities on very favorable terms. Bodin regarded this capital flow as a healthy development that could be strengthened by an increase in the size of the banking sector.

The influx of gold and silver raised prices everywhere, though certainly not enough to produce uniform inflation rates in different countries. The other causes of inflation, while not negligible, were, in practice, of less significance. The importance of monopolies, in both the goods and the labor markets, was restricted by law, at least in principle (68). With regard to exports, it was true that these could raise the price level because they both reduced aggregate supply and (since food was paid for in monetary metal) increased aggregate demand. But Bodin, as we shall see, had an understanding of the benefits of trade that was unusually sophisticated for both his time and his country, and he clearly did not think that this effect, on its own, could produce sustained inflation.

His identification of fashionable demand for luxuries as the fourth cause of high prices may in part reflect the fact that Bodin "had in his make-up a large measure of Puritanical censoriousness" (Sabine 1951,

280   History of Political Economy 32:2 (2000)

343), which has been evident to the commentators on his political philosophy. Clearly, on its own such demand could explain relative price
effects (which would certainly impinge on popular consciousness of
dearness) but not sustained inflation. It is, however, interesting that in
analyzing the demand for luxuries, Bodin (69–72) used precisely the
approach in terms of relative scarcity that underpinned not only his
development of the quantity theory but the preceding Scholastic analysis of the Just Price.

   Bodin understood perfectly well that part of the rise in prices was to
be attributed to debasement. He also understood well—unlike some of
the more recent defenders of Malestroit—that this was more than a
change in the unit of account. The very process of debasement imposed
forced saving upon the private sector, at least in the short run. But it
was not the fundamental explanation for high prices, for two reasons.
Firstly, after the state had captured resources, the subsequent long-run
equilibrium would indeed represent no more than a change in the unit
of account; secondly, it would not explain the *sustained* inflation peculiar to the sixteenth century, given that debasement itself was a well-
established European practice.

   Nonetheless, Malestroit himself had attempted to explain all the rises
in price by this fifth cause, debasement. Bodin was able to show that
Malestroit's demonstration was faulty both because his understanding
of the complex history of French currency was inadequate and because
he had biased his results by selecting particular years. "It is, therefore,
a mistake to take as the basis of our calculations a year when money
was strongest and to set aside the years when money was weakest,
which were incomparably more frequent than the good years" (79).
Malestroit's attempt to explain price increases in terms of debasement
was thus fundamentally flawed; the rise in prices had to be determined
by the combined effect of debasement and the change in the relative
values of commodities and the precious metals. Thus while Malestroit
explained a fivefold price increase by debasement, Bodin's estimate of
the rise in prices of different commodities involved figures of 10, 12, or
even 20 times (80–81), as already noted.

   Bodin himself had identified five causes of *high prices*. As we have
seen, he was not convinced that all five causes explain sustained *inflation*. This is true of cause 3, exports. But Bodin's unwillingness to attach
significance to the exports argument stemmed in turn from a view of
the gains from trade that requires examination.

4. Bodin's Wider Analysis

Exports and the Gains from Trade

In analyzing Bodin's claims to economic sophistication, it is important to understand that Bodin showed an appreciation of the gains from trade that was extraordinary both for the time of his writing and for the fact that his work appeared in the most mercantilist country in Europe. Although the nineteenth-century economist J. R. McCulloch was aware of this aspect of Bodin's writings—McCulloch owned a copy of Richard Knolles's 1606 translation of the *Republic* as well as Baudrillart's 1853 study of Bodin (McCulloch 1862, 37)—this aspect of Bodin's work seems to have attracted much less attention since McCulloch's day, even though it is integral to the argument.

Once again, we need to look at the Scholastic writers to understand the background. The earlier Christian writers, even up to the twelfth century, were suspicious of trade and of individuals engaged in it. As late as 1078 a church council held that merchants (like soldiers) could not hope for eternal salvation (Gordon 1975, 172). But this attitude, which stemmed from Aristotle, was gradually relaxed from the time of Aquinas, who cautiously accepted trade as an occupation that could legitimately be pursued (G. O'Brien 1920, 145–55). The discussions in the Scholastic literature would, for the reasons already given, have been well known to Bodin, who, apart from his novitiate and his decade at Toulouse, was prodigiously well read. But Bodin went much further than the Scholastics. Indeed, he presented a remarkable case for the wealth-creating effects of trade.

Because France was able to trade with the Near East directly, France was now wealthier, Bodin argued (66). Like those economists in the 1950s who were emancipating themselves from the sterile, general equilibrium interpretation of the work of Eli Heckscher and Bertil Ohlin (Kravis 1956), Bodin argued that trade made goods available that would not otherwise be obtainable. In turn, he believed that this was in accordance with natural law, reflecting God's provision: "God has with admirable foresight made provision, for He has distributed His favours in such a way that there is no country in the world so well provided for as not to lack many things" (86). This, in turn, implied that trade bound nations together in mutual benefit. Indeed, in contradiction of all accepted mercantilist tenets, Bodin argued that imports, by reducing shortages, could be positively beneficial in their effect on the price level.

282   History of Political Economy 32:2 (2000)

It would be too much to expect that Bodin was entirely consistent in his treatment of trade and its beneficial effects. For there are undoubtedly mercantilist traces in his writings, as others have observed (MacIver 1930). It is not the fact that Bodin (88–89) recommended export duties that gives rise to this view; even the nineteenth-century English classical economists, favorable to freedom of trade, were prepared to countenance these (D. P. O'Brien 1975, 190). Rather, it is the argument that imports from Italy were unnecessary, given French natural resources, and that they involved luxury items (Bodin [1568/1578] 1997, 69); thus Bodin's puritanism surfaced again. In turn, this may reflect the fact that Bodin, for all his generally benevolent attitude toward foreigners (Bodin de St. Laurent [1907] 1970, pt. 2, chap. 2, is titled "Bodin xénophile"), disliked Italians. Perhaps this reflected some unfortunate experiences in Toulouse or, more probably, the grasping nature of Italian merchants (Boyer-Xambeu, Deleplace, and Gillard 1994, 22); for Bodin, while arguing that foreigners should be treated with kindness, explicitly excluded from this recommendation rogues from Italy (86).

Gresham's Law

Bodin's claims to economic sophistication are further enhanced when we examine his treatment of the proposition that has become known as Gresham's Law. The idea that goes by this name long predates Sir Thomas Gresham (1519–1579), in whose oeuvre it is not found. The misattribution is the work of the late-nineteenth-century writer H. D. MacLeod, who as one commentator has stated, "was endowed with a marvelous ability for reading into a text what is not there" (De Roover 1949, 91). Gresham's Law can be found in classical Greek writing, notably in Aristophanes' play *The Frogs*. But thirteenth-century scholastic writings were associated with a Greek revival, so it is hardly surprising that the idea is found therein, not only in the work of Nicholas Oresme but in that of earlier writers (Seligman 1930, 61–62).

Bodin understood the law not in the sense that it later had—that it is not possible to maintain a bimetallic currency with a fixed mint ratio, which must necessarily diverge from the relative world price of gold and silver—but in terms of the effects of debasement (Bodin [1568/1578] 1997, 114–15). In this context the law is summarized by the phrase "bad money drives out good." Debased coinage, which still has the same *legal* value as undebased coinage, will remain in circulation while the undebased coinage (with a higher *market* value) flows abroad to take advantage of its greater purchasing power in world markets.

Bodin's understanding of the law, in the context of debasement but not in the context of a bimetallic currency, is important in two ways. First, since the debate with Malestroit involved the issue of debasement, this was the most direct application of the law. But it also had the important implication (though Bodin does not spell this out) that the law in this application explained the shortage of specie in France in the fifteenth century, to which Bodin did indeed draw attention. For successive debasements of gold and silver coin would have driven out the full-weight coin, leaving France short of the precious metals. This would indeed explain why, as Bodin noted, despite successive debasements, on which Malestroit relied for his case, prices had actually fallen in the preceding century. Second, because Bodin did not appear to understand the law in the context of a bimetallic currency, he failed— unlike Navarrus—to appreciate that it was not possible to have a fixed silver/gold price ratio of 12:1. Here Bodin's historical methodology and his enormous reading seem to have combined to mislead him; he advocated the retention of a 12:1 ratio on the grounds that this had been the world price ratio for more than 2,500 years (Bodin [1568/1578] 1997, 109–10). In truth the ratio was changing even as Bodin wrote, as Navarrus showed himself to be aware:

> If there is a shortage of gold coins their value may well increase, so that more coins of silver or other metal are given in exchange for them. Thus we now see that because of the great scarcity of gold money some people will give 23, and even 24 and 25 *reales* for a [gold] doubloon, which according to the law and price of the kingdom is worth only 22. Similarly, if silver money becomes scarce its value may rise, so that more gold or metal money is given in exchange for it. (Navarrus 1556, extracted in Grice-Hutchinson 1952, 95).

Since Bodin understood perfectly well the analysis of relative scarcity employed here, he should have appreciated that his preference for the historic 12:1 ratio was ill-founded. It has been suggested that his preference reflected a philosophical theory about numbers as the basis for a philosophy of human society (Spooner 1972, 94), but at all events his position sat ill with his analysis of relative scarcity and the effects of changes in the *supply* of money. However, in order to complete our

284   History of Political Economy 32:2 (2000)

understanding of Bodin's analysis, it is also necessary to look at his treatment of the *demand* for money.

The Demand for Money

For Bodin to be regarded as having a special claim to a pioneering statement of the quantity theory of money, it is desirable that he should have paid attention to the question of the demand for money. For the quantity theory does not, except in a very simplified form, imply that the change in price level resulting from an increase in the money supply should be exactly proportional. Such a position can only be sustained by treating the demand for money as of unit elasticity with respect to the price level; correspondingly, an analysis of the demand for money is required if such proportionality is to be recognized as simply a special case.

Some commentators have argued that Bodin neglected this issue (Monroe [1924] 1966, 198; Schumpeter 1954, 312–14). But a careful reading of the *Response* indicates clearly enough that Bodin understood that the demand for money—and thus the velocity of circulation —was related to the stage of economic development. He was clear that more developed economies would exhibit a greater demand for transactions balances (67). Thus an increase in the money supply would have a smaller effect on the price level than if balances were unimportant. Again, however, this is entirely consistent with Bodin's understanding of the importance of relative scarcity—the demand for balances affected the relative scarcity of money. Thus it is clear, once again, that his analysis of the value of money—commodity money in this context—falls within the general (Scholastic) treatment of value.

Whatever the nature of the demand for money, however, it was undeniable that changes in the supply would affect the price level and that these effects were likely to be harmful. Bodin both paid attention to the precise nature of the harm and suggested possible remedies.

5. Inflation: Effects and Remedies

The Harm of Inflation

The prevalence of debasement by medieval monarchs led the Scholastic writers, from Aquinas onward, to explain that the consequent price changes confuse markets and injure trade. This insight was further developed by Copernicus (Monroe [1924] 1966, 69). As the inheritor of this tradition, Bodin emphasized the harmful effects of rising prices in his *Response*; both the public and private sectors suffered from the economic uncertainty when the standard of value was no longer stable: "For if money, which ought to govern the price of everything, is changeable and uncertain no one can truly know what he has: contracts will be uncertain, charges, taxes, wages, pensions and fees will be uncertain, fines and penalties fixed by laws and customs will also be changeable and uncertain; in short, the whole state of finances and of many public and private matters will be in suspense" (102). Following the Scholastic analysis, Bodin here directed his remarks at debasement, although the application is much wider.

It was debasement, however, that Bodin believed to be the only *remediable* cause of inflation. The other causes could not be countered without doing more harm than good. There was no sense in trying to drive out the precious metals; experience showed that both monopoly and extravagance would be tolerated in practice, and insofar as exports were inflationary, the gains from trade had also to be taken into account. But debasement could be attacked, even though this would limit the freedom of the sovereign, which Bodin elsewhere argued was absolute (Sabine 1951, 345–50).[12]

Currency Reform

Debasement made it impossible to stabilize prices (Bodin [1568/1578] 1997, 110–14). It introduced difficulties into foreign exchange markets and trade, since equilibrium exchange rates ultimately depended on metallic content, but these would take some time to achieve following debasement (112–13, 117). To avoid such effects, a reform of the coinage was necessary.

In discussing this issue, Bodin was able to draw on his extensive reading and to display an astonishing understanding of the extremely complicated background of European coinage (Hauser 1932, xxvii–

---

12. Bodin did, however, discuss some inherent limitations on sovereignty, notably natural law (Sabine 1951, 347–50), and, as Bodin de St. Laurent has pointed out ([1907] 1970, 78–84), debasement, to which Bodin was fundamentally opposed, was regarded as a legitimate exercise of sovereignty by other writers both before and after Bodin.

286   History of Political Economy 32:2 (2000)

xxxi). He addressed his discussion to both private and governmental debasement. The free-enterprise version of debasement was subject to horrific penalties that, however, failed to achieve their end (Bodin de St. Laurent [1907] 1970, 77). Bodin's solution, which anticipates that of Thomas Joplin in the nineteenth century (D. P. O'Brien 1993, 24), was to make forgery unprofitable rather than either impossible or too terrifying to undertake. Were it made unprofitable, it would be reduced to a very low level (Bodin [1568/1578] 1997, 94–97, 118–19). It could be made unprofitable by a reform of the coinage that ensured that ordinary transactors were not easily fooled because the coinage was regular, stable, and easily recognized.

Quantitatively, the major problem was not forgery and private debasement but the activity of government in debasing the coinage systematically (just as twentieth-century forgery of paper currency is of minuscule importance compared with the activities of governments in inflating the money supply). Kings fell prey to the urgings of their courtiers, who recommended debasement (98–99), and, apparently in search of increased revenues, monarchs carried out this activity on a huge scale (110–14) and with little public condemnation. What the public sector gained in command over resources was correspondingly lost by the private sector, so that before account is taken of the disruption of markets, what was under consideration was at best a zero-sum game (120, 124–25). But the confusion engendered by debasement actually benefited the monarchs engaged in this activity. By undermining public awareness of the characteristics of full-weight coins, the monarchs could more easily pass off debased coinage at full value.

Despite his general defense of the absolute nature of sovereignty—a defense that other writers extended even to debasement—Bodin instead argued that the coinage should be reformed. What was required was a full-weight coinage without alloy. The ratio between silver and gold should be 12:1 (pp. 99–108). Such a reformed coinage would make it harder for monarchs to pass off coins with a significant proportion of alloy in future. "We will also, by these means, prevent all falsification of the coinage; and even the most stupid and ignorant will know the worth of any coin by the sight, the sound, and the weight, without fire, graving-tool or touchstone" (107). The full-weight coin should also have milled edges, to prevent clipping, and it should be cast rather than hammered (121–23). Such a reform would securely establish the value of gold and silver coinage and would leave inflation to be determined only by unavoidable increases in the quantities of the precious metals.

Thus the high-value coinage (gold and silver) would be established on a firm footing. However, there was a further difficulty: the question of the composition of low-value coinage for use in retail transactions by poorer people. The problem of the composition of the "Billon" was a perpetual dilemma for Renaissance governments (Spooner 1972, 102, 140–42). Perhaps it is not surprising that Bodin was not able to solve a problem that had defeated these governments; indeed, there are inconsistencies in the treatment in the *Response* that are sufficiently serious to suggest that the process of revision between 1568 and 1578 involved some prolonged tinkering with the original text. At one point Bodin even suggested that small-value coinage should be phased out (102–3), while at another he recommended copper coins (or very small silver ones) for the poor (107–8). Yet he took the (not unusual) view that copper was not suitable for coinage because it was of varying value, not merely through history but also between different countries (108–9). Again, toward the end of the *Response* he seemed to have veered back toward the view that no Billon should be issued (120).

Unsatisfactory though these vacillations may be, the issue was, from Bodin's point of view, rather minor compared with the need to stabilize the standard of value. Though the poor certainly needed some kind of token for retail transactions, the agricultural sector as a whole was able to use barter to a remarkable extent. Indeed, as English experience demonstrated (97–98), there was no easy solution; finding a suitable medium for retail transactions in an economy characterized by subsistence agriculture and barter was extremely difficult.

6. Bodin's Achievement

It should be clear from the account of Bodin's thought given here that Bodin did indeed formulate a recognizable version of the quantity theory of money in his *Response to Malestroit*. He went on to employ this in his *Republic*, as Bodin de St. Laurent has pointed out ([1907] 1970, 31), in turn incorporating parts of the *Republic* into the second edition of the *Response*. It seems clear that Schumpeter's judgment of Bodin's achievement was substantially correct. In fact, some reservations that Schumpeter subsequently expressed about Bodin and the quantity theory more narrowly defined (he suggested that Bodin failed to distin-

288   History of Political Economy 32:2 (2000)

guish clearly enough between currency—which could then include
paper—and precious metals as commodities [Schumpeter 1954, 313])
seem unnecessary. Bodin's analysis does contain the idea of a demand
for money relating to the existing price and income level (treated as the
stage of development); a discussion of the supply of money, distinguishing money in coined form; an understanding that the money
market clears, with causality running from changes (primarily) in the
money supply to changes in the price level; and an appreciation of the
operation of markets at both national and international levels. Indeed,
Bodin shows considerable sophistication in his development of the
analysis.

Perhaps the clearest testimony to the originality and nature of his
contribution is the extent in turn to which his work not only exercised
a very considerable, acknowledged influence, especially in England,
but also the extent of its unacknowledged influence—in a word, plagiarism. His influence in England was particularly marked, as his
French editor has noted (Hauser 1932, lxvi). Although no trace has
been found of a sixteenth-century English translation referred to by
Bodin's publisher, when the second edition appeared (G. A. Moore
[1948, vii–viii] made extensive and scholarly inquiries about the existence of such a translation, at the time of his now extremely rare translation of the second edition), Bodin himself did go to England in 1581
and may have been there two years earlier (Bodin de St. Laurent
[1907] 1970, 44; Baudrillart 1853, 128–29). In England, too, the process of plagiarism began early. In 1581 his ideas were appropriated by
the anonymous editor of the *Discourse of the Common Weal of this
Realm of England*, originally written by John Hales (or Sir Thomas
Smith; see Palliser 1992, 457–58) (Monroe [1924] 1966, 59; Schumpeter 1954, 166). Both his descendant Jean Bodin de St. Laurent ([1907]
1970, 40–51) and his French editor, Henri Hauser (1932, lxix–lxxv),
noted the extent of the plagiarism that he suffered in France. During
the next century his influence became widespread, and it has been
traced in considerable detail by Bodin de St. Laurent ([1907] 1970,
40–51) and by Monroe ([1924] 1966, 90, 93–95, 99, 101, 113, 117,
120, 144). Monroe (1951, 132–41) also published a partial translation of the *Response*. A particularly interesting manifestation of his
impact during the next century is the incorporation of his *Response*,
in abstracted form, into Gerard de Malynes's *Englands View, in the*

Unmasking of Two Paradoxes (1603). Malynes actually took the argument further; as commentators have noted (De Roover 1949, 247n; Silk 1972), Malynes makes the excellent point that what is interesting about the quantity theory in the context of international flows is the lagged response of prices across countries.

Both the acknowledged influence and the plagiarism are testimony to the fact that Bodin's achievement was considerable. He had provided, as early as the mid-sixteenth century, both the first proper analysis and the first clear documentation of that century's inflation. His statement was not in any sense a piece of casual pamphleteering; it drew on a highly developed Scholastic background and reflected intelligence, intellectual training, and scholarship. He showed himself fully aware of the implications, in the context of debasement, of Gresham's Law; he not only analyzed the effects of changes in the money supply in terms of the Just Price analysis of relative scarcity but also related the demand for money to the degree of economic development; and he capped these accomplishments with an appreciation of the benefits of trade that was indeed remarkable, not only for that century but even for the next. When the question of his attainment is related directly to a detailed examination of the content of his *Response*, as has been done here, the extent of his achievement seems undeniable.

References

Baudrillart, H. 1853. *Jean Bodin et son temps*. Paris: Guillaumin.

Bodin, J. 1568. *La Response de Maistre Jean Bodin Advocat en la Cour au paradoxe de monsieur de Malestroit, touchant l'encherissement de toutes choses, & le moyen d'y remedier*. Paris: Martin le Jeune.

——. 1578. *Les Paradoxes du Seigneur de Malestroict, Conseiller du Roy, & Maistre ordinaire de ses comptes, sur le faict des Monnoyes, presentez à sa Majesté, au moys de Mars, M.D.LXVI. Avec la responce de Jean Bodin aus dicts Paradoxes*. Paris: Jacques du Puys.

——. [1568/1578] 1997. *Response to the Paradoxes of Malestroit*. Translated by H. Tudor and R. W. Dyson. Bristol: Thoemmes.

Bodin de Saint Laurent, J. [1907] 1970. *Les Idées monétaires et commerciales de Jean Bodin*. New York: Burt Franklin.

Boyer-Xambeu, M. T., G. Deleplace, and L. Gillard. 1988. Métaux d'Amérique et monnaies d'Europe. *Annales Economies Sociétés Civilisations* 43:959–67.

——. 1994. *Private Money and Public Currencies: The Sixteenth-Century Challenge*. Translated by A. Azodi. New York: M. E. Sharpe.

290   History of Political Economy 32:2 (2000)

Chiang, A. C. 1984. *Fundamental Methods of Mathematical Economics*. 3d ed. London: McGraw Hill.

D'Avenel, G. 1894. *Histoire économique de la propriété, des salaires, des denrées et de tous les prix en général depuis l'an 1200 jusqu'en l'an 1800*. Paris: Imprimerie Nationale.

Davies, G. 1994. *A History of Money*. Cardiff: University of Wales Press.

Dempsey, B. W. 1935.The Historical Emergence of Quantity Theory. *Quarterly Journal of Economics* 50:174–84.

De Roover, R. 1949. *Gresham on Foreign Exchange*. Cambridge: Harvard University Press.

———. 1953. *L'Evolution de la lettre de change, XIVe–XVIIe siècle*. Paris: Colin.

Franklin, J. H. 1968. Jean Bodin. In vol. 3 of *International Encyclopaedia of the Social Sciences*, edited by D. L. Sills. New York: Macmillan.

Gazier, M., and B. Gazier. 1978. *Or et monnaie chez Martin de Azpilcueta*. Paris: Economica.

Gillard, L. 1994. Y a-t-il Étalon-or à la Renaissance? In *Or, monnaie, échange dans la culture de la Renaissance*, edited by A. Tournon and G.-A. Pérouse. St. Etienne: University of St. Etienne.

Gómez Camacho, F. 1998. Later Scholastics: Spanish Economic Thought in the Sixteenth and Seventeenth Centuries. In *Ancient and Medieaval Economic Ideas and Concepts of Social Justice*, edited by S. Todd Lowry and B. Gordon. Leiden: Brill.

Gordon, B. 1975. *Economic Analysis before Adam Smith*. London: Macmillan.

Grice-Hutchinson, M. 1952. *The School of Salamanca: Readings in Spanish Monetary Theory, 1544–1605*. Oxford: Clarendon.

———. 1978. *Early Economic Thought in Spain, 1177–1740*. London: Allen and Unwin.

Hamilton, E. J. 1934. *American Treasure and the Price Revolution in Spain*. Cambridge: Harvard University Press.

Harsin, P. 1928. *Les Doctrines monétaires et financières en France du XVIe au XVIIIe Siècle*. Paris: Félix Alcan.

Hauser, H., ed. 1932. *La Response de Jean Bodin*. Paris: Librairie Armand Colin.

Heaton, H. 1948. *Economic History of Europe*. Rev. ed. New York: Harper.

Hegeland, H. 1951. *The Quantity Theory of Money*. Göteborg, Sweden: Elanders Boktryckeri.

Humphrey, T. M. 1993. *Money, Banking, and Inflation*. Aldershot, England: Edward Elgar.

Jevons, W. S. 1863. *A Serious Fall in the Value of Gold Ascertained and Its Social Effects Set Forth*. London: Stanford.

Kravis, I. 1956. Availability and Other Influences on the Commodity Composition of Trade. *Journal of Political Economy* 64:143–55.

Letwin, W. O. 1963. *The Origins of Scientific Economics*. London: Methuen.

Lowry, S. Todd. 1996. Review of M. T. Boyer-Xambeu, G. Deleplace, and L.

Gillard, *Private Money and Public Currencies: The Sixteenth Century Challenge.* (New York: M. E. Sharpe, 1994). *HOPE* 28:310–13.

McCulloch, J. R. [1862] 1995. *A Catalogue of Books, the Property of a Political Economist.* London: Routledge/Thoemmes.

MacIver, R. M. 1930. Jean Bodin. In vol. 2 of *Encyclopaedia of the Social Sciences,* edited by E. R. A. Seligman, with Alvin Johnson. New York: Macmillan.

Malynes, G. de [1603] 1972. *Englands View, in the Unmasking of Two Paradoxes.* New York: Arno Press.

Monroe, A. E. [1924] 1966. *Monetary Theory before Adam Smith.* New York: A. M. Kelley.

———, ed. 1951. *Early Economic Thought: Selections from Economic Literature prior to Adam Smith.* Cambridge: Harvard University Press.

Moore, G. A. 1948. Introduction to *The Response of Jean Bodin to the Paradoxes of Malestroit and the Paradoxes.* Chevy Chase, Md.: Country Dollar Press.

Morineau, M. 1985. *Incroyable Gazettes et fabuleux métaux.* Paris: Maison des Sciences de l'Homme.

O'Brien, D. P. 1975. *The Classical Economists.* Oxford: Clarendon.

———. 1993. *Thomas Joplin and Classical Macroeconomics.* Aldershot, England: Edward Elgar.

———. 1997. Introduction to Bodin [1568/1578] 1997.

O'Brien, G. 1920. *An Essay on Mediaeval Economic Teaching.* London: Longman.

Palliser, D. M. 1992. *The Age of Elizabeth.* London: Longman.

Peronnet, M. 1994. De l'or splendeur immortelle . . . . In *Or, monnaie, échange dans la culture de la Renaissance,* edited by A. Tournon and G.-A. Pérouse. St. Etienne: University of St. Etienne.

Phelps Brown, E. H. and S. V. Hopkins. 1959. Builders' Wage-rates, Prices, and Population: Some Further Evidence. *Economica* 27.101:18–29.

Popescu, O. 1998. Latin American Scholars. In *Ancient and Medieaval Economic Ideas and Concepts of Social Justice,* edited by S. Todd Lowry and B. Gordon. Leiden: Brill.

Reynolds, B. 1945. Introduction to *Method for the Easy Comprehension of History,* by J. Bodin. New York: Columbia University Press.

Sabine, G. H. 1951. *A History of Political Theory.* 3d ed. London: Harrap.

Schumpeter, J. A. 1954. *History of Economic Analysis.* London: Allen and Unwin.

Seligman, E. R. A. 1930. Bullionists. In vol. 3 of *Encyclopaedia of the Social Sciences,* edited by E. R. A. Seligman, with Alvin Johnson. New York: Macmillan.

Servet, J.-M. 1994. Les Paradoxes des *Paradoxes* de Malestroit. In *Or, monnaie, échange dans la culture de la Renaissance,* edited by A. Tournon and G.-A. Pérouse. St. Etienne: University of St. Etienne.

Silk, M. 1972. Introduction to *Englands View, in the Unmasking of Two Paradoxes,* by G. de Malynes. New York: Arno Press.

Spiegel, H. W. 1991. *The Growth of Economic Thought.* 3d ed. Durham, N.C.: Duke University Press.

Spooner, F. C. 1972. *The International Economy and Monetary Movements.* Cambridge: Harvard University Press.

Tooley, J. 1955. Introduction to *Six Books of the Commonwealth,* by J. Bodin. Oxford: Blackwell.

Vilar, P. 1976. *A History of Gold and Money, 1450–1920.* Translated by J. White. London: NLB.

Part IV
Religion

[12]

Religious Views in His Works

The Relationship of the *Colloquium heptaplomeres* to the *Universae naturae theatrum* and *De la démonomanie des sorciers*

Marion Leathers Daniels Kuntz

WHAT were Bodin's religious views? This difficult question can perhaps be answered more readily from his works than from the facts of his life. During his life he had been accused of being a Jew, a Calvinist, a heretical Catholic, an atheist. Bodin seemed to be none of these, surely not the latter; indeed, it is impossible to read Bodin's works and not to sense the profoundly religious nature of the man. True religion to Bodin was an extremely personal matter practiced in his search for God and the eternal praise of His Majesty. True religion, he felt, requires no church; in fact, the church often impedes true worship. True religion cannot be controlled by the state, for to forbid men the private exercise of their religion is to make them oftentimes atheists. Although Bodin was tolerant of all religions, the one thing he could not abide was atheism. "So the greatest superstition that is, is not by much anything so detestable as Atheisme. And truly they (in mine opinion) offend much, which think that the same punishment is to bee appointed for them that make many gods, and them that would have none at all: or that the infinitie of gods admitted, the almightie and everliving God is thereby taken away. For that superstition how great soever it be, doth yet hold men in feare and awe, both of the laws and of the magistrats, as also in mutuall duties and offices one of them towards another; whereas meere Atheisme doth utterly root of mens' minds all the fear of doing evill."[40]

[40] Bodin, *Six Bookes* p. 539.

INTRODUCTION

A thorough understanding of Bodin's religious thinking can be attained only by a careful analysis of his last three works. In the *Universae naturae theatrum* he gives a detailed account of the universe and God's relation to this theater of nature. In *De la démonomanie des sorciers* he expands his theory of the universe to include the world of spirits, both angelic and demonic. In the *Colloquium heptaplomeres* he incorporates his ideas about the universe and the spirit world, but he expands these concepts into a full view of man in the universe, who is searching for his own personal relationship to the cosmos and a comprehension of true religion.

In the *praefatio* of the *Universae naturae theatrum* Bodin explains why he turns to the theater of universal nature to explore the question of God. Man's laws are often irrational and full of error, but the laws of nature are logical and fixed, for God himself is their author. The contemplation of nature is of prime importance, for it often leads a man to thoughts of God.[41] "And indeed the Theater of Nature is nothing other than the contemplation of those things founded by the immortal God as if a certain tablet were placed under the eyes of every single one so that we may embrace and love the majesty of that very author, his goodness, wisdom, and remarkable care in the greatest matters, in moderate affairs, in matters of the least importance. For as Aristotle writes, the one who doubts whether there is a God or not must be refuted by no weak arguments."[42] Nature not only brings pleasure to the beholder but also such a desire for the Founder that we, though unwilling, are seized, stupefied, and amazed at the love of Him.[43] All the ornaments of the world, the more beautiful manifestations of the angels, and the immortal spirits show the work of the Master Builder.

God is the prime mover of the universe, and creation is so unique to the prime cause that it is communicable to no creature.[44] God is the principle that sets the universe in motion. "The ultimate principle is eternal, and nothing can be previous to it, nothing like it,

[41] In the *Theatrum*, Bodin's views on nature are quite close to the tenets of Stoicism.
[42] Jean Bodin, *Universae naturae theatrum* (Lyon, 1596), pp. 3–4.
[43] *Ibid.*, p. 4.
[44] *Ibid.*, pp. 16–17.

RELIGIOUS VIEWS IN BODIN'S WORKS

nothing contrary to it, and nothing equal to it."[45] "Principle is singular nor can it be more than one, and it is without beginning; for if anything was before the principle, it can not even deserve to be called the principle, since it owes its origin to another, either from nature or time: but principle ought to be of this sort, according to the teaching of Aristotle himself, so that things arise neither from themselves nor from others, but from the principle."[46] The principle is eternal; if it were not, "it would be necessary that God either have his origin from another, or from himself; it could not be from another, because it would not be a principle; not from himself because nothing can be made from itself . . . therefore it is necessary that principle be eternal."[47]

God, the principle, the prime mover, alone is infinite and eternal. In things eternal there is no first cause, no last. The world has a first cause; consequently it is not eternal. Nothing can be eternal in its own nature whose first cause is voluntary, and since the first cause of the world is voluntary, and its station and conditions depend on the will of another, the world is not eternal.[48]

Cause cannot precede principle; God, the principle, created the universe not from necessity but from free will. Causes proceed from the first cause in a fixed order, as though a golden chain had been let down from heaven, but causes are not unchangeable because God alone is changeless.

It is impossible for the human mind to comprehend the principle because the principle cannot be known by comparison. Although Bodin states that man cannot understand God, he presents three views of the origin of the world. The Chaldaeans and Hebrews say that it was created and came into action from pure privation and that it will return to nothingness. The Academicians, Stoics, Epicureans, ancient Latins, and some Arabs, except Averroës, say that it was not created but came into being from misshapen matter and that it will perish and all things will return to chaos. Aristotle says that it has neither beginning nor end but existed from eternal

---

[45] *Ibid.*, p. 16.   [46] *Ibid.*, p. 22.   [47] *Ibid.*, p. 58.
[48] *Ibid.*, p. 37; cf. also Jean Bodin, *Colloquium heptaplomeres de rerum sublimium arcanis abditis,* edited by Ludovicus Noack (Schwerin, 1857), p. 27.

INTRODUCTION

time and would exist forever. Bodin's own views are similar to the Chaldean-Hebraic interpretation, although he states that matter cannot be corrupted because nothing is corrupted which was not born; so all things in this way will return where first they were begun and will return to their own beginnings.[49] There can be nothing in the middle between being and nonbeing.[50]

The world and all that is in it is corporeal and therefore *divisibile, patibile, ac dissolubile est.*[51] Bodin cites Psalm 101 and Isaiah 65 to substantiate the claim that the Master Builder (*opifex*) has decreed that at some time or other the universe will perish. God alone is incorporeal and the Hebrews call "God, maqom, that is, place, because above the sky his divine majesty and essence embrace the universe. They do not say that God is in the world, but the world is in God, since He is not inclosed in the world nor shut out from the world, although the sky is called the abode of God."[52]

God's relation to the universe and to man is emphasized by the epithets Bodin used to describe Him. God is called *conditor, rex, opifex, architectus, deus optimus maximus, principium,* and *lux sempiterna.* God is without body and indivisible and is able to communicate no part of his essence to another. "For if a creature should have any part of the divine essence he would be God completely because God does not have parts nor is divided into parts."[53] Because man is finite, he can never grasp the infinite mind and goodness of God. Man may question the phenomena of nature and the dire happenings on earth, but he should be ever mindful that God made

[49] Bodin, *Theatrum,* p. 83. Bodin in the same section describes matter as a *meretrix* who puts on and takes off forms.

[50] *Ibid.,* p. 71. On being and nonbeing Bodin says: "Because nothing can be fashioned in the middle between being and nonbeing: For we see the beginning of generation is made in the natural body, with matter and form attendant, as in an end from which, and this generation extends itself into the completed body: indeed the change [*mutatio*] which precedes generation has a foundation residing in its own matter and form; consider the embryo, or blood or seed or roots of plants or buds or the beginnings of fossils or metals, all of which have their own form and matter; wherefore that figment, which Aristotle in his thinking imagined between being and nonbeing [*non-ens*], never existed in nature, moreover cannot even be captured in thinking."

[51] *Ibid.,* p. 41.   [52] *Ibid.,* p. 107.   [53] *Ibid.,* pp. 629–30.

RELIGIOUS VIEWS IN BODIN'S WORKS

all things good. Evil is nothing else than the privation or the lack of good. As jailers, magistrates, and judges are necessary in states, so in this state of the world "God himself for the generation, care, and safeguarding of things has placed angels in all places, in states, provinces, families, as leaders and moderators, and also he placed avengers in all places who do nothing and punish in no way except ordered by God."[54] Though man may not understand, God is ever planning for his welfare. When God noticed that man was carried by base desires away from the contemplation of intelligible things, He willed for man to be involved in agriculture and the care of animals so that this concern would lessen man's mad desires.[55] Indeed, there is a marvelous power of nature placed in the minds of men which inspires them to piety, justice, and virtue. But how do they follow divine knowledge unless God has given them the breath of life?[56]

God alone is simple and can impart no part of his infinity to any creature. How then can God the Creator, eternal principle, without cause, be known? Bodin's answer is Platonic-Augustinian: there are ideas shared between the Creator and the things created. "God had created every seed of the field before it was in the land, which cannot be interpreted in any other way than as the archetype and eternal example in the mind of the Creator."[57] Other values are not all equally remote from God, for there is a chain of being. Next to God in created nature are two Seraphs which stand by the eternal Creator and have six wings and eyes in all parts of the body.

Although knowledge of created things is known through cause, as the Aristotelians said, God is known in a different way, through his creative influences. "God cannot be known from higher causes or antecedent causes, which are none, but can be known only from the rear, that is, from effects."[58] God used good and bad angels, the stars, and other natural causes to bring about all things, and there is no action, no calamity, which has not come from God.[59] Although

---

[54] *Ibid.*, p. 632. [55] *Ibid.*, p. 273. [56] *Ibid.*, p. 207.
[57] *Ibid.*, p. 630. [58] *Ibid.*, p. 633.
[59] Jean Bodin, *De magorum daemonomania* (Basel, 1581), pp. 13-15, 36-38, 92-94. The Latin edition, translated by Franciscus Junius, was used for all the citations from this work.

INTRODUCTION

man can never know "who and what God is . . . ,"[60] Bodin constantly emphasizes that nature is the key to understanding God. In
the conclusion of the *Universae naturae theatrum* Bodin says that
he wrote about nature so that we might grasp even a shadowy recognition of the Creator and "break forth in his praises with so much
force that at length we might be carried on high by these steps;
which indeed is the highest and final good of man."[61]

God created the universe through the exercise of His free will,
and He bestowed free will on man. "But if this world is ruled by
the highest fairness, also we must confess that the wicked are punished by right, nor is any necessity for sinning due to the higher
causes, but free will is granted to man by which he may be higher not
only than the lascivious desires but also than the stars."[62] Man was
made a little lower than the angels, and since angels are good and
devils bad, man also has a free choice to be good or bad.[63] Citing
Deuteronomy 30, Bodin presents God's words:

> I have placed before your eyes good and evil, life and death; choose
> therefore the good and you will live. . . . After God created man,
> he gave him free will and said 'If you wish, you will keep my com-
> mandments; and they will preserve you; I have given fire and
> water to you, you can direct your hand to one and to the other; you
> have good and bad, life and death, and whatever you wish, you
> will have.'[64]

In 1578 Bodin presided as judge in a case of witchcraft brought
against Joanna Harvilleria. Bodin found the woman guilty as
charged and condemned her to death. In the *praefatio* of *De la démonomanie* (1580) Bodin explains the charge and the penalty, and
with the witchcraft case as a starting point, Bodin unfolds in the
rest of the book his concept of the world of spirits. He defines a
magician as one who is wise and prudent in the ways of the devil
and so perverts the law. The devil has devised superstitions and im-
pieties and has taught these to his slaves, the magicians, for the

---

[60] Bodin, *Colloquium heptaplomeres*, p. 42.
[61] Bodin, *Theatrum*, p. 633.
[62] *Ibid.*, p. 32.   [63] *Ibid.*, pp. 14–15.   [64] *Ibid.*, p. 16.

RELIGIOUS VIEWS IN BODIN'S WORKS

destruction of the human race. Lest anyone be doubtful concerning the spirit world, Bodin cites the philosophers and the sacred writings to prove that spirits do exist. Good spirits are called angels, and evil spirits are known as demons, according to the opinion of the Sorbonne in September 1398. From the beginning of the universe God created angels and that great Satan whom the Scripture calls Behemoth and Leviathan. On the nature of demons Bodin cites ancient authorities who believed demons were of two orders, good and bad, but he follows the opinion of the theologians in believing that all demons are bad.

In discussing the association of spirits with men, Bodin reiterates his view stated in the *Universae naturae theatrum* that the *anima* of men is between demons and angels, placed in the middle as it were, and since men are created a little lower than angels, men have the choice of following angelic or demonic natures. Magicians are filled with evil spirits who deceive in two ways, either openly with expressed pacts with the devil or by idolatry in the guise of religion. Magicians pretend that they can foretell the future, but true divination comes from God who speaks to His prophets in dreams, in visions, or through angels. All other divination is human and diabolic. The hymns of Orpheus call upon the oracles of Pan, which is Satan to the Hebrews. Plutarch calls Pan the great leader, and Caesar and Pompey relied on Pan and soothsayers, but all these are human predictions.

Bodin says that in pursuing legitimate goals men often find no help from nature or human faculty but, instead of turning to God who can help most of all, turn to magicians who invoke the devil. Bodin details the several kinds of diabolic divinators: (1) people who send their children through fire; (2) judges who judge with money and priests who divine with silver; (3) sorcerers who rely on lots and numbers; (4) those who fool the eyes of men; (5) those who beg the oracles of evil spirits or consult the devil hidden in bones of beasts; (6) those who consult the dead. All these divinators are abominations to God.[65] God ordained natural divination from

---

[65] Martin Luther was also strongly opposed to magicians and astrologers. See Carlo Ginzburg, *Il nicodemismo: simulazione e dissimulazione religiosa nell' Eu-*

INTRODUCTION

the creation of the universe, as the Cabala shows, in secret intelligence of divine miracles and in allegories woven throughout sacred scripture. The sacred writings show that it is not necessary to insist on literal interpretation because God speaks in allegories and parables, and His secrets hang as if from a chain let down from heaven. Since God is the first and eternal cause, all things, all spirits and divinations come from him.

Bodin places astrologers in the same category as magicians, and he says it is wrong to trust in astrologers since God is above all. Astrologers are unworthy to make judgments about spirits, virtues, merits, or punishments, and it is most unworthy for astrologers or anyone, for that matter, to argue about religion. Bodin does not deny that magicians are able to cause storms, sickness, sterility, and to kill men and flocks, but he cites Augustine who says that demons have no power of themselves, but God has given them power for punishing men. He continues by saying that God has thousands of ways for vengeance: first through Himself, then through angels, then through demons, men, and beasts, and finally through nature. God brings about all things by means of angels, demons, stars, and other natural causes. He increases our plenty through good servants and punishes us through evil agents.

Through this often tedious book Bodin constantly emphasizes that magicians are shrewd men who are under Satan's power, yet Satan himself can do nothing except what God wills. With this as his major theme he returns at the end of the book to the case of Joanna

ropa del '500 (Turin, 1970), p. 30: "In 1520 Luther had published a comment to the decalogue, including among the violators of the first commandment also magicians, necromancers, and astrologers. Luther's hostility toward astrology was great; moreover, this anti-astrological polemic on a religious basis was widespread enough as was the traditional, contrary attempt to show—if the words of Psalm 18 are recalled, 'The heavens declare the glory of God'—the religious legitimacy of astrology. But, coming from a heretic such as Luther, this new attack on astrology could very easily be turned around. Laurent Fries, a physician and astrologer of Colmar, intervened in defense of the science of the stars with a short work (*Ein kurtze Schirmred der Kunst Astrologie* . . . [A Brief Defense of the Art of Astrology . . .], J. Grüninger, Strasburg, 1520) written in the form of a dialogue between Fries himself and Luther. In this work Fries tried to show that astrology was, from a Christian point of view, perfectly orthodox and not therefore, as Luther had maintained, a pagan science."

RELIGIOUS VIEWS IN BODIN'S WORKS

Harvilleria. He defends the death penalty for magicians and sorcerers because they have allied themselves on the side of Satan, whose aim is to destroy the works of God.[66]

In the *République* Bodin had said that prevention of crime was a more proper remedy than punishment; however, he theorizes, in keeping with the premises of canon law, that the principal benefit derived from punishing crime is that citizens succeed in appeasing God's wrath, and they gain God's benevolent care for the good of the whole commonwealth. Sorcerers, then, must be punished because their crime is aimed at God's majesty. "As Bodin had stated elsewhere, it is not customary for jurists to make codes of law for the sake of vindicating the theories of philosophers, but rather for the sake of serving those practical ends at which the majority of people wish to arrive. Expediency is thus a matter of principle for our author. Had he not explained this to us, we might have considered that in estimating sorcery as the most heinous of crimes, he was making an undue and hypocritical concession to God."[67]

Although it may seem strange that a man of Bodin's erudition and legal training would believe in witchcraft and magic, he was not unlike many of his age in this belief. The spirit world to which angels and demons belonged was a vital part of Bodin's religious thought; consequently, magicians and sorcerers were part of his world view.[68]

The key to Bodin's religious thought is found in the *Colloquium heptaplomeres*, the intriguing work which Bodin completed in 1588[69]

---

[66] For Bodin's place in the history of magic, see Lynn Thorndike, *History of Magic and Experimental Science*, VI (New York, 1941), pp. 525–27. Thorndike stated that few people were as credulous regarding the powers of witches as Bodin, yet Bodin distinguished "natural means of knowing secret things" from witchcraft.

[67] H. E. Mantz, "Jean Bodin and the Sorcerers," *The Romanic Review* 15 (1924), 174–75.

[68] Bodin's view was surely not uncommon in the sixteenth century. See Daniel P. Walker, *Spiritual and Demonic Magic from Ficino to Campanella* (London, 1958).

[69] Diecmann and Guhrauer believed that 1593 was the correct date because at the end of Bibliothèque Nationale fonds latin 6564 and other manuscripts the letters H.E.J.B.A.S.A.AE. LXIII seem to indicate that Bodin wrote the *Colloquium* when he was 63 years old, that is, in 1593. See E. Guhrauer's introduction to *Das Heptaplomeres des Jean Bodin, zur Geschichte der Kultur und Literatur im Jahrhundert der Reformation* (Berlin, 1841). However, 1593 is not the correct date

INTRODUCTION

but did not publish. Guhrauer believed that Bodin never intended the
book to be published during his lifetime because he knew his age
too well. The German scholar stated that the *Colloquium heptaplomeres* should be regarded as Bodin's religious testament for a
later age, which he worked out only for his inner satisfaction.[70]
Contrary to Guhrauer's statement, I believe that Bodin would have
published the *Colloquium heptaplomeres* had he lived longer. In
spite of the dangers involved,[71] Bodin must have felt a great need
to publish the *Colloquium heptaplomeres* because this work is truly
the key to the other two works and, perhaps to all his works.

The *Colloquium heptaplomeres* expresses the basic ideas of the *Universae naturae theatrum* and *De la démonomanie* and then advances
a step farther. In the *Colloquium heptaplomeres* Bodin presents the
problems of the creation of the universe, which constituted a great
portion of the *Theatrum*, and of God's revelation of Himself through
the order of nature and through the spirit world, the theme of
De la démonomanie. Then he advances to the problem of man in the
natural world, in the world of spirits, and in his quest for God or,
as Bodin poses the problem, his quest for true religion.

The *Colloquium heptaplomeres* is a dialogue between men of
seven different faiths or points of view. Coronaeus, at whose home
the conversations take place, represents the Catholic viewpoint, Salomon the Jewish, Toralba the philosophic naturalist, Fridericus the
Lutheran, Curtius the Calvinist, Senamus the Skeptic, and Octavius
the Islamic. In the *Theatrum* Bodin uses a pseudodialogue form, but
the dialogue is soon forgotten for the exposition. In the *Colloquium
heptaplomeres* the dialogue form is maintained throughout, each
man presenting his opinions on the various points under discussion.

In Book II of the *Colloquium heptaplomeres* the men, with Toral-

---

because a manuscript of the *Colloquium* which I discovered in the Bibliothèque
Mazarine (Bibliothèque Mazarine fonds latin 3527) carries the date 1588. This
evidence opens up many new problems for Bodin scholars. Either Bodin was not
born in 1530 (for he could not have been 63 years old in 1588), or A.AE. LXIII
(anno aetatis LXIII) does not refer to his chronological age. An article by the author
on this manuscript and Bibliothèque Mazarine fonds latin 3529 is now in progress.

[70] Guhrauer, *Das Heptaplomeres*, p. 6.

[71] The *Methodus*, the *République*, and *De la démonomanie* had already been
placed on the Index.

RELIGIOUS VIEWS IN BODIN'S WORKS

ba dominating the conversation, debate the causes of things. Toralba points out that God did not create the universe from necessity, which is one of the central arguments of the *Theatrum*. Toralba says: "Still nothing is more foolish than to say that the first cause is the producer and preserver of all things and to find this same first cause by servile obligation and necessity and yet to assign to oneself free will. . . . That God is immutable is agreed by all natural scientists and theologians. But they think that higher causes are checked by the force and power of lower causes. More credible is the opinion of the poets, who, in their fictions, profess that Jupiter is loosed from the power of lower gods but still is bound by the higher laws of Nemesis. . . . Augustine thinks that fate applies to God alone or to no one."[72] Salomon agrees with Toralba and says that fate is God who receives all things within himself and encompasses all things with free will. Toralba then proffers an opinion which contains much of the thought of the *Theatrum* and *De la démonomanie*: "Natural things do not happen by chance, at random, or in blind sequence but proceed uniformly according to the same laws, so that given the cause the effect follows, unless they are kept from doing so by the divine will in all things or human will in some or by the power of demons in many."[73]

Throughout the *Colloquium heptaplomeres* Bodin emphasizes that demons and angels are emissaries from God to man, and just as in the *Démonomanie*, he cites numerous examples of strange events that happen apart from nature and consequently must be a result of demonic power. He constantly repeats, however, that demons have no power of themselves and can do nothing unless ordered by God.

Bodin reiterates the fact that God alone is eternal, and he departs from Aristotle's teaching that the world is eternal. In the *Universae naturae theatrum* Bodin also states this idea and adds that the world cannot be eternal of its own nature since it depends on the will of another.[74] In contrast man has been granted free will by God. If a

[72] *Colloquium heptaplomeres*, Book II, p. 20.

[73] *Ibid.*, p. 24.

[74] "Nothing can be eternal in its own nature, whose first cause is voluntary: the first cause of the world is voluntary; therefore, the world cannot be eternal in its own nature, since its state and condition depend on the freedom and will of another." *Universae naturae theatrum*, p. 37.

INTRODUCTION

man chooses the good, he will live; if he chooses evil, he will suffer punishment. Man is also free to obtain knowledge of the good. If man chooses to find God, God reveals Himself by a process of emanation rather than by any particle of God being implanted in man, which would be impossible because it would destroy the Unity which alone is eternal.[75] Bodin posits a certain kind of immortality for the soul and envisions a life after death in which the just will be rewarded and the unjust punished. To Bodin, however, punishments are not infinite.[76]

The ideas which are expressed in the first three books of the *Colloquium heptaplomeres* are paralleled by the same ideas in the *Universae naturae theatrum*. The main theme of the *Theatrum* is that God can best be known from the theater of universal nature,[77] and

[75] *Ibid.*, pp. 629–30. Bodin's concept of free will reflects the influence of St. Augustine. Cf. Augustine's *On the Free Choice of the Will*, Book I and Book III, chapters XI–XVIII. The emanation theory which Bodin emphasizes in the *Colloquium heptaplomeres* reflects the influence of the Neoplatonic "stages" and also the emanation theories of the Cabalists. In the *Theatrum* and *De la démonomanie* Neoplatonic influence is more apparent; in the *Colloquium* there is increased attention to Cabala. For a concise statement concerning Neoplatonic and Cabalistic theories of emanation, note Gershom G. Scholem, *Major Trends in Jewish Mysticism* (New York, 1954), pp. 208–209. "According to the Kabbalists, there are ten such fundamental attributes to God which are at the same time ten stages through which the divine life pulsates back and forth. The point to keep in mind is that the Sefiroth are not secondary or intermediary spheres which interpose between God and the universe. The author does not regard them as something comparable to, for example, the 'middle stages' of the Neoplatonists which have their place between the Absolute One and the world of the senses. In the Neoplatonic system, these emanations are 'outside' the One, if it is possible to use that expression. There have been attempts to justify an analogous interpretation of the theology of the Zohar and to treat the Sefiroth as secondary stages or spheres outside of or apart from the divine personality. . . . True the Zohar frequently refers to the Sefiroth as stages, but they are plainly regarded not as the steps of a ladder between God and the world, but as various phases in the manifestation of the Divinity which proceed from and succeed each other."

[76] See *Colloquium heptaplomeres*, pp. 102–103, 342–43, 344–46. Also *Universae naturae theatrum*, pp. 536–41. For a recent treatment of the question of eternal torment in the seventeenth century, see Daniel P. Walker, *The Decline of Hell* (Chicago, 1964).

[77] "In this elegant allegory it is indicated that God cannot be known from higher or antecedent causes, which are none, but only from behind, that is, from effects . . . and He placed man not in a hidden recess but in the middle of the world, so that he might contemplate more easily and better than if he were in the heaven the universe of all things and all His works, and from the wealth of His works man

RELIGIOUS VIEWS IN BODIN'S WORKS

Toralba, who dominates Books II and III of the *Colloquium hepta-plomeres,* constantly expresses this view. In fact, many passages are so similar that only a few words are changed. Bodin was fascinated by certain stories, and he repeated them in both books. He was so impressed with accounts of Egyptian mummies, their powers of stirring up storms, and their powers of healing that he repeated this story in all three of these works.[78]

More important still for an understanding of Bodin's thought is the discussion of harmony with which he begins Book IV and which is also developed in the *Universae naturae theatrum* (pp. 143 ff.). He begins by showing the harmony in numbers, as in geometric progressions, then the harmony in musical systems, then the harmony most perfectly expressed in nature. Harmony in nature includes harmony in religion and toleration, which is central to Bodin's thinking. The harmony of nature is based on multiplicity, which is the aspect of creation in the world. The unity of Divinity is apart, however, from every multiplicity.[79] Bodin calls upon the concept of harmony to show that, as there is need for multiplicity in nature, so also there is need of this multiplicity in religion. When the dialogue ends with the statement that no further discussions will be held on religion, the concept of harmony takes on additional significance. There is no rejection or acceptance of any one religion, but rather a recognition of the divine descent of all religious beliefs

---

might probingly view the Sun, that is, God Himself." *Universae naturae theatrum,* p. 633. For Toralba's identical view compare his speeches throughout Books II and III.

[78] *Colloquium heptaplomeres,* pp. 66 ff., *Universae naturae theatrum,* pp. 143–44, *De magorum daemonomania,* p. 197.

[79] For an excellent discussion of the *Colloquium heptaplomeres* see Giorgio Radetti "Il problema della religione nel pensiero di Giovanni Bodin," *Giornale critico della filosofia Italiana,* VI, fasc. 4–5 (1938), 277–94. On the question of harmony he says: "As in nature the elements are comparable to voices, to notes which, even though diverse and, in fact, for this very reason, form a harmony ('From whence the sweetest elements, etc.'—cf. *Universae naturae theatrum,* p. 143). So in the human world the state has as its goal the foundation of this harmony among men; the last page of the *Republic* is a complete exaltation of the harmony which regulates and unifies the universe. Cf. *De la rép.,* p. 1060, cf. *Methodus,* p. 294. Moreover, the same doctrine of climates is bound to this doctrine of universal harmony," p. 293.

INTRODUCTION

and a universal brotherhood of men in the worship of divinity and in a moral life and a free conscience for everyone.[80]

Bodin's emphasis upon harmony and toleration, coming as it did in the midst of an age of religious conflicts, makes him an innovator in the religious thinking of the Cinquecento, because the complete tolerationists' view that Bodin was offering was not held by anybody before Uriel da Costa and Spinoza. In contrast to da Costa and Spinoza, who developed a tolerationist attitude because they had given up any historical religion, Bodin remained religious throughout his life.[81]

To summarize, the relationship of the *Colloquium heptaplomeres* to the *Universae naturae theatrum* and *De la démonomanie* is that of a synthesis to its parts: each of the other works contains many of the same ideas as the *Colloquium heptaplomeres*, but the *Colloquium heptaplomeres* contains *all* the ideas inherent in the other two. The first three books of the *Colloquium* reflect the emphasis in the *Theatrum* on the theater of nature as the work of the Master Builder. The laws of nature reflect the wonder of their Creator. The first three books of the *Colloquium* also reflect the spirit world of *De la démonomanie*. Everything which does not happen from God or through the laws of nature must happen because of the action of demons or angels.

The line written at the end of the *Theatrum* gives a clue to another strong relationship between the three works. Bodin says that he wrote the book when all France was burning with civil war. ("*Finis Theatri Naturae, quod Io. Bodinus Gallia tota bella civili flagrante conscripsit.*") The point that Bodin seems to be making is that France is burning because she has not applied the harmonious laws of nature

---

[80] Radetti, "Il problema della religione," p. 294. Bodin had already stated in the *République* that a man of no religion could not be obedient to the law, yet he stressed in the *Colloquium heptaplomeres* the fact that no one can be forced to believe. His plea for toleration was witnessed as early as 1576 by his conduct in the Estates General of Blois as representative of the third estate. See Joseph Lecler, *Toleration and the Reformation* (New York, 1960), pp. 179–85.

[81] Professor Richard H. Popkin called to my attention the relationship of Bodin, da Costa, and Spinoza in regard to toleration. It might be added that Guillaume Postel (1510–1580) expressed tolerationist views that were very similar to those expressed in the *Colloquium heptaplomeres*.

RELIGIOUS VIEWS IN BODIN'S WORKS

to the question of religious toleration, and France (and the world) will continue to burn until the harmony of nature becomes a symbol for universal harmony, especially in the area of religion. This is, of course, the theme of the *Colloquium heptaplomeres*. The last three books of the *Colloquium* are concerned with the question of true religion. The harmony of nature and the spirit world which reflects the higher Unity of God serve, then, as a base upon which Bodin builds the main structure of the *Colloquium heptaplomeres*: the nature of true religion, which reveals and accepts the multiplicity of ways to approach God and the multiple revelations of God to man. True religion is tolerant, for it sees the harmonious multiplicity of religions. No religion is true whose point of view is not universal, whose expression is not free, whose center does not reflect the intimate harmony of God and nature. The *Démonomanie* reflects this emphasis on true religion and so is related not only to the first part, but also to the second part of the *Colloquium heptaplomeres*. Bodin says in his book on witchcraft that true religion is the recognition of God, and that God has revealed himself in multiple ways through miraculous allegories which we read in the Cabala.

It is interesting to note also the progression in form of presentation through the three works. In *De la démonomanie* Bodin uses pure exposition. The dialogue appears, to a limited degree, in the *Universae naturae theatrum*. The *Colloquium heptaplomeres* then shows the full development of the dialogue style, while incorporating all his religious and philosophical thought.

When one looks back from the *Colloquium heptaplomeres* to his earlier work, one realizes that the *Politique* of 1576 has become progressively more liberal in his religious views. When Bodin published the *République* in 1576, it was difficult to determine precisely what his religious views were, but he maintained in 1559 in his *Discours au senate et au peuple de Toulouse* that people should be brought up publicly in one religion, as an indispensable element in the cohesiveness of the state; he also avowed that care should be taken to preserve religious unity, and religion should not be cast in doubt by becoming a subject for disputation. Religion, according to Bodin in 1576, provides the unity of the state and underlies the king's power,

INTRODUCTION

the execution of the laws and respect for the laws, and obedience of
the subjects.[82] Between 1580 and 1596 his liberal views became even
more apparent, until they reach a climax in the *Colloquium hepta-*
plomeres, in which his religious opinions seem to have developed
into a kind of theism which leaves each man's religion, provided he
has some, to his own personal conscience. In the *Colloquium hepta-*
plomeres atheism alone is intolerable to Bodin.

Scholars have held diverse opinions concerning which speaker
represents Bodin's thinking. Baudrillart, Noack, Guhrauer, and with
some limitation, Dilthey think Toralba speaks for Bodin; Huet and
Guttmann say Salomon does; Chauviré seems to choose Salomon
and Toralba, and Mesnard points to Coronaeus.[83] Nearer to the
truth, I believe, is the view that all the speakers represent Bodin's
thinking at one time or another. No one represents his thinking
exclusively, but Bodin is sympathetic to some views of each as the
dialogue develops. The point seems to be, however, that regardless
of Bodin's approval or disapproval of the religious views represented
in the dialogue, he constantly stresses the need for toleration of all
religions.

Coronaeus the Catholic, the gentle peacemaker who does not want
to offend anyone, represents authority and tradition. Salomon the
Jew, who commands respect by his erudition and his advanced age,
displays a vast knowledge of the Cabala and the Old Testament.
The other speakers find it very difficult to refute Salomon. Octavius,
a convert from Catholicism to Islam, points out that Muslims have
ideas common to both the Jewish and Christian religions. He believes that many religions can be received by a state. Octavius also
describes exotic places and strange customs in the East, and he has
a good knowledge of demons and angels. Curtius, the Calvinist, represents the Reformed religion with its emphasis on inner piety. He
holds fast to his belief in the Incarnation, the Virgin birth, and the
immortality of the soul, but he is not nearly so dogmatic as the
Lutheran Fridericus, a mathematician who displays a wide knowledge of demonology. Fridericus is the least tolerant of the seven.

---

[82] *République*, Book IV.
[83] See Radetti, "Il problema della religione," p. 278.

RELIGIOUS VIEWS IN BODIN'S WORKS

Senamus is the skeptic who questions the beliefs of all but says that all religions are good. He also displays a subtle wit, which may reflect a trait of Bodin, who was said to possess a genial disposition and a lively wit.[84] Toralba believes that true religion consists in the simple adoration of God and following the laws of nature. He thinks rites and ceremonies are unnecessary. Salomon disagrees with him on this point, but both agree that the oldest religion is the best, the religion of the earliest man and the patriarchs, Adam, Enoch, Job, Abraham, Isaac, and Jacob.

Perhaps some additional remarks are in order concerning Coronaeus' role in the dialogue. Although fewer speeches are allotted to Coronaeus than to the other speakers, his position is central for a proper balance among the various opinions. The importance of his role gradually evolves as the dialogue progresses, until Coronaeus becomes the mediator, as it were, between the non-Christians (Salomon, Toralba, Octavius, and Senamus) and the Christians (Curtius, Fridericus, and, of course, himself). He often remarks that he believes in the authority of the church, but his belief does not keep him from an appreciation of the non-Christians nor does he answer the harsh words of Curtius and Fridericus in kind but with love.

The role of Coronaeus is more representative of the *Colloquium* in its entirety than is that of Senamus, who is also tolerant. Senamus approves of all religions and pays homage to all, but his skepticism does not allow a real belief in any. On the other hand, Coronaeus' tolerance leads him to agree even with some points that the non-Christians bring forth, yet he is firm in his Catholic faith. If Bodin himself could not possess the certainty of Coronaeus' faith, he, nevertheless, seemed inspired by his portrayal of a liberal sixteenth-century Catholic, who in several ways resembles the eminent Cardinal Gasparo Contareni.

We may say then, in summary, that the *Colloquium heptaplomeres* is one of the great expressions of religious synthesis. There is an

---

[84] Senamus cleverly misquotes Horace (*Graecia capta ferum victorem cepit*, *Epist.* II. 1. 156) as an answer to Salomon, who has been pointing out the superiority of the Jewish religion. Senamus says: "Judaea capta ferum victorem cepit." (Captured Judea captured the savage conqueror.) *Colloquium heptaplomeres*, p. 201.

INTRODUCTION

essence shared by all historical faiths but never exhausted by any
one. Hence in the great tradition of universalism we find a sixteenth-
century voice. It was not left to the later centuries to have this message
expressed by Shaftesbury, Locke, Spinoza, Hume, or Lessing. The
very age that bred rancor and bloodshed also produced its opposite,
harmony and toleration.

The *Colloquium heptaplomeres* and the Sixteenth Century

THE relation of the *Colloquium heptaplomeres* to the intellectual currents of the sixteenth century is as involved and complicated as everything else about the work. The colloquy requires opposing participants, and truth is preserved by conflict and resolution of diverse opinions. This dialogue form was a favorite literary type, and there are many Renaissance examples. Perhaps the form was popular during the Renaissance and Reformation period because the dialogue provided a *persona* for the author whose views might not find favor with the authorities; he could always say the speakers in the dialogue said it, not he. Although the *Praise of Folly* is not a dialogue, Erasmus used "Folly" as such a *persona* to criticize the social scene and the church. The *Praise of Folly* is also similar to the *Colloquium heptaplomeres* in that no real conclusion is reached but rather the problem is boldly displayed.

The setting of Bodin's dialogue reflects the ideal societies depicted in Renaissance utopias. The home of Coronaeus is a utopia that provides all the aspects of life dear to the well-versed man of the Renaissance—intelligent conversation, polished manners, wit, good food, music, indeed all the arts. Coronaeus' home recalls Castiglione's *Courtier* and looks forward to Bacon's *New Atlantis*.[85]

[85] The enlightened atmosphere of Coronaeus' home also recalls the well-ordered and tolerant government of the Khazars, whose king in 960 A.D., could boast of a broad-minded and just administration when fanaticism, ignorance, and anarchy reigned in Western Europe. Those who were persecuted because of their religion could find refuge there. The supreme court of justice was composed of seven judges,

INTRODUCTION

In the sense in which "Renaissance," describing an individual man, signifies universal breadth of interest, the *Colloquium heptaplomeres* is truly a Renaissance book. The philosophical orientation of the work is Neoplatonic, especially of the Florentine variety. Bodin is close to Ficino in his admiration for the "divine" Plato, whose *Timaeus* and *Phaedo* he constantly cites. To Bodin, as to Ficino, Plato represents the perfection of an ancient tradition of theology. Bodin, following Numenius, calls Plato the Attic Moses.[86] In the introduction to his translation of the *Corpus hermeticum* Ficino writes:

Mercurius Trismegistus was the first philosopher to raise himself above physics and mathematics to the contemplation of the divine. . . . Therefore he was considered the original founder of theology. Orpheus followed him and held second place in ancient

two of whom were Jews, two Mohammedans, two Christians, and one pagan. The "Khazari Letters," which detailed the affairs of this tolerant state, were first published in 1577 by Isaac Aqrish into whose hands these documents had fallen while on a journey from Egypt to Constantinople. Cf. also A. Garosci, *Jean Bodin* (Milan, 1934), p. 110, note 4: "This reminds us of the *Book of the Khazars*, where a Rabbi, a Mohammedan, and a Natural Philosopher converse in the presence of a King. But it is not credible that Bodin had directly imitated Jewish sources. Rather, it is evidently the imitations of the anti-Christian discourse of the Rabbi in Celsus, preserved in Origen, *Contra Celsum*." For a thorough and fascinating account of the Khazars see D. M. Dunlop, *The History of the Jewish Khazars* (Princeton, 1954). *The Khazar* was written originally in Arabic in A.D. 1140, by Judah ha-Levi and later translated into Hebrew. Dunlop states, p. 116, that ha-Levi's work is "a defense of Rabbinic Judaism cast in the form of a dialogue which is represented as having taken place in Khazaria 400 years before the author's own time. In this dialogue the interlocutors are the Khazar and others. Ha-Levi is not concerned to enlarge on the setting, his main interest being theological not historical, but he regards the conversion of the king to Judaism at this date as an accepted fact." The Khazari Letters, which were in existence in ha-Levi's time, were supposedly an interchange of letters between Hasday ibn-Shaprut, a well-known Jew in Spain, and Joseph, king of the Khazars. Dunlop points out that the expression "books of the Khazars" is not applicable to the letters and important details given by ha-Levi are not in the letters. Where Isaac Aqrish obtained the text of the Khazari Letters is unknown. As to the authenticity of the letters, Dunlop, p. 130, states: "If anyone thinks that the Khazar correspondence was first composed in 1577 and published in *Qol Mebasser*, the onus of proof is certainly on him. He must show that a number of ancient manuscripts, which appear to contain references to the correspondence, have all been interpolated since the end of the sixteenth century. This will prove a very difficult or rather an impossible task."

[86] *Colloquium heptaplomeres*, p. 187.

THE *Colloquium* AND THE 16TH CENTURY

theology. Aglaophemus was initiated into the Orphic mysteries. Aglaophemus' successor in theology was Pythagoras, and his pupil was Philolaus, the master of our divine Plato. So six theologians, in wonderful order, formed a unique and coherent succession in ancient theology, beginning with Mercurius and ending with the divine Plato.[87]

Throughout the *Colloquium heptaplomeres* Bodin shows admiration for this ancient tradition and these ancient theologians.

With Pico, Bodin shares perhaps an even greater affinity. The *Colloquium heptaplomeres* is surely a work in which the right of the individual to intellectual and spiritual freedom is proclaimed. Pico's philosophy is pervaded with emphasis on the right and duty of man to search freely in the intellectual and spiritual world. "Pico rejects any inquisition, in the domain of knowledge as in that of faith. For him there are no heretics of the intellect. The intellect can be moved to accept a determinate proposition only when it produces the conviction of that proposition in itself; and this conviction must be founded on determinate grounds."[88] Bodin also reflects Pico's thinking on the question of original sin and the Fall. Bodin speaks of the golden age of man transmitted through the noble heroes of our ancestors, and he does not look back to Adam but to those after the Fall, namely, Abel, Enoch, Noah, Abraham, Job, Isaac, and Jacob.[89] To Pico also man's sin and consequent Fall do not stand "as an indelible stain upon his nature; for in it he sees nothing but the correlate and counterpart to something other and higher. Man must be capable of sin, that he may become capable of good."[90] Pico defends the teaching of Origen, whom Bodin also cites, that there can be no eternal punishment. "An eternity of punishment would imply a form of finality which according to Pico's basic con-

[87] Quoted by Paul Oskar Kristeller, *The Philosophy of Marsilio Ficino* (Gloucester, Mass., 1964), pp. 25–26.

[88] Ernst Cassirer, "Giovanni Pico della Mirandola," *Journal of the History of Ideas* 3 (1942), 328.

[89] *Colloquium heptaplomeres*, p. 172 and throughout.

[90] Cassirer, "Pico della Mirandola," p. 329.

INTRODUCTION

ception would contradict the real meaning of human existence."[91]
Bodin presents the same view, which has been referred to earlier in
this introduction.

Bodin's Neoplatonism also has its roots in Plotinus, Augustine,
Proclus, and Dionysius the Areopagite. Nor is he completely separated from the medieval theological tradition, for he shows great
admiration for St. Thomas, even when he allows one of the speakers
to refute him. Bodin shows the same respect for Aristotle and Averroës, whom he often refutes. Pico also displayed profound respect for
Averroës, although he disagreed with him.

In addition to the religious views discussed earlier, the *Colloquium
heptaplomeres* represents many of the ideas of the Brethren of the
Common Life, the Christian humanists, such as Erasmus, who emphasized inner religion and true piety, and the Reformers. Curtius
in the *Colloquium heptaplomeres* expresses the Reformed concern
with the worship of saints, "idols," and with other "empty rites."

The rising interest in science during the Renaissance appears in
the *Colloquium heptaplomeres*. Reference is made to gunpowder,
new stars that have appeared, and the scientific investigation of nature. Geography, travel, and the studies of navigation which flourished in Portugal and Spain were of keen interest to the man of the
Renaissance as they were to the scholars at Coronaeus' house.

The role of a Renaissance prince as portrayed by Machiavelli also
concerns Bodin's scholars, for Octavius says that it is sometimes
justifiable for physicians and princes to lie.

Senamus with his constant doubting and questioning reflects the
revival of Skepticism in the sixteenth century. Perhaps the most
significant influence of Pyrrhonism was on the theological disputes
of the period. "This initial version of this style of argumentation was
intended to show that as soon as the Reformers had admitted that the
church could err, thus denying the traditional rule of faith, they
could then be reduced to skeptical despair. If the alternative criterion
of true faith is Scripture, then, according to St. Francis de Sales,
Cardinal du Perron, Pierre Charron, Bishop Camus and others, no

[91] *Ibid.*, p. 330.

1

THE *Colloquium* AND THE 16TH CENTURY

one can tell by Scripture alone what it says or means. All the Reformers have to offer are the dubious opinions of Luther, Calvin, and Zwingli."[92] Montaigne and Charron tried to undermine the reasoning abilities of man and consequently cast doubt upon the reasons of the Protestants for their faith. Although Senamus represents the skeptic point of view, all of Bodin's speakers agree that it is wicked for a person to destroy a man's religious beliefs and have nothing to put in their place.

Bodin favors the "new learning" of the Renaissance, and he has Toralba say that the more he knows, the more he knows that he does not know. Curtius says that this is characteristic of most learned men and that when a man can freely view the lands and heavenly bodies from the top of a mountain, he is struck by his old earth-bound ignorance. He also explains that many have refused to learn because of the power of empty authority.

Closely connected with the "new learning" was the Renaissance idea of wisdom, which the *Colloquium heptaplomeres* develops throughout the work. Though the "new learning" reflected wisdom on one level, to most Renaissance men true wisdom was the "knowledge of divine things," as Ficino said. True wisdom was mysterious and veiled from the eyes of the profane. Pico said that God created from eternity the *prima mens*, wisdom, and from this divine intellect or wisdom come all the ideas or forms by which God created all things. "It is because a knowledge of Ideas is the result of divine illumination that wisdom is said to come from God. Not only do the sacred texts of Jews and Christians say that only God can teach wisdom, and that it can only be got by faith, hope, and charity, but Plato also tells how he daily asked God for wisdom. This is the divine meaning hidden in the Orphic fable of the birth of Minerva from the head of Zeus. Explained by Ficino and his followers, who were themselves following Boccaccio, the myth meant that all wisdom has its origins in God and is mysteriously infused in us by God. . . . At this crucial point Ficino joins Nicholas of Cusa and the

---

[92] Richard H. Popkin, *The History of Scepticism from Erasmus to Descartes* (Assen, 1960), p. 69.

INTRODUCTION

Christian mystics; wisdom is a gift of the Holy Spirit, a supranatural infusion of divine light."[93]

The *Colloquium heptaplomeres* emphasizes this Renaissance concept of wisdom perhaps more than any other single idea, as the complete title of the work suggests. Salomon is repeatedly asked to explain these secrets of divine things which were hidden from the average man. Salomon professes that he "drinks from the same springs" as everyone else, yet he does unfold some mysteries that he says are locked in the divine words of the Old Testament and the Cabala. By the numerous discussions that the participants in the dialogue have about allegories which the untutored never comprehend, Bodin reveals his interest in Renaissance wisdom. Salomon says that the Old Testament is filled with allegories so that the secrets of God may not grow stale in their commonness. "Therefore we must exercise our mind on rather obscure divine words so that we may not only abstain from faults and embrace true glory but also seek the body's health, the mind's prudence and wisdom, and the closest union with immortal God."[94]

Many Renaissance figures agreed that the Bible held secrets for the wise. Pico said that the Bible had a literal meaning and a secret meaning; the literal meaning can be grasped by the *vulgus*, but the secret meaning needs the expert intellect. Savonarola also believed in the hidden meaning of the Bible. Sebastian Franck called the Bible a book sealed with seven seals. Campanella pointed out the scriptures' ambiguous character.[95] To these men and to Bodin the ambiguous nature of the scriptures was part of their idea of wisdom, but there were other factors which colored their premises. "They were inspired by very diverse motives: Pico della Mirandola by his desire to reconcile pagan philosophy with Christian faith, Savonarola by his efforts aimed at a fundamental reform of the Church, and Cam-

[93] Eugene F. Rice, Jr., *The Renaissance Idea of Wisdom* (Cambridge, Mass., 1958), p. 67.

[94] *Colloquium heptaplomeres*, pp. 74–75; Eng. transl. below, pp. 96–98 f. Bodin begins Book III with the question of the allegory, and he develops thoroughly the idea of wisdom in this book.

[95] See Edward E. Lowinsky, *Secret Chromatic Art in the Netherlands Motet* (New York, 1967), p. 137.

THE *Colloquium* AND THE 16TH CENTURY

panella by his enthusiasm for the new science. Since they remained in the Roman Catholic camp and had to justify their views, they had to resort to the theory of an esoteric meaning of the Scriptures which would support their beliefs."[96] All these diverse motives seem applicable to Bodin and help explain his emphasis on secret meanings.

Bodin begins Book IV, as he did Book III, in the *Colloquium heptaplomeres* with a discussion that reflects this hidden meaning. The conversation begins with comments on geometrical progressions and then develops into a discussion of musical theories and practices; from music the discussion drifts into the nature of harmonies (nonmusical), and if one looks at the last book of the *Colloquium heptaplomeres*, the hidden meaning of the musical discussion becomes clear. It was appropriate for Bodin to use music as a springboard for broader questions of harmony. The musical world of the latter part of the Cinquecento was very different from the early years of the era, and the revolutions in religion, science, and philosophy may be compared to that in music.[97]

Lowinsky, in his excellent study of Renaissance music,[98] points out that the new chromaticism in the music of the Renaissance met with a hostile attitude from the church. "The defense of the diatonic system of the Ecclesiastical modes against the rising wave of chromaticism presents one of the most fascinating chapters of Renaissance

[96] *Ibid.*, pp. 137–38.

[97] The fifteenth century is called by Donald F. Tovey "the Golden Age" of music. It began with the inherited "modes" and ended with the basis of the modern major and minor scales. Thus the very concept of harmony changed, and what had been rejected, even regarded as illegal and blasphemous, became the very norm. Whereas we think of Palestrina's masses as the most appropriate and fitting music for the Sistine Choir to sing in St. Peter's, the Council of Trent discussed whether to permit polyphony. We may well link Bodin's problem of harmonizing the new religious and philosophic thoughts with Palestrina's problem of how to incorporate the experiments in disharmony. Tovey asks the question if there is anything deeper in the use of A♯ than "a desire for a sensational variety of harmony." The problem was to find limits to the novelty. When the *Colloquium heptaplomeres* was written (1588), the great careers of Orlando de Lasso and Palestrina were almost finished; both died in 1594. Josquin des Prés and Monteverde were flourishing. When Monteverde introduced discords and experimented with new rhythmic principles, his problem was like Bodin's, whether the old styles could establish order in the new materials. Article "Music," *Encycl. Brit.* (11th ed.), XIX, 75–77.

[98] Lowinsky, *Secret Chromatic Art*; see also his article, "Music in Renaissance Culture," *Journal of the History of Ideas* 15 (1942), 509–53.

INTRODUCTION

theory. A study of the material available reveals with the utmost clarity that the Church took a most lively and serious interest in the matter of preserving the old diatonic system of modes."[99]

The question of Renaissance wisdom and secret meanings leads us to the secret meaning in the *Colloquium heptaplomeres*, and for this we must turn our attention to Hermes Trismegistus and the Cabala. As Frances Yates has pointed out,[100] the core of the Renaissance Neoplatonism was Hermetic. The core of the *Colloquium heptaplomeres* is also Hermetic. Bodin's concept of man who can be in tune with God and the cosmos by the demonic agents of God is very similar to the Hermetic concept of man. Yates says: "Contrast this Hermetic Adam with the Mosaic Adam, formed out of the dust of the earth. It is true that God gave him domination over the creatures, but when he sought to know the secrets of the divine power, to eat of the tree of knowledge, this was the sin of disobedience for which he was expelled from the Garden of Eden. The Hermetic man in the 'Pimander' also falls and can also be regenerated. But the regenerated Hermetic man regains the dominion over nature which he had in his divine origin. When he is regenerated, brought back into communion with the rule of 'the all' through magico-religious communion with the cosmos, it is the regeneration of a being who regains this divinity. One might say that the 'Pimander' describes the creation, fall, and redemption not of a man but of a magus. . . ."[101]

This concept of man who is in tune with the mysteries of the universe is a theme that runs throughout the *Colloquium heptaplomeres*, not specifically stated by one of the participants but gathered from

---

[99] *Ibid.*, p. 111.

[100] Frances E. Yates, "The Hermetic Tradition," in Charles S. Singleton, ed., *Art, Science, and History in the Renaissance* (Baltimore, 1967), p. 255. See also Frances E. Yates, *Giordano Bruno and the Hermetic Tradition* (Chicago, 1964).

[101] Yates, "Hermetic Tradition," p. 257. Jean Thenaud, a sixteenth-century Franciscan, wrote a book about the Cabala (*La saincte et trescrestienne cabale*), in which he condemns as superstitious the use of the Cabala by believers in magic. "He disapproves particularly of the attribution of 'superstitions, curious writings, and vain fictions' not only in philosophy but even in theology, to great men of past ages and of the consideration of Moses as 'prince of magic.' Among the books which he censures are the Hebrew *Raziel* and the works of Hermes Trismegistus." Cited by Joseph Leon Blau, *The Christian Interpretation of the Cabala in the Renaissance* (New York, 1944), p. 95.

THE *Colloquium* AND THE 16TH CENTURY

the conversations of all, and especially articulated by Salomon and Toralba. The emphasis is on man after the Fall, who by all the magico-religious forces of the cosmos can unfold the secrets of divine things and thereby regain a harmony with the universe and with God.[102] Bodin follows Trismegistus' theory of the emanation of the divine presence into man.[103] There are repeated references to the Cabala and to Hermes, whom the Neoplatonists believed to be an Egyptian priest, perhaps prior to Moses, from whom much of the ancient wisdom flowed to Plato. Salomon gives lengthy explanations about how the Hebrews came in contact with the Cabala, which was an oral tradition for many centuries. Salomon places the Cabala as equal in divine revelation to the Old Testament and other prophetic writings. The references to Hermes and the Cabala in the *Colloquium heptaplomeres* are too numerous to cite. Bodin thus places himself in the midst of one of the most important aspects of Renaissance Neoplatonism, the Hermetic tradition.

[102] This concept is very akin to Pico's use of the Cabala as one element in a universal synthetic system of thought. Franciscus Georgius of Venice, a follower of Pico in Cabalistic thought, published *De harmonia mundi totius cantica tria* in 1525 and therein revealed that the harmony of which he spoke was the nature of Pico's synthesis of all philosophies. For an excellent study of the Christian use of the Cabala, see Blau, *The Christian Interpretation of the Cabala*. Other illuminating works on the Cabala and Jewish mysticism are Gershom G. Scholem, *On the Kabbalah and Its Symbolism* (New York, 1965); Gershom G. Scholem, *The Messianic Idea in Judaism* (New York, 1971); Gershom G. Scholem, *Major Trends in Jewish Mysticism* (New York, 1954); Wolfgang S. Seiferth, *Synagogue and Church in the Middle Ages: Two Symbols in Art and Literature* (New York, 1970). Also, Joseph Leon Blau, "Postel and the Significance of Renaissance Cabalism," *Journal of the History of Ideas* 15 (1954), 218–32; François Secret, "Les Jesuites et le Kabbalisme Chrétien à la renaissance," *Bibliothèque d'humanisme et renaissance* 20 (1958), 542–55; P. Zambelli, "Il «De auditu Kabbalistico» e la tradizione lulliana nel Rinascimento," *Atti e mem. dell'Accad. Toscana . . . «La Colombaria»* 30 n.s. 16 (1965), 113–247.

[103] Bodin's theory of emanation was also very close to that of the Spanish Cabalists. See Scholem, *The Messianic Idea in Judaism*, p. 44. "To the question of how the world came into being the Spanish Kabbalists had proffered their doctrines of emanations. From the abundance of His being, from the treasure laid up within Himself, God 'emanated' the *sefirot*, those divine luminaries, those modes, and stages through which He manifests Himself externally. His resplendent light emanates from stage to stage, and the light spreads to ever wider spheres and becomes light evermore thickened. Through the descent of the lights from their infinite source all the worlds were emanated and created; our world is but the fast and outward shell of the layers of divine glory."

INTRODUCTION

Bodin's use of the Cabala in the *Colloquium* is analogous to the
Cabalistic thinking of his learned and strange countryman, Guillaume Postel (1510–1581). Of all the famous Renaissance Cabalists,
Postel was perhaps the only one who had read all the Cabalistic
writings in the original tongue. Whereas Pico had relied mainly on a
commentary on the *Zohar* for his knowledge, and Reuchlin's sources
were chiefly pre-Zoharic, Postel was acquainted with all the major
documents of the Cabala. Bouwsma says that "of all the intellectual
strains with which Postel was acquainted, this comes closest to a
source for him in the most literal sense. No doubt the Cabala rein-
forced tendencies already present in his mind. But Postel so vener-
ated the authority of Cabalistic writings that they constantly influenced the development of his ideas (after 1545) and the manner of
his expression."[104]

There were three elements of Cabalistic thinking that were especially dear to Postel, and they appear throughout his writings.[105]
They are the sacredness of the Hebrew language, cosmic sexual dualism, and universal harmony. This is not to say that other Renaissance
Cabalists did not also display keen interests in these areas. Postel,
however, emphasized these aspects and centered much of his thought
around them. This is of particular interest when one observes that
these ideas are the major Cabalistic themes expressed by Bodin in
the *Colloquium*.[106]

The Hebrew language had special significance for Postel, as indeed
did all language which enabled man to communicate with the ultimate source of truth. Postel shared the Cabalistic view of Hebrew
as the holy tongue and the original common language for communication between God and man. Hebrew was reverenced, almost

---

[104] William J. Bouwsma, *Concordia Mundi: The Career and Thought of Guillaume
Postel* (Cambridge, Mass., 1957), p. 138. Cf. also Blau, *Christian Interpretation of
the Cabala*, pp. 97–98.

[105] For the most complete account of Postel's writings, see François Secret, *Bibliographie des manuscrits de Guillaume Postel* (Geneva, 1970). I have read a number
of Postel's major works, and it is indeed striking how often Postel's ideas reappear
in Bodin's *Colloquium*, and also to a lesser degree, in the *Theatrum* and the
Démonomanie.

[106] These themes appear very often in the *Colloquium*.

THE *Colloquium* AND THE 16TH CENTURY

worshipped, by Postel, as the key to wisdom and sublime things. "It thus represented ultimate human order, and its recovery by Renaissance scholarship therefore signified far more to Postel than an impressive academic feat; it suggested to him the approaching reunion of the human race under God."[107]

Similarly, in the *Colloquium* Bodin's Salomon, perhaps the most important of the seven speakers, and certainly the most learned, constantly reminds his friends that ignorance of the holy tongue has led to many errors in translation and interpretation of scripture and therefore separates man from divine wisdom. In explaining the works by which eternal God is indicated, Salomon says "this secret lies hidden to those unskilled in the holy tongue."[108]

The holy tongue is related to numbers, especially the number four. Salomon in the *Colloquium* shows a marked preference for the number four because the holy, most sacred name of God, which cannot be uttered by man, the sacred tetragrammaton, contains four letters. Bodin's Salomon prefers the number four to the number three, and he reminds his friends that the voice of God repeated the four names of God to Moses.[109] Postel earlier had shown an affinity for the number four. "Four indeed eventually supplanted

[107] Bouwsma, *Concordia Mundi*, p. 105.

[108] *Colloquium heptaplomeres*, p. 184; "quod arcanum latet imperitos linguae sanctae."

[109] *Ibid.*, pp. 282–83. "It would be much more likely to contrive a quaternity from the name tetragrammaton than a trinity, as did Basilides the evangelist, whose opinion the Noetians and Lombard himself, the Master of the Sentences, seem to follow, as Abbot Joachim wrote, because, in addition to three persons, they substituted a fourth which they called *hypokratora*. The Pythagoreans seem to have held this opinion. They had been accustomed to swear to a holy quarterity. Timaeus Locrensis indicated that by means of a tetragonal pyramid this quaternity held many thousands of worlds together. The powerfully sagacious reasoning by the Master of the Sentences concerning the quaternity either established the quaternity or overturned the trinity, because he opposed the two relations of things produced to the two relations of things producing, namely, the thing begetting, the thing begotten, the thing breathing, the thing neither begotten nor begetting nor breathing. The four wheels would be appropriate to this opinion, and also the four animals of divine vision, and that voice of God repeating to Moses the four divine names, namely, the God of your father, the God of Abraham, the God of Isaac, the God of Jacob." Emphasis upon the number four and the sacred tetragrammaton pervade the *Colloquium*.

INTRODUCTION

three in Postel's thought as the number for God Himself, whom Postel analyzed into essence, unity, truth, and goodness, of which the first three find fulfillment in the fourth."[110]

Cosmic sexual dualism was a key to Postel's concept of the universe. The idea of a masculine and feminine principle in the universe is ancient and widespread, and Postel had many sources from which to draw, especially from the Neoplatonists and the Cabala. A sexual dualism is fundamental to the Cabalistic picture of the universe. That basic Cabalistic text, the *Zohar*, is permeated with a concern to establish the masculine and feminine identities of things: rich and poor, right and left, sun and moon, heaven and earth. Ultimately the work conceives of God Himself in terms of a sexual dualism which explains His generative power. "From the Neo-Platonists Postel absorbed suggestions about the order prevailing among the masculine principle, the feminine principle, and God; he conceived of the sexual principles as emanations from God which correspond to the common Neo-Platonic principles of the universal Mind and, following from it, the universal soul."[111] Postel saw these sexual principles working throughout the universe, and this concept of sexual dualism is a dominant force in Postel's thoughts. In *De Etruriae regionis . . . originibus* Postel says that after Noah's arrival in Etruria this dualism was revealed in names attributed to the goddesses.[112] Postel was so absorbed with cosmic dualism that his ideas

---

[110] Bouwsma, *Concordia Mundi*, p. 107. See Guillaume Postel, *De Etruriae regionis, quae prima in orbe Europaeo habitata est, originibus institutis, religione, et moribus et imprimis* (Florence, 1551), pp. 145–53, 188 ff.; for a lengthy discussion of the primacy of the number four also see Postel [Elias Pandocheus], *De nativatate mediatoris ultima* (s.l., s.d.), pp. 31 ff.

[111] Bouwsma, *Concordia Mundi*, p. 109.

[112] Postel, *De Etruriae regionis . . . originibus*, p. 104. "From Noah . . . the wife of Noah and the mother of the world, preserved from the line of Cain, assumed various names in Italy. She has been called Vesta, Rheack, Maiach, Arezia, from the property of the four elements," pp. 106–107. "The fiery Spirit is the basis of a rational nature and because it has been fastened on matter, it is accustomed to be ascribed to the feminine: . . . For it is altogether necessary that, just as in the whole nature of things we see Form, which is the image of the masculine and is called Mind, and Matter which gives its basis to the feminine and to mothers. . . ." Also note p. 144. "The higher are Idea, Mind, Masculine, Agent Intellect, and Man turned

THE *Colloquium* AND THE 16TH CENTURY

on this subject even appear in his letters to friends. For a restitution of all things Postel believed there was need for a double spirit. One for the higher part, paternal and mental, was for the restitution of souls (*animorum*). The other for the lower part, maternal and spiritual, was for the restitution of spirits (*animarum*).[113]

In the *Colloquium* Bodin has Salomon explain in a lengthy passage the allegorical meaning of male and female elements. I quote only a brief section: "woman in an allegorical sense everywhere means body. . . . The word man indicates natural form, and woman indicates matter, which also is often called in Proverbs *Meretrix* (harlot), since as a harlot takes pleasure in a number of men, so matter delights in a number of forms."[114]

Universal harmony is the central theme of the *Colloquium heptaplomeres*, and in this concept Bodin's thought reveals great similarity to that of Postel. Postel's belief in the unity of all things led him to stress the similarities of people's beliefs. In *De Orbis Concordia* Postel said that all men were brothers,[115] and he emphasized the fraternity

---

inward; the lower are Similitude, Spirit, Feminine, Passive Intellect and Man exterior and apparent."

[113] *Alia Postelli Epistola ad D.C.S.*, 1553, bound in Guillaume Postel, *Absconditorum a constitutione mundi clavis, qua mens humana tam in divinis, quam in humanis pertinget ad interiores velaminis aeternae veritates* (Amsterdam, 1646), p. 107. "There is need for a dual Spirit in the restitution, . . . one for the higher part, paternal and mental, in the understanding, for the restitution of [masculine] souls: and this was given to the Apostles. The other, for the lower part, maternal and spiritual (For the mind and spirit are as masculine and feminine) in the heart, for the restitution of [feminine] souls. Let it be and seem to be spiritual which was a living being." This letter was written by Postel on 14 August 1553 while he was staying in the house of the Giunti.

[114] For the complete passage, see Salomon's second speech, *Colloquium heptaplomeres*, p. 73. Also see Salomon's reference to the Greeks who gave their gods male characteristics, and the Latins who gave theirs feminine characteristics, p. 119.

[115] *De orbis terrae concordia* (Basel, 1544), p. 276. "If then we ought to be moved especially by the example of the highest divine will, we who will be sons against brothers . . . in so fierce a soul: in addition, he who hurls back injury in that he condemns in another what he approves in himself." Also note p. 275, "also from the example of the supreme God who is exceedingly kind toward all (even ungrateful and wicked men), He orders and persuades us to honor with kindnesses not only friends, but also enemies and to condone their injuries: He wishes that this be done because of fear of our eternal damnation, or desire of everlasting happiness, or, that which is most excellent, the example of God and the love of virtue: it

INTRODUCTION

among men when he proclaimed that all men believe in God.[116] In the *praefatio* of *De nativitate mediatoris ultima* he said that divine truths have been revealed from many sources such as the Targum, Zohar, Midrash, and Rabboth, and God's providence toward mankind is so great that His truths were made known to all people so that they might know Him.[117] Differences among men are the result of ignorance or difficulty of understanding, but God does not condemn mankind because of ignorance.[118] God is the same God for all men, and all men must be as one. All men who do good are acceptable to God.[119]

The title of Bodin's work, *Colloquium heptaplomeres de rerum sublimium arcanis abditis*,[120] indicates the primacy of harmony in Bodin's thought and also suggests a relation to the theory of universal harmony which was dear to Postel. The Greek word *heptaplous* means "seven times" and the noun, *meros* means "part." Seven speakers say their parts in the freedom of Coronaeus' home, and although the seven often disagree, they respect the others' opinions, and recog-

---

cannot be allowed that anything greater can be imagined for the preservation of nature."

[116] *Panthenòsia* (s.l., s.d.), p. 10. "And so let us rejoice, O sons, brothers, fathers, daughters, sisters, mothers, in this alone, that Turks, Jews, Christians, Heretics, Pagans, and all the nations of the world believe that God is, and all either have or seek Jesus."

[117] *De nativitate mediatoris ultima* (s.l., s.d.), p. 9. "They exist in the Targum, Zohar, Midrash, Rabboth, and in many other interpreters. One must not think that the providence of God is so small toward the human race that the people pardoned by the blessing of Ismael are deprived of their truths by which God, the giver of light, forgave them in their darkness."

[118] *Ibid.*, pp. 150–51. "All men are harmonious in principles, but they only disagree in manner. Still it is true that all men seek the good in order that not only men but all things created with them, with nature as guide, may accomplish this. . . . Wherefore, whatever difference there is among men, it resides in ignorance alone or in the difficulty of understanding. . . . For what parent would condemn a son because of his true ignorance?"

[119] *Ibid.*, pp. 151–52. "But since God and man are one in Christ, it is then necessary that both gentiles and Israelites become one. . . . For he who does good in every nation, this one has been accepted by That One, whether he is excellent or not in the practice of sacred rites."

[120] The *Colloquium heptaplomeres* may reveal by its title the influence of two earlier works whose themes are compatible with the ideas of the *Colloquium heptaplomeres*. They are the *Heptaméron* of Margaret of Navarre and the *Heptaplus* of Pico della Mirandola.

THE *Colloquium* AND THE 16TH CENTURY

nize the right that each man has to state his opinion and live according to his own religious beliefs. These seven "parts" indicate Bodin's insistence upon harmony among all religions. The seven parts may also refer to the seven-branched candelabra of Moses, which Postel used in his book, *Candelabri typici in Mosis tabernaculo . . . interpretatio*, to indicate the universal significance of Israel and France in establishing the kingdom of heaven on earth.[121]

The prophet Elias has a very prominent place in Zoharic writings and in the eschatology of the Cabalists; Elias was assigned the task of bringing world peace and religious harmony to men. Elias is the prophet who, along with Isaiah, is most frequently quoted in the *Colloquium*. Postel identified himself with Elias as the preacher of eternal truth and the one to bring universal harmony. He took the

[121] Antoine Teissier in his additions to the *Histories* of Jacques-Auguste de Thou (1553–1617) suggested a relationship between Bodin and Postel. In *Éloges des hommes savants, tirés de l'histoire de M. de Thou, avec des additions*, edited by Antoine Teissier (Leyden, 1715), pp. 210–11, he made this very important statement concerning the *Colloquium* and its relation to Postel:

> Henri Etienne assures us that he saw Postel at Venice publicly proclaiming that if one wished to have a good religion, it would be necessary to compose a religion from those of the Turks, the Jews, and Christians. Moreover, Mr. Naudé said that at the time when Postel was at Venice there were four men who gathered twice every week to discuss with complete freedom all the religions of the world and that Postel wrote what took place in their discussions. After the death of Postel, these writings fell into the hands of Bodin and became the material for the book entitled, *About the Hidden Secrets of Sublime Things. . . .*

In 1684, Diecmann made a similar statement in *De naturalismo*, p. 3:

> And so it was pleasing to arrange his whole scene with Bodin as chorus-leader so that any religion might be applauded more than the Christian religion, or that religion might be mingled by Samaritan confusion with Jewish and Turkish treachery; that he seems to have wished to unite himself clearly to the intention of his most insane citizen, Guillaume Postel, whom Henricus Stephanus heard saying publicly now and then at Venice that whoever wishes to fashion a form of good religion ought to blend this from those three—the Christian, Jewish, and Turkish religions. I am not at all deceived in this conclusion which I learned not so long ago from a certain French manuscript which mentioned that Guy Patin, physician and royal professor at Paris, had heard from Gabriel Naudé, whom he knew very intimately, that there had been at Venice four men who had met twice a week for the purpose of establishing philosophical discussions about the various religions. Among those were Coronaeus of Rouen and the one whom I mentioned, Guillaume Postel, who acted as a stenographer. His [Postel's] manuscripts, after he had died at Paris in 1584, came into the hands of Bodin and were used to complete this work.

INTRODUCTION

pseudonym Elias Pandocheus and published the *Panthenōsia* under
this name. Bodin named his first son Elias, and Bodin also published
a book, *Sapientiae moralis epitome quae bonorum gradus ab ultimo
ad summum hominis extremumque bonum continua serie deducit*
under the name of Elias Bodin. In the *Colloquium heptaplomeres*
Bodin makes a striking reference to Elias which may, indeed, refer
to Postel. Salomon has been speaking of the prophet Elias and his
struggle with the priests of Bahal. Then Bodin has Fridericus say:
"I would wish that now a certain Elias would give proof from
heaven in view of kings and people to explain what is the best among
so many and so great religions."[122]

Although the answer to this question is never formulated in the
Colloquium heptaplomeres, harmony with its handmaiden, toleration, is from the beginning of the *Colloquium* posited as the real
answer to religious questions and indeed all questions concerning the
cosmos. The home of Coronaeus and the attitude of the seven men
toward each other provide a harmonious setting from the outset. Although all were well trained in the liberal arts, "each seemed to surpass the other in his unique knowledge."[123] However, they lived together with such harmonious understanding that "no one so much
resembled himself as all resembled all."[124]

Music as a reflection of the music of the spheres, the divine harmony, is central to Bodin's concept of harmony in the *Colloquium
heptaplomeres*. At the close of each day's discussion Coronaeus summoned the boys "who were accustomed to soothe their spirits by
sweetly singing divine praises with a harmony of lyres, flutes, and
voices."[125] The blending of voices and instruments in praise of God
serves to bring the seven speakers back into a harmonious relationship
with each other after their divergent opinions have been expressed.
The harmony of the seven-stringed lyre reminds the seven of the
divine music which is a leitmotif of the *Colloquium*.

Although the new chromaticism in the music of the Renaissance
met with a hostile attitude from the church, Coronaeus reflects Bodin's belief that a Catholic should be able to entertain opinions

---

[122] *Colloquium heptaplomeres*, p. 132.
[123] *Ibid.*, p. 2.   [124] *Ibid.*   [125] *Ibid.*, p. 19.

THE *Colloquium* AND THE 16TH CENTURY

which differ from the church's when he finds delight in chromatic systems. No longer does the single mode reign supreme; a contrapuntal scheme with voices pitched against each other entails a harmony to which the "enlightened" (*auribus eruditis*) can truly respond. When there is no harmonious blending of sounds (or opinions), one overpowers the other, and "the dissonance offends the delicate senses of wiser men."[126]

All participants in the discussion agree on a concept of harmony that envisions a unity based on multiplicity (*concordia discors*), and one may safely say that this is the only subject discussed in the *Colloquium heptaplomeres* in which the scholars share a common opinion. From the question of musical harmonies Bodin directs the discussion toward harmony in the natural world. Toralba, the natural philosopher, dominates this conversation and adds a new dimension to the concept of harmony when he states that there is a basic harmony in each harmonious element. Toralba later remarks that things which are contrary to each other in nature herself cannot be mingled by design but only blended or united so that they seem to be one. This statement is revealing for the question, which is posed later in the dialogue, whether it is proper for men to discuss religion, since opinions on this subject show such variance. Yet, as Toralba cogently states, the opposites in nature, when united with certain interventions in their midst, safeguard the remarkable harmony of the universe, which would perish if it were all fire or moisture.[127]

Even in a well-ordered state, Toralba continues, men of justice, integrity, and virtue would not be perceived unless wicked men were mingled with the good, sane with the mad, brave with the cowardly, rich with the poor, low with the noble. Senamus rejoins that a state would be happier if all wicked men were driven out. Curtius counters that "as the variances of individual matters combine for the harmony of one universe, so also do the hostilities of individual citizens foster the harmony of all peoples."[128]

[126] *Ibid.*, p. 112. In addition to Lowinsky's studies on chromaticism already cited, see Kathi Meyer-Baer, *Music of the Spheres and the Dance of Death* (Princeton, 1970).

[127] *Colloquium heptaplomeres*, p. 114.

[128] *Ibid.*, p. 116.

INTRODUCTION

There can be no doubt that Bodin believed that many factions protect the harmony and stability of the state because a state split into two opposing camps would fall prey to civil wars such as France was suffering during Bodin's lifetime. From the consideration of political factions Bodin directs attention to the question of the multiplicity of religious opinions, and the question of religious harmony dominates the last two books of the *Colloquium*.

The reconciliation of all citizens and foreigners in a remarkable harmony, even though they differ among themselves and with the state in matters of religion, is achieved, according to Octavius, when the state admits every kind of religion. Coronaeus prays that there be a harmony of all mortals about divine matters and one religion, provided it is the true religion. Although one may assume that Coronaeus was referring to the Catholic religion, he never makes this plain but only posits the statement, which leads to a lengthy discussion of the true religion. The role of Coronaeus in the *Colloquium heptaplomeres* is important in that he typifies an enlightened Catholic position in the Cinquecento. Of the seven, Coronaeus is the peacemaker, the harmonizer. When the discussions become harsh because of the conflicting opinions of the speakers, Coronaeus speaks conciliatory words which indicate some validity for every contradictory opinion. Although Bodin does not give the shrewdest or the lengthiest speeches to Coronaeus, the importance of his harmonizing role cannot be minimized, for it is at the home of Coronaeus that these discussions with seven different points of view take place.

The statement that Adam had been instructed in the best religion and had worshipped eternal God to the exclusion of all others stands unrefuted. The argument becomes intense, however, when the question of rites is mentioned. The discussants share no harmonious opinion on the true function of a sacred rite. Nor can they agree on the meaning of Jesus as Messiah or the unity in the Trinity. Yet at the end of the *Colloquium* Bodin says that the seven scholarly friends continued to cherish the integrity and piety of life by their common interests and manner of living with a remarkable harmony (*mirabili concordia*). Although they never discussed religion again, each protected his own religion through the greatest holiness of life.

THE *Colloquium* AND THE 16TH CENTURY

The dialogue ends without rejection or acceptance of any one religion but rather with recognition of the divine descent of all religious beliefs and the universal brotherhood of men in the worship of divinity and in a moral life and free conscience for everyone.[129] As the harmony of nature is based on multiplicity, and the oldest religion is the natural religion of the parents of the human race, so there is need for the harmony of nature, based on multiplicity, to be applied to questions of religion and therefore a tolerance of all religions.[130] Atheism alone is detestable to Bodin.

The harmony which Bodin focuses upon in the *Colloquium heptaplomeres* implies much more than mere toleration. Toleration is an important theme, especially religious, but it is a by-product of harmony. The harmony of nature must be a pattern for world harmony which will permeate the lives of all men. Men who live in harmony, as Bodin conceived it, must of necessity be tolerant of each other.

Until the harmony of nature becomes an exemplar for earthly

[129] Bodin had already stated in the *République* that a man of no religion could not be made to obey the law, yet in the *Colloquium* he stresses the fact that no one can be forced to believe.

[130] For additional sources on the religious questions in the *Colloquium heptaplomeres*, see Friedrich von Bezold, "Jean Bodins Colloquium Heptaplomeres und der Atheismus des 16. Jahrhunderts," *Historische Zeitschrift*, 113 (1914), 3F.17, 260–315; George Holland Sabine, "The Colloquium Heptaplomeres of Jean Bodin," in *Persecution and Liberty. Essays in Honor of G. L. Burr* (New York, 1931), pp. 271–309; Ernst Benz, "Der Toleranz-Gedanke in der Religionswissenschaft (Über den Heptaplomeres des Jean Bodin)," *Deutsche Vierteljahresschrift* 12 (1934), 540–71; Pierre Mesnard, "La pensée religieuse de Bodin," *Revue du seizième siècle* 16 (1929), 77–121; Roger Chauviré, "Grandeur de Bodin," *Revue Historique* 188–89 (1940), 378–97; Lucien Febvre, "L'universalisme de Jean Bodin," *Revue de sythèse*, 7–8 (1934), 165–68; Georg Roellenbleck, *Offenbarung, Natur und Jüdische Überlieferung bei Jean Bodin. Eine Interpretation des Heptaplomeres* (Studien zur Religion, Geschichte und Geisteswissenschaft, 2) (Gütersloh, 1964); Joseph Lecler, *Toleration and the Reformation* (New York, 1960); Don Cameron Allen, *Doubt's Boundless Sea* (Baltimore, 1964), pp. 97–110; Ernst Gustav Vogel, "Zur Geschichte des ungedrückten Werks Colloquium Heptaplomeres," *Serapeum* 1 (1840), 113–16; also the very important article of Giorgio Radetti, "Il problema della religione nel pensiero di Giovanni Bodin." Although the following articles do not deal with the *Colloquium* specifically, they are very useful for an understanding of the religious aura of the *Colloquium*. See Paul Oskar Kristeller, "The Myth of Renaissance Atheism and the French Tradition of Free Thought," *Journal of the History of Philosophy* 6 (1968), 233–43; also Hubert Jedin, "Gasparo Contarini e il contributo veneziano alla riforma cattolica," in *La civiltà veneziana del Rinascimento*, edited by Diego Valeri (Venice, 1958), pp. 103–24.

lxv

INTRODUCTION

harmony, a harmony based on multiplicity, the lives of men may
necessarily reveal contradictions if the state or society or religion
allows no multiplicity (*concordia discors*), no blending of opposites,
no dissonant sounds.

Perhaps the poem of Curtius in which he proclaims the contrariety
in all things tempered by immortal God reveals most clearly Bodin's
concept of harmony in the *Colloquium heptaplomeres*:

> Creator of the world three times greatest of all,
> Three times best parent of the heaven,
> Who tempers the changes of the world,
> Giving proper weight to all things,
> And who measures each thing from His own ladle
> In number, ratio, time,
> Who with eternal chain joins with
>   remarkable wisdom two things opposite in every way,
>   preparing protection for each,
> Who, moderating melody with different sounds and
>   voices yet most satisfying to sensitive
>   ears, heals sickness, has mingled cold with heat
>   and moisture with dryness,
> The rough with the smooth, sweetness with pain,
>   shadows with light, quiet with motion,
>   tribulation with prosperity,
> Who directs the fixed courses of the heavenly
>   stars from east to west,
> West to east with contrary revolutions,
> Who joins hatred with agreement,
> A friend to hateful enemies.
> This greatest harmony of the universe though discordant
>   contains our safety.[131]

[131] *Colloquium heptaplomeres*, pp. 114–15.

Bibliography

Primary Sources

Agrippa, Henry C. *De incertitudine et vanitate scientiarum et artium atque excellentia verbi dei declamatio* (s.l., 1530).

Bellarminus, Robertus. *Disputationum de controversiis Christianae fidei, adversus huius temporis haereticos*, II (Venice, 1721).

Bodin, Jean. *Colloquium heptaplomeres de rerum sublimium arcanis abditis*, edited by Ludovicus Noack (Schwerin, 1857).

———. *Consilia Johannis Bodini Galli, & Fausti Longiani Itali, de principe recte instituendo*, translated by Johann Bornitius (Erfurt, 1603).

———. *Das Heptaplomeres des Jean Bodin, Zur Geschichte der Kultur und Literatur im Jahrhundert der Reformation*, edited by Dr. E. Guhrauer (Berlin, 1841), abridged edition.

———. *De la démonomanie des sorciers* (Paris, 1580).

———. *De magorum demonomania*, translated by Franciscus Junius (Basel, 1581).

———. *Le colloque de Jean Bodin des secrets cachez des choses sublimes,'* edited by Roger Chauviré (Paris, 1914), abridged edition.

———. *Les six livres de la république* (Paris, 1576).

———. *Method for the Easy Comprehension of History*, translated by Beatrice Reynolds (New York, 1965).

———. *Methodus ad facilem historiarum cognitionem* (Paris, 1566).

———. *Six Books of the Commonwealth*, translated by M. J. Tooley (Oxford, 1955).

———. *The Six Bookes of a Commonweale*, translated by Richard Knolles, edited by Kenneth D. McRae (Cambridge, Mass., 1962).

———. *Universae naturae theatrum* (Lyon, 1596).

Grotius, Hugo. *Epistolae Hugonis Grotii* (Amsterdam, 1687).

Haywood, William. *The Hierarchie of the Blessed Angells* (London, 1635).

Paolini, Fabio. *Hebdomades* (Venice, 1589).

Pico, Giovanni della Mirandola. *On the Dignity of M⌐n; On Being and the One; Heptaplus* (New York, 1965).

INTRODUCTION

Postel, Guillaume. *Absconditorum a constitutione mundi clavis, qua mens humana tam in divinis quam in humanis pertinget ad interiores velaminis aeternae veritatis* (Amsterdam, 1646).

———. *Candelabri typici in Mosis tabernaculo iusso divino expressi brevis ac dilucida interpretatio* (Venice, 1548).

———. *De Etruriae regionis, quae prima in orbe Europaeo habitata est, originibus institutis, religione, et moribus et imprimis* (Florence, 1551).

——— [Elias Pandocheus]. *De nativitate mediatoris ultima, nunc futura et toti orbi terrarum in singulis ratione praeditis manifesta, quae in theosofiae et filosofiae arcanis hactenus fuere* (s.l., s.d.).

———. *De orbis terrae concordia* (Basel, 1544).

———. *De rationibus spiritus sancti* (Paris, 1543).

———. *Descriptio Alcahirae urbis quae Mizir et Mazar dicitur*, edited by Angela Codazzi (Varese, s.d.).

———. *Guillaume Postel (1510–1581) et son interprétation du candélabre de Moyse*, edited by François Secret (Nieuwkoop, 1966).

———. *Panthenōsia* (s.l., s.d.).

Secondary Sources: Books

Albert-Buisson, François. *Michel de l'Hôpital* (Paris, 1950).

Allen, Don Cameron. *Doubt's Boundless Sea; Skepticism and Faith in the Renaissance* (Baltimore, 1964).

———. *The Legend of Noah* (Urbana, 1963).

———. *The Star-Crossed Renaissance* (Durham, 1941).

Allen, John William. *History of Political Thought in the Sixteenth Century* (New York, 1928).

Amphoux, Henri. *Michel de l'Hôpital et la liberté de conscience au xvi siècle* (Paris, 1900).

Baron, Salo Wittmayer. *A Social and Religious History of the Jews*. XVIII, *Inquisition, Renaissance, and Reformation*; XIV, *Catholic Restoration and Wars of Religion* (New York, 1969).

Baudrillart, Henri. *Bodin et son temps; tableau des théories politiques et des idées economiques du seizième siècle* (Paris, 1853).

Bayle, Pierre. *A General Dictionary Historical and Critical: A New and Accurate Translation of that of the Celebrated Mr. Bayle*, translated by J. B. Bernard, Thomas Birch, John Lockman (London, 1735).

Blau, Joseph Leon. *The Christian Interpretation of the Cabala in the Renaissance* (New York, 1944).

Boas, George. *The Happy Beast in French Thought of the Seventeenth Century* (Baltimore, 1933).

Bouwsma, William J. *Concordia Mundi: The Career and Thought of Guillaume Postel (1510–1581)* (Cambridge, Mass., 1957).

———. *Venice and the Defense of Republican Liberty. Renaissance Values in the Age of the Counter Reformation* (Berkeley, 1968).

Brush, Craig B. *Montaigne and Bayle* (The Hague, 1966).

BIBLIOGRAPHY

Bury, John B. *The Idea of Progress* (London, 1920).

Butler, Sir Geoffrey. *Studies in Statecraft* (Cambridge, 1920).

Cassirer, Ernst. *Descartes, Corneille, Christine de Suède* (Paris, 1942).

———. *Individuo e cosmo nella filosofia del Rinascimento* (Florence, 1935).

Charbonnel, J. Roger. *La Pensée italienne au xvie siècle et le courant libertin* (Paris, 1919).

Chauviré, Roger. *Jean Bodin, auteur de la république* (Paris, 1914).

Church, Frederic C. *The Italian Reformers 1534–1564* (New York, 1932).

Church, William F. *Constitutional Thought in Sixteenth Century France* (Cambridge, Mass., 1941).

De Chaufepié, Jaques George. *The Life of Servetus, Being an Article of his Historical Dictionary*, IV, translated by James Yair (London, 1771).

Diecmann, Ludovicus J. *De naturalismo, cum aliorum, tum maxime Jo. Bodini, ex opere ejus MSC anekdotō, de abditis rerum sublimium arcanis* (Leipzig, 1684).

Dunlop, D. M. *The History of the Jewish Khazars* (Princeton, 1954).

Febvre, Lucien. *Le Problème de l'incroyance au xvie siècle* (Paris, 1942).

Franklin, Julian H. *Jean Bodin and the Rise of Absolutist Theory* (Cambridge, 1973).

———. *Jean Bodin and the Sixteenth-Century Revolution in the Methodology of Law and History* (New York, 1963).

Fulton, John F. *Michael Servetus, Humanist and Martyr* (New York, 1953).

Garin, Eugenio. *Scienza e vita civile nel Rinascimento italiano* (Bari, 1965).

Garosci, Aldo. *Jean Bodin, politica e diritto nel Rinascimento francese* (Milan, 1934).

Gentile, Giovanni. *Studi sul Rinascimento* (Florence, 1936).

Ginzburg, Carlo. *Il nicodemismo: simulazione e dissimulazione religiosa nell' Europa del '500* (Turin, 1970).

Hoefer, Dr., ed. *Nouvelle biographie général* (Paris, 1855).

Hofmann, John J. *Lexicon universale* (Leyden, 1693).

Jones, Percy M. *French Introspectives from Montaigne to André Gide* (Cambridge, 1937).

Jones, Rufus M. *Studies in Mystical Religion* (London, 1919).

Katz, Jacob. *Exclusiveness and Tolerance. Studies in Jewish-Gentile Relations in Medieval and Modern Times* (New York, 1961).

Kelley, Donald R. *Foundations of Modern Historical Scholarship: Language, Law, and History in the French Renaissance* (New York, 1970).

Kristeller, Paul Oskar. *Iter Italicum* I, II (Leiden, 1965, 1967).

———. *The Philosophy of Marsilio Ficino* (Gloucester, Mass., 1964).

———. *Studies in Renaissance Thought and Letters* (Rome, 1956).

Lecler, Joseph. *Toleration and the Reformation* (New York, 1960).

Levron, Jacques. *Jean Bodin et sa famille* (Angers, 1950).

Lowinsky, Edward E. *Secret Chromatic Art in the Netherlands Motet* (New York, 1967).

McRae, Kenneth D. "The Political Thought of Jean Bodin" (Ph.D. dissertation, Harvard, 1953).

INTRODUCTION

Merritt, Arthur Tillman. *Sixteenth-Century Polyphony* (Cambridge, Mass., 1954).

Mesnard, Pierre. *L'Essor de la philosophie politique au* xvie *siècle* (Paris, 1951).

———. *Oeuvres philosophiques de Jean Bodin*, I (Paris, 1951).

Meyer-Baer, Kathi. *Music of the Spheres and the Dance of Death* (Princeton, 1970).

Mondolfo, Rodolfo. *Figure e idee della filosofia del Rinascimento* (Florence, 1963).

Morhof, Daniel G. *Polyhistor* (Lubeck, 1732).

Olgioti, Francesco. *L'anima dell' umanesimo e del Rinascimento* (Milan, 1924).

Ong, Walter J. *Ramus, Method, and the Decay of Dialogue* (Cambridge, Mass., 1958).

Owens, John. *The Skeptics of the Italian Renaissance* (New York, 1893).

Picot, Émile. *Les Français italianisants au* xvie *siècle* (Paris, 1906).

Popkin, Richard H. *The History of Scepticism from Erasmus to Descartes* (Assen, 1960).

Possevino, Antonio. *Iudicium de nuae militis Galli scriptis, quae ille discursus politicos et militares inscripsit, de Joannis Bodini methodo historiae: Libris de republica et demonomania* (Roma-Vaticana, 1592).

Prevost, and Roman D'Amat, eds. *Dictionnaire de biographie française* (Paris, 1954).

Puteanis, Petro and Jacobo, eds. *Catalogus bibliothecae Thuanae* (Paris, 1679).

Rekers, B. *Benito Arias Montano (1527–1598)* (London, 1972).

Reynolds, Beatrice. *Proponents of Limited Monarchy in Sixteenth Century France: Francis Hotman and Jean Bodin* (New York, 1931).

Rice, Eugene F., Jr. *The Renaissance Idea of Wisdom* (Cambridge, Mass., 1958).

Robertson, J. M. *A History of Free Thought, Ancient and Modern to the Period of the French Revolution*, I, II (London, 1969).

Roellenbleck, Georg. *Offenbarung, Natur und Jüdische Überlieferung bei Jean Bodin. Eine Interpretation des Heptaplomeres* (Studien zur Religion, Geschichte und Geisteswissenschaft, 2) (Gütersloh, 1964).

Rosenthal, Franz. *Knowledge Triumphant. The Concept of Knowledge in Medieval Islam* (Leiden, 1970).

Scharbau, M. Henrico. *Judaismus Detectus in quo vindicantur et restituuntur, qui vel injuste inter Judaeos relati, vel ex Judaeorum numero immerito exclusi sunt* (Lübeck, 1722).

Scholem, Gershom G. *Major Trends in Jewish Mysticism* (New York, 1954).

———. *The Messianic Idea in Judaism* (New York, 1971).

———. *On the Kabbalah and Its Symbolism* (New York, 1965).

Secret, François. *Bibliographie des manuscrits de Guillaume Postel* (Geneva, 1970).

Seiferth, Wolfgang S. *Synagogue and Church in the Middle Ages: Two Symbols in Art and Literature* (New York, 1970).

BIBLIOGRAPHY

Simone, Franco. *The French Renaissance: Medieval Tradition and Italian Influence in Shaping the Renaissance in France*, translated by H. Gaston Hall (London, 1969).

Singleton, Charles S. *Art, Science and History in the Renaissance* (Baltimore, 1967).

Spink, J. S. *French Free-Thought from Gassendi to Voltaire* (New York, 1960).

Taylor, Henry Osborn. *Thought and Expression in the Sixteenth Century*, I, II (New York, 1920).

Tetel, Marcel. *Marguerite de Navarre's "Heptameron": Themes, Language, and Structure* (Durham, N.C., 1973).

Thorndike, Lynn. *Alchemy during the First Half of the Sixteenth Century* (London, 1938).

———. *History of Magic and Experimental Science*, V, VI (New York, 1941).

Thou, Jacques-Auguste de. *Les Éloges des hommes savants, tirés de l'histoire de M. de Thou*, edited by Antoine Tessier (Leyden, 1715).

———. *Historiarum sui temporis* (n.p., 1620), V, liber CXVII, 701.

Von Tieghem, Paul. *La Littérature latine de la renaissance: étude d'histoire littéraire européenne* (Geneva, 1966).

Walker, Daniel P. *The Decline of Hell* (Chicago, 1964).

———. *Spiritual and Demonic Magic from Ficino to Campanella* (London, 1958).

Yates, Frances E. *The French Academies of the 16th Century* (London, 1947).

———. *Giordano Bruno and the Hermetic Tradition* (Chicago, 1964).

Articles

Bainton, Roland H. "Wylliam Postell and the Netherlands," *Nederlandsch Archief voor Kerkgeschiedenis* 24 (1931), 161–72.

Baldwin, Summerfield. "Jean Bodin and the League," *Catholic Historical Review* 23 (1937–38), 160–84.

Baudrillart, Henri. "Jean Bodin et l'heptaplomeres" in his *Publicistes modernes* (Paris, 1862), pp. 229–40.

Bauer, Robert J. "A Phenomenon of Epistemology in the Renaissance," *Journal of the History of Ideas* 31 (1970), 281–88.

Beinart, Haim. "The Records of the Inquisition. A Source of Jewish and Converso History" in *Proceedings of the Israel Academy of Sciences and Humanities* II (Jerusalem, 1968), 211–27.

Belladonna, Rita. "Sperone Speroni and Alessandro Piccolomini on Justification," *Renaissance Quarterly* 25, no. 2 (1972), 161–72.

Benz, Ernst. "Der Toleranz-Gedanke in der Religionswissenschaft. (Über den Heptaplomeres des Jean Bodin)," *Deutsche Vierteljahresschrift* 12 (1934), 540–71.

Bezold, Friedrich von. "Jean Bodins Colloquium Heptaplomeres und der Atheismus des 16. Jahrhunderts," *Historische Zeitschrift* 113 (1914) 3F.17, 260–315.

INTRODUCTION

Blau, Joseph Leon. "Postel and the Significance of Renaissance Cabalism," *Journal of the History of Ideas* 15 (1954), 218–32.

Boas, George. "Recent Books in the History of Philosophy," *Journal of the History of Ideas* 19 (1958), 581–84.

Buonaiuti, Ernesto. "La filosofia religiosa del Rinascimento," *Religio* 15 (1939), 335–55.

Bouwsma, William J. "Postel and the Significance of Renaissance Cabalism," *Journal of the History of Ideas* 15 (1954), 218–32.

Bredvold, Louis Ignatius. "Milton and Bodin's Heptaplomeres," *Studies in Philology* 21 (1924), 399–402.

Cassirer, Ernst. "Giovanni Pico della Mirandola," *Journal of the History of Ideas* 3 (1942), 123–44, 319–46.

———. "On the Originality of the Renaissance," *Journal of the History of Ideas* 4 (1943), 49–56.

Chauviré, Roger. "Grandeur de Bodin," *Revue Historique* 188–89 (1940), 378–97.

Clive, H. P. "The Calvinist Attitude to Music," *Bibliothèque d'humanisme et renaissance* 20 (1958), 79–107.

De Chaufepié, Jaques George. "Guillaume Postel" in his *Nouveau dictionnaire historique et critique* 3 (Amsterdam, 1750), 215–36.

Drake, Stillman. "Renaissance Science and Music," *Journal of the History of Ideas* 31 (1970), 483–500.

Droz, E. "Le Carme Jean Bodin, hérétique," *Bibliothèque d'humanisme et renaissance* 21 (1959), 453–67.

Durand, Dana B. "Tradition and Innovation in 15th Century Italy," *Journal of the History of Ideas* 4 (1943), 1–20.

Febvre, Lucien. "L'universalisme de Jean Bodin," *Revue de synthèse* 54 (1934), 165–68.

Ferguson, Wallace K. "Renaissance Tendencies in the Religious Thought of Erasmus," *Journal of the History of Ideas* 15 (1954), 499–508.

Gianturco, Elio. "Bodin's Conception of the Venetian Constitution and His Critical Rift with Fabio Albergati," *Revue de littérature comparée* 18 (1938), 684–95.

Gray, Hanna H. "Renaissance Humanism," *Journal of the History of Ideas* 24 (1963), 497–514.

Hirsch, Elisabeth F. "Erasmus and Portugal," *Bibliothèque d'humanisme et renaissance* 32 (1970), 540–49.

Hughes, Merritt Y. "Spenser's Acrasia and the Renaissance Circe," *Journal of the History of Ideas* 4 (1943), 381–99.

Jedin, Hubert. "Gasparo Contarini e il contributo veneziano alla riforma cattolica," in *La civiltá veneziana del Rinascimento*, edited by Diego Valeri (Venice, 1958), pp. 103–24.

Keller, Abraham C. "Zilsel, the Artisans, and the Ideas of Progress in the Renaissance," *Journal of the History of Ideas* 11 (1950), 235–40.

BIBLIOGRAPHY

Kristeller, Paul Oskar. "The Humanist Bartolomeo Facio and His Unknown Correspondence," in *From the Renaissance to the Counter-Reformation: Essays in Memory of Garrett Mattingly*, edited by C. H. Carter (London, 1966), pp. 56–74.

———. "The Myth of Renaissance Atheism and the French Tradition of Free Thought," *Journal of the History of Philosophy* 6 (1968), 233–43.

———. and Randall, John H., Jr. "Study of Renaissance Philosophies," *Journal of the History of Ideas* 2 (1941), 449–96.

Levron, Jacques. "Jean Bodin, Sieur de Saint-Amand," *Bibliothèque d'humanisme et renaissance* 10 (1948), 69–76.

Linder, Robert D. "Pierre Vinet and the Sixteenth Century French Protestant Revolutionary Tradition," *Journal of Modern History* 38 (1966), 125–37.

Lowinsky, Edward E. "Music in Renaissance Culture," *Journal of the History of Ideas* 15 (1942), 509–53.

Mantz, Harold E. "Jean Bodin and the Sorcerers," *The Romanic Review* 15 (1924), 153–78.

Marongiu, A. "Jean Bodin e la polemica sulle «assemblee di stati»," in *Gouvernés et gouvernants,* 3ᵉ partie, I (Brussels, 1966), 49–70.

McRae, Kenneth D. "A Postscript on Bodin's Connections with Ramism," *Journal of the History of Ideas* 24 (1963), 569–71.

———. "Ramist Tendencies in the Thought of J. Bodin," *Journal of the History of Ideas* 16 (1955), 306–23.

Mesnard, Pierre. "La Démonomanie de Jean Bodin," in *L'Opera e il pensiero di G. Pico della Mirandola*, II (Florence, 1965), pp. 333–56.

———. "Jean Bodin à la recherche des secrets de la nature," in *Umanesimo e esoterismo* (1960), 221–34.

———. "Jean Bodin fait de l'histoire comparée la base des sciences humaines," *Organon* 3 (1966), 181–84.

———. "La Pensée réligieuse de Bodin," *Revue du seizième siècle* 16 (1929), 77–121.

Michel, François. "Adrien de Thou et l'heptaméron de Marguerite de Navarre," *Bibliothèque d'humanisme et renaissance* 5 (1938), 16–36.

Monter, E. William. "Inflation and Witchcraft: The Case of Jean Bodin," in *Action and Conviction in Early Modern Europe*, edited by Theodore K. Rabb and Jerrold E. Seigel (Princeton, 1969), pp. 371–89.

Morandi, Carlo. "Botero, Campanella, Scioppio e Bodin," *Nuova Rivista Storica* 13 (1929), 342–50.

Moreau-Reibel, J. "Bodin et la ligue d'après des lettres inédites," *Humanisme et renaissance* 1–3 (1934–35), 422–40.

Ong, Walter J. "Peter Ramus and the Naming of Methodism," *Journal of the History of Ideas* 14 (1953), 235–48.

———. "System, Space, and Intellect in Renaissance Symbolism," *Bibliothèque d'humanisme et renaissance* 18 (1956), 222–39.

Pineas, Rainer. "Polemical *Exemplum* in Sixteenth Century Religious Controversy," *Bibliothèque d'humanisme et renaissance* 28 (1966), 393–96.

INTRODUCTION

Pines, Shlomo. "The Jewish Christians of the Early Centuries of Christianity According to a New Source," in *Proceedings of The Israel Academy of Sciences and Humanities,* II (Jerusalem, 1968), 237–309.

Planchenault, N. "Études sur Jean Bodin," *Mémoires de la société académique de Maine et Loire* I (Angers, 1857), 11–105.

Ponthieux, A. "Quelques documents inédits sur Jean Bodin," *Revue du seizième siècle* 15 (1928), 56–99.

Popkin, Richard H. "Skepticism and the Counter-Reformation in France," *Archiv für Reformationsgeschichte* 51 (1960), 59–87.

Radetti, Giorgio. "Il problema della religione nel pensiero di Giovanni Bodin," *Giornale critico della filosofia Italiana,* VI, fasc. 4–5 (1938), 277–94.

Randall, John H., Jr. "The Development of Scientific Method in the School of Padua," *Journal of the History of Ideas* 1 (1940), 177–206.

Reynolds, Beatrice. "Shifting Currents in Historical Criticism," *Journal of the History of Ideas* 14 (1953), 471–92.

Sabine, George Holland. "The Colloquium Heptaplomeres of Jean Bodin," in *Persecution and Liberty. Essays in Honor of G. L. Burr* (New York, 1931), pp. 271–309.

Screech, M. A. "The Illusion of Postel's Feminism," *Journal of the Warburg and Courtauld Institute* 16 (1953), 162–70.

Secret, François. "Jean Macer, François Xavier et Guillaume Postel, ou un épisode de l'histoire comparée des religions au xvie siècle," *Revue de l'histoire des religions* 170 (1966), 47–69.

———. "L'Emithologie de Guillaume Postel," *Archivio di Filosofia, Umanesmo e Esoterismo,* nos. 2–3 (1960), 381–437.

———. "Les Jésuites et le kabbalisme chrétien à la renaissance," *Bibliothèque d'humanisme et renaissance* 20 (1958), 542–55.

———. "Notes pour l'histoire des juifs en France," *Revue des études juives* 125, fasc. 1–3 (1966), 233–43.

———. "Notes sur les hébraisants chrétiens," *Revue des études juives* 123, fasc. 1–2 (1964), 141–68.

———. "Notes sur les juifs d'Avignon à la renaissance," *Revue des études juives* 121 (1962), 178–87.

Tindall, William Y. "James Joyce and the Hermetic Tradition," *Journal of the History of Ideas* 15 (1954), 23–39.

Tuve, Rosemond. "Imagery and Logic; Ramus and Metaphysical Poetics," *Journal of the History of Ideas* 3 (1942), 365–400.

Ulph, Owen. "Jean Bodin and the Estates-General of 1576," *Journal of Modern History* 19 (1947), 289–96.

Vogel, Ernst Gustav. "Zur Geschichte des ungedrückten Werks Colloquium Heptaplomeres," *Serapeum* 1 (1840), 113–16.

Wagner, Robert L. "Le vocabulaire magique de Jean Bodin dans la demonomanie des sorciers," *Bibliotheque d'humanisme et renaissance* 10 (1948), 95–123.

BIBLIOGRAPHY

Walker, Daniel P. "The Prisca Theologia in France," *Journal of the Warburg and Courtauld Institute* 17, nos. 3–4 (1954), 204–59.

Weisinger, Herbert. "Ideas of History during the Renaissance," *Journal of the History of Ideas* 6 (1945), 415–35.

Wilson, Harold S. "Some Meanings of 'Nature' in Renaissance Literary Theory," *Journal of the History of Ideas* 2 (1941), 430–48.

Zambelli, P. "Il «De auditu Kabbalistico» e la tradizione lulliana nel Rinascimento," *Atti e mem. dell' Accad. Toscana . . . «La Colombaria»* 30 n.s., 16 (1965), 113–247.

Zilsel, Edgar. "The Origins of William Gilbert's Scientific Method," *Journal of the History of Ideas* 2 (1041). 1–22.

[13]

Jean Bodin's Daemon and his Conversion to Judaism

Christopher R. Baxter

Introduction

In the *Démonomanie* Jean Bodin describes in vivid and circumstantial detail the apparition of a daemon to an unnamed acquaintance.[1] As long ago as 1910 von Bezold argued that the acquaintance was Bodin himself.[2] His extremely thorough article has had surprisingly little impact on the interpretation of Bodin's thought. Neither von Bezold himself, in his substantial article on the *Heptaplomeres*,[3] nor subsequent critics, have carried his arguments much further. Mesnard ignored the subject of Bodin's daemon completely.

In his book on Bodin's religious system, Roellenbleck is cautious.[4] He usefully underlines the Judaic atmosphere of the narrative, and concludes guardedly, from Bodin's treatment of the functions of daemons elsewhere, that it is «sehr wahrscheinlich, daß Bodin seine eigenen religiösen Erlebnisse in diesem Sinn verstand, und sich des Umgangs mit einem Engel gewürdigt fand». He remains uneasy about the details of the narrative: «Die wunderlichen spiritistischen Züge stechen befremdend heraus.»[5] This defensiveness is a long way removed from the traditional reaction to supposing that Bodin is describing his own daemon, as expressed with Enlightened impatience by Grosley.[6] Yet the continuing note of apologia,

---

[1] *La Démonomanie des Sorciers*, Paris 1580, Bk. I, ch. 2 (foll. 10–13). All references are to this edition [10.1].

[2] F. v. BEZOLD, Jean Bodin als Okkultist und seine Demonomanie, *Historische Zeitschrift* (105) 1910 [70].

[3] Das Colloquium Heptaplomeres und der Atheismus im 16. Jahrhundert, *Historische Zeitschrift*, 113/1914, 114/1915.

[4] G. ROELLENBLECK, Offenbarung, Natur und jüdische Überlieferung bei Jean Bodin, Kassel 1964 [239].

[5] ROELLENBLECK, [239], 120.

[6] «Grosley n'a pu se persuader que Bodin eût écrit sérieusement de telles rêveries.» Reported by L. DEVISME in *Magazin Encyclopédique de Millin*, 40 (1801), 46 [18].

Christopher R. Baxter

the urge to screen the disturbing potential of Bodin's demonology, remains insidiously pervasive of even the best interpretations of Bodin.

In a recent article Monter has countered some traditional attitudes to the *Démonomanie*, showing ways in which it is typical of Bodin's writing.[7] His rehabilitation is less concerned however with what Bodin says than with how he says it. Consequently we hear nothing of Bodin's daemon, and only some tentative suggestions about the role of daëmons in Bodin's philosophical system. This is somewhat surprising in view of Monter's insistence on the interlocking relations between Bodin's works.

I shall argue in this paper that we can date fairly precisely the time when Bodin's daemon became part of his everyday consciousness, profoundly modifying his religious and philosophical development. I shall argue that Bodin's total vision owes its definitive structure to this daemonic experience, and that the daemon converted Bodin to the «simplified, archaic Judaism» succinctly described by Walker,[8] and which Roellenbleck's book systematically investigates.

The Daemonic Narrative

A useful place to start is at the beginning of the narrative itself.

« Je puis asseurer d'avoir entendu d'un personnage, qui est encores en vie, qu'il y avoit un esprit qui luy assistoit assiduellement, et commença à le cognaitre, ayant environ trente sept ans ... ce qui luy advint comme il dict, ayant un an au paravant continué de prier Dieu de tout son cueur soir et matin, à ce qu'il luy pleust envoyer son bon Ange pour le guider en toutes ses actions, et apres et devant la priere il employoit quelque temps à contempler les œuvres de Dieu ... et à lire la Bible, pour trouver laquelle de toutes les religions debatues de tous costez estoit la vraye, et disoit souvent ces vers (psaume 143)

> ‹Enseigne moy comme il faut faire,
> Pour bien ta volonté parfaire,
> Car tu es mon vray Dieu entier,
> Fais que ton esprit debonnaire
> Me guide et meine au droict sentier.›

Blasmant ceux-là, qui prient Dieu qu'il les entretienne en leur opinions, et continuant cette priere, et lisant les sainctes escriptures, il trouva en Phi-

---

[7] E. W. MONTER, Inflation and Witchcraft: The Case of Jean Bodin, in Action and Conviction in Early Modern Europe, Princeton, 1969, 371–389 [268].

[8] D. P. WALKER, Spiritual and Demonic Magic from Ficino to Campanella, London 1958, [193], 171.

Bodin's Daemon and his Conversion to Judaism 3

lon Hebrieu au livre des sacrifices, que le plus grand et plus agreable sacrifice, que l'homme de bien, et entier peut faire à Dieu, c'est de soy mesme, estant purifié par luy. Il suivit ce conseil, offrant à Dieu son ame. Depuis il commença comme il m'a dict, d'avoir des songes, et visions pleines d'instruction: et tantost pour corriger un vice, tantost un autre, tantost pour se garder d'un danger, tantost pour estre resolu d'une difficulté . . . non seulement des choses divines, ains encores des choses humaines.»[9]

The daemonic narrative here describes religious attitudes strikingly like those expressed by Bodin in the *Methodus* of 1566,[10] and in his letter to Bautru des Matras, which is generally ascribed to the early sixties.[11] It seems to be the letter on an unorthodox Protestant, still wishing to describe himself as holding a version of Christianity (something he is nowhere else found doing), and able to conceive of changing his religious opinions by rational discussion.[12] He refers to previous correspondence in which he had written that «the true religion is none other but a sincere turning toward God of an cleansed spirit», an opinion he twice records in the *Methodus*.[13] In the *Methodus* Bodin is scrupulously neutral in describing his proposed book on comparative religion.[14] This neutrality derives in part from his own religious position – he was still genuinely searching to find which religion *was* true; in part from his persistent care never to appear offensively unorthodox, and thereby sow doubt in the minds of others; and in part from the generally secular frame of reference of the *Methodus*. On the other hand the *Methodus* has quite a strong Protestant flavour. Bodin refers very favourably to Calvin, Luther and

---

[9] *Dém.*, Bk. I, ch. 2, fol. 10–10v.

[10] *Methodus ad facilem historiarum cognitionem*, Paris 1566. All references are to the translation by Beatrice REYNOLDS, New York 1945 [4.23], followed in brackets by the page and column in MESNARD's French translation (see note 11).

[11] Printed in the *Appendix* to R. CHAUVIRÉ, Jean Bodin, auteur de la République, Paris 1914, 520–524 [76]. As a member of the Paris Parlement, Bodin took an oath of Catholicism in the summer of 1562. MESNARD makes this the *terminus ante quem* for dating the letter (e.g. in his introduction to the Œuvres Philosophiques de Jean Bodin, Paris 1951, XVI) [4.22]. But in previous correspondence with Bautru, written before December in an unspecified year, Bodin had already discussed the cause of the civil war. Mesnard's argument would make the dating of this improbably *precede* the war! Here as elsewhere Mesnard will not allow that Bodin could well be a Catholic, without necessarily being a Christian.

[12] «I beg and beseech you to make me of your opinion or to follow me in mine.»

[13] *Methodus*, 25, 33; (285 B, 290 A).

[14] *Meth.*, 25; (285 B).

Christopher R. Baxter

Melanchthon. His historiography is inspired in part by Protestant historians,[15] and he always quotes the psalms in Protestant translations.[16]

The Bautru letter violently attacks what Bodin calls the worship of saints, of statues and of the Eucharist. His objection is the Calvinistic one – that to worship the «wafer-God» is to idolise bread, αϱτολατϱεια. Similarly, he sees the religious wars as involving «the murder and persecution of good men who are trying to overthrow the most shameful idolomania»: ειϑωλομανειαν – a coining significantly reminiscent of a later neologism which stuck, *Démonomanie.* He puts himself and Bautru amongst the persecuted; perhaps in this like the daemon informant with his singing of psalm 143, which in Marot's translation is headed: «C'est la prière qu'il fit (sc. David), quand par crainte de Saul il se cacha en une fosse, où il s'attendoit d'estre prins, dont il estoit en grande angoisse».

Already then, Bodin's position is intransigently monotheist. Christ is seen as one of a whole line of prophets, which includes most Greek philosophers with the notable exception of Aristotle, who have been sent from heaven to recall men to the worship of the one God. «And then Christ, seizing the sacred fires of the eternal Pallas, as with Prometheus' rod, came down from heaven to earth, so that he might cleanse the world, sullied by a host of debaucheries and crimes, and lead mankind, enslaved by execrable superstition, to the true worship of Almighty God». This reference to Christ is uniquely favourable in Bodin's writing, though even here he seems to be prophet rather than saviour.

Commentators on the *Methodus* often express surprise at the progressive intrusion into this mainly secular, empirical and analytical work of a moral even teleological dimension. Beatrice Reynolds put it this way: «As we read on into the last chapter, on the origin of races, we may well wonder if he (Bodin) had not become a convert to Judaism.»[17] For reasons which will be discussed below. I think this is unlikely, but Miss Reynolds' remark does point to the impending crisis.

Bodin's friend had his daemonic experience when thirty seven, after a year of prayer and contemplation along lines which correspond to Bodin's own religious preoccupations in the *Methodus*, notably his sense that the discovery of religious truths is essentially a private affair, to be sought less in the scientific, objective study of religious systems, than in «frequent prayers and the turning of a clean mind toward God».[18] Some

---

[15] See J. L. BROWN, The Methodus ad Facilem Historiarum Cognitionem of Jean Bodin, a critical study, Washington 1939 [140].

[16] Such clear indications of Protestant feeling are less obvious in the *République.*

[17] In the introduction to her translation of the *Methodus*, XXVI.

[18] *Methodus*, 25; (285 B).

Bodin's Daemon and his Conversion to Judaism 5

twelve months or so after completing the *Methodus* Bodin himself was thirty seven. [19], [20]

Bodin's Daemon

In the year 1567 Bodin first seems to have become involved in the investigation of daemonic phenomena. A relevant passage occurs in a chapter of the *Démonomanie* which considers forms of protection against magic. Bodin thinks that the man who gives alms to the poor, for instance, is immune from *maleficia*.

«De faict j'ay sçeu estant à Poictiers aux Grands Jours parmi les substituts du Procureur general, qu'il y eust deux sorciers qui demanderent l'aumosne en une riche maison. On les refusa: ils jetterent là leur sort, et tous ceux de la maison furent enragés et moururent furieux ... estans meschans et n'ayans pitié des pauvres, Dieu n'eut point pitié d'eux. Aussi l'Escripture Saincte appelle l'aumosne צדקה (shedakah), et au lieu que nous disons donnez l'aumosne, ils disent donnez la Justice, comme estant l'une des choses qui justifie plus le meschant.»

Several Old Testament instances of this usage follow. As Bodin already believed that Hebrew words expressed the ultimate meanings of the things they designated, this equivalence would have revelatory force for him. He now continues with a striking assertion.

«Brief toute l'Escriture saincte n'est pleine d'autre chose. Voila peut estre l'un des plus grands et des plus beaux secrets qu'on puisse remarquer pour oster à Satan, et a tous les Sorciers la puissance de nuire ... Toutefois le plus asseuré moyen et qui passe tous les autres c'est de se fier en Dieu, et s'asseurer de luy comme d'une forteresse treshaute et inexpugnable (a reference to psalm 91): c'est dit Philon, le plus grand et le plus agreable sacrifice qu'on sçaurait faire à Dieu, et pour lequel Abraham receut tant de benedictions, et duquel l'Escripture dit qu'il se fia en Dieu, et qu'il luy fut imputé à justice.»[21]

In these lines, where Bodin is elucidating his own experiences at the age of thirty seven, with the help of the Old Testament, we meet in close proximity three similarities to the daemonic narrative. Firstly, there is the crucial sacrifice passage from Philo. Secondly, there is the Hebraic emphasis – for so Bodin considers it – on the beneficial value of almsgiving. His informant had told him that «il estoit souvent adverty de donner l'aumosne, et alors que plus il donnait l'aumosne, plus il sentoit que ses

---

[19] Bodin was born in 1529 or 1530.

[20] Bezold does not pursue this coincidence of age.

[21] *Dém.*, Bk. III, ch. 1, foll. 124v–125. Bodin's interest in *naement d'auguillette* while at Poitiers is described at length *Dém.*, Bk. II, ch. 1, foll. 57v–58.

affaires prosperoit.» And thirdly, there is the allusion to psalm 91, which
the daemon had instructed the informant to recite. «Et apres avoir
eschapé le danger, il dict qu'il ouyt en dormant une voix qui disoit: Il
faut bien dire ‹Qui en la garde du haut Dieu pour jamais se retire.› » Later
in this same chapter about the Poitiers witches Bodin again refers to the
use of psalm 91 as an antidote to magic, quoting it at considerable length.

In fact all this chapter is very closely related to the daemonic narrative
chapter. We read that Bodin's informant «employoit un jour de la
sepmaine autre que le Dimenche (pour les debauches qu'il disoit qu'on
faisoit ce jour là) pour lire en la Bible, et puis meditoit, et pensoit à ce
qu'il avoit leu ... pui après il prenoit plaisir à louer Dieu, d'un Psalme
de louange.»

Words like these are closely paralleled by Bodin's counsel that «Chacun
doit instruire sa famille à prier Dieu matin et soir ... (et) donner pour le
moins une ou deux heures en un iour de la sepmaine à faire lire la Bible
par le chef de la famille»[22] and by his declaration that: «le Dimenche ...
est souillé de toutes des desbauches et folies dont on se peut aviser au
grand deshonneur de Dieu.»[23]

The heavily paternalistic tone of the first quotation is in turn matched
in the daemonic narrative, where two of the informant's visions concern
his father. In one instance the informant had asked God to bless him, and
was rewarded with the vision of his human father giving his benediction,
a vision which strikingly concludes the whole narrative.

These coincidences between the two chapters can hardly be merely
coincidental. They are all the more noteworthy in view of the limited
information given as to the exact form the daemon's religious teaching
took. Roellenbleck goes so far as to say that we are not told of any
theological information imparted by the daemon.[24] But this will hardly
do. It is to overlook the rigorously simplified nature of Bodin's theology,
the strongly ethical bias of his religion. Bodin insists that the daemon did
explain difficulties «non seulement des choses divines, mais encores des
choses humaines» and that the friend «avoit les songes veritables de ce
qu'il devoit faire ou croire». The daemon's advice about almsgiving,
psalm-singing, early morning prayer, is advice about «choses divines»,
and has theological implications. Thus in the *Heptaplomeres* the seven
participants do have one form of worship in common, psalm-singing,
because of its exclusively monotheistic orientation.

The main ground for Bodin's reticence – and anonymity – in the daemonic narrative is probably his conviction that few people are granted

---

[22] *Dém.*, Bk. III, ch. 1, fol. 123.

[23] *Dém.*, fol. 127.

[24] *Dém.*, 118.

Bodin's Daemon and his Conversion to Judaism   7

communication with a good daemon. The *Démonomanie* is dedicated to persuading its readers that large numbers of people invoke bad ones. For Bodin, white daemonic magic does not exist, nor for that matter does natural magic. He believes that the concept of good daemons is almost always used as a cover for Satan worship. «Satan a tousjours cherché de beaux mots comme d'Esprit familier, et blance Daemon, et Petitmaistre, parce que le mots de Satan et Diable sont odieux.»[25] Moreover, as the daemonic narrative tells us, the main and much-needed activity the daemon exercised was to save Bodin's friend from danger. Bodin would hardly want to increase the danger by revealing his friend's identity. All the more so in view of the highly dubious orthodoxy of the «friend's» religion, even before 1567.

The chapter in which the narrative occurs itself has radically anti-Christian implications. It starts off by describing man's intellectual soul as a mean between bad daemons and angels. This curious, neo-Platonising cosmology is given an apparently Christian gloss by maintaining that Adam's fall broke the continuity between God and Creation. The Christian gloss should continue to say that Christ restored the broken continuity. For Bodin the restoration is effected by prayer, and he explains later that «Les Hebrieux tiennent en leur Theologie secrette que l'Ange faict oblation à Dieu des âmes des esleus.»[26] Christ then seems to be replaced as mediator by the good daemon, who offers up souls in sacrifice. At the end of the daemonic narrative, Bodin goes on to make two observations of its significance, which show that the daemonic narrative is central to the origin and purpose of the whole book. Firstly, the circumstantially authenticated experience of a man communicating with a good daemon is a guarantee that communication with bad daemons is not some highly improbable conjecture.[27] And secondly, the physical phenomena

---

[25] *Dém.*, Bk. II, ch. 3, fol. 78v, and cf. Bk. II, ch. 1, fol. 52.

[26] *Dém.*, Bk. II, ch. 5, fol. 90.

[27] Johann WEYER's arguments against witchcraft persecution are largely based on the assertion that such communication with bad daemons is a case of melancholic delusion. Bodin's fury against Weyer, his certainty that Weyer was a Satanic double agent, was much intensified by this assertion that what Bodin experienced as fact was mere fancy. MONTAIGNE's too wellknown doubts about persecution (*Essais*, Bk. III, ch. 11) derive from humanitarian impulses, rather than, as MONTER asserts ([268], 389) from systematic scepticism. Montaigne did not, in fact, maintain his earlier disbelief in the reality of witchcraft, since such a denial would be to set limits to God's unknowable powers – a sceptical argument frequent in the *Démonomanie*. (*Essais*, Bk. I, ch. 27). There is a nicely ironic chassé-croisé here, for Montaigne, who much admired the *Methodus*, criticised Bodin for being too sceptical about prodigies in it. (*Essais*, Bk. II, ch. 10). This was a scepticism which Bodin was very soon to jettison.

reported by his informant match phenomena described in the Old Testament, and thus guarantee the daemon's reliability as a source of religious and moral enlightenment.

The *Démonomanie* is organised around this dual reference, empirical and scriptural. The scriptural reference is entirely to the Old Testament, which Bodin generally refers to as the «Loy de Dieu», particularly where the Pentateuch is concerned. Book One describes the «moyens divins naturels et humains de prévoir et de prévenir les choses futures». It exhaustively explores the nature of prophecy with the help of the Old Testament and confirms the prophetic status of the daemonic experience.[28] The second book described the unlawful practices of witches, which are proscribed by the Law of God. It is characterised by the fullness of Bodin's first hand researches into contemporary daemonic phenomena. Most of the third book, on means to combat magic, is taken up with the chapter in which, as we have seen, Bodin develops the religious implications of the daemonic narrative. The last book discusses means of exterminating witchcraft, using the rigorous legislation of Deuteronomy against idolatry, blasphemy and witchcraft (which involves the other two crimes). The devastating skill with which Bodin uses the double reference to Scripture and experience in the refutation of Johann Weyer, which follows as a lengthy appendix, has been well described by Monter.[29]

Bodin's conversion

From this point I shall refer to the daemon as Bodin's own.[30] I want to

---

[28] *Dém.*, Bk. I, ch. 4, foll. 23–24, especially where Bodin distinguishes different degrees of prophetic illumination, drawing heavily on Maimonides. He argues in the same chapter that the strictest monotheism is a sign of the true prophet, fol. 27, and that «les enfans d'Israel (sont) tous ceux qui se fient en Dieu», fol. 30v. Such views obviously facilitated his identification with the Hebraic outlook.

[29] MONTER is less convincing in comparing the organisation of the *Démonomanie* and the *Malleus Maleficarum* ([268], 386). There are closer comparisons to make with more recent Protestant writers on witchcraft, including WEYER. Thus PEUCER's *Commentarius de praecipuis divinationum generibus*, Wittenberg 1553, discusses witchcraft within the framework of divination, of which prophecy in one species, rather as the *Démonomanie* does. It begins by discussing lawful divination (fol. 9) then unlawful divination (fol. 13) then prophecy. Bodin had discussed lycanthropy with Peucer, and was interested in pursuing the question whether this was a natural or divine phenomenon (*Methodus*, 79).

[30] There is much additional justification for this in Bezold's article on the *Démonomanie*.

Bodin's Daemon and his Conversion to Judaism 9

apply to his experience of the daemon seven characteristics which Nock refers to in his discussion of intellectual conversion.[31]

1. Conversion is generally preceded by a period of doubt and of searching. Thus we have seen Bodin seeking in his soul and in the Bible to find the true religion, whilst the avowed aim of his projected study of human, natural and divine affairs was to help men to «that intimate relationship which we have with God . . . and again be united closely to him.»[32]

2. In many conversions a single phrase seems to alluminate the whole Bible or a mere image to bring peace and assurance to the soul. In Bodin's case the phrase from Philo about sacrifice seems to have played a crucial role in confirming Bodin's conviction of an impending resolution of his spiritual uncertainty. An uncertainty whose final resolution involves the intimate certainty of God as a tower of spiritual strength: thus the repeated use of psalm 91. A key to the whole Bible is provided for Bodin by the equivalence of the words charity and justice in Hebrew.[33]

3. Conversion comes to a person as something unforeseen, as a blinding revelation of something new. Even the notion of familiar spirits, of good daemons, is absent from Bodin's writings before 1567. The felt immediacy of the daemon's presence is abundantly clear in Bodin's conversion, especially in the miraculous escapes from danger which it facilitated. An observer can often trace the seeds and development of such revelation. Bodin himself writes of the daemonic voice that «luy sembla avoir ouy la voix de Dieu en dormant, qui luy dist, ‹Je sauveray ton ame: c'est moy qui t'ay apparu par cy devant›», a remark which suggests a previous history of spiritual intimations.

4. The sense of fresh understanding and of a new spiritual well being is often accompanied by psychosomatic disorders. The daemon would twitch Bodin's left and right ears, and even strike from his hands any «bad» book he might be reading. And the daemon also appeared to Bodin as a bright circle of light. In one case Bodin saw on his bed «un jeune enfant vestu d'une robe blanche changeant en couleur de pourpre, d'un visage de beauté esmerveillable.»

5. A conversion leads to a definite change in the conduct of one's daily

---

[31] A. D. Nock, Conversion, London, 1933, esp. chapter I.

[32] *Methodus*, 16; (282 A).

[33] Bodin's discussion of justification in the *Heptaplomeres* is a re-working of this *Démonomanie* passage (*Dém.*, Bk. III, ch. 1, foll. 124v–125). Roughly speaking, Bodin replaces the doctrine of justification by a doctrine of *reward*. Compare the passage about political «justification» in the *République*, Bk. VI, ch. 1, referred to below, p. II, which is also based on the notion of reward and punishment.

life. It led Bodin to rise very early to pray. His feelings about the pollu-
tion of the Sabbath probably led him to keep the Sabbath. He certainly
put into practice in his own family the Judaic paternalism which he
advocates in the *Démonomanie.*[34]

6. Conversion frequently turns a man into a prophet, with a message
to deliver and a policy to pursue, and

7. Conversion means turning one's back on something.

The larger implications of the last two points are the subject of what
follows. In particular we shall be concerned with the policies advocated
in the *République,* and with Bodin's rejection of the basic Christian
mysteries, along with the Christian ethics of forgiveness.

The Law of God

References to the New Testament are as infrequent in the *République*
(1576) as in the *Methodus,* and when they occur are for purposes of
illustration. They never have prescriptive force. The normative use of
the Old Testament, the Law of God, on the other hand, has become all
pervasive, dominating the discussion at every important point. The conclusion to the chapter concerning sovereignty, the concept on which Bodin's fame is based, affirms with epigrammatic vigour that the Law of
God provides the pattern of all justice.

«For if iustice be the end of the law, and the law is the worke of the
prince, and the prince is the lively image of almightie God; it must needes
follow, that the law of the prince should be framed unto the modell of
the law of God.»[35]

Bodin specifically identifies the natural and divine law, which he
normally couples in the one phrase. Interestingly, in the final chapter of
the first book, concerning the attributes of sovereignty (which are most
easily exercised in a monarchy), Bodin refers only to the Law of God.
And in chapters six and seven of the following book, concerning the
characteristics of aristocràties and democracies, he refers to neither natural

---

[34] In his partial edition and translation of the *Heptaplomeres,* Berlin, 1841,
GUHRAUER prints a letter of Bodin about the education of his children: «Je leur
ai dressé trois cent sentences morales ... et pour leur apprendre les principales
congruités et concordances je leur ai appris ces mots: Ego cupio vehementer
laudare opificem mundi optimum et potentissimum omnium.» [23], 254.

[35] *The Six Books of a Commonweale,* ed. K. D. McRAE, Harvard 1962, Bk. I,
ch. 10, p. 113 [7.44]. All references are to his edition, followed by the page in
the 1583 edition. Sometimes this is less full than the Knolles translation edited
by McRae, which uses the later Latin version.

Bodin's Daemon and his Conversion to Judaism   11

nor divine law. For his concern in the *République* is almost exclusively with kings.

Time and again, Bodin insists that sovereign power can only be exercised within the constraining limits of the Law of God. On the other hand, as far as civil law goes, the sovereign has complete liberty of action. He cannot be bound by any charge or condition «except that such charge or condition ... be directly comprehended within the lawes of God and nature.»[36] In this sense a king is absolute, and for this reason Bodin roundly attacks whose who would «subject him to the generall estates, or to the councell ... (or) to his lawes ... Under this colour they make a mixture and confusion of civill lawes with the lawes of nature, and of both joyntly with the lawes of God.»[37] These assertions are flat contrary to a phrase like the following from the *Methodus*: «The more you can take from the power of the prince (and on this point one cannot go wrong) the more just will be the rule and the more stable for the future.»[38]

Discussions of the reasons for this change usually refer to the deterioration of the political situation in France between the appearance of the two works, and growth of the *politique* attempts at bolstering up Valois power. And it is quite true that, unlike the *Methodus*, the *République* comments directly about the French situation, and recommends remedies. But what sort of comments, and what sort of remedies?

Bodin ascribes the weakness of France at the beginning of the religious wars to Henry II's failure to punish the wicked and protect the poor, thereby breaking the Law of God.[39] Describing the lamentable state of the royal finances under Charles IX, Bodin refers to «the calamitie of those times when as children and women ruled», a punishment, he later explains, which is threatened in the Old Testament.[40] These calamities would have continued «if God had not sent our King Henrie 3 from heaven to restore it to the first beautie.»[41] Moreover Henry's rule, providentially thus established, against numerological law, is maintained by special divine favour.[42]

It will be obvious from these examples that it is not sufficient to point only to the contemporary situation to explain the concept of sovereignty

---

[36] *République*, Bk. I, ch. 8, p. 89; (128).

[37] *Rép.*, Bk. VI, ch. 4, p. 717; (965).

[38] *Methodus*, 256; (405 B).

[39] *République*, Bk. II, ch. 4, p. 217; (295); Bk. VI, ch. 2, pp. 677; (898), 681; (901).

[40] *Rép.*, Bk. VI, ch. 2, p. 679; (ef. 901); Bk. VI, ch. 4, p. 714; (960).

[41] *Rép.*, Bk. VI, ch. 2, p. 654; (863).

[42] *Rép.*, Bk. IV, ch. 2, p. 463; (567), and McRae's note.

in the *République*, but also to take into full account the moral and religious nature of its recommendations for restoring political stability. The naturalistic analysis of the *Methodus* has largely gone. Praise of Machiavelli has turned into vituperation, for having «laid down as the twin foundations of Commonweals impiety and injustice, and (having) condemned religion as hostile to the state ... as for justice, if Machiavelli had cast his eye ever so lightly over good authors, he would have found that Plato calls his *Republic* the books of justice, this being one of the firmest supports of all Commonweals.»[43]

In the *Methodus* Bodin confesses that he is so far relatively ignorant of Hebraic legal literature,[44] and nowhere does he suggest that Hebraic law is universally normative. We have moved a long way from this in the discussion of justice which climaxes the *République*. Here Bodin defines justice as essentially a strict system of rewards and punishments.

«(This justice) the Hebrewes by a strange word call *Credata*: for the difference betwixt this and the other Iustice given unto men by God, whereby we are justified, which they call *Tsedaca*. For that by these, as by most certain guides, wee must enter into this most religious and stately temple of Iustice.»[45]

Bodin argues at some length that justice should be implemented harmonically. He believes that this harmonic justice is exemplified only in the Law of God,[46] and in Hebraic legislation. The *lex talionis*, for example, is to be understood as describing this harmonic justice, rather than as demanding, with some naive arithmetic, one eye for one eye, one tooth for one tooth. «And so the auntient Hebrewes, the best interpreters of God his law, have understood it, expounded it, and also practised it: as is in their Pandects to be seene in the *Title of Penalties*.»[47]

A moral universe

Is it possible to see a development towards these ideas in the *Methodus*? There is no mention of divine law in the epistolary dedication, and in the discussion of the *Form of Monarchy*[48] neither natural or divine law are mentioned. In the section curiously headed *Form of Government in*

---

[43] *Rép.*, Preface of 1576, A 70.
[44] *Methodus*, 3; (274 A).
[45] *République*, Bk. VI, ch. 6, p. 755; (1014).
[46] *Rép.*, 784; (1049).
[47] *Rép.*, 781; (1045).
[48] *Methodus*, 201–206; (375 A–378 B)

Bodin's Daemon and his Conversion to Judaism   13

Marseilles Bodin mentions the «loftiest knowledge of heavenly and natural things» possessed by the Druids, only to add tersely: «I discuss only the state», meaning that his investigation of political systems is solely concerned with *res humanae*.[49] A new pages later however he does criticise the gynocratic rule of Mary and Elisabeth I for contravening divine and natural laws.[50]

Only in the closing pages of this extremely long chapter on different types of political system, when Bodin discusses the Hebrews, does the notion of divine law become important.[51] Moses ordered that the Hebrews should be ruled by divine law. The history of his people is said to show that royal power was pleasing to God. And it is, significantly, immediately following this discussion that Bodin affirms monarchy to be the best political system.[52] The whole chapter concludes with a brief discussion on religion as the *fundamentum regni*, which seems extraordinarily slight after the massive weight of empirical political analysis which has come before.[53] Nevertheless it is indicative of a tension in Bodin's mind.

The rigid distinctions which Bodin's methodology sets up between human, natural and divine history in the *Methodus*, his attempt to construct a secularised *summa*, is under great strain at many points. The *Methodus* derives its fascination – and its unsatisfactoriness – from the sense it gives of a powerful mind gripped by enormous visions of intellectual investigation, but as yet unsure of the direction in which it will ultimately move. The observer can see that this direction is in fact towards a Hebraically inspired, morally organised universe. Bodin will abandon his triple concept of history and substitute for it a triple concept of Law – human, natural and divine. The Hebraic aspect of this development has its seeds in the notion of Moses as the first, divinely inspired lawgiver and supreme philosopher,[54] of the Hebrews as the best interpreters of natural and divine things [55] and as the fountainhead of all existing religions.[56] The moral emphasis is present in Bodin's assertion that to reject the tes-

---

[49] *Meth.*, 250; (402 AB). The assertion that he is studying only *res humanae* is repeated throughout the first half of the work (cf. pp. 1, 8, 14, 16, 42, 44, 153).

[50] *Meth.*, 253; (404 A).

[51] *Meth.*, 279–282; (418 B–420 A).

[52] *Meth.*, 282; (420 A).

[53] «Argomentazioni che appaiono come l'appendice posticcia di un rigoroso discorso politico» says COTRONEO, Bodin teoretico della storia Napoli 1966, [246], 169.

[54] *Methodus*, 201, 303, 340; (375 B, 431 B, 451 B). This view of Moses coexists with the argument that the *least* reliable witnesses are those closest to the events they describe.

[55] *Meth.*, 111, 130, 317; (327 A, 337 A, 438 B).

[56] *Meth.*, (463 B).

timony of Moses is eroneous, impious and immoral.[57] It is especially
apparent in the penultimate chapter, where Bodin argues that all the
peoples of the world are fundamentally one, and that the historical
process demands «that the peoples should unite their possessions and
ideas in mutual commerce».[58] The crucial notion – crucial for Bodin's
later development – occurs here. Divine vengeance is invoked to describe
the process by which «the Greeks were subject for a time to the Latins . . .
and in turn the Latins . . . to the Goths». The chapter concludes – and it
is followed only by the bibliography – that the only Jewish tribe which
had preserved a separate identity disappeared from history «not without
marked evidence of divine vengeance».[59] Yet these indications of a moral
universe, it is clear, go against, they do not constitute, the main purpose
of the *Methodus*.

Divine Retribution

If, as the *République* maintains, the king is bound by the Law of God,
it follows that he cannot allow his subjects to break it with impunity.
One of the fiercest notes in the *République* is the ringing denunciation
of pardon, especially for those who have transgressed God's laws:

«The wilfull murderer ‹You shall take him (saith the law) from my
sacred altar, neither shalt thou have pitie on him, but cause him to dye
the death: and afterwards I will stretch forth my great mercies upon
you›. Nevertheless the Christian kings on that day which they commaund
to bee most holy kept, as on Good Friday, use for the most part to pardon
some one man or other, condemned of most horrible and notorious
crime.»[60]

Or again: «the law of God expressly forbiddeth to have any pitie of
the poore in judgement.»[61] Rewards and punishments are essential for
maintaining the state, its two principal foundations,[62] and the fatal
weakness of democratic systems is the unwillingness of men to condemn
and punish their peers.[63] The corresponding advantage of monarchy is

---

[57] *Meth.*, (448 B).

[58] *Meth.*, (449 A).

[59] It is curious that Bodin does not apply the idea of retribution in discussing
the history of the Hebrews.

[60] *République*, Bk. I, ch. 10, p. 174; (240), with marginal reference to *Deuteronomy*, 19 and 21.

[61] *Rép.*, Bk. III ch. 5, p. 341; (449), Bk. IV, ch. 6, p. 509; (622). See also
Bk. V, ch. 3, 582; (725) and Bk. V, ch. 4, pp. 593, 595; (729, 742).

[62] *Rép.*, 584; (729).

[63] *Rép.*, 592; (742), also Bk. VI, ch. 4, p. 704; (943).

that rewards can be administered by the king and punishments by his ministers.[64]

Supposing the king does grant impunity to criminals, what sort of sanction can there be? The checks on sovereign power in the *Methodus* were constitutional, immanent ones. As a consequence (or is it a cause?) of the removal of these political safeguards in the *République*, the checks on the sovereign are necessarily religious, transcendental.[65] Thus, «pardons granted to such villaines (e.g. murderers) drawe after them plagues, famine, warres, and ruines of Commonweales: and that is it for which the law of God saith. That in punishing them that have deserved to dye, they shall take away the cause from among the people».[66]

All this is exactly the theory of the *Démonomanie*, which the critical tradition has unnecessarily separated from the *République*.

It is not the function of the *République* to describe in detail the mechanism of divine retribution. This fact is explained with lucid brevity in the chapter dealing with the *conversiones rerumpublicarum*. «The chaunges and ruines of Commonweales are human (e), or naturall, or divine.» «Politicians and astrologers» study the first two types of causation, and «divines» the third. Nevertheless, Bodin does sketch in the outlines of the mechanism of retribution. «The Divine constantly affirmeth all plagues, wars, dearth, destructions of cities and nations, to proceed from the contempt of God.»[67]

Now, just as with the monarch, who should not himself punish, but delegate the task to others, so with God, who acts «by meane causes and the ministerie and power of angels».

«In this all divines... wholly agree, none of all these things to bee done by almightie God, as by an efficient cause: but by permission onely, and to bee from him divided, but as from a not letting cause: which cause the manner of the Hebrew phrase everie where signifieth by the word Hiphil, ordinarily used, when it speaketh of the vengeance of God.»[68]

Bodin reserves a full treatment of such «divine causes» to the *Démonomanie*, which explains the daemonic mechanism of the *conversiones rerumpublicarum*, a mechanism set in motion by the willed impiety of witches.

---

[64] *Rép.*, Bk. IV, ch. 6; (625). Bk. V, ch. 4, p. 593; (730).

[65] God may act through foreign rulers or a specially appointed subject. Otherwise tyrannicide is forbidden; see the 1578 Preface (A 70) and Bk. II, ch. 5.

[66] *Rép.*, Bk. I, ch. 10, p. 174; (240) and see Bk. IV, ch. 2., p. 438; (542). Bk. IV, ch. 6, p. 512; (625).

[67] *Rép.*, Bk. IV, ch. 2, pp. 437, 438; (542).

[68] *Rép.*, Bk. IV, ch. 6, p. 512; (625).

The Daemonic Machinery

We saw above that the *Methodus* moves only fitfully towards a providential doctrine of history. At one point, in defining «natural» history,
Bodin even slips into a form of words which seems to deny the existence
of a continually active providence. «Natural history presents an inevitable and steadfast sequence of cause and effect unless it is checked by
divine will or for a brief moment abandoned by it.»[69] In later works,
Bodin will assert that all non-regular or violent natural phenomena
are under providential control, being produced by daemonic agents. The
Methodus on the other hand is virtually innocent of demonology. But
not quite. In two places Bodin refers in passing to «animi immortales».[70]
And in refuting the doctrine of the eternity of the world, Bodin counters
the argument of Proclus that, in creating the world, God must have been
«carried from rest to action (which) involves a change ... which is very
far from that everlasting mind» by referring to Christ's assertion that
«He might have, if He wished, twelve legions of angels for a guard.
From this He wished to imply that this world is full of immortal souls
(animorum immortalium) whose service God uses like that of servants».[71]
These incidental references do not begin to constitute a theory of daemonic activity, and in any case, Bodin's later demonology almost totally
ignores the rich material in the New Testament. The *Methodus* is not a
«superstitious» book. Bodin is often sarcastically critical of stories of
miracle and prodigy,[72] an attitude noticeably absent from works written
after his daemonic experience.

In the *Theatrum Naturae*[73] Bodin does indeed insist that scientific
truth is to be sought by reason and experiment – «experience«. But since
Hebrew is the language of truth, and since the Hebrews are obviously
best qualified to interpret their own books, a more certain – and a corroborative – method is to rely on Hebraic exegesis of the Law of God.
So Bodin's science turns out to be the revealed science of the Book of
Genesis and the Psalms. The main speaker in the *Theatrum* is called
Mystagogus, a word which Bodin uses when explicating his daemonic
experience in the *Démonomanie*, by quoting an anonymous Greek verse
(actually Menander) which says: «To every man there is given a guide
of his life, a mystagogue». Probably Bodin conceives of his daemon as
having initiated him into the secrets of the universe.

---

[69] *Methodus*, 17; (282 A).
[70] *Rép.*, 11, 30; (279 A, 288 A).
[71] *Rép.*, 310, 311; (435 AB).
[72] *Rép.*, 57, 77; (301 A, 310 B).
[73] *Universae Naturae Theatrum*, Lyon 1596 [13.1].

Bodin's Daemon and his Conversion to Judaism   *17*

At all events, Bodin is utterly persuaded of the omnipresence of the daemonic machinery in the physical world, and deeply concerned, in the *Démonomanie* and *Heptaplomeres*, to warn against adoration, or fear, of these spirits. In the first three books of the *Heptaplomeres* Bodin rejects the Aristotelean, mechanistic universe in favour of a moral universe (i.e. a rewarding and punishing one) operated by daemons on behalf of a totally transcendent deity. But these daemons, as mere creatures, must not be worshipped. To worship them, as witches, do, is an impious threat to strict Hebraic monotheism. The last three books of the *Heptaplomeres* are written to show that all versions of Christianity contain the same idolatrous threat. The doctrines of the incarnation, of atonement, of the forgiveness of sins, are absurdities: how can a finite creature have any contact with an infinite creator; how can one creature atone for the sins of others? The forgiveness of sins is incompatible with Bodin's Hebraic system of rewards and punishments, which he bases on an uncompromising voluntarism. There is no eternal damnation, merely annihilation for the very wicked. However, in spite of the idolatrous nature of Christianity, no blasphemy is involved in the worship and belief of most Christians, who, unlike witches, are merely mistaken in their religion. Witches, by rejecting the Christianity which they believe to be true, are not rejecting the true God, but they *are* rejecting God. And, since any sincere religion, even the most superstitious, is welcome to God, it is the duty of all princes to maintain the traditional religion, even Christianity, and to punish backsliders. If they do not do it, God will.[74]

Bodin conceives of divine rewards and punishments operating, in Hebraic fashion, in this world, though he does believe that the very best men turn into stars when they die. Now God, who punishes through the daemonic machinery, also rewards through it. In the *Paradoxon*[75] a treatise on the *summum bonum*, Bodin describes the highest reward of virtue as the gift of prophecy: prophets are those men «qui ont la communication du bon ange, que les autres appellent l'intellect actuel, de la splendeur duquel les gens de bien sont instruits par songes et visions de

---

[74] *Colloquium Heptaplomeres*, ed. L. NOACK, Schwerin, 1857 [16.2] Bodin has a very acute insight into the historically conditioned interrelations of social and religious institutions, and is acutely apprehensive about the moral and religious confusion attendant on violent cultural change. Without the belief in a rewarding and punishing God, society will collapse. Any religion maintains this belief to some extent. Hence Bodin's resolute religious conformism.

[75] *Paradoxon, quod nec virtus ulla in mediocritate, nec summum hominis bonum in virtutis actione consistere possit*, Paris 1596 [14.1]. I quote from Bodin's French translation, *Le Paradoxe de Jean Bodin*, Paris 1598 [14.2].

tout ce qu'il faut suivre et fuir, et d'advertir les princes et les peuples de
la volonté de Dieu.»[76]

Revelation

Bodin's own prophetic activity – his revealing to others of God's will –
was partly a matter of foretelling the political future. This he did frequently, and with some success[77]. More interestingly, there is evidence
to suggest that Bodin intervened personally to try to ensure the success
of prophecies in which he had a vested interest. Some of the murkier
parts of his career may conceal activities of this sort[78]. His most important prophetic activity was literary, notably the *Démonomanie*, and
the *République*. The *Démonomanie*, which more than any other work
was responsible for the European witch scare of the late sixteenth century[79], was extremely effective in securing the implementation of the Law
of God, though by magistrates acting on their own initiative, rather than
under royal guidance, as Bodin had intended. The *République* had a
curious fate. It was an enormous publishing success, and became a land-
mark in intellectual history. But as far as Bodin's specific, Biblically-
derived proposals were concerned, the voice of the prophet cried in a
wilderness of unconcern. His proposals on alms-giving[80], on Sabbath
observance[81], on the powers of the father, and husband[82], on the institut-
ing of moral «censors»[83], on the abolition of usury[84], for all the vehe-
mence with which they were uttered, fell on deaf ears, and have played
little part in subsequent appreciation of his work.

---

[76] *Paradoxe*, [14.2] 31. Bodin's daemonic machinery has high ergonomic
efficiency. Daemons reward individuals by the gift of prophecy, and prophets
by their teaching ensure political stability. Daemons punish those who worship
them, and by causing wars, plagues, etc., ensure political chaos. In either case
society is recalled to that fear of God on which political prosperity is based.
(Witches are in fact deluded in believing that they *control* their daemon. This
delusion is an Satanic double-cross to gain their allegiance.)

[77] See Bezold [70].

[78] See J. MOREAU-REIBEL, Bodin et la Ligue d'après des lettres inédités,
Humanisme et Renaissance 2 (1935), 422–440 [124], and S. BALDWIN, Jean
Bodin and the League, *Catholic Historical Review*, 23 (1937/38), 160–184 [136].

[79] Cf. R. MANDROU, Magistrats et Sorciers en France au XVIIᵉ siècle, Paris
1968, ch. 2.

[80] *République*, Bk. VI, ch. 2, p. 676; (897).

[81] *Rép.*, Bk. I, ch. 1, p. 7; (69); Bk. IV, ch. 2, pp. 461, 462; (566).

[82] *Rép.*, Bk. I, ch. 4, pp. 20, 22, 27; (30, 32, 38).

[83] *Rép.*, Bk. VI, ch. 1, p. 644; (835); Bk. VI, ch. 6, p. 771; (1030).

[84] *Rép.*, Bk. V, ch. 2, p. 572; (707).

In the 1572 edition of the *Methodus* Bodin refers to several works, *De Decretis, De Jure Imperio, De Imperio*, which have not survived[85]. As they are not mentioned in the 1566 edition, it is possible they could have helped us reconstruct the shift from the secular *Methodus* to the religious *République*.[86] In another 1572 addition, Bodin prefaces the discussion of the Hebrew monarchy by asserting that «Philo the Jew, in the book about the creation of a prince, taught that the rule of one prince had been established by the command of God.[87]» Now, Philo consistently interprets the Jewish history of political instability, breakdown, and exile as the result of divine retribution. Turnebus had published a Greek edition of Philo in 1552 and Gelenius a Latin edition in 1554 – the one Bodin used. In 1575, Pierre Bellier published a French translation of most of Philo's works[88]. The dedication of this translation contains what is almost a summary (minus the daemons) of the Hebraic political system of the *République* and the *Démonomanie* as I have described it in this paper. For this reason it is worth quoting at some length, since it illustrates how Philo is, almost certainly, a major new intellectual influence at work in the development of Bodin's political thought after the *Methodus*[89].

---

[85] *Methodus*, 355, 357, 360, 361. Cf. PIERRE BAYLE's article on Bodin (MESNARD, Œuvres Philosophiques de Jean Bodin, vol. I, p. XXXVI) [4.20]. The *De Decretis* and the *De Imperio* are specifically mentioned as having been burnt, at Bodin's death bed request. Mesnard thinks they were written in the fifties.

[86] In this connection it is interesting that Bodin begins to introduce the notions of justice and charity into his notion of legitimate political authority in the *Réponse aux paradoxe de M. de Malestroit*, Paris 1568. (Cf. HAUSER's edition, Paris 1932, 33.) [5.9]. It is even more significant that Bodin introduces comments on the contemporary political situation into the 1572 edition of the *Methodus*, and that after 1567 he was to involve himself very actively in political affairs. The crisis of 1566/67 is psychological, moral and intellectual. We have seen its origins in the letter to Bautru des Matras on the causes of the civil wars. But when the wars draw to their close in the 1590's, and Bodin returns to the less immediately committed, encyclopaedic, academic atmosphere of the *Methodus*, his works remain «religious» in the sense used here, and are only indirectly the fulfilment of the philosophic summa envisaged in his first major work.

[87] *Methodus*, 279, (418 B).

[88] *Les Œuvres de Philon Juif*, Paris 1575.

[89] I said that Bellier's words omit the daemon here. Yet it is worth noting the inspired, almost lyrical tone of this passage in which Philo is made to come alive again, and address the privy councillor Philippe Hurault directly. The fear of blasphemy and the attraction of retributionist political theories in this period are quite common. I discuss some of these matters in my chapter on Problems of the Religious Wars in J. CRUICKSHANK, ed., *French Literature and its Background*, vol. I, London, 1968, 166–185. For the Protestant use of retributionist

«J'ai seulement sur la fin à vous dire un mot de sa part (sc. de Philon):
c'est qu'il vous prie bien fort de faire votre rapport d'une petite requeste
verbale au conseil du Roy: petite dis-je en paroles mais de fort grande
consequence, estant question de la paix et repos de toute la pauvre
France, affligee des maux envoiés d'en haut, pour les execrables blas-
phemes prononcés journellement contre l'honneur de Dieu. Elle tend à
ce que, pour les moyens et raisons au long desduites en son traitté du
second commandement du Decalogue, l'Edit du ... Roy Francois ...
contre ceux qui preignent le nom de Dieu en vain, et le blasphement,
soit renouvelé ... et qu'avec ce le Dimanche sacré et jour du repos fut
deuement ... solenizé, il y auroit esperance que Dieu feroit la paix avec
nous ... il nous bailleroit la tant desirée paix: au lieu de stérilité abon-
dacne de biens: au lieu de maladie santé, au lieu de peste un bon et salubre
aer ... et ne se commettroient journellement tant de meurtres, lesquels
sans doute, suivant la parole de Dieu, ne proviennent que desdits blas-
phemes, comme dit Moyse.»

In the *Heptaplomeres*, Philo, together with Moses Maimonides, is the
most important Jewish authority. Maimonides is used rather more, in
detail. But it is Philo who appears to afford the general frame. Guttmann's
erudite essay on Bodin's Judaism [90] contains little mention of Philo. Philo
was essentially a Greek in culture, and represented an extremely liberal
form of Judaism. Briefer histories of Judaism are rather disparaging about
him, if only because he played a considerable part in the development of
early Christian thought.

For Bodin, however, Philo's Judaism is not in doubt. We have seen that
it was the reading of Philo which led Bodin to an awareness of his daemon.
It was probably Philo who provided Bodin with the main outlines of his
religious system – above all its strict monotheism and its doctrine of
daemons who, by carrying out divine rewards and punishments in this
world, safeguard the absoluteness of God. Bodin is heavily dependent on
Philo's efforts to unite philosophy and revelation, the secular and the
religious, through allegorical exegesis of the Bible. Ultimately, no doubt,
all effort to unite reason and revelation is doomed to failure, and commentators will continue to comment on the inadequacy of Bodin's
attempts to do so.

Yet in the continually fascinating *Heptaplomeres* Bodin seems aware of
the hopelessness of the task. The gap between Senamy the naturalist, and
the six other speakers, is not meant to be bridged. Senamy shares *some*

---

ideas see V. DE CAPRARIIS, Propaganda e Pensiero Politico in Francia durante le
guerre di religione, Napoli 1959, 32 and passim [195].

[90] J. GUTTMANN, Jean Bodin in seinen Beziehungen zum Judentum, *Monats-
schrift für Geschichte und Wissenschaft des Judentums*, 1905 [59].

assumptions with the other speakers. He believes, like the Bodin of the *Methodus*, in «piety to God, reverence to parents, charity to individuals, and justice to all».[91] It is a refrain, which, with some modifications, is found in most of Bodin's works. But Senamy, though he believes in one God, and possibly in a moral universe, does not believe it is run by daemons, nor does he believe in revelation. He is the pre-daemonic, neutral Bodin, who planned the almost entirely secular *Methodus*.

But shortly after the *Methodus* was written revelation, and the activity of daemons in the world, became facts of experience for Bodin. It was not a position Bodin argued himself into. It just happened. What the profoundly autobiographical *Heptaplomeres* communicates, above all else, is the awareness that rational debate is not the mode through which religious insight is achieved. Thus, after the end of the *Heptaplomeres*, the speakers continue to meet as friends. «Mais on ne parla jamais plus de religion.» For revelations are sacred.

---

[91] *Methodus*, 11; (279 A).

[14]

BODIN AND JUDAISM*

Maryanne Cline Horowitz

Jean Bodin (1529/30-1596) is a French Renaissance thinker who contributes to historiography, jurisprudence, comparative religion, demonology, natural theology, political philosophy, and economics.[1] In the tradition of treatises on human dignity associated with the Italian Renaissance, Bodin is one of the strongest advocates of human dignity and of the freedom of the will (both God's will and human will).[2] Clues to the unity and distinctiveness of Bodin's thought are his application of the ancient Stoic «seeds of virtue and knowledge» to epistemology throughout his works[3] and an empathy to Judaism very rare among sixteenth-century Christian scholars of Hebraica; in all of Bodin's usages of «seeds of virtue and knowledge», he does not modify the phrase by mention of original sin. Agreeing with the Stoics that sages are few, Bodin exhibits a high assessment of human potential – as in his citation of the Stoicizing and Platonizing allegorical commentaries on Genesis of Philo of Alexandria (before the codification of Rabbinic law) and of *De libero arbitrio* (Augustine's book on free will before his debate with Pelagius and before his refinement of the doctrine of original sin). To Bodin, how might a God who provided all of nat-

---

* I appreciate permission to publish here revised sections of Chapter 8 of MARYANNE CLINE HOROWITZ, *Seeds of Virtue and Knowledge* (Princeton, New Jersey, Princeton University Press, 1998). The book traces from ancient Stoicism through the seventeenth century the notion that the human mind cultivates God-given seeds of virtue and knowledge into a blossoming garden of all the sciences and virtues.

[1] The following is a brief list of Bodin's works in the chronological order of their first publication *Oratio* (1559), *Methodus* (1566); *Response...à M. de Malestoict* (1568); *République* (1576); *Distributio* (1580); *Démonomanie* (1580); *Epitome* (1588); *Paradoxon* (1596); *Le Paradoxe* (1598); *Theatrum* (1596); manuscript «Colloquium Heptaplomeres».

[2] See the brief summary of Bodin as a natural theologian in FRANÇOIS BERRIOT, *Athéismes et athéistes au XVᵉ siècle en France*, 2 vols. (Université de Lille, Éditions du Cerf, 1984), II, pp. 775-797. Paul Lawrence Rose reveals that Bodin's view of natural goodness is especially evident in the *Paradoxon*: see *Bodin and the Great God of Nature: The Moral and Religious Universe of a Judaiser* (Geneva, Librairie Droz, 1980).

[3] For an excellent Italian edition of ancient Stoic sayings, that is seeds of knowledge intended for transplantation from sage to student, see MARGHERITA ISNARDI PARENTE, *Stoici antichi*, 2 vols. Classici della Filosofia (Torino, UTET, 1989).

ure with its sources for growth and development not provide the human soul with the seeds for its flowering? Our attention here will focus on Bodin's merger of Stoicism and Judaism in the figure of Salomon in Bodin's ecumenical conversation *Colloquium heptaplomeres*;[4] often I shall bring in evidence from Bodin's book of natural philosophy *The Theatrum* that supports Bodin's criticism of Christianity.[5]

Jean Bodin's life and religion have been a matter of controversy partly because his name is a common one in the historical records.[6] There is general agreement among historians that born in Angers, Bodin studied in a Carmelite house in Paris in the mid-1540s. Like Erasmus, Lèfevre d'Étaples, and Calvin, Bodin sought proficiency in the trilingual humanist curriculum of Latin, Greek, and Hebrew texts. Documents published in 1933 indicate his family's background was Catholic,[7] and Bodin took an oath to Catholicism in 1562, joined the Catholic League briefly the same year as Charron, 1589, and received a Catholic burial in 1596. On one hand, one might argue from such evidence that Bodin's knowledge of Judaism

---

[4] JEAN BODIN, *Colloquium of the Seven about Secrets of the Sublime*, ed. and trans. Marion Leathers Daniels Kuntz (Princeton, N. J., Princeton University Press, 1975), XV-XXVIII, especially notes 5-6, 25-15. JEAN BODIN, *Colloquium heptaplomeres de rerum sublimium arcanis abditis*, ed. L. Noack (Schwerin, 1857). My references to Colloquium will be to Kuntz's translation followed by page number in Noack's Latin with Hebrew and Greek text. JEAN BODIN, *Colloque entre sept scavans*, ed. François Berriot with Katherine Davies, Jean Larmat and Jacques Roger (Geneva, Droz, 1984) follows a 1923 French manuscript with variants; an international team of scholars currently is working on a critical edition. For source study, see G. ROELLENBLECK, *Offenbarung...und juedische Ueberlieferung bei Jean Bodin* (Gütersloh, 1964). For posthumous criticism of Bodin, see PIERRE BAYLE, selection from *Dictionnaire historique et critique* (1734) in JEAN BODIN, *Oeuvres*, ed. and trans. Pierre Mesnard (Paris, Presses Universitaires de France, 1951), pp. XXIII-XXXVII, especially XXXIII; also MESNARD'S *Vers un portrait de Jean Bodin*, VII-XXI. I have examined aspects of the religious issue in *La religion de Bodin reconsiderée: Le Marrane comme modèle de la tolérance*, in *Jean Bodin: Actes du Colloque Interdisciplinaire d'Angers*, 2 vols. (Angers, Presses de l'Université d'Angers, 1985), I, 201-215, and II, 568-573, and *Judaism in Jean Bodin*, «The Siteenth Century Journal», 13, 1982, 109-113.

[5] *Universae naturae theatrum: in quo rerum omnium effectrices causae & fines quinque libris discutiuntur autore Jean Bodino* (Lyon, Jacques Roussin, 1596). References will be to the 1596 edition, followed by an additional reference to volume, chapter, and page in French translation by Fougerolles. I have also consulted the Frankfurt: Wechel, 1605 edition. Fougerolles, next note, numbers the topic changes as chapters and inserts in the text the numbered chapter headings. ANN M. BLALR'S, *Restaging Jean Bodin: The 'Universae Naturae Theatrum' (1596) in its Cultural Context* (Princeton University Dissertation, 1990), revised form forthcoming at Princeton University Press, makes a major contribution to the history of this book. See also Pierre Bayle's discussion of the *Theatrum* in his article on Bodin, reprinted in *Oeuvres*, p. XXII, XXIV, and W. H. GREENLEAF, *Bodin and the Idea of Order*, in *Jean Bodin* (Munich, 1973), pp. 23-38, especially 23-25.

[6] For example, a Jean Bodin was tried as a heretic in Paris in 1548; a Jean Bodin was noted in the marital records of Geneva in 1552.

[7] EMILE PASQUIER, *La famille de Jean Bodin*, «Revue d'histoire de l'église de France», 19, 1933, 457-462.

might be attributed to his reading of Hebrew texts; on the other hand, very few Christian students of Hebraica gained from reading alone such a closeness to a Jewish view of the patriarchs of Genesis. Already in the 1580s, Bodin's books received criticism for unorthodoxy, and several of his books appeared on the Index of Prohibited Books.[8] Some contemporaries reported that Bodin's mother was a Jewish refugee from Spain, and seventeenth-century readers of the *Colloquium* often identified Bodin with the position of the Jewish speaker Salomon. That was a very reasonable interpretation, for Bodin's breadth of views on history are in fact very distant from a Christological viewpoint on human history.[9] His ability to criticize Christianity from the points of views of non-Christian speakers is unusual among those who only learned their Hebrew from the tri-lingual curriculum.[10] Not surprisingly, Bodin's manuscript of ecumenical conversation was highly valued among the *libertins érudits*, including Gabriel Naudé, librarian to cardinals in Rome as well as to Richelieu and Mazarin.[11]

Bodin's view that God has provided human nature with the potentiality for virtue, truth, and piety is the inner functional epistemology upon which his human, natural, and divine types of history attain unity. In the *Epitome, Methodus, République,* and *Paradoxon,* where Bodin examines reason and experience in human life, Bodin trusts in the seed of virtue as the source for prudence or *honnesté.*[12] In the *Theatrum,* God-given seeds of knowledge enable humans to distinguish truth from falsity in natural philosophy; yet Bodin also has hopes that the seed of knowledge will make comparative study of law, history, and government into a science

---

[8] Books on the Index: *De Republica libri VI,* 1592; *De Daemonomanie,* 1594; *Methodus,* 1596, Index of Clement VIII; *Universae naturae theatrum,* 1633. For examination of documents showing the criticism that leads to book condemnation, see BERRIOT, *La fortune du 'Colloquium heptaplomeres',* in *Colloque entre sept scavants,* XVIII-XXIV.

[9] JEAN BODIN, *Methodus ad facilem historiarum cognitionem* (Paris, Martinus Juvenes, 1572), in BODIN, *Oeuvres,* ed. and trans. Pierre Mesnard; modern French translation, *Oeuvres,* pp. 278-473. JEAN BODIN, *Method for the Easy Comprehension of History,* trans. Beatrice Reynolds (N.Y., Norton & Company, 1945).

[10] For the negative views of Judaism prevalent among Christian Hebraicists, see FRANK E. MANUEL, *The Broken Staff: Judaism through Christian Eyes* (Cambridge, Harvard University Press, 1992). For the best analysis of deliberate resistance of Christian Hebraicists to Jewish viewpoints, see JEROME FRIEDMAN, *The Most Ancient Testimony: Sixteenth-Century Christian Hebraica in the Age of Renaissance Nostalgia* (Athens, Ohio, Ohio University Press, 1983).

[11] See praise for Bodin conspicuously near recommendation to read minor works of great authors and to read unpublishable contemporary manuscripts in GABRIEL NAUDÉ, *Advis pour dresser une bibliothèque* (Leipzig, VEB, 1963), discussed in MARYANNE CLINE HOROWITZ, *Toleration and Skepticism in the French Free-Thinkers in the First Decades of the Edict of Nantes,* in *Early Modern Skepticism and the Origins of Toleration,* ed. Alan Levine (forthcoming).

[12] *La catégorie de l'honnesté dans la culture du XVIᵉ siècle* (Université de Saint-Étienne, Institut d'Études de la Renaissance et de L'Age Classique, 1965).

(*Distributio, Methodus, République*). From his first publicly delivered and published oration to his secret manuscript copied for private reading, we shall see Bodin's confidence that, despite human disagreements on specific doctrines or rituals, the seeds of religion may be cultivated to create piety and civic harmony.

In the *Colloquium*,[13] we meet the Catholic host Coroaneus who conforms to the Council of Trent, a strict Lutheran Fridericus, a moderate Calvinist Curtius, a Jew Salomon, a natural philosopher and advocate of natural theology Toralba, a congenial doubter and religious universalist Senamus, and a tolerant convert to Islam Octavius. Non-Christians outnumber Christians in a discussion which concludes with a criticism of religious persecution and an agreement to nourish their piety in peaceful harmony (Kuntz 471; Noack 358).

In the conversation at the close of the dialogues, Senamus declares the minimum beliefs shared by all present necessary for religion – that God is the parent of all gods and creator of nature, and that prayer with a good heart to God will please God and lead to knowledge of true religion (465; 354-355). In the criticism there of the persecution of the Jews in Spain and Portugal emerges the notion that religious belief cannot be forced, but must stem from freedom of the will. Senemus in some ways expresses the spirit of the work in declaring «But I, lest I ever offend, prefer to approve all the religions of all rather than to exclude the one which is perhaps the true religion» (465; 354).

Encouraged by Senamus' seeking a common religion, Toralba and Salomon agree with him that the oldest religion is the best, and they cite the religion of the biblical patriarchs (182-183; 1140-1142). Utilizing a Stoic cluster of terms – «reason», «light», «innate», «planted» – Toralba views the law of nature commanding the worship of one God: «Indeed as I view the almost infinite variety of sects, Christians differing with Ismaelites [Muslims] and pagans differing among themselves, no standard of truth seems more certain than right reason, that is, the supreme law of nature, planted in men's minds by immortal God» (337; 257; also 185; 142). This view meets the approval of the Calvinist and the Catholic. Later Toralba adds «Indeed reason, which is divine light, innate to the mind of each man, sees, feels, and judges that which is right, that which is wrong, that

---

[13] For the influence of this manuscript, see BERRIOT, *La fortune de 'Colloquium heptaplomeres'*, in *Colloque*, XV-L, and RICHARD POPKIN, *The Dispersion of Bodin's Dialogues in England, Holland, and Germany*, «Journal of the History of Ideas», 49, 1988, 157-160, and *The Role of Jewish Anti-Christian arguments in the Rise of Scepticism*, in *New Perspectives on Renaissance Thought*, ed. John Henry and Sarah Hutton (London, Duckworth, 1990), pp. 5-8.

which is true, that which is false» (359; 259). After a debate about the doctrine of reward and punishment in an afterlife, Senamus suggests tolerance
to disagreement, and Toralba concludes «is it not better to embrace that
most simple and most ancient and at the same time the most true religion
of nature, instilled by immortal God in the minds of each man from which
there was no division (I am speaking of that religion in which Abel, Enoch,
Lot, Seth, Noah, Job, Abraham, Isaac, and Jacob, heroes dearest to God,
lived) than for each one to wander around uncertain?» (462; 351-352).

A fuller discussion by Toralba, Senamus, and Salomon of this ancient
religion focuses on the Decalogue, that is the Ten Commandments. Salomon suggests a correspondence between the divine laws and hidden secrets of nature, as have been revealed by Philo Hebraeus, Abraham Ibn
Ezra, King Solomon, and Leone Hebreus, and cites Ezra for the Decalogue
as natural law (191; 147).[14] Ezra's (1089-1140) biblical commentaries are
known to reveal «secrets». Toralba confirms that the two tablets are the
law of nature, and all the commands except the resting on sabbath are
common to other nations (193; 148). Toralba boldly declares a Pelagian
view: «If true religion is contained in the pure worship of eternal God, I
believe the law of nature is sufficient for man's salvation» (225; 172).
Against Curtius's citation of Paul «The law was given by Moses, but grace
has been given through Jesus Christ», (410; 311) both the Jew and the
Muslim argue for the benefits of obeying divinely granted law (Mosaic
law or the Koran respectively) for attaining a life of virtue and a life worthy
of salvation (415, 420; 315, 319). Toralba and Senamus go further into free
thinking in suggesting that neither revealed law nor faith in Jesus Christ is
necessary. Toralba avows the outstanding virtues of ancient philosophers,
and denies they could be eternally suffering (421; 319). Speaking the civic
religion of Bodin's *Oratio*, Senamus suggests that those most natural and
worthy are religious to the gods, pious to their country, loyal to their parents, charitable to their neighbors, and kind to those in need (422; 320-

---

[14] A possible source for Bodin's knowledge of Ibn Ezra is a book by a Hebraicist with
whom Bodin studied in Paris: JEAN MERCIER, *Aseret ha-Devarim Decalogus*, containing commentary by Abraham Ibn Ezra, Hebrew and Latin (Lyon, 1566-1568). ISAAC HUSIK, *Medieval Jewish
Philosophy* (New York, Macmillan, 1916) p. 194, confirms that Ibn Ezra (1089-1164) holds that
the Decalogue, with the exception of the seventh day of rest, consists of laws planted by God in
the minds of rational beings; that is exactly the consensus of Bodin's seven speakers. Technically,
while recognizing that the Decalogue is acknowledged by the intelligent of all nations, Ibn Ezra
does not refer to it as natural law. The first Jewish philosopher to introduce into Hebrew the
term *dath tiv ith*, «natural law» is Joseph Albo (d. 1444). JOSEPH ALBO, *Sefer ha-Ikkarim*, trans.
I. Husik (Philadelphia, Jewish Publication Society of America, 1946) and J. GUTTMANN, *Towards
a Study of the Sources of the Book of Principles*, in *Dat u-Maddah* (Jerusalem, 1955), 169-181 (in
Hebrew).

321). Putting Christians on the defensive, the new Muslim Octavius argues that Muslims are superior to Christians in acts of virtue (426; 323-324). Salomon proclaims:

> What lawgiver was ever so cruel that he commanded his people to do something which was impossible?...It is so far removed from God's nature for Him to command anything which cannot be done as for Him to blame a man for breaking all the law when he had erred from one commandment, and even a man who has violated all the commands of the law and returned to honor after repentance, attains pardon for all his sins (430; 327).[15]

Salomon on several occasions indicates God's praise for people after Adam such as Noah, Enoch, and Moses (VI, p. 407). However, to Toralba's plea for that natural religion, Salomon suggests that common folk, and even the educated, hold more constant in religion through rites and ceremonies (462-463; 352). As in Philo's *The Decalogue*, Salomon views the Mosaic law code as a detailing of the four commandments of worship to God and of the six commandments of duty to other humans (186-187; 143).[16] Toralba does not find those special laws necessary and other participants reject some details of Jewish law. By Bodin's categories of law in the *Distributio*, Bodin is categorizing the Decalogue as *ius gentium*, the Decalogue excepting the sabbath command is *ius naturale*, and the specific laws as particular *ius civile* of one historical people. Thus Bodin is suggesting that all that humans need for living a good life – the natural law indicating that one should worship God and treat other human beings well – is contained in the divine law and explicitly in the divinely-revealed Decalogue.

In the *Colloquium*, the doctrine of original sin receives refutation, not only from a Jew and a Muslim, and doubter, but also from a natural philosopher expounding principles declared in the *Theatrum*. When Philo Judaeus comes up for discussion, Salomon corrects the church fathers' formative Christianization of Philo, refusing to identify Philo's *logos*, the word, with Jesus (368-369; 279-380). Likewise Bodin gives Philo's allegory of Genesis 1-2 to explain Adam's sin as the turning of the intellect (Adam)

---

[15] Salomon takes a position of full divine mercy for evildoers, a libertarian Jewish position of the Arabic period and libertarian Muslim philosophers; see HARRY AUSTRYN WOLFSON, *Repercussions of the Kalam in Jewish Philosophy* (Cambridge, Harvard University Press, 1979), 198-233. See also BODIN, *Paradoxe*, in *Selected Writings on Philosophy, Religion, and Politics*, ed. Paul L. Rose (Geneva, Droz, 1980), p. 54, discussed in ROSE, *Jean Bodin and the Great God of Nature*, pp. 145-147.

[16] PHILO, *De decalogo; De specialibus legibus*, trans. F. H. Colson (London, Heinemann, 1937), XXIX, pp. 82-93 and 100-101.

away from contemplation toward temptations of the senses (Eve) and of pleasures (serpent). This time the allegory is an opportunity to argue that neither sins nor virtues are passed down from parents to children and that «there is no original sin» (392-393; 297).

Coronaeus cites the Council of Trent anathema against those who would deny original sin, identifying that view as the Pelagian heresy; Fredericus cites Augustine's support for orginal sin; Curtius cites the Jewish and Christian Scriptures. However, in support of Salomon, the Muslim Octavius and the naturalist Toralba argue that the doctrine would credit to the Creator evil in a newborn infant (392-396; 296-300). The natural philosopher cites Christians, Muslims and Hebrews for concurring that the soul is created clean and pure from God (396-402; 299-305). Toralba's denial of the possibility of original sin passing from generation to generation utilizes principles found in *Theatrum*: sin originates not in the body but in decisions in the soul; the human soul does not come in the seed but is directly created by God (Aristotle, *De gen. animal.* II. 3 736b. 28); sin therefore cannot be passed down from parent to child (399-400; 302-303). *Theatrum* IV, ch. 11, cites Augustine's *De libero arbitrio* for the argument that each has freedom of the will, the power within to control passions; not only can one prevent evil deeds, but also restrain one's eyes and thoughts.[17] Fredericus cites Augustine to argue that the contagion of the flesh defiles the souls, but, as we already know from *Theatrum*, Bodin denies evil in matter.

What follows next from the natural philosophy of Toralba, which is consistent with the principles of the *Theatrum*, is an argument against the possibility of the union of the Divine and human in Jesus. Toralba views God as «eternal essence, one, pure, simple, and free from all contact of bodies, of infinite goodness, wisdom and power» (325; 248). The gap between Creator and created is too great for a union of infinite immaterial Divine and the finite bodily human (351; 267). Likewise Salomon borrows the same technique from Bodin's *Methodus* to suggest how religion can corrupt humankind: «All this discussion about the Fall of origin, which I think is no fall, has its beginnings in the leaders of the Christian religion ...Hence the seeds of errors began to creep far and wide through men's minds». (404-405; 306).[18] He then refers to God ordering Noah after

---

[17] AUGUSTINE, *The Free Choice of the Will*, in *The Teacher, The Free Choice of the Will–Grace and Free Will*, trans. Robert P. Russell (Washington, D.C., Catholic University of America Press, 1968). Bodin is influenced by Augustine's Stoicizing phrase «eternal law impressed upon our nature», p. 85. Augustine praises human free will and dignity, pp. 178-179.

[18] See *Methodus*, in *Oeuvres*, ed. Mesnard, pp. 163-164.

the flood to be good as commanding only what is possible (430; 327). The dialogue on evil takes on an arborescent flavor. Lutheran Fredericus argues: «...with whatever color the root is imbued, it imbues the trunk, branches, leaves, flowers, and fruits with the same flavor, odor, color, and poison. So it is with the nature of man, overturned from the foundation, seems to have no spark of any good or virtue» (396; 299). Returning to Philo of Alexandria's allegory, Salomon discusses Adam's recovery as mind regaining control over senses. That clue to Philo's allegory reminds us of the passage in the *Theatrum* where the teacher Mystagogue describes the human soul as a garden, containing fruit trees of virtue and knowledge: «Likewise we recognize that the seeds of all the virtues and sciences have been Divinely sown in our souls from their origins, in order to permit humans to live delightfully, as in the middle of a garden odiferous with flowers and trees, and most abundant of all sorts of fruits».[19] Fredericus' argument, although evocative of trees of vice derived from the gospel of Matthew, would not hold up with Mystagogue.

Salomon goes on. Capable of fathering a child in God's image and perpetuating humanity, Adam has the ability to enjoy and perpetuate the tree of life, that is contemplation of true wisdom (Prov. 3:13-18) (405; 306). Fredericus reinterprets the tree as referring to the cross (505; 306-307), but Salomon proclaims that anyone may repent and God will help restore their right reason (405-406; 307) and Octavius reads a verse in which «the wrong doing of the father does not harm the son »and «the figure of trees displays this secret of hidden wisdom» (406-407; 307-308). Octavius suggests a metaphor of ascent to the Divine that is pleasurable, like a Muslim paradise: through love of God, one «plucks the sweetest fruits of happiness. This is that faith, or rather a unique trust in God, which, having embraced all virtues, nourishes and safeguards them» (422; 320).

For all their tolerance amid diversity of belief, all seven agree that if a storm breaks out on the Mediterranean sea and a nearby ship carries on board a mummy from an Egyptian tomb, it would be wise to throw the mummy overboard to be rid of the demons.[20] In fact, Bodin's natural phi-

---

[19] «sic etiam in animis nostris, virtutum ac scientiarum omnium semina divinitùs spārsa fuisse, ut quasi in hortis odoratissimis, floribus & arboribus, ac frugum omnium copia abundantissimis, homini iucundissimè vivere liceret. Nam modicè culta mens abūndanti fertilitate luxuriat». *Theatrum*, p. 475.

[20] *Colloquium*, pp. 73, 58; *Theatrum*, pp. 143-144, as well as *Démonomanie*. Kuntz, p. XLI, note 78. Montaigne points out that Bodin does not apply his own critical methods of the Methodus to the so-called «witnesses» of demonic activity: MARYANNE CLINE HOROWITZ, *Drogue médicinale ou vieux conte: l'histoire et la justice chez Montaigne, Bodin et saint Augustin*, in *Montaigne et l'histoire*, ed. Claude G. Dubois (Bordeaux, Université de Bordeaux Press, 1991).

losophy consistently differs from Aristotle's in not attributing storms, earthquakes, or plagues to natural causes but to divine punishment (66-67; 51). Thus Bodin need not burden the laws of natural causation with all the haphazard and troublesome happenings of nature.[21] Demons represent no Manichaean evil force separate from God's providence and creation; rather they are instruments of God's justice. Likewise, as in the Hebrew Bible, God can intervene to reward individuals or whole societies. Bodin refers to Aristotle and Theophrastus to support his belief that plants and animals sometimes grow without seed as by spontaneous generation,[22] and Curtius proclaims that some fish are grown from the sea without seed (67; 51). In the *Response*, Bodin tries to get the French to eat more fish, as God has blessed their seas with such abundance. Bodin's biblical view that the created universe and the work of the sixth day, human beings, are «*tov meod*» is the fundamental source for his need to explain natural disaster and human wrongdoing as brought about by demons.

Bodin emphasizes free will in achieving virtue, and the belief that divine help would be given to anyone who turned to God. In assessing that human beings have full capacity to choose between right and wrong, Bodin, satirizing Aristotle, attributes full free agency to God. «Yet what more impious, more arrogant, finally, more mad than to give free will to himself, but wish to take it from God? The consequence is that God cannot stay the course of the sun, or check the power of the celestial stars, or change anything in universal nature; nor even the impulses and the volitions of man can He impel whither He wishes».[23] One of the reasons for Bodin's reluctance to cite Stoics in the context of free will and virtue is his rejection of their doctrine of determinism. God might have created humankind to pursue virtue always, and the world so that in no mind or matter could exist a seed of evil (*semen malorum*); but God chose to grant humans the greater good of free will.[24]

A short ethical treatise published at the end of Bodin's life confirms his distance from an acceptance of original sin and the consequent need for

---

[21] JEAN CÉARD, *La nature et les prodiges: L'Insolite au XVIe siècle en France* (Genève, Droz, 1977).

[22] *Theatrum*, pp. 272-275; *Methodus*, 210 b.

[23] JOSEPH DAN, *No Evil Descends from Heaven' – Sixteenth Century Jewish Concepts of Evil*, in *Jewish Thought in the Sixteenth Century*, ed. Bernard Cooperman, (Cambridge, Mass., Harvard University Center for Jewish Studies, 1983), 89-105, citing p. 93, thirteenth-century *Sefer ha-Yashar* (Venice, 1544) for the natural process by which thorns are created with the rose and dirt with fruitful seed of wheat. Bodin, likewise, views all aspects of nature, including poisons, as beneficial from the perspective of the totality of nature.

[24] *Methodus*, VIII, 231 b 1-10; Reynolds, p. 310.

Jesus Christ and his closeness to a merger of ancient ethics with a Hebrew biblical perspective (key achievement of Philo of Alexandria). Bodin's *Paradoxon* (written 1591) is published in 1596 and his French translation (1596) is published in 1598 when the *politique* movement is culminating in King Henry IV's Edict of Nantes, which legally establishes freedom of conscience and public office for Calvinists throughout France and allows public Calvinist religious services in some areas of Catholic France.[25] Like neo-Stoic Du Vair, Bodin in his dedicatory letter indicates that he is providing a moral discipline that might serve well in time of civil war.[26] Unlike Du Vair's *La constance* (1594), Bodin's *Paradoxe* does not Christianize his philosophical ethic, but presents it in a way suitable to individuals of not only different Christian denominations but of different world religions, as would become apparent to readers of the manuscript *Colloquium*. Bodin very succinctly presents a moral system based on ancient moral philosophy.

The dialogue form proceeds in a conversation between father and son. In answer to the question whether the virtues and vices are in our souls, the father responds:

Nature has not planted vices in us: that is why the wise would say that he was well born, and that his soul being good will find a body pure and dry: but all the Hebrews and Academics have held for an assured thing, that we have souls inseminated by a Divine seed of all virtues,[27] that we can lead very close to the very happy life, if we allow that they take their development: and for the proof, we see that tender minds, which have never before learned, suddenly conceive the principles and foundations of all fields: and also the earth is filled naturally with an infinity of plants, metals, minerals, and precious stones that which she produces without seed and without labor, the sea produces the fish, which are sustained by celestial influences: thus it is that the soul which is inseminated by an infinitude of beautiful sciences and virtues, which being aroused by the divine influence produce the sweet fruits which grow to be trees of prudence and of knowledge: but one should not stop at the fruits of prudence, but one should go farther to the fruits of life, that wisdom.

---

[25] King Henry IV, *Edict du Roy & Declaration sur les precedents Edicts de Pacification* (Paris?, Royal Press, 25 February 1, 1599). The king signs the edict in April 1598, but it not published by the Parlement of Paris until February 1599. G. A. ROTHROCK, *The Huguenots: A Biography of a Minority* (Chicago, Nelson-Hall, 1979), pp. 124-126.

[26] *Paradoxon quod nec virtus ulla in mediocritate, nec summum hominis bonum in virtutis actione consistere possit; Le Paradox de Jean Bodin Angevin qu'il n'y a pas une seule vertu en mediocrité, ny au milieu de deux vices*, Dedicatory letter p. 37, in *Selected Works*, ed. Rose, p. 54; commentary pp. VII-X. ROSE, *Jean Bodin and the Great God of Nature*, pp. 145-147. For an overview, emphasizing its view of salvation for non-Christians, see MESNARD, *Jean Bodin et la morale d'Aristote*, «Revue Thomiste», 49, 1949, pp. 542-562.

[27] «mais tous les anciens Hebrieux & Academiques ont tenu pour chose asseurée, que nous auons les ames parsemees d'une semence divine de toutes vertus....» *Le Paradox*, p. 65, in *Selected Writings*, ed. Rose, pp. 63-64. ROSE, *Jean Bodin and the Great God of Nature*, p. 108.

Here, Bodin sums up his view that the natural world including human nature is good, basing his claim on the two ancient fountains of wisdom – the Hebrew scriptures and the Platonic Academy (to which Bodin attributes the Stoic phrases *seeds of virtue* and *seeds of knowledge*). That argument by authority supports the reality of the seeds of virtue and knowledge in the human soul. Further proof is a child stating fundamental principles, as in the geometry lesson in Plato's *Meno*. Bodin declares that the observation of nature shows that the earth and sea can produce without seed as well, demonstrating the Creator's continuing active providence. Readers may differ in interpreting the relative impact of the God-given seeds, the natural sunlight, the celestial astrological influence, or divine aid. Nevertheless, in this garden-in-the-soul passage, Bodin emphasizes both God's original creation and God's continuing influence in the growth of the trees of virtue and knowledge in the human mind. Bodin views the ultimate goal to be wisdom, symbolized as in the Hebraic tradition as the tree of life; Leone Hebreus and Philo view archetypal Adam in Paradise and Adam whose reason is in proper order as comprehending the wisdom of the tree of life.[28] What is evidently apparent is the coalescence in the mature Jean Bodin's thought of Hebraic, Platonic, and Stoic imagery of the goodness within human nature.

A fundamental viewpoint of Bodin is that nature, including human nature, is good. Bodin's view of the goodness of all of nature and of God's creation is founded fundamentally on Genesis, on a traditional Jewish reading of Genesis, common to Philo, the rabbinical tradition, and Kabbalists, that contrasts with Augustine's creation of the doctrine of original sin and the Fall of humanity evident in *The City of God*.[29] While the rabbinical Jewish tradition discusses free will as choice between good and evil inclinations in human nature, Bodin tends to omit discussion of the evil inclination. Gen. 1:12, 18, 21, and 24 declare «And God saw that it was good». Bodin cites that passage at the conclusion of his *Theatrum*, and after recalling the candelabra of seven lights and the analogous seven

---

[28] LÉONE HÉBREU, *Dialogues d'amour*, trans. Pontus de Tyard (Lyon, 1551), ed. T. Anthony Perry (Chapel Hill, University of North Carolina Press, 1974). The other edition's publications indicate extensive popularity: LÉONE HÉBREU, *Dialogues d'amour*, trans. Denys Sauvage (Lyon, 1551), rpt. 1559, 1577, 1580, 1595. See ARTHUR LESLEY, *The Place of the 'Dialoghi d'amore'* in *Contemporaneous Jewish Thought*, and EVA KUSHNER, *Pontus de Tyard entre Ficin et Léon l'Hébreu*, in *Ficino and Renaissance Neoplatonism* (Toronto, University of Toronto Press, 1968), 71-86.

[29] See ELIZABETH A. CLARK, *Vitiated Seeds and Holy Vessels: Augustine's Manichean Past*, and ELAINE PAGELS, *Adam and Even and the Serpent in Genesis 1-3*, in *Images of the Feminine in Gnosticism*, ed. Karen L. King (Philadelphia, Fortress, 1988).

planets, Bodin cites in Latin the culminating repetition in Genesis 1:31 after God saw his creation of human nature: «all that God had made was very good» and adds that the Hebrews said it elegantly «*tova me'od*», «very good».[30]

MARYANNE CLINE HOROWITZ

---

[30] «...cùm disertè scriptum sit, 'omnia quae Deus fecerat optimà fuisse', quod Hebraei elegantiùs dicunt, *tova me' od*». *Theatrum*, p. 631; V, 12, pp. 914-915.

[15]

THE ENIGMA OF BODIN'S RELIGION

Paul Lawrence Rose

a) Remarks on Methodology

The traditional ways of dealing with the writings of major figures in the history of thought, particularly political thought, have their weaknesses. Recently Quentin Skinner has voiced dissatisfaction with the "textualist" practice of simply reading the relevant works of an author in a close fashion without any reference to the context in which they were originally written. [1] Professor Skinner proposes a more genuinely "historical" approach to the history of political thought which would rather be a history of ideologies embracing the major works themselves, those less distinguished writings by contemporaries which form part of the same discussion, and the social and political context of the period in which those major works were composed.

While recognising the weakness of traditional accounts and the force of Prof. Skinner's methodology, I must confess that I do not think that his suggestions are sufficient to obtain a full understanding of a number of major thinkers. It seems to me that Prof. Skinner's proposals for reforming the historiography of ideas go only half way in that they help us to grasp better how Bodin's contemporaries understood the *République,* but do not really tell us how Bodin himself understood his writings or for what purpose he intended them to serve. In the *République* Bodin may have used the same words and examples as many of his contemporaries; but it seems to me that his intentions and meaning were very remote from what the other writers of his time could have accepted or even comprehended.

In order to mount an exploration of Bodin's mind I should like to propose a somewhat different methodology based on two principles: (1) the completeness or integrality of Bodin's thought and writings and (2) the integration of Bodin's ideas and personality.

Some readers may think that any attempt to understand what goes on inside anyone else's head — particularly one dead these 400 years — is a

---

[1] Q. Skinner, *Foundations of Modern Political Thought* (Cambridge, 1978), I, introduction.

chimerical undertaking.   I should not myself wish in the least to deny the power and reality of individualism and idiosyncrasy which is so much in evidence in each of us and our acquaintances, not to say our dogs.   Yet most writers are publicists and write, not only out of vanity or for profit, but to enlighten and convince their readers.   Such persuasion may not always be manifest and blatant; sometimes indeed plain speaking may be impossible for reasons of censorship.   Yet the writings of a major thinker like Bodin are sufficient in variety and bulk to allow us to grasp his thought in the round and as a whole.

I am not advocating here any Straussian thesis which sees all great authors as having hidden messages which they are obliged to conceal for fear of persecution (although it happens that Bodin was compelled to be devious because his ideas were wildly heretical and destructive of Christianity).   My main suggestion is simply that, rather than divide the thought of someone like Bodin into separate compartments, one should endeavour to understand his total vision and then his individual writings on politics, history, law and so forth in the light of that vision.   If this is done then what appear to scholars who read no further than the *République* to be contradictions, confusions and paradoxes, very often will disappear.

No amount of reading in the everyday political literature of the later sixteenth century is really going to tell us how Bodin understood or intended his own work.   What may guide us into Bodin's mind is a knowledge of *all* his writings and of the vision which they represent.   Many sentences in the *République* may appear pretty straightforward but if one tries to analyse a single one of them without first understanding Bodin's general purpose, only distortion of greater or lesser degree can result.

How then are we to grasp Bodin's vision?   If there is one area of belief that embodies human thinking about the most fundamental aspects of life it is religion.   Religion conveys the most general perceptions of reality, for example, in its particular doctrines of divinity, creation, transcendence and immanence; it formulates ideas of man through such doctrines as free will and sin; it expresses the sensibility of the individual man in his predilection for harsh religious attributes such as judgement, retribution, and suffering, or softer ones such as mercy, repentance and compassion.   *La religion, c'est l'homme.* [2]

It should be clear by now that I believe that intellectual history cannot be written simply as the history of abstracted ideas. Ideas must first be set in the general context of a writer's religious vision; but I would go further and state that the religious vision itself cannot be understood as a purely intellectual system. The emotional charge is vital to an individual's religion and this takes us into the realm of personality.

There is a long-standing orthodoxy that in writing intellectual history, whether it be the history of political thought or the history of science, one must

---

[2] For an appreciation of the theological premises of Locke's political thought see J. Dunn, *The Political Thought of John Locke. An Historical Account of the Argument of the Two Treatises of Government* (Cambridge, 1969), pp. xi, 87ff.

at all costs keep separate the *thought* and *personality* of a thinker. Nothing seems to me to be such a dead hand on the study of thinkers of the past or present than this prescription. Of course it is difficult to integrate thought and personality without slipping into banalities yet this is hardly a reason for not trying. Let me cite two examples from the biography and thought of Bodin. In 1569 Bodin was arrested for heresy and spent the next year unrepentant in prison even though a simple recantation and oath of Catholicism such as he had sworn in 1562 (and swore again in 1589) would have sufficed to gain his release. Surprising conduct, one would agree, for a reputed *politique*. My second example adds to the confusion for it apparently contradicts the former one; it is Bodin's apparently zealous subscription to the Catholic League and support of the League's claimant to the throne in 1589-90. This episode has proved a major thorn in the side of conventional interpretations of Bodin, yet I believe that it, like the paradoxical imprisonment of 1569, can be understood if one has first grasped the nature of Bodin's religion. Hidden in the pages of Bodin's writings are details of a conversion to prophetic religion, indeed of the author's own transfiguration as a prophet. It was this transfiguration that provoked Bodin's stubbornness in 1569 and twenty years later convinced him that the Catholic League was the instrument of God's retribution on France. In this conversion and its resultant effects on Bodin's thought and behaviour we may see clearly illustrated the interplay of religion, politics and personality.

My account of Bodin's conversion (or rather conversions, for the phenomenon was enacted in three stages) will be found in Chapter VIII. I wish it could have been less conjectural but Bodin is an elusive thinker and the sources are not as full as one would like. Nevertheless, I have tried to construct an account which might shed some light on some of the central riddles of conversion: what are the constants in thought and personality which are present in the convert before and after conversion?; what are the particular sources of psychic unrest before conversion?; how is the convert restored to inner peace? Any study of a conversion-experience must take us to the heart of the convert's religion and raises in an acute form the problem of the relationship between thought and personality.

The methodology I propose does not seek to "prove" anything. Historical proof is not the same as legal proof, and belongs to a different category of demonstration altogether; intellectual history is a different animal again from political and social history and the most that can be hoped for is a certain plausibility and persuasiveness of argument. In the case of figures like Bodin that plausibility must, it seems to me, depend on whether the general picture of his thought holds together. If one has got Bodin's "religion" right then one should be able to pick virtually any page of his works and understand and clarify it in the light of his religion; equally one should be able to interpret any biographical fact by reference to his religion. It seems to me that there is no point in taking isolated phrases about sovereignty out of the *République* and seeking to understand their meaning unless one already has a clear idea of where those sentences belong in the general structure of Bodin's thought. This kind of purely logical dissection leads inevitably to our misconceiving the meaning of Bodin's political ideas no matter how publicly and directly they may seem to be expressed.

b) Categories

This study began as an attempt to solve the problem of reconciling Bodin's religious vision with his reputedly naturalistic and secular thinking on politics and history. It soon emerged that it was a misconception to contrast, or even to separate, his religious and secular thought for even in Bodin's most apparently secular writings such as those on politics and economics there is a religious aura permeating the whole work. Bodin certainly uses such categories as "natural" and "divine" but it would be wrong to suppose that these reflect a basic dichotomy in his mind between what we would call religious and secular thought. "Natural" and "divine" refer more to the modes in which Bodin's religious sense organises itself; history, politics, law and economics are natural disciplines, whereas theology is a divine discipline. There is no opposition in Bodin between nature and religion for nature is part of religion. Thus it is that Bodin is able to speak of the Decalogue as "the revealed law of nature"; the Ten Commandments are *divine* law in that they are promulgated by God but they also represent *natural* law. Bodin in this way distinguishes formally between natural and divine law, but in essence both kinds of law really are different manifestations of what one may call a fundamentally *religious* understanding of law. For these reasons it is ill-conceived to think of Bodin's political theory as falling into our modern categories of secular or religious thought. Such categories are not even separate ones in Bodin but rather interpenetrating.

At several points in his political career Bodin actually put into practice this religious perception of politics, most notoriously in his decision to join the Catholic League in 1589. As our last chapter will explain, Bodin's writings on the League not only reveal how unhistorical it is to apply such artificial categories to Bodin as "religious" and "secular", but also discredit the seemingly concrete labels of *politique* and *ligueur*. Bodin himself was simultaneously *politique* and *ligueur* and his understanding of the entire political problem was dictated by a profusion of political, legal, natural and above all, moral and religious ideas. Politics, ethics and religion, far from forming separate categories, were fused by Bodin into unaccustomed and dynamic modes of thought.

As one reads Bodin in this light then a great deal of what appears to be confused and obscure in his writings begins to make sense. It seems indeed that many of the charges of muddled thinking laid by modern critics against Bodin have arisen out of applying traditional Greek and Christian categories or those of jurisprudential thinkers of the seventeenth and later centuries to this uniquely original philosopher. Bodin was not a Hobbesian, nor a Lockean, nor a "predecessor of Montesquieu". And if Bodin was neither an absolutist nor a liberal theorist, neither can he be said to fall into the mainstream of Christian theocratic thought. Bodin's categories were not those of Calvin, nor of Aquinas, nor even those of the Gospels. Bodin's categories and religious vision stemmed, it will be argued, from the Jewish tradition represented by the works of Philo and Maimonides. In the case of his political philosophy Bodin built upon these foundations but constructed his edifice to take account of the shifts in terrain which a thousand years of political and legal development had produced. It is Bodin's shrewdness in grafting the realities of

4

French history on to a Jewish theocratic vision that explains both the genius of his works as well as their enduring capacity to be interpreted in misconceived categories.

c) Judaising

The term Judaiser has a long history in Christianity. The original Judaisers were those Christian adherents of St. Peter who against St. Paul urged conformity to Jewish ritual law. Later the term came to be applied to Christian heretics like the fourth century Byzantine Photinus or the Russian "Judaisers" of the fifteenth century who denied the Trinitarian divinity of Christ though admitting Him as the Redeemer and as such as a part or mode of the Father.

The European Reformation saw an extension of Judaising activity in such forms as an increasing knowledge of Hebrew and a reawakened interest in the Old Testament. [3] In general the Protestant Reformation's simplifying attack on traditional doctrines and ecclesiastical organisation had the effect of an unconscious Judaising campaign. It was, however, the more radical reformers who found themselves denounced by the Lutherans and Calvinists as "Judaisers"; the radicals were taxed with advocating a modern Pharisaic legalism based upon the New Testament and denounced for trying to reproduce in Christian form various aspects of Hebraic conduct and belief, or merely for refusing to consider the Old Testament superseded by the New.

The phenomenon of Judaising in the sixteenth century still awaits a full investigation but from existing studies we can see already how Judaisers of the period seized upon new categories of thought which had been purposely excluded from Christian tradition, or indeed (as in the case of Bodin) had simply been unthinkable to the minds of Christians. Such new modes of thought were exploited to the full for their ability to open up new dimensions of religious and moral philosophy. [4] Pico della Mirandola and Guillaume Postel availed themselves of the Jewish mystical Kabbala in order to achieve a reform of Christianity which would transform the Christian religion into a universal creed. Michael Servetus and Lelio and Fausto Sozini, on the other hand, applied their Judaising so as to destroy the creedal doctrines of the Trinity and the divinity of Christ. These radical Judaising tactics scarcely met with magisterial approval. Calvin shuddered that "it is indeed an abomination to see how this miserable man Servetus excuses the Jew's blasphemies

[3] In general see S.W. Baron, *A Social and Religious History of the Jews* (2nd ed., New York, 1952-   ), XIII, chs. 47 and 48. L.I. Newman, *Jewish Influence on Christian Reform Movements* (New York, 1925). G.H. Williams, *The Radical Reformation* (Philadelphia, 1967), pp. 834-39. J. Friedman, *Michael Servetus. A Case Study in Total Heresy* (Trav. d'Hum. et Rena., 163, Geneva, 1978), ch. 12.

[4] J.L. Blau, *The Christian Interpretation of the Cabala in the Renaissance* (New York, 1944). W.J. Bouwsma, *Concordia Mundi. The Career and Thought of Guillaume Postel (1510-81)* (Cambridge, Mass., 1957). F. Secret, 'Un cheval de Trois dans l'église du Christ: La Kabbale chrétienne', in *Aspects du libertinisme au seizième siècle*, éd. J. de Boisset and A. Stegmann (Paris, 1974), pp. 153-166. Friedman, *Servetus*.

against the Christian religion". Yet Servetus' Judaising strategy was directed towards the restoring of Christianity to its original purity of doctrine; no wonder he countered Calvin's accusations by charging the theologian with "Jewish legalism" in *his* preference for the "irrational, impossible, Mosaic law" over that of the New Covenant of Christ. "You have shocked me with your true Jewish zeal", Servetus sadly remarked.[5]

Some Socinians went further than Servetus in their Judaising and argued that Christ's death had restored freedom of the will to man and so expurgated original sin.[6] They admitted, however, that original sin had been incurred by Adam whereas Jewish belief held that there never had been a transmissible original sin but only the Fall of Adam. Yet for all the wildness of their heresies the Socinians and other Christian Judaisers remained Christians. Christ may not have been accepted by them as part of the divine godhead itself but He was still more than a mere man and was superhuman in nature. Moreover, their thought is almost always characterised by the presence of such concepts as "justification" (by faith or belief in Christ if not by His death itself) or "redemption" (in which Christ has greater or lesser functions). All these Judaisers who sought to use Jewish concepts to revolutionise Christianity were actually heretics *within* Christianity.

Not so Bodin who Judaised, not to reform Christianity, but to refute its claim to be the true religion. It was a largely discredited Christianity that was to be absorbed into Bodin's vision of a universal *vera religio*, a true religion closer to Judaism than to any other positive religion.

Bodin's Judaising took various forms. In his published writings he made no secret of his extensive knowledge of Jewish sources (though he occasionally concealed some of his most radical Judaising in such printed works as the *Paradoxe* by citing a Christian source rather than a Jewish one).[7] Nor did Bodin seek to hide a generally sympathetic attitude towards the Jews. He was ready to tolerate them as a minority on account of their antiquity, their unconcern about gaining converts and their abstention from politics.[8] These were political reasons for a Judaeophile policy but there were much deeper

[5] 'Accusation et procès de Michel Servet (1553)', in *Registres de la compagnie des pasteurs à Genève au temps de Calvin*, eds. R.M. Kingdon, J.-F. Bergier, A. Dufour (Tr. Hum. Ren., 55, Geneva, 1962), II. Cf. Baron, *History*, XIII, 283f. Friedman, *Servetus*, for bibliography.

[6] E.M. Wilbur, *A History of Unitarianism* (Boston, 1945). Williams, *Radical Reformation*, pp. 742f, 839.

[7] For Bodin's knowledge of Jewish sources see F. Bezold, 'Jean Bodin als Okkultist und seine *Démonomanie*', *Historische Zeitschrift*, CV (1910), 1-64 (pp. 50ff). J. Guttmann, 'Jean Bodin in seinen Beziehungen des Judentums', *Monatschrift für Geschichte und Wissenschaft des Judentums*, XLIX (1905), 315-348; 459-489. M. Isnardi-Parente, 'Le volontarisme de Jean Bodin: Maimonide ou Duns Scot?', in *Verhandlungen der internationalen Bodin Tagung in München*, ed. H. Denzer (Munich, 1973), pp. 39-51, takes Bodin's public reliance on Duns too literarily, to my mind. See below, Chapters IV and V.

[8] Baron, *History*, XV, pp. 94ff.

reasons of a religious nature governing Bodin's attitude. Judaism was for him the source of all religions :

> Such is the religion of the Jews from which all others save demonolatry seem to derive their origin. Whence Judaism is called by Chrysostom the mother of the gentiles. [9]

(Note the typical use of a Christian source to validate what is in fact a Judaising statement). And in the *Heptaplomeres* :

> But the purest and simplest religion of the Hebrews has no impurity mingled within it and no heresies attached; it knows the worship of the one true God. [10]

This archetypal quality of Judaism was to prove irresistible to a religious thinker engaged in the discovery of a universal *vera religio* who held no special brief for Christianity.

Yet in dealing with Bodin's religious ideas one immediately runs up against the problem caused by sixteenth century censorship. In a major religious work like the *Paradoxe* Bodin had to step very cautiously indeed in advancing a theory of religious virtue which effectively repudiated Christian doctrines of theological virtue and grace in favour of a Judaised approach portraying faith, hope and charity as natural virtues. Such opinions, if made explicit, would have quickly brought Bodin to the stake. Bodin, therefore, was forced to express his radical ideas in ambiguous terminology and in a form which appears full of logical errors and confusion. Each sentence may read simply but paragraphs rarely make sense unless the reader has first fully appreciated the whole Judaising tendency of Bodin's thought. My treatment of the *Paradoxe* in Chapter V may appear to make Bodin's writing more straightforward than it is but it seemed essential to attempt to unravel some of the involutions of this cryptic text.

If Bodin's printed works do not easily yield up information about his religion, nor can we go direct to the clandestine and startlingly original *Heptaplomeres* in search of straightforward indications. It is true that the speeches of the Jew Salomon in the *Heptaplomeres* put forward some forthright Judaising opinions, but any work written in dialogue form presents numerous difficulties of interpretation. Above all the form of the *Heptaplomeres* precludes us from easily assuming that the remarks of Salomon or any other participant unequivocally express Bodin's own ideas. In order to be able to use the *Heptaplomeres* as evidence of Bodin's authentic religious views we must first carry out a methodological sieving of the work. Two kinds of filters suggest themselves. In the first place we may ascertain his religious beliefs from

---

[9] *Republica* (1586), p. 344: "Qualis est Iudaeorum religio, a qua caeterae praeter demonolatria origines duxisse videntur; quam propterea Chrysostomus gentium matrem appellat."

[10] *Heptaplomeres*, ed. Noack, p. 197 (trs. p. 258): "Sed Hebraeorum purissima ac simplicissima religio nihil impuri admistum habet, nullas haereses adjunctas, nullum praeterquam unius Dei cultum agnoscit." For Bodin's use of Jewish ideas see G. Roellenbleck, *Offenbarung, Natur und jüdische Überlieferung bei Jean Bodin* (Gütersloh, 1964), pp. 97-113. C.R. Baxter, 'Jean Bodin's Daemon and his Conversion to Judaism', in *Verhandlungen*, ed. Denzer, pp. 1-21.

other sources such as the *Paradoxe* and the *Démonomanie* and use this knowledge as a control upon the ambiguities of the *Heptaplomeres*. In the second
place we may use an internal filter, examining his statements in the *Heptaplomeres* on some key themes such as prophecy, ethics and happiness, ascer-
taining the extent of agreement among speakers on these themes, and using
thë resulting knowledge to control the disputation by the participants upon
other themes. One of the main objectives of this book has been to design a
fruitful method for the decoding of that enigmatic work — perhaps the first
masterpiece of comparative religion — the *Heptaplomeres*. (I hope to apply
the method more extensively in a future work).

From this method it results that Bodin *largely* agreed with the sentiments
he put into the mouth of Salomon, but not *completely* so; Bodin did not
become a Jew but remained a Judaiser. This circumscription did not, however,
save Bodin from being condemned as a secret Jew by some contemporaries,
or from being derogatorily accused of being of Jewish ancestry in later centuries,[11] or from having his religion described as "Judaism" by modern
writers.[12] (In fact Bodin seems to have been descended from a French provincial family although it would be unwise to rule out entirely the remote
possibility of some Marrano ancestry).[13] For Bodin the real attraction of
Judaism was that it supplied him with new ways of thinking about universal
religion which broke out of the old constricting arena of Christian theology;
for Bodin to have adhered to Judaism proper and to have observed Jewish
rites would have meant renouncing that very universalism towards which his
whole Judaising strategy was directed.[14]

Bodin originally Judaised in order to achieve a universal *vera religio*
but by the time of the *Paradoxe* and *Heptaplomeres* his religious vision had
become so thoroughly Judaised that it entailed the destruction of the fundamentals of Christian doctrine. Only this purged Christianity could be admitted
as a constituent of *vera religio*. Bodin's Judaising eventually accomplished
a critique of Christianity which repudiated Christian doctrines of grace, original
sin, theological virtue, justification and redemption. All these themes came to
seem to Bodin to be fallacious categories of Christian thought which obstructed
the path to true religion. Man, for example, cannot in any sense ever be
justified, concluded Bodin; this was a Christian category and any discussion
of justification is futile. But, said Bodin adopting Jewish categories, man
can be made *happy* or *blessed* by the gift of divine prophetic illumination.
Man's natural powers enabled him to prepare himself for this divine illumi-

---

[11] Baron, *History*, XV, 94ff, 420f, for bibliography on these charges. P. Mesnard,
'La conjuration contre la renommée de Jean Bodin: Antoine Tessier (1684)', *Bulletin de
l'Association Guillaume Budé*, XVIII (1959), 535-559. R. Chauviré, *Jean Bodin, auteur
de la République* (Paris, 1914), pp. 158ff.

[12] E.g., by Roellenbleck, *Offenbarung*. Baxter, 'Bodin's Daemon'. D.P. Walker,
Spiritual and Demonic Magic from Ficino to Campanella (London, 1958), p. 171. See
below, Chapters VIII, note 141.

[13] J. Levron, *Jean Bodin et sa famille. Textes et commentaires* (Angers, 1950).
Cf. P. Mesnard, 'État présent des études Bodiniennes', *Filosofia*, XI (1960), 687-696.

[14] P. Mesnard, 'Jean Bodin et la critique de la morale d'Aristote', *Revue Thomiste*,
LVII (1949), 542-562, comes close to grasping the nature of Bodin's Judaising. But see
Chapter V. (In his later articles Mesnard lost sight of this Judaising theme).

nation through cultivating the virtues of righteousness, faith, hope and charity; precisely this natural self-preparation or purification constituted the subject of moral philosophy and ethics. It was thanks to the new categories of understanding made available to him by Jewish thought that Bodin was able to formulate this unusual conception of religion and ethics.

The anti-Christian thrust of Bodin's Judaising sets him apart from the Christian Judaisers of the sixteenth century and the uniqueness of his position becomes apparent if the attitudes of Bodin and Servetus towards their Jewish mentors are compared. One of Servetus' motives for Judaising Christianity was to attract Jewish converts by abolishing the obstacle of the Trinity which prevented Jewish acceptance of Christ as the messiah. Bodin, on the contrary, never sought to convert the Jews and indeed saw no reason why they should forsake their pure monotheism for the rather unsatisfactory doctrines of Christianity which he regarded as tainted with superstition. Again Servetus generally corrupted Jewish ideas to make them fit his idiosyncratic conception of Christianity, while Bodin left the concepts of Jewish theologians intact and remained faithful to their spirit and content. This applies particularly to the cardinal Judaising themes which Bodin expounded in his writings as the foundations of *vera religio*, namely the Decalogue, the Deuteronomic choice of good and evil, and purification and prophecy.

d) Bodin's Judaised Religion. Purification, Prophecy and the Great God of Nature

Bodin's vision of *vera religio* was Judaised in its very structure — its two poles of purification and prophecy were also the pillars of Philo's Judaism. For Bodin purification and prophecy are more than a mere formula; they are ideas embodied in the actuality of his religious biography. As a youth Bodin had been trained in a Carmelite spirituality which also revolved around purification and prophecy but his quest for a universal religion isolated him from these religious feelings on account of their Christian setting. It was only after Bodin had subsequently encountered purification and prophecy in a quite alien Jewish context that he was able to resume them so as to fill a troubling vacuum in his religious sensibility. Thanks to this Judaising of purification and prophecy Bodin was eventually able to reconcile his earlier Carmelite spirituality with his leanings towards a universal religion devoid of Christian specificity. These developments comprise the first two stages of Bodin's conversion to true religion. The first of these — the shift away from Christianity to universal religion — I would date to before 1559; the second, in which Bodin embraced a Judaised religion based upon purification and prophecy, had occurred, it seems, by 1566. The third and final stage was to be marked by Bodin's own transfiguration as a prophet, an illumination that took place probably in 1567-68. The analysis of the third stage (Chapter VIII) reveals just how Bodin's religious ideas of purification and prophecy were fulfilled biographically in the sequence of his conversions; having first purified himself by the cultivation of religious virtue, Bodin was prepared to receive a prophetic illumination which was indeed not denied to him.

9

For Bodin, all the virtues are religious, not just the theological virtues of faith, hope and charity. [15] This is because all the virtues contribute to the purification of the soul which is the first part of *vera religio* and the prelude to prophecy. Ethics is, therefore, one of the two great sectors of Bodin's religion. It is vitally important here to recognise that Bodin has adopted a Judaised understanding of ethics. Greek and Christian ideas of ethics tend to be abstract and systematic in contrast with the concrete and practical nature of Jewish ethics. The difference is to be seen in the appeal of Greek and Christian moral philosophy to a systematic psychology; in Jewish tradition all virtue was the manifestation of a general " righteousness " which in a unitary soul depended entirely on free will. This concrete view of virtue as "righteousness" is quite foreign to the Christian tradition of seeing virtue as an abstract concept rooted in ideas of "the good" and depending, furthermore, on the operation of divine grace. Grace itself in Christian thought is an abstract metaphysical concept whereas in Judaism grace refers rather to particular acts of God's will and love.

The concreteness of Jewish ideas of virtue, free will and grace is likely to create confusion in the mind of a reader accustomed to the categories of Greek or Christian thought. In Christian thought free will is a religious concept but in Judaism it is both religious and "naturalistic" since it is intrinsic to man and not limited by the constant Christian control of grace. For this reason Jewish ethics seems to be a confused mixture of naturalistic and religious thinking, yet it is really a religious theory which incorporates naturalistic elements.

According to Bodin's Judaised theory of ethics, virtue is achieved by the natural powers of man. This is not the naturalistic theory it appears to be for it is set within a religious framework. To Greek, Christian and modern secular ways of thinking Bodin's ethics may seem even contradictory, a mixture of the religious and the natural. But viewed in the context of Jewish religious and ethical thought, Bodin's moral philosophy shapes itself into a lucid and coherent theory of ethics.

Ethics in fact occupies a pivotal position in Bodin's thought, uniting politics with religion. "Righteousness" for example is not merely an ethical or a religious notion but incorporates moral virtue, the pursuit of justice and the worship of God. Righteousness in its role as justice lies at the heart of Bodin's political thought just as it animates that of Philo and Maimonides. In the Jewish tradition taken up by Bodin politics are neither autonomous nor secular but rather are conducted within a moral and religious universe. It is within this Judaised context that Bodin's political thought, whether as expressed soberly in the *République* (Chapter II below) or more luridly in the writings on the Catholic League (Chapter IX), must be understood. For all their naturalistic appearances Bodin's political writings are ultimately moral and religious.

The integration of Bodin's ethical and religious thought means that our knowledge of one of these spheres is essential for an understanding of the other. In particular the ideas of virtue outlined in the *Paradoxe* have great significance for Bodin's religion. Bodin's belief that man has a natural capacity

---

[15] I have not used the term "moral theology" to describe Bodin's religious ethics since that term connotes a particular Christian theory.

for virtue carries the implication that man's will is not flawed by original sin and this in turn means that man has no need of a redeeming saviour. We therefore find embedded in Bodin's moral philosophy the roots of his non-Christian religious beliefs in free-willed Deuteronomic choice and the redundancy of any sort of Christian redeemer. Although Bodin for purposes of formal convenience dealt with moral philosophy in the *Paradoxe* and religious doctrine in the *Heptaplomeres* the two works are intimately linked and cannot really be read in isolation from another.

Bodin's ethics also throws a great deal of light on his religious conversions. For it is the *free-willed* purification of the soul and the achievement of virtue that paved the way for his final prophetic conversion. The virtuous purification of the soul, according to both Philo and Bodin, is not an end in itself but rather prepares the soul to receive that rarest gift of prophetic illumination which God bestows only upon His elect.

Bodin's religion hinges on prophecy for it is prophecy which unifies the crucial theophanies of *illumination* and *revelation*. Following Philo and Maimonides, Bodin argued that prophecy was the result of the influx of divine light or spirit into the soul, a light communicated by means of the active-intellect of the universe and the various angelic intelligences. Prophecy was conferred by God's will alone on selected men whose purification had prepared them to receive the gift which their free will, however, could not secure. For Philo, Maimonides and Bodin perfect happiness consisted in the ecstatic vision, knowledge, love and enjoyment of God which the prophetic light produced in the soul. It is clear from the manner in which Bodin expunged the terminology of grace in his later writings that he understood prophecy as based not on a Christian idea of divine grace but rather upon Judaised notions of "extraordinary divine help" (Chapters V and VI).

In its other function prophecy is the vehicle of divine revelation. The first purpose of revelation is to communicate God's will to men but revelation also serves an ethical purpose in recalling men to virtue. Here again we may see how misconceived it is to impose on Bodin the conflicting categories of nature and revelation. For Bodin revelation is the natural law; it is required only because men stray from nature. In the *Heptaplomeres* Bodin cites Philo to the effect that "the Ten Commandments depart not at all from nature... the tables of Moses contain nothing but the law of nature and the life of our ancestors".[16] Bodin's notion of a "revealed law of nature" may seem paradoxical but it was no paradox in the Jewish tradition which he adopted.

Bodin's theory of prophetic revelation has a yet more pregnant role to play in Bodin's religion in that it provides the key to his solution of the fundamental problem of how the transcendent and immanent aspects of God are to be reconciled: The active intellect and angels who transmit to human prophets the commands of a transcendent God are immanent spirits inhabiting the universe of nature.

[16] *Heptaplomeres*, pp. 190f (249).

If God is extrinsic to nature how does He manifest Himself in the natural universe? Philo's solution was that "God is everywhere in His powers, nowhere in His essence". According to Philo the chief of these immanent powers or spirits is the *logos* which he sees as the directing immanent executive of God's commands. The *logos* is emphatically not God Himself as it is in Christianity (though Philo may have been responsible for influencing the early Christian adoption of the term). Below Philo's *logos* are ranged the angels (who transmit prophecy and other forms of good to men) and the demons (who inflict evil as punishment for the sins committed by human free will). These immanent spirits are "natural" in that they are part of the natural universe rather than divinity but they are "supernatural" in being spirits.

Philo's general approach to the problem of immanence was followed by later Jewish thinkers although for obvious reasons his Christian term *logos* was replaced by such terms as *shekina* in rabbinical writers, by *active-intellect* in Maimonides, and by *sefirot* or emanations in the Kabbala. This was also to be Bodin's line. Rather than accept the Trinitarian solution of Christianity which saw the Holy Ghost as the bridge between transcendence and immanence and envisioned Christ as the reconciler of the rift between God and nature, Bodin turned to Philo and a Judaised vision of God and nature. God and nature are different in quality but God acts in nature through the immanent powers and spirits which are always under His control. This attempt to explain divine immanence led Philo and Bodin to understand God's law as the law of nature. For both thinkers God Himself is not part of nature but His law *is*.

God's revealed law comprehends the law of nature:

> God wished to renew (*for Moses*) that same law of nature by His own word and comprehend it in the Decalogue... When men grew deaf to the law of nature the divine voice was required so that those who contemned nature might hear the Father of nature proclaiming His words. [17]

Divine and natural law are thus different sides of the same coin. The Hebrews, says Bodin in the *Démonomanie,*

> were not ignorant of the difference between the works of God and of nature. For Solomon remarked in his allegories that the wise son obeys the commands of his father and does not forget the law of his mother. That is, he heeds the commands of God and the law of nature. [18]

Thanks to this essentially religious vision of law Bodin's natural universe becomes a moral universe. The moral and the natural are held together by two major bonds — one is free will, which is a fact of nature making moral choices; the other is the immanent powers of the angels and demons which by rewarding good and punishing evil operate the whole system of divine

---

[17] *Ibidem.* Latin quotation given below in Chapter VII.

[18] *Dèmonomanie,* I, fol. 37: "Ce n'est pas que les Hébrieux ayent ignoré la différence des œuvres de Dieu et de nature: car Salomon l'a souvent remarqué, quand il dict aux allégories, 'L'enfant est sage, qui obeist aux mandemens du père, et n'oublie pas la loy de la mère.' Il entend les commandemens de Dieu, et la loy de nature". See Chapter VIII.

cosmic justice. It is impossible to divorce Bodin's idea of the moral from his notion of the natural: both are facets of his religious understanding of God and nature. [19]

That understanding is summed up in the formulae connecting God and nature which recur in Bodin's writings — "the Father of nature", "this great prince of nature", "this great legislator of nature", "the sovereign of nature", "the Great Great God of Nature". [20] This God is not part of nature but nature cannot be considered, cannot exist, without constant providence. It is this God who maintains the peace and justice of nature, preservative functions dimly and imperfectly reflected in the actions of His earthly counterparts, the sovereign kings. According to Bodin, the universe and all its parts including political states are inherently unstable; there is in all things which are part of universal nature an intrinsic tendency to degenerate, and it is only the preserving power of God which averts the collapse of all orderly structure and a return to chaos. [21]

For Bodin the triumph of God's preserving power over a degenerative universe is attested by the astonishing harmony of the natural universe:

> For one sees how this great God of Nature has bound all things by means which reconcile the extremes and compose the harmony of the intelligible, celestial and elemental universe through indissoluble powers and links. Just as harmony perishes if the opposite voices are not joined by the middle voices, so too it is with the world and its parts. [22]

This universal harmony is the cosmic justice of the Great God of Nature.

Bodin's idea of the Great God of Nature suggests that it is wrong to enquire whether he was a follower of theistic or of natural religion. In Bodin the two forms of religion are not exclusive of one another but rather are mixed together. Most of the modern inclination to keep these categories separate stems from those Enlightenment thinkers who had opposed *natural* theology to *revealed* theology and opted for the former to the exclusion of the latter. Aquinas had distinguished between natural and revealed theology but, accepting natural theology as dependent on a revealing God, he had taken both theologies as complementary modes of perceiving God. In this perspective natural religion does not appear as necessarily deistic although it has often been taken as

---

[19] See Chapter V.

[20] E.g., *Methodus*, ed. Mesnard, p. 114 (trs. p. 15); *République*, I, i, p. 5; *Démono-manie*, fol. 7 (see below); *Paradoxe*, p. 33; *Heptoplomeres*, p. 190 (249). See Chapters II, V and VII.

[21] This comes through most clearly in the *Theatrum Naturae* which I hope to treat in detail in a future work.

[22] *Démonomanie*, fol. 7: "Car on void que ce grand Dieu de nature a lié toutes choses par moyens, qui s'accordent aux extremitez, et composé l'harmonie du monde intelligible, celeste et élémentaire par moyens et liaisons indissolubles. Et tout ainsi que l'harmonie périroit, si les voix contraires n'estoyent liées par voix moyennes, ainsi est il du monde, et de ses parties".

such since the eighteenth century. Aquinas and Bodin were able to conceive of such a thing as theistic natural religion without regarding it as a glaring contradiction in terms such as it has subsequently become. Yet they apprehended this mixture of theism and natural religion in ways that differed profoundly. Bodin refused to allow Aquinas' ideas of grace and redemption; instead he embraced a *vera religio* whose combination of nature and revelation was founded not on Christ but on a Judaised theory of prophecy. The revelation of a revealing God is communicated by means of prophecy which reinforces and explains nature.

In prophecy then lies the heart of Bodin's *vera religio* for it is prophecy that transmutes natural religion into *vera religio*.[23] Bodin's true religion was neither Christianity, nor deistic natural religion, nor even Judaism; it was in fact a Judaised religion whose fusion of elements of nature and revelation was achieved by recourse to an exalted idea of prophecy.

e) Synopsis

This book attempts to examine Bodin's ideas on religion, ethics and politics at various levels. The difficulty of the material and complexity of the argument has led me to adopt what may be a confusing and possibly a tedious method of exposition which will involve the patient reader in going over some texts as many as three times. In extenuation the author would like to think that each circuit is made on a deeper level of understanding. Nevertheless readers who find themselves bored by the first tour (Chapters I - III) might find themselves revived if they proceed to the second section where the proper deciphering of Bodin's enigmatic religion begins. I wish I could have dispensed with these dry opening chapters yet they seem essential if the reader is to gain an impression of the significance of Bodin's concept of virtue for all aspects of his thought.

Part A (Chapters I - III) offers a straightforward, summary account of the role of virtue in Bodin's political and educational thought. For the most part I have not tried to indicate here the Judaised character of his ethics and moral philosophy. That virtue is a major concern of Bodin's from 1559 until his last writings suggests that his reputed shift from political thought to religion and ethics in his later life is not as real as it appears. Ethical and religious preoccupations inform all Bodin's works including the *Methodus* and the *République;* this is the point which the rather cursory treatment of these two works in Chapter II is intended to make.

The discussion of a little-known group of Bodin's educational writings in Chapter III (the *Epître à son neveu,* the *Consilium* and the *Sapientia*) brings to the surface further aspects of Bodin's sense of the connections between society, ethics and religion. In the social sphere Bodin saw education as

---

[23] An important article by P. Mesnard, 'La pensée religieuse de Bodin', *Revue du Seizième Siècle*, XVI (1929), 77-121, drew attention to the prophetic theme in Bodin's religion but I hope to have explored more deeply the nature of Bodin's idea of prophecy by interpreting it as a salient feature of his Judaising.

inculcating moral and intellectual virtue which served to promote amity and peace. At the same time education was seen to have a vital religious function which consists in showing men the relation between father and son, or teacher and pupil, so prescribing the proper relation between God and man. Before God the adult always remains a minor and the relationship between man and God is seen by Bodin as based on an unequal love which is further mixed on the side of man with fear and reverence. Adult wisdom consists of this recognition of human pupillage.

Part B (Chapters IV-VII) is an exposition of the systematically Judaised character of Bodin's moral and religious philosophy. Adopting the Philonic idea of religion as purification and prophecy Bodin perceived ethics in its guise of purification as essentially religious and indeed as the prelude to prophecy. If Bodin's religion can be used to elucidate his ethics the reverse process is also feasible. Our investigation of the religious basis of Bodin's ethics has presented an opportunity to penetrate the ambiguities of the *Heptaplomeres* by using the *Paradoxe* as a control on certain key passages in the clandestine work.

Part C (Chapters VII-VIII) adds a biographical dimension to the religion of Bodin and examines the evolution of his religious thought. The main framework for this religious biography is a study of Bodin's successive conversions. Chapter VIII seeks to understand the psychological motives of these experiences and perhaps to shed some light on the general phenomenon of conversion. The study of conversions is one of the most fertile fields of biographical interpretation for these transfigurations are accompanied by intense dynamic interaction between the ideas and personality of the convert. The impulse for conversion seems to come from a psychic disturbance in the personality, but the disturbance is expressed and formulated in theological terms. With Chapter VIII I hope to have clarified the fascinating and difficult problem of Bodin's conversions and also to have demonstrated how vital for an understanding of Bodin's religious biography is an awareness of his Judaising strategy.

The last chapter illustrates the impact of Bodin's religion on other aspects of his biography. In this account of Bodin's political conduct at Laon after 1589, one may see again how ideas and biography interact and at the same time how Bodin's Judaised prophetic religion directed his political behaviour.

The present book is intended merely as *prolegomena* to a more rounded intellectual biography of Bodin. But I hope it is sufficient to vindicate the effectiveness of the two methodological principles announced at the beginning of this introduction: (1) That Bodin's thought must be comprehended in its completeness if any one compartment of his thought is to be understood without distortion, and (2) That a true understanding of Bodin can only be achieved through the integration of his thought with his personality and biography. If these principles are to be observed, we have need of a full understanding of Bodin's religion. The Judaising programme which Bodin pursued so unflinchingly is the key to that enigmatic religion.

[16]

Dialogues of Toleration: Erasmus and Bodin

Gary Remer

The article examines two different types of "tolerant" dialogues, represented by Desiderius Erasmus and Jean Bodin. Erasmus offers a traditional conception of dialogue, in which the speakers are engaged in a common search for truth. This search for truth justifies toleration. To discover truth, the speakers must be free to question the other speakers' views, as well as their own. And they must respect each other because civility promotes the discovery of truth. Bodin, by contrast, presents an alternative version of the tolerant dialogue in his *Colloquium heptaplomeres*, a dialogue between representatives of seven different religions. While the Erasmian dialogue presupposes that (1) there is a single truth and that (2) the greater the consensus, the more successful the dialogue, in Bodin's *Colloquium*, the speakers do not pursue a common truth. Rather, they offer up their own particular versions of truth, unwilling to change their positions. The speakers do not agree on the truth because truth—especially religious truth—is complex, and each speaker represents a different facet of that multifaceted truth. And though the speakers remain firm in their initial convictions, they gain from the dialogue a clearer perception of their own opinions. By comparing their views with one another, the speakers come to better understand their separate truths, the sum of which constitutes the whole truth.

Introduction

There is no necessary link between dialogue and toleration. First, not all defenders of toleration value dialogue. Mystics and spiritualists, for example, justify toleration on the ground that truth is internal and cannot be forced. But because they view truth as a matter of the spirit, not reason, they eschew dialogue. As one Dutch Anabaptist states: "The Christian faith is not a word pronounced by the mouth, but a true eternal force, a divine operation . . . which no one can know but he who receives it. It does not consist . . . in words outwardly pronounced, but in the experience of the living, true, just and eternal God and his Christ."[1] Second, not all dialogues are tolerant. Some are didactic, where the speaker possessing knowledge instructs his unenlightened

I would like to thank Professors Marion Leathers Kuntz, Eric Gorham, Martyn Thompson, Anthony Cummings, and Gordon Schochet for their helpful comments.
1. David Joris, *Een suyverlijcke bewijsreden*, as cited in Roland Bainton, *David Joris. Wiedertäufer und Kämpfer für Toleranz im 16. Jahrhundert* (Leipzig, 1937), p. 80.

306   THE REVIEW OF POLITICS

interlocutor. For example, Thomas More's *Dialogue Concerning Heresies* is not an investigative dialogue between peers, but a didactic, authoritarian dialogue between More, who knows the truth, and the messenger, a youth in danger of being lost to the Lutheran heresy, who is ignorant of the truth. In this case, dialogue becomes More's vehicle to reclaim the youth. There is no toleration of heterodoxy here, no question that anything besides More's opinion is legitimate.[2]

Nevertheless, although dialogue and toleration **can** be distinct, there has been, in fact, a long-standing connection between the two concepts. Thus, while dialogue is not significant to all arguments for toleration, it remains central to the most famous defenses of toleration, like John Milton's *Areopagitica* (1644) and John Stuart Mill's *On Liberty* (1859). For both Milton and Mill, toleration promotes discussion, which, they believe, will lead to the discovery of more truths. The same nexus between toleration and dialogue is found in the U.S. Supreme Court's "marketplace of ideas" theory, which assumes that free speech should be protected because truth will emerge from the free interchange of ideas.

Dialogue has also traditionally been defined as tolerant. For example, Socrates' claims of ignorance, in contrast to More's profession of knowledge, suggests that his dialogue's conclusion has not been predetermined and that interlocutors in the Socratic conversations are truly free to express their opinions. And Cicero explicitly defends, in his dialogues, the liberty of speakers to state their opinions and to form their own judgments. "But let everyone defend his views," Cicero writes in the *Tusculan Disputations*, "for judgment is free: I shall cling to my rule and without being tied to the laws of any single school of thought which I feel bound to obey."[3] Alluding to the tolerant nature of the Socratic and

---

2. See Rainer Pineas, "Thomas More's Use of the Dialogue Form as a Weapon of Religious Controversy," *Studies in the Renaissance* 7 (1960):200-201. See also *The Complete Works of St. Thomas More*, ed. Thomas M. C. Lawler, Germain Marc'hadour, and Richard C. Marius (New Haven: Yale University Press, 1981), vol. 6, part 2, pp. 440-41.

3. Cicero, *Tusculan Disputations* 4. 4. 7. See also *Ibid.* 2. 26. 63-64; 5. 29. 83; Cicero, *De natura deorum* 1. 7. 17; Cicero, *De finibus* 5. 26. 76. All citations from Cicero, unless otherwise indicated, are from the Loeb Classical Library editions (Cambridge, MA: Harvard University Press).

ERASMUS AND BODIN 307

Ciceronian dialogues, Rudolf Hirzel argues in his classic *Der Dialog* that real dialogue, like that found in democratic Athens, presupposes freedom of thought and speech.[4]

The relationship between dialogue and toleration is the focus of this article. I examine here how two different thinkers in the sixteenth century, Desiderius Erasmus (1466-1536) and Jean Bodin (1530-1596), develop theories of religious toleration based on the model of dialogue. While both view dialogue as a model for toleration, I argue that each presents a different version of dialogue from which he derives a separate theory of toleration. In the section on Erasmus, I discuss Erasmus's "tolerant" dialogue, which is best exemplified by *De libero arbitrio, diatribe sive collatio* (*On Free Will: A Disputation or Comparison*), a one-sided conversation with (and refutation of) Martin Luther, published in 1524. Erasmus offers in *De libero arbitrio* a traditional conception of dialogue, in which the speakers are engaged in a common search for the truth. I show that Erasmus looks backward to Cicero in developing his conception of dialogue. Erasmus, however, also anticipates Milton and Mill's case for toleration, which deems toleration a means to truth. The expression of opposing opinions, for Erasmus, allows the listener to compare viewpoints and to decide which is the most probable. Like the present-day "marketplace of ideas" approach, the Erasmian dialogue requires that the speakers adopt a certain degree of skepticism.[5] Although the interlocutors have their own opinions and argue for them, each speaker must entertain the possibility that he may be mistaken and, consequently, that he may ultimately adopt another position. Lacking certainty, the speakers in the Erasmian dialogue must tolerate other views. They must also respect each other because, Erasmus argues, civility promotes the discovery of truth.

In the section on Bodin, I argue that Bodin puts forward an alternative version of the tolerant dialogue in the *Colloquium heptaplomeres de rerum sublimium arcanis abditis* (*Colloquium of the Seven about Secrets of the Sublime*), which was finished in 1588, but

---

4. Rudlof Hirzel, *Der Dialog: Ein Literarhistorischer Versuch*, 2 vols. (Leipzig: 1895; reprint ed.; Hildesheim: Georg Olms, 1963), 2: 43.

5. Justice Holmes writes in his *Abrams* dissent: "Time has upset many fighting faiths." *Abrams v. U.S.*, 250 U.S. 616 (1919). Erasmus's skepticism, however, is far more limited than the Supreme Court's.

circulated in manuscript form until the first complete printed edition was published in 1857.[6] Like the Erasmian dialogue, this dialogue between representatives of seven different religions is open: speakers are permitted to state their opinions and to decide for themselves. In fact, Bodin's dialogue is less restricted than any of Erasmus's because, in contrast to Erasmus's dialogues, the *Colloquium* includes non-Christian speakers, who are presented as every bit the equal of the Christian participants. But while diversity of opinion is found in both forms of dialogue, the speakers' goals—and the dialogues'—differ. In the Erasmian dialogue, or the Socratic and Ciceronian for that matter, the goal is to work together to find the truth, or at least to move closer to it.[7] Implicit in this vision of dialogue are the assumptions that (1) there is a single truth and that (2) the greater the consensus, the more successful the dialogue. In the *Colloquium*, however, these assumptions are rejected. The speakers do not pursue a single, common truth. Rather, they offer up their particular versions of the truth, unwilling to change their own positions.

From the perspective of the first dialogue, Bodin's *Colloquium* is a failure; the speakers do not even try to agree. But I argue that Bodin's dialogue is successful when judged on its own terms. The speakers do not agree on the truth, the *Colloquium* suggests, because truth—especially religious truth—is complex, and each speaker represents a different facet of that multifaceted truth. And though the speakers remain firm in their initial convictions, they gain from the dialogue a clearer perception of their own opinions. By comparing their views with one another, the speakers come to better understand their separate truths, the sum of which constitutes the whole truth.

The difference between these two forms of dialogue has practical implications for toleration. A traditional dialogue like Erasmus's, with its monistic conception of truth, is exclusive. It presumes that if x is true, then y must be false. And it only tolerates in areas that are not yet known. Thus Milton, the oft-

---

6. Marion Leathers Daniels Kuntz, *Colloquium of the Seven about Secrets of the Sublime* (hereafter cited as Kuntz, *Colloquium*) (Princeton: Princeton University Press, 1975), p. xxxvii.

7. On the Socratic dialogue as a "common search" for the truth, see W. K. C. Guthrie, *Socrates* (Cambridge: Cambridge University Press, 1971), p. 129.

ERASMUS AND BODIN 309

presumed herald of contemporary freedom of speech and press, would have banned Catholicism because it conflicted with "known" truths.[8] As long as truth is in doubt, according to Milton, debate must be permitted: "To be still searching what we know not, by what we know, still closing up truth to truth as we find it . . . this is the golden rule in *Theology*."[9] But, Milton reasons, we **can** know that Scripture is absolutely and solely authoritative, and because Roman Catholicism denies this proposition, it should be proscribed. Regardless of whether the opinion in question is Protestantism or liberal democracy, however, the message implicit in the first kind of dialogue is that once a conviction is held with certainty, there is no reason to tolerate competing ideas. Because dialogue aims at truth, then dialogue and diversity's *raison d'être* ceases when truth is known. By contrast, Bodin's dialogue accepts a pluralistic conception of truth. It notes that simply because x is true, does not mean that y cannot also be true. Therefore, this second type of dialogue can tolerate contradictory opinions, even when the opposing sides are convinced of their own truth. Truth, in the *Colloquium*, is not a monopoly maintained by force, but a shared commodity divided between different, mutually tolerant persuasions.

Erasmus

HUMANISM, DIALOGUE, AND SKEPTICISM

Desiderius Erasmus was born in Holland, the illegitimate son of a priest. He rose during his lifetime to become a celebrity of international stature based on his far-ranging scholarship in biblical, classical, and theological studies. And to this day, Erasmus is the best known humanist of the sixteenth century.[10] His reputation as "prince of the humanists" is rightly deserved. His vast corpus bespeaks an intense interest in the endeavors and studies characteristic of the Renaissance revival of the *studia humanitatis*

---

8. See John Milton, *Areopagitica, Complete Prose Works of John Milton*, 7 volumes (New Haven: Yale University Press, 1953-74), 2: 565; Leonard Levy, *Emergence of a Free Press* (New York: Oxford University Press, 1985), pp. 95-96.

9. *Areopagitica*, 2: 551.

10. Roland H. Bainton, *Erasmus of Christendom* (New York: Crossroad, 1969), p. 3.

known as humanism.[11] But above all, Erasmus demonstrates the humanist's concern with rhetoric, the most distinctively humanistic area of study.[12] All Erasmus's writings, including those not specifically devoted to rhetoric, are composed with an eye to their persuasiveness. It is with this attention to oratory that he writes of himself: "Erasmus taught nothing except eloquence."[13]

An important rhetorical tool for Erasmus was dialogue, a common *genus* during the Renaissance. The Quattrocento humanists had favored dialogue as a literary genre, and Erasmus followed their example.[14] There is an important difference, however, between the dialogues of Erasmus's predecessors and his own. The Quattrocento humanists' dialogues did not generally concern religious issues. The Reformation had not yet brought doctrinal matters to the fore. But Erasmus did make use of the dialogue to deal with religious issues, especially after the Reformation had begun.

Erasmus did not discuss all religious issues in dialogue form. He reserved the religious dialogue for nonessential doctrines. For Erasmus, the fundamentals of faith could not be discussed. These doctrines that were essential to salvation had to be accepted without question. Nonessential doctrines, however, were not obligatory and could be questioned. These nonessentials were adiaphoral, literally "things that make no difference."[15] There-

11. The five traditional humanistic studies are grammar, rhetoric, history, poetry, and moral philosophy. On defining Renaissance humanism, see Paul Oskar Kristeller, *Renaissance Thought: The Classic, Scholastic, and Humanist Strains* (New York: Harper and Row, 1961), pp. 9-10; Craig Thompson, "The Humanism of More Reappraised," *Thought* 52 (September 1977): 233.

12. As Paul Oskar Kristeller has observed, Renaissance humanism "must be understood as a characteristic phase in what may be called the rhetorical tradition in Western culture." *Renaissance Thought*, pp. 11-13.

13. Erasmus, *Opus Epistolarum Des. Erasmi Roterodami* (hereafter cited as EE), ed. P. S. Allen, H. M. Allen, and H. W. Garrod, 12 vols. (Oxford: Clarendon Press, 1906-57), 1:30. 1-3 (letter to John Botzheim, 30 January 1523).

14. Recent discussions of the humanist dialogue include: David Marsh, *The Quattrocento Dialogue: Classical Tradition and Humanist Innovation* (Cambridge, MA: Harvard University Press, 1980); J. F. Tinkler, "Humanism and Dialogue," *Parergon: Bulletin of the Australian and New Zealand Association for Medieval and Renaissance Studies* 6 (1988): 197-214; and K. J. Wilson, *Incomplete Fictions: The Formation of English Renaissance Dialogue* (Washington, D. C.: The Catholic University of America Press, 1985).

15. On the historical development of the concept "adiaphora," see Bernard J.

ERASMUS AND BODIN 311

fore, dialogue could be applied to them. As long as the speakers could agree on the fundamentals of faith, they were permitted to disagree on other beliefs. Erasmus makes this point in *Inquisitio de fide* ("An Examination Concerning Faith"). In this colloquy between a Catholic and a Lutheran, the Catholic discovers that the Lutheran, though reputed to be a heretic, adheres to the Apostle's Creed and is, therefore, orthodox. Erasmus suggests through this dialogue that Catholic and Lutheran can retain their beliefs and discuss their differences because the two only differ on nonessentials.

When the issues debated are not essential to salvation, the speakers may adopt a skeptical attitude toward their own beliefs. In the colloquy *Convivium religiosum* ("The Godly Feast"), Erasmus depicts an intellectual exchange between nine educated laymen who interpret Scripture without impinging on the fundamentals of faith. As the character Eusebius says there of his own scriptural interpretation: "Whether it's correct I don't know; I'm satisfied that the idea isn't irreverent or heretical." The interlocutors do not claim certainty. They only seek the most probable scriptural interpretation.[16] Similarly, in his *Disputatiuncula (Little Disputation)*, Erasmus uses the form of dialogue with a missing interlocutor (his friend John Colet) to investigate an adiaphoristic question: whether or not Jesus suffered in anticipation of his crucifixion. Responding to Colet, who maintains that Jesus' divinity precluded him from actually feeling pain, Erasmus takes the position that Jesus, because of his human nature, did indeed experience dread, fear, and sadness before his death. Because his debate with Colet does not concern an essential of faith, however, Erasmus concedes the possibility of error. Erasmus claims that he would even prefer being mistaken, since his mistakes offer him the opportunity to learn.[17] In these dialogues, Erasmus acknowl-

Verkamp, *The Indifferent Mean: Adiaphorism in the English Reformation to 1554*, Studies in the Reformation, vol. 1 (Athens, Ohio and Detroit, Michigan: Ohio University Press and Wayne State University Press, 1977), pp. 20-25.

16. *Convivium religiosum* (1522), *The Colloquies of Erasmus*, trans. Craig R. Thompson (Chicago: University of Chicago Press, 1965), pp. 58, 61; Marjorie O'Rourke Boyle, *Erasmus on Language and Method in Theology* (Toronto: University of Toronto Press, 1977), p. 138.

17. See Erasmus, *Desiderii Erasmi Roterodami Opera Omnia* (hereafter cited as LB), ed. J. Clericus, 10 volumes (Leyden: 1703-6), 5: 1265D-E (*Diputatiuncula de*

edges the legitimacy of doctrinal diversity, but he reveals the full potential of his tolerance in *De libero arbitrio*, another dialogue with a missing interlocutor.

After much papal pressure to repudiate Luther, Erasmus wrote *De libero arbitrio*, a rejection of Luther's position on the freedom of man's will. Against Luther's assertion that a person's will cannot affect his salvation, Erasmus replies that free will plays some role in human redemption. Erasmus composed *De libero arbitrio* in the form of a *diatribē*, a kind of philosophical dialogue, and not a bitter, abusive denunciation, as a diatribe is defined today. In fact, Erasmus most commonly referred to his piece not as *De libero arbitrio*, but as *Diatriba*. The genre's roots are in classical antiquity, where it developed as a popularization of the philosophical dialogue, designed to investigate moral issues like the nature of good and evil or the sufficiency of virtue for happiness. It can be distinguished, formally, from other genres of dialogue by its use of a fictional interlocutor, whose personality remains sketchy in the debate.[18]

In debating free will, Erasmus and Luther do not only disagree about the reality of free will; they also disagree about (1) whether it is essential to take a position on free will and (2) what degree of knowledge is necessary (and possible) in the matter. Luther contends that belief in the nullity of free will is a necessary doctrine.[19] And Luther asserts that certainty, not skepticism, is required of the believer in an essential doctrine like free will.[20] Erasmus maintains that free will is adiaphoral. The best advice for most men, he writes, is that they "not waste their time or

---

taedio, pavore, tristitia Jesu, instante supplicio crucis: deque verbus, quibus visus est mortem deprecari, 'Pater, si fieri potest, transeat a me calix iste' [*Little Disputation on the Dread, Fear, and Sadness of Jesus, when the Punishment of the Cross was pressing upon him. . . .*]).

18. On the classical use of *diatribē*, see André Oltramare, *Les Origines de la Diatribe Romaine* (Geneva: Imprimeries Populaire, 1926), especially pp. 9-17, 116-25; Marjorie O'Rourke Boyle, *Rhetoric and Reform: Erasmus' Civil Dispute with Luther* (Cambridge, MA: Harvard University Press, 1983), pp. 6-8.

19. E. Gordon Rupp and Philip S. Watson, eds., *Luther and Erasmus: Free Will and Salvation* The Library of Christian Classics: Icthus Edition. (Philadelphia: Westminster Press, 1969), pp. 116-117.

20. *Ibid.*, p. 109. See Boyle, *Rhetoric and Reform*, particularly pp. 43-66.

ERASMUS AND BODIN 313

talents on labyrinths of this kind."[21] Implicit in this statement is the belief that it is unnecessary to determine the status of free will. Erasmus maintains that he is free to assume the role of skeptic in this debate: "So far am I from delighting in 'assertions' that I would readily take refuge in the opinion of the Skeptics, wherever this is allowed by the inviolable authority of the Holy Scriptures and by the decrees of the Church."[22] To which Luther responds: "Let Skeptics and Academics keep well away from us Christians, but let there be among us 'assertors' twice as unyielding as the Stoics themselves."[23]

Erasmus expresses his skepticism about free will in the method he adopts to analyze it: argument *in utramque partem*. In this method of argumentation, perfected by the Academic skeptic Carneades (c. 213-129 B.C.E.), the speaker argues on either side of the question. That the same issue could be argued from either side, the ancient Skeptics reasoned, shows the impossibility of epistemological certainty. The implications of argument *in utramque partem*, however, are not solely negative. Although it was used to deny certain knowledge, it was also used by the Academic skeptics to determine probability, the closest approximation of truth. By arguing the strengths and weaknesses of each position, the Skeptic could compare the different opinions and decide which one is most probable.[24]

As a dialogue with the missing Luther, *Diatriba* is structured as an argument *in utramque partem*. Like the Academics, Erasmus considers both sides of the issue to arrive at the most probable conclusion. He divides the body of *Diatriba* between scriptural passages supporting free will and passages seeming to oppose free will. Because the biblical texts are ambiguous, Erasmus hopes

21. LB 9:1218B-C (*De libero arbitrio*). See also LB 10:1663B (*Spongia adversus adspergines Hutteni*); Desiderius Erasmus, *Collected Works of Erasmus* (hereafter cited as CWE), still in progress (Toronto: University of Toronto Press, 1974-), 8: 280. 358-60 (Letter to Pierre Barbier, 13 August 1521).

22. *Luther and Erasmus: Free Will and Salvation*, p. 37. Cf. CWE 27:118 (*Praise of Folly*).

23. *Luther and Erasmus: Free Will and Salvation*, p. 106.

24. Cicero, *De officiis* 2. 2. 8. See also *Tusculan Disputations* 2. 3. 9; Cicero, *Academica* 2. 3. 7-8; Alain Michel, *Rhétorique et Philosophie chez Cicéron: Essai sur les Fondements Philosophique de l'art de Persuader* (Paris: Presses Universitaires de France, 1960), pp. 158-73.

that he will arrive at probability through a "comparison of Scriptures [*collatione Scripturarum*]"; as M. O. Boyle notes, Erasmus refers to his *De libero arbitrio* as a *collatio*, a comparison.[25] Erasmus's method of *collatio* finds its classical precedent in Cicero, who defines comparison as one of the subdivisions of probability. "A parallel [*collatio*]," Cicero writes, "is a passage putting one thing beside another on the basis of their resemblances."[26] Since Scripture has only a single author, Erasmus's form of *collatio* must ultimately end with textual reconciliation.[27] Thus, he harmonizes the texts in favor of the existence of free will, which he finds the more probable opinion. In particular, Erasmus finds "highly probable [*satis . . . probabilis*]" the opinion of those who "attribute most to grace and almost nothing to free will, yet do not deny it altogether," since this view "allows man to study and strive, but does not permit him to make any claims for his own powers."[28]

The skepticism of *De libero arbitrio*—its argument *in utramque partem*, its tentativeness, and its probabilism—may have been radical for its time, but Erasmus's conception of the skeptical dialogue was not new. It had its source in the tradition of classical rhetoric, particularly in Cicero's vision of the philosophical dialogue. Cicero distinguished between the rhetoric of philosophical dialogue, which he referred to as "the rhetoric of philosophers," and the rhetoric "we use in the lawcourts."[29] One characteristic that distinguished this rhetoric of philosophers from legal rhetoric, Cicero suggests, is its skepticism. Although legal rhetoric generally involves matters that cannot be demonstrated with certainty,[30] Cicero believed that philosophical dialogue was more closely tied to skepticism than was legal oratory. First, the uncer-

25. Boyle, *Rhetoric and Reform*, pp. 20-21, pp. 43-46; *Luther and Erasmus: Free Will and Salvation*, p. 47; LB 9:1220F (*De libero arbitrio*); LB 10:1312C-D (*Hyperaspistes* I).

26. Cicero, *De inventione* 1. 30. 47-49.

27. LB 9:1241D (*De libero arbitrio*).

28. LB 9:1224C (*De libero arbitrio*); See *Ibid.* 1241C; LB 10:1327B-C (*Hyperaspistes* I).

29. *De finibus* 2. 6. 17; *Tusculan disputations* 1. 47. 112.

30. Although judicial oratory concerns past facts that are, in theory, ascertainable and could not be other than they were, the judicial genre still deals with matters that are, at least in the present, under contention. See M. Fabius Quintilian *Institutione Oratoria* 5, chaps. 1-7.

ERASMUS AND BODIN 315

tainty of legal cases is ended by the jury's decision. Philosophical debates, however, have no resolution, since they have no authoritative arbiter to settle the question.[31] Second, the subject-matter of judicial oratory concerns real facts that have occurred, most likely, in the not-too-distant past. So that even if orators, in judicial matters, can usually present credible arguments on both sides of the case, they are limited in their arguments by evidence. The link between philosophical dialogue's subject-matter, which concerns abstract ideas, and the facts, however, is far more tenuous. Therefore, there are fewer restraints on what position a speaker can take in dialogue. In contrast to the concreteness of legal oratory, philosophical dialogue is "something involved in boundless uncertainty."[32] Skepticism, Cicero concludes, is a persistent attribute of philosophical dialogue.[33]

That philosophical dialogue is skeptical does not in-and-of-itself make philosophical dialogue tolerant. Skepticism does not necessarily lead to toleration. A traditional response to doubt, for example, has been conformity to convention, not toleration of diversity.[34] Philosophical dialogue is tolerant, however, because toleration is thought to facilitate discovery of truth or, at least, discovery of the most probable truth. No person in the dialogue can claim certain knowledge, but all believe that their discussion moves them closer to truth. And for Erasmus, as for Cicero, each person must decide for himself. Erasmus concludes *Diatriba* with the words: "I have completed my discourse; now let others pass judgment."[35] The judgment Erasmus refers to here is individual

31. John Tinkler also observes that while Academic skepticism is generally characteristic of rhetoric, in judicial oratory the orator is not, himself, permitted to speak skeptically. In public, he is expected to argue, unambivalently, either for or against a position. See John F. Tinkler, "Renaissance Humanism and the *genera eloquentiae*," *Rhetorica: A Journal of the History of Rhetoric* 5 (1987): 295.

32. *De oratore* 2. 19. 78; *De natura deorum* 1. 6. 14. See also Hirzel, *Der Dialog*, 1: 531.

33. Thus, Cicero, despite his disdain for Epicureanism, concedes that he may be in error: "'many men, many minds'—so it is possible that I am mistaken" (*De finibus* 1. 5. 15).

34. Richard Tuck, "Scepticism and toleration in the seventeenth century," *Justifying Toleration: Conceptual and historical perspectives*, ed. Susan Mendus (Cambridge: Cambridge University Press, 1988), p. 25.

35. *Luther and Erasmus: Free Will and Salvation*, p. 97.

and does not preclude further debate. It is the judgment of philosophical dialogue about which Cicero writes in the *Tusculan Disputations*, "judgment is free."[36] Erasmus believed that many theological debates, like the debate over free will, cannot be decided.
They are questions, like Cicero's philosophical questions, "which
do not admit of resolution."

As I have already stated, Erasmus does not permit debate on
all theological matters. Doctrinal adiaphora can be discussed in a
tolerant dialogue, not the fundamentals of faith. But Erasmus's
list of doctrinal adiaphora is lengthy, while the doctrines that he
enumerates as articles of faith are limited: "The sum and substance of our religion is peace and concord. This can hardly
remain the case unless we define as few matters as possible and
leave each individual's judgment free on many questions."[37] Only
doctrines that have a clear scriptural source are defined as essential.[38] But most doctrines, according to Erasmus, do not have a
plain basis in Scripture. For example, although Erasmus declares
the doctrine of the Trinity to be essential, he views most related
doctrines as adiaphoral.[39] Likewise, Erasmus thinks that the doctrine of the Immaculate Conception, the divine right claims of the
Church hierarchy—pope, cardinals, and bishops—and most questions about the sacraments are all adiaphoral.[40] The consequence
of Erasmus's strict standard for the fundamentals of faith is greater

36. See above, note 3.

37. CWE 9:252. 232-234 (Letter to Jean de Carondelet, 5 January 1523). See
also *Ibid.* 250. 172-51. 188; 253. 244-46.

38. LB:10 1335C (*Hyperaspistes* I). See also CWE 7:126. 235-45 (Letter to Jan
Slechta, 1 November 1519).

39. LB 10:1259F-1260A (*Hyperaspistes* I, 1526).

40. LB 6:696C-D (Note on I Cor. 7:39, *Novum Testamentum*, 1519); CWE 9:264.
649-651 (Letter to Jean de Carondelet, 5 January 1523); LB 10:1663A-B (*Spongia
adversus adspergines Hutteni*, 1523); LB 6:926-928 (*In Epistolam ad Timotheum I*);
Desiderius Erasmus, *Ausgewählte Werke*, ed. Hajor Holborn with Annemarie
Holborn (Munich: C.H. Beck, 1933), p. 193, lines 9-28 (*Ratio verae theologiae*); LB
5:1079B (*Ecclesiastes*); CWE 66:11, cited in Cornelis Augustijn, *Erasmus: His Life,
Works, and Influence*, trans. J. C. Grayson (Toronto: University of Toronto Press,
1991), pp. 78-79. See also CWE 7:126. 235 - 127. 260 (Letter to Jan Slechta, 1
November 1519); Bainton, *Erasmus of Christendom*, pp. 185-186; Joseph Lecler,
Toleration and the Reformation, trans. T. L. Westow, 2 vols. (New York: Association
Press, 1960), 1: 126-27; and Craig R. Thompson, *Inquisitio de Fide*, rev. ed. (Hamden,
Connecticut: Archon Books, 1975), pp. 39-48.

ERASMUS AND BODIN 317

toleration. The fewer the articles of faith, the greater latitude there is for religious diversity, and the fewer people there are to be labelled heretics. Not only is Erasmus unwilling to label Luther a heretic, he even intimates that the followers of the heresiarch Arius (died 335) were not heretics.[41]

Limiting fundamentals, however, cannot be equated with full toleration since Christians are still held accountable for essential beliefs. And Erasmus, though he urges the prince to use restraint and choose persuasion over coercion whenever possible, does ultimately permit capital punishment against heretics "in the most necessary cases."[42] The state, Erasmus concedes, can execute heretics who pose a threat to civil order.[43] But Erasmus does not support capital punishment as a common recourse to heresy, since, in practice, he never condones a single heretic's execution.[44]

THE DECORUM OF DIALOGUE

Because of its relationship to dialogue, Erasmus's theory of toleration addresses more than just the question of **what** can be discussed. An important element of Erasmian toleration is also **how** something should be discussed. Erasmus justifies toleration because he believes it will reveal more truth. But as a rhetorician he understands that how a speaker expresses himself is as important as the idea he expresses.[45] It is a fundamental principle of rhetoric that speakers, to be successful, must be mindful of propriety or *decorum*. "I shall begin by approving of one who can observe what is fitting," Cicero writes. "This, indeed, is the form of wisdom that the orator must especially employ—to adapt himself to occasions and persons."[46] Although the principle of *decorum* is common to all types of rhetoric, the rules of *decorum* will vary depending on the type of speech in question. Thus, philosophical dialogue, with its particular characteristics, possesses its own rules of *decorum*, distinct from the three major

41. EE 5:465. 1-468. 155 (Letter to William Warham, 1 June 1524); CWE 9:261. 526-36 (Letter to Jean de Carondelet, 5 January 1523).
42. LB 9:1059E (*Apologia adversus Monachos quosdam Hispanos*, 1528).
43. LB 10:1576B-C (*Epistola contra quosdam qui se falso jactant evangelicos*).
44. Bainton, *Erasmus of Christendom*, p. 257.
45. Cicero, *Orator* 22. 72.
46. *Orator* 35. 123.

genres of public oratory: deliberative, judicial (forensic), and epideictic (demonstrative).

The *decorum* of philosophical dialogue is tolerant in a way that is distinct from the *decorum* of public oratory. Public oratory addresses matters that the public-at-large can understand and decide: political issues (deliberative); the innocence or guilt of the accused (judicial); and a man's personal character (epideictic). As a consequence of public oratory's popular character, rhetoricians have traditionally viewed emotional appeals as a necessary part of its *decorum*.[47] The result of public oratory's emotionalism is that while the audience's decisions are not physically coerced, speech still takes place in an intolerant atmosphere. This intolerance is manifested in the orator's emotional manipulation of the audience. Because public oratory addresses the common people, the classical rhetoricians presume that the orator must compel his audience, emotionally, to arrive at the proper decision. Thus, Quintilian writes: "unless we [orators] force, and occasionally throw them [the audience] off their balance by an appeal to their emotions, we shall be unable to vindicate the claims of truth and justice.[48] By manipulating his audience's emotions, the orator signals his lack of respect for his listeners. They, in his mind, are an unthinking mass that must be moved. Even the good orator (*vir bonus dicendi peritus*) does not acknowledge his listeners' abilities to discover and understand truth and justice. Instead, he assumes that if the claims of truth and justice are to be vindicated, he must maneuver his audience into doing what is right.[49]

The *decorum* of philosophical dialogue, however, is different from public oratory in its lack of emotionalism and attending intolerance. It is possible to avoid emotional appeals in philosophical dialogue because of the nature of the participants. Public oratory, the classical rhetoricians argue, is addressed to large, popular audiences incapable of finding truth for themselves. But philosophical dialogue takes place in the context of a small, elite group, presumed competent to discuss such difficult matters. For Cicero, the masses are antiphilosophical, which absolutely pre-

47. Quintilian 3. 4. 15; Cicero, *Brutus* 80. 279.
48. Quintilian 5. 14. 29.
49. Quintilian 12. 1. 1.

ERASMUS AND BODIN 319

cludes a popular setting for philosophical discussion.[50] In line with Cicero, Erasmus in *Diatriba* designates his audience as the learned elite. The investigation he conducts in *De libero arbitrio*, Erasmus writes, "has always been considered most proper for scholars."[51] The *Diatriba*'s limited audience contrasts with the popular audience of ancient deliberative oratory (the political assembly) and of Erasmus's own version of the deliberative genre (preaching) which was addressed to all classes of society.[52]

Cicero and Erasmus assumed that because philosophical dialogue was limited to a learned elite searching together for truth, *decorum* required that the interlocutors eschew emotional manipulation. Unlike public oratory, which is marked by "extreme energy and passion," and a "vigorous style," Cicero writes that philosophical dialogue should be serene and restrained.[53] And while, for Erasmus, emotional manipulation is sometimes appropriate for public oratory—preaching—it is not suitable for scholarly dialogue: "in the disputing of truth, . . . it is moderation which pleases."[54] Cicero and Erasmus exclude classical rhetoric's two nonrational proofs, *ethos* and *pathos*, from philosophical dialogue.[55] *Ethos*, the appeal to the speaker's authority, is eliminated because relying on someone else's opinion, substitutes blind faith for reason.[56] Likewise, *pathos*, the eliciting of the audience's passions, is rejected in philosophical dialogue because the passions "conflict with deliberation and reason," thereby preventing the interlocutors from arriving at the truth or its closest approxima-

---

50. *Tusculan Disputations* 2. 1. 4. Cf. Plato *Republic* 494a.

51. *Luther and Erasmus: Free Will and Salvation*, p. 36.

52. LB 5:858E-859A, 870D-881C (*Ecclesiastes*). See James Michael Weiss, "*Ecclesiastes* and Erasmus: The Mirror and the Image." *Archiv für Reformationsgeschichte* 65 (1974):100-101; John O'Malley, "Content and Rhetorical Forms in Sixteenth-Century Treatises on Preaching," *Renaissance Eloquence: Studies in the Theory and Practice of Renaissance Rhetoric*, ed. James J. Murphy (Berkeley: University of California Press, 1983), p. 244.

53. *De oratore* 1. 59. 255; *De officiis* 1. 1. 3.

54. *Luther and Erasmus: Free Will and Salvation*, p. 96.

55. Aristotle established, and subsequent rhetoricians have accepted, three modes of persuasion: *ethos, pathos*, and logical proof. Aristotle, *Rhetoric* 1356a 1-4; 1358a 3-13; 1356a 13-19; 1356a 19-21.

56. Cf. Cicero's *De natura deorum* 1. 5. 10 and Erasmus's *Hyperaspistes I*, LB 10:1305F.

tion.[57] To ensure that the interlocutors' emotions are kept in check, Cicero and Erasmus go so far as to control the dialogue's external environment. Thus, the setting for Cicero's dialogues is almost always his gardens and villa, like his villa at Tusculum, a relaxed milieu, distant from the agitation of the city.[58] And Erasmus, in his colloquy *Convivium religiosum*, locates discussion in the garden of a countryside villa, limiting the number of interlocutors to nine, "the number of muses."[59]

By adopting Cicero's *decorum* of dialogue, Erasmus creates an environment for theological debate that is tolerant in more than its absence of persecution. It is possible to refrain from physical abuse and still be intolerant. As I noted above, emotional manipulation does not involve force yet is coercive. Looking solely at the physical side of intolerance ignores the fact that intolerance often has a psychological dimension or sometimes has **only** a psychological dimension to it, as in the example of the Amish, who oppose any external punishment for religious error, but exact psychological payment from dissenting members through the practice of social avoidance or "shunning" (*Meidung*).[60] Erasmus shows concern for psychological intolerance because it is a person's state of mind, not physical condition per se, that affects his ability to discover truth. Therefore, Erasmus maintains, that to arrive at truth, the interlocutors must treat each other respectfully. He describes his disputation with Luther as "temperate . . . for the purpose of eliciting the truth." He writes that he pursues the matter without recrimination, "because in this way the truth, which is often lost amid too much wrangling may be more surely perceived." He uses gentle words in *Diatriba*, "so that truth might

57. *Tusculan Disputations* 5. 15. 43; 4. 28. 61; 4. 21. 47-48.

58. *Academica* 2. 3. 9; *De natura deorum* 1. 6. 15; Michel Ruch, *Le Preamble Dans Les Oeuvres Philosophiques De Ciceron: Essai sur la Genese et l'art du Dialogue* (Paris: Belles Lettres, 1958), pp. 80-82; Introduction to Loeb Classical Library edition of *De finibus*, trans. H. Rackham, p. xvi.

59. See *Colloquies*, p. 49; p. 78; Lawrence V. Ryan, "Erasmis Convivia: The Banquet Colloquies of Erasmus," *Medievalia et Humanistica: Studies in Medieval and Renaissance Culture*, new series 8 (1977): 205; Boyle, *Erasmus on Language and Method in Theology*, p. 139.

60. See John A. Hostetler, *Amish Society* (Baltimore: The Johns Hopkins University Press, 1990), pp. 33-41, 86-89; Donald B. Kraybill, *The Riddle of Amish Culture* (Baltimore: The Johns Hopkins University Press, 1989).

shine forth more unfalteringly." Erasmus denies that he is engaged in gladiatorial combat with Luther. Combat, he explains,
will only obstruct the search for truth.[61] Like Cicero, Erasmus
concludes that truth is furthered by a more harmonious relationship between interlocutors.

Bodin

THE PURPOSE OF DIALOGUE: BODIN'S ALTERNATIVE
    Like Erasmus, the French-born Jean Bodin was trained as a
humanist, although Bodin's humanism had a more practical bent
than Erasmus's. Reflecting the late, particularly French, humanists' interest in academic jurisprudence, Bodin studied law at the
University of Toulouse and composed his magnum opus, the *Six
livres de la république* (1576), as a systematic explanation of French
and universal public law. Bodin was impelled to consider the
question of religious toleration in the *République* because he composed the work during the French Wars of Religion. Between
1562 and 1593, France was torn apart by a series of wars between
the majority Roman Catholics and the minority Calvinists known
as the Huguenots. During this period of religious conflict, which
saw the massacre of over ten thousand Huguenots on St.
Bartholomew's Day 1572, the practice of toleration was rare. In
the *République*, Bodin took a progressive stand on toleration, supporting the *Politiques*, those Catholic moderates in the War that
believed the question of religious toleration should be determined by what best furthered political order. Ideally, the *Politiques*
argued, the state should enforce outward religious uniformity
because confessional differences might lead to civil unrest. But in
states, such as France, where a religious minority has grown too
large to be easily suppressed, toleration should be granted. In his
later work, the *Colloquium heptaplomeres*, Bodin takes a more radical stand in favor of religious toleration, supporting the protection of almost all religious convictions.
    The *Colloquium heptaplomeres* is a series of conversations, di-

---

61. *Luther and Erasmus: Free Will and Salvation*, pp. 36-37; LB 10:1287C
(*Hyperaspistes* I). In contrast to *Diatriba*, Erasmus's stance in *Hyperaspistes*—responding to Luther's combative *De servo arbitrio*—is more contentious. See, for
example, LB 10:1312A; 1364D-E.

vided into six books, between men of seven different religions: Paulus Coronaeus, a Catholic; Fridericus Podamicus, a Lutheran; Antonius Curtius, a Calvinist; Salomon Barcassius, a Jew; Octavius Fagnola, a Moslem; Diegus Toralba, a proponent of natural religion; and Hieronymus Senamus, a skeptic. The participants discuss a wide variety of topics, but the *Colloquium*'s central discussion, which takes place mostly in Book 4, concerns the question of the true religion.

Like Erasmus, Bodin creates a dialogue in which the interlocutors observe the rules of *decorum*. Their conversation is courteous, even affectionate at times. They were united by "innocence and integrity." And "they were not motivated by wrangling or jealousy but by a desire to learn; consequently they were displaying all their reflections and endeavours in true dignity." Again, like Erasmus, who maintained that philosophical and theological debate should be limited to a small educated elite, Bodin portrays the seven interlocutors in the *Colloquium* as "exceptionally well trained in the disciplines of the liberal arts," with "each seem[ing] to surpass the others in his unique knowledge." The dialogue's setting was designed to foster moderate, learned discussion. The group meets in the Venetian home of Coronaeus. Venice, as is noted in the *Colloquium*, offers its people "the greatest freedom and tranquillity of spirit," and Coronaeus's home itself "was considered a shrine of the Muses and virtues." To encourage scholarly conversation, Coronaeus had filled his home "not only with an infinite variety and supply of books and old records, but also instruments either for music or for all sorts of mathematical arts."[62] And to calm the spirits of the interlocutors, Coronaeus arranged for choirboys to sing divine praises at the end of each day's discussion.[63]

Although the *Colloquium* is similar to Erasmus's dialogues in its *decorum*, when judged by the goals of Erasmian dialogue, it is a failure. It is this traditional conception of dialogue that most

---

62. Kuntz, *Colloquium*, pp. 3-5.

63. *Ibid.*, p. 15. See also Marion Leathers Kuntz, "The Home of Coronaeus in Jean Bodin's Colloquium Heptaplomeres: An Example of a Venetian Academy," *Acta Conventus Neo-Latini Bononiensis*, Proceedings of the Fourth International Congress of *Neo*-Latin Studies, Bologna, 26 August to 1 September 1979, pp. 278-79.

ERASMUS AND BODIN 323

scholars implicitly accept when they brand the *Colloquium* a failed dialogue.[64] In Georg Roellenbleck's words, "[t]he *Heptaplomeres* is the protocol of a failure, a failure of dialogue, a failure of rational discussion of religious material."[65] For Erasmus, as for Socrates and Cicero before him, the participants in a dialogue work together to discover the truth. And the closer the participants approach the truth, the more they will agree. But the interlocutors in Bodin's *Colloquium* do not agree. In fact, the dialogue's characters are never able to move any of their fellow speakers from their original beliefs. As Quentin Skinner explains, the participants recognize in their inability to persuade the futility of religious discussion. It is because religious discussion is useless, Skinner argues, that we are told in the dialogue's conclusion that "afterwards they held no other conversation about religions."[66] Similarly, Joseph Lecler writes that the speakers' lack of consensus signals Bodin's belief that "the old policy of colloquies, which had once been advocated by the Christian humanists, had been finally condemned by experience."[67]

Bodin's *Colloquium*, however, is only a failure if we accept the traditional conception of dialogue. Roellenbleck declares the *Colloquium* a failure because he presupposes this conception, even though he concedes that the participants in the dialogue have "learned a lot."[68] This benefit does not count, for Roellenbleck, because "in the end, nothing has changed. . . . Nobody has been convinced or has modified his position." But what if, *pace* Roellenbleck et al., "learning a lot" does matter, learning both about others' beliefs and, through them, about your own? Then the participants lack of unity would not, by itself, indicate a failed dialogue.

---

64. An exception is Marion Leathers Kuntz. Professor Kuntz graciously shared with me her views on the *Colloquium* as anything but a failed dialogue. See expresses some of these ideas in her soon-to-be-published essay "Structure, Form and Meaning in the *Colloquium Heptaplomeres* of Jean Bodin."

65. Georg Roellenbleck, "Les Poèmes Intercalés dans L'Heptaplomeres," *Jean Bodin: Actes du Colloque Interdisciplinaire d'Angers, 24 au 27 Mai 1984*, 2 vols. (Angers: Presses de l'Universite D'Angers, 1985), 2: 448.

66. Kuntz, *Colloquium*, p. 471; Quentin Skinner, *The Foundations of Modern Political Thought*, 2 vols. (Cambridge: Cambridge University Press, 1979), 2: 249.

67. Lecler, *Toleration and the Reformation*, 2: 180.

68. Roellenbleck, "Les Poèmes Intercalés dans L'Heptaplomeres," 2: 448.

The inability of Bodin's interlocutors to agree on religion stems from their differing assumptions. Unlike Erasmus's dialogues on doctrinal adiaphora, the conversations in Bodin's *Colloquium* revolve around the fundamentals of faith and there is no consensus among the interlocutors about the fundamentals. The Jew, the Moslem, and the follower of natural religion reject Christ as Lord. The Christians' proofs derived from New Testament citations are meaningless to them. Yet for Christians, as Coronaeus explains, "If you reject the evangelical testimonies, it is as if you denied the principles of the sciences, without which not even the geometricians will have any proof."[69] Unable to agree on the basic proofs of argument, the interlocutors lack the tools of persuasion. Accordingly, Senamus states: "I think those discussions about religion will come to nothing."[70]

Paradoxically, although Bodin's characters discuss religion, they, like Erasmus, criticize discourse between religions because it may lead to skepticism. In line with Erasmus, they believe that questioning the fundamentals of faith imperils one's soul. And reflecting Bodin's own political ideas, the characters in the *Colloquium* fear the effects of religious skepticism on the state's stability.[71] Thus, Toralba observes that people should keep away from religious discussion lest it cause a believer "to abandon the religion of his ancestor," tearing him away from the faith "which God has bestowed from his bountiful goodness." Salomon declares that "according to our laws and customs we are prohibited from discussing religion . . . lest divine laws seemed to be called into doubt"—doubt that "produces the opinion of impiety." Senamus, citing Siena's ban on "discussions about divine matters and the decrees of the popes," links the prohibition on religious disputes to civil peace. Similarly, Octavius proclaims the danger of religious debate—"dangerous enough in private but even more so in public." According to Octavius, "if it is not permissible to argue about human laws [in the Florentine republic and in ancient Sparta] so that there will be no approach for breaking the

69. Kuntz, *Colloquium*, p. 292.
70. *Ibid.*, p. 170.
71. *Ibid.*, pp. 165-70. Cf. Jean Bodin, *The Six Bookes of a Commonweale*, ed. with Introduction Kenneth Douglas McRae (Cambridge, MA: Harvard University Press, 1962), pp. 535-36.

laws through disputation, how much less should this be done about divine laws." And Curtius states that the ancient prophets thought it laudable to abstain from discussions about one's own religion with outsiders. Therefore, Curtius continues in a relativist fashion, "Christians should not cast doubt on the articles of their own faith, nor should Jews among each other or Mohammedans among each other."

Even Coronaeus, who favors religious dialogue and who, along with Fridericus, implores Salomon to enter the discussion about religion, concedes that he is unwilling to question his own religious doctrines. Religious discussion, for him, is a means to lead non-Christians into the proper pathway. But Coronaeus opposes Christians discussing the tenets of their faith among themselves, for fear that they become "hopelessly entangled by doubtful considerations and involved in various errors."[72] Coronaeus wants others to question their religions, but as for himself, he states: "I shall not allow myself to be carried away by the arguments of any one or to be separated from the accepted religion of the Roman pontiffs."[73] Only the dogmatic Fridericus, so confident that his faith cannot be shaken, unequivocally supports religious dialogue. The rest assert that it is wrong to engage in any activity that casts doubt on their own dogmas.

The speakers find support for their fears in the fact that religion is inherently uncertain. "Religion," Toralba explains, "will be grounded either in knowledge or opinion or faith." Knowledge cannot be the sole basis of religion, since true knowledge requires "proof based upon the surest principles and fortified by necessary conclusions," and the different religions have not provided such proof. We are left, therefore, with opinion and faith, neither of which is certain. "If religion depends on opinion, that ambiguous opinion wavers between truth and falsehood and totters during hostile discussion." And faith, which is "pure assent without proof," can be lost. For if we receive our faith from our trust in another person's word, when "we reject this opinion of his uprightness or erudition, we lose faith."[74] And if faith is

72. Kuntz, *Colloquium*, p. 170.
73. *Ibid.*, p. 205.
74. Cf. Thomas Hobbes, *Leviathan*, ed. C. B. Macpherson (London: Penguin Books, 1968), pp. 132-34; 179-83.

granted by divine infusion, it can, by definition, be lost: any belief that is "inevitable and fixed so that it cannot be lost . . . is force, not faith."[75]

Despite agreeing that religious dialogue is dangerous, the characters of the *Colloquium* still go on to discuss religion; they reject the traditional model of dialogue in which everyone's beliefs are open to scrutiny, but are still willing to present their religious views. The *Colloquium*'s speakers reconcile their criticism of religious discussion with their participation in it by creating a kind of dialogue that does not bring about the skepticism they dread. In contrast to the traditional dialogue, their conversations reinforce their original beliefs. The final words of the *Colloquium* confirm this deepening of opinions. The speakers, the text states, spoke no more about religions, "although each one defended his own religion with the supreme sanctity of his life."[76]

How can a dialogue across religious lines strengthen the believer's faith? Toralba provides the answer. Anticipating an argument made centuries later by John Stuart Mill, he contends that we understand ourselves only by way of contrast with others. Justice, integrity or virtue would not be perceived, "unless wicked men mingled with the good, sane with the mad, brave with the cowardly, rich with the poor, low with the noble. . . . Indeed, these discussions which Coronaeus began would offer no purpose or pleasure unless they took lustre from opposing arguments and reasons."[77] The exercise of defending his religious beliefs against those of the others clarifies each speaker's views to himself. What is initially held as an unreflected prejudice is retained, after discussion, as an intellectually defensible—if not fully demonstrable—opinion.

Instead of giving up on religious discourse, as most commentators contend, Bodin suggests that religious discussion moves the participants to a higher level of understanding. He expresses the dialogue's maturational powers in musical terms. During the

75. Kuntz, *Colloquium*, p. 169. Cf. *The Six Bookes of a Commonweale*, p. 535.
76. *Ibid.*, p. 471.
77. *Ibid.*, p. 148. Cf. John Stuart Mill, *On Liberty*, in *Collected Works of John Stuart Mill*, ed. J. M. Robson, with an Introduction by Alexander Brady, vol 18: *Essays on Politics and Society* (Toronto: University of Toronto Press, 1977), pp. 244-45.

course of the dialogue, the speakers traverse the range of musical *genera*, from the diatonic, which allows only seven tones, to the chromatic, which allows tones and half tones equalling twelve, to the more complex enharmonic *genus*. Coronaeus alludes to this progression in a song, based on Psalm 133, sung at the conclusion of the *Colloquium*: "Lo, how good and pleasing it is for brothers to live in unity, arranged not in common diatonics or chromatics, but in enharmonics with a certain more divine modulation."[78] Like the advancement of musical *genera* in Coronaeus's song, the participants in the *Colloquium* have moved through the dialogue to a higher level. Because enharmonics is the more refined and arcane *genus*, it represents, for Bodin, greater understanding. As Nicolo Vicentino argues in his *L'antica musica ridotta alla moderna prattica* (1555), enharmonics is reserved "for the few—for people with cultivated taste, not for the common folk."[79] And Bodin, influenced by "the Hermetic belief that the deepest truths cannot be revealed to the multitude," equates the esoteric with the deeper truth.[80] It is because the speakers in the *Colloquium* have reached a higher level, that they hold no further conversations about religion.[81] They have achieved their goal.

Although Bodin values dialogue for elucidating a speaker's opinion to himself, this benefit alone is insufficient to justify toleration. St. Thomas Aquinas, for example, allowed that heresy played a positive role in the search for truth since it permitted the faithful to contrast truth with error. Nevertheless, St. Thomas supported the death penalty for heretics. To Aquinas, their error was not essential to the discovery of truth.[82] Why, then, does

---

78. *Ibid.*, p. 471. The general argument that the movement in song suggests a higher understanding is made by Kuntz in "Structure, Form and Meaning in the *Colloquium Heptaplomeres*," pp. 26-27. On the ancient Greek understanding of enharmonic music, see *Ancient and Oriental Music*, ed. Egon Wellesz, *New Oxford History of Music*, vol. 1 (New York: Oxford University Press, 1957): 387-90.

79. Edward E. Lowinsky, *Secret Chromatic Art in the Netherlands Motet*, trans. Carl Buchman (New York: Russell and Russell, 1946), p. 90.

80. Frances E. Yates, "The Hermetic Tradition in Renaissance Science," in *Art, Science, and History in the Renaissance*, ed. Charles S. Singleton (Baltimore: The Johns Hopkins Press, 1967), p. 264. On Bodin's ties to Hermeticism and other mystical traditions, see Kuntz, *Colloquium*, pp. liv-lvi.

81. See Kuntz, "Structure, Form and Meaning in the *Colloquium Heptaplomeres*," p. 28.

82. St. Thomas Aquinas, *Summa theologiae*, 2, 2, q. 11, art. 3.

Bodin grant his characters the opportunity to promote their religions, when none of his contemporaries do so? Even Erasmus,
who supported limited toleration, does not grant equal status to
heretics and non-Christians, because he believes their errors to be
damnable. The key to Bodin's exceptionalism is his conception of
religious truth.

THE NATURE OF TRUTH

Bodin sees religious truth as a complex whole—what Marion
Daniels Kuntz refers to as "a unity based on multiplicity (*concordia
discors*)"[83]—with each religion forming a part of the greater whole.
Bodin, however, does not view these elements as thoroughly
consistent with each other, but as subsisting in a state of tension.
Taken together, the different religions express the unity of truth,
yet each particular religion conflicts with the others. Once again,
Bodin relies on a musical metaphor to convey his idea. In a
conversation about harmonic theory that he initiates, Coronaeus
opines that the sweetest harmony is achieved "with the full system of the highest tone blended with the lowest, with the fourth
and fifth interspersed." In contrast, "harmonies in unison, in
which no tone is opposite, are not pleasing to the trained ear."[84]
This idea that harmony or truth inheres in different opposing
elements is voiced by other speakers. Toralba observes that what
is most pleasing to the senses is "a harmony which depends on
the blended union of opposites."[85] And Curtius recites a poem
praising God for His universe based on opposites: "This greatest
harmony of the universe though discordant contains our safety."[86]

Nature's blending of opposites does not destroy the individual components. The elements retain their separate identities.
The opposing elements of nature, Toralba explains, are forms,
like the contrary forms of fire and water. And "things which are
contrary to each other in nature herself cannot be mingled by

83. Marion Daniels Kuntz, "Harmony and the Heptaplomeres of Jean Bodin,"
Journal of the History of Philosophy 12 (1974): 35-36.
84. Kuntz, *Colloquium*, p. 144. See also "Harmony and the Heptaplomeres of
Jean Bodin," pp. 35-36; "The Home of Coronaeus in Jean Bodin's *Colloquium
Heptaplomeres*," pp. 279-80.
85. Kuntz, *Colloquium*, p. 145.
86. *Ibid.*, p. 147.

design, but only blended, joined, or united so that they seem to be one."[87] Like nature, religious truth is also composed of distinct elements whose differences cannot be ignored. Although tolerant of different religions, Octavius still declares: "Truly we ought to despise the blending of sacred rites."[88] We cannot treat opposing religions as if they are the same. Similarly, Salomon rebukes Senamus, who adopts the practices of all religions: "I would prefer that you were hot or cold rather than lukewarm in religion, Senamus. And yet, how is it possible to defend the religions of all at the same time."[89] Salomon's fellow participants follow his advice, remaining steadfast in their convictions. Each person believes that by doing so he protects the purity of his faith, which alone reveals the full truth. Bodin, however, does not identify with any single religion. He recognizes the divine descent of all religious beliefs.[90] Thus for him, religious differences should not be retained for the sake of any single religion, but because they, collectively in their opposition to each other, contain the whole truth. The variety of religions mirrors the contrariety of the universe. In Curtius's words, it is "the variant natures of individual things [that] combine for the harmony of one universe."[91]

Bodin emphasizes that the opposition of individual elements must be kept within limits, that the contrariety of extremes must be curbed. The participants in the *Colloquium* point to intervening elements as a moderating force. In music, "extreme opposites are brought together by intermingling of the middle tones (Fridericus)." In nature, opposites are "united by the interpolation of certain middle links." These links "present a remarkable harmony of the whole which would otherwise perish completely if this whole world were fire or moisture (Toralba)." And among philosophic schools, the opposite camps of Epicureans and Stoics were joined, as if by certain bonds, midway by the Academicians and Peripatetics (Toralba)." Such intermediate schools were necessary, for "if one opposite were joined to another opposite with no middle ground between, there would necessarily be continual

87. *Ibid.*, p. 146.
88. *Ibid.*, p. 157.
89. *Ibid.*, p. 465.
90. *Ibid.*, pp. xli-xlii.
91. *Ibid.*, p. 149.

battle." It is also safer when a political office is divided between three persons instead of two. "For a third party forces two opposing factions toward harmony, when the others have allied themselves (Coronaeus)." Finally, a state split into two factions, divided about laws, honors, or religion, is bound to destroy itself. "If, however, there are many factions, there is no danger of civil war, since the groups, each acting as a check on the other, protect the stability and harmony of the state (Curtius)."[92]

To moderate conflict, Bodin does not construct the *Colloquium* as a bipolar dialogue between extremes. Instead, he includes in the *Colloquium* a spectrum of religious opinions. The opposition between the three Christians, who believe in divine revelation and in Christ as the son of God, and the natural philosopher and skeptic, who deny or question these beliefs, is mediated by the Jew and the Moslem, who believe in divine revelation, but deny Christ's divinity. Bodin also curbs the opposition between speakers by following the rhetorical rules of *decorum*. As noted earlier, the *decorum* of the *Colloquium* resembles the *decorum* of Erasmus's dialogues. Unlike Erasmus, however, Bodin does not follow these rules for the purpose of finding the one truth. For Bodin, the rules of *decorum* represent the unity of the parts within the whole. Like the opposing elements of nature, the interlocutors in the *Colloquium* are part of a common universe and conflicts between them must be restrained. Despite their differences, they are described at the end of the dialogue as brothers living in unity.[93]

Consistent with the view that each religion possesses some aspect of truth, all the participants call for toleration. Coronaeus assures his guests "the greatest freedom in speaking about religion."[94] For Toralba, "the law of nature and natural religion which has been implanted in men's souls is sufficient for attaining salvation."[95] Presumably, therefore, all religions that adhere to the natural law should be tolerated. Curtius, as already seen, argues that many sects can live together more peacefully than two. He also cites the Church Fathers and the Church Councils as sup-

92. *Ibid.*, pp. 146-51.
93. "Lo, how good and pleasing it is for brothers to live in unity" (*Ibid.*, p. 471).
94. *Ibid.*, pp. 165-66.
95. *Ibid.*, p. 186.

ERASMUS AND BODIN 331

porting the principle of toleration: "'It is not for religion to compel, which ought to be undertaken of one's own accord, not by force.'"[96] Senamus holds up the example of Jerusalem, where eight Christian sects, Jews, and Moslems coexisted, each group tolerating the rest.[97] Likewise, Octavius applauds the tolerance of the kings of the Turks and Persians and the religious freedom of Venice.[98] And Salomon affirms that no "more serious insult against God can be conceived than to wish to force anyone to obey Him." Because religion should not be coerced, he explains, Jews do not force their religion on gentiles—although Salomon is unwilling to tolerate Jewish apostates.[99] By the conclusion, even Fridercus, the most dogmatic of the interlocutors, agrees that faith cannot be compelled. The Emperor Theodoric's opinion, he states, "is worthy to be inscribed in golden letters on the door posts of princes. . ., that we are unable to command religion because no one can be forced to believe against his will."[100]

THE ARGUMENT FROM CONSCIENCE

I have until now discussed what I see as Bodin's primary argument for religious toleration: that each religion represented in the *Colloquium* should be tolerated because it is a part of the truth. Bodin, however, offers another, seemingly more modern justification for toleration that does not depend on a religion's veracity: the argument from conscience. According to this argument, any person that is genuine in his beliefs, even if wrong, will be saved. Octavius, the most consistent defender of conscience in the *Colloquium*, includes sincere idolaters and polytheists among the saved, despite his strict monotheism, because "with pure heart and soul and an upright conscience, they were thus instructed and trained by the priests and thus worship the divinity that was known to them and related to them." Octavius finds support from the other non-Christian interlocutors. Salomon, who

96. *Ibid.*, p. 468. See also *ibid.*, pp. 469-71.
97. *Ibid.*, pp. 465-66.
98. *Ibid.*, pp. 151, 467. Octavius, however, also praises the Persians and Turks for forbidding discussions about religion because they lead to civil unrest (p. 167). The key for Octavius is that religious discussion must not degenerate into violence.
99. *Ibid.*, pp. 468-69.
100. *Ibid.*, p. 471.

like Octavius is repelled by the Christian doctrine of the Incarnation, concedes that "even worship which is offered in good faith to a clay god is not unpleasing to eternal God."[101] And Toralba and Senamus, agree that "a just error is erased by a just excuse" and that all religions practiced "not with faked pretense but a pure mind" are "not unpleasing to eternal God."[102] The Christian, particularly the Protestant, interlocutors, however, have less regard for the sincere conscience. While Octavius cites both St. Thomas Aquinas and St. Augustine as respecting the erroneous conscience,[103] the Protestant participants—like the Catholic Aquinas—do not believe that heretics are capable of sincere error. Fridericus denies that there can be a just error for impiety. And Curtius does not excuse ignorance of divine law because it "has been manifested so often and so long throughout the world." They assume that once someone is shown the truth, then any departures from it must be willful and perverse.[104]

Although the arguments on behalf of the erring conscience focus on the otherworldly question of salvation, they have temporal implications. The argument from conscience undermines the orthodox Christian justification of religious persecution, which states that the heterodox must be punished for their damnable errors. First, some theologians, like St. Augustine, argued that heretics should be punished for their own good, hoping that punishment would help them question their errors and put them on the road to salvation.[105] Second, other theologians, like St. Thomas Aquinas, justified persecution because of the enormity of the heretic's crime. Heretics were viewed as an insidious, corrupting force within the body of the faithful.[106] Despite their

---

101. *Ibid*, p. 241. See also *Ibid.*, p. 243.

102. *Ibid.*, pp. 243, 251.

103. *Ibid.*, pp. 157-58.

104. Kuntz, *Colloquium*, p. 163; Lecler, *Toleration and the Reformation*, 2: 180-181. St. Thomas Aquinas did not consider that heretics may honestly be mistaken; to him the heretic always chose to disbelieve. See *Summa theologiae* 2, 2, q. 11, a. 1.

105. See St. Augustine, *Letters*, vol. 4, *The Fathers of the Church: A New Translation*, trans. Sister Wilfrid Parsons (New York: Fathers of the Church, Inc., 1955), pp. 161-62; Herbert Deane, *The Political and Social Ideas of St. Augustine* (New York: Columbia University Press, 1963), pp. 204, 217, 197.

106. *Summa theologiae*, 2, 2, q. 11, a. 3.

ERASMUS AND BODIN 333

differences, both arguments presume that a belief in orthodox doctrines is necessary for salvation. Bodin's argument from conscience, however, denies this assumption. And once this assumption is denied, both justifications of persecution are weakened, if not overturned. The argument that a heretic must be persecuted for his own good no longer makes sense if he can gain salvation, in spite of his objective errors. Similarly, once it becomes possible to respect sincere error, even on the fundamentals of faith, it becomes difficult to accept the image of the heretic as the ultimate malefactor, who must be eradicated for his crimes.

If Bodin tolerates not only the seven religions of the *Colloquium*, but any sincere faith, does he tolerate all religious opinions? The answer is yes, with one exception—atheism. For Bodin, atheists are a threat to society. Thus Coronaeus restates in the *Colloquium* what Bodin himself argues in the *République*. Believers in any religion, no matter how superstitious, are "kept by this awe of the divine in a certain way within the bounds of duty and of the laws of nature. The atheist, on the other hand, who fears nothing except a witness or a judge, necessarily rushes headlong toward every crime."[107] This assumption that atheists are a danger to social order was unquestioned during Bodin's time. Even a century later, John Locke argues, in his *Letter Concerning Toleration*, that atheists are not to be tolerated, since "[p]romises, covenants, and oaths, which are the bonds of human society," can have no hold over them.[108]

Bodin's unwillingness to tolerate atheists is based on more than his political concerns. It fits with his general defense of religious toleration. Bodin's defense is premised, first, on the idea that each religion possesses some element of truth. Bodin, however, dismisses the possibility that atheism has any truth. Judging atheism by the standard of consensus, which has been used as a criterion of truth since the ancient Greeks,[109] Bodin finds that all

107. Kuntz, *Colloquium*, p. 239. Cf. *The Six Bookes of a Commonweale*, pp. 539-40.

108. John Montuori, *John Locke on Toleration and the Unity of God* (Amsterdam: J. G. Gieben, 1983), p. 93.

109. Klaus Oehler, "Der Consensus omnium als Kriterium der Wahrheit in der antiken Philosophie und der Patristik," *Antike und Abendland* 10 (1961): 103-129.

people agree that there is a God. Belief in God, Toralba says, "seems to have been planted, as it were, by nature herself in the hearts and minds of all men."[110] And while Senamus notes that many recognize other divinities besides God, he states that "[a]ll men recognize that God is the Parent of all gods, as far as I know."[111] Rejecting atheism as an objective possibility, Bodin also denies the atheist's subjective claims to conscience, thereby negating the second justification of toleration. Like Aquinas, who assumes that all heretics are maliciously motivated, Bodin assumes that no atheist is truly sincere. Whatever religious doubts people entertain can never genuinely extend to the existence of the Deity. To emphasize this point, Bodin has the skeptic, Senamus, equate atheism with deceit. There are four groups of atheists, according to Senamus, which range from those who dissemble for self-interest to those who avow their atheism, publicly and privately mocking at everyone's religion.[112] Senamus supposes that all four types of atheists have bad intentions. And therefore, these persons who act out of bad conscience cannot assert a liberty based on a right to conscience.

Conclusion

I have presented in this article two different models of dialogue and the theories of toleration derived from them. The first kind of dialogue, exemplified by Erasmus's *De libero arbitrio*, aims at a common discovery of the truth or the closest approximation of it. In this type of dialogue, the speakers may have tentatively arrived at their own points of view, but because they are still searching for the truth, they adopt a skeptical stance toward the issue under discussion. They also treat each other and each other's opinions respectfully, not only because it is wrong to persecute another when you yourself are uncertain of the truth, but because civility promotes the discovery of truth. The theory of toleration implicit in this type of dialogue is nothing short of an early version of the argument from truth, that is, the argument that free speech should be safeguarded because it leads to the discovery of

110. Kuntz, *Colloquium*, p. 325.
111. *Ibid.*, p. 465.
112. *Ibid.*, pp. 236-37.

truth. Of course, Erasmus does not apply this full toleration to all religious opinions—only the nonessentials; and he does not grant this freedom of discussion to all individuals—only the learned elite. Nevertheless, Erasmus establishes a theory of toleration that will eventually be expanded beyond these limitations.

The second type of dialogue is represented by Bodin's *Colloquium heptaplomeres*. In contrast to the interlocutors in Erasmus's dialogue, the participants in the *Colloquium* do not want to reconsider their own opinions. Indeed, they must overcome their fears that a dialogue about religion may lead them to skepticism. What Bodin's interlocutors want from a dialogue, and what they get in the end, is a confirmation of their beliefs. By defending their beliefs against the criticisms of others, the *Colloquium*'s speakers emerge from the dialogue with a fuller understanding of and faith in their respective religions. Bodin allows each speaker to retain his initial beliefs because, for Bodin, each speaker represents a part of the truth. And to achieve the full religious truth, the multiplicity of religions must be presented. As the characters in the *Colloquium* explain, truth is a complex whole composed of contradictory elements. Bodin supports toleration because he believes that no one religion has a monopoly on the truth. In addition, Bodin offers the argument from conscience as another justification of toleration. He contends that sincere worship, even of false gods, should be protected. The true God, the *Colloquium*'s characters say, accepts heartfelt, albeit mistaken, worship. Only atheists are denied their right to conscience. Like his contemporaries, Bodin assumes that atheists are threats to their society, and he denies that they can ever be sincere in their convictions.

Finally, I suggested in the Introduction that one practical difference between the two types of dialogue is that Erasmus's is more restrictive than Bodin's. Implicit in Erasmus's dialogue is a monistic conception of the truth that excludes from discussion ideas that contradict accepted truths. In contrast, Bodin's dialogue accepts a multiplicity of truths and can, therefore, permit discussion of ideas that contradict what is already "known" to be true. This difference between the two types of dialogue, however, only affects the question of what should or should not be legally tolerated. But the difference between these two types of dialogue concerns another practical implication more subtle than that of

legal toleration. It raises the question of whether, in tolerant
societies, dialogues between fundamentally divergent persons or
groups are beneficial. For it is possible to accept the Erasmian
conception of dialogue—that the purpose of discussion is to work
together to find the truth—and to still call for full toleration, if one
accepts a number of nontruth-related rationales for toleration and
freedom of speech, like the arguments that freedom of speech
promotes dissent,[113] self-fulfillment,[114] and that censorship im-
pairs the dignity and equality of the silenced speaker.[115] The
willingness to tolerate diverse opinions, however, does not mean
that controversial dialogue in a pluralistic society should be valued as a normative good. From the Erasmian perspective, only
dialogues that move the interlocutors toward agreement are useful. Thus, academic, political, or religious discussions in which
the participants seek the most plausible theory, a common answer, or some compromise is legitimate. But if agreement is the
goal, a dialogue between persons holding fundamentally different opinions will be futile. To take an example from our own
society, if we accept Erasmus's point of view, a dialogue between
supporters and opponents of abortion rights, euthanasia, or any
other debate whose basic assumptions are irreconcilable, would
be senseless. Bodin's *Colloquium* suggests, however, that such
dialogues may be beneficial. Conversation, even with an inflex-
ible "other" offers the speakers the advantages of both self-dis-
covery and of possibly learning another aspect of a greater, more
complex truth.

113. Steven H. Shiffrin, *The First Amendment, Democracy, and Romance* (Cambridge, MA: Harvard University Press, 1990).

114. Thomas Emerson, *The System of Freedom of Expression* (New York: Random House, 1970); Edwin E. Baker, *Human Liberty and Freedom of Speech* (New
York: Oxford University Press, 1989).

115. Dworkin, *A Matter of Principle* (Cambridge, MA: Harvard University
Press, 1985), p. 386.

Part V
Natural Philosophy and Method

[17]

Humanist Methods in Natural Philosophy: the Commonplace Book

Ann Blair

As new evidence for the interaction between humanism and science in the Renaissance I will trace the use among natural philosophical authors of a quintessentially humanist method of reading and storing information—through the commonplace book. In this method of reading (which I will call the method of commonplaces) one selects passages of interest for the rhetorical turns of phrase, the dialectical arguments, or the factual information they contain; one then copies them out in a notebook, the commonplace book, kept handy for the purpose, grouping them under appropriate headings to facilitate later retrieval and use, notably in composing prose of one's own. Strictly defined the commonplace book is a humanist innovation, but like most Renaissance practices it adapted a concept with a glorious ancient pedigree to suit contemporary, in this case pedagogical, needs. Ancient rhetoric, from Aristotle's *Topics* to Quintilian's *Institutio oratoria*, had developed a list of the places or *loci* of use to the orator: including "seats of arguments" (from effects, from circumstances, from greater or lesser, for example) and rhetorical embellishments (amplification, *captatio benevolentiae*, and so on). In the Middle Ages florilegia and sermon manuals supplemented those theoretical guides to good arguing with substantive material which could be copied directly: moral sentences or in the case of medical handbooks, "commonplace" medical recipes, compiled for easy access.[1]

In the Renaissance the notion of "place" continued to expand, as pupils throughout Europe were taught to keep their own commonplace books while in school and afterwards through a lifetime of reading. Guarino da Verona, Erasmus, and Vives among other pedagogues wrote specific instructions for keeping such notebooks. Alongside memorable rhetorical idioms the commonplace book was to record, often in a separate

---

[1] Sister Joan Marie Lechner, *Renaissance Concepts of the Commonplaces* (New York, 1962), 62, on medical compilations.

notebook, a wide range of *realia* or interesting bits of general information
sorted under appropriate subject headings according to the topics and
themes addressed.[2] Travellers in particular were admonished to keep notebooks of this kind to record all the things that they encountered.[3] The
commonplace book thus encompassed all the aspects of *inventio,* or the
gathering of material for an argument, and became the crucial tool for
storing and retrieving the increasingly unwieldy quantity of textual and
personal knowledge that guaranteed copiousness in speech and writing.
The commonplace book thus spread as widely in Renaissance Europe as
the Erasmian ideal of eloquence through *copia rerum* or abundance of
material.[4] Historians of literature have indeed amply shown how minor
and major literary figures, most notably Shakespeare and Montaigne,
relied for their writing on commonplace books, both on personal notebooks and on the printed cribs designed to supplement (or in the case of
the lazy writer, to replace) them.[5]

What is less well known and what I will argue here is that natural
philosophical writers in the sixteenth and early seventeenth centuries
relied equally heavily on books of commonplaces, specifically natural
commonplaces. My main example will be a little-known encyclopedia of
natural philosophy, the *Universae naturae theatrum (Theater of all nature)*
first published in 1596 by the French political philosopher Jean Bodin.[6]
Bodin is primarily known for his theory of sovereignty expounded in his
Six livres de la république (1576), for his rabid manual of witchhunting
or *Démonomanie* (1580), and for his elusive position on religious toleration
associated with a work left in manuscript, the *Colloquium heptaplomeres.*[7]

[2] Zachary Schiffman, "Montaigne and the Rise of Skepticism in Early Modern Europe:
A Reappraisal," *JHI,* 45 (1984), 504-5.

[3] See for example J. H. Alsted: "Qui peregrinatur, conficiet sibi adversaria, in quibus
obvia via quaeque consignabit. Domum reversus singula rediget in certum ordinem. Qui
certo in loco commoratur, sequentes monitiones notabit." *Orator* (Herborn, 1616), 302-3.

[4] Terence Cave, *The Cornucopian Text: Problems of Writing in the French Renaissance*
(Oxford, 1979), section I, ch. 1.

[5] See for example T. W. Baldwin, *William Shakspere's Small Latine and Lesse Greeke,*
2 vols. (Urbana, 1944). On Montaigne, see Francis Goyet, "A propos de 'ces pastissages
de lieux communs' (le rôle des notes de lecture dans la genèse des *Essais*)," *Bulletin de la
Société des Amis de Montaigne,* 5-6 (1986), 11-26, and 7-8 (1987), 9-30. I am grateful to
Francis Goyet for useful conversations about commonplaces in the Renaissance, on which
he is preparing a French *thèse d'état.* One example of a printed commonplace book
is Theodor Zwinger's *Theatrum vitae humanae* (1565), on which see Walter J. Ong,
"Commonplace Rhapsody: Ravisius Textor, Zwinger and Shakespeare," in R. R. Bolgar
(ed.), *Classical Influences on European Culture 1500-1700* (Cambridge, 1976), 91-126.

[6] There is unfortunately no complete intellectual biography of Jean Bodin since René
Chauviré, *Jean Bodin, auteur de la République* (La Flèche, 1914); for a recent study of
his later thought see Paul Lawrence Rose, *Bodin and the Great God of Nature* (Geneva,
1980).

[7] These texts are easily available: *Six Livres de la République* (Lyon, 1593) reprinted
(Paris, 1986); *De la Démonomanie des sorciers* (Paris, 1587) in facsimile (Paris, 1984);

But Jean Bodin was also a humanist, author of a Latin translation with commentary of Oppian's *Cynegetica* (On the hunt, 1555), and of a *Method for the easy comprehension of history* (or *Methodus*, 1566).[8] Finally, he was a natural philosopher: the *Theatrum* is a 633-page work of physics (in Bodin's own words) which discusses the natural world from its first principles through the stages of the chain of being—rocks and metals, plants and animals, souls, angels and heavenly bodies.[9] The *Theatrum* appeared soon after its publication on the reading lists of university professors of natural philosophy in the German-language area, which is sufficient evidence that, although today we consider Jean Bodin almost exclusively for his political philosophy, his *Theatrum* was read and perceived by contemporaries as a significant contribution to natural philosophy. In tracing how Bodin used his sources and how his work was used in turn by its readers we can follow traditional natural philosophy in the making through a seemingly unending cycle of textual selection and assessment which the method of commonplaces can usefully illuminate.

The evidence for Bodin's use of a book of natural commonplaces in composing the *Theatrum* is only indirect: Bodin provides almost no discussion of his methods in the *Theatrum*; furthermore no autograph manuscripts survive.[10] We cannot know, therefore, exactly what form Bodin's notebook might have taken: how many entries, of what type, accumulated over how many years and so on. Bodin's use of such a notebook seems quite probable, however, not only because the method was widely taught in Renaissance schools but also because Bodin seems to have followed his own precepts enounced in the *Methodus* of 1566. In chapter 3 entitled "how properly to establish the places of histories" Bodin explains:

The abundance and variety of histories is so great that they cannot be clearly understood nor retained in the memory for long unless they are distributed into certain established categories. . . . So for that reason I think we must follow this order in providing an account of all places in three books: in the first of human matters; in the second of the natural events that happen often in history; in the third of divine things.

Colloque entre sept sçavans. . . , ed. François Berriot (Geneva, 1984) and *Colloquium of the Seven. . .* , tr. Marion L. Kuntz (Princeton, 1975).

[8] See Bodin, *Cynegetica* (Paris, 1555); *Methodus ad facilem historiarum cognitionem*, ed. and tr. Pierre Mesnard in *Oeuvres philosophiques de Jean Bodin* (Paris, 1951), English translation by Beatrice Reynolds (New York, 1945). Unless otherwise specified all translations are my own.

[9] For a study of this work see Ann Blair, "Restaging Jean Bodin: the *Universae naturae theatrum* in its Cultural Context" (Ph.D. dissertation Princeton University 1990 and forthcoming Princeton University Press).

[10] For a bibliography of Bodin's extant writings see Roland Crahay, Marie-Thérèse Isaac and Marie-Thérèse Lenger, *Bibliographie critique des éditions anciennes de Jean Bodin* (forthcoming).

Bodin goes on to describe these commonplace books in more detail, in particular:

The second book will embrace with the appropriate divisions the histories of the natural things which occur most often in reading historians: first on the principles of nature, on time and place, birth and death, and motion and change more generally; on the elements and their nature; on imperfect bodies, metals and stones; on the genus of plants, on animals divided into three orders, on the celestial bodies, on the shape and size of the world.[11]

That is, at an interval of thirty years, an excellent description of the *Theatrum*.

Like a commonplace book, the *Theatrum* is an aid to the memory: its title evokes contemporary memory theaters, and Bodin's *Theatrum* can be interpreted as a bookish contribution to that tradition[12] Bodin explicitly adopts the form of a dialogue between master and pupil "because nothing is more efficacious for the memory."[13] Secondly, like the commonplace book that Bodin describes, the *Theatrum* is about the natural things "that happen fairly often in history" or "that occur fairly often in reading historians."[14] Bodin's purpose is to make natural philosophy out of natural history by offering new causal explanations for a myriad natural "facts" culled from his reading. Why is the goat dumbfounded by eating an eryngius plant? (294) Why is a smaller seed more potent than a larger one? (276) The facts embedded in these questions appear in the natural histories of Pliny and Theophrastus respectively[15] evidently for Bodin they are already so well established by virtue of their being asserted there that they do not need to be stated in the *Theatrum* before they are explained. The goat is dumbfounded by the eryngius plant because of a natural antipathy, and smaller seeds are more potent than larger ones not, as Theophrastus claimed, because they are formed more rapidly but because their virtue is more concentrated. The *explananda* have become "commonplaces" in the technical as well as the colloquial sense: in being selected from their original source and entered into the commonplace book they have become self-evident truths. Bodin's task then is to create natural philosophical knowledge by providing causal understanding of these undisputed facts.

[11] Jean Bodin, *Methodus*, in Pierre Mesnard, *Oeuvres philosophiques*, 119, 122.

[12] See Frances Yates, *The Art of Memory* (Chicago, 1966).

[13] Jean Bodin, *Universae naturae theatrum*, 2nd ed. (Frankfurt, 1597), 7. All further references to this work will be given in parentheses in the text.

[14] History and the accounts of historians seem here to be interchangeable for Bodin, in a kind of conflation which is analogous to his confusion of nature and natural philosophy in the prefatory praise of the *Theatrum*. I argue that this slippage reveals Bodin's assumption that the textual representation of nature, or history, is transparent.

[15] Pliny, *Natural history*, VIII, ch. 50, also Plutarch, *Moralia*, "De sera numinis vindicta," 558E; Theophrastus, *De causis plantarum*, II, ch. 17.

Bodin uses the commonplace book as an arsenal of "factoids," tidbits of knowledge which he divorces from their original context in order to suit his own purposes. In his lifetime Bodin was reputed for the abundance of beautiful things (*pulcherrimarum rerum copia*) that he could command in conversation;[16] his writings also display the range and depth of his notebooks. In the *Theatrum* Bodin draws on his wide reading which is perhaps not as wide, however, as the 250 authors whom he cites by name would suggest: many of these citations were no doubt culled from an intermediate source which became invisible when they passed through the commonplace book, as I am able to demonstrate in a few cases.[17] Bodin also includes direct personal experience; for example, an observation from his daily life as a student in Toulouse that salt water fish are larger and have more taste than fresh water fish, a fact that he uses to show that salt water is purer than fresh water (333), or an observation that required motivated investigation, of a 20-cubit crocodile, which he contrasts with the no doubt bookish fact that terrestrial crocodiles do not exceed three cubits, this time to show the greater fertility of water over air (394). Bodin gathers information from acquaintances like one "Alacris" of Clermont who showed him wood that had petrified while floating in a certain fountain in the center of France (228) and, in a uniquely Renaissance fashion, from consulting with practitioners of various manual professions (see for example the description of the sauna below). The commonplace book thus accumulates "facts" from an indefinitely large and disparate range of sources and treats each fact, whether traditional or of recent origin, bookish or directly observed, as equivalent to every other. Bodin specifies cases of personal experience but not in order to stress the greater validity of directly observed over bookish knowledge[18] rather Bodin consistently mentions those sources, including bookish ones, which fall outside the ordinary canon of classical texts and with which his reader would probably not be familiar.

The flexibility of the dialogue form allows the *Theatrum* to follow the structure of the commonplace book and to combine the two conflicting organizational principles of topic and theme. The headings in the com-

---

[16] See the comment by de Thou as quoted in Pierre Bayle, *Dictionnaire historique et critique*, "Bodin," note (E), also reprinted in Pierre Mesnard, *Oeuvres philosophiques*, xxvii.

[17] For example a list of Thomist doctors cited on the question of the location of angels ("Durandus et Bernardus de Guagnaco in impugnationibus, Henr. quolib. 2., Thomas Anglicus in quolib., Henr. [sic for Herv.] Brito in 2. sentent., Ioan. Paris. in Correctorio" *Theatrum*, 514) is lifted from Pico della Mirandola, *Apologia* in *Opera omnia* (Basel, 1567), I, 128-29. I am grateful to Jean Céard for help in tracking down this source.

[18] This attitude contrasts with that of the early experimenters who boasted of their superior reliability and of that of their witnesses; cf. Peter Dear, "*Totius in verba*: the Rhetorical Constitution of Authority in the Early Royal Society," *Isis*, 76 (1985), 145-61; or Steven Shapin and Simon Schaffer, *Leviathan and the Air-Pump: Hobbes, Boyle and the Experimental Life* (Princeton, 1985).

monplace book can vary indefinitely and arbitrarily: those which Bodin suggested in the *Methodus* were primarily topical (elements, plants, animals, and so on), and in broad outline the *Theatrum* follows the topics and order specified there, ascending the chain of being step by step. But the way in which Bodin brings together topically unrelated material in adjacent questions or within the answer to one question suggests that he also used thematic headings, a practice that was commonly advocated, along with cross-references or multiple entries of the same material under different headings. Bodin can thus gather entries under a thematic heading to pursue a general pattern of nature; for example, when he sets out to explain why the heat of the summer is greater in areas on either side of the tropics than in the tropics themselves, although the rays of the sun are more oblique there. He first establishes the fact by citing cases reported in two works of recent history of the spontaneous combustion of the northern countryside under the summer heat.[19] He then explains that the summer air in Northern regions like Muscovy is dense with humidity and thus hotter than the drier air in Southern climes. Bodin corroborates this conclusion with the common observation that fire burns hotter in wood than in straw and in metal than in wood, and he further illustrates his point by describing the practice of the sauna:

Those who want to heat baths rapidly at moderate expense pour water on the stones at the bottom of the bath which have been heated by fire: in a moment the closed room fills with the densest vapor, from which a violent heat is spread in the thick air: from which it is clear that the thickness of the air, excited by the vapor of the water, keeps the heat, while earlier it could not because of its fineness. (212)

Bodin never actually states the principle that denser things hold heat better than finer ones, but he amasses an original array of material on that theme and lays the foundation for a general "law" of nature, which he nonetheless never makes explicit.[20]

The *Theatrum* moves seamlessly from one topic to the next through the intermediary of themes or less substantive rhetorical devices, pursuing each topic or theme until the *copia* on that issue is exhausted. In Bodin's *République* and *Methodus* one can also detect the legacy of a commonplace book in the material that Bodin has gathered, but there he marshals his

---

[19] Bodin cites his sources here again because they are not well known: "Thomas Cromer in historia Polonica lib. 17; Sigismundus libr. in historia Moschovitarum." He is referring, with a number of minor errors, to Martin Cromer, *Polonia sive de origine et rebus gestis Polonorum libri XXX* (Cologne, 1589), XXVIII, 412; and Sigismund of Herberstein, *Rerum Moscovitarum commentarij* (Basel, 1556), 61.

[20] Bodin's reluctance to generalize to a "law of nature" as we might expect him to here and his unwillingness to dismiss reported facts as impossible because in violation of such laws (as we would be tempted to in many cases that he accepts) probably result in part from his strict adherence to the principle of divine omnipotence.

copia in support of a few general arguments or themes born no doubt from his professional experience and lifelong reflection on questions of government and human history. In natural philosophy, where Bodin has less personal expertise, the shape of the original note-taking is more apparent in the final product: Bodin provides little overarching framework in which to relate his causal explanations one to the other. As a result he does not always confront his topical material thematically: contradictory explanations thus coexist in different parts of the work, as a few attentive contemporary readers pointed out. On page 284, for example, Bodin explains that grafted trees yield more and sweeter fruit because of the more abundant sap called up to repair the wound, although a few pages earlier he had explained that older trees yielded sweeter fruit precisely because they were less full of sap (279). Is it the abundance or the absence of sap which causes sweetness in fruit? Bodin never addresses the general principle but provides contradictory evidence in the answers to different questions. Here Bodin's commonplace book, with its idiosyncratic set of interests, served to hide rather than uncover a thematic link.

The method of commonplaces can thus explain some of the puzzling features of traditional natural philosophy beyond the specific case of the *Theatrum*.[21] Even if not all authors of traditional natural philosophy kept actual notebooks, the method serves as a metaphor for their way of creating physical knowledge. Although originally designed for notes from reading, the commonplace book easily accommodates material from non-bookish sources. It may record the origin of a fact (whether bookish or reported by a witness or an artisan) but treats each entry independently of its source, as potentially useful knowledge equivalent to every other entry. "Credulity" can therefore coexist with observation, new facts with traditional ones, without generating any internal tension. Similarly, the method of commonplaces explains how critical judgment can coexist with blatant inconsistencies. In sorting incoming information, the commonplace book offers opportunities for new critical confrontation of material; on the other hand the indefinite multiplication of separate headings can easily harbor contradictions which seem to belie the very critical faculties demonstrated elsewhere. As a tool for composition which opens many possibilities but requires none in particular, the commonplace book is

[21] In its general outline what I have called the method of commonplaces is as old as bookish natural philosophy itself: Pliny's *Natural History* offers a prime example of a source continually recycled through generations of texts, which is itself constructed from the compilation of primarily bookish tidbits of natural knowledge. On the origins and career of this classic of "notebook science," see G.E.R. Lloyd, *Science, Folklore and Ideology: Studies in the Life Sciences in Ancient Greece* (Cambridge, 1983), 139-44 and Charles Nauert, "Humanists, Scientists and Pliny: Changing Approaches to a Classical Author," *American Historical Review*, 84 (1979), 72-85.

supremely tolerant of cognitive dissonance. And this tolerance is, I would argue, the key to the long survival of traditional natural philosophy.[22]

Just as Bodin's *Theatrum* grew out of a book of commonplaces, so too it served in turn as material to be entered in the commonplace books of its readers; the reception of Bodin's *Theatrum* through the first half of the seventeenth century is testimony to the continued vitality of the method. Three annotated copies which I have found show how diligent readers assigned topical and thematic headings to paragraphs and pages in their copies of the *Theatrum*, possibly as a first step toward entering the material into their notebook, in any case as a convenient index for future reference.[23] One reader was especially attentive to Bodin's judgments of other authors: whom he praised and whom he criticized. All of them were alert to interesting "facts" which they flagged in the margin: both bookish (that the beams of the temple of Utica lasted 1200 years, probably taken from Pliny [278]) and garnered from direct experience (like the case of William of Orange who lost his sense of taste from a head wound, which Bodin reports having learned from William himself [460]). All of them also show some of the work of the commonplace book in the margins of their text: linking Bodin's passage to passages on the same topic in contemporary works that they had read (like Scaliger, Cardano, or the natural historians), to other passages in Bodin (thus pointing out contradictions like the one above), or to their own direct experience (when Bodin calls hares the fastest quadrupeds, one reader notes: "but when they are tired, dogs catch up with them" [405]). These marginalia reveal how the "facts" in Bodin's *Theatrum* were selected and absorbed into the mental networks of contemporary readers.

Some of Bodin's readers went on to cite the *Theatrum*—unfortunately not those whose annotations I have found. But citations of the *Theatrum* in the fifty years after its publication reveal the same process of selecting and reusing discrete facts from the text, as if through a commonplace book: the German natural philosophers who cite Bodin's *Theatrum* and recommend it to students for further reading starting in 1598 (notably Rodolph Goclenius, Bartholomäus Keckermann, and Clemens Timpler)[24]

---

[22] Cf. Edward Grant, "Aristotelianism and the Longevity of the Medieval World View," *History of Science*, 16 (1978), 93-106.

[23] These copies were annotated by Nicolas Granius, professor of natural philosophy at the universities of Rostock then Helmstedt (active at least 1596-1608) (at the Herzog August Bibliothek in Wolfenbüttel), by Isaac Casaubon (1559-1614) (at the British Library), and by an anonymous reader (in the personal library of Jean Céard). For the complete transcription of this last, richest set of marginal annotations see the appendix to my dissertation. I am most grateful to Jean Céard for the opportunity to study these notes.

[24] Rodolph Goclenius, annot. *Physicae seu naturalis philosophiae Institutiones Cornelii Valerii Ultrajectini* (Marburg, 1598); Bartholomäus Keckermann, *Systema physicum* (Danzig, 1610); Clemens Timpler, *Physicae ... systema* (Hanau, 1605). For more on these figures and their colleagues see Joseph Freedman, *European Academic Philosophy in the*

were especially interested in including Bodin in their doxographies on traditional Aristotelian subjects and dwell on Bodin's unusual anti-Aristotelian positions on the causes of underground springs or comets or earthquakes. Like that one annotator, they selected primarily doxographical facts into their notebooks. On the other hand, natural historians like Johann Jonston used the *Theatrum* as a source of material for their own work. Both with and without naming his source Jonston takes numerous interesting "factoids" from Bodin: such as the distance of the reference star Prima Arietis from the equinox as reported by past astronomers, or the fact that vinegar penetrates the inner recesses of iron or that large emeralds are to be found in Lyon and Prague—Bodin had actually mentioned only Genoa and Magdeburg, but Jonston wrongly attributes these examples to Bodin.[25] These natural facts are recycled almost fifty years after the publication of Bodin's *Theatrum* in Jonston's *Thaumatographia naturalis* which was reedited as late as 1665.

The cycle of textual natural philosophy, processed through the commonplace book, thus continues unabated well into the seventeenth century. In the 1610s, for example, Alsted and Keckermann discuss the best ways to keep commonplace books. Keckermann in particular addresses Bodin's recommendations in the *Methodus*:

In the second book [Bodin] wants to contain the histories of natural things. His advice abut the physical commonplaces is skillful and fruitful. . . . Nonetheless his advice about the places of natural history is not free from confusion, in addition to the fact that the physical places are confused with those of astronomy and geography: just as the sciences are distinct from one another, so they each have their boundaries and peculiar method.[26]

Not for Keckermann then the potential which Bodin leaves for confronting material from different disciplines through thematic combinations; Keckermann recommends instead notebooks that mirror the academic disciplines, according to the Aristotelian principle that to each discipline its own method and material. The debate between what one might hastily call humanist and neo-scholastic visions of the commonplace book only reinforces my argument for the fundamental role of the method in the practice of traditional natural philosophy in this period.

But the method of commonplaces was not simply a tool of bookish

---

Late Sixteenth and Seventeenth Centuries: the Life, Significance and Philosophy of Clemens Timpler (2 vols.; Hildesheim, 1988).

[25] Jan Jonston, *Thaumatographia naturalis* (Amsterdam, 1633), I, ch. 3, 14 (cf. *Theatrum*, 563); IV, ch. 31, 196 (cf. *Theatrum*, 256); IV, ch. 21, 174 (cf. *Theatrum*, 233).

[26] Bartholomäus Keckermann, "De locis communibus in genere et in specie de historicis recte concinnandis, epistola scripta ad . . . Dn. Gualterum ab Holden," appended to *Gymnasium logicum. Lib. secundus*, in *Opera omnia quae extant* (2 vols.; Geneva, 1614), I, 498. For Alsted's discussion of commonplaces see his *Orator* as cited above and the section on Didactica in his *Encyclopedia* (Herborn, 1630).

natural philosophy that disappeared—later than some have thought, but which disappeared nonetheless—with the rise of "modern" science during the seventeenth century. Indeed the core of the method lives on, I would argue, in Francis Bacon's precepts for a new science. It would be foolish to ignore the very real differences between Bodin and Bacon: Bacon deplores for example precisely the cycle of bookish natural philosophy that we can trace in the making and reading of Bodin's *Theatrum* when he complains that by "superinducing and engrafting new upon old . . . we would revolve forever in a circle with mean and contemptible progress."[27] But what Bacon offers in place of traditional natural philosophy is a method of commonplaces applied in principle at least to the world itself rather than to books.

Bacon praises the practice in the *Advancement of learning*:

For the disposition and collocation of that knowledge which we preserve in writing, it consisteth in a good digest of common-places; . . . I hold the entry of common-places to be a matter of great use and essence in studying, as that which assureth copie of invention, and contracteth judgement to a strength. But this is true, that of the methods of common-places that I have seen, there is none of any sufficient worth: all of them carrying merely the face of a school, and not of a world; and referring to vulgar matters and pedantical division, without all life or respect to action.[28]

The *New Organon* presents Bacon's new tool for scientific investigation, which turns out to be just such a method of commonplaces "carrying the face of a world" and designed for "action." The first step is to collect and present to the understanding all known instances of a phenomenon, combined with instances where it is absent or present to varying degrees; the next step, induction, proceeds by the systematic confrontation of the material arranged in tables: the prerogative instances revealed in this confrontation help to reach flawless general principles. Bacon's ideal is a method of natural commonplaces derived from direct observation which abides by strict guidelines for the thematic sorting and confrontation of material gathered topically.[29] In practice, however, Bacon was in too great a hurry to follow his rules carefully: the result is an unfinished work which shares with Bodin's *Theatrum* a close proximity to the commonplace book from which it derives, and it is a traditional Renaissance commonplace book at that. As Graham Rees has shown, Bacon's last work, the *Sylva sylvarum* (1626), juxtaposes bookish with directly observed facts, com-

[27] Francis Bacon, *New Organon*, ed. Fulton H. Anderson (Indianapolis, 1960), I, aphorism 31, 46.

[28] Francis Bacon, *The Advancement of Learning*, ed. Arthur Johnston (Oxford, 1974), Book II, ch. 14, 129-130.

[29] For a similar point see Paolo Rossi, *Francis Bacon, from Magic to Science* (Chicago, 1968), ch. 6, especially 207-14; on Bacon's method more generally see Lisa Jardine, *Francis Bacon: Discovery and the Art of Discourse* (Cambridge, 1974), ch. 4.

bines credulity and experimentation, critical judgment and what appear to us as the most obvious inconsistencies.[30] While the *New Organon* places the method of commonplaces at the center of a bold new program for natural investigation, the *Sylva sylvarum*, one of the most widely reprinted of Bacon's works (and regrettably the least studied by historians of science), reveals the long career of the Renaissance book of natural commonplaces as exemplified in Jean Bodin's *Universae naturae theatrum*.[31]

Harvard University.

---

[30] Graham Rees, "An Unpublished Manuscript by Francis Bacon: *Sylva Sylvarum* Drafts and Other Working Notes," *Annals of Science*, 38 (1981), 377-412; see also Mordechai Feingold and Penelope Gouk, "An Early Critique of Bacon's *Sylva sylvarum*: Edmund Chilmead's Treatise on Sound," *Annals of Science*, 40 (1983), 139-57, e.g. 151.

[31] In addition to the debts acknowledged above, I am grateful to Anthony Grafton for many helpful readings of this work and to Roger Chartier for the opportunity to present it at the Centre Alexandre Koyré in Paris.

[18]

Ann Blair

As a young law student frequenting the markets of Toulouse in the 1550s, Jean Bodin came to the conclusion that salt-water fish tasted better than fresh-water fish. As an older man, looking back on a checkered but prolific career, through some forty years of civil war, he reflected that the saltiness of the ocean was a divine gift that preserved it from impurity, and made the fish there grow bigger and tastier. The received, Aristotelian explanation for the saltiness of the sea from earthly exhalations was absurd; instead, Bodin proposed an explanation informed by critical reflection, but also by "true piety" and a sense of the proper limits of reason. Filled with discussions of this kind, Bodin's last major work, the *Universae naturae theatrum* or "theater of all of nature" (1596), grew out of a traditional practice of natural philosophy, based on the compilation and explanation of "facts" drawn largely from books, but which increasingly in the Renaissance also incorporated "experience" of various kinds. At the same time, Bodin's natural philosophy was motivated by an irenicist agenda, which he shared with other late humanists, to demonstrate for the agreement of all the greatness and providence of God; as in his more famous *République* and *Démonomanie*, Bodin hoped to restore much-needed order to society and to stem a rising tide of impiety, notably by inspiring everyone to worship the Creator. On both counts the *Theatrum* opens a new window onto the methods, motivations and difficulties of a kind of natural philosophy not often studied by historians of science.

Since its beginnings as a discipline, the history of science has tried to explicate in the early modern period the remarkable changes in the conceptions of nature and of natural philosophy grouped for convenience as the "Scientific Revolution." By now we have a number of detailed and illuminating accounts of the major figures and institutions that contributed to the development of "modern science." What we still lack, however, is a serious understanding of the more widely diffused conceptions of nature and natural philosophy that preceded and often persisted concurrently with these new developments. We need to look beyond the forward-looking few to a broader set of educated but nonspecialist authors and readers of natural philosophy to elucidate the context of the Scientific Revolution. However bold their declarations of a revolutionary break with the past, however exceptional and specialized their individual talents, the innovators were trained in, often continued to draw from, and, in any case, were responding to a range of more "ordinary" practices of natural philosophy. By studying these we can sharpen our sense of what was revolutionary about the Scientific Revolution, and of the process by which new ideas and practices developed and coexisted with, and ultimately supplanted the old. Bodin's *Theatrum* offers a fine point of departure from which to examine traditional natural philosophy at its height in the late Renaissance (ca. 1550–1630).

While historians of science once considered the Renaissance to be indifferent if not hostile to the study of nature, it now increasingly appears as a period of ex-

4   •*INTRODUCTION*•

plosion in natural knowledge, gathered from newly recovered ancient texts as
well as newly discovered lands. On the one hand Renaissance humanists accumulated and transmitted the greatest legacy of texts to date—ancient, medieval
and modern—complete with elaborate commentaries and attempts at synthesis.
On the other hand, the sheer mass and diversity of the textual legacy and a new
interest in empirical observations served gradually to dislocate received opinion
and authorities, by uncovering contradictions and offering alternatives, no single
one of which prevailed. The breakdown of Christendom into devastating wars of
religion further motivated the search for, and increased the difficulty of finding,
grounds for philosophical consensus. Recent studies have taken a number of approaches to chart areas in this rich and varied field: focusing, for example, on the
commentaries on a canonical text (notably the *Canon* of Avicenna), or on a theme
in contemporary literature (the prodigious and the marvelous); on the widespread practice of natural historical collecting, or on the life and works of individuals, ranging from a lesser-known alchemist to a well-known philosopher like
Gassendi.[1]

I have chosen a single book, a kind of encyclopedia of nature, from which to
explore avenues in late Renaissance science—through comparison with various
other contemporary works,[2] through a study of the text itself, its structure and
composition, its motivations and metaphors, its arguments and conclusions (both
the idiosyncratic and the more typical ones), and, finally, through its reception in
the century following its publication. Rather than filming change over time, I
offer mostly a detailed still picture of what it meant to "do physics" for Jean Bodin
and various near-contemporaries, even as a first, moderate phase of the Scientific
Revolution was under way and a second, more radical one was about to begin
(starting, say, in the 1620s and 1630s). I have organized my own book around
three major themes, which I introduce in chapter 1 in presenting the *Theatrum*
and its context: the bookish methods and practice of "physics" (chapters 2–3), the
religious motivations for the study of nature (chapter 4), and the problem of ordering a vast and ever-increasing stock of knowledge (chapter 5). Chapter 6
traces the reception of the *Theatrum*, from a survey of extant copies, from the citations and marginal annotations of readers of the three Latin editions (1596,
1597, 1605), and from its two vernacularizations—a French translation by the
Lyonnais doctor François de Fougerolles (1597), which appealed to a limited, educated readership, and a popular German adaptation of the *Theatrum* entitled
Problemata Bodini, by Damian Siffert, whose careful selection of themes from
Bodin's original gave them their longest life, down to a final edition in 1679. I
conclude with an epilogue that sketches some of the continuities and disconti-
nuities between the traditional natural philosophy of Bodin and the revolutionary call of Francis Bacon to replace the old system of knowledge with a new
method of investigation.

With the exception of the mathematical sciences which followed a separate set
of ancient models and methods,[3] natural philosophy consisted primarily, for over
two thousand years, in the transmission and criticism of authoritative texts and
their successive commentaries. To make natural knowledge was to transmit, sort,

explain, and modify the definitions, facts, and arguments accumulated previously, producing texts that following generations of scholars would process in much the same way. This seemingly unending cycle of "literary empiricism" or "humanistic science" culminated in the late Renaissance, as scores of new texts, ancient and modern, poured into the pool of available material.[4] Already ancient scholars had devised methods to manage and collate vast quantities of material: erudition at the library of Alexandria (founded by Ptolemy I [323–285 BCE]) produced catalogues of books and their contents, doxographies (that is, lists of the opinions of authorities) and numerous scholarly devices for collecting and comparing material stored in hundreds of thousands of papyrus rolls;[5] on natural topics in particular, Pliny the Elder, in the preface to his *Natural history* (ca. 70 CE), boasted of having gathered twenty thousand pieces of information (no doubt he had the help of amanuenses, but we have no details about the methods they used).[6] During the Middle Ages, encyclopedias and florilegia made available summaries of knowledge and quotations from authorities arranged according to various organizational principles. The problem of sorting and storing knowledge for future reference was thus hardly new to the Renaissance, and previous methods of note-taking no doubt inspired the solution advocated by humanist pedagogues which became widespread in Renaissance scholarship in many fields, including natural philosophy.

In chapter 2, I argue from an analysis of the printed text (unfortunately no manuscripts of Bodin's survive) that the *Theatrum* was composed from a commonplace book, a practice of note-taking taught in Renaissance schools and advocated by Bodin himself in his first major work, the *Methodus ad facilem historiarum cognitionem* (*Method for the Easy Comprehension of History*—1566). This was a personal notebook in which each schoolboy (and later, adult reader) was taught to enter and sort under subject headings interesting turns of phrase, opinions, or facts of all kinds encountered in reading, travel, and daily life, for later retrieval and use. As a warehouse of information the commonplace book was indefinitely expandable and flexible, able to accommodate new and disparate material without internal tension, including the results of direct observation and empirical investigations. By divorcing its contents from their original contexts, the commonplace book tended to reduce to equal status "facts" of all categories; by breaking down natural knowledge into hundreds of separate issues requiring causal explanation, it required neither consistency nor a totalizing answer. Bodin's reliance on a book of natural commonplaces in composing the *Theatrum* can help to account for features peculiar to this work, such as its way of explaining facts that are taken for granted or its juxtaposition of discrete particulars according to loose thematic and topical links, and features which have puzzled modern assessments of Renaissance natural philosophy more generally, like the coexistence of traditional with "modern" elements, of critical judgment with "credulousness" and contradictions.

As a method of managing information, the commonplace book was perfectly suited to handle the explosion of knowledge in the late Renaissance without cognitive dissonance. What Edward Grant has argued of medieval Aristotelianism, that its longevity was due to its great flexibility and to the atomization of scholastic literature, also holds for this method of traditional natural philosophy, which survived what might otherwise have been fatal internal tensions and succumbed only to external attacks.[7] Judging from the scholarly reception of the *Theatrum*, this cycle of producing natural knowledge from texts continued at least through the first half of the seventeenth century, with no hint of an imminent demise. Given their versatility, these bookish methods cannot in themselves account for the forms of Bodin's arguments. In chapter 3 I examine the uses to which Bodin put the method of commonplaces: notably, his unusually eclectic choice and treatment of sources, and his construction of arguments less often from the "demonstrative reasons" that he announces, than from a mix of looser, dialectical arguments characteristic of sixteenth-century legal reasoning—arguments from authority, experience, and religious principle, even from highly idiosyncratic allegorical interpretations.

In chapter 4 I pursue in more depth the peculiarities of Bodin's agenda. The *Theatrum* is part of a surge of natural theological works in late sixteenth-century France, prompted by widespread fears of a generalized loss of faith during the virtually continuous civil wars of religion between 1562 and 1598 and designed to show from rational, philosophical arguments the truth of key religious tenets. Developed as an argument against the Epicurean denial of divine governance of this world, and touted during the Middle Ages as a method for converting Jews and Muslims (e.g., by Peter Abelard and Ramon Lull), in the late Renaissance natural theology offered grounds for agreement among the warring religious parties by demonstrating from reason alone a common core of piety. In addition, for Bodin, natural theology put philosophy back on its proper, pious track, and showed the absurd falsity of those philosophies, including Aristotelianism, Epicureanism, and natural magic, which did not sufficiently acknowledge the providence, free will, and omnipotence of God, or the limits of human reason. The *Theatrum* thus tackles some of the oldest problems in the Judeo-Christian tradition, of reconciling faith and biblical authority with the attractive elements of ancient pagan philosophies. By the mid-sixteenth century, both the philosophy and the religion that Thomas Aquinas had so powerfully reconciled had exploded into multiple alternatives; Bodin's attempt at a new reconciliation is one among many such attempts during this period, which include Gassendi's Christianized Epicureanism or Lipsius's Christianized Stoicism.

Although Bodin, too, maintains that religion and philosophy cannot contradict one another, the synthesis he proposes is quite unique. His natural philosophy is a largely anti-Aristotelian concoction of different (e.g., Stoic, Neoplatonic, and Judaized) elements, and the "piety" he defends is so devoid of confessional features that it omits any reference even to the major Christian doctrines (e.g., redemption) that were standard in contemporary natural theologies. Others have expertly explicated Bodin's private, Judaized religion.[8] My purpose is rather to follow his supraconfessional strategy in the *Theatrum*. In Books I and IV Bodin claims to demonstrate from philosophy key religious principles: that the world is not eternal (against Aristotle), and, against the Epicureans, Averroës and most recently the Italian Aristotelian Pomponazzi, that the personal soul is immortal (and, he shows in the process, corporeal). In the natural-historical Books II and III, Bodin brings back myriad particulars of nature to the providence of God, with careful emphasis on the limits of human reason in understanding phenomena that are in fact supernatural and carried out by the activity of demons. Bodin's project in *Theatrum* to build basic religious consensus from the study of nature shows that the tradition of natural and physico-theologies, which is well known from the late seventeenth to the early nineteenth centuries, began well before then.

My final major theme is the struggle characteristic of the late Renaissance of bringing order and coherence to ever-increasing quantities of knowledge—what Roger Chartier has aptly called the "tension between the exhaustive and the essential."[9] On the one hand, Renaissance pedagogy and dialectic emphasized the importance of correct ordering for learning and research; on the other hand, the breakdown of medieval disciplinary boundaries, for both intellectual and institutional reasons, the multiplication of new sources of knowledge, and the accelerated circulation of texts through printing could only overwhelm idealized schemas of knowledge. Solutions to the problem of order ranged from self-consciously disordered miscellanies which justified themselves by reference to ancient models and the pleasure derived from their variety, to rigidly structured textbooks or charts, which touted their utility, but preserved order at the expense of content. Between these extremes, authors attempted all kinds of systematic, topical arrangements, and some resorted to the inferior, because merely arbitrary, alphabetical arrangement, found for example in most dictionaries and a few commonplace books. The universal refrain was the need to balance utility with pleasure, the unity of order with the variety of the material. Like so many contemporaries, Bodin starts off by proclaiming the dignity of order and the unique validity of his arrangement in the *Theatrum*, but in practice (as I show in chapter 2), the details succeed one another according to a fairly arbitrary (although often elegant) chain of thought.

In chapter 5 I explore Bodin's double use of the metaphor of the "theater." First, nature is a theater or a spectacle laid out by God for human contemplation, which is both beautifully varied and perfectly ordered by its Creator. Second, Bodin unself-consciously conflates the theater of nature that is his subject with the "Theater of Nature" that is the book he has written, in which Bodin, too, tries to match variety with unifying order. In the first part of the chapter, I trace the widespread use of the "theater of nature" among contemporary natural philosophical authors. In the second part, I take as a point of departure Bodin's statements in the *Theatrum* in which he describes his book entitled "theater" as a kind of table (*tabula*) presenting a vast and complex subject matter in a clear and synthetic order, to consider works entitled "theater" across many disciplines in the period 1550–1700. Although I do not claim to have exhausted the vast number of works entitled "theater," I offer a rough typology of the various forms and functions that authors signaled for their works by the use of this title. With the exception of "laments" which play off the better-known topos of the *theatrum mundi*

8 •INTRODUCTION•

to explose the tragicomedy of human existence, the title most often connotes, as in Bodin's *Theatrum*, the ambition of treating a large subject systematically, as if in a tabular fashion. As a result, it applies to works that implement this contradictory task in different ways—from skeletal charts to anthologies in which complex organizational schemes yield to simple accumulation of a mass of material. I present this brief survey of a vast topic—my own attempt at a "theater"—as a prelude to a larger project on encyclopedism in early modern Europe.

This book is informed by a number of historiographic perspectives. In the history of science recent scholarship has begun to compensate for the long-standing emphasis of the discipline on the modern aspects of sixteenth- and seventeenth-century science and to refine our understanding of Renaissance natural philosophy, once dismissed as stagnant. Charles Schmitt has established that Aristotelianism did not impose a narrow dogmatism in the Renaissance (if ever it did), but embraced an eclectic and heterogeneous array of sources, interpretations, and direct criticisms of the Philosopher.[10] The old assumption that the humanist movement with its literary emphasis was antithetical to the development of "science" is also being overturned. Recent work on Kepler, Mersenne, and Gassendi reveals the impact of humanist disciplines such as philology, dialectic, or the history of philosophy on well-known contributors to the emergence of modern science.[11] My aim in bringing to light Jean Bodin's natural philosophy is not to argue that he should be included among these canonical figures, but to extend the range of authors and texts included in the history of science. Bodin's type of natural philosophy generated more texts and more readers in its time than those authors who have been singled out as forward-looking; to study it is to shed light not only on the context in which the writers of the "avant-garde" wrote and were first received, but also on the assumptions and expectations that they shared with lesser-known but more representative contemporaries. That Jean Bodin is, of course, no "ordinary" author, given his reputation in political philosophy and his various idiosyncratic views, adds a further dimension of interest to the *Theatrum* without making it less revealing (to careful analysis) of its cultural context.

Historians of literature are also branching out from their own set of canonical figures to consider natural philosophical texts. Scholars of the French Renaissance in particular have produced ground-breaking studies on the monstrous and prodigious, the occult and text-based cosmography.[12] Considerations of composition, structure, and metaphor have yielded valuable insights for my study of Bodin's *Theatrum*. My argument for the use of commonplace books in natural philosophy, for example, is inspired by recent work on Montaigne and Shakespeare.[13] In turn I hope that the metaphor of the "theater of nature" that I explicate in Bodin and many other natural philosophical authors will become recognized as a widespread and distinct counterpart to the well-known topos of the "theater of the world" traced by literary historians. Furthermore, my survey of the metaphor of the book as theater is designed as a complement to the studies of medieval and Renaissance "mirrors."[14]

As cultural history, this study is especially influenced by new developments in the history of the book and of reading. A whole range of questions concerning the book as physical object and commercial commodity and the reader as consumer and appropriator has added intellectual depth to the traditional pleasures of bib-liophilia.[15] Combining the focus of the history of the book with the model of "total" studies of specific places pioneered by the Annales school, I propose what one might call an "histoire totale" of one book. I follow the *Theatrum* from its origins in the printshop (where a dispute concerning the publication of the French translation has left traces in the archives) and in the commonplace books of the author, to its resting point in the notes and citations of its readers. Its reception by erudite and both cultivated and popular vernacular audiences illuminates the different rhythms and forms of appropriation of a text as physical book: the original Latin text with few aids to the reader made its greatest impact in the years after its initial publication; the French translation tried to enhance the consultability of the work and to reach a wider cultivated audience, without much success in its day (but more among today's historians); while the popular adaptation of the *Theatrum* to cheap editions of *problemata*, imitated from the classical question-and-answer form, had the longest staying power of all, past the death of traditional natural philosophy in learned circles.

Of course this book is also about Jean Bodin, who, despite an abundant literature,[16] remains an elusive figure on historical as well as intellectual grounds,[17] ranging from the banality of his name[18] to the heterodoxy of his thought. He was born in 1529 or 1530 in Angers to a moderately well-off family (his father was a master tailor; his maternal relatives included a *procureur*). His mother, Catherine Dutertre, was from Anjou, and neither Marrano nor Jewish, as a persistent myth has maintained.[19] He was sent for his education to a Carmelite monastery in Angers, then probably on to Paris (ca. 1545–48). He may have matriculated at the University of Paris;[20] even if he did not, he probably attended public lectures introducing him to the main intellectual currents of the day, such as those of Petrus Ramus on dialectic and rhetoric, or Adrien Turnèbe on Greek philology, from whom he was accused of plagiarizing in his first publication, a Latin verse translation with commentary of Oppian's *Cynegetica* (1555).[21] He may have been the "Jehan Baudin" tried for heresy in Paris in 1548 whose fate is unknown. In any case he was released from his vows as a Carmelite (taken while under age) in 1548.[22] He turned to the study of law, first in his home town, then in Toulouse.[23] Despite lingering uncertainty concerning his whereabouts in the early 1550s (possibly Geneva in 1552),[24] Bodin earned his law degree at Toulouse, where humanistic reforms in legal education had already been introduced, although the law faculty there remained more conservative than others. Bodin strove to find a position for himself at the university,[25] or as headmaster in one of the new humanist collèges planned in Toulouse, delivering for the latter purpose an eloquent speech hailing the rebirth of letters under Francis I.[26] After the failure of these attempts, Bodin can next be traced taking the oath of Catholicity required for admission as an *avocat* at the Parlement of Paris in 1562. In 1570 he was appointed commissioner for reform of forest tenures in Normandy, with the task of reviving a royal privilege fallen into disuse.[27]

Given the difficulty of identifying him, we know Bodin best by his publications.[28] Already in 1566, the *Methodus*, one of the important humanist treatises on how to read, evaluate, and write histories, also included a tripartite plan of study

• *I N T R O D U C T I O N* •

of things human, natural, and divine, and announced his polymathic interests.[29] It was followed by reflections on the inflation experienced in sixteenth-century Europe,[30] and an attempt at systematizing law, the *Juris universi distributio* (1578), probably based on a manuscript finished much earlier.[31] Bodin achieved national and European renown with his *Six livres de la République* (1576).[32] In this long, often rambling work, Bodin replaced Aristotle's notion of governments that "mix" elements of the democratic, aristocratic, and monarchical forms with a notion of sovereignty that is necessarily indivisible and absolute, and ideally vested in a hereditary monarch. He based his arguments on a comparative study of governments through history, gathered from his wide-ranging erudition, and on his horror of the civil disturbances that convulsed France from 1562 on: for Bodin, the monarch is bound by his conscience to govern according to the "law of God and of nature," and to act in all things to preserve the state, but, whatever his decisions, the subjects (including the nobility and magistrates) have no right to resist, even on religious grounds.[33] For laying the theoretical foundations of absolutism, Bodin was hailed in his own day, and since, as one of the principal modern authorities in political philosophy.

Meanwhile Bodin had settled in Laon, where he married Françoise Trouillart, the widow of a controller of the royal domain and the sister of a royal *procureur*. In 1576 Bodin participated in the Estates General, as a representative of the Third Estate from Vermandois. Bodin argued for peace and resisted the king's desire to alienate royal lands in order to fund continued war against the Protestants, drawing from his own theory that the fundamental duty of kings was to preserve the state (starting with the royal demesne).[34] In so doing, he alienated himself from the king, whose favor he seemed to be courting, and spent the rest of his life in retirement from the center of politics, taking over his brother-in-law's office as *procureur du roi* in Laon at the latter's death in 1587 and returning to his writing. In 1580 he published the *De la démonomanie des sorciers*, which was widely reprinted and translated into Latin, German, and Italian, in which he railed against the growing worship of Satan and called for the persecution of suspected witches by all means necessary.[35] Alfred Soman has shown that, although Bodin was a prosecutor, he probably never tried a witchcraft case, and was considered extreme among his colleagues, whom he openly accused of sympathizing with witches for prosecuting them too leniently.[36] He also prepared a second French edition of the *République* and a significantly revised Latin translation (published in 1586), from which translations into other vernaculars were made.

From roughly 1571 to 1584, Bodin served in the household of the king's youngest brother, François duc d'Alençon, who became duc d'Anjou in 1576. Alençon was at the center of a group of malcontents who formed the core of the *politique* party favoring religious toleration to end the civil wars.[37] As part of Alençon's retinue, Bodin participated in the delegation that welcomed the Polish ambassadors come to greet their new king Henry of Anjou in Metz in 1573,[38] and traveled to England in 1581 in the advance party charged with negotiating a marriage contract between François and Queen Elizabeth (which failed); he accompanied François to Flanders in 1582–83 in a military attempt to drive out the

Spaniards (also a failure). Bodin's hopes for reward in the duke's household were dashed at the latter's death in 1584. Bodin also performed odd legal services for noblemen, including the marquis de Moy (1580–93) and Henry of Navarre.[39] By the 1580s Bodin had two sons, Jean and Elie, who both died before adulthood, and a feeble-minded daughter, Antoinette, who lived under tutelage and died without issue.[40] He was constantly in financial straits, which may help to explain (along with intellectually consistent reasons advanced by Paul Rose) why he continued to serve in his office when the city of Laon was governed by the Catholic League after 1588.[41] In 1594 Bodin slipped out of the city to meet the royal troops come (successfully) to bring Laon under the control of the new king, Henry IV.[42] It is at this point, I would suggest, that Bodin met Jacques Mitte de Chevrières, a lieutenant to the king in the Lyonnais who had accompanied Henry in his Northern campaign, and to whom Bodin dedicated the *Universae naturae theatrum*.[43] Two references in the text (pp. 560, 563) indicate that the *Theatrum* was composed in 1590; the preface is dated March 1, 1596. By early June of the same year Bodin had died of the plague.

Bodin left a will, last seen by Gilles Ménage in the late seventeenth century, in which he reportedly asked that a number of his manuscripts be burned, and that he be buried in the Church of the Franciscans.[44] Jacques Gillot refers to a final poem that Bodin composed on his death bed, in which he made no reference to Jesus Christ and concludes that "the naughty man . . . died a Jew."[45] This and other comments, along with peculiar biases in Bodin's works, have raised questions about Bodin's religious position and relation to Judaism that continue to be discussed.[46] Bodin's beliefs have been so elusive precisely because he veiled heterodox views under conventional practice and preferred to rally readers to the cause of a "piety" which he cautiously left mostly unspecified. A manuscript on religion generally attributed to Bodin was circulated clandestinely until its first publication in the mid-nineteenth century;[47] the *Colloquium heptaplomeres* or "conversation of the seven wise men," portrays a debate between seven men, who each argue for a different religion (including some scathing attacks on Christianity), before deciding to abandon the topic and live harmoniously together without further discussion.[48] Although the dialogue form here (unlike in the *Theatrum*) is exploited for ambiguity, and the author's intention has been much debated, the *Colloquium* is noted for its implicit call for religious toleration and indifference to matters of ritual.[49] In addition, Bodin published in 1596 another, short dialogue concerning ethical questions, his *Paradoxon* or "paradox that there is no virtue in the middle way" which he also translated into French.[50]

Unlike most late humanists, Bodin comes down to us as a solitary figure, who left practically no manuscript correspondence,[51] and was frequently marginalized and harassed. He was arrested in 1568–69, possibly preventively (to guard him against more violent vigilante attacks), on suspicion of heterodoxy (presumably of Protestant leanings);[52] under the League in Laon he was denounced twice as heterodox, his house searched, and a number of his books burned.[53] He fell out of favor with Henry III, after participating for a few months in his academy,[54] never reaped any significant rewards from his service to Alençon (who was sus-

12   •*INTRODUCTION*•

pected of plotting against his brother Henry III and was therefore allowed little
power), and died early in Henry IV's reign. He was remembered as a mediocre
lawyer, who was not well liked by his colleagues.[55] Nonetheless, Bodin was not
only a prolific and original author, but unusually widely read and engaged in issues of immediate contemporary significance. Bodin's works are often the richest source of biographical details, in particular of the personal contacts which
were crucial to the exchange of ideas as well as natural specimens (and books).[56]
The *Theatrum* reveals, for example, that Bodin met William of Orange and the
renowned cartographer Abraham Ortelius (presumably during his trip to the
Netherlands in 1582–83). Bodin also met with John Dee, according to the latter's
diary for 1581, and has an entry in Janus Dousa's *liber amicorum*.[57] Furthermore,
Auger Ferrier, engaged in a bitter fight with Bodin over astrological conclusions
and scholarly reputation, reveals in passing that Bodin traveled to Italy some time
before 1580.[58]

The *Universae naturae theatrum*, which has recently begun to be studied,[59] does
not so much provide grounds for a major reinterpretation of Bodin, as force us to
take seriously the wide range and the internal coherence of his thought. Instead
of parceling out his contributions to different disciplines and evaluating them
separately, we should consider his works as he did, as parts of a single program
of study. Although Bodin has often been described as Janus-faced, torn between
the modern insights of the *République* and the superstitions of the *Démonomanie*,[60]
Paul Rose has rightly emphasized that the apparent paradoxes in Bodin's thought
arise more from a modernizing interpretation of his work than from his arguments themselves.[61] Bodin consistently envisions God as active in both nature and
human affairs, to reward, punish, and govern the world, often acting through the
intermediary of demons at his command. To worship these demons (or Satan,
their leader) is to deny the greater glory of God; such idolatry and impiety is at
the root of the moral degeneration of society, and of the civil wars, famines, and
other disturbances permitted by God in vengeful wrath. To restore order Bodin
calls for the obedience of subjects (in the *République*), the eradication of witchcraft (in the *Démonomanie*), and the universal acknowledgment (in the *Theatrum*)
of a few core religious principles—divine omnipotence, providence, and justice.
In his political as well as his natural philosophy Bodin seeks grounds for stability
across doctrinal differences as a solution to the wars that plagued most of his
adult life, and to which he refers repeatedly in his later works.[62]

Bodin is also consistent in his methods of engaging a vast array of sources to
support his argument. Bodin was admired by contemporaries, even by the king
(despite the latter's displeasure with him), for his abundant wit and "the quantity
of wonderful things (*pulcherrimarum rerum copia*) that he drew from his acute
memory on all subjects."[63] Whether he actually kept commonplace notebooks as
he advocates in the *Methodus*, at the very least his mind operated like a set of notebooks, storing up information from his encyclopedic reading among ancient and
modern writers. He would retrieve the material according to the topic at hand,
often accumulating multiple examples to make a point so thoroughly as to drown
it out (as in the *République*), or juxtaposing different cases with little connective

argument (as in the *Theatrum*). Bodin also reuses the same material, and in his last work cites nearly every one of his earlier publications.[64] His articulation of evidence with argument is more effective in the *République*, where he selects facts to support specific conclusions, honed no doubt by his experience in politics and the legal profession. In the *Theatrum*, his argument that God is provident and omnipotent could be equally served by any natural phenomenon, so that his choice of evidence inevitably seems arbitrary. In both cases the dialectical skills of the lawyer predominate over any systematic or logical structure. Finally, Bodin worked fast, often from tacit intermediate sources, generating errors at the same rhythm as the massive erudite volumes that are the hallmark of late humanist polymathy.

My contributions to a better understanding of Bodin's thought are mostly a by-product of a fine-grained analysis of the *Theatrum* undertaken in the first instance in order to examine, through its example, the methods and practices of traditional natural philosophy in the late Renaissance. To consider the *Theatrum* in this cultural context is not only to take a new approach to old questions in the history of science about the persistence of tradition and the emergence of the modern, but also to show how, despite its idiosyncrasies, Bodin's work was typical of a number of trends in natural history, natural theology, and encyclopedism in the late Renaissance.

Part VI
Theories of History

[19]

THE MAJOR THEMES OF THE METHODUS

John L. Brown

In analyzing the several elements which have entered into the composition of the *Methodus*, we have already discussed portions of its subject matter. The dedicatory epistle, as it has been remarked, deals largely with the necessity of the union between legal and historical studies. The Italian artes account for the rhetorical material found in the Proemium and in the first few opening chapters. The German historians and theorists provoked the refutation of the theory of the Four Monarchies, the defence of Hebrew chronology, and the discussion of the origin of peoples.

However, there are other, and more important, themes in the *Methodus* which have not yet been considered, and which do not owe their inspiration to any preceding historical art. I have isolated some of these and traced their occurrence throughout the work. Although this method makes for compactness and clarity, it is employed at the risk of minimizing the fundamental confusion and lack of organization which marks the *Methodus* as well as the *République*. There is an *implied* organization in the *Methodus*, but it is frequently obscured by a mass of superfluous and often irrelevant detail. These are the themes which I have chosen to consider as "major:"

(1) The naturalistic basis of history
(2) *Respublica mundana*
(3) The idea of progress
(4) The historicity of myths
(5) Philology as historical evidence
(6) Judgments on preceding historians
(7) Political ideas.

Bodin's organization of the *Methodus*, of course, does not follow these lines. The dedicatory epistle, as I have said, concerns itself with legal questions. The *proemium de facilitate, oblectatione, et utilitate historiarum*, the first chapter, *Quid historia sit et quotuplex,* the second, *De ordine historiarum* (the correct order in which histories should be read), and part of the fourth, *De historicorum delectu,* dealing with the writing of history, stem from the elegant humanist tradition.   The fifth, *De recto historiarum iudicio,* where Bodin establishes his theory of climate and of the psychology of peoples as the naturalistic basis of history, and the sixth, *De statu rerumpublicarum,* where he states his political ideas, are *sui generis;* many contend that the latter chapter has no rightful place in an *ars historica* at all.   As I have pointed out, the last three chapters, *Confutatio eorum qui quatuor monarchias aureaque saecula statuunt, De Temporis universi ratione,* and the *Qua ratione populorum origines haberi possint* spring, directly or indirectly, from Bodin's contact with German Protestant historiography.   The final chapter, the tenth, consists of a bibliography of universal history, *De historicorum ordine et collectione,* similar in nature, (but more complete in detail) to those found in Baudouin and Chytraeus.

A naturalistic view of history is at the foundation of Bodin's methodology.[1]   Where, in the ever-changing flux, in the constantly shifting complex of human institutions, human religions, human laws can the theoretician of history find a solid basis on which to make his generalizations?   Is it possible to discover in history any stable and unchanging point of reference?   This is assuredly a difficult problem, and, in his consideration of it, Bodin tends slightly toward the historical pyrrhonism[2] which was to assert itself so strongly during the seventeenth and eighteenth centuries :[3]

> Atque id paulo aliter faciendum nobis est, quam Diodorus, Volterranus, Caelius, Sabellicus, Boemus; qui de populo- rum variis legibus, religionibus, epulis, institutis levissime scripserunt, de quibus, tamen, quod in infinita sunt

---

[1] Although, as we shall see, this naturalistic approach is obscured and compromised by all sorts of concessions to astrology, numerology, etc.   Nor can we overlook Bodin's deep sense of religiosity, his feeling of the mystery of human destiny.

[2] Cf. Meta Scheele, *Wissen und Glaube in Geschichtswissenschaft. Studium zum historischen Pyrrhonismus in Frankreich und Deutschland,* Heidelberg, 1930.   Bodin's historical scepticism is touched on briefly, pp. 17-19.

[3] *Methodus,* 117.

The Major Themes of the Methodus

> varietate ac paulo momento per sese vel principium arbi-
> trio mutabilia, nihil certum statui potest.

Bodin, realizing the necessity "of proceeding in a slightly
different fashion," does believe, however, that a reasonably certain
basis for historical theorizing can be established.[4]

> Quaeramus igitur illa quae non ab hominum institutis,
> sed a natura ducuntur, quoque stabilia sunt, nec umquam
> nisi magna vi, aut diuturna disciplina mutantur; & mutata
> nihilominus ad pristinam redeunt naturam, quo de genere
> nihil a veteribus scribi potuit, cum regionum ac locorum,
> quae ita pridem patuerunt, penitus assent ignari.

In the uncertainty and chaos of human history, therefore, the
one sure criterion of historical generalization must be found in a
study of natural influences, which are stable and unchanging and
have a dominant role in molding the personality, physique, and
historical character of peoples. On this basis, Bodin intends to
analyze the nature (perhaps we would use the term *national
psychology*) of the peoples of the South; then those of the North;
then of those of the East and the West. Having determined the
"national psychology" of these races, their historical destiny may
be studied with more accuracy and understanding.

From this basic concept of a naturalistic history, stem several
other significant ideas. First of all, the ancients, unacquainted
with the vast tracts of land which had been so recently discovered,
were not able to determine the nature of peoples, since they lacked
the necessary data. Bodin thus touches on the question of the
Ancients and the Moderns (already much discussed, as we shall
see[5] in the sixteenth century) and favors the modern camp. Any
belief in the superiority of the moderns over the ancients brings
with it as a necessary consequence some vague idea of progress.
With Bodin, the theory of progress is not treated as a definite,
affirmative concept; rather he approaches it negatively, by attack-

---

[4] *Ibid.*, pp. 118-119.

[5] Cf. *Methodus*, chap. VII, and also Hubert Gillot, *La querelle des anciens
et des modernes en France*, Paris, 1914.

ing the old idea of a golden age in the past and constant degeneration since. His fundamental assumption, moreover, that the
primary influences in history are natural influences presupposes
the conception of human progress. Nature is stable and unchanging. It follows, therefore, that nature produces men in the present
who are just as capable as those it produced two thousand years
ago—perhaps more capable.[6]

One of the boldest consequences of Bodin's naturalistic view of
history is his opposition to the old world-scheme of the Four
Monarchies and his setting up of a new historical periodization,
based on geographical and climatic factors and on the movement
of civilization from South to North. In this fifth chapter, he sets
up his outline of three great epochs: the first dominated by the
Oriental, southeastern peoples; the second, dominated by the
Mediterranean peoples; and the third, dominated by the Northern
peoples. Each of these epochs he designates as two thousand years
in length.[7]

Investigation of the nature of peoples, furthermore, reveals
that all races have particular capabilities, particular weaknesses;
none is a complete whole within itself, but rather a part of the
macrocosm of the *respublica mundana*. Bodin advances many
reasons in favor of the necessity of the *respublica mundana*:
economic interdependence, inter-relationship of peoples. One of
the most important, however, is this: each people, with its characteristic qualities, is a part of the macrocosm—the Southerners,
with their mental powers represent the brain; the Northerners,
with their manual dexterity, the arms, etc. The *respublica mundana* must result from the necessary co-operation of its separate
parts. The structure of the chapter has an inner unity from its
dependence on the fundamental idea that history is largely determined by natural forces. From this, the other themes (idea of
progress, *respublica mundana*) spring naturally, like branches from
a central trunk.

---

[6] Cf. J. B. Bury, *The Idea of Progress* (New York, 1932), pp. 37-39 and
also Jules Delvaille, *Essai sur l'histoire de l'idée du progrès jusqu 'à la fin
du XVIIIe siècle*, Paris, 1910.

[7] Cf. *Methodus*, 178.

90   *The Major Themes of the Methodus*

This "theory of climates" as it has been styled, expressed in the fifth chapter of the *Methodus*, is one of the most widely known ideas of Bodin. Sketched in the *Methodus*, it was amplified in the *République*.[8] It has often been considered the basis of the later speculations of Montesquieu on the same theme.[9] Anton Meuten has published a dissertation on *Bodins Theorie von der Beeinflüssung des politischen Lebens der Staaten durch ihre geographische Lage*.[10] Bodin, of course, owes much to the ancients, such as Hippocrates, as it is evident from the classical illustrations he employs to prove some of his contentions,[11] and much to near contemporaries,[12] notably Jean Cardan; but he gave the idea more final expression, more definite form.[13]

Here, as elsewhere in the *Methodus*, we find a disconcerting mixture of credulity and critical acumen, of thought-provoking ideas coupled with the stale cant of astrology. Improbable stories accepted on faith occur on the same page with sharp observations which Bodin had made personally. Strange scraps of miscellaneous pseudo-scientific information—why goats never have sore eyes, whether the right-hand side or the left is more lucky, the problem of "interior heat," of bile and humors—very akin to the *Pseudo-*

---

[8] Cf. especially Bk. V, chap. i, "Du reiglement qu'il faut tenir pour accomoder la forme de Republique a la diversite des hommes: and le moyen de cognoistre le naturel des peuples."

[9] Cf. E. Fournol, *Bodin, prédécesseur de Montesquieu. Etude sur quelques théories politiques de la République et de l'Esprit des Lois* (Thèse), Paris, 1896.

[10] Inaugural-Dissertation, Bonn, 1904.

[11] Classical authors cited in this chapter include: Varro (170, 174); Livy, (180); Galen (119); Ptolmey (118); Strabo (120); Posidonius (120); Pliny (*passim*); Hippocrates (124, 148); Aristotle (127, 156); Tacitus (139, 149, 158); Columella (144); Caesar (149, 179); Plato (170); Plutarch (171).

[12] Among near contemporaries cited we find: Machiavelli (157, 175); Boemus (167); Munster (167, 184); Copernicus (177); Sleidan (179); Julius Scaliger (180); Ziegler (184); Agricola (195); Cardan (195, 221).

[13] Cf. A. Garosci, *Jean Bodin: politica e diritto nel Rinascimento francese* (Milan, 1934), pp. 147 ff. where he notes Machiavelli and Conrad Celtes as precursors, as well as passages in C. H. Agrippa's *De incertitudine et vanitate scientiarum* and especially J. Cardan, *De rerum varietate*. Cf. also Moreau-Reibel, *op. cit.* pp. 69 ff.

doxia Epidemica of Sir Thomas Browne[14]—obscure the main
lines of the argument and often blind the casual reader to its real
value. Even the periodization of history is supported by Bodin's
belief in the efficacy of the number three and its mystical connota-
tions.[15]

No knowledge, then, is more important for the correct interpretation of universal history than an acquaintance with the nature
of peoples, based on the theory of climates and natural influences.
Bodin believed that natural influences had a good deal to do with
human history—but not everything to do. There are shades to
his opinions and even, here and there, contradictions. There are
many factors modifying the effect of natural surroundings. Bodin
was not an out-and-out determinist, like Cardan or Pontus de
Tyard, who admitted no possibility of modification.[16] Man is not
solely the result of his environment and (a characteristic touch,
mixing the superstitious and the rational) the astrological signs
under which he was born. Man can overcome the "law of nature"
by the help of God and by the strength of his own disciplined
will.[17]

The men of the North are usually large in stature and of high
color, as Bodin has observed in the person of his friend Holsterus[18]

---

[14] This relationship does not seem to have been remarked. Browne refers
to Bodin often in his *Pseudoxia Epidemica*. Cf. *Works of Sir Thomas
Browne,* ed. Charles Sayle (Edinburgh, 1928), II, 174-175, 179, 275, 288.

[15] Cf. *Methodus,* 177.

[16] Cf. Henri Busson, *Les sources et le développement du rationalisme dans
la littérature française de la Renaissance* (Paris, 1924), p. 547.

[17] Cf. *Methodus,* 118. "Sed imprimis illud statuo nullam esse locorum
aut caelestium syderum tantam vim, quae necessitatem sit allatura (quod
ne cogitare quidem fas est) ab iis tamen homines sic affici, ut naturae legem
nisi ope divina, aut diuturna disciplina superare non possint." Cf. also
République (ed. 1583), p. 666: ". . . et la difference des hommes mon-
taignars à ceux qui demeurent en la plaine, ou és lieux marescageux, ou
battus des vents impetueux: après nous dirons aussi combien la discipline peut
changer le droit naturel des hommes: en reiectant l'opinion de Polybe et de
Galen, qui ont tenu que le païs et la nature des lieux emporte necessité aux
moeurs des hommes."

[18] *Ibid.,* p. 124. Cf. *République* (ed. 1583), p. 668, where he repeats this
information and adds that Holster was "commisaire des guerres natif d'Ostol-
come en Suede."

who is broad shouldered and red haired. Hubert Languet[19] the noted traveler also gives the same testimony. Northerners, with much "internal heat" are fiercer and stronger than those from the South.[20] Consequently, the great invasions have usually been made from the North; and the strongest empires have been propagated from the North toward the South, and never in the opposite direction. Rome conquered the Carthaginians, but was unable to advance beyond the Danube. The internal heat and the humors of the Germans account for their strength, for their heroic eating and drinking, and for their warlike habits.[21] The people of the South are intellectually gifted, those of the North, physically. Men of the North have the physical force to conquer empires, but lack the ability to maintain them.[22] There is a certain divine wisdom in the fact that crafty nations are physically weak and the physically strong are wanting in guile.[23] Bodin defends the fecundity of the northern races, disputing the judgment of Hippocrates that the Scyths (a vague term which Bodin seems to use for all the Northern races) were impotent, because of excessive physical activity.[24]

The southern peoples (because of their abundance of black bile) tend to be melancholy and contemplative; they were the authors and chief practitioners of the beaux arts; unravelled the mysteries of nature; invented the mathematical sciences. Northerners, abounding in blood and humors, are not suited for contemplation, but possess a mechanical dexterity. The men of the temperate zone have their own special capabilities. They are gifted as executives and statesmen.[25]

---

[19] *Ibid.*

[20] Cf. *République* (ed. 1583), p. 673.

[21] Cf. R. Charbonnel, *La pensée italienne au XVIe siècle* (Paris, 1919), p. 243. Cf. also C. Cremonini, *De calido innato,* Leyden, 1634 and *République* (ed. 1583), p. 668 et passim.

[22] Cf. *Methodus,* 138 and *République* (ed. 1583), p. 671: "Et la sagesse de Dieu a si bien distribué ses graces qu'elle n'a iamais uni la force grande avec une grande ruse d'esprit, ny aux hommes, ny au bestes."

[23] *Methodus,* 139.

[24] *Ibid.,* 147. Cf. also *Gargantua et Pantagruel* (Bk. II, Chap. 30) where Rabelais uses the same argument of Hippocrates.

[25] *Ibid.,* 162.

The Northerners are more fickle than the men of temperate or southern regions. Childlike, they are easily angered and easily appeased. Examples of the inconstancy of the Germans are numerous, Bodin remarks, but nothing is more revelatory of this than their attitude toward religion. Bodin's account of the Reformation gives an interesting sidelight on his attitude toward Protestantism.[26] He begins:

> Bohemia and Saxony were the first to fall away from the Roman rite; how wisely they acted is not a question that I shall discuss here. They had many serious and erudite men, who revealed the frauds of the popes.[27] These men having meditated about the matter for a long time, finally made a decision and undertook a movement of the greatest difficulty. I am speaking rather of the common people, who associated themselves in the movement without understanding it in the least.

He remarks the widespread revolt and the consequent rise of hundreds of confusing, conflicting sects:[28]

> If, having rejected the old religion, the Germans could have made up their mind about another and remained in agreement about it, they would have been able to persuade others much more easily. Rather, in a short time, all Germany was a tangle of conflicting religious opinions. Not only were there Hussites and Lutherans, but also a countless crowd of other sects; Anabaptists, Zwinglians, Waldensians, Adamites, and many others.

In discussing this question of constancy and fickleness, Bodin inserts an aside which expresses his own personal opinion of these matters. For him, constancy is a thing of moderation, not of unyielding rigidity. His is not the heroic attitude of a man who takes an uncompromising position, which he will defend with his life. It is rather the attitude of Montaigne, the attitude which insists that no conviction is worth shedding blood for. This was

---

[26] *Methodus,* 184.
[27] The Magdeburg Centuriators.
[28] *Methodus,* 185.

The Major Themes of the Methodus

the feeling of most of the *Politiques* at a time when wisdom consisted in trimming the sails to catch the wind of circumstance. Bodin's entire life was adjusted to this end and his religious views, so confusing otherwise, become more comprehensible in this light.[29] There is the note of personal conviction in this confession of moderate faith of a *politique*:[30]

> Ego vero sic existimo esse in hominum dictis & factis, ut in rebus omnibus, auream mediocritatem quae constantia dicitur; quaeque inter levitatem & pertinacem medium tuetur; nec sapientibus unquam laudata est in una sententia perpetua permansio; sed ut in navigando tempestati obsequi artis est, etiamsi portum tenere nequeas, tum vero gubernaculum ad omnem caeli faciem torquere, ac saepius velificationem mutare, summae prudentiae iudicatur.

In concluding his remarks on the influence of natural conditions, Bodin points out that the nature of peoples is much affected by windy, mountainous, or swampy places.[31]   Mountaineers are sturdy and robust, such as the Swiss are.   Hot and swampy places produce languid, disease-ridden inhabitants.   Seafaring races become fierce and aggressive through the constant battering of wind and wave.

A very potent influence in changing and shaping the nature of a people is interbreeding.   This accounts for the wide divergence from type that is found among races.[32]   Bodin enlarges on this theme in his ninth chapter, where he uses it to prove that all claims of "pure descent" and "unmixed blood" are quite unfounded.

As I have already pointed out, the idea of the *respublica mundana* is intimately connected with Bodin's naturalistic conception of his-

---

[29] Cf. also L. J. Diecmann, *De naturalismo . . . cum aliorum, tum maxime Jo. Bodini* . . . . (Leipzig, 1684), p. 3; and for a different view, Summerfield Baldwin, "Jean Bodin and the League," in *Catholic Historical Review*, XXIII (1937), 160-184.

[30] *Methodus*, 187.   Cf. also passage of same tenor, repeated almost verbatim, in *République*, Bk. V, chap. I.

[31] *Ibid.*, 204.

[32] *Ibid.*, 212 ff.   "Non parum etiam mores hominum et naturam immutant confusiones populorum."

tory and develops naturally from it. It is a theme which recurs throughout the *Methodus* and under the most diverse aspects: as an argument against "economic isolationism" and against the vanities of "national origins; in connection with the theory of correspondences and of the macrocosm and the microcosm; and as an aspect of the *ius gentium.* It is treated most fully in the fifth chapter in the course of the discussion of national psychology. This conception of a *respublica mundana* (an ideal of world unity, no longer based, however, on the mediaeval ideal of the *respublica christiana*) was common enough at the time among jurists and philosophers.[33]

Every citizen performs his part in the state, according to his capabilities. In turn, as Bodin has shown, each people has its own psychology, its own particular aptitudes: the sum of these, united to form a complete and co-ordinated whole, goes to make up the *respublica mundana.* And the *respublica mundana,* in its turn, has its place in the series of cosmic and celestial correspondences.[34] Bodin re-states the theme in terms of the macrocosm and the microcosm, one of the favorite subjects of Renaissance philosophizing, to which he will later devote a chapter in his *Universae naturae theatrum,* from, however a slightly different approach:[35]

There is a "correspondence" between the human body and the *respublica mundana*: the philosophers are the brain, the

---

[33] Cf. Otto Gierke, *J. Althusius und die Entwicklung der naturrechtlichen Staatstheorie,* Breslau, 1880. He includes references to Oldendorp, Connan, Winkler, Cantiuncula, although he claims that Bodin does not treat the theme.

[34] *Methodus,* 169. "Quod igitur de una civitate, idem quoque de mundana Republica iudicandum relinquitur, ut distributis populorum muneribus, Australium sapientia, Scytharum robur, mediorum prudentia quomodo propria sit. id quod etiam in animae partibus videre est. etenim mens ipsa monet, ratio iubet, sensus autem veluti satellites ad exequendum adhibentur."

[35] *Ibid.,* pp. 169-170. "Et in triplici animae facultate, animali, vitali, et naturali: una quidem a cerebro motum & sensum: altera spiritum a corde vitalem: tertia ab hepate vegetationem. neque enim melius, opinor, insita populo cuique natura intelligi potest, nec de historia quaque iudicium certius ac verius fieri, quam si microcosmus hic magno homine, id est, cum mundo conferatur."

The Major Themes of the Methodus

military men are the heart, "quod illic irascendi vis posita sit,"[36] and the workmen and the farmers perform the function of the liver, which supplies nourishment and manufactures blood for the body.[37] After establishing the correspondences between the human body and the *respublica mundana,* Bodin proceeds to demonstrate a like relationship between the *respublica mundana* and the planets.[38]

The threefold division of peoples, Northern, Temperate, and Southern, corresponds also to a threefold scheme of the world: the intellectual world of the mind; the celestial world of the stars; and the "elemental" world of the birth and death of things.[39]

Bodin's periodization of history (also outlined in this rich and germinal fifth chapter) into three great epochs is compounded of the diverse, but related materials which have been pointed out here. His division results from his theories of national character as formed by natural influence, of the *respublica mundana* and from his belief in the significance of the number three.[40] The first two-thousand-year period has been dominated by the Southern peoples and has been marked by the development of religion and philosophy, for which the contemplative southern temperament is especially fitted. The next two thousand years belong to the people of the temperate zone and are characterized by the rise of governments and of the political arts. The third period is one in which

---

[36] Cf. *Methodus,* 170.

[37] Cf. R. Charbonnel, *op. cit.,* p. 194: "Partant de ce principe que chaque monde trouve la raison de ses lois dans un monde supérieur, que la constitution de l'homme n'est que l'image de la constitution de l'univers, puisque le ciel est la cause formelle de la nature, de son organisation, des types génériques, et spéciaux qui s'y rencontrent, l'astrologie et toutes les sciences qu'elle embrasse s'efforcent de mettre en relief les correspondances . . .

[38] Cf. *Methodus,* 176. Cf. also E. Fournol, "Quelques traites du droit public," *Nouvelle revue historique du droit,* XXI (1897), 308-309.

[39] Cf. *Methodus,* p. 177.

[40] *Ibid.* p. 178. "Ita quoque duobus annorum millibus homines religione ac sapientia praestiterunt . . . duobus item annorum millibus in constituendis civitatibus, in legibus sanciendis, in coloniis deducendis occupati fuerunt . . . ab Australibus ad mediae regionis homines imperia sunt delata. consequentibus annorum millibus id est a Christe morte, variae artes antea incognitae, & opificia in lucem venerunt . . . atque imperia . . . abrogata et ad Scythas Martis alumnos translata fuerunt."

The Major Themes of the Methodus   97

the Northern peoples, the children of Mars, take the ascendancy
and bring with them mechanical inventions and warfare. It is a
periodization of history which recalls Hegel's division into
Oriental, Greco-Roman, and Germanic cultures. It has even more
affinity, however, with Vico's schema in the *Scienza nuova*. Both
are organized on the basis of the number three. Vico, however, extending the division by threes farther than Bodin,
establishes the three different types of natures, of customs, of
natural laws, of government, of language, of jurisprudence, etc.[41]

The *respublica mundana* also has its economic ramifications.
Bodin's arrangement of the *loci* of history in his third chapter
reveals to what extent he conceived of history in economic terms.[42]
He points out, moreover, the economic interdependence of the
various nations. None can produce everything it needs for itself;
economic necessity builds up an association among nations, a sort
of commercial *respublica mundana*.[43] He enlarges on this idea in
his ninth chapter in combatting the degeneration-idea. Vaunting
the achievements of the moderns, Bodin signalizes certain inventions, such as the magnetic needle, which have enabled men to
extend their geographical horizons far beyond the dreams of the
ancients. These have made possible great commercial advances,
which, in turn have strengthened the *respublica mundana*. It is
not the mediaeval ideal of world unity based on a common faith,
but rather a unity based on business practices and trade.[44] This
praise of trade (never respected during the Middle Ages) reflects

---

[41] Cf. *Scienza nuova*, ed. F. Nicolini (Bari, 1931), Bk. IV, section iv.

[42] Bodin's interest in economic problems becomes more evident in the
famous *Réponse à M. de Malestroit* (1568) and in certain passages of the
République notably in Bk. VI, chap. iii, *De re numaria*. . . . Cf. Henri
Hauser's edition of the *Réponse* (Paris, 1932), with an excellent introduction. He well notes (p. xxxvi): "Et plus loin, il (Bodin) esquisse . . .
une théorie . . . qui annonce déjà l'optimisme manchesterien, ou si l'on
préfère cette formule, la théodicée cobdenienne.

[43] Cf. *Methodus*, 36.

[44] *Ibid.* p. 479: "ex quo non modo mercatura (quae antea sordida vel non
satis erat cognita) abundans et quaestuosa evasit, verumetiam omnes
homines secum ipsi et cum respublica mundana velut in una eademque civitate
mirabiliter conspirant."

98   *The Major Themes of the Methodus*

a significant social trend; already the saint of the new order, the businessman, is in the process of canonization.[45]

There is yet another aspect under which Bodin conceives of the *respublica mundana*. The king of Spain, he says, rules over the most diverse territories, separated from each other by great physical distances, by differences of race, religion, and language, but which are, nevertheless, welded into union by the binding force of a common sovereignty. There is, moreover, among all men a certain common law of reason, a *ius gentium*, which all recognize. The world should be like one state, since all men are bound together by the *ius gentium* and by bonds of blood. But this sovereignty of reason is not absolutely binding on anyone and consequently the *respublica mundana* remains in the realm of the ideal.

One of the principal obstacles in the way of the realization of the *respublica mundana* is national vanity or pride in national origin. In his ninth chapter, Bodin seeks to deflate this illusion, by showing how all peoples have been inextricably intermingled by migration, inter-breeding, etc. There is no such thing as purity of blood. He states that his principal aim in writing about the origin of nations was to show that all men were consanguineous.[46]

> cum enim multa divinitus ad origines scribendas Mosem impulerunt, tum illud etiam, opinor, ut omnes homines ad quos ea fama pervenisset, plane intelligerent se esse consanguineos, & eadem generis coniunctione sociatos.

There is a genuine eloquence in Bodin's words on international relationship. Whoever boasts of being self-sufficient, of being of "pure stock" is breaking the chain of brotherhood which binds human society together. Such was the contempt of the Egyptians for the Hebrews; of the Greeks for the Latins; once for the Roman, the name of *peregrinus* was the synonym for enemy; and Germans call foreigners (with great scorn) *Valchi*. How much better it is to associate with the foreigner on friendly terms since

---

[45] Cf. H. J. Laski, *The Rise of Liberalism: The Philosophy of a Business Civilization* (New York, 1937), p. 2.

[46] *Methodus*, 535-536.

all men are joined by common bonds?[47] How unwise were those
laws of Plato and Lycurgus, which cut citizens off from all contact with outsiders. What is this, but depriving men of human
associations? Moses decreed that foreigners should be treated
with all respect and that injuries done to them should be punished
more severely than those done to citizens. This inter-relationship
of nations is emphasized by Almighty God, says Bodin, repeating
a point he has already made, since He made no region so fertile
that it was economically independent.[48]

It is in the seventh chapter of the *Methodus* that Bodin, after
refuting the German pretensions relative to the Four Monarchies,
demolishes another of the myths created partly by the prophecy
of Daniel and partly by classical poets and philosophers: the myth
of the Golden Age.[49] Thus the statue in Daniel was supposed
to represent five epochs: the head of gold represented the first;
the chest of silver, the second; the thighs of bronze, the third;
the legs of iron, the fourth; and the feet of clay, the fifth. Bodin
opposes this opinion:[50]

> nam si quis historicorum, non poetarum excutiat intelli-
> gentiam, profecto iudicabit parem esse in rebus humanis,
> atque in omnium rerum natura conversionem.

In opposing the myth of the golden age, Bodin enunciates his
theory of progress. With him it is not yet a clear-cut concept.
He approaches it from the negative side, by denying the degeneration of man, denying the superiority of the past over the present.
Rather than a theory of progress, as Gillot[51] has correctly seen,
it is more correctly designated as a contribution in favor of the
moderns in the nascent struggle between the Ancients and the
Moderns which was to be waged so vigorously for the next two
centuries. Bodin—as well as some of the keenest of his con-

---

[47] *Ibid.*, p. 537.

[48] *Ibid.*

[49] Cf. also G. Atkinson, *Les nouveaux horizons de la Renaissance française*
(Paris, 1935), pp. 346 ff.

[50] *Methodus*, p. 470.

[51] H. Gillot, *op. cit.*, p. 142, *et passim*.

temporaries—was a standard bearer in the camp of the sixteenth century modernists.[52]

The Golden Age? Compared with the present age, asserts Bodin, it was rather an Iron Age. Everyone knows that the flood was sent because of the wrong-doing of men. In the Golden Age, they say, Saturn and Cameses were flourishing: and it is clear that Cameses was the son of Noah and Saturn was Nimrod.[53] But Cameses criminally violated the modesty of his father. And the nature of Nimrod, the founder of the Golden Age, is indicated by his name alone, which means rebel in Hebrew. Moses calls him the "strong hunter" (robustus venator), a term which everywhere designates robbers. Aristotle places thieves in the classification of hunters. And there was Jupiter Belus, who cast out his own father. There are many "Joves" (at least three hundred were worshipped in antiquity) but each one is characterized by the deposition of his father and is further known for parricide, for incest, and for every sort of lust. The "golden age" was also marked by the revolt of the giants against heaven; by the chaos following the building of the Tower of Babel, by the confusion of the tongues.[54] This then, says Bodin, is the period which has been held up as worthy of emulation! Manethon was correct when he rated Hercules as "the greatest of pirates," and one addicted to all sorts of lust. But if these accounts seem fabulous, consult the histories of Thucydides.[55] He writes that shortly before his time the land was filled with robbers and the sea with pirates. There was no disgrace in the "profession" of

[52] Among these was Loys le Roys, Regius professor of Greek at the Collège de France, whose ideas invite comparison with Bodin's on many points. Cf. especially his *Douze livres de la vicissitude ou la varieté des choses* (Paris, 1575) and the thesis of H. Becker, *Louis LeRoy,* Paris, 1897.

[53] Another example of Bodin's gropings toward a "comparative mythology."

[54] Cf. *Methodus,* 470 ff. See especially p. 474: "haec fuerunt aurea et argentea secula, quibus homines ferarum more in agris ac silvis dispersi, tantum haberent, quantum per vim et nefas retinere possent, quousque paulatim ab illa feritate ac barbarie sunt ad hanc quam videmus morum humanitatem ac legitimam societatem revocati."

[55] *Ibid.,* p. 473.

brigand. *Ius* lay in force of arms. This was the way men lived in the golden age which has been sung by the poets![56]

If the human race were constantly degenerating, as the proponents of the Golden Age assert, it would have "struck bottom" long since. But since the men of the "gold and silver" ages could sink no lower, they were driven on by shame or by necessity and assisted by the grace of God, they gradually began to improve, little by little.[57]

This is Bodin's cautious and incomplete statement of the "theory of progress." He obviously did not conceive of "progress" in the modern sense, as an ever-mounting straight line, the doctrine of necessary advancement and Panglossian optimism which hypnotized the nineteenth century. He did not think of "progress" in those terms at all. For him, it was simply an aspect of the constant changes (*conversiones*) to which all things are subject. A culture flourishes and then decays; but the culture that follows may attain a higher level of civilization, thanks to the achievements of that which preceded. "Progress" was not a value in itself, as it was later to become. However, Bodin's conviction that mankind is not constantly degenerating; that, through a long series of *conversiones,* some slight advances must necessarily appear; that the achievements of his own day were equal and superior to those of the ancients all pointed to the crystallization of the concept in later thinkers.

Social habits have improved.[58] Human sacrifices are no longer offered and the revolting wild-beast shows of the Romans have disappeared. Ancient heroes are surpassed by modern counterparts. And there are changes (*conversiones*) in the arts as well as in civil government. They spring up, attain a mature flowering,

---

[56] *Ibid.,* p. 474.

[57] *Ibid.* "Quod si res humanae in deterius prolaberentur, iampridem in extremo vitiorum ac improbitatis gradu constitissemus: quo quidem antea perventum esse opinor. sed cum flagitiosi homines nec ulterius progredi, nec eodem loco stare diutius possent, sensim regredi necesse habuerunt, vel cogente pudore, qui hominibus inest a natura: vel necessitate, quod in tantis sceleribus societas nullo modo coli poterat: vel etiam, quod verius est, impellente Dei bonitate."

[58] *Ibid.,* p. 475.

and disappear. Greece, once supreme, is in dust. Latin culture crumbled under the barbarian assaults, but from its ashes sprang the vigorous civilization of his own day. Bodin devotes the rest of the chapter[59] to a panegyric of the present.[60]

> ad nostra tempora relabor, quibus multo postquam literae toto pene terrarum orbe conquierant, tantus subito scientiarum omnium splendor affulsit, tanta fertilitas extitit ingeniorum, ut nullis unquam aetatibus maior.

Even the Germans, weighed down as they are by "humors" have shared in this movement, as it has been demonstrated by Olaus Magnus, Holster and others. It would seem that fate decreed that the Goths, who had once dealt the death blows to learning, should help in resuscitating it. All of these facts indicate a certain cycle (*conversio*). Doubtless, the same process takes place in the spirit of man as in the fields, which produce better, after having lain fallow for a time.[61]

It may be said that the ancients were the inventors of the arts and therefore deserving of more credit. But the moderns have invented devices quite unknown to the ancients, such as the magnetic needle, which Bodin styles "divine," and which made possible the discovery of new worlds.[62] In war, ancient weapons now appear ridiculous. And the invention of printing alone is worth all the achievements of the ancients. Nevertheless, Bodin, always moderate in his views, warns that those who claim all credit for the present are just as wrong as those who unreservedly support the ancients. Each age makes its own peculiar contribution and nature is an inexhaustible treasury, from which no one epoch can draw all the knowledge.[63]

---

[59] *Ibid.*, pp. 476-479.

[60] *Ibid.*, p. 478.

[61] Cf. *Ibid.* For a bibliography on the cyclic conception of history, see P. Sorokin, *Social and Cultural Dynamics*, vol. II, *Fluctuation of Systems of Truth, Ethics, and Law* (New York, 1937), p. 381.

[62] *Ibid.*, p. 479: "Cum enim magnete nihil sit admirabilius in tota rerum natura, usum tamen eius plane divinum antiqui ignorarunt: & cum illi sese alveo mediterraneo continerent, nostri quotannis terrarum orbem crebris navigationibus obeunt & in alium orbem, ut ita dicam, colonias deducunt, iam ut intimos Indiae recessus apertos habemus."

[63] *Ibid.*, p. 480.

In his discussion of "national psychology" and its various correspondences, Bodin sought to establish a relation between the
several human types and the planets. Saturn and Venus correspond
to the Southern peoples; Jove and Mercury to those of the temperate zone; to the North, Mars and the Moon. This further
demonstrates the unity of nature: for the Chaldeans claimed that
Saturn presides over contemplation; Jupiter over execution, and
Mars over the manual arts.[64] After setting up these correspondences, Bodin proceeds to utilize them in a fashion which strikingly
recalls Vico's theories on the historicity of myths. The poets have
written that Saturn was overthrown by Jove. This indicates an
actual social change, although expressed in figurative and symbolic
language. Poetry, which was composed long before history was
written, is a valuable aid in reconstructing primitive history. In
the earliest times, the priests and the philosophers were chosen as
kings:[65]

> ac fortasse illud est quod a poetis iactatur; Saturnum ab
> Jove de imperio deturbatum id est religiosos ac sapientes
> homines primis temporibus iustitiae fruendae causa reges
> esse creatos.

That is to say, Saturn, representing the Southern peoples, the
philosophico-religious type, was dominant in the earliest days.
But, men unfortunately are not kept in order by piety alone and
must be constrained by stronger means. Thus "Saturn" was
deposed by "Jove," and the philosophical races of the South were
displaced by the races of the temperate zone. And Bodin implies
(by the later development of the chapter) that Jove was then
displaced by Mars, and the Northern races became dominant:[66]

> sed cum sola pietate homines in officio continere se posse
> arbitrarentur, neque tamen id praestare possent, cum
> scilicet plerique nec metu divino, nec ulla religione
> ducerentur, prudentiores arrepta potestate Rempublicam
> regere.

---

[64] This attribution of certain qualities to the different planets is treated
by R. Charbonnel, *op. cit.*, pp. 196 ff.

[65] *Methodus*, 168.

[66] *Ibid.*

Significant, too, is Bodin's stand that pagan mythology is only
a distorted version of Christian truths: another aspect of his
recognition of the inherent historicity of the myth. He states
definitely: the old poets translated into the form of fables the
ancient truths which they received from their ancestors.[67] The
belief that pagan mythology was an imperfect representation of
Christian doctrine motivated his attempt to synchronize this
mythology with the Old Testament story. What Sacred Scripture
relates of Cham, who violated the modesty of his father, is reproduced by the Greeks in the figure of Jove.[68] The Greek Saturn
was only the Biblical Nimrod under another name.[69] These
speculations, fragmentary as they are, clearly adumbrate the more
extensive treatment of the myth in the *Scienza Nuova*.[70] Bodin
did not approach mythology in the fashion of most of his contemporaries simply as a collection of pleasant but mendacious
tales. Rather he saw in it, and in ancient poetry as well, a figurative and symbolic treatment of actual social and economic history.
He would have viewed myths in much the same light as the
modern anthropologist, except for his passion for reducing them
to Old Testament terms.[71]

Mythology, then, concludes Bodin, is one of the auxiliary sciences of history . . . and there are still others, as yet little utilized,

---

[67] *Methodus*, 512: "Omitto quod veteres Poetae rei veritatem a maioribus
acceptam ad fabulas inanes transtulerunt."

[68] *Ibid.*, 513.

[69] *Ibid.*, 470.

[70] Cf. G. Vico, *La scienza nuova* (Bari, 1928), I, Section 2, Paragraph 43,
p. 89: "Questa stessa degnitá con l'antecedente che ne dánno prima tanti
Giovi, dappoi tanti Ercoli tralle nazioni gentili—oltreché né dimonstrano
che non si poterono fondare senza religione né ingrandire senza virtú,
essendono elle ne' lor incominciamentio selvagge e chiuse, e perciò non
sappiendo nulla l'una dell'altra, per la degnitá che 'idee uniformi, nate tra
populi sconosciuti, debbon aver un motivo commune di vero,'—ne dánno di
piú questo gran principio: che le prime favole dovettero contenere veritá
civili, e perciò essere state le storie de' primi populi."

[71] Cf. Paul Hazard, *La crise de la conscience européenne* (Paris, 1935),
III, 37-38, where he quotes a letter of Bossuet to D. Huet: "Il faut, Mon-
seigneur, être ennemi de la raison et du bon sens pour mépriser les avantages
que la véritable religion tire des fables dont les anciens ont enveloppé les
traditions primitives du genre humain."

such as philology.   Language and linguistic changes, he asserts,
provide valuable historical evidence for those who know how to
make use of them.   He is especially interested in linguistic evidence
as a tool in the research concerning the origin of peoples :[72]

> illud tamen quod nostri originum scriptores non satis
> aperuerunt, scilicet linguarum vestigia, in quibus praeci-
> puum est originis argumentum. . . .

The linguistic knowledge of his day was not sufficiently developed to lend the support of scientifically correct illustrations
to his remarkably sound general principles.   Here, as elsewhere
in Bodin, we discover a disconcerting mélange of the sound and
the silly.   He lays down fundamental principles of *Sprachwissens-
chaft* worthy of a Vossler, of a Meillet: then backs them up with
examples akin to some of Isidore's etymologies.   The skeleton of
his linguistic theories is impressive, when viewed as a skeleton.
Taken undiluted, in the chapter *Qua ratione populorum origines
haberi possint,* they are confused, bogged down with verbiage and
etymological blunders, such as the derivation of the term *Ouallones*
(Walloons) from "où allons-nous."   His views are further in-
validated by the fact that he has a thesis to prove: the Germans,
he contends, derived their language and their general culture from
the ancient Celts, who lived in Gaul.   I have chosen to emphasize
the soundness of his general linguistic principles, minimizing the
untenable details.

The problems he considers indicate the validity of his basic
ideas: the historical significance of place names and personal
names; the causes of linguistic change; the linguistic conservatism of rural areas; words as an index of social organization and
as a means of tracing the history of institutions.

Linguistic changes tend to occur, he remarks,[73] on account of
three principal reasons: First of all, the passage of time alters all
things.   The songs, of very ancient composition, sung at Roman
religious festivals were understood by very few on account of the
changes in the language.   Thus, all languages of all peoples tend

---

[72] *Methodus,* 540.
[73] *Ibid.,* p. 548.

106 *The Major Themes of the Methodus*

to change somewhat in a slow and gradual fashion.[74] Another cause for linguistic change and one that brings about a more rapid alteration of language, is the intermingling of various peoples by colonization, migration, and invasion. Italy and Greece preserved the purity of their speech, claims Bodin, for many generations; after the incursions of the Goths and the Scyths, it was changed beyond recognition. A final cause for change in languages resides in the very nature of the region in which it is spoken. The people of the North employ a vocabulary full of consonants, which are emitted harshly and forcibly—due to their abundance of "interior heat" and the rigor of the climate.[75] Southerners pronounce less harshly, with a greater abundance of vowels, due to their lack of interior heat. For example, when Charlemagne led his colony of Saxons into Belgium, they pronounced *Pfert,* while the Flamands, brought up in a more temperate climate, said *Pert.*

The science of place names, asserts Bodin, has been much neglected in France, despite its value as historical evidence. He has gathered his information about the subject from various sources, including several of his friends: Jerome Chandieu, (Hieronymus Chando)[76] "secretarius regius, non minus eruditione quam generis splendore clarus," and "Philibertus Barjotus, praetor Maconensis." Caesar, moreover,[77] had tried to establish the fact that the Britons were descended from the Belgian Gauls, since the place names of the two people were similar.

Significant, too, are Bodin's remarks about linguistic conservatism. "Country people," he wisely remarks, "did not take kindly to Latin words;" large towns and districts closest to Italy showed the most pronounced Latinization of speech.[78] In fact, in Southern Gaul, the language became almost the same as Latin. But in the rest of the country, it was clear that the Roman soldiers did not impress their language on the populace. Traces of the old Celtic speech are still to be noted in French. German is still more rich in them, since Rome established few colonies in Germany outside

---

[74] *Ibid.,* p. 549.
[75] *Ibid.,* p. 549-550.
[76] *Ibid.,* p. 567.
[77] *Ibid.,* p. 547.
[78] *Ibid.,* p. 571.

of Constance and Trèves. Among the Celtic survivals, Bodin notes[79] *alauda,* etc. and many suffixes, such as *-magus, -dunus, -marc,* etc. He claims that the Germans lacked the suffix *-magus,* since it signified "city" and they had none at this period. Since the word does not exist, he argues, neither does the institution. The social development of a culture may be gauged by the growth of its vocabulary. *Land,* he claims is another Celtic word[80] which the Germans use as a general term and which, among the French, (*lande*) signifies a waste place, such as "all Germany was in the earliest times." After pointing out various other similarities, Bodin draws the desired conclusions from his linguistic investigations: German speech was derived from Celtic sources, and the Germans owe their origin, their laws, and their civilization to the Gauls.[81] Bodin's further claim (following Bovillus and Picart) that the ancient Celtic language was derived from the Greek[82] is simply another manifestation of the Renaissance passion for tracing the national vernaculars back to the purest classical sources. Such pseudo-linguistic acrobatics were tiresomely common throughout the period. The rather truculent nationalism which is the dominating tone of Bodin's philological discussions clashes with the pleas for the brotherhood of man and for the realization of the *respublica mundana* which he expressed elsewhere in the same chapter. Contradictions, however, are common enough, both in the *Methodus* and in the *République.*

This group of ideas which we have just considered, scattered throughout the *Methodus,* forms the basis, properly speaking, of Bodin's philosophy of history, if such a term may be applied to the loosely integrated series of concepts. To marshal them in logical sequence (as Bodin himself took little care to do) we might sum them up rather in this fashion: the basis for historical theoriz-

---

[79] *Ibid.,* p. 570.

[80] *Ibid.,* p. 575.

[81] *Ibid.,* p. 576: "Perspicuum esse opinor Germanicam linguam, magna sui parte e purissimis Celtarum fontibus derivari. Quod si ita est, sequitur illud quoque originem, arma, leges, humanitatem denique Gallis deberi: ac vehementer labi Lazius qui maiores nostros a Germanos oriundos esse affirmat."

[82] *Ibid.,* p. 550.

ing must rest on a knowledge of natural conditions, since these, in a large measure, determine the psychology and the cultural destiny of peoples. These natural conditions are constant and unvarying; they produce men in the present who are as gifted and capable as those of the so-called "Golden Age." Mankind is not constantly degenerating. History consists of a series of *conversiones,* of cycles, which result in a slow, upward movement, in slight, but undeniable, progress. This theoretical statement is supported, as ·is customary in Bodin, (and this is one of his most valuable contributions to scientific methodology) by a comparative investigation which seeks to prove by the marshalling of historical fact that the "Golden Age" was actually a cruel and primitive period. Natural conditions, moreover, whether they be economic, social, psychological, point toward the necessity for a *Respublica mundana,* the union of various peoples, and the abolition of national prejudices. History cannot be narrowly national; it must be international and universal in its point of view. In studying history, many "auxiliary sciences" have been overlooked; Bodin urges the utilization of evidence derived from the historical and comparative study of myths (as figurative expression of actual events) and of language (as indicative of social organization and the nature of institutions), especially in throwing light on primitive periods, when written records are rare. More important, perhaps, than these conclusions themselves, is the method which leads Bodin to them: the method of the comparison of historical fact, applied haltingly and gropingly to be sure, but which will be used on a more impressive scale in the *République,* and which is of a real significance in the development of modern scientific procedure.

One sizeable bloc of material in the *Methodus* is that inspired by the writings of Bodin's predecessors in historical theory, whether Italian humanists or German reformers; another, as we have just seen, consists of that devoted to an exposition of the fundamentals of a "philosophy of history." There remain two other major groups of ideas—Bodin's judgments on previous historians, a critical labor incidental to, but still indicative of, his main concepts about history and its composition; and a second group stating his political doctrines, interesting as a preparatory sketch for the *République,* but out of place, as his critics have remarked, in an *ars historica*. It is to the section devoted to criticisms of individual historians that we shall now give our attention.

*   *   *   *   *   *

F. Baudouin in his *De instituenda historia* concerns himself with a critical evaluation of preceding historical writers, and Bodin, perhaps following his lead, devotes a part of the fourth chapter, *De historicorum delectu,* to the same purpose. Most of the later *artes historicae* likewise undertake the task. Several of Bodin's judgments are extremely provocative, especially those on Guicciardini, Paulus Jovius, and Tacitus.

Montaigne knew this chapter of the *Methodus* well and utilized it in the composition of the essay *Des Livres*. This essay, in its criticisms, is full of Bodinian echoes. There is a common admiration for Caesar; there is a preference in each for an historical style, which, as Montaigne says, is *nue et informe*. Both agree that the perfect historian should be well-versed in actual affairs and that more than scholarship is necessary in his formation. Finally, Montaigne dismisses further discussion of historiographical problems by pointing out that these things have been well handled by Bodin:[83]

> Vrayement la conoissance que nous avons de nos affaires est bien plus lasche. Mais cecy a este suffisamment traicte par Bodin, et selon ma conception.

He does not agree, however, with Bodin's judgment on Plutarch, one of the longest critiques in the chapter, and the one which is probably the most known, thanks to Montaigne's refutation of it in the essay *Défense de Sénèque et Plutarche*.[84] Bodin observes that, treating history by the biographical method, Plutarch assumes the office of a "censor of princes" rather than of the true historian. "Est autem quod in eo miremur liberum de re quaque iudicium, ut non tam historicus quam principum censor esse videtur."[85] He concludes, nevertheless, that if anyone is suited for this task, Plutarch

---

[83] *Essais,* Book II, Chap. X.
[84] *Ibid.,* Book II, Chap. XXXII.
[85] *Methodus,* 85.

is. He quarrels with the construction of Plutarch's work and claims that the system of "parallel lives" often leads to unhappy results, since men are handled side by side who are not comparable in any sense of the word.[86] Furthermore, Plutarch did not know Latin sufficiently well (as he admits himself) to treat of Roman[87] subjects with accuracy. He made several mistakes in his remarks on Greek and Roman coinage, which led Guillaume Budé astray in the composition of the *De Asse*.[88] Bodin, moreover, cannot believe, in view of the strictness of the old Roman laws concerning adultery, the statement made by Plutarch that the exchange of wives was permitted among the Romans.[89] It is here that parenthetically he points out what he believes to be an error of Cujas in the interpretation of certain terms relating to Roman adultery laws.[90] This however is the criticism that aroused Montaigne:

saepe incredibilia & plane fabulosa narrat, sed utitur verbo ne quis temere assentiatur. Ut in Lycurgo scribit puerum Lacedaemonium crudelissimam lacerationem & iliorum distractione ad necem usque pertulisse, ne vulpis furtum detegeretur.

Montaigne counters:

Venons à Plutarque. Jean Bodin est un bon autheur de nostre temps et accompagne de beaucoup plus de jugement que la tourbe des escrivailleurs de son siecle et merite qu'on le juge et considere. Je le trouve un peu hardy en ce passage de sa *Méthode,* ou il accuse Plutarque non seulement d'ignorance surquoy je l'eusse laisse dire, car cela n'est pas de mon gibier, mais aussi en ce que cet autheur escrit souvent des choses incroyables et entierement fabuleuses (ce sont ses mots) . . . .

---

[86] *Methodus*, 86: "idque facile intelligi potest in comparatione Demosthenis ac Ciceronis: Catonis and Aristidis . . . quid autem aliud est Agesilaum Pompeio, quam muscam Elephanto conferre?"

[87] *Ibid.* "Interdum etiam in Romanorum antiquitate labitur: quod in homine Graeco, qui se linguam Latinam non satis intellexisse in vita Demosthenis confitetur, mirum videri non debet."

[88] *Ibid.,* 87. "Librae minam aequavit in vita Fabii and Antonii. id quod Budaeo magnam praebuit errandi occasionem."

[89] *Ibid.*

[90] *Ibid.,* p. 86.

Montaigne does not find the illustration of the Spartan boy at all incredible, since he is so thoroughly imbued in the spirit of those times :[91]

> Je suis si imbu de la grandeur de ces hommes la que non seulement il ne me semble, comme a Bodin, que son conte soit incroyable, que je ne le trouve seulement rare et estrange.

One of the most significant of Bodin's judgments is his evaluation of Tacitus. Tacitus was the very storm center of an intellectual movement (connected intimately with the *ragion di stato*) which raged in western Europe during the sixteenth and seventeenth centuries. G. Toffanin has well interpreted it in his *Machiavelli e il Tacitismo*.[92] It was by no means limited to Italy, however, and the Tacitus-problem was hotly discussed in France[93] and Spain[94] as well. Schanz-Hosius[95] gives an excellent, succinct sketch of the varying fortunes of Tacitus' work and the various interpretations applied to it from the Middle Ages through the

---

[91] Sir Thomas Browne, however, in the *Pseudodoxia Epidemica* (Bk. VI, cap. xviii) agrees with Bodin: "The relation of Plutarch of a youth of Sparta that suffered a Fox concealed under his robe to tear out his bowels . . . is, I perceive, mistrusted by men of judgment."

[92] Padua, 1921.

[93] Among French commentators of Tacitus, Amelot de la Houssaye (1634-1706), the translator of Gracián, is outstanding. Cf. his *Tibère, discours politiques sur Tacite* (Amsterdam, 1683) and his *Morale de Tacite* (Paris, 1686).

[94] Tacitus, like Machiavelli, was sharply attacked in Spain. Cf. especially Pedro de Ribadeneyra (1527-1611), *Tractado de la religion y virtudes que debe tener el Principe Christiano para gobernar y conservar sus estados, contra lo que Nicolás Machiavelo y los Políticos de este tiempo enseñan* (Madrid, 1788), vii: "Estas son las fuentes de que beben los Políticos de nuestro tiempo: estas las guías que siguen: estos los preceptores que oyen, y la regla con que regulan sus consejos. Tiberio, viciosisimo y abominable Emperador; Tácito, Historiador Gentil y enimigo de Christianos; Machiavelo, Consejero impío; Lanúe, Soldado Calvinista; Mornéo, profano; Bodíno (por hablar de él con modestia) ni enseñado en Teología, ni exercitado en piedad."

[95] Schanz-Hosius, *Geschichte der römischen Literatur* in *Handbuch der Altertumswissenschaft*, VIII[2] (Munich, 1935), pp. 639-643.

Renaissance. In the sixteenth and seventeenth century, he was generally regarded as an a-moral apologist for tyranny. In the eighteenth century, there was a counter-movement which hailed him as a Republican. The general position of Tacitus at the end of the sixteenth century is made clear by a statement issued by the Senate of Venice, refusing a request to print Boccalini's commentaries on Tacitus :[96]

> It is the teaching of Tacitus that has produced Machiavelli and the other bad authors, who would destroy public virtue; we should replace Tacitus by Livy and Polybius, historians of the happier and more virtuous times of the Roman Republic, and by Thucydides, the historian of the Greek republic, who found themselves in circumstances like those of Venice.[97]

Thus it is clear that Machiavelli and Tacitus were closely linked: condemnation of Tacitus had its genesis in the fact that he was considered as the intellectual parent of the author of the *Prince,* synonym for all that was to be condemned.[98] And Bodin's defence of Tacitus, which flies in the face of the accepted criticism of the time, is largely due, in my opinion, to his favorable attitude toward Machiavelli,[99] expressed in the *Methodus.* Many critics of Bodin

---

[96] Cf. A. Rinaldi, *Traiano Boccalini e la sua critica letteraria* (Venice, 1933), pp. 62-64.

[97] Quoted by F. Sclopis, "Montesquieu et Machiavel," in *Revue historique de droit français et étranger,* II (1856), 25. Also quoted in Sandys, *History of Classical Scholarship* (Cambridge, 1908), II, 88.

[98] The distortion of Machiavelli by later writers has an extensive bibliography. For England, cf. Mario Praz, *Machiavelli and the Elizabethans* (London, 1928) ; for France, G. Waille, *Machiavel en France* (Paris, 1884), and also the more modern but mediocre *La pensée de Machiavel en France* by Albert Cherel (Paris, 1935). There is no satisfactory treatment to my knowledge of the diffusion of Machiavelli in Spain, where, nevertheless, a great deal of commentary on his work was produced. The *Anti-Machiavel* of Innocent Gentillet, with its enormous diffusion, was the most widely accepted interpretation of Machiavellian thought (first ed. 1576).

[99] If Bodin does not overwhelm Machiavelli with praise, at least he does not curse him as atheistic, immoral, etc., as was the habit of his contemporaries, especially after the work of Gentillet.

have denied any real influence of Machiavelli on him, except for the fact that he derived his information on the art of war (used in the *République*) almost entirely from Machiavelli's *Arte della guerra*. Reading the *République* and taking Bodin at his word, they have believed that he was a rabid anti-Machiavellian. But a careful perusal of the *Methodus* reveals that his attitude toward Machiavelli in 1566 was quite different from his attitude in 1576. This shift in position and the problems which it raises should receive examination.

In the *Methodus*, Machiavelli is mentioned twenty times. Bodin cites him with praise as the first author, who, after a lapse of two thousand years, applied himself to the study of politics.[100] He mentions him, as we have seen, along with Guicciardini and Polybius, as one of those historians best versed in the *principum arcana*.[101] Machiavelli's *History of Florence* was one of the principal sources for Bodin's treatment of the changes in the Florentine state contained in Chapter VI of the *Methodus*.[102] He declares that Machiavelli is too severe in his judgments of Southern peoples.[103] Most acute of all, however, is Bodin's keen perception that Machiavelli was not an apologist for tryanny as most of his contemporaries believed; rather he saw in Machiavelli a Republican, who believed that the *stato misto* (with a democratic bias) was the best form of the state. In taking this position, Machiavelli was open to attack from Bodin on two sides: in the first place, Bodin believed that the popular state was the least satisfactory of all forms of government; secondly, he insists (in the teeth of all the conventional political theory of the Renaissance) that the *stato misto*, far from being the ideal form of the state, is instead a

---

[100] *Methodus*, 230: "Post Aristotelem, Polybius, Dionysius Halicarnassus, Plutarchus, Dio, Tacitus (eos omitto, quorum scripta interciderunt) multa de Repub. praeclare et graviter in historiis dispersa relinquerunt. multa quoque Maciavellus, primus quidem, ut opinor, post annos mille circiter ac ducentos quam barbaries omnia cumularat, de Republica scripsit, quae omnium ore circunferuntur: nec dubium est quin multo plura verius ac melius scripturus fuerit, si veterum philosophorum et historicorum scripta cum usu coniuxisset."

[101] *Ibid.,* p. 70.

[102] *Ibid.,* pp. 384 ff.

[103] *Ibid.,* p. 157.

The Major Themes of the Methodus

wholly mythical creation, since sovereignty, which cannot be divided, must necessarily reside in one person or in one group of persons. After describing the popular state as a form of anarchy, he remarks :[104]

> Etenim N. Maciavellus argumentis ac rationibus praestantissimum esse persuasum habet. sed in eo genere minus illi credendum puto praesertim cum evertat suae disputationis fundamenta. Nam in Principis institutione, statim initio duos duntaxat posuit imperii status: monarchiam et rempublicam. Idem ad Livium, Venetorum rempublicam omnium praestantissimam esse affirmat, quam tamen putat esse popularem: cum libri III status populares semper laudabiliores fuisse scripserit; contra philosophorum et historicorum, contra omnium magnorum virorum probatam opinionem.

It is hard to see, Bodin observes, how Machiavelli could support the popular state after he had seen the calamities which fell upon his native Florence as a result of this regime.[105] Bodin brands the *stato misto* as absurd :[106]

> Absurdum quoque. . . . debet videri quod Polybius affirmat, reipublicae summum imperium partim in populo, partim in Senatu, partim in consulibus fuisse: ac propterea imperium temperatum videri ex optimatibus, regno, ac populo. Quàm opinionem Dionysius ac Cicero arripuerunt; deinde Maciavellus, Contarenus, Th. Morus. Garimbertus, Manutius vehementer probarunt.

On p. 282 Bodin repeats his reproof to Machiavelli, for having been taken in by the error of Aristotle and· Polybius in supporting the *stato misto*.

In spite of this disagreement with Machiavelli on several points, there is nowhere in the Methodus what might be called the conventional "Anti-Machiavellian" feeling: Bodin had *read* Machiavelli[107] (unlike most of his contemporaries) and knew him, not

---

[104] *Methodus,* 422.

[105] *Ibid.,* p. 427.

[106] *Ibid.,* p. 270.

[107] An account of the influence of Machiavellian thought on the work of Bodin may be found in the mémoire of M. Guillaume Cardascia, presented

The Major Themes of the Methodus   115

only as the author of the *Prince,* but also as the author of the *Florentine History,* of the *Arte della guerra,* of the *Discorsi,* and even of the *Ritratto delle cose della Francia.*[108] Consequently, Bodin was equipped to judge more sanely than most of the French political writers of his time. This sanity of judgment is reflected in the calm tone of his remarks in the *Methodus.*

In the *République* all is changed. Bodin seems to have forgotten all that he knew of Machiavelli and indulges in conventional vituperation against him. The preface contains a violent attack :[109]

> Nous avons pour exemple un Machiavel, qui a eu la vogue entre les couratiers des tyrans & lequel Paul Jove ayant mis au rang des hommes signalez, l'appelle neantmoins Atheiste & ignorant des bonnes lettres : quant a l'Atheisme, il en fait gloire par ses escrits : et quant au scavoir, ie croy que ceux qui ont accoustume de discourir doctement, peser sagement, & resoudre subtilement les hauts affaires d'estat s'accorderont qu'il n'a iamais sonde le gue de la science politique, qui ne gist pas en ruses tyranniques, qu'il a recherchees par tous les coins d'Italie & comme une douce poison coulee en son livre du Prince, ou il rehausse jusqu'au ciel & met pour un parangon de tous les Roys, le plus desloyal fils de Prestre qui fust onques. . . .

Other passages of a like tone are found in the *République,* which indicate a definite "anti-Machiavellian" feeling. What are the reasons for this volte-face? Had Bodin "forgotten" what he knew about Machiavelli? I think it more probable, that, bending before public opinion in France which was becoming more and more hostile to things Italian, Bodin had deliberately "forgotten" in order to conform to public taste and to escape censure.

---

for the *Diplôme des Etudes supérieures d'Italien* (1937) : *L'Influence de Machiavel sur Jean Bodin et les auteurs politiques français du XVIe siècle.* Parts of this fine unpublished study may appear in *Humanisme et Renaissance.*

[108] The judgment of C. Benoist in his article *Bodin et Machiavel* in the special "Numero consacré à Bodin" of the *Province d'Anjou* (November, 1928) is rather unhappy, since he claims that Bodin had only a second-hand, sketchy knowledge of Machiavelli's work.

[109] *République* (Ed. 1578), p. 596.

116   *The Major Themes of the Methodus*

Recalling Bodin's position toward Machiavelli as expressed in the *Methodus* and the conventional linking of Machiavelli and Tacitus in the political ideology of the day, his praise of the latter becomes more comprehensible. But, in addition, Tacitus possessed qualities which made him attractive to Bodin. He fulfilled the Polybian ideal of having been a man of action as well as an historian. He had served as praetor and proconsul in Germany, where he not only gained military experience but also had a sharp eye for geographical and ethnographical details. Hence his authority on matters German.[110] His brief, epigrammatic style is admirable, especially effective for delineating character.[111] As a political guide, he is invaluable.[112]

> nullus profecto historicus magistratui ac iudici utilior videtur.

Consequently it distresses Bodin to see Tacitus attacked so generally and unfairly:[113]

> sed me lacerat & conficit quorundam reprehensio, quae refutatione minus egeret, nisi auctoritate plurimum valerent. nam ausus est Alciatus historiam illam plane divinam senticeta vocare in ea epistola quam ad Iovium scripsit.

Many reject Tacitus because his style is difficult; others condemn him for his "anti-Christian" leanings. Bodin defends him on these two counts.[114]

After mentioning Suetonius, Velleius Paterculus, and Guillaume de Bellay (whom he heaps with praise)[115] Bodin devotes

---

[110] *Ibid.*

[111] *Ibid.*

[112] *Ibid.*

[113] *Ibid.*

[114] *Ibid.*

[115] Guillaume du Bellay, brother of Cardinal du Bellay, ambassador of the French king to the German princes. Cf. V. L. Bourilly, *Guillaume du Bellay, Seigneur de Langeais*, Paris, 1904. Bodin says of him (*Methodus*, p. 99): "sed ne quis meum civem (fuit enim natione Andegavus) a me plus aequo laudari putet, multo plura Sleidanus qui cum hominem omni genere laudum cumulavisset, tum vero Gallicae nobilitatis decus appellavit."

several enthusiastic pages to Guicciardini. In order to make his qualities still more brilliant, he compares him with the unlucky Paulus Jovius, whom he had already soundly drubbed in comparing him with Polybius.[116] Guicciardini has a certain "passionate zeal in searching out the truth."[117] This is one of the most striking differences between him and Paulus Jovius. Guicciardini goes back to the original sources, while Paulus Jovius simply indulges in "declamationes scholasticorum in modum."[118] Guicciardini is particularly skilled in describing the evolution of the state, since there is no country where changes in government occur more frequently than in Italy.[119]

Bodin considers the mediaeval chronicles as full of *nugae* but he tempers his judgment because of the barbarism of the times in which they were written. He includes a respectable list of these chronicles, which is repeated, with greater detail, in the tenth chapter of the *Methodus*.

Bodin cites only two authorities for the history of the Tartars: Marco Polo (Paulus Venetus) and Hayto.[120] He considers neither of them very reliable, refusing to swallow Polo's tale that the Caspian Sea never has fish in it except in times of fast, when, providentially, it swarms with them. Father Alvarez[121] both

---

[116] *Methodus,* p. 79: "Ille (Polybius) in sua Respublica princeps; hic (Paulus Jovius) privatus; ille imperator; hic medicus; ille magnam Europae partem, oram Africae et Asiam minorem, ut populorum intellegeret, peragravit; hic annos septem et triginta, ut ipse gloriatur in Vaticano consedit." Is this "hic medicus" the phrase which suggests to Montaigne his "medecin traictant de la guerre" in the essay *Des Livres* (Bk. II, Chap. x)?

[117] L. Ranke, *Zur Kritik neuerer Geschichtschreiber* (Leipzig, 1884), p. 74 disputes this judgment of Bodin, mentioning him by name and quoting the *Methodus.* Ranke can think of no place more suitable for an historian to sit than in the Vatican archives. Cf. also *Methodus,* 80: "Cuius (Guicciardini) scripta si cum Jovio conferantur, non magis congruent quam rotunda quadratis."

[118] *Ibid.,* p. 102. Bodin uses the same expression on p. 80, also in reference to Paulus Jovius.

[119] *Ibid.,* p. 103.

[120] Hetoum, Prince of Gorigos, *Liber historiarum partium orientis, sive Passagium terrae sanctae Haythono autore, scriptus anno 1300,* Hagonoae, 1529.

[121] R. P. Alvarez, *Historiale description de l'Ethiopie,* Fr. trans. Antwerp, 1558.

writes very well and also gives a dependable account of the people and customs of Ethiopia. Likewise Ziegler, Krantz, Cromer, and Olaus Magnus[122] carry information on the hitherto unknown territories of the Saxons, the Belgians, the Poles, and the Danes.[123] Olaus sometimes indulges in tall tales, which are, nevertheless, confirmed by other historians and travelers such as Gaspar Peucer and Hubert Languet, both famed for their erudition.[124]

A writer of the same sort as Alvarez, Leo Afer, is known for his description of Africa. Bodin classes Alvarez, Leo, and some of the ancient geographer-travelers in a special group, which he calles the *geographistorici*.[125] Bodin gives a thumb nail sketch of Leo Afer, who enjoyed a wide vogue in the sixteenth century.[126] A Moor by birth, a native of Spain, a Mohammedan, then a Christian, a traveler in Africa, in Asia Minor, and Europe, he was given to Pope Leo after having been captured by pirates; under the patronage of the Pope, he wrote (in Arabic) his geographical treatise on Africa, which he then translated into Tuscan. Afterward it was translated into Latin and French.[127] It was an extremely popular book, and Bodin borrowed much from it, not only for use in the *Methodus* but especially for the *République*.[128] Ranking with Leo Afer as *geographistorici* are E. Leandro[129] and

---

[122] Complete information on these, as well as other German geographers, will be found in the thesis of L. Gallois, *Les géographes allemands de la Renaissance,* Paris, 1890.

[123] Cf. Thor Beck, *Northern Antiquities in French Literature,* Vol. I, *Vagina gentium and the Liberty Legend,* New York (Institute of French Studies), 1934.

[124] Cf. *Methodus,* 109: "hoc enim Gaspar Peucerus vir magnae eruditionis et minime vanus, tum etiam Linguetus non minus doctrina quam diuturna totius Europae peregrinatione clarus."

[125] *Ibid.*

[126] There is an excellent modern edition, *Description de l'Afrique, Tierce Partie du Monde . . .* edited with an introduction by C. Schefer, Paris, 1896.

[127] The Latin translation appeared at Antwerp, 1556; the French, at Lyons and Antwerp, 1556.

[128] Its influence may be noted on other French erudite writing of the sixteenth century, especially after the translations of 1556. J. C. Scaliger borrowed from it for the fifth book of his *Exotericae exercitationes* (1557); Thevet used it in his *Cosmographie universelle.*

[129] Bodin evidently refers to F. Leandrus Albertus, whose *Descrittione di tutta Italia* was published at Bologna in 1550.

Munster[180] the former because of his geographical studies of Italy, the other of Germany.

Another special group of historians may be called the *Philosophistorici*[181] because they "rerum gestarum narrationem cum sapientiae praeceptis cumularunt." In this class Xenophon, Josephus, and Plutarch are outstanding. Moses is the finest of them all;[182] no one gives a more dependable account of human origins. He furthermore proves that the Hebrews surpassed all other peoples in faith, integrity, and antiquity. From the writings of Moses, it is easy to refute all the vain fables of Diodorus, Herodotus, and Justin.[183]

An unusual feature of Bodin's criticism of various historians is his defence of Julian the Apostate against the attacks of Christian historiographers. While deploring his rejection of the Christian faith and his return to superstition, Bodin insists, however, on the qualities which the man possessed: his continence, his fortitude, his justice, and his courage. He insists that Julian should not simply be passed over in silence by historians. The passage is particularly interesting, since, as Villey[184] points out, Montaigne wrote a like defence of the Apostate in his *De la liberté de conscience,*[185] which follows the same line as Bodin and may have owed its inspiration to the *Methodus.* Louis Cons touches on Montaigne's indebtedness to Bodin in this essay in his article *Montaigne et Julien l'Apostat.*[186]

Bodin concludes his critical excursus with a short list of recommended national historians, among whom we find Polydore Vergil; Beatus Rhenanus; Paulus Emilius and Gauguin for France; Guicciardini, among others, for Italy.

---

[180] Munster, *Cosmographia* (French translation by Belleforest in 1575).

[181] *Methodus,* 111.

[182] Compare the like position of Baudouin and most of the German historians.

[183] *Methodus,* 112.

[184] *Les sources et l'evolution des Essais de Montaigne* (Paris, 1914), I, p. 322.

[185] *Essais,* Bk. II, Chap. xix.

[186] *Humanisme et Renaissance,* IV (1937), 411-420.

[20]

BODIN AND THE MEDIAEVAL THEORY OF CLIMATE

By MARIAN J. TOOLEY

No ONE who has written about Republics, says Bodin, has considered the fundamental problem of how the form of a Republic should be adapted to the natural
aptitudes of its people. Failure to appreciate this principle, and the attempt to
frame laws by absolute standards has only brought great states to ruin. He therefore proceeds to the enquiry himself.[1] A modern reader, investigating the theory
of 'climate,' or environment as it applies to politics, which he proceeds to expound, must be struck by the fact that some of his most important statements —
the distribution of the temperaments, for instance — appear to be made quite
arbitrarily, for no explanations are given. This in itself suggests that his theory
was not 'proles sine matre,' but that he was drawing upon some common stock of
scientific notions familiar to his contemporaries. The suggestion becomes certainty when he cuts short his illustration of a particular point with the remark
that he need not go into particulars which are matters of common knowledge,
and easily accessible in the sources from which he himself had got them.[2]

But what were those sources? He does not say. He does, of course, frequently
cite authority for his facts. This authority is of two sorts, either the writers of the
ancient world such as Aristotle, Ptolemy, Galen, Caesar, Tacitus, Livy, or contemporary historians and travellers. He uses Commines and Guicciardini on the
Italians, Sigismund d'Heberstein's history of the Muscovites, Francesco Alvarez
on Ethiopia, and Las Casas on the American Indians. He also repeats conversations with the Polish ambassador from Lithuania,[3] Henry II's French ambassador
to the English Court,[4] and reports of the French ambassadors who negotiated a
settlement of the Italian question with the Emperor Charles V.[5]

But, although it is clear that he drew his facts from these sources, only suggestions are to be found in them of the theories about environment that he
thought the facts illustrated. It has in consequence been very generally assumed
that his theories were original, and possibly his most important contribution to
political thought, though subject to the qualification that he mixed incongruously
penetrating observations on the consequences of such natural influences as temperature on the physical and moral constitution of men with much superstitious

---

[1] *Six Livres de la République*, v, i (Paris, 1608), p. 665. There are three versions of this chapter. The
first draft appeared in the *Methodus ad facilem historianum cognitionem*, v, published in 1566; in it
all the general principles are stated, but not particularly related to contemporary politics. This relation was made in the *Six Livres de la République*, v, i, of 1576. In 1586 Bodin published his own Latin
version, *De Republica Libri Sex*, which is a free translation of the French, but with a few significant
additions. All references are to the French version unless otherwise indicated.

[2] *Meth.*, [Geneva, 1610], p. 139.

[3] *Rep.*, p. 668.

[4] *Rep.*, p. 669. In the Latin version (Frankfort, 1609), p. 777, he refers to a visit which he himself
had made to England, where he noted the weather.

[5] *Rep.*, p. 676.

matter about the occult influence of the stars.[6] But if he was indeed 'l'initiateur de la théorie des climats,'[7] one would expect him to give most attention where in fact he gives least, to the discussion of the grounds of his general statements about the effects of environment. The fact that he assumes their obviousness, and devotes all his energies to a wealth of illustration, suggests that it was the illustrative matter that was new, but the general principles too familiar to need exposition.

Fortunately the activities of the sixteenth-century printers and publishers are evidence of the taste of the reading public. Judging by the number of editions that appeared, there was a considerable and steady demand for mediaeval cosmological writings, especially of the more popular encyclopaedic and informative type. Twenty-four editions of Sacrobosco's *De Sphaera* appeared before 1500 and many others followed in the sixteenth century. It was also the subject of numerous commentaries[8] and translated into French, German, Spanish, Italian and English. Ten editions of the Latin text of Bartholomaeus Anglicus, *De Proprietatibus Rerum*, and four editions of the French translation appeared before 1500, and further editions in both tongues followed during the sixteenth century.[9] There were six editions of the *Cuer de Philosophie* between 1507 and 1534, and others followed.[10] There were four editions of Guido Bonatti's *De Astronomia Tractatus*, and at least four of Vincent of Beauvais' *Speculum Naturale.*

A man of Bodin's wide reading could hardly have been unfamiliar with this literature. In fact there is incontrovertible evidence that his scientific thought was formed in these traditions. His *Universae Naturae Theatrum* is an exposition of his system of the world, and despite occasional divergencies on particular points it is fundamentally mediaeval. That is to say, his cosmology is based on Ptolemy, his physics on Aristotle, and his physiology on Galen, interpreted in the light of their great Arab commentators such as Haly and Avicenna. From the fusion of these traditions Bodin inherited from his mediaeval predecessors the doctrine of a geocentric universe composed of the four elements of matter, and astrologically controlled. Moreover, in this work he betrays his acquaintance not only with the traditional doctrines, but with the actual writings of the Schoolmen, for he freely cites among others Aquinas, Albertus Magnus, Duns Scotus and

[6] R. Chauviré, *Jean Bodin, auteur de la République* (Paris, 1914), p. 359. For opinions on his importance and originality in this respect see also J. W. Allen, *A History of Political Thought in the Sixteenth Century* (London, 1928), pp. 431–438; P. Mesnard, *L'Essor de la philosophie politique au XVIᵉ siècle* (Paris, 1936), pp. 530–538; J. Moreau-Reibel, *Bodin et le droit publique dans ses rapports avec la philosophie de l'histoire* (Paris, 1933), pp. 69–102. A. Garosci, *Jean Bodin, politica e diritto nel rinascimento francese* (Milan, 1934), pp. 149–153, draws attention to the currency of similar ideas in the fifteenth century, but without discussing their origins.

[7] E. Fournol, *Bodin prédécesseur de Montesquieu* (Paris, 1896), p. 117.

[8] P. Duhem, *Le Système du monde*, III, 2 (Paris, 1913), 239.

[9] Fourteen French versions by 1556; see Ch. V. Langlois, *La Connaissance de la nature et du monde au moyen âge* (Paris, 1911), p. 123.

[10] For a description of this work see E. Renan *Le Livre des Secrets aux Philosophes*, in *Hist. litt. de la France*, XXX, 567–595.

66 *Bodin and the Mediaeval Theory of Climate*

Henry of Malines. It is in this work, then, that one must look for the physical theories that underlay his theory of climate.

Bodin starts by repeating the doctrine that the physical universe is constituted out of matter and form,[11] and the unending process of alteration to which it is subject is the consequence of the perpetual transmutation of matter from one form to another.[12] Form, he says, can be either simple, as are the rudimentary forms of the four elements, or 'mixed,' as in the case of all things into whose composition enter two or more elements.[13] All four elements are present in living bodies. Hence the doctrine, associated with Galen, of the four radical complexions, according as earth, fire, air or water predominates in the composition. Bodin does not expound this doctrine in a work devoted to physics, but he habitually assumes it when writing of the physique of men. As a peripatetic physicist, however, he holds that, though matter is capable of receiving all forms, it possesses in itself no active principle enabling it to assume form spontaneously.[14] An extrinsic efficient cause is required to accomplish this process. Outside and enveloping the world of material transmutations are the heavens, in ceaseless motion. If nature does nothing in vain, what is the purpose of this activity? To Bodin, as to his mediaeval predecessors, the conclusion was inescapable; it must be the stars in their courses that govern the mutations of matter.[15] Moreover, for Bodin, since he rejected the doctrine that form is latent in matter and the stars merely elicit it,[16] the stars are actually the source from which the multiplicity of forms immediately proceeds.[17]

In treating of the structure of the heavens, he follows Ptolemy in supposing a series of revolving spheres, enveloping the motionless core of the material world. First are the spheres of the seven planets, the Moon, Mercury, Venus, the Sun, Mars, Jupiter, Saturn, and beyond these the eighth sphere of the fixed stars, or Signs of the Zodiac. What followed was a matter of less universal agreement. Bodin decides for two more spheres to explain the double diurnal and annual movement of the heavens.[18] The movement of the ninth sphere is the origin of the west to east circuit of the planets on the poles of the Zodiac in their several periods of time. The tenth sphere is the source of the most regular and most rapid of all movements, the diurnal revolution of the whole heaven from east to west.[19] Each planet and star has its formal properties, long fixed by a tradition going back to Ptolemy's Arab followers. How these properties are transmitted

[11] 'Naturale corpus est ens mutabile materia formaque coagmentatum,' *Universae Naturae Theatrum*, I (Lyons, 1596), 13.

[12] Pp. 52–54.

[13] P. 74.

[14] P. 53.

[15] He constantly asserts this, e.g., pp. 15–16, or p. 53, when he puts the 'caelestia corpora' first in the order of efficient causes of generated things.

[16] P. 67.

[17] Pp. 15–16, 'tota natio philosophorum formas omnes a prima causa fluentes per caelestium causarum ordines distribui tradunt;' see also p. 97.

[18] Pp. 554–556.

[19] The structure of the heavens is the subject of the whole of Book V.

Bodin and the Mediaeval Theory of Climate

through space Bodin does not say, though he argues that a cause can be remote from its effects, and instances the control of the moon over the tides.[20] But the matter had been very fully discussed in the thirteenth century, and scientific doctrine on the subject fixed. In performing their revolutions the heavenly bodies communicate their several 'virtues' by emitting rays equally in all directions. Each point on the earth's surface, therefore, is at the center of the total radiation of that part of the heavens contained within its horizon, and the intensity of the influence of each particular star depends upon the angle of incidence at which its rays fall upon the recipient.[21] Thus all individuals, 'les creatures qui sont cy aval soit herbes, ou arbres, ou vermines, ou bestes, poissons, oyseaux, hommes et femmes,'[22] are the product of, and perpetually subject to an influence at once complex and perpetually modifying, as the tempering influence of the stars upon one another changes with the change in their relative positions. In this way the almost infinite variety of individuals in the world of matter and the endless mutability of things terrestrial were explained.

It will be seen that in this system of ideas the principles of astrology had to be assumed to explain the functioning of the universe. Moreover, they seemed to be confirmed by such observations as the relation between the cycle of life and the circuit of the sun, and between the movements of the tides and the phases of the moon. Astrology was fundamental to all the natural sciences. All occurrences from the flora of a district to the history of its inhabitants must be determined by the virtue of the presiding stars, and explained by reference to their influence. The astrological system of the world was therefore universally accepted in the later Middle Ages,[23] and expounded in literature at all levels of scholarship, whether the work of constructive thinkers such as Albertus Magnus,[24] or popular encyclopaedias in the vulgar tongue such as the *Image du Monde* of Maître Goussouin.[25]

In Bodin's day this system was, of course, challenged. He was aware of it, and considered with some care Copernicus' new and disruptive hypothesis of a heliocentric system. He dismisses it for reasons that anyone in the fourteenth century might have given: it is contrary to the evidence of the senses, to the authority of the Scriptures, and incompatible with Aristotelian physics.[26] One could hardly

[20] Pp. 152–153.

[21] Most clearly expounded by Roger Bacon, *Opus Maius* (ed. Bridges, Oxford, 1897), ii, 112–115. See also Albertus Magnus, *De Natura Locorum*, i, v, or Bartholomaeus Anglicus, *De Proprietatibus Rerum*, xiv, i. Hereafter in these notes these three works are cited merely by the names of the authors.

[22] *Cuer de Philosophie* (Paris, 1514), xlvi r⁰.

[23] This doctrine of the governance of the stars over matter is not found in such writers as Sacrobosco who were not familiar with Aristotle's physical works. It is expounded or assumed by all those who were, from the thirteenth century onwards.

[24] 'Contrarietas non est ex materia, quia materia non est causa virtutis et formae, oportet ergo quod sit ex loco informato a figuratione radiorum stellarum,' *De Natura Locorum*, i, v.

[25] 'Par li ciels et les estoilles . . . corrompt et naist toute riens qui est en cest monde et qui a fin et commencement,' *Image du Monde* (ed. H. O. Prior, Paris, 1913), vi, 173. This is the prose redaction of the later thirteenth century. The original version was in verse, and appeared in 1246.

[26] *Univ. Nat. Theat.*, pp. 580–583.

68   *Bodin and the Mediaeval Theory of Climate*

have better evidence of the deliberateness with which Bodin adhered to the mediaeval system.

It is obvious that a doctrine of the influence of environment is implicit in this system of ideas. Its situation or *locus* determines the celestial influences to which the body occupying it is exposed, and therefore the constitution of that body. Moreover it was widely believed, on Galen's authority, that physical constitution determines moral aptitudes, and moral aptitudes determine behavior. Bodin himself sums up the doctrine in a couple of sentences. 'Elementa vi coelestium agitantur. In elementa vero corpus humanum continetur, sanguis in corpore, spiritus in sanguine, anima in spiritu, mens in anima.'[27]

What, then, are the fundamental constituents of place? Long before Bodin said so, it was established that they are latitude, longitude, and configuration. Of these latitude is by far the most important, as it defines place in relation to the path of the sun. The property of the sun is to radiate heat, and heat is the first principle of life. The astrological virtue of the sun therefore is to impart vitality; 'ad generationem sensibilium corporum committitur, et ad vitam ea movet, nutrit, et auget, et perficit, et purgat ac renovat.'[28] Bodin emphasizes its importance as the source of life when he says it imparts heat 'non causaliter sed formaliter.'[29] It is therefore the universal planet whose virtue reaches everywhere.[30]

But its virtue is not equally potent everywhere, for the obliquity of its rays is not everywhere the same. Ptolemy's division of the world into arctic, temperate, and tropic zones suggested three fundamental types of climate, frigid, temperate and torrid. It is clear, however, in all discussions of climate, that the lines of demarcation were not thought of as coinciding with the circles. Indeed, the Arctic and the Tropics were believed to be uninhabitable, and the hot and cold and temperate climates refer to the habitable earth only, though where the dividing lines came was never defined by mediaeval writers. The only precise divisions they recognized were the seven climates, lying between 12°N. and 50°N., into which Ptolemy divided the inhabited earth known to him, i.e., the area between Scythia and the African desert, the Pillars of Hercules and India. Regions beyond these limits were, he thought, populated by very primitive and savage tribes, inhabitants of the ante-climata and ultra-climata of his mediaeval successors.[31]

As knowledge of these extremes increased, the seven climates lost their peculiar importance. This may be the reason why Bodin never divides the world in this way, but considers only the three fundamental types of climate — hot, cold, and temperate. But he was no longer content with the old vagueness about their limits, and defines them precisely for the first time by dividing the hemisphere

[27] *Meth.*, p. 95.

[28] Vincent of Beauvais, *Speculum Naturale*, xv, iv. See also Bartholomeaus, viii, xxviii.

[29] *Univ. Nat. Theat.*, p. 578.

[30] *Rep.*, p. 690, and *Meth.*, p. 103.

[31] The seven climates are defined in Sacrobosco, *op. cit.*, iii, and in all descriptions of the earth's surface thereafter. Bacon, p. 297, adds three ante-climata to the south and ultra-climata between the seventh climate and the polar circle.

equally, first into three zones of 30 degrees of latitude each, and then into six subdivisions of 15 degrees, of which he believes only the most southerly and the most
northerly to be uninhabitable.[32] He does not, however, observe these neat divisions in differentiating the peoples of Europe and the Mediterranean basin, for
they did not coincide with the political divisions he wished to explain. He remarks
in the *Methodus* that what may be classed as hot climates extend to 40°N.;
the temperate is that which lies between 40°N. and 50°N.; north of 50°N. the
climate is cold or very cold. Therefore, he classes England and Scotland, Denmark and North Germany as cold; France, South Germany, North Spain, Italy,
and Macedonia as temperate; South Spain, Sicily, the Peloponnese, and North
Africa as hot.[33] Scandinavia beyond the sixtieth parallel, a remote region on the
fringes of the world, provides the fourth very cold type.

The sun, however, is only one of the planets, and radiation of their proper
virtues proceeds from all, not only of the planets but the signs as well. But
though the principle might be universally agreed upon, not so its precise interpretation. 'In what manner the signs and the planets are to be assigned to the
different regions of the world is difficult to determine, for the authorities do not
agree,' says Bacon, and does not make the attempt.[34] But others, notably Guido
Bonatti, Henry Bate of Malines and Pierre d'Ailly did. They had two problems
to consider. In the first place ever since Ptolemy's day the signs had been associated with another sort of division of the earth's surface — that into the four
quarters of the inhabited earth indicated by the four cardinal points of the compass. The signs were grouped in units of three to make the four triplicities, and
each triplicity was associated not only with one of the four quarters, but with one
of the four elements of matter;[35] their astrological significance was therefore
identified with the element to which they were attributed in each case. But
which triplicity belonged to which quarter? Was for instance the north or the east
under the hot and active triplicity of fire? Ptolemy and Albumazar disagreed.
D'Ailly in his *Tractatus de concordantia discordantium astronomorum super sig-
nificationibus triplicitatum* discussed the problem at length,[36] and reported Henry
of Malines as having done so before him.[37] Its solution affected the second problem of the planets, for they in their turn were associated with the triplicities. Did
Mars the bringer of war, conjoined with the triplicity of water, have dominion
over the west as Ptolemy said, or over the north as Albumazar said?

Bodin was not concerned with the problem of planetary influence in this particular form. Indeed, he rejected Ptolemy's doctrine that each of the signs reigns

---

[32] *Rep.*, p. 667, and *Meth.*, p. 82.

[33] *Meth.*, p. 89.

[34] VII, iv, p. 381.

[35] The system is fully explained by Bartholomaeus, VIII, ix–xxi; or *Cuer de Philosophie*, p. lxiv–
lxvi v°.

[36] Published in a collection of texts of which sixteen are by d'Ailly and five by Jean Gerson. There
is no date, title, place of publication or pagination. But it is known to have come from the press of
John of Westphalia at Louvain, in 1480.

[37] This work of Henry of Malines is only known through d'Ailly's report of it; see Wallerand,
Henri Bate de Malines (in *Les Philosophes belges*, II [1931], 18).

Bodin and the Mediaeval Theory of Climate

over a particular locality.[38] In any case, Bodin was not so much interested in this division of the earth into quarters as in the division into zones, because he attached a much greater importance to latitude than to longitude as a determinant of the nature of place. In considering planetary radiation, therefore, what was useful to him was the tradition that the planets were independently associated with the divisions of latitude. The almost universal rule was to follow Ptolemy in assigning the seven planets to the seven climates in order, as does, for instance, the author of the *Cuer de Philosophie*,[39] or d'Ailly,[40] or Bonatti.[41] However, this method of distribution did not suit Bodin, for that part of the inhabited earth that interested him did not fall exclusively within the framework of the seven climates. Instead he adopted the much rarer practice of assigning the planets to the zones. One writer at any rate in the thirteenth century had done so. Guido Bonatti ascribed one of the three outer planets, and one of the three inner to each zone — Saturn and Luna to the frigid, Jupiter and Mercury to the temperate, and Mars and Venus to the torrid.[42] Bodin follows the principle but changes the order. He transposes Mars and Saturn, thus placing the frigid zone under Mars and Luna, and the torrid under Venus and Saturn.[43] This is extremely arbitrary of him, for it involves the linking of a hot with a cold planet in each case, and sacrifices the principle of similarity between a climate and its planets. The only reason he gives for this distribution is not its logic, but its conformity with observed effects (d'Ailly had already observed that this must be the final test[44]), and he thought he observed the warlike influence of Mars in the north, and the contemplative virtue of Saturn in the south.[45]

For Bodin, therefore, differences of latitude subject the human organism to more complex influences than merely the effects of heat. The occult influences of the planets proper to each zone emphasize divergencies, and environment in one zone is highly differentiated from that in another.

Bodin's second constituent of place, longitude, everyone was agreed was far less important. East is east and west is west, for the sun is in the ascendant and therefore more potent over the one, and in declension and therefore feebler over the other.[46] But the distinction is less marked, *occultior*. Neither the dividing line, nor the principle of differentiation had ever been defined.[47] Bodin agrees that it is

---

[38] *Meth.*, pp. 135–138. See also *Univ. Nat. Theat.*, pp. 621–624.

[39] cvii. v⁰.

[40] *Ymago Mundi*, x. Bodin treats of his various works on astrology at some length in *Rep.*, IV, ii.

[41] *De Astronomia Tractatus*, IV, viii.

[42] *Op. cit.*, IV, vii. I have not found that anyone else did this, but Bonatti attracted attention in France and Charles V commissioned a translation (C. Jourdain, 'Nicholas Oresme et les astrologues de la Cour de Charles V,' in *Revue des Questions Historiques*, XVIII [1875]).

[43] *Rep.*, pp. 691–692, and *Meth.*, pp. 102–103.

[44] *De Concordantia Discordantium Astronomorum.*

[45] I have not been able to find that he had any precedent for this arrangement. But the spheres of influence of the planets seem to have been a matter of some uncertainty. Bodin's contemporary, Auger Ferrier, whom he cites on occasion, gives a quite different distribution according to the points of the compass in his *Des jugements astronomiques sur les nativitez*.

[46] Pierre d'Ailly, *De Concordantia Discordantium Astronomorum.*

[47] Bacon, p. 250, and Pierre d'Ailly, *Ymago Mundi*, xii.

Bodin and the Mediaeval Theory of Climate   71

impossible to say in this case where the division comes, and does not attempt that precision he achieved in the case of latitude. But he is sure about the extremes, which he shifts eastwards to the Moluccas and westwards to the Canaries. Circumnavigation of the world has not destroyed for him the notion of an eastern and western quarter of the globe, each with its fixed site, and specific quality.

But there was something more in the determination of the nature of place than the stellar radiation to which it was exposed. It was an axiom of Aristotelian physics that the communication of form is conditioned by the aptness of the material to receive it. As Albertus Magnus expressed it, the nature of all generated things depends first on radiation (*radius*) and second on site (*locus continens*),[48] for from the one proceeds heat, which is the first principle of life and, within the other is contained moisture, which is the first principle of growth.[49] In other words the counterpart of stellar radiation is regional geography, which Vincent of Beauvais analyses as altitude, humidity, the proximity of mountains and the sea, the quality of the soil;[50] for it is all these things that determine the balance between heat and moisture. In high altitudes the atmosphere is cool, thin and dry, and in low-lying places, especially near the sea, damp, warm, and heavy. It follows that mountainous districts are more northerly in their climate than the latitude indicates, and sheltered valleys more southerly. Great importance was also attached to the prevailing winds, for Ptolemy had said bodies are conditioned by the air which contains them. The number was fixed at twelve and their several qualities determined.[51] For this reason it was agreed that the situation of mountains matters as much as their altitude; it affects not only the temperature of the adjacent territories by exposing them in one direction and protecting them in another, but determines the prevailing winds. These were the considerations which informed Aquinas's discussion of a suitable site for a city.[52] It was not merely a question of health either, for health and energy profoundly affect behavior. Aquinas remarked on the demoralizing effect of too fertile a soil and too soft an air, for there pleasure comes easily and exertion is not necessary.[53] On the other hand, it was generally agreed that places liable to great winds and storms were especially noxious, because the agitation of the atmosphere disturbs the mind and distorts the judgment.[54]

When Bodin discusses configuration as the third constituent of environment, he selects the same features as important, mountains — especially their aspect — marshes and tempestuous winds;[55] and he finds therein the explanation of many of the differences between the people of one province and another. The Pyrenees

---

[48] Albertus, II, i.

[49] Albertus, II, ii.

[50] IV, cxii. What follows is common form, and can be found, for instance, in Albertus, I, xiii, and Bartholomaeus, XIV, i and ii.

[51] For the number and quality of the winds see Bartholomaeus, x, iii, and d'Ailly, *Ymago Mundi*, lx.

[52] *De Regimine Principum*, II, ii.

[53] *De Regimine Principum*, II, iv.

[54] Vincent of Beauvais, *op. cit.*, IV, ix.

[55] *Rep.*, p. 668, and *Meth.*, p. 131.

exaggerate the differences in latitude between France and Spain, by exposing Frenchmen to northerly influences only, and Spaniards to southerly; and the Appennines have the same effect in emphasizing the distinction between Tuscan and Lombard.[56] Rough prevailing winds make the people of Britain, Portugal, Thrace, and Persia turbulent, whereas the Italians and the inhabitants of Asia Minor, living in approximately the same latitudes are humane by reason of the soft airs that blow over them; and it is the wind that makes Gascons more intractable than Belgians, despite their more southerly situation.[57] Florence, built in mountainous country, is an energetic and turbulent city, and its citizens, like those of the Swiss Cantons, impatient of government; Venice, being a city of the plain, is stable because is inhabitants are more pacific and amenable to good counsel.[58] He ascribes the prosperity of Genoa or Ghent to the opportunities of a maritime situation, but the prosperity of Nuremberg he thinks is due to the infertility of the soil, which had compelled its inhabitants to exert themselves in other ways to assure their subsistence.[59] For the same reason Attica was the mother of all the arts.[60]

Environment reacts on men through their bodies in the first instance; for temperature and humidity, which are the fundamental properties of place, are also the fundamental properties of the four elements of which body is composed. Hence the four radical complexions in men are characterized by the physical properties of the predominating element; the phlegmatic, like water, is cold and moist; the sanguine, like air, hot and moist; the choleric, like fire, hot and dry; the melancholic, like earth, cold and dry. A causal connection was therefore traced between place and radical complexion. But, as d'Ailly pointed out, this is the result of a process not of assimilation, but of reaction; cold climates produce men of hot temperaments, and hot climates, cold temperaments.[61] External heat, it was believed, draws out the moisture of the body, and with that the 'spiritus' or breath of life that courses with the blood through the veins; internal heat and moisture is thereby lost, the temperature of the body reduced and vitality lowered. External cold and drought, on the other hand, conserve internal heat and moisture by closing the pores of the skin and so checking evaporation. Extreme cold or drought, however, have the opposite effect; by preventing any evaporation at all they lower the temperature of the body by conserving too much moisture, and so diminish its vitality.[62]

[56] *Rep.*, p. 692.

[57] *Rep.*, p. 696. The reference to the Gascons and the Belgians appears only in the Latin version, p. 808.

[58] *Rep.*, p. 664.

[59] *Rep.*, p. 697.

[60] *Meth.*, p. 130.

[61] *De Concordantia Discordantium Astronomorum*. See also Aquinas, *In Libris Politicorum*, VII, lect. V. (This section of the Commentary on the *Politics* is probably not Aquinas' own work — see M. Grabmann, 'Welchen Teil der aristotelischen Politik hat der hl. Thomas von Aquin selbst commentiert,' *Philosophisches Jahrbuch der Görres-Gesellschaft*, XXVIII, 3 (Fulda, 1915). I have used Aquinas' name for the sake of brevity.)

[62] These doctrines are fully expounded by Bartholomaeus, IV, i–xi. They are in part stated, or implied, in any discussion of complexion, e.g., Albertus, II, ii, or Vincent of Beauvais, *op. cit.*, IV, cix–cxi.

These physiological notions were used to explain what Ptolemy and Avicenna had said about the physique both of northern races and negroes. In the north, where the air is cold and dry, the natives are physically vigorous; they are strong, tall, broad and long-lived; moreover, internal heat means a large appetite and rapid digestion. Those who live in a hot climate, from the dissipation of their vital forces, are small and feeble, of weak digestion and small appetite. Certain characteristic appearances were also observed with great regularity. In cold climates the coloring is fair and the texture of the skin and hair fine; voices are soft and deep in tone, the effect of damp on the throat. In hot countries the sun draws the blood to the surface and darkens the skin — in extreme heat blackens and coarsens it — dries and frizzles the hair. Drought makes voices high-pitched and harsh.[63]

The distribution of the temperaments according to climate was therefore obvious. It was generally agreed that the peculiarities of the cold dry temperament, the melancholic, were to be observed in the dark and puny inhabitants of the extreme south. It was also agreed that the races of the far north exhibited the characteristics of the phlegmatic complexion, the cold and damp, for the men there are large, fair and slow-moving. In the less rigorous climate of the temperate regions, where the temperature was such as to conserve the heat of the body without preventing the evaporation of surplus moisture, occurred the better-balanced, choleric, and sanguine types.

These physiological theories were not, however, the only principle on which the distribution of the temperaments was determined. There was also the tradition associating the complexions with the triplicities presiding over the four quarters of the inhabited earth. But this was a matter of much greater uncertainty than the agreed effects of temperature; the authorities, as has been observed, differed as to their distribution, thus presenting their mediaeval disciples with a problem of reconciliation that exercised all their ingenuity. The tradition that apparently became current in France — for it is found in that repository of commonplaces, the *Cuer de Philosophie* — was Albumazar's; the phlegmatic complexion, under the triplicity of water, is assigned to the north, the melancholic under that of earth to the south, the choleric under that of fire to the east; and the sanguine under that of air to the west.[64]

It is this tradition which explains Bodin's apparently arbitrary arrangement of the temperaments in order from north to south, phlegmatic, sanguine, choleric and melancholic — though his is a distribution according to latitude, rather than to quarters. But the two methods are not unrelated. The northern quarter falls in the frigid regions and the southern in the torrid. The extremes of east and west are both included in the temperate zone, as d'Ailly had already observed;[65] but the cold damp of the west causes that quarter to have affinities with the north, whereas the warmth of the east relates it more nearly to the south. So Bodin could assume the obviousness of the arrangement when he said that Scandi-

---

[63] See Albertus, II, iii; Bartholomaeus, IV, i–iv; Vincent of Beauvais, *op. cit.*, IV, cix–cxi.

[64] P. lxvi. v⁰.

[65] *Ymago Mundi*, xii.

74   *Bodin and the Mediaeval Theory of Climate*

navians are phlegmatic, Germans sanguine, Frenchmen choleric, and Spaniards melancholic.[66] It followed the accepted order of the triplicities, and was consistent with the agreed effects of temperature; for the sanguine temperament, being moist, is proper to a more northern climate than the choleric, which is dry.

But — and this was the crux of the matter for Bodin — it was an accepted doctrine that, as Bacon says, 'upon their radical complexions depend men's dispositions in respect of morals, of learning and languages, of all crafts and occupations.'[67] The conclusion was based upon the account of the functioning of an animal organism in the *De Motibus Animalium* attributed to Aristotle, and his analysis of intellectual processes in the *De Anima*. All spontaneous activity springs from impulses which are organic in origin, because such activity is a consequence of appetite, and appetite follows the excitement of some sense located in an organ of the body. Therefore the involuntary activities of any living creature are conditioned absolutely by its physical constitution.[68] Animals, says William of Auvergne, of necessity follow their radical complexions.[69] The vegetative and the sensitive soul — i.e., the principles of growth and of sensation — is each, says Vincent of Beauvais, 'obligata materiae.'[70] Moreover those activities of men which are deliberate are also, though indirectly, affected by temperament. Even the intellective soul, Vincent of Beauvais adds — and Aquinas agrees with him — is conditioned by the body it inhabits 'secundum quid.' Aquinas explains by paraphrasing the third book of the *De Anima;* all knowledge is begotten upon the organs of sense, for the subjects of thought are the fantasmata or sensible species abstracted from the multitude of primary sense impressions.[71] From this it was argued that the more acute the sense impressions the more penetrating the consequent processes of thought. But the acuteness or otherwise of sensatory experience depends on physical constitution; for sense impressions are conveyed to the brain by 'spirit' which circulates, with the blood, through the veins; hot blood is thick and impedes the operation of spirit and so only permits dull perceptions; but thin blood facilitates fineness of perception by allowing 'spirit' to course freely.[72]

These premises accepted, there was very general agreement as to their particular consequences. The primary physical bases of character are blood and spirit. Hot blood means energy and *animositas* — the quality that makes men confident and assertive, impatient, magnanimous, greedy of honor and power. The 'hot-tempered' northerner therefore is a great fighter, brave because con-

[66] *Rep.*, p. 677.

[67] Bacon, p. 138.

[68] 'Organicas partes quoque preparant ydonee passiones ut cito moveantur ad dilectabilem consecutionem' (d'Ailly, *De Concordantia Discordantium Astronomorum*).

[69] *De Universo*, i, xlvi.

[70] *Op. cit.*, iii, xxxiv.

[71] Aquinas, *In Libris Politicorum*, vii, lect. v.

[72] The doctrine of the processes of sensation came from the *De differentia spiritus et animae* attributed to Constabulinus, (or Costa ben Luca). It was included in the collected works of Constantine Africanus published in Basel in 1536.

temptuous of wounds — he does not fear loss of blood because he can well spare it. But as a necessary defect of these virtues he is intellectually dull. Southerners on the other hand, being thin-blooded, are timid, and vengeful and cruel in consequence. But their 'spirit' being unimpeded in its operation, they are characterized by *subtilitas* or fine impressions and speculative acuteness. They excel, therefore, in the sciences, especially the occult, in religion and the liberal arts. In extreme cases the vividness of their imaginations leads the melancholic into delusions and madness. In practical affairs they compass their ends by guile and not by force; their cruelty is the cruelty of artists not of brutes.[73]

When Bodin particularizes about 'la diversité des hommes,' he selects precisely the same characteristics for discussion. He too compares men in respect of size, the type of energy in which they excel, their coloring, the quality of their voices, the nature of their cruelty, and their characteristic forms of madness; and he finds all the old generalizations substantially true.[74] From the ambassador from Lithuania he learned that the Muscovites of the far north were very fair, like Ptolemy's albinos;[75] and on the testimony of Las Casas he noticed that Magellan had found the Patagonians of the southern hemisphere very large and very simple;[76] and the West Indians, especially the Brazilians, like other southern races, he ascertained were extremely cruel.[77] Moreover he found in mediaeval medicine the answer as to why all these things should be so; it is always 'radical complexion.' It is the black bile of the melancholic temperament that predisposes southerners to contemplation, religion and the occult sciences. Such men are reposeful and docile, and whereas divine illumination is given to all, it is most fully effective in the quiet mind, just as light is mirrored most brightly in still waters.[78] The yellow bile of the choleric temperament makes men energetic, practical in their activities, apt to undertake great enterprises. Such is the disposition of the French. The Germans, on the other hand, though active, are unstable; it is a consequence of the sanguine complexion, of the hot blood that makes men robust and gay, but unreliable and at the mercy of impulse because too thickwitted to plan and keep to a course of action. He remarks in parentheses that tyrants have always drawn their bodyguards from northern races, not only for their strength and courage, but also because of their inaptitude for intrigue.[79] When such people become deranged, their madness is not the self-tormenting frenzy of the melancholy, but a mere folly of dancing and singing. The phlegmatics of the far north,

---

[73] Albertus, II, iii, Aquinas, *In Libris Politicorum*, VII, v. and *De Regimine Principum*, II, i; Vincent of Beauvais, *op. cit.*, IV, cx and cxi; Bartholomaeus, xv, *l*; *Cuer de Philosophie*, pp. cxi, v⁰–cxii, r⁰; d'Ailly *De Concordantia Discordantium Astronomorum*. There is more detail in some than in others, but no disagreements, for there is a common literary parentage, chiefly Ptolemy, Haly and Avicenna. D'Ailly's discussion is the fullest.

[74] *Rep.*, p. 673, and *Meth.*, p. 90.

[75] *Rep.*, p. 688.

[76] *Rep.*, p. 671.

[77] *Rep.*, p. 680.

[78] *Rep.*, p. 687, and *Meth.*, p. 105.

[79] *Rep.*, p. 678, and *Meth.*, p. 92.

condemned by nature to be chiefly remarkable for their stupidity, do not interest him very much, and have only a small place in the discussion. Mental disorder with them takes the form of senile obliviousness.[80]

Other influences, to his mind, enhanced these characteristics. In the first place, the four radical complexions were habitually associated with the four ages of man, the sanguine complexion with childhood, the choleric with adolescence, the melancholic with maturity and the phlegmatic with old age.[81] This means, he thought, that the first type is eager but erratic, the second adventurous, the third conservative and reflective, and the fourth physically and mentally lethargic.[82]

In the second place there was the influence of the presiding planets.[83] Saturn predisposes to contemplation and Venus to idleness and licentiousness, and as they are, according to Bodin, the planets of the southern regions, they confirm the predisposition of the melancholic to religious fervor and loose morals, and explain why genius is so often allied to wickedness. He illustrates by citing Alvarez on the Ethiopians and Livy on the Carthaginians. The temperate zone is under the beneficent planet Jupiter, whose subjects are of good physique and good morals, and concerned with the operations of the practical intellect, such as law and jurisprudence; his associate, Mercury, also disposes to useful activities, rhetoric, business and commerce. Here as well, therefore, the tendencies of the dominant temperament, the choleric, are confirmed. The sanguine north is under Mars, who not only makes men warlike, but apt at all crafts, especially those that have to do with metal and fire. His partner, the Moon, makes men chaste, and also great hunters.[84]

Bodin emphasizes his thesis by considering what happens when men migrate. Albertus had noticed that plants and animals in general grow larger or smaller as they are moved from one climate to another,[85] and he thought that if Ethiopians settled in the north their skins would become fair in a few generations.[86] Here again, Bodin accepts the mediaeval doctrine as substantially true because he thought it explained what had occurred in his own times. He ascribed the conquest of Spain by the Moors, and the victories of the Spanish troops taken to Germany by Charles V, to the improvement in their military energy when they removed to a more northerly country. On the other hand, the German *Lanzknechts* who went south to Italy under the Constable of Bourbon and Frönsberg suffered a corresponding decline; and the French armies under Philibert of Orange failed before Naples as the Cimbrians and the Gauls had failed before Rome.[87] But, though he thought climate operated immediately upon men's

---

[80] *Rep.*, pp. 677–682 and 698–699; *Meth.*, pp. 95, 114.

[81] By analogy with the association of the four seasons with the four elements of matter. The table of correspondencies appeared in Sacrobosco *De Computo Ecclesiastico*.

[82] *Rep.*, p. 686.

[83] For the qualities of the planets see Bartholomaeus, viii, xxiii–xxx; Guido Bonatti, *op. cit.*, iii, i–vii; *Cuer de Philosophie*, p. lxvii, v°.

[84] *Rep.*, pp. 690–691.

[85] Albertus, ii, i.

[86] Albertus, ii, iii.

[87] *Rep.*, p. 670.

Bodin and the Mediaeval Theory of Climate   77

energies, it takes time for their dispositions to be permanently altered, for men do not respond to environment as quickly as do plants which suck their nourishment directly from the soil. But given time, men will, he thought, become acclimatized, mentally and morally as well as physically, as happened to the Saxons Charlemagne transplanted to the Low Countries.[88]

What probably first suggested the application of these physiological ideas to the study of politics was that chapter in the *Politics*[89] in which Aristotle observed that northern races are naturally independent but undisciplined; southern races intelligent but slothful, and thus the predestined subjects of tyrants; while those occupying a middle situation have energy enough for independence and intelligence enough to rule not only themselves but others. Mediaeval commentators saw quite clearly that this passage was explained by reference to the effects of climate on men's capacities. It was glossed in this way, for instance, in the commentary on the *Politics* attributed to Aquinas.[90]

As one would expect, Bodin kept to this traditional framework in distinguishing political types. But he very much enlarged its positive content by considering the effects not only of temperature on the human constitution, but of total stellar radiation. This enables him to draw conclusions about laws, occupations, forms of government, and the tendencies of international relationships. Because cold makes men physically vigorous and brave, the best soldiers are produced in the north. Therefore, all the great invasions have come from that direction — of the Goths, Vandals, Franks, Normans, Tartars. For this reason the more northern race will always overcome the more southerly in war; Rome had her greatest triumphs in the Levant and North Africa, but even in her best days could not penetrate northwards beyond the Danube.[91] The English had never conquered the Scots, but habitually defeated the French.[92] Because Mars disposes to manual skill as well as war, from the north come the best craftsmen, Flemings, Germans and English.[93] But because none of these influences are evocative of intelligence, northerners are inaccessible to all appeal save that of the senses, and all arguments save those of force. He uses Caesar, Tacitus, and Solinus to show that among them the ruler is powerless who is not armed with the sword, and he collects evidence about the brutality of their punishments.[94] For this reason, too, though conquerors come from the north, such have not founded permanent empires, for they lack both the intelligence and perseverance to hold what they overrun.[95]

The proper virtue of those who live in the temperate zone is prudence, or the

---

[88] *Rep.*, p. 698.

[89] VII, vii.

[90] *In Libris Politicorum*, VII, v. Pierre d'Ailly also interprets the passage in this way in his *De Concordantia Discordantium Astronomorum.*

[91] *Rep.*, p. 672, and *Meth.*, p. 91.

[92] *Rep.*, p. 676.

[93] *Rep.*, p. 690, and *Meth.*, p. 103.

[94] *Rep.*, p. 679.

[95] *Meth.*, p. 91.

right functioning of the practical intellect, which results from that union of intelligence and skill that a moderate climate, and the beneficent planets of Jupiter
and Mercury induce. Such people excel in business and politics. Hence all the
great systems of law — Greek, Roman, and French — have been evolved in these
regions. Here also have arisen all the great empires the world has ever known —
Assyrian, Median, Persian, Parthian, Greek, Roman, and Celtic. The great
historians, orators, and poets have come from these regions. Here men are
governed not by force but reason; they reach their conclusions by discussion,
and prefer the method of negotiation to war.[96]

The children of Saturn, the visionaries of the south, are preoccupied with the
problems of abstract truth rather than good conduct, and all the great systems of
religion have arisen first in these parts. It is not reason but faith by which they
are ruled, and they appeal to oracles rather than arguments. The enervating
effects of a hot climate make them wretched soldiers, but they prevail, nevethe-
less, in virtue of their superior cunning.[97] The more southerly race, therefore,
has always excelled over its northern neighbors in matters of diplomacy. Bodin
quotes with approval Commines' remark that though the French have usually
been defeated by the English, they have always secured advantageous terms by
the peace settlements that have followed war; though they, in their turn, rightly
complain that they are habitually beaten at the diplomatic game by the Spaniards, who have got the better of them in every settlement for the last hundred
years or more.[98]

And the moral? Bodin concluded boldly that certain modes of conduct are not
altogether within the province of human volition; if Leo Africanus and Francisco
Alvarez had realized this, he says, they would not so have praised Africans for
their abstemiousness — it is the simple consequence of a feeble appetite. Similarly, the chastity of northerners is not to be particularly admired, for it comes
of the weakness of the sexual impulse in those of a phlegmatic temperament;
nor is the licentiousness of the south to be blamed, for it is equally the mark of
the melancholic complexion.[99] The apparent virtuousness of the Germans comes
from their lack of imagination; it takes 'spirit' to make men either greatly good
or greatly bad, and Livy should not, therefore, have blamed Hannibal for his
vices, for they were inseparable from his genius.[100] But more important to Bodin
than these criticisms of other writers is the practical conclusion he draws. Statesmen must frame their policy in accordance with these unalterable facts of the
situation; to try and subject southerners to the laws proper to the temperate
regions, or accustom northerners to legal processes will only bring all to ruin.[101]
He ascribes the failure of the Spaniards in the Low Countries in his own day to

---

[96] *Rep.*, p. 687, and *Meth.*, p. 105.
[97] *Rep.*, p. 690, and *Meth.*, p. 105.
[98] *Rep.*, p. 676.
[99] *Rep.*, p. 671, and *Meth.*, p. 113.
[100] *Rep.*, p. 685; and *Meth.*, p. 102.
[101] *Rep.*, p. 689.

their attempt to impose regulations suitable to Spain on a people living 12 degrees of latitude further north.[102] At least one of Bodin's mediaeval predecessors had anticipated him in thinking that the relativity of standards of conduct among men was a governing factor in practical politics. In the first years of the fourteenth century another Frenchman, John of Paris, rejected on these grounds the possibility of creating a universal temporal state. 'Diverse modes of life and diverse forms of policy occur in those regions where the climate and the character of the people are different, and what one community of men esteem as highly virtuous, another does not consider virtuous at all.'[103]

Such thoughts were dangerous. By seeming to call in question the moral responsibility of the individual, they struck at the root of the Christian ethic.[104] When therefore in 1277 the Bishop of Paris held an enquiry into heterodox teaching in the university, among the 217 propositions anathematized were those that embodied the views of the extremists, or Averroists, among natural philosophers on this subject of environment — that the world is subject in all its occurrences to the order of necessity — that diversity of place determines absolutely the course of events — that the will of the individual is under the compulsion of the stars, and is as much necessitated by cognition as is the appetite of brutes — that diversity in men in respect not only of temporal but spiritual qualities is the consequence of the diverse figure of the heavens.[105]

But even the most orthodox could not entirely reject the implied system of ideas. To believe in the validity of the reason at all was to accept the cosmology of the astrologers; and those who could not, as did the Averroists, postulate a conflict between the truths of faith and the truths of reason, were concerned to find a means of reconciling religion and science. The position taken up was always the same. As Aquinas saw very clearly, the theory of the influence of the stars was a theory explaining the transmutations of matter. In so far as they have bodies, men are, like all things compounded of matter, fashioned by that influence. Physically they are the product of environment, and those impulses which come from sensuous experience are spontaneous because the senses are a property of body. But their immaterial souls cannot be directly subject to these forces which move matter, though they may be indirectly through the desires of the flesh. The uncompromising Averroist held that this indirect influence is as absolute as the direct one because conduct is determined by appetite. But Albertus and Aquinas, and all who adopted their views, were emphatic that the will is not, like sense, inherent in any organ of body and therefore remains free; a rush of blood to the heart excites anger, but the soul is not thereby under compulsion to violence.[106] In the last analysis men can and on occasions do, resist

---

[102] *De Republica Libri Sex*, p. 770. This passage does not appear in the French.

[103] *De Potestate Regali et Papali*, cap. iii, in Goldast, *Monarchia S. Imperii Romani*.

[104] Alexander Neckham, *De Naturis Rerum*, i, vii (ed. T. Wright, *Rerum Brittanicarum Medii Aevi Scriptores*, London, 1863) already put this quite clearly (p. 39). See also Aquinas, *Ad Fratrem Reynaldum de Judiciis Astrorum*.

[105] Denifle-Chatelain *Chartularium Universitatis Parisiensis*, i, No. 473, pp. 543 ff. Arts: 21, 142, 162, 159, 143.

natural impulses — in other words escape the empire of the stars. One can never, then, predict of any individual how he will act on any given occasion, and horoscopes and particular prognostications thereby stand condemned. Nevertheless, because most men most of the time follow their natural impulses, one can arrive at tolerably accurate conclusions as to how different types of men in the mass will behave in certain situations. Bacon, for instance, asserted that the astrologer can confidently make general judgments about communities of men, and useful observations on their manners and customs, religions and wars, whereas he has far less certainty in pronouncing on the activities of individuals.[107]

Those who held such views saw in the actual variety of law and custom the record of the deliberate effort of men to correct those natural imperfections peculiar to their several situations. Dante, while justifying universal temporal monarchy, rejected the desirability of a universal system of law, on the grounds that men living under different conditions need different kinds of discipline. 'Nations, kingdoms and cities have their special conditions which ought to be regulated by different laws. For law is a rule to direct life, and naturally the Scythians who live outside the seventh climate . . . must needs be regulated in a different way from the Garamantes who live under the equinoctial circle.'[108] Bodin was emphatically of this opinion. He explicitly rejects the belief, which he attributes to Polybius and Galen, that men's conduct is determined absolutely by the influence of the stars; men, he says, by an effort of will, by an exercise of reason, or by discipline, can overcome the impulses of their natures.[109] Indeed, he had said his object in making this detailed study of the effects of climate was to show 'combien la discipline peut changer le droit naturel des hommes.' He thought the development of the Germans from the primitive tribes Tacitus described to the civilized people of his own day a case in point.[110] But discipline relaxed, men relapse quickly into the mere creatures of environment. 'Vrai est que si les lois et coustumes ne sont bien entretennus, le peuple retournera bien tost à son naturel.'[111] Discipline and its decay was, he holds, the secret of the rise and fall of Rome. The very same view had been expressed in the commentary on the *Politics* attributed to Aquinas.[112]

So Bodin concludes, it is the business of a good statesman to apply through law and government that discipline which corrects the defects of nature, but in doing so he must, like a good architect, use the materials locally available; he must apply that sort of discipline that the local inhabitants are capable of undergoing, with profit to themselves. Bodin goes further than Dante in thinking that

---

[106] Free will is affirmed in relation to the influence of climate by Aquinas, *In Libris Politicorum*, VII, lect. v. The problem is more fully argued by Albertus, *Summa Theologiae*, I, q. 68; and Aquinas, *Summa Theologica*, I, q. 115; Ia II ae q. 9. After the great controversy it was usual to add a saving clause about free will in all discussions of the influence of environment.

[107] Bacon, pp. 249 ff.

[108] *De Monarchia*, I, xiv.

[109] *Rep.*, p. 669 and *Meth.*, p. 50.

[110] *Rep.*, p. 697 and *Meth.*, p. 133.

[111] *Rep.*, p. 698.

[112] *In Libris Politicorum*, VII, v.

this principle governs not only forms of law, but also forms of government — 'estat' — 'L'un des plus grands, et peutestre le principal fondement des Republiques est d'accomoder l'estat au naturel des citoyens et les edicts et les ordonnances à la nature des lieux, des personnes et des temps.'[113] The determination of the measures appropriate in any given situation Bodin left to the practical politician; his own task was completed when he had described 'la nature des lieux' upon which policy must be based.

These comparative studies of the capacities of men inevitably raised the question as to which was the nation most favored by nature. The Schoolmen had no hesitation as to the principle of selection. Aristotle had lent his immense authority to the opinion that it is the middle and not the extreme situation which is to be preferred, because the union of northern vigor and southern intelligence corrects the defects of either. Controversy arose, however, over the identification of the middle situation. Aristotle had said the Greeks occupied it. Ptolemy held, on the other hand, that the fourth climate was the best, i.e., the area lying approximately between 28°N. and 34°N. Haly agreed, but thought that its eastern regions were the most excellent; for the fourth climate occupies a central position among the seven climates, and the east of the world is on the right hand, partakes of the nature of the sun (which is there in the ascendant), is masculine, and under the most majestic of the triplicities, that of fire.[114] These considerations made the Arabs the most fortunate of races. His authority carried great weight; Albertus accepted it,[115] and Pierre d'Ailly quoted it with respect.

But for all their great reverence for the opinions of their teachers, western Christians found it difficult to accept without question the natural superiority of the infidel Arab. Even Albertus in one passage argues on the evidence, and despite the opinion of the 'philosophers,' in favor of the superiority of the inhabitants of the sixth and seventh climates.[116] After his time and as a result of the self-conscious nationalism fostered by the government of Philip IV, the Greek and the Arab were deposed in favor of the Frenchman. John of Jandun explicitly claims for the French precisely the superiority Aristotle claimed for the Greeks.[117] Pierre Dubois expresses similar views. In the *De Recuperatione Terre Sancte,* while pressing for a French crusade, he warns the king not to lead it in person, but stay in France and beget and educate children there, 'for those born and brought up in the kingdom of France greatly excel those born in other regions in their manners, constancy, courage and beauty.'[118] In the *De Abbreviatione Guerrarum et Litium* he argues in favor of a sort of universal French empire, because 'as everybody knows, the Franks excel the people of all other regions and kingdoms . . . they make a much greater and better use of their judgment than any other nation; they do not give way to irrational anger, nor resist the

[113] *Rep.*, p. 666.

[114] This is how Pierre d'Ailly summarizes Haly, *Ymago Mundi*, xiii.

[115] Albertus, II, ii.

[116] Albertus, I, xi.

[117] *De Laudibus Parisiis*, II, viii, in Le Roux de Lincy et Tisserand, *Paris et ses historiens au XIVᵉ et XVᵉ siècles* (Paris, 1867), p. 60.

[118] Acad. des Inscr.: *Collection de textes pour servir à l'étude de l'histoire*, No. 9 (Paris, 1891), p. 139.

82 *Bodin and the Mediaeval Theory of Climate*

dictates of right reason — characteristics which we do not observe in other people.'[119] This is clearly for him a question of climate, for he adds that if Frenchmen migrate they lose this excellence, though he considered that it takes three or even four generations' domicile in foreign parts to corrupt entirely the virtues of a Frenchman. Pierre Dubois is content to affirm; the author of the popular *Cuer de Philosophie* attempts proof by relating the superiority of the French to the superexcellence of the stars above their heads. If we consider, he says, the most noble movement of the universe, the movement of the spheres upon the poles of the zodiac, we perceive that the Arctic pole is above the Antarctic, the west the right hand of the world. Furthermore, there is a greater multitude of more beautiful stars in the quarter of the heavens towards the Arctic pole than towards the south. Therefore the northwest regions of the inhabited earth are the 'most noble.' 'Nous Latins . . . nous habitons vers occident et vers la pole arctique,' he concludes, and leaves the reader to make his own inferences.[120]

Bodin shares these convictions, but does not express them with quite such simple dogmatism. He accepts the principle that the middle situation is the best, and formally awards the palm to Italy, as being midway between Scandinavia and Ethiopia, Spain and Arabia.[121] But he makes nothing of it, and draws no conclusions. On the other hand, he is very much preoccupied with the natural advantages the French enjoy over their neighbors. He, too, thinks the northwest quarter of the inhabited earth is to be preferred. In the *Methodus* he discusses with some care the important question, which of the four quarters is on the right hand of the world. Astrologers divided all natural agents into those that were masculine and dominant, and those that were feminine and subservient, the one symbolized by the right hand and the other by the left. He rejects the claims of the east, west and south, whatever the supporting authority, and decides in favor of the north, on the grounds that according to the most excellent (because the most rapid) motion of the world, the diurnal from east to west, the north is on the right, the south on the left hand.[122] Furthermore, the west is similarly dominant in relation to the east because its affinities are with the north in respect of its coldness, whereas the east is related to the south; 'all the ancients agree,' he alleges, 'that the facts support this, for they describe the east as more docile and submissive than the west.'[123] The northwest corner of the world, then, is that most favored by nature.

More precisely, in the concluding passages of the chapter in the *Republic*, he claims for the French that preeminence that Aristotle claimed for the Greeks, but on the grounds supplied by mediaeval glossators of the *Politics*, that the complexion characteristic of those latitudes is the best. According to Galen, irresponsibility is the mark of the sanguine temperament and, like the childhood

[119] This pamphlet has not been edited; but M. Langlois has printed long extracts from it in his edition of the *De Recuperatione Terre Sancte*. This passage is quoted on p. 129.
[120] P. civ, r⁰.
[121] *Rep.*, p. 677.
[122] *Meth.*, p. 109, and *Rep.*, p. 691.
[123] *Rep.*, p. 691.

with which it is associated, comes from uncertainty of purpose. This is illustrated by the inconstancy of the barbarians in the past to the faith they so readily adopted, and the multiplication of sects among the Germans and the English in his own time. In contrast, the melancholy temperament of the south, associated with middle life, makes men obstinate in perseverance. He gives the Jews as an example, momentarily forgetful that if his climate theory holds, their migrations should long ago have changed their radical complexion, and with that their persistent adherence to the religion of their fathers. But the impetuosity Caesar ascribes to the Gauls he identifies with the energy and enterprise — 'allégresse' — of youth, characteristic of the choleric disposition. In fact the French, in virtue of their environment, exhibit in their conduct the firmness and energy that is the happy mean between levity and obstinacy.[124] He not only agrees with Pierre Dubois and John of Jandun but he agrees with them for reasons which they would thoroughly have understood and approved.

Certain conclusions emerge very clearly from this comparison of Bodin's observations on climate with those of his mediaeval predecessors. In the first place, his theory is coherent in all its parts, because it derives logically from the mediaeval conception of the system of the world, and so shares its consistency. In the second place, Bodin added nothing substantially new; he drew every one of his main ideas from accepted traditions very generally held. Nevertheless, he did not leave the doctrine exactly as he found it. For one thing, he assembled within the compass of a single discussion, not only all that had been said on the subject, but also what had hitherto only existed in fragmentary form, as scattered observations arising incidentally out of some other topic. He thereby reduced to coherent form material till then unordered. For another thing, though he found no reason to modify any of the ideas he inherited, he greatly enriched their content by adducing a mass of new evidence, independently observed. The Schoolmen were primarily interested in the philosophical problem of establishing by ratiocination a single system of ideas from the various traditions they inherited. If they illustrated at all, they were content to repeat examples hallowed by age and use. Bodin took the system for granted, and gave all his attention to its practical implications. He was therefore most original where they were least so, in the handling of evidence. He did what they did not do, systematically surveyed the contemporary scene to show how the laws of environment actually worked. More important still, in doing this he gave the doctrine a quite new emphasis. The Schoolmen were provoked to discuss the influence of environment because they saw it raised the moral problem of the free will of the individual. Bodin was not so much interested in the problems raised, as in the use that could be made of the science by the statesman. A true understanding of the laws of environment, he thought, was the inevitable starting point of all sound policy, all good laws, all beneficial institutions. His claim to originality rests on this re-orientation of traditional beliefs, to serve a useful purpose. He applied the science.

BEDFORD COLLEGE, UNIVERSITY OF LONDON

[124] *Rep.*, p. 698 ff., and *Meth.*, p. 116.

Name Index

Abelard, Peter 384
Afer, Leo 427
Africanus, Leo 443
Aglaophemus 257
Agustín, Antonio 128
Alacris of Clermont 373
Albumazar 434
Alciato, Andrea 23, 54, 126, 127, 133
Allen, J.W. 6, 13, 180
Alsted, J. 377
Althusius, Johannes 35, 36, 37, 102, 122
Alvarez, R.P. 426, 427
Alvarez, Francisco 441, 443
Andreae, Johannes 122
Aquinas, St. Thomas 11, 215, 226, 332, 357, 362, 364, 430, 436, 439, 444
Aristotle xvii, 25, 44, 45, 62, 66, 85, 98, 99, 102, 144, 247, 313, 315, 384, 408, 423, 429, 446, 448
Arnisaeus, Henning 35, 37, 43, 44, 45, 49, 50, 61, 122
Arthur, Duke of Brittany 159
Augustine, Saint 244, 247, 258, 313, 317, 362
Austin, John xiii, 3, 6, 11, 12, 13, 15, 17
Averroës 384
Avicenna 438

Bacon, Francis 378, 379, 382, 445
Baldus 110, 112, 114, 115, 122, 164
Barclay, William 160, 174
Barjotus, Philibertus 415
Baron, Eguinaire 137, 138
Bartholomew, Saint 144
Bartolus 110, 113, 114, 115, 122, 133, 145
Bate, Henry 434
Baudouin, François 128, 129, 130, 139, 140, 142, 143, 396, 418
Baudrillart, Henri 147, 223, 230, 252
Baxter, Christopher R. xvi, 151, 285–305
Beaumanoir, K.L. 145
Becker, Carl 147
Bellièvre, Privy Councillor 205
Belus, Jupiter 409

Besold, Christopher xiii, 46, 47, 48, 49, 49, 51, 57, 61, 122
Beza (de Bèze), Theodore 74, 76
Blair, Ann xvii, 369–79, 381–91
Boccaccio 259
Boccalini 421
Bodin de St. Laurent, Jean xi–xvii, 210, 214, 217, 224, 228, 229, 230
Bodin, Elias 270
Bodin, Elie 389
Bodin, Jean (son) 389
Bonatti, Guido 430, 434, 435
Bornitius 99, 122
Botero, Giovanni 194
Bouwsma, William J. 264
Boyer-Xambeau, M.T. 212, 224
Boyle, M.O. 344
Bracton, Henry 3
Brecht, Arnold 11
Brown, John L. xvii, 395–428
Browne, Sir Thomas 400
Brutus, Junius 37
Budé, Guillaume 125, 126, 128, 137, 419

Cabot, Vincent 32, 37
Caesar, Julius 15, 46, 74, 243, 415, 429, 442
Calvin, John 73, 74, 259, 287, 308, 323
Camacho, Gómez 215, 216
Campanella 260, 261
Camus, Bishop 258
Capet, Hugh 75
Cardan, Jean 399, 400
Cardano, F. 376
Carlyle, A.J. 4
Carneades 343
Casas, Las 429
Castiglione 255
Chandieu, Jerome 415
Charlemagne 415, 442
Charles V 74, 429, 441
Charles IX 72, 73, 79, 295
Charron, Pierre 258, 259, 308
Chartier, Roger 385